DAT

DATE	ISSUED TO

HOOVER'S
TOP 2,500
EMPLOYERS

Hoover's
BUSINESS
PRESS

Austin, Texas

Hoover's
BUSINESS PRESS

Copyright © 1996 by Hoover's, Inc. All rights reserved. No part of this book may be reproduced or transmitted in any form or by any means, electronic or mechanical, including by photocopying, facsimile transmission, recording, rekeying, or using any information storage and retrieval system, without permission in writing from Hoover's, except that brief passages may be quoted by a reviewer in a magazine, in a newspaper, online, or in a broadcast review.

10 9 8 7 6 5 4 3 2 1

Publisher Cataloging-In-Publication Data

Hoover's Top 2,500 Employers

    Includes indexes.

    1. Business enterprises — Directories. 2. Corporations — Directories.

HF3010   338.7

Company information and profiles from the *Hoover's* series of handbooks, guides, and directories are also available on America Online, Baseline, Bloomberg Financial Network, CompuServe, LEXIS-NEXIS, Microsoft Network, Reuters NewMedia, and on the Internet at Hoover's Online (www.hoovers.com), CNNfn (www.cnnfn.com), Farcast (www.farcast.com), IBM InfoMarket (www.infomkt.ibm.com), InfoSeek (www.infoseek.com), IBM Infosage (www.infosage.ibm.com), Pathfinder (www.pathfinder.com), PAWWS (www.pawws.com), and Wall Street Journal Interactive (www.wsj.com).

A catalog of Hoover's products is available on the World Wide Web (www.hoovers.com).

ISBN 1-57311-013-2

This book was produced by Hoover's Business Press using Claris Corporation's FileMaker Pro 3.0, Quark, Inc.'s Quark XPress 3.32, EM Software, Inc.'s Xdata 2.5, and fonts from Adobe's Clearface, Futura, and Myriad families. Cover illustration is by Jennifer Hewitson. Electronic prepress and printing were done by Quebecor Printing (USA) Corp. in Fairfield, Pennsylvania. Text paper is 60# Postmark White.

US AND WORLD DIRECT SALES
Hoover's, Inc.
1033 La Posada Drive, Suite 250
Austin, TX 78752
Phone: 512-374-4500
Fax: 512-374-4501

US BOOKSELLERS AND JOBBERS
Little Brown and Co.
200 West Street
Waltham, MA 02154
Phone: 800-759-0190
Fax: 617-890-0875

US WHOLESALER ORDERS
Warner Publisher Services
Book Division
9210 King Palm Drive
Tampa, FL 33619
Phone: 800-873-BOOK
Fax: 813-664-8193

EUROPE
William Snyder Publishing Associates
5, Five Mile Drive
Oxford OX2 8HT
England
Phone & fax: +44-186-551-3186

HOOVER'S, INC.

Founder: Gary Hoover
Chairman, President, CEO, and Publisher: Patrick J. Spain

Senior Managing Editor — Production: George Sutton
Senior Managing Editor — Editorial: James R. Talbot
Senior Contributing Editors: Alta M. Campbell, Alan Chai
Senior Editor: Thomas Trotter
Associate Editor: William Cargill
Editorial Coordinator: Ken Little
Assistant Editorial Coordinator: Melanie Lea Hall
Editors: Chris Barton, Paul Mitchell, Anthony Shuga
Research Manager: Sherri M. Hale
Desktop Publishing Manager: Christina Thiele
Senior Researchers: Sarah Hallman, Jim Harris, Brian Pedder, David Ramirez
Researchers: Lynn Monnat, Patricia Pepin
Research Assistants: Leslie Navarro, Erica Taylor
Senior Writers: Joy Aiken, Stuart Hampton, Diane Lee, Barbara M. Spain, Jeffrey A. Twining
Writers: Rosalind Conway-Ahmed, Michael Daecher, Jennifer Dean, Joshua Hinsdale,
Charles Homer III, Lisa C. Norman, Cory Walton, Chris Wilson
Financial Editors: Jenny Hill, Dennis L. Sutton
Copy Editors: Dawn Albright, Casey Kelly Barton, Calvin Cahan, Allan Gill, Jeanne Minnich,
Patrice Sarath, John Willis
Fact Checkers/Proofreaders: Ramalakshmi Bollini, Kelly Seiler Borsheim, Robyn Gammill,
Rowena M. Holden, Michael G. Laster, Elizabeth Gagne Morgan, Nancy Nowlin, William J. Rice,
Carole Sage, Marianne Tatom, John F. Waukechon, Andrea Winkler
Database Editors: Tweed Chouinard, Yvonne A. Cullinan, Karen Hill, Britton E. Jackson
Desktop Publishers: Michelle de Ybarrondo, Trey Colvin, Kevin Dodds, JoAnn Estrada,
Gregory Gosdin, Elena Hernandez, Holly Hans Jackson, Louanne Jones
Database Entry: Ismael Hernandez Jr., Eldridge N. Goins, Danny Macaluso, Scott A. Smith

Director, Hoover's Online: Matt Manning
Senior Brand Manager: Leslie A. Wolke
Online Production Manager: Richard Finley
Online Content Editor: Martha DeGrasse
Online Editors: Kay Nichols, Perrin Patterson
Electronic Media Producers: Chuck Green, Rick Navarro

Senior Vice President, Sales and Marketing: Dana L. Smith
VP Finance and Administration and CFO (HR): Lynn Atchison
Vice President, Electronic Publishing: Tom Linehan
Director, Corporate Communications: Jani F. Spede
Controller: Deborah L. Dunlap
Systems Manager: Bill Crider
Fulfillment Manager: Beth DeVore
Office Manager: Tammy Fisher
Direct Marketing Manager: Marcia Harelik
Sales Manager: Shannon McGuire
Advertising Sales Manager: Joe McWilliams
Customer Service Manager: Rhonda T. Mitchell
Shipping Coordinator: Michael Febonio
Advertising Coordinator: Michelle Swann
Communications Coordinator: Angela Young
Customer Service Representatives: John T. Logan, Darla Wenzel
Administrative Assistant: Margaux Bejarano
Publicity Assistant: Becky Hepinstall

HOOVER'S MISSION STATEMENT

1. To produce business information products and services of the highest quality, accuracy, and readability.
2. To make that information available whenever, wherever, and however our customers want it through mass distribution at affordable prices.
3. To continually expand our range of products and services and our markets for those products and services.
4. To reward our employees, suppliers, and shareholders based on their contributions to the success of our enterprise.
5. To hold to the highest ethical business standards, erring on the side of generosity when in doubt.

CONTENTS

ABOUT *HOOVER'S TOP 2,500 EMPLOYERS*

With the possible exception of what to wear to the interview, the most vexing question facing job hunters has always been: Where are the jobs? With all the news reports of downsizing, corporate restructuring, and belt-tightening, the question seems even more pertinent today.

Yet, in fact, companies both large and small are hiring people everyday.

So where do you look to find out who's hiring? You could start with this book. If you added up the employees of the companies listed here, starting with the chemists at Abbott Labs in Abbott Park, Illinois, and ending with the modem makers at Zoom Telephonics in Boston, you'd find that the companies in *Hoover's Top 2,500 Employers* employ nearly 35 million people. In the last year alone, these companies have added almost 2.5 million more workers to their payrolls.

CHOOSING THE COMPANIES

To compile the information in this book, we began by researching more than 10,000 companies, both public and private. We studied annual reports and other company documents, faxed requests for information, and made countless telephone calls. We consulted lists in publications such as *Forbes, FORTUNE, Business Week*, and *Inc.* As the data began to take shape, we developed a sliding scale of which employers we wanted to include in this book; that is, which ones were "large" and which ones were "fast-growing." In order to qualify for inclusion, a company must have (a) registered employee growth of 25% or more over the past year, (b) added 200 or more jobs, or (c) employed more than 5,000 people. No companies with fewer than 50 employees are included.

You will also find companies in *Hoover's Top 2,500 Employers* that have eliminated jobs. At first glance, it might seem surprising to find companies with shrinking work-

forces in a book of leading employers. In fact, numerous companies listed dropped *thousands* of employees over the past year. Why did we include them? Because no matter how many jobs large corporations like GTE and DuPont drop, they are still leaders in hiring new workers.

We also believed it was important to include these large corporations because the percentage change in their total number of employees is not always directly related to hiring and firing. Often the changes in a major corporation's workforce is due to its sale of a subsidiary or merging with another company. For example, Columbia/HCA Healthcare Corp. added 83,000 jobs last year. The reason? It acquired the 117-hospital Healthtrust. Over the same period, General Mills dropped 115,818 jobs. A disastrous year? Hardly. General Mills had simply spun off a major segment of its business, Darden Restaurants.

We've also included a group of large, privately held companies for which we could not determine the number of employees added or dropped in the last year. Private companies tend to be more, well, private about such information. But whether they want to keep it a secret or not, these are large corporations you would be wise to consider as future employers. We also included a number of large universities. Often overlooked by job seekers, universities are among the largest and most active employers in the nation.

ORGANIZATION OF THIS BOOK

To help you find a job close to home (or as far away as possible, depending on your state of mind), we have organized the companies by state and have indexed them by metropolitan area. We've also included an index of companies by industry. And if your future employer is revealed to you — but not its location — through a vision or by a psychic, don't fret, because we have an alphabetical list of companies as well. We have included each company's headquarters location, although many of the larger companies have offices across the nation (IBM, for instance, has an office or two outside its Armonk, New York, home). We did not bend our rules to ensure an equal sampling for each state — California, as would be expected, has many more entries than Hawaii. But in every state except Alaska, we were able to uncover at least one, if not a handful of companies, that met our guidelines. We hope that in the next edition we will be able to cover all 50 states.

We have also included telephone and fax numbers, brief industry descriptions, and the names of chief executives and senior human resources officers. Some companies reported to us that they did not have one person in charge of personnel, that hiring was done at a departmental level; their entries have been marked accordingly. In these cases, you should call or fax the company to find out to whom you should send a résumé.

JOB-HUNTING RESOURCES

This section provides some further tools for your job search. First, we've excerpted a selection from *NetJobs* that covers online tools for conducting a job search. For new college graduates who have joined the job-hunting ranks, we have included an article, "Grad Seeks Job," reprinted from *Internet World*. Next, we have a list of Web sites created by corporations specifically for job seekers. The information contained at these sites can be useful in selecting companies to contact and in preparing for your interview. Finally, knowing that we can't provide you with all the information you might need (however hard we try), we've included a list of other useful books on job hunting that will help you with a variety of job-search skills, such as crafting a perfect résumé and preparing yourself for an interview.

The temporary-employment industry has grown fat off other industries' attempts to stay lean and mean. Many now offer health plans and paid vacations and special-ize in servicing particular industries. We have included capsule profiles of 20 of the leading firms to familiarize you with these businesses. These 20 temp agencies presently employ more than 4 million contract workers. Many provide training for their employees and should be given serious consideration, especially if you are entering the job market for the first time.

LISTS

This section begins with the top 500 companies in this book listed by total employees, by one-year absolute employee growth, and by one-year percentage employee growth. The employee information in the book is taken from the most current available sources and reflects data for the companies' 1995 or 1996 fiscal years. The other lists in this section have been excerpted from a variety of sources to provide you with additional viewpoints on the American employment scene.

A DIGITAL GUIDE TO JOB HUNTING

The Internet is a fantastic resource for job seekers. Why wait for the Sunday paper to check the want ads? Career Mosaic on the Internet has lists of jobs that are immediately available at large and small companies alike: 3Com, Citibank, NEC, and Sprint, to name just a few.

Thousands of corporations have established Web sites on the Net where they will tell you all about themselves. Check out the list of Web addresses for companies that maintain job information sites. Throughout the book, we've interspersed home pages and addresses of other online employment information you might find helpful.

Hoover's Online, which can be found at www.hoovers.com, is packed with information about more than 10,000 companies and contains links to many company Web sites as well as other business and job information. For more in-depth information — including company history, officers, products, key competitors, and financial history — Hoover's Online subscribers can access profiles of many of the companies found in

Hoover's Online — http://www.hoovers.com

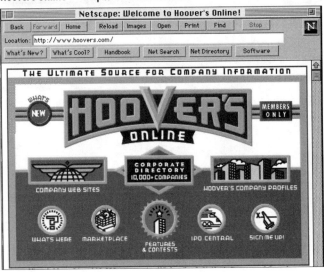

Hoover's Top 2,500 Employers. (These companies are marked by a 📖 icon.)

Hoover's company information also can be found on America Online, Baseline, Bloomberg Financial Network, CompuServe, LEXIS-NEXIS, Microsoft Network, and Reuters NewMedia. On the Internet, you can also find it on Farcast (www.farcast.com), IBM InfoMarket (www.infomkt.ibm.com), InfoSeek (www.infoseek.com), IBM Infosage (www.infosage.ibm.com), Pathfinder (www.pathfinder.com), PAWWS (www.pawws.com), and Wall Street Journal Interactive (www.wsj.com).

THE SOFTWARE

To make sending out résumés a snap, we've included a free CD-ROM for Windows and Macintosh that contains all 2,500 companies in an easy-to-use database. Developed in Claris's FileMaker (a run-time copy of which is part of our software package), the program combines a simple intuitive interface (no user manual required) with a flexible search engine. You can use the software to export the data into other applications, such as word processors, spreadsheets, or other databases. Printing cover letters and mailing labels for your prospective employers will be a snap.

Finally, we would like to mention other Hoover's titles from our list of handbooks, guides, and directories that might be of help. *Hoover's Handbook of American Business*, *Hoover's Handbook of Emerging Companies*, *Hoover's Guide to Media Companies*, and *Hoover's Guide to Computer Companies* all provide in-depth profiles of companies. A series of regional guides covers companies in Texas, the Bay Area, Southern California, Chicago, and the New York area. A complete catalog is available at www.hoovers.com.

Happy Hunting!

The Editors
Hoover's, Inc.
August 1996

Hoover's Company Profiles...

COLUMBIA/HCA HEALTHCARE

OVERVIEW

A string of acquisitions has Columbia/HCA blue in the face. Headquartered in Nashville, the company is the #1 health care provider in the US. It owns and/or operates hundreds of hospitals, outpatient surgery centers, and other health care facilities throughout the US, in the UK, and in Switzerland.

Columbia/HCA is acquiring additional hospitals all over the country. When taking over a facility, the company upgrades the equipment and adds new services to make the hospital more attractive to doctors and prospective patients. It also develops such related facilities as outpatient, diagnostic, and acute-care clinics in the area to create an all-encompassing network of health care providers.

Chairman Rick Scott — named by Time magazine in 1996 as one of the 25 most influential Americans — has been the leader of an industry-wide trend toward consolidation. With his powerful empire, Scott demands discounts from suppliers, which are then passed on to consumers.

In what would be its first venture into health insurance, Columbia/HCA agreed to acquire 85% of not-for-profit insurer Blue Cross & Blue Shield of Ohio, although the deal has been challenged by Blue Cross's governing association and the Ohio attorney general. The purchase would give Columbia/HCA a new way to direct more patients into its network of hospitals.

WHEN

In 1987 Scott (a Dallas lawyer) and Fort Worth financier Richard Rainwater founded Columbia Hospital Corp. to buy 2 hospitals in El Paso for $60 million. The pair began renovating the run-down hospitals, pleasing doctors by responding quickly to their demands and needs. The partners eventually sold 40% of the hospitals to local doctors, hoping that ownership would motivate physicians to increase productivity and efficiency. However, some critics claimed the practice would lead to overcharging.

The company entered the Miami market the next year and by 1990 had 4 hospitals in operation. After merging with Smith Laboratories in 1990, Columbia went public. With the merger Columbia acquired Sutter Laboratories (orthopedic products). By the end of 1990, it had 11 hospitals. Sales grew, driven not only by new hospital revenues, but also by increased same-hospital sales.

In 1992 Columbia entered the Fort Myers, Florida, market with the purchase of Basic American Medical, Inc., which operated 8 hospitals. The company bought additional facilities that year, including several in the Miami area and a psychiatric hospital in El Paso.

In 1993 Columbia merged with Galen Health Care, which operated 73 hospitals. Galen had been spun off from health plan operator Humana earlier in the year. The merger provided Columbia with about 15 new markets and linked Columbia's respected name with Galen's strength in numbers.

Columbia and Hospital Corporation of America (HCA) merged in 1994. It was Scott's 2nd try at grabbing HCA; he had originally made a bid for the hospital operator in 1987.

HCA was founded in 1968 by Thomas Frist, his son Thomas Frist Jr., and Jack Massey (founder of Kentucky Fried Chicken Corporation) in Nashville. It started with a single Nashville hospital but grew rapidly. By 1973 the company ran 50 hospitals, and by 1983 it owned 376 hospitals in the US and 7 other countries.

Changes in Medicare reimbursement procedures (paying on fixed schedules rather than a percentage basis) and the advent of HMOs began to cut into hospital occupancy rates. HCA began paring operations in the late 1980s, including selling 102 of its rural hospitals to an employee stock ownership plan. In 1989 Frist Jr. led a $5.1 billion LBO of the company. To pay down debt, he continued to sell assets, and in 1992 Frist took the company public once again.

Columbia/HCA in 1994 acquired the US's largest operator of outpatient surgery centers, Dallas-based Medical Care America. The next year it completed the $3.45 billion takeover of 117-hospital HealthTrust, constituting the largest hospital merger to date in the US. Also in 1995 the company agreed to enter into a 50/50 joint venture with HealthONE, the biggest health care provider in Colorado.

In 1996 Columbia/HCA agreed to purchase most of Blue Cross & Blue Shield of Ohio, with plans to become joint venture partners in an integrated insurance and health care service alliance.

Hospital acquisitions remained a major part of Columbia/HCA's 1996 strategy, with the company negotiating some 150 separate transactions. Completed purchases include 3 Houston-area hospitals and a 462-bed facility in Tulsa.

Columbia/HCA Healthcare added more employees to its payroll than any other company in Hoover's Top 2,500 Employees. Read the whole story about Columbia/HCA and

...tell the whole story

WHO

Chairman, President, and CEO: Richard L. Scott, age 43, $858,000 pay (prior to promotion)
COO: David T. Vandewater, age 45, $737,000 pay
President, International Group: Donald E. Steen, age 49, $528,000 pay
SVP and General Counsel: Stephen T. Braun, age 40
SVP and Treasurer (Principal Financial Officer): David C. Colby, age 42
SVP Financial Operations: Samuel A. Greco, age 44
SVP Marketing/Public Affairs: Lindy B. Richardson, age 49
SVP Development: Joseph D. Moore, age 49
SVP Columbia Sponsored Networks: Richard A. Schweinhart, age 46
SVP Human Resources/Administration: Neil D. Hemphill, age 42
SVP: Victor L. Campbell, age 49

WHERE

HQ: Columbia/HCA Healthcare Corporation, One Park Plaza, Nashville, TN 37203
Phone: 615-327-9551
Fax: 615-320-2222
Web site: http://www.columbia.net

Columbia/HCA operates hospitals, outpatient surgery centers, and home health agencies in 38 US states, Switzerland, and the UK.

WHAT

	1995 Health Care Network Facilities No.
Home health agencies	200
Skilled nursing units	156
Ambulatory surgery centers	135
Psychiatric units	117
Rehabilitation units	60
Comprehensive outpatient rehabilitation facilities	17
Total	**685**

	1995 Sales % of total
Medicare	36
Medicaid	6
Other	58
Total	**100**

Selected Services

Cardiology
Diagnostic services
Emergency services
General surgery
Home health care
Internal medicine
Neurosurgery
Obstetrics
Oncology
Orthopedics
Outpatient surgery

KEY COMPETITORS

American Medical
Beverly Enterprises
Catholic Healthcare
Charter Medical
Daughters of Charity
Detroit Medical Center
Healthsouth
Holy Cross Health System
Horizon/CMS Healthcare
Integrated Health Services
Kaiser Foundation Health Plan
Mayo Foundation
Mercy Health Services
New York City Health and Hospitals
OrNda HealthCorp
Sisters of Charity Health Care
Tenet Healthcare
UniHealth
Universal Health Services

HOW MUCH

NYSE symbol: COL
Fiscal year ends: December 31

	Annual Growth	1986	1987	1988	1989	1990	1991	1992	1993	1994	1995
Sales ($ mil.)	134.8%	—	—	45	153	290	499	807	10,252	11,132	17,695
Net income ($ mil.)	141.6%	—	—	2	6	10	15	26	507	630	961
Income as % of sales		—	—	4.4%	4.1%	3.4%	3.0%	3.2%	4.9%	5.7%	5.4%
Earnings per share ($)	20.6%	—	—	—	—	0.84	0.92	1.18	1.50	1.80	2.14
Stock price – high ($)		—	—	—	—	15.50	18.75	22.00	33.88	45.25	54.00
Stock price – low ($)		—	—	—	—	10.00	9.75	13.75	16.25	33.25	35.38
Stock price – close ($)	34.0%	—	—	—	—	11.75	17.00	21.25	32.88	36.25	50.75
P/E – high		—	—	—	—	18	20	19	23	25	25
P/E – low		—	—	—	—	12	11	12	11	18	17
Dividends per share ($)	40.4%	—	—	—	—	0.00	0.00	0.00	0.12	0.12	0.12
Book value per share ($)	109.8%	—	—	—	—	2.93	6.40	10.25	10.31	13.87	15.99
Employees		—	—	—	—	5,900	6,300	13,300	131,600	157,000	240,000

1995 YEAR-END:
Debt ratio: 50.9%
Return on equity: 14.5%
Cash (mil.): $232
Current ratio: 1.53
Long-term debt (mil.): $7,137
No. of shares (mil.): 446
Dividend
Yield: 0.2%
Payout: 5.6%
Market value (mil.): $22,625

STOCK PRICE HISTORY HIGH/LOW/CLOSE

1986 1987 1988 1989 1990 1991 1992 1993 1994 1995

Top 2,500 Employers

Job-Hunting Resources

Getting On Track

Reprinted by permission from *NetJobs*. Copyright © 1996 by Wolff New Media.

I wish there were a big career placement center in the sky, a place that had everything.

Would you settle for Cyberspace? Enormous virtual career centers have set up shop on the Net. Like college career centers or the employment centers in public libraries, the online versions are full service. But virtual career centers take the job search to the next level. They update their mammoth collections of searchable job listings daily; feature personality assessment tests and walk-throughs of resume writing; link to company home pages and corporate research centers; and offer internship directories (no torn pages), cover letter guides, and even listings of work opportunities overseas. But unlike their offline cousins, the virtual career centers are not just for the job seeker; they're also for employers. One of the biggest draws of a virtual career center is its resume bank. You can submit a resume, tag it with keywords that describe your qualifications and interests, and post it for thousands of potential employers. Companies can then search for the candidates that are right for them. You may not feel the need to go elsewhere to job search online, but *NetJobs* recommends using these virtual career centers as home bases, places to return to over and over again as you network, shop your resume around, and find job opportunities in the far corners of Cyberspace.

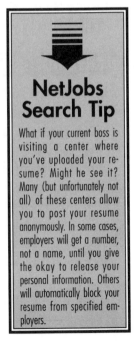

NetJobs Search Tip

What if your current boss is visiting a center where you've uploaded your resume? Might he see it? Many (but unfortunately not all) of these centers allow you to post your resume anonymously. In some cases, employers will get a number, not a name, until you give the okay to release your personal information. Others will automatically block your resume from specified employers.

Career Centers

Adams JobBank Online

Adams Media Corporation publishes guide books and software to assist job seekers. Recently the company opened a BBS with job listings, a forum on eWorld, and a Website. On eWorld, Adams offers support for the company's products, general job search discussions on the message boards, issues of the *Career Moves* newsletter (job tips, wacky jobs of the month, and job listings with companies nationwide), and software to log on to the company's BBS. The Website is built around a searchable database that lets job seekers plug in a job title and location and get a list of companies with openings. The Website also features profiles of companies advertising jobs on the site, articles on the workplace for women and minorities, and a resume bank.

WORLD WIDE WEB
> **URL** http://www.adamsonline.com

Career Center

Every college and university, most libraries, and many community centers and churches offer career guidance and resources to assist job seekers. America Online's Career Center can compete with the best of them. The Career Center has so many resources it's hard to imagine spending time here and not finding a job. Where do you begin? To help situate the newbie, the Center publishes monthly articles about trends in the job market and online job searching. For those not sure what they want do with their lives (or what they can afford to do), an online database based on the *Occupation Outlook Handbook*, a federal publication, lists descriptions, average earnings, and entrance qualifications for over 250 of America's most popular occupations. When you've narrowed your interests, but need to find employers, the Center's Employer Contact Database provides info on thousands of American companies, and it's an excellent place to prepare for an interview. You won't get the interview without a good resume, however, and if you need help preparing a resume, head to the Resume Templates and Cover Letter Library for examples. Is there such a thing as too many job opportunities? The Center includes the Help Wanted USA database with descriptions of over 10,000 current job openings in the U.S. and the Federal Employment Service area with a huge selection of Federal jobs. In addition, AOLers can submit their resumes to the Talent Bank with the hopes that when they're offline doing something else employers and head hunters will be online searching for them. The Center can even assist you with your offline job search; it maintains a database with contact information on local employment agencies. Although AOL rivals most competitors with its job listings and databases, its counseling services give it a huge edge. You can visit the Career Counseling area and chat live with a group of other job seekers and a professional counselor, or, for more personal career advice, you can schedule a one-on-one meeting with a counselor. Many professional (and costly) career guidance companies also use the Center to hold meetings and to sell their services.

AMERICA ONLINE
Keyword career

Career Magazine

The resources here are truly impressive. That's probably why close to 200,000 people visit the site every month. They come to search the site's listings of thousands of jobs (mostly for engineers and programmers) which are updated daily; shop for new employees; drop off resumes in the resume bank; research one of the close to 200 hundred companies listed in the site's Company Profiles section; and read employment-related articles on subjects ranging from job fairs to head hunters to interviews.

WORLD WIDE WEB

URL http://www.careermag.com

Career Mosaic

The elegant graphics make this site, which is divided into six sections, easy and fun to use. A Career Resource Center offers tips on creating the ultimate resume and acing an interview. A calendar of Online Job Fairs invites you to "come to the hire happenings." The CollegeConnection collects job listings and internship opportunities for students and recent graduates. In ResumeCM you can post your resume, or, if you're an employer, you can search for the candidate to fill your job opening. An a-to-z list of companies lets visitors familiarize themselves with important companies. Finally, a searchable database of jobs lets you look for hot jobs in over 60 different fields.

WORLD WIDE WEB

URL http://www.careermosaic.com/cm

careerWEB

CareerWEB has only been around since May of 1995, but already it has assembled an impressive collection of employment resources. Besides a growing number of job listings in a wide range of fields (transportation, sales, marketing, engineering, and computers, among others), the site also offers a list of about 50 company profiles, and a job-search newsletter called *Connections* (which is packed with online job-search tips). Best of all, careerWEB recognizes that job searching can be a bit depressing at times, so they offer a Career Readiness Inventory, which is a thinly-veiled job-search pep talk. Ready, set, go!

WORLD WIDE WEB

`URL` http://www.cweb.com/welcome.html

E-Span

One of the most complete and omnipresent job-search services in Cyberspace, E-Span features career advice, resume-building assistance, interviewing suggestions, and job listings. The heart of E-Span is its database of job listings, which can be searched by occupation, location, or a related keyword. Employers listing jobs range from Sony to the state of Wisconsin; while job postings are voluminous, they favor the computer and financial industries. Listings remain on E-Span for up to four weeks and are updated weekly. If you've found a job you're interested in, send your response directly to the potential employer. E-Span, however, is happy to accept resumes for its online resume bank. With over 6,000 new job listings going up each week (the database is updated every Monday) and its comprehensive career research support, E-Span must be counted among the heavyweights of job resources in Cyberspace.

AMERICA ONLINE
Keyword jobs

COMPUSERVE
Go espan

WORLD WIDE WEB
URL http://www.espan.com/js/js.html

Heart

Heart's slogan "Connecting employers and candidates throughout the world...or around the corner" lends the comforting suggestion that your job search will be a short one. The site has a database of job openings in about 75 fields which you can search by company, location, or discipline. Heart also sponsors regular online job fairs with leading companies like Unisys Corporation and Fidelity Investments; visit the site for a calendar of upcoming fairs. Hint to users: Heart is heavily geared towards college students.

TELNET
URL telnet://career.com

WORLD WIDE WEB
URL http://www.career.com/PUB/heart.html

JobWeb

Yet another general job resource with separate sections for college students, recent graduates, experienced job seekers, and human resources professionals. Click into the appropriate category for

career counseling, job databases, career fairs, and bibliographies.

WORLD WIDE WEB
`URL` http://www.jobweb.org

Monster Board

Looking for a job is scary. Monsters are scary. But never fear, this monster is here to help. In fact, this accommodating monster has assembled a collection of job-hunting resources that will take the bite out of looking for a job. The main attraction of the page is its job database, and with over 48,000 job listings, it's a job force to be reckoned with. To add job listings to the database, potential employers should first read the directions on the page. The Monster Board also maintains a resume bank called Resume City; instructions at the Website will tell job seekers how to develop and submit their resumes for perusal by employers. But it's not all work and no play at the Monster Board—a section of the board dedicated to the "next generation" offers links to music and film sites.

★★★★

WORLD WIDE WEB
`URL` http://www.monster.com

NationJob

NationJob has everything a good job site should have: an extensive, searchable database of jobs, a searchable database of company profiles, and links to other job resources. But it also has one thing that sets it apart from other sites: P. J. Scout. The free (P)ersonal (J)ob Scout service is like having a friend shop for a job for you. Just fill out a form with your name, email address, and job criteria, and P. J. Scout sends you descriptions of job

★★★

and P. J. Scout sends you descriptions of job opportunities you might be interested in.

WORLD WIDE WEB
`URL` http://www.nationjob.com

Online Career Center

This well-designed site is a not-for-profit cooperative that provides career counseling and a growing database of about 8,000 jobs and resumes. Thousands of private and public institutions list their job openings with the Online Career Center. (Those companies wishing to post their jobs should visit the site for subscription rates.) Participating employers include giants like AT&T, Bank of America, Eastman Kodak, Kraft, Unisys, and the CIA, and smaller concerns like the Akron Public School System. The job openings range from trading-room support on Wall Street to emergency-room nurses in Ohio to marketing executives in Zurich. In addition to the large number of entry-level positions for the Net-savvy college crowd, the OCC lists opportunities for experienced professionals. Both job listings and resume banks are searchable. OCC also offers articles on employment-related topics such as choosing a career or understanding what to expect from professional career advisors. You can even access a calendar of local offline career fairs and professional conventions at OCC. If job searching is on your agenda, then OCC's address should definitely be one of your bookmarks.

WORLD WIDE WEB
`URL` http://www.occ.com/occ

Virtual Job Fair

Fancy graphics, good organization, and high-quality information make the Virtual Job Fair a must-see site for job seekers. Currently 400 U.S. companies list over 9,000 job opportunities at the page, and over half of them are in the computer industry. This searchable database of job listings is updated every month. There's also a Resume Center that helps candidates create a password-protected resume; if a company is interested in a resume, the candidate is contacted through the site, ensuring complete confidentiality. The site is also closely associated with the magazine *High Technology Careers*, and it offers a link to the full text of the publication. Rounding out the Virtual Job Fair is a collection of links to other employment-related job sites.

★★★★★

WORLD WIDE WEB

`URL` http://www.careerexpo.com

Indexes

Best Bets on the Net

Best Bets weeds the Net's garden and leaves only the flowers standing. For four different fields—Education & Academe, Humanities & Social Sciences, Science & Technology, and Business & Government—the page offers its choices for the best sites on the Net. And if that weren't enough, it also features a detailed description of each job site and provides a link to it. If it has to do with

★★★★

finding a job on the Net, it's a good bet you'll
find it here.

WORLD WIDE WEB
`URL` http://asa.ugl.lib.umich.edu/chdocs/employment

CareerNet

Although the site offers hundreds of links, its
greatest asset is its clear and easy access to the federal job boards in each state.

★★

WORLD WIDE WEB
`URL` http://www.careers.org

The Catapult

Links to over 400 career and job-related resources
on the Net.

★★★

WORLD WIDE WEB
`URL` http://www.jobweb.org/catapult/catapult.htm

Employment Resources on the Internet

Steve Lodin, the site's creator, has penned an essay
on finding jobs on the Net and assembled a collection of job links that is astounding in its size
and reach. Everything from the Career Shop to
uk.jobs.wanted has a link to the page. Hats off to
Steve!

★★★★

WORLD WIDE WEB
`URL` http://www.cs.purdue.edu/homes/swlodin/jobs.html

Job Link

The creators of this site have done more than
organize resume databases and collect a massive
number of job-related links; they've annotated
them to assist in narrowing your search. Job
Finders is also one of the best gateways to infor-

★★★

mation on colleges and universities in the U.S.
and throughout the world.

WORLD WIDE WEB
`URL` http://infonext.nrl.navy.mil/job.html

Job Hunt

A cavalcade of job links all under one roof. The
first section of the site organizes its links into
three categories: Academia; General; and Science,
Engineering, and Medicine. For those shopping
for a job by location, Job Hunt collects links to
the help-wanted sections from eight major newspapers (the *Philadelphia Inquirer*, *San Jose Mercury
News*, *Boston Globe*, and *Chicago Tribune* are
among them). Hundreds of recruiting agencies
online can be reached from this page via the links
in the Recruiting Agencies topic. Job seekers who
know the company they want to work for can
check the company's latest job listings using the
links in the Companies section; those looking for
any kind of job in any state in the nation can
look under the Newsgroup section which features
links to misc.jobs.offered, misc.jobs.misc, and
misc.jobs.offered.entry. Links to resume banks
and other meta job lists round out this incredible
employment page.

★★★★

WORLD WIDE WEB
`URL` http://rescomp.stanford.edu/jobs

Job Opportunities

Another access ramp to the major employment
services and large academic and government job
databases. Link to listings from major employers
like Oak Ridge National Laboratory, the Library
of Congress, and Integrated Computer Solutions,
or connect to E-Span, the Online Career Center,

★★

or connect to E-Span, the Online Career Center, and other national job databases.

WORLD WIDE WEB

`URL` http://ageninfo.tamu.edu/jobs.html

Riley Guide

The grandmother of resources for job seekers, whose full title is actually Employment Opportunities and Job Resources on the Internet, is affectionately known as the Riley Guide. This index of links breaks down the Net's copious job offerings into easy-to-use categories like Academe Jobs, Engineering Jobs, Social Sciences Jobs, Resources for Jobs in Each State of the U.S., Resources for Jobs in Canada, and Career Planning Services and Resources. The Guide is easily one of the best collections of job links in Cyberspace.

★★★★

WORLD WIDE WEB

`URL` http://www.jobtrak.com/jobguide.html

The Virtual Press

The Virtual Press links to general job boards, recruiters, job databases, and regional job resources. If you're just starting a job search, it can be a great launching pad.

★★★

WORLD WIDE WEB

`URL` http://tvp.com/vpjic.html

Pounding the Cyberpavement

I'm ready to begin the search. I guess I should be checking the Sunday paper for jobs.

Don't bother. Print classifieds are for yesterday's job seeker. Every newspaper that means anything (the *Chicago Tribune*, the *Los Angeles Times*, *The New York Times*) is now on the Net, and the online world works a futuristic magic with the antiquated job listings. First of all, job data can be isolated, sorted, and sifted with powerful search engines; if you're looking to be a doctor in DeKalb or a programmer in Peoria, you can hone in on only the relevant listings. But online classifieds go beyond newspapers. With the network of newsgroups, commercial services, industry-specific home pages, and large online career centers, the Net has collected huge sets of job listings all its own. You won't find them in your local daily. You won't find them in national magazines. You won't find them in the trade papers. You'll only find them online.

Across the Nation

America's Help Wanted

Thousands of jobs are posted here by hundreds of employers nationwide. Search the database and see if any company in America wants your help.

★★

WORLD WIDE WEB
`URL` http://www.jobquest.com

America's Job Board

With its links to the Employment Services of all 50 states, this board offers a job database of close to 250,000 listings. There is no cost either to the job seekers or employers who utilize this service (America's Job Board is funded through the Unemployment Insurance taxes paid by employers). Those looking for work can choose to browse the listings under the Military Specialty, Job Code, or Federal Opportunities sections; or they can execute a self-directed search by choosing from a detailed menu of job criteria (industry, title, location). America's Job Board also maintains links to the job boards of about 100 companies from ADEPT, Inc. to Zeitech, Inc.

★★★

WORLD WIDE WEB
`URL` http://www.ajb.dni.us

biz.jobs.offered

Scanning the job listings on this newsgroup almost makes you want to sing "Yankee Doodle Dandy"—thousands of openings in just about every state in the Union are posted here, including openings for network developers, programmers, engineers, technical writers, and clinical applications specialists. There's so much job

★★★★

action that professional recruiters often post here hoping to pick up business. Post your own job listing, look for a job, and get into the fray.

USENET
biz.jobs.offered

CareerPath.com

After filling out a brief registration form, you'll be able to search the help-wanted section of 14 major dailies around the country, including the *Boston Globe*, the *Chicago Tribune*, the *Los Angeles Times*, *The New York Times*, the *San Jose Mercury News*, and *The Washington Post*. You'll be thankful for the site's powerful search engine—the page carries an average of 110,000 job listings per week!

WORLD WIDE WEB
URL http://www.careerpath.com

The Classifieds

★★★★★

Think about it. How large would a newspaper classifieds section be if it contained over 6,000 detailed descriptions of jobs in over 25 fields? Too heavy to carry with you on the subway in the morning! But thanks to The Classifieds on America Online, you don't need to worry about managing a mountain of paper. The listings are neatly organized by job field. Of course, the Computers section contains the most listings, but even a lesser Cyberspace-related occupation like mechanic has close to 100 ads. So stand back *New York Times*, *Chicago Tribune*, and *Los Angeles Times*, The Classifieds is here and bigger than all of 'ya put together!

AMERICA ONLINE
Keyword classifieds→Employment Ads→Employment Classified Board

D.I.C.E. National Network

BBS

This California-based BBS has a good selection of contract and permanent jobs, mostly within the computer industry.

★★

BBS
408-737-9339

Help Wanted USA

Large California hospital seeks transplant specialists. Small Wisconsin company seeks accountants. Brooklyn school department seeks teacher to work with AIDS children. This database claims up to 4,000+ job listings each week, collected by private consultants nationwide, and while there aren't always jobs listed in Arkansas (sorry, Bill), larger states are usually well represented. Broader in appeal than the job newsgroups, this database offers a good selection of computer-related jobs, along with large numbers of medical, social service, and business positions. Search the database by specific terms (obstetrics RN) or by general terms (sales and marketing). Updated every Wednesday.

★★★

AMERICA ONLINE
Keyword help wanted

Internet Employment Network

A somewhat limited resource with a few listings for jobs in around 60 different fields. The most valuable resources here are the capsule descriptions of each company that posts a listing.

★★

GOPHER
URL gopher://gopher.msen.com/11/vendor/napa

The Job Board

Warning: check into the Rules and Suggestions section of this site before responding to any of the job descriptions posted here—the people who run the board state very clearly that the volume of responses they receive is too high to bother with any that cause processing problems. So get with the program and make yourself a candidate for any of the hundreds of job openings (mostly computer related) posted here. The service collects resumes and cover letters and then reports back to you if anyone's interested.

WORLD WIDE WEB
`URL` http://www.io.org/~jwsmith/jobs.html

JOBBS!

Send your resume to sysop Bill Griffin and he'll add it to his database of 30,000+ candidates. The system also provides information on employers, companies, applicants, and career lifestyles.

BBS
770-992-8937

misc.jobs.misc/misc.jobs

Many, many, many jobs are advertised on these newsgroups, and for a change, some of them are not computer related. A company in California is currently looking for entrepreneurs to distribute its line of sunglasses; home health care workers are urgently needed in Utah; and telemarketers are sought to work in Kansas. There are also plenty of keyboard jobs for computer-minded personnel.

USENET
misc.jobs.misc • misc.jobs

misc.jobs.offered

Are 5,000 opportunities enough for you? There is frequent discussion on the Net about splitting this unwieldy newsgroup because of its volume. But if you're seeking a job in the computer industry, misc.jobs.offered provides the most bang for the buck, assuming you can make your way through the huge number of listings. Large corporations and start-up firms post their needs here for systems managers, programmers, and analysts. Outside the computer industry, pickings are slimmer—lots of opportunities, of course, to become a millionaire through telemarketing.

★★★★★

USENET
misc.jobs.offered

misc.jobs.resumes

Thousands of people a week post their occupational profiles on this newsgroup. The trick to success is undoubtedly making yourself stand out among all the other programmers and engineers. "Willing to relocate," "Japanese bilingual," or "MARKETING" catch the eye. You'll find a great variety of job skills here—from aquaculturists and actuaries to wireless tech engineers and semiconductor specialists. Potential employers respond privately.

★★★★

USENET
misc.jobs.resumes

GRAD SEEKS JOB

By Aaron Weiss

Reprinted with permission from *Internet World,* September 1996.
Copyright © 1996 Mecklermedia Corp.

It's soon after graduation, and the party's over — literally. You've got whatever money wasn't spent on beaujolais and kazoos to live on — that's about eight minutes' worth. You need a job. Fortunately, there are many folks out there who would like to give you one. Unfortunately, they don't know who or where you are. But today there are electronic forums through which you can shout to the employers of the world, "Here I am, a graduate full of spunk and vinegar! Hire me!" And if grovelling like that doesn't work, you can even send them a résumé.

The first stop on our tour of job-hunting sites for shiny new grads is JobDirect (**www.jobdirect.com**). As with most of the job-search sites on the Net, the ambition of this service is to pair up hungry employers with even hungrier employees. JobDirect is oriented towards matching companies that recruit soon-to-be graduate students with applicants.

If you're a student in want of work, you first enter JobDirect's Student Zone, where you register and receive a log-in name. Once logged in, the site walks you step-by-step through a résumé template wherein all relevant details of your accomplishments and achievements are stored. The résumé writing process is fairly detailed. Not only do you put in the typical content, but you are asked to select areas of interest and applicable "keywords" that describe yourself.

All of this is intended to facilitate searches and match you up with compatible employers. You can have the site send you e-mail when a new job posting matches your résumé, or an employer can e-mail you directly if your résumé catches their eye. The site also allows you to edit your résumé at any time, or search through the job database on criteria you specify, whether or not they match your personal résumé. All these services are entirely free for the student job-hunter (the service charges the employers).

That said, there are some deficiencies of JobDirect. First, there is no way to browse the entire job database. While many applicants may enjoy having JobDirect select positions matching specified criteria, some users might prefer the old-fashioned method of reading every job listing themselves.

Second, the job postings in the JobDirect database are heavily skewed towards computing and technology positions. Someone looking to be a reference librarian, for instance, is less likely to find success here than someone interested in programming network communications. This technological bias applies to most of the Internet-based job-hunting services, but it's still worth a few minutes to put your résumé into as many databases as possible, whatever the field of interest (especially when it costs nothing).

Less personalized but more comprehensive than JobDirect is JobWeb (**www.jobweb.org**). This site, maintained by the National Association of Colleges and Employers, contains thousands of postings and almost 50 links to additional career-related information. Unlike JobDirect, JobWeb does not offer users the chance to enter their own résumé information. Rather, you only can search the job database via descriptive keywords and geographic location. But there are many job postings to be found here, and the keyword search is flexible, allowing for complex searches using Boolean operators ("and," "or," "not," etc.).

Also sporting flexible Boolean searches — plus a gaggle of other features — is the graphics-heavy CareerMosaic (**www.careermosaic.com**). Here, you can perform the typical search of job listings using keywords, and according to additional criteria such as geographic location. There are a variety of job sites in CareerMosaic's listings, but again they are biased towards fields related to technology.

A number of Usenet newsgroups also carry job postings (which we'll look at shortly), and CareerMosaic offers one-stop shopping to search all of its current Usenet postings. You can enter your résumé into CareerMosaic's "Resume-CM" service, and it will be posted automatically to newsgroups in which employers are most likely to scout out provective prodigies. This well-rounded site is entirely free and is certainly worth a few clicks of your time.

Similar to CareerMosaic is a job search site called E-Span (**www.espan.com**). It also offers flexible keyword searches of its listings in the CareerPro MasterFile Database as well as the opportunity to post your résumé to the ResumePro Database. E-Span suggests matches between your résumé and available positions. A passcode lets you edit your résumé to keep it current or delete it.

Yet another comprehensive employment service is Jobtrak (**www.jobtrak.com**). With a claimed 2,000-plus new listings per day, Jobtrak offers résumé and keyword-search services similar to the previously described sites. The difference is that Jobtrak listings — although free to access — are restricted to students or alumni of universities, and you need to use a password to view the listings. Generally, university career centers can tell you the Jobtrak password for your school.

JobCenter (**www.jobcenter.com**) also offers keyword searches of job listings and résumé posting facilities ($20 for 6 months). JobCenter can e-mail you anytime a new job listing appears that matches your criteria.

IntelliMatch (**www.intellimatch.com**) is another service designed to match résumés with employers. To make best use of it, you must complete a detailed résumé — a standardized form that a number of employers have agreed to review via IntelliMatch service. Most of the employers are technology- and business-related firms, and this free service is worth a shot for anyone interested in those fields. Unlike JobDirect, you can browse all available postings on IntelliMatch without filling out the résumé.

As mentioned earlier, there are a number of newsgroups in which employers routinely post help wanted ads. In fact, there are so many of them that listing them all here is not feasible. Some of them — such as **biz.jobs.offered** (business-related jobs), **comp.jobs**, and **comp.jobs.offered** (computer-related jobs) — cover general fields of interest. Most of the newsgroups are regional — such as **alabama.jobs**, **can.jobs** (Canada), **houston.jobs**, **nyc.jobs**, and so forth. Thus, you can either use your newsreader to search for all newsgroups with "jobs" in their name or check within the hierarchies of your field of interest or region.

For an overview of job-related newsgroups, check the listing at **www.collegegrad.com/jobs/usenet.html**. Of course, with so many groups, sifting through the list can be quite a pain on the eyes, nerves, and backside. Fortunately, there are several Web sites that regularly index the contents of many job newsgroups. They allow you to conduct quick keyword searches through a multitude of postings.

Besides the already-mentioned CarreerMosaic, this type of newgroup searching is offered by the Monster Board Newsgroup Search (**www1.monster.com/b/search/func=news**). Career Magazine (**www.careermag.com/careermag/news/**)

offers the most detailed keyword search, allowing queries by location, skills, and job title.

Here's a novel idea: Compile want ads from newspapers across the United States. CareerPath.com (**www.careerpath.com**) has already thought of this, and that's exactly what it offers. Want ads are selected from nine city newspapers, including the *Boston Globe*, *Chicago Tribune*, *New York Times*, and *Washington Post*. You select fields of employment and newspapers to search, and voilà! Although you have to register on the main page to gain search access, registration is free.

JobNet (**www.westga.edu/~coop/**) is a potpourri of job postings collected from the nooks and crannies of the Internet. It's not necessarily the cleanest, best-organized, or most comprehensive job site, but if you like the idea of finding postings that may not have appeared on all the big-name sites, JobNet may be worth a look. The job postings are mostly managerial positions, and a variety of employees — from hospitals to

computer firms — post here. There also is a link to a listing of free services on the Internet where you can post a résumé.

Another mixed bag of job-hunting resources, especially résumé distribution , is the Web-based magazine Tripod (**www.tripod.com**). In its "Work & Money" section is a subsection called "Services" where you can find career counseling, internships, and most notably, a résumé builder and distributor.

Also chock full of advice, job links, and some postings for new jobseeking graduates is College Grad Job Hunter at **www.collegegrad.com**. Although it has a few links to mostly technology-oriented job postings, this site mainly offers suggestions for new grads, such as not to wear nose rings to an interview. This is a good place to get an overview of what the employers look for, and it provides links to more detailed job-posting sites oriented towards students.

Some job hunters have a set goal and know which company or companies they

Job Direct — http://www.jobdirect.com

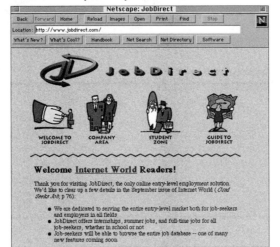

want to work for. College Grad Job Hunter and Tripod assume a college grad is looking for an open position with any company.

Most of the job hunting sites already mentioned offer links to the Web pages of employers participating in the service. For example, on CareerMosaic's main page you can click on a link entitled Employers that brings up a large list of participating firms. Clicking on any one of these will take you to that company's Web site, where you can often find the company's own listings of available positions. This is a good strategy for keeping an eye on openings at particular companies.

Like any employment service, Internet-based job resources don't guarantee you'll find instant and fulfilling employment. However, they do make it easier to sift through pages of openings and to distribute résumés far and wide. And there have been an increasing number of reports of the success of these online services. So give it a shot. It only can only increase your visibility and chances.

Aaron Weiss is a freelance writer based in Canada.

This material originally appeared in *Internet World* magazine, Volume 7, Number 9, September 1996, pp. 76-79. Copyright© 1996 Mecklermedia Corporation, 20 Ketchum Street, Westport, CT 06880; 203-341-2802; info@mecklermedia.com; http://www.iworld.com.

Job-Hunting Resources for New Graduates

MAILING LISTS

CARE
For job issues
To: majordomo@igc.org
Body: info care

Career-Forum
For the discussion of job-search anecdotes
To: majordomo@cedar.cic.net
Body: info career-forum

JobPlace
Self-directed job search techniques and placement issues
To: listserv@news.jobweb.org
Body: info jobplace

USENET NEWSGROUPS WITH JOB LISTINGS
ab.jobs
alt.jobs
atl.jobs
au.jobs
austin.jobs
az.jobs
ba.jobs
ba.jobs.contract
ba.jobs.direct
ba.jobs.misc
ba.jobs.offered

ba.jobs.resumes
balt.jobs
bc.jobs
bermuda.jobs.offered
bionet.jobs
bln.jobs
can.jobs
cit.jobs
cle.jobs
cmh.jobs
comp.jobs
comp.jobs.offered
conn.jobs.offered
cv.jobs
dc.jobs
dfw.jobs
dod.jobs
eunet.jobs
euro.jobs
geoinfonet.job-market
hepnet.jobs
houston.jobs.offered
hsv.jobs
in.jobs
la.jobs
mi.jobs
milw.jobs
misc.jobs
misc.jobs.misc
misc.jobs.offered
misc.jobs.resumes

nb.jobs
ne.jobs
nm.jobs
nv.jobs
nyc.jobs.offered
oh.jobs
ont.jobs
osu.jobs
ott.jobs
pdaxs.jobs.computers
pdaxs.jobs.resumes
pgh.jobs.offered
phl.jobs.offered
qc.jobs
relcom.commerce.jobs
sat.jobs
sdnet.jobs
seattle.jobs.offered
stl.jobs
su.jobs
sudbury.jobs
swnet.jobs
telemail.gte.jobsd
tnn.jobs
tor.jobs
triangle.jobs
tx.jobs
uiuc.misc.jobs
us.jobs.contract
us.jobs.resumes
utah.jobs

Source: *Internet World*, September 1996

JOB WEB SITES FOR COMPANIES LISTED IN THIS BOOK

3Com Corporation
http://www.3com.com:80/0files/jobs/index.html
7th Level, Inc.
http://dallas009.7thlevel.com:80/sevlinfo/personnel
Abbott Laboratories
http://www.jobweb.org/employer/abbott.htm
Access Health, Inc. http://www.access-
Health.com/employ/hr2.htm
Active Voice Corporation
http://www.activevoice.com/avhome/aboutav/jobop.htm
Adaptec, Inc. http://www.adaptec.com/hr/hr_main.html
ADC Telecommunications, Inc. http://www.ps-
mpls.com/ADC/CORP_DIR.html#employment
Addison-Wesley Longman/Penguin http://www.aw.com/hrd
Adobe Systems Incorporated
http://www.adobe.com/JOBS.html
ADTRAN, Inc. http://www.adtran.com/employ.html
Advanced Engineering & Research Associates, Inc.
http://www.aera.com/jobs.htm
Advanced Micro Devices, Inc.
http://www.careermosaic.com/cm/amd/amd3.html
Aetna Inc. http://www.aetna.com/opp.htm
A.G. Edwards, Inc.
http://www.agedwards.com/aboutage/jobopps.htm
Ag Services of America, Inc.
http://www.agservices.com/work.html
Air Products and Chemicals, Inc.
http://www.airproducts.com/employ/emplinfo.html
ALLTEL Corporation
http://www.is.alltel.com/opportun.html
Altera Corporation
http://www.altera.com/html/hr/employ.html
Amdahl Corporation
http://www.amdahl.com/doc/employment
American International Group, Inc.
http://www.aig.com/career/Careers.html
American Management Systems, Incorporated
http://www.amsinc.com/career/career.htm
American Power Conversion Corporation
http://www.apcc.com/jobopps.htm
AmeriData Technologies, Inc.
http://www.ameridata.com/info/jobs.3.html
Ames Department Stores, Inc.
http://www.http://205.161.53.12/hiring.html
Amgen Inc. http://www.bio.com/hr/job/amgen_1.html
Amoco Corporation
http://www.amoco.com/what_we_do/ss/hr/
job_listings/index.html
AMP Incorporated http://www.amp.com/jobs/jobs.html
AMR Corporation http://www.americanair.
com/aa_home/aa_hr/a_wide_ variety.html
Amway Corporation
http://www.amway.com/amway/opportun/
Analog Devices, Inc.
http://www.analog.com/about/jobops/jobops.html
Analysts International Corporation
http://www.analysts.com/jobs/index.html

Andersen Consulting
http://www.ac.com/careers/c_frcareer_1.html
Andersen Worldwide
http://www.arthurandersen.com/firmwide/recruit/cl0.htm
Andrew Corporation http://www.andrew.com/hrsg0001.htm
Anixter International Inc.
http://www.anixter.com/career.html
Aon Corporation
http://www.aon.com/aon/employment/hrjobs.html
APAC TeleServices, Inc. http://www.http://job.apac.com
A+ Network, Inc. http://www.aplsnet.com/jobs.htm
Apple Computer, Inc.
http://www.http://www2.apple.com/employment/default.html
Applied Materials, Inc.
http://www.appliedmaterials.com/html3/employment/index.
html
ARAMARK Corporation http://www.aramark-uniform.com/
employment/
Archer-Daniels-Midland Company
http://www.jobweb.org/employer/archer-b.htm
Ariel Corporation http://www.ariel.com/jobs.htp
Armstrong World Industries, Inc.
http://www.armstrong.com/company/employment.html
Arris Pharmaceutical Corporation
http://www.arris.com/Career_Opps/Career_Opportunities
Ascend Communications, Inc.
http://www.ascend.com/aboutascend/jobs/jobsindex.html
Aspen Technology, Inc.
http://www.aspentec.com/~aspentec/jobs
AT&T Corp. http://www.careermosaic.com/cm/att/att6.html
Atmel Corporation
http://www.atmel.com/atmel/career/career1.html
Attachmate Corporation
http://www.atm.com/corpinfo/cooljob/cooljob1.htm
Automatic Data Processing, Inc.
http://www.careermosaic.com/cm/adp/adp4.html
AutoZone, Inc. http://www.autozone.com/hr/index.html
Avant! Corporation http://www.avanticorp.com/employ.html
Ball Corporation
http://www.ball.com/aerospace/jobhome.html
Bally Total Fitness Holding Corporation
http://www.ballyfitness.com/employment.html
Banc One Corporation http://www.bankone.com/careernet
BankBoston Corporation
http://www.http://helpwanted.com/company/bkb/bkbhp.htm
Bankers Trust New York Corporation
http://www.bankerstrust.com/hr/hr.html
Barnett Banks, Inc. http://www.barnett.com/jobs.htm
Baxter International Inc.
http://www.jobweb.org/employer/baxter.htm
Bay Networks, Inc.
http://www.baynetworks.com/Corporate/Employment
BBN Corporation http://www.bbn.com/bbnjobs/jobsrch.htm
BDM International, Inc.
http://www.bdm.com:80/bdm/l1_car.htm
BellSouth Corporation
http://www.bst.bls.com/java/jemployment-main.html

Boatmen's Bancshares, Inc.
http://www.nationjob.com/boatmen
The Boeing Company http://www.nationjob.com/boeing
Booz, Allen & Hamilton Inc.
http://www.bah.com/shared/careers.html
Boston Technology, Inc.
http://www.bostontechnology.com/employ.htm
Brite Voice Systems, Inc.
http://www.brite.com/html/netscape/employ.html
Broderbund Software, Inc.
http://www.broder.com/company/jobs.html
BTG, Inc. http://www.btg.com/jobs
BTU International, Inc. http://www.btu.com/career.htm
Burlington Coat Factory Warehouse Corporation
http://www.coat.com/jobs.html
Burlington Industries, Inc.
http://www.jobweb.org/employer/burlingt.htm
Cabletron Systems, Inc. http://www.cabletron.com/jobs
Cadence Design Systems, Inc.
http://www.cadence.com/employment.html
Caliber System, Inc.
http://www.calibersys.com/technlgy/employ.htm
Cambridge Technology Partners, Inc.
http://www.ctp.com/EmployOpp
Cargill, Incorporated http://www.cargill.com/
cgi-bin/htimage/images/s0.map?414,109
Carpenter Technology Corporation
http://www.cartech.com/comp05.htm
Cascade Communications Corp.
http://www.casc.com/employment/index.html
Caterpillar Inc.
http://www.caterpillar.com/envision/opport.htm
Ceridian Corporation
http://www.ceridian.com/ar_index.html
Chrysler Corporation http://www.occ.com/chrysler
The Chubb Corporation http://www.chubb.com/hr.html
CIBER, Inc. http://www.occ.com/ciber
Cincinnati Bell Inc. http://www.occ.com/cbis
Circuit City Stores, Inc. http://www.occ.com/circuit
Cirrus Logic, Inc. http://www.cirrus.com/career
Cisco Systems, Inc.
http://www.cisco.com/public/employment.html
CKS Group, Inc. http://www.cks.com/connect/507.html
Claremont Technology Group, Inc.
http://www.clrmnt.com/Employment/index.html
Comerica Incorporated
http://www.jobweb.org/employer/comerica.htm
Compaq Computer Corporation
http://www.monster.com/companies/Compaq.html
Computer Associates International, Inc.
http://www.cai.com/img/mainmenu.conf?113,303
Computer Horizons Corporation http://www.occ.com/chc
Computer Sciences Corporation
http://www.csc.com/career.html
Computer Task Group, Incorporated
http://www.ctg.com:80/nuxcarer.htm
Compuware Corporation http://www.occ.com/compuware
ConAgra, Inc. http://www.occ.com/conagra
The Continuum Company, Inc.
http://www.http://world.hire.com/
continuum/jobindex.html
Coopers & Lybrand L.L.P.
http://www.colybrand.com/clwww30.html

Cummins Engine Company, Inc.
http://www.occ.com/cummins
Cypress Semiconductor Corporation
http://www.careermosaic.com:80/
cm/cypress/cypress2.html
Cyrix Corporation http://www.cyrix.com/hr/hrhp.htm
Dallas Semiconductor Corporation
http://www.dalsemi.com/HR/index.html
Data General Corporation
http://www.dg.com/info/jobs.html
Data Translation, Inc. http://www.datx.com/datxjobs.html
Datastream Systems, Inc.
http://www.dstm.com/pages/employ.htm
Davidson & Associates, Inc.
http://www.Davd.Com/jobs/jobs.html
Dayton Hudson Corporation
http://www.careermag.com/employers/mervyns/index.html
Dell Computer Corporation
http://www.careermosaic.com/cm/dell/dell3.html
Deloitte Touche Tohmatsu International
http://www.dttus.com/dttus/hr/dthr1.htm
Diebold, Incorporated http://www.occ.com/diebold
Digital Equipment Corporation
http://www.digital.com:80/.i/info/careers
The Dow Chemical Company
http://www.dow.com:80/recruit/index.html
Dow Jones & Company, Inc. http://www.wsj.com/careers
DSC Communications Corporation
http://www.dsccc.com/job.htm
The Dun & Bradstreet Corporation
http://www.careermosaic.com/cm/dnb
DynCorp http://www.dyncorp.com/jobs.htm
Eastman Chemical Company
http://www.eastman.com/hr/index.shtml
Eastman Kodak Company
http://www.kodak.com/aboutKodak/corpInfo/employment
Ops/employmentOps.shtml
Eaton Corporation
http://www.jobweb.org/employer/eaton.htm
Edify Corporation
http://www.edify.com/edify/jobs/jobs.htm
Edison International
http://www.edisonx.com/html/news/jobs/jobs.htm
Elcom International, Inc.
http://www.elcom.com/elcintad.htm
Electronic Arts Inc. http://www.ea.com/topten.html
Electronic Data Systems Corporation
http://www.eds.com/careers/ejc00000.html
Eli Lilly and Company
http://www.lilly.com/career/index.html
Entergy Corporation
http://www.careermosaic.com/cm/entergy/e2.html
Enterprise Rent-A-Car http://www.erac.com/joblist.html
EPIC Design Technology, Inc.
http://www.epic.com/products.html
Ernst & Young LLP http://www.ey.com/EYI/CAREER.HTM
Essex Corporation http://www.essexcorp.com/jobs.htm
Ethan Allen Interiors Inc.
http://www.ethanallen.com/adspecial.html
Excalibur Technologies Corporation
http://www.excalib.com/jobs.html
Exide Electronics Group, Inc.
http://www.careermag.com/employers/exide/index.html

Federated Department Stores, Inc.
http://www.careermag.com/employers/macys/index.html
Fifth Third Bancorp http://www.53.com/bancorp/hr/jobs
Finlay Enterprises, Inc.
http://www.helpwanted.com/hwdocs/company/finlay
/jobs/ffjchp.htm
First Union Corporation
http://www.firstunion.com/careers/careers.html
First USA, Inc. http://www.careermosaic.com/cm/first-
usa/first4.html
FMC Corporation
http://www.fmc.com/Career/careerHome.html
FMR Corp.
http://www.http://helpwanted.com/hwdocs/company/fidelit
y/jobs/fideljob.html
Ford Motor Company http://www.ford.com/careercenter
FORE Systems, Inc.
http://www.fore.com/html/hr/index.html
Forte Software, Inc.
http://www.forte.com/forte/coinfo/jobs/employment.html
Fritz Companies, Inc.
http://www.fritz.com/hr/position/position.htm
FTP Software, Inc. http://www.ftp.com/hr/index.html
Funco, Inc. http://www.funcoland.com/fyi.html
Fusion Systems Corporation
http://www.fusn.com/fusn_job.htm
Gateway 2000, Inc.
http://www.gw2k.com/employ/employ.htm
General Dynamics Corporation http://www.occ.com/gdls
General Electric Company
http://www.careermosaic.com/cm/ge/ge1.html
General Instrument Corporation
http://www.gi.com/employ/employ.htm
General Magic, Inc. http://www.genmagic.com/extjob.html
General Mills, Inc. http://www.http://jobs.genmills.com
General Motors Corporation
http://www.gm.com/edu_rel/careers/career.htm
Genome Therapeutics Corporation
http://www.cric.com/htdocs/corporate/jobs/index.html
Gensym Corporation
http://www.gensym.com/companycontacts/contactpeople.
html
Glenayre Technologies, Inc.
http://www.glenayre.com/jobs.html
Global Village Communication, Inc.
http://www.globalvillag.com/joblist.html
The Goldman Sachs Group, L.P.
http://www.gs.com/recruiting
The Good Guys, Inc.
http://www.thegoodguys.com/General/Employ.html
GPU Inc. http://www.gpu.com/cgi-bin/jobs_index.pl
Granite Broadcasting Corporation http://www.k-
eyetv.com/info/jobs.html
Great Lakes Chemical Corporation
http://www.jobweb.org/employer/great_la.htm
Greyhound Lines, Inc.
http://www.greyhound.com/jobs.html
Group Health Cooperative of Puget Sound
http://www.ghc.org/about_gh/employ/hr_ads.html
GTE Corporation
http://www.gte.com/Working/working.html
Hallmark Cards, Inc. http://www.occ.com/hallmark

HarperCollins Publishers, Inc.
http://www.harpercollins.com/jobopps.htm
Harris Corporation http://www.harris.com/employment
H. E. Butt Grocery Company
http://www.http://hookem.com/htm/ads/heb/jobs.htm
Hewlett-Packard Company http://www.jobs.hp.com
Hillenbrand Industries, Inc. http://www.occ.com/hillrom
Hyperion Software Corporation
http://www.hysoft.com:80/career/career.html
ICF Kaiser International, Inc.
http://www.icfkaiser.com/icfpage/ICFJOBS.htm
Information Storage Devices, Inc.
http://www.isd.com/jobs.html
Informix Corporation
http://www.informix.com/informix/corpinfo/inside/hr/
jobs.htm
Infoseek Corporation
http://www.infoseek.com/doc/Jobs.html
Integrated Device Technology, Inc.
http://www.idt.com/jobs.html
Integrated Systems, Inc.
http://www.isi.com/Latest/JobOpenings.html
Intel Corporation
http://www.careermosaic.com/cm/intel/intel11.html
International Business Machines Corporation
http://www.empl.ibm.com
International Data Group
http://www.idg.com/welcome/jobs/jobs.html
International Rectifier Corporation
http://www.irf.com/~ir/career
Intuit Inc. http://www.intuit.com/int-human-resources/
career-opportunities/index.html
Iomega Corporation
http://www.careermosaic.com/cm/iomega/i5.html
Itron, Inc. http://www.itron.com/career.html
ITT Corporation http://www.espan.com/spot/itt/itt.html
J. C. Penney Company, Inc.
http://www.jcpenney.com/careers/woo
J.D. Edwards & Company
http://www.jdedwards.com/career/index.htm
John H. Harland Company
http://www.careermag.com/employers/jharland/index.html
Johnson & Johnson
http://www.jnj.com/recruit/recruit.htm
Johnson Controls, Inc. http://www.jci.com/bg/employ.htm
J.P. Morgan & Co. Incorporated
http://www.jpmorgan.com/CorpInfo/Careers/Home_Page.
html
Keane, Inc. http://www.keane.com/careers
KEMET Corporation http://www.kemet.com/corp/jobs.htm
Kimball International, Inc.
http://www.jobweb.org/employer/kimball.htm
KLA Instruments Corporation
http://www.http://hrweb.kla.com/empl/employ.htm
Koch Industries, Inc. http://www.nationjob.com/koch
KPMG Peat Marwick LLP http://www.us.kpmg.com/career
The Kroger Co.
http://www.foodcoop.com:80/Kroger/kc/co.html
Kulicke and Soffa Industries, Inc.
http://www.occ.com/kands
Lear Corporation http://www.lear.com/recruit
Lockheed Martin Corporation
http://www.lockheed.com/jobs.html

Logicon, Inc. http://www.logicon.com/employ.html
Long John Silver's Restaurants, Inc.
http://www.jobweb.org/employer/ljsilver.htm
Loronix Information Systems, Inc.
http://www.http://loronix.com/company/jobs.html
Louisiana-Pacific Corporation
http://www.lpx.com/jobs.html
Lowe's Companies, Inc.
http://www.lowes.com:80/empopps
LucasArts Entertainment Company
http://www.lucasarts.com/pages/TopIndexJobDescription.
main.html
Lucent Technologies Inc.
http://www.att.com/gbcs/employment
Manugistics Group, Inc.
http://www.manugistics.com/html/career.html
MAPCO Inc. http://www.mapcoinc.com/employ.html
MapInfo Corporation http://www.occ.com/mapinfo
Massachusetts Mutual Life Insurance Company
http://www.massmutual.com/viewtop/ifmar1.html
Mattson Technology, Inc.
http://www.mattson.com/jobs.htm
The May Department Stores Company
http://www.maycompany.com/College/index.html
Mayo Foundation http://www.mayo.edu/career/career.html
McAfee Associates, Inc.
http://www.mcafee.com/corp/jobs/jobs.html
MCI Communications Corporation
http://www.mci.com/about/jobs/home.shtml
McKee Foods Corporation
http://www.mckeefoods.com/jobs.html
Measurex Corporation
http://www.measurex.com/employ/employ.htm
Medtronic, Inc.
http://www.medtronic.com/public/medtronic/employment
Mellon Bank Corporation
http://www.mellon.com/brochure/EMPLOY.HTM
MEMC Electronic Materials, Inc.
http://www.memc.com/job.htm
Merck & Co., Inc. http://www.merck.com/careers
Metamor Technologies LTD
http://www.metamor.com/pages/jobs.htm
Microcom, Inc. http://www.microcom.com/jobs/jobs.htm
Micron Technology, Inc.
http://www.micron.com/mti/hr/hrcareer.html
Microsemi Corporation
http://www.microsemi.com/jobs.htm
Microsoft Corporation http://www.microsoft.com/Jobs
Milliken & Co.
http://www.jobweb.org/employer/millkn.htm
Millipore Corporation
http://www.millipore.com/corporate/hr/index.html
Modine Manufacturing Company
http://www.jobweb.org/employer/modine.htm
Molex Incorporated http://www.molex.com/jobs.html
Molten Metal Technology, Inc.
http://www.mmt.com/company/employ/emp1.htm
Mustang Software, Inc.
http://www.mustang.com/public/jobs/jobs.htm
Mylex Corporation http://www.mylex.com/careerop.htm
National Semiconductor Corporation
http://www.nsc.com/hr/index.html
National Steel Corporation
http://www.jobweb.org/employer/Natsteel.htm

Natural MicroSystems Corporation
http://www.nmss.com/nmsweb/jobs.htm
NETCOM On-Line Communication Services, Inc.
http://www.netcom.com/jobs
Netscape Communications Corporation
http://www.http://home.mcom.com/people/index.html
Nichols Research Corporation
http://www.nichols.com/cgi-bin/show_jobs.pl
NIKE, Inc.
http://www.careermag.com/employers/nike/index.html
Norfolk Southern Corporation http://www.occ.com/
cgi-bin/dfind?jobs.all:and:key:xnorfolkx
Northern Trust Corporation
http://www.ntrs.com/jobs/index.html
Novell, Inc. http://www.http://corp.novell.com/job
Oak Technology, Inc.
http://www.oaktech.com/employmt.html
Oracle Corporation
http://www.oracle.com/corporate/hr/html/index.html
Orbit Semiconductor, Inc.
http://www.orbitsemi.com/job.html
Orbital Sciences Corporation
http://www.cweb.com/orbital/welcome.html
Pacific Enterprises
http://www.pacent.com/class/emplops.html
Pacific Gas and Electric Company http://www.occ.com/pge
PacifiCare Health Systems, Inc.
http://www.phs.com/phs_hr/cgi-win/phs_hr.exe/all
Papa John's International, Inc.
http://www.iglou.com/pjpizza/career.html
Parametric Technology Corporation
http://www.ptc.com/hr/hr.htm
Paychex, Inc.
http://www.paychex.com/paychex/jobs/jobs.html
PCA International, Inc. http://www.pcam.com/hr-gen.htm
PeopleSoft, Inc. http://www.peoplesoft.com/jobs.htm
PETsMART, Inc.
http://www.petsmart.com/petsmart/jobs.htm
Philip Morris Companies Inc.
http://www.occ.com/occ/member/cppmusa.html
Pinnacle Micro, Inc.
http://www.pinnaclemicro.com/employ.html
Pinnacle Systems, Inc.
http://www.pinnaclesys.com./pinnacle/career.html
PRC Inc. http://www.prc.com/career.html
The Procter & Gamble Company
http://www.pg.com/index9.html
The Progressive Corporation http://www.auto-
insurance.com/employ1.htm
Proxima Corporation http://www.monster.com/proxima
The Prudential Insurance Company of America
http://www.prudential.com/career0.html
PSINet, Inc. http://www.psi.net/jobs.html
QUALCOMM Incorporated
http://www.qualcomm.com/HR/hr2.html
Quantum Corporation
http://www.quantum.com/hr/hr.html
Quarterdeck Corporation
http://www.http://arachnid.qdeck.com/jobs/
QuikTrip Corporation
http://www.nationjob.com:8080/news/progs/
compcat-qutr.html
Rainbow Technologies, Inc.
http://www.rnbo.com/HR.HTM

Raytheon Company http://www.raytheon.com/jobs.html
Read-Rite Corporation
http://www.readrite.com/aahtml/hr.htm
Revco D.S., Inc. http://www.revco.com/emp-op-main.htmld
The Reynolds and Reynolds Company
http://www.reyrey.com/employ.html
Reynolds Metals Company
http://www.rmc.com/employ.html
RJR Nabisco Holdings Corp.
http://www.nabisco.com/townhall/jobs
Rocket Science Games Inc.
http://www.rocketsci.com/jobops.html
Rockwell International Corporation
http://www.rockwell.com/rockwell/careers
R. R. Donnelley & Sons Company
http://www.careermag.com/employers/rrdon/index.html
RWD Technologies, Inc.
http://www.occ.com/occ/member/cprwd.html
Ryder System, Inc. http://www.http://ryder.inter.net/ryder/
html/employment.html
S3 Incorporated http://www.s3.com/corporate/jobs/
Salomon Inc http://www.salomon.com/recruit
SBC Communications Inc.
http://www.sbc.com/swbell/credits/jobs/opportunity.html
Scangraphics, Inc.
http://www.scangraphics.com/scang/employ.htm
Schlumberger Limited http://www.slb.com/recr/career-
page.html
Scientific-Atlanta, Inc. http://www.sciatl.com/D/b/index.html
Seagate Technology, Inc.
http://www.careermosaic.com/cm/seagate/seagate7.html
Sequent Computer Systems, Inc.
http://www.sequent.com/cgi-bin/jobs
ServiceMaster Limited Partnership
http://www.svm.com/F2.html
Silicon Graphics, Inc.
http://www.sgi.com/Misc/Jobs/getajob.html
Softdesk, Inc. http://www.softdesk.com/jobops.htm
SoftKey International Inc.
http://www.softkey.com/html3/hr/index.html
Software Spectrum, Inc. http://www.http://netsrv.
swspectrum.com/txt/empl/pointer.htm
Soligen Technologies, Inc.
http://www.PartsNow.com/about/06-05.shtml
Southwire Company, Inc.
http://www.southwire.com/sw/jobs/jobs.htm
Sprint Corporation http://www.sprintopps.com
Spyglass, Inc. http://www.spyglass.com/company/jobs.html
Stanford University http://www.http://www-
leland.stanford.edu/group/employment
Storage Technology Corporation
http://www.stortek.com/StorageTek/stkjob1.html
Sun Healthcare Group, Inc.
http://www.sunh.com/sundance.html
Sun Microsystems, Inc.
http://www.careermosaic.com/cm/sun/sun5.html
Symantec Corporation
http://www.careermosaic.com/cm/symantec/sym1.html
System Software Associates, Inc.
http://www.ssax.com/careers/career.htm
SystemSoft Corporation
http://www.systemsoft.com/~imagemap/
mainswitchboard?359,56

Tandem Computers Incorporated
http://www.careermosaic.com/cm/tandem/tm1.html
Target Therapeutics, Inc.
http://www.tget.com/jobs/index.html
TCSI Corporation http://www.tcsi.com/Working
Technology Solutions Company
http://www.techsol.com/careers/index.htm
Tektronix, Inc. http://www.tek.com/Tektronix/Careers
Tellabs, Inc. http://www.tellabs.com/about/career.html
Teradyne, Inc. http://www.teradyne.com/hr/tocindex.html
Texas Instruments Incorporated
http://www.ti.com/recruit/docs/recruit.htm
Travelers Group Inc. http://www.occ.com/travelers
Tribune Company http://www.
tribune.com/employment/index.html
TRW Inc. http://www.trw.com/careers/seg/seg_careers.html
UnionBanCal Corporation
http://www.careermosaic.com:80/cm/union_bank/ub6.html
Unisys Corporation http://www.unisys.com/Career
United States Cellular Corporation
http://www.uscc.com/corp/hr/scripts/hr_home.html
United Technologies Corporation
http://www.utc.com/workingatutc.html
United Waste Systems, Inc. http://www.uwst.com/jobs.html
U. S. Bancorp http://www.usbank.com/usb16000.html
U.S. Robotics Corporation
http://www.occ.com/occ/member/cpus-r.html
U S WEST Communications Group
http://www.careermosaic.com/cm/uswest/usw7.html
U.S. Xpress Enterprises, Inc.
http://www.usxpress.com/RECRUIT.HTM
UUNET Technologies, Inc. http://www.uu.net/jobs.html
Vanstar Corporation
http://www.occ.com/occ/member/cpvansta.html
Videonics, Inc. http://www.videonics.com/Employment.html
VideoServer, Inc. http://www.videoserver.com/htm/jobs.htm
Wabash National Corporation http://www.
nlci.com/wabash/emplymnt.htm
Walgreen Co.
http://www.occ.com/occ/member/cpwalgreen.html
Walker Richer & Quinn Inc.
http://www.wrq.com/employ/joboppor.htm
Wallace Computer Services, Inc.
http://www.jobweb.org/employer/wallace.htm
Wal-Mart Stores, Inc. http://www.wal-mart.com/cgi-
bin/htmldisp?ci:5
Western Digital Corporation
http://www.wdc.com:80/employment
Whirlpool Corporation
http://www.whirlpool.com/html/corp/career
WMS Industries Inc.
http://www.pinball.wms.com/employment.html
XcelleNet, Inc.
http://www.xcellenet.com/about/employment/index.html
Xerox Corporation
http://www.careermosaic.com/cm/xerox/xerox3.html
Xilinx, Inc. http://www.xilinx.com/jobs.htm
Xircom, Inc.
http://www.xircom.com/Happenings/Jobs/index.html
Xpedite Systems, Inc. http://www.xpedite.com/jobs.htm
Youth Services International, Inc.
http://www.youthservices.com/ysijobd.htm
Zoom Telephonics, Inc. http://www.zoomtel.com/jobs.html

ACCUSTAFF INCORPORATED

6440 Atlantic Blvd.
Jacksonville, FL 32211
Chm, Pres & CEO: Derek E. Dewan
Dir HR : Andrea Giggetts

Phone: 904-725-5574
Fax: 904-725-8513

For Branch Office Locations, call: 800-852-2281

General office personnel

INTERIM SERVICES INC.

2050 Spectrum Blvd.
Fort Lauderdale, FL 33309
Pres & CEO: Raymond Marcy
VP Admin: Thomas L. Mirgon

Phone: 954-938-7600
Fax: 954-938-7780

For Branch Office Locations, call: 954-938-7600

Legal, light industrial, clerical, administrative & medical employee personnel

ADIA SERVICES, INC.

64 Willow Place
Menlo Park, CA 94025
CEO: John P. Bowmer
VP Worldwide Quality & HR: Barbara LaTour

Phone: 415-610-1000
Fax: 415-610-1076

For Branch Office Locations, call: 800-836-7423

General office personnel

KELLY SERVICES, INC.

999 W. Big Beaver Rd.
Troy, MI 48084
Pres & CEO: Terence E. Adderley
SVP HR: Joanne E. Start

Phone: 810-362-4444
Fax: 810-244-4853

For Branch Office Locations, call: 810-362-4444

Office & professional, technical, light industrial & electronic assembly personnel

ADMINISTAFF INC.

19001 Crescent Springs Dr.
Kingwood, TX 77339
CEO: Paul Sarvadi
VP HR: Jim Wilkes

Phone: 713-358-8986
Fax: 713-358-3354

For Branch Office Locations, call: 800-237-3170

General staff leasing services

MANPOWER INC.

5301 N. Ironwood Rd.
Milwaukee, WI 53217
Chm, Pres & CEO: Mitchell S. Fromstein
Mgr HR: Sharon Rooney

Phone: 414-961-1000
Fax: 414-961-3255

For Branch Office Locations, call: 800-885-9925

Industrial, medical, office & clerical personnel

CAREER HORIZONS, INC.

177 Crossways Park Dr.
Woodbury, NY 11797-2047
Pres & CEO: Walter W. Macauley
Asst VP HR: Robert Sabatino

Phone: 516-682-1400
Fax: 516-496-1008

For Branch Office Locations, call: 516-682-1400

Medical & health care, financial & administrative personnel

NORRELL CORPORATION

3535 Piedmont Rd. NE
Atlanta, GA 30305
Pres & CEO: C. Douglas Miller
VP HR: Peter Rosen

Phone: 404-240-3000
Fax: 404-240-3312

For Branch Office Locations, call: 800-274-1431

Medical, clerical, light industrial, accounting & financial, technical, computer & administrative personnel

CORESTAFF, INC.

4400 Post Oak Pkwy., Ste. 1130
Houston, TX 77027-3413
Chm, CEO & Pres: Michael T. Willis
EVP Fin & Admin: Austin P. Young

Phone: 713-961-3633
Fax: 713-963-9711

For Branch Office Locations, call: 713-961-3633

Temporary & contract support & information technology services for businesses, professional & service organizations, manufacturers, institutions & government agencies

THE OLSTEN CORPORATION

175 Broad Hollow Rd.
Melville, NY 11747-8905
Chm & CEO: Frank N. Liguori
SVP HR: Martin Gelerman

Phone: 516-844-7800
Fax: 516-844-7011

For Branch Office Locations, call: 800-225-8367

Office & clerical, accounting & health care personnel

PAYROLL TRANSFERS, INC.

3710 Corporex Dr., Ste. 300
Tampa, FL 33619
Pres: Marc Moore
Dir HR: Carol Ryals
Phone: 813-664-0404
Fax: 813-621-6816

For Branch Office Locations, call: 800-343-5099

Accounting & financial employee leasing services

TAD RESOURCES INTERNATIONAL, INC.

639 Massachusetts Ave.
Cambridge, MA 02139
Pres & CEO: James S. Davis
No central personnel officer
Phone: 617-868-1650
Fax: 617-492-1432

For Branch Office Locations, call: 800-767-5776

Technical & engineering personnel

PERSONNEL GROUP OF AMERICA, INC.

6302 Fairview Rd., Ste. 201
Charlotte, NC 28210
CEO: Edward P. Drudge Jr.
Dir HR: Laurine Thompson
Phone: 704-442-5100
Fax: 704-334-4922

For Branch Office Locations, call: 704-442-5100

General office personnel

TTC, ILLINOIS

50 Meadowview Ctr.
Kankakee, IL 60901
CEO: Michael McCafferty
No central personnel officer
Phone: 815-935-8100
Fax: 815-936-3098

For Branch Office Locations, call: 815-935-8100

Employee leasing services for financial & technical personnel

REMEDYTEMP, INC.

32122 Camino Capistrano
San Juan Capistrano, CA 92675
Pres & CEO: Paul W. Mikos
VP HR & Risk Mgmt: Jeffrey A. Elias
Phone: 714-661-1211
Fax: 714-661-2972

For Branch Office Locations, call: 800-491-8367

Clerical & light industrial personnel

THE VINCAM GROUP, INC.

2850 Douglas Rd.
Coral Gables, FL 33134
Chm, Pres & CEO: Carlos A. Saladrigas
VP HR: Tom Simmons
Phone: 305-460-2350
Fax: 305-460-2399

For Branch Office Locations, call: 800-962-4404

Professional office & technical personnel

ROBERT HALF INTERNATIONAL INC.

2884 Sand Hill Rd., Ste. 200
Menlo Park, CA 94025
Chm, Pres & CEO: Harold M. Messmer Jr.
Dir HR: Susan Rhodes
Phone: 415-854-9700
Fax: 415-854-9735

For Branch Office Locations, call: 800-804-8367

Accounting & finance (Accountemps, Robert Half), administrative & office (OfficeTeam), paralegal & legal (The Affiliates) & information technology (RHI Consulting) personnel

VOLT INFORMATION SCIENCES, INC.

1221 Avenue of the Americas
New York, NY 10020-1579
Chm, Pres & CEO: William Shaw
VP HR: Norma Kraus
Phone: 212-704-2400
Fax: 212-704-2424

For Branch Office Locations, call: 800-292-0120

Engineering, design, data processing, scientific & technical support personnel

STAFF BUILDERS, INC.

1983 Marcus Ave.
Lake Success, NY 11042
Chm, Pres & CEO: Stephen Savitsky
VP: Don Ramsey
Phone: 516-358-1000
Fax: 516-358-1036

For Branch Office Locations, call: 516-358-1000

Home health care & supplemental staffing services for health care institutions

WESTERN STAFF SERVICES, INC.

301 & 303 Lennon Ln.
Walnut Creek, CA 94598-2453
Chm & CEO: W. Robert Stover
VP HR: Beverly D'Elena
Phone: 510-930-5300
Fax: 510-934-5489

For Branch Office Locations, call: 800-872-8367

Clerical, light industrial & medical personnel

 An in-depth profile of this company is available
to subscribers on Hoover's Online at www.hoovers.com.

31

USEFUL BOOKS ON JOB-HUNTING

The 100 Best Companies to Work for in America, Robert Levering and Milton Moskowitz, 2nd ed., Doubleday, 1993.

The 100 Best Jobs for the 1990s & Beyond, Carol Kleiman, Dearborn Financial Publishing, Inc., 1992.

101 Dynamite Questions To Ask On Your Job Interview, Richard Fein, Impact Publications, 1996.

200 Letters for Job Hunters, William S. Frank, Ten Speed Press, 1993.

The Adams Jobs Almanac 1995, Bob Adams, Inc., 1995.

Alternative Careers, John Wiley & Sons, Inc., 1995.

Beyond Blue Suits and Resumes: Proven Methods Insure Your Job Finding Success, Annette L. Segall, York Publishing Company, 1995.

The Career Coach, Carol Kleiman, Dearborn Financial Publishing, Inc., 1994.

Change Your Job, Change Your Life! High Impact Strategies For Finding Great Jobs In The 90s, Impact Publications, Ronald L. Krannich.

Cover Letters That Knock 'Em Dead, Martin John Yate, Bob Adams, Inc., 1995.

Damn Good Resume Guide, 3rd ed., Yana Parker, Ten Speed Press, 1996.

Electronic Job Search Revolution: How To Win With The New Technology That's Reshaping Today's Job Market, Joyce Lain Kennedy and Thomas J. Morrow, John Wiley & Sons, Inc., 1994.

Electronic Resume Revolution: Creating A Winning Resume For The New World Of Job Seeking, Joyce Lain Kennedy and Thomas J. Morrow, John Wiley & Sons, Inc., 1995.

Electronic Resumes for the New Job Market, Peter Weddle, Impact Publications, 1995.

Every Woman's Essential Job Hunting & Resume Book, Laura Morin, Bob Adams, Inc., 1994.

From College to Career: Entry-Level Resumes for Any Major, Donald Asher, Ten Speed Press, 1992.

Help! My Job Interview is Tomorrow! How To Use The Library To Research An Employer, Mary Ellen Templeton, Neal-Schuman Publishers, 1991.

How To Create The Job You Want, Raymond Gerson, Enrichment Enterprises, 1996.

How to Get a Job in 90 Days or Less, Matthew J. DeLuca, McGraw-Hill, Inc., 1995.

I Could Do Anything If I Only Knew What It Was: How To Discover What You Really Want And How To Get It, Barbara Sher and Barbara Smith, Delacorte Press, 1994.

Interviewing, Arlene S. Hirsch, John Wiley & Sons, Inc., 1995.

Job Smarts for Twentysomethings, Bradley G. Richardson, Vintage Books, 1995.

Knock 'Em Dead: The Ultimate Job Seekers Handbook, Martin John Yate, Bob Adams, Inc., 1996.

National Business Employment Weekly Jobs Rated Almanac, Les Krantz, 3rd ed., John Wiley & Sons, Inc., 1995.

NetJobs, Mary Goodwin, Deborah Cohn, and Donna Spivey, Michael Wolff & Company, Inc., 1996.

Resumes That Knock 'Em Dead, Martin John Yate, Adams Publications, 1995.

What Color Is Your Parachute? 1996, Richard Nelson Bolles, Ten Speed Press, 1996.

TOP 2,500

A List-Lover's Compendium

EMPLOYERS

Top 500 Companies by Employees in
Hoover's Top 2,500 Employers

Rank	Company	Employees	Rank	Company	Employees
1	United States Postal Service	753,384	51	H&R Block, Inc.	91,000
2	General Motors Corporation	745,000	52	ConAgra, Inc.	90,871
3	Wal-Mart Stores, Inc.	675,000	53	Little Caesar Enterprises, Inc.	90,000
4	PepsiCo, Inc.	480,000	54	The Great Atlantic & Pacific Tea	
5	Ford Motor Company	346,990		Company, Inc.	89,000
6	United Parcel Service of		55	The Goodyear Tire & Rubber	88,790
	America, Inc.	332,000	56	AlliedSignal Inc.	88,500
7	Kmart Corporation	307,000	57	Flagstar Companies, Inc.	88,000
8	AT&T Corp.	299,300	58	BellSouth Corporation	87,600
9	Sears, Roebuck and Co.	275,000	59	Citicorp	85,300
10	Columbia/HCA Healthcare	240,000	60	Xerox Corporation	85,200
11	International Business		61	Hughes Electronics Corp.	84,000
	Machines Corporation	225,347	62	Beverly Enterprises, Inc.	83,000
12	General Electric Company	222,000	63	Rockwell International	
13	Dayton Hudson Corporation	214,000		Corporation	82,671
14	McDonald's Corporation	212,000	64	Johnson & Johnson	82,300
15	J. C. Penney Company, Inc.	205,000	65	Andersen Worldwide	82,121
16	The Kroger Co.	205,000	66	Exxon Corporation	82,000
17	Marriott International, Inc.	179,400	67	Viacom Inc.	81,700
18	United Technologies Corp.	170,600	68	International Paper Company	81,500
19	Lockheed Martin Corporation	160,000	69	Albertson's, Inc.	80,000
20	Philip Morris Companies Inc.	151,000	70	The Home Depot, Inc.	80,000
21	Sara Lee Corporation	149,100	71	BankAmerica Corporation	79,916
22	Blue Cross and Blue Shield	146,000	72	UAL Corporation	79,410
23	Motorola, Inc.	142,000	73	Emerson Electric Co.	78,900
24	ARAMARK Corporation	140,000	74	Westinghouse Electric Corp.	77,813
25	University of California	133,000	75	RJR Nabisco Holdings Corp.	76,000
26	Lucent Technologies Inc.	131,000	76	Kaiser Foundation Health Plan	75,000
27	Goodwill Industries		77	Cargill, Incorporated	73,300
	International, Inc.	130,000	78	Raytheon Company	73,200
28	The May Department Stores	130,000	79	WMX Technologies, Inc.	73,200
29	IGA, Inc.	128,000	80	The Chase Manhattan Corp.	72,695
30	Chrysler Corporation	126,000	81	Aluminum Company of America	72,000
31	Domino's Pizza, Inc.	125,000	82	KPMG Peat Marwick LLP	72,000
32	Darden Restaurants, Inc.	124,730	83	State Farm Mutual Automobile	
33	Winn-Dixie Stores, Inc.	123,000		Insurance Company	71,437
34	American Stores Company	121,000	84	Electronic Data Systems	
35	Federated Department Stores	119,100		Corporation	71,000
36	Safeway Inc.	114,000	85	The Walt Disney Company	71,000
37	AMR Corporation	110,000	86	Minnesota Mining and	
38	Federal Express Corporation	107,000		Manufacturing Company	70,687
39	GTE Corporation	106,000	87	Coopers & Lybrand L.L.P.	70,500
40	The Boeing Company	105,000	88	American Express Company	70,347
41	E. I. du Pont de Nemours		89	Food Lion, Inc.	69,345
	and Company	105,000	90	Carlson Companies, Inc.	69,000
42	The Limited, Inc.	104,000	91	Ernst & Young LLP	68,452
43	Hewlett-Packard Company	102,300	92	Walgreen Co.	68,000
44	The Prudential Insurance		93	TRW Inc.	66,500
	Company of America	100,000	94	NYNEX Corporation	65,800
45	The Procter & Gamble Co.	99,200	95	Time Warner Inc.	65,500
46	Borg-Warner Security	96,974	96	Ameritech Corporation	65,345
47	Melville Corporation	96,832	97	Meijer, Inc.	65,000
48	Eastman Kodak Company	96,600	98	American Home Products	64,712
49	Publix Super Markets, Inc.	95,000	99	Tyson Foods, Inc.	64,000
50	Woolworth Corporation	94,000	100	VF Corporation	64,000

Top 500 Companies by Employees in
Hoover's Top 2,500 Employers (continued)

Rank	Company	Employees	Rank	Company	Employees
101	McDonnell Douglas Corp.	63,612	151	Burlington Northern Santa Fe Corporation	45,655
102	Daughters of Charity National Health System	62,300	152	Anheuser-Busch Companies	45,529
103	Bell Atlantic Corporation	61,800	153	Whirlpool Corporation	45,435
104	Digital Equipment Corporation	61,700	154	Norwest Corporation	45,404
105	U S WEST Communications	61,047	155	Merck & Co., Inc.	45,200
106	The Gap, Inc.	60,000	156	ABM Industries Incorporated	45,000
107	Tenet Healthcare Corporation	60,000	157	Blockbuster Entertainment Group	45,000
108	Tenneco Inc.	60,000	158	Nabisco Holdings Corp.	45,000
109	Toys "R" Us, Inc.	60,000	159	Northwest Airlines Corp.	45,000
110	Delta Air Lines, Inc.	59,717	160	Ogden Corporation	45,000
111	Texas Instruments	59,574	161	SUPERVALU Inc.	44,800
112	SBC Communications Inc.	59,300	162	CIGNA Corporation	44,707
113	Johnson Controls, Inc.	59,200	163	Eckerd Corporation	44,600
114	Deloitte Touche Tohmatsu International	59,000	164	Lowe's Companies	44,546
115	ITT Industries, Inc.	59,000	165	First Union Corporation	44,536
116	NationsBank Corporation	58,322	166	Ryder System, Inc.	44,503
117	The TJX Companies, Inc.	58,000	167	The Allstate Corporation	44,300
118	Halliburton Company	57,300	168	Fleming Companies, Inc.	44,000
119	Textron Inc.	57,000	169	MTA New York City Transit	44,000
120	Baxter International Inc.	56,580	170	Pfizer Inc.	43,800
121	Kimberly-Clark Corporation	55,341	171	Campbell Soup Company	43,781
122	Montgomery Ward Holding	55,000	172	Chevron Corporation	43,019
123	Caterpillar Inc.	54,352	173	American Standard Companies Inc.	43,000
124	Seagate Technology, Inc.	53,000	174	Browning-Ferris Industries	43,000
125	CPC International Inc.	52,500	175	Dole Food Company, Inc.	43,000
126	Eaton Corporation	52,000	176	NCR Corp.	43,000
127	Price/Costco, Inc.	52,000	177	Amoco Corporation	42,689
128	Schlumberger Limited	51,000	178	Family Restaurants, Inc.	42,500
129	Mobil Corporation	50,400	179	H. J. Heinz Company	42,200
130	MCI Communications Corporation	50,367	180	New York City Health and Hospitals Corporation	41,711
131	Abbott Laboratories	50,241	181	Fluor Corporation	41,678
132	Honeywell Inc.	50,100	182	Consolidated Freightways, Inc.	41,600
133	The Dun & Bradstreet Corporation	49,500	183	Intel Corporation	41,600
134	Union Pacific Corporation	49,500	184	Ingersoll-Rand Company	41,133
135	Tandy Corporation	49,300	185	Corning Incorporated	41,000
136	Bristol-Myers Squibb Company	49,000	186	Metropolitan Life Insurance Company	41,000
137	State University of New York	48,300	187	R. R. Donnelley & Sons Co.	41,000
138	Sprint Corporation	48,265	188	AMP Incorporated	40,800
139	Army & Air Force Exchange Service	48,219	189	Cooper Industries, Inc.	40,400
140	Pacific Telesis Group	48,062	190	Dillard Department Stores, Inc.	40,312
141	Hilton Hotels Corporation	48,000	191	Aetna Inc.	40,200
142	CSX Corporation	47,965	192	DHL Worldwide Express	40,000
143	Travelers Group Inc.	47,600	193	H. E. Butt Grocery Company	40,000
144	Georgia-Pacific Corporation	47,500	194	Restaurant Co.	40,000
145	Hyatt Corporation	47,000	195	The Dow Chemical Company	39,537
146	Pinkerton's, Inc.	47,000	196	Weyerhaeuser Company	39,431
147	Wendy's International, Inc.	47,000	197	Gannett Co., Inc.	39,100
148	Banc One Corporation	46,900	198	USAir Group, Inc.	39,000
149	Merrill Lynch & Co., Inc.	46,000	199	Wackenhut Corporation	39,000
150	Dana Corporation	45,900	200	The Salvation Army	38,999

Top 500 Companies by Employees in
Hoover's Top 2,500 Employers (continued)

Rank	Company	Employees	Rank	Company	Employees
201	Andersen Consulting	38,000	251	Dean Witter, Discover & Co.	30,779
202	Cox Enterprises, Inc.	38,000	252	Parker-Hannifin Corporation	30,590
203	ITT Corporation	38,000	253	The Southland Corporation	30,523
204	The University of Michigan	38,000	254	The University of Wisconsin	
205	Levi Strauss Associates Inc.	37,700		System	30,410
206	Brinker International, Inc.	37,500	255	The Dial Corp	30,100
207	Unisys Corporation	37,400	256	Owens-Illinois, Inc.	30,100
208	Colgate-Palmolive Company	37,300	257	Living Centers of America, Inc.	30,000
209	Nordstrom, Inc.	37,000	258	Universal Corporation	30,000
210	Northrop Grumman Corp.	37,000	259	The Vons Companies, Inc.	30,000
211	Warner-Lambert Co.	37,000	260	Reynolds Metals Company	29,800
212	American Greetings Corp.	36,800	261	KeyCorp	29,563
213	Alco Standard Corp.	36,500	262	Shoney's, Inc.	29,500
214	Circuit City Stores, Inc.	36,430	263	The Black & Decker Corp.	29,300
215	Chiquita Brands International	36,000	264	Litton Industries, Inc.	29,100
216	First Data Corporation	36,000	265	Bechtel Group, Inc.	29,000
217	Ruby Tuesday, Inc.	36,000	266	Jewel Food Stores, Inc.	29,000
218	Rite Aid Corporation	35,700	267	Pathmark Stores, Inc.	29,000
219	First Chicago NBD Corp.	35,328	268	Loral Corporation	28,900
220	Interstate Bakeries Corp.	35,000	269	Monsanto Company	28,514
221	Lear Corporation	35,000	270	Bob Evans Farms, Inc.	28,300
222	Loews Corporation	34,700	271	Texaco Inc.	28,247
223	Yellow Corporation	34,700	272	SYSCO Corporation	28,100
224	American International Group, Inc.	34,500	273	Los Angeles County Department of Healthcare Services	28,000
225	IBP, inc.	34,000	274	The Marmon Group, Inc.	28,000
226	ServiceMaster Limited Partnership	34,000	275	Mars, Inc.	28,000
227	Tyco International Ltd.	34,000	276	Rhone-Poulenc Rorer Inc.	28,000
228	Computer Sciences Corp.	33,850	277	Pitney Bowes Inc.	27,723
229	Best Buy Co., Inc.	33,500	278	American Brands, Inc.	27,700
230	The Gillette Company	33,500	279	General Dynamics Corp.	27,700
231	Deere & Company	33,400	280	Bally Entertainment Corp.	27,600
232	Fruit of the Loom, Inc.	33,300	281	Borden, Inc.	27,500
233	Coca-Cola Enterprises Inc.	33,000	282	Nationwide Insurance Enterprise	27,476
234	Ashland Inc.	32,800	283	First Interstate Bancorp	27,200
235	TCI Communications, Inc.	32,500	284	Sun Healthcare Group, Inc.	27,100
236	Continental Airlines, Inc.	32,300	285	Aon Corporation	27,000
237	The Coca-Cola Company	32,000	286	Fred Meyer, Inc.	27,000
238	Revco D.S., Inc.	32,000	287	James River Corp. of Virginia	27,000
239	The Southern Company	31,882	288	The Ohio State University	27,000
240	Ralston Purina Company	31,837	289	The Penn Traffic Company	27,000
241	Avon Products, Inc.	31,800	290	Norfolk Southern Corporation	26,944
242	Mercantile Stores Company, Inc.	31,700	291	Service Merchandise Company	26,850
243	Dresser Industries, Inc.	31,500	292	Eli Lilly and Company	26,800
244	PPG Industries, Inc.	31,200	293	Harris Corporation	26,600
245	Thrifty PayLess Holdings, Inc.	31,200	294	HEALTHSOUTH Corporation	26,427
246	American Red Cross	31,000	295	Cracker Barrel Old Country Store, Inc.	26,299
247	Manor Care, Inc.	31,000	296	Heritage Media Corporation	26,200
248	Office Depot, Inc.	31,000	297	Hoffmann-La Roche, Inc.	26,000
249	Fleet Financial Group, Inc.	30,800	298	Roadway Express, Inc.	26,000
250	Intimate Brands, Inc.	30,800	299	Stone Container Corporation	25,900
			300	The City University of New York	25,800

Top 500 Companies by Employees in
Hoover's Top 2,500 Employers (continued)

Rank	Company	Employees	Rank	Company	Employees
301	Foodmaker, Inc.	25,785	351	Ames Department Stores, Inc.	22,000
302	Caliber System, Inc.	25,700	352	Atlantic Richfield Company	22,000
303	The University of Maryland		353	Dollar General Corporation	22,000
	System	25,690	354	Harrah's Entertainment, Inc.	22,000
304	Bruno's, Inc.	25,600	355	Life Care Centers of America	22,000
305	Giant Food Inc.	25,600	356	Louisiana State University	
306	Mayo Foundation	25,433		System	22,000
307	McDermott International, Inc.	25,400	357	OrNda HealthCorp	22,000
308	PNC Bank Corp.	25,400	358	Pacific Gas and Electric Co.	22,000
309	Dover Corporation	25,332	359	Randall's Food Markets, Inc.	22,000
310	Automatic Data Processing, Inc.	25,000	360	The Times Mirror Company	21,877
311	CNA Financial Corporation	25,000	361	Navy Exchange System	21,854
312	Marsh & McLennan Companies	25,000	362	Consolidated Stores Corp.	21,633
313	Mattel, Inc.	25,000	363	The University of Florida	21,500
314	Shaw Industries, Inc.	25,000	364	Barnes & Noble, Inc.	21,400
315	Edison Brothers Stores, Inc.	24,600	365	The Yucaipa Companies	21,230
316	Laboratory Corporation of		366	Illinois Tool Works Inc.	21,200
	America Holdings	24,600	367	Kohl's Corporation	21,200
317	Times Mirror Professional		368	OfficeMax, Inc.	21,171
	Information	24,500	369	Advocate Health Care	21,145
318	Club Corporation International	24,480	370	National Service Industries	21,100
319	Cummins Engine Company, Inc.	24,300	371	Shell Oil Company	21,050
320	Mellon Bank Corporation	24,300	372	USX-Marathon Group	21,015
321	Premark International, Inc.	24,300	373	ITT Hartford Group, Inc.	21,000
322	Champion International Corp.	24,129	374	KinderCare Learning Centers	21,000
323	National Railroad Passenger		375	Brunswick Corporation	20,900
	Corporation	24,100	376	USX-U.S. Steel Group	20,845
324	Berkshire Hathaway Inc.	24,000	377	National City Corporation	20,767
325	The Caldor Corporation	24,000	378	Furniture Brands International,	
326	Payless ShoeSource, Inc.	24,000		Incorporated	20,700
327	Sisters of Mercy Health System-		379	The Circle K Corporation	20,566
	St. Louis	24,000	380	Pampered Chef Ltd.	20,550
328	Compaq Computer Corp.	23,884	381	Masco Corporation	20,500
329	Trans World Airlines, Inc.	23,628	382	Science Applications	
330	Conrail Inc.	23,510		International Corporation	20,500
331	Echlin Inc.	23,400	383	The University of Pennsylvania	20,500
332	Read-Rite Corporation	23,074	384	Crown Cork & Seal Company	20,409
333	BJC Health System	23,000	385	Hannaford Bros. Co.	20,400
334	Integrated Health Services, Inc.	23,000	386	AutoZone, Inc.	20,200
335	Liberty Mutual Group	23,000	387	Circus Circus Enterprises, Inc.	20,200
336	Newell Co.	23,000	388	Ruddick Corporation	20,200
337	The University of Iowa	23,000	389	Barnett Banks, Inc.	20,175
338	Freeman Cos.	22,800	390	Schering-Plough Corporation	20,100
339	Knight-Ridder, Inc.	22,800	391	Allina Health System	20,000
340	MacAndrews & Forbes Holdings	22,800	392	Borders Group, Inc.	20,000
341	The University of Washington	22,655	393	Capital Cities/ABC, Inc.	20,000
342	Springs Industries, Inc.	22,600	394	Catholic Healthcare West	20,000
343	Burlington Industries, Inc.	22,500	395	Hechinger Company	20,000
344	Duke University	22,500	396	Intermountain Health Care, Inc.	20,000
345	Genuine Parts Company	22,500	397	Metromedia Company	20,000
346	Host Marriott Services Corp.	22,400	398	National Council of Young Men's	
347	National Semiconductor Corp.	22,400		Christian Associations of the	
348	FMC Corporation	22,164		United States of America	20,000
349	Staples, Inc.	22,132	399	The Texas A&M University	20,000
350	Allegiance Corporation	22,000	400	The University of Illinois	20,000

Top 500 Companies by Employees in
Hoover's Top 2,500 Employers (continued)

Rank	Company	Employees
401	University of Minnesota	20,000
402	Southwest Airlines Co.	19,933
403	Smith's Food & Drug Centers, Inc.	19,859
404	Service Corporation Intl.	19,824
405	The Stanley Works	19,784
406	The Interpublic Group of Companies, Inc.	19,700
407	Wells Fargo & Company	19,520
408	Airborne Freight Corporation	19,500
409	Bethlehem Steel Corporation	19,500
410	The Hertz Corporation	19,500
411	Hollinger International, Inc.	19,500
412	ShopKo Stores, Inc.	19,500
413	SunTrust Banks, Inc.	19,415
414	Omnicom Group Inc.	19,400
415	Michaels Stores, Inc.	19,330
416	Deluxe Corporation	19,286
417	Steelcase Inc.	19,200
418	Southern Pacific Rail Corp.	19,089
419	Advance Publications, Inc.	19,000
420	Kinko's, Inc.	19,000
421	Sisters of Charity of the Incarnate Word Health Care	19,000
422	Sonoco Products Company	19,000
423	SSM Health Care System Inc.	19,000
424	Trump Organization	19,000
425	Waban Inc.	19,000
426	York International Corporation	19,000
427	The University of Missouri	18,997
428	Eastern Mercy Health System	18,982
429	U.S. Industries, Inc.	18,640
430	Perdue Farms Incorporated	18,600
431	American Electric Power Company, Inc.	18,502
432	Asplundh Tree Expert Co.	18,500
433	Family Dollar Stores, Inc.	18,500
434	Health Care and Retirement Corporation	18,500
435	Arkansas Best Corporation	18,459
436	The Sherwin-Williams Company	18,458
437	California State University	18,454
438	Union Camp Corporation	18,258
439	Praxair, Inc.	18,222
440	Interstate Hotels Company	18,200
441	Becton, Dickinson and Company	18,100
442	Mercy Health System	18,100
443	Payless Cashways, Inc.	18,100
444	Zenith Electronics Corporation	18,100
445	Belk Stores Services, Inc.	18,000
446	Fleetwood Enterprises, Inc.	18,000
447	FMR Corp.	18,000
448	The Johns Hopkins University	18,000
449	Long John Silver's Restaurants, Inc.	18,000
450	Teledyne, Inc.	18,000

Rank	Company	Employees
451	Sisters of Providence Health System	17,956
452	Hills Stores Company	17,900
453	Vishay Intertechnology, Inc.	17,900
454	BankBoston Corporation	17,881
455	Boise Cascade Corporation	17,820
456	Microsoft Corporation	17,801
457	Russell Corporation	17,766
458	Apple Computer, Inc.	17,615
459	The Pep Boys	17,591
460	Eastman Chemical Company	17,500
461	WestPoint Stevens Inc.	17,500
462	Lefrak Organization Inc.	17,400
463	Phillips Petroleum Company	17,400
464	Owens Corning	17,300
465	Occidental Petroleum Corporation	17,280
466	Fabri-Centers of America, Inc.	17,200
467	Federal-Mogul Corporation	17,200
468	Duke Power Company	17,121
469	Unicom Corporation	17,045
470	The Timken Company	17,034
471	Boatmen's Bancshares, Inc.	17,023
472	A.C. Nielsen Co.	17,000
473	American Retail Group, Inc.	17,000
474	Apple South, Inc.	17,000
475	DynCorp	17,000
476	Federal Prison Industries, Inc.	17,000
477	Henry Ford Health System	17,000
478	Indiana University	17,000
479	Musicland Stores Corporation	17,000
480	The Quaker Oats Company	17,000
481	University of Southern California	17,000
482	Oracle Corporation	16,882
483	Holy Cross Health System	16,856
484	Whitman Corporation	16,841
485	Humana Inc.	16,800
486	Penske Corporation	16,700
487	Associates First Capital Corporation	16,647
488	Leggett & Platt, Incorporated	16,600
489	Maytag Corporation	16,595
490	Consolidated Edison Company of New York, Inc.	16,582
491	Columbia University in the City of New York	16,565
492	Tennessee Valley Authority	16,559
493	FRD Acquisition Co.	16,500
494	Genesis Health Ventures, Inc.	16,500
495	The Principal Financial Group	16,500
496	Square D Company	16,500
497	Weis Markets, Inc.	16,500
498	Edison International	16,434
499	Northwestern Healthcare	16,427
500	Doubletree Corporation	16,400

Top 500 Companies by One-Year Absolute Employee Growth in Hoover's Top 2,500 Employers

Rank	Company	Absolute Growth	Rank	Company	Absolute Growth
1	Columbia/HCA Healthcare Corp.	83,000	51	Intel Corporation	9,000
2	Lockheed Martin Corporation	77,500	52	PepsiCo, Inc.	9,000
3	Wal-Mart Stores, Inc.	53,000	53	Intimate Brands, Inc.	8,800
4	General Motors Corporation	52,200	54	Apple South, Inc.	8,600
5	The Chase Manhattan Corp.	30,565	55	Corporate Express, Inc.	8,366
6	McDonald's Corporation	29,000	56	Best Buy Co., Inc.	8,200
7	United States Postal Service	24,440	57	H&R Block, Inc.	8,200
8	Tenet Healthcare Corporation	21,200	58	Tyson Foods, Inc.	8,200
9	Interstate Bakeries Corporation	21,000	59	HEALTHSOUTH Corporation	8,004
10	Dayton Hudson Corporation	20,000	60	Genesis Health Ventures, Inc.	7,877
11	The TJX Companies, Inc.	20,000	61	Staples, Inc.	7,566
12	First Chicago NBD Corporation	17,698	62	Federated Department Stores, Inc.	7,400
13	Bally Entertainment Corporation	16,400	63	PNC Bank Corp.	7,400
14	Marriott International, Inc.	15,960	64	Ernst & Young LLP	7,165
15	H. E. Butt Grocery Company	15,000	65	Sisters of Mercy Health Systems-St. Louis	7,100
16	Burlington Northern Santa Fe Corporation	14,944	66	ARAMARK Corporation	7,000
17	First Data Corporation	14,000	67	Lowe's Companies	6,991
18	Revco D.S., Inc.	14,000	68	Furniture Brands International,	6,900
19	ITT Corporation	13,000	69	Hughes Electronics Corporation	6,900
20	Raytheon Company	13,000	70	Sun Healthcare Group, Inc.	6,900
21	The Home Depot, Inc.	12,700	71	Norwest Corporation	6,604
22	First Union Corporation	12,678	72	Arkansas Best Corporation	6,583
23	Kimberly-Clark Corporation	12,634	73	Carlson Companies, Inc.	6,500
24	Hollinger International, Inc.	12,280	74	H. J. Heinz Company	6,500
25	Living Centers of America, Inc.	12,200	75	Whirlpool Corporation	6,419
26	Time Warner Inc.	12,200	76	Dana Corporation	6,400
27	United Parcel Service of America, Inc.	12,000	77	The Yucaipa Companies	6,213
28	Viacom Inc.	11,700	78	Technitrol, Inc.	6,159
29	International Paper Company	11,500	79	Walgreen Co.	6,100
30	Nine West Group Inc.	11,299	80	Doubletree Corporation	6,045
31	The May Department Stores Co.	11,000	81	Andersen Consulting	6,000
32	Winn-Dixie Stores, Inc.	11,000	82	Browning-Ferris Industries, Inc.	6,000
33	Lear Corporation	10,960	83	Federal Express Corporation	6,000
34	Rockwell International Corp.	10,780	84	The Walt Disney Company	6,000
35	CPC International Inc.	10,600	85	Northwestern Healthcare	5,982
36	AMP Incorporated	10,400	86	Alco Standard Corporation	5,900
37	Aluminum Company of America	10,300	87	Rhone-Poulenc Rorer Inc.	5,900
38	Domino's Pizza, Inc.	10,000	88	U S WEST Media Group	5,721
39	Motorola, Inc.	10,000	89	Applebee's International, Inc.	5,700
40	Seagate Technology, Inc.	10,000	90	Wingate Partners	5,700
41	Tyco International Ltd.	10,000	91	Lone Star Steakhouse & Saloon	5,600
42	Compaq Computer Corporation	9,512	92	International Business Machines Corporation	5,508
43	CNA Financial Corporation	9,400	93	Comcast Corporation	5,500
44	Andersen Worldwide	9,399	94	Manor Care, Inc.	5,500
45	MCI Communications Corp.	9,367	95	Outback Steakhouse, Inc.	5,500
46	Fleet Financial Group, Inc.	9,300	96	RJR Nabisco Holdings Corp.	5,400
47	Loews Corporation	9,300	97	Club Corporation International	5,280
48	Darden Restaurants, Inc.	9,212	98	Borg-Warner Security Corp.	5,276
49	Ford Motor Company	9,212	99	Ingersoll-Rand Company	5,201
50	Aon Corporation	9,000	100	Penske Corporation	5,200

Top 500 Companies by One-Year Absolute Employee Growth in Hoover's Top 2,500 Employers (continued)

Rank	Company	Absolute Growth	Rank	Company	Absolute Growth
101	Boston Scientific Corporation	5,162	151	Hewlett-Packard Company	3,900
102	Circuit City Stores, Inc.	5,017	152	ConAgra, Inc.	3,871
103	Chrysler Corporation	5,000	153	Parker-Hannifin Corporation	3,860
104	DHL Worldwide Express	5,000	154	Gateway 2000, Inc.	3,858
105	Emerson Electric Co.	5,000	155	Republic Industries, Inc.	3,692
106	The Gap, Inc.	5,000	156	The Texas A&M University System	3,633
107	The Kroger Co.	5,000	157	Kohl's Corporation	3,600
108	Office Depot, Inc.	5,000	158	Frontier Corporation	3,597
109	Price/Costco, Inc.	5,000	159	Mayo Foundation	3,577
110	Publix Super Markets, Inc.	5,000	160	General Dynamics Corporation	3,500
111	Restaurant Co.	5,000	161	Tandy Corporation	3,500
112	Tenneco Inc.	5,000	162	Anthem Inc.	3,490
113	Universal Corporation	5,000	163	U. S. Bancorp	3,471
114	Diamond Shamrock, Inc.	4,850	164	Danka Business Systems PLC	3,420
115	Oracle Corporation	4,824	165	FMR Corp.	3,400
116	Humana Inc.	4,800	166	Owens-Illinois, Inc.	3,400
117	NIKE, Inc.	4,740	167	Cincinnati Milacron Inc.	3,395
118	Read-Rite Corporation	4,602	168	Borders Group, Inc.	3,300
119	Blockbuster Entertainment Group	4,600	169	IBP, inc.	3,300
120	GranCare, Inc.	4,600	170	Omnicom Group Inc.	3,300
121	Laboratory Corporation of America Holdings	4,600	171	Texas Instruments Incorporated	3,241
122	Proffitt's, Inc.	4,600	172	Sara Lee Corporation	3,200
123	Grey Advertising Inc.	4,582	173	Southwest Airlines Co.	3,115
124	Food Lion, Inc.	4,505	174	Gannett Co., Inc.	3,100
125	Cracker Barrel Old Country Store	4,503	175	PETsMART, Inc.	3,100
126	American Standard Companies	4,500	176	York International Corporation	3,100
127	Bob Evans Farms, Inc.	4,500	177	Baxter International Inc.	3,080
128	Colgate-Palmolive Company	4,500	178	Apple Computer, Inc.	3,023
129	R. R. Donnelley & Sons Company	4,500	179	ABM Industries Incorporated	3,000
130	Solectron Corporation	4,481	180	American Stores Company	3,000
131	Johnson Controls, Inc.	4,400	181	Automatic Data Processing, Incorporated	3,000
132	Hollywood Entertainment Corp.	4,312	182	Coca-Cola Enterprises Inc.	3,000
133	McCrory Corporation	4,300	183	CUC International Inc.	3,000
134	Chiron Corporation	4,226	184	Ingram Industries Inc.	3,000
135	Thermo Electron Corporation	4,166	185	J. C. Penney Company, Inc.	3,000
136	The Southern Company	4,056	186	Mattel, Inc.	3,000
137	Schnuck Markets Inc.	4,042	187	Newell Co.	3,000
138	Applied Materials, Inc.	4,040	188	Pfizer Inc.	3,000
139	Albertson's, Inc.	4,000	189	Ruby Tuesday, Inc.	3,000
140	ASARCO Incorporated	4,000	190	Schlumberger Limited	3,000
141	Dollar General Corporation	4,000	191	Star Enterprise	3,000
142	Hilton Hotels Corporation	4,000	192	Wendy's International, Inc.	3,000
143	Manufactured Home Communities, Inc	4,000	193	The Gymboree Corporation	2,924
144	MBNA Corporation	4,000	194	MTA New York City Transit	2,914
145	Safeway Inc.	4,000	195	Anheuser-Busch Companies, Incorporated	2,907
146	Textron Inc.	4,000	196	UGI Corporation	2,886
147	American Medical Response, Inc.	3,998	197	Boatmen's Bancshares, Inc.	2,854
148	Central and South West Corp.	3,945	198	AutoZone, Inc.	2,800
149	Foundation Health Corporation	3,918	199	Echlin Inc.	2,800
150	Hannaford Bros. Co.	3,900	200	Harnischfeger Industries, Inc.	2,800

Top 500 Companies by One-Year Absolute Employee Growth in *Hoover's Top 2,500 Employers* (continued)

Rank	Company	Absolute Growth	Rank	Company	Absolute Growth
201	Corrections Corp. of America	2,772	251	Werner Enterprises, Inc.	2,148
202	Weyerhaeuser Company	2,766	252	Coopers & Lybrand L.L.P.	2,140
203	Nellcor Puritan Bennett Inc.	2,704	253	Value Health, Inc.	2,132
204	Ceridian Corporation	2,700	254	Airborne Freight Corporation	2,100
205	The Charles Schwab Corporation	2,700	255	Journal Communication Inc.	2,100
206	Citicorp	2,700	256	Mothers Work, Inc.	2,074
207	Fisher Scientific International Inc.	2,700	257	ICN Pharmaceuticals, Inc.	2,040
208	Mariner Health Group, Inc.	2,700	258	Fiserv, Inc.	2,027
209	The Procter & Gamble Company	2,700	259	Carmike Cinemas, Inc.	2,022
210	Science Applications International Corporation	2,700	260	Berkshire Hathaway Inc.	2,000
211	Schwegmann Giant Super Markets	2,646	261	Bradlees, Inc.	2,000
212	Micron Technology, Inc.	2,630	262	Dell Computer Corporation	2,000
213	Seaboard Corporation	2,617	263	Family Dollar Stores, Inc.	2,000
214	Amdahl Corporation	2,600	264	Fleetwood Enterprises, Inc.	2,000
215	Cargill, Incorporated	2,600	265	Health Care and Retirement Corporation	2,000
216	MaxServ, Inc.	2,600	266	Medaphis Corporation	2,000
217	Union Pacific Corporation	2,600	267	Nordstrom, Inc.	2,000
218	Westinghouse/CBS Group	2,600	268	OrNda HealthCorp	2,000
219	Edward D. Jones & Co.	2,582	269	Pinkerton's, Inc.	2,000
220	Nabors Industries, Inc.	2,577	270	Sensormatic Electronics Corp.	2,000
221	Microsoft Corporation	2,544	271	Toys "R" Us, Inc.	2,000
222	American International Group	2,500	272	The Vons Companies, Inc.	2,000
223	The Dun & Bradstreet Corp.	2,500	273	BJ Services Company	1,997
224	Lexmark International Group	2,500	274	Maxxim Medical, Inc.	1,979
225	Spiegel, Inc.	2,496	275	America Online, Inc.	1,954
226	Dillard Department Stores, Inc.	2,480	276	Silicon Graphics, Inc.	1,943
227	Movie Gallery, Inc.	2,441	277	Consolidated Stores Corporation	1,934
228	American General Corporation	2,400	278	Columbia University in the City of New York	1,926
229	Deloitte Touche Tohmatsu International	2,400	279	Circus Circus Enterprises, Inc.	1,925
230	Foster Poultry Farms Inc.	2,400	280	Commercial Metals Company	1,919
231	Hometown Buffet Inc.	2,400	281	Eckerd Corporation	1,900
232	NACCO Industries, Inc.	2,400	282	Eli Lilly and Company	1,900
233	Catholic Healthcare West	2,382	283	Genuardi Super Markets	1,900
234	American Freightways Corp.	2,361	284	SYSCO Corporation	1,900
235	Dover Corporation	2,340	285	U.S. Robotics Corporation	1,896
236	Cox Communications, Inc.	2,320	286	Michaels Stores, Inc.	1,890
237	Harveys Casino Resorts	2,310	287	Fluor Corporation	1,871
238	Dean Witter, Discover & Co.	2,304	288	Smith's Food & Drug Centers	1,859
239	Dresser Industries, Inc.	2,300	289	OfficeMax, Inc.	1,857
240	Springs Industries, Inc.	2,300	290	Caremark International, Inc.	1,850
241	TRW Inc.	2,300	291	Sonat Inc.	1,840
242	American Biltrite Inc.	2,235	292	Alleghany Corporation	1,812
243	Oxford Health Plans, Inc.	2,230	293	BREED Technologies, Inc.	1,800
244	E-Z Serve Corporation	2,216	294	Consolidated Products, Inc.	1,800
245	John Q. Hammons Hotels, Inc.	2,200	295	ICF Kaiser International, Inc.	1,800
246	Merrill Lynch & Co., Inc.	2,200	296	Integrated Health Services, Inc.	1,800
247	Universal Health Services, Inc.	2,200	297	Knight-Ridder, Inc.	1,800
248	WLR Foods, Inc.	2,200	298	Landry's Seafood Restaurants	1,800
249	First Alert, Inc.	2,192	299	Quorum Health Group, Inc.	1,800
250	AirTouch Communications, Inc.	2,150	300	Sinclair Oil Corporation	1,800

Top 500 Companies by One-Year Absolute Employee Growth in Hoover's Top 2,500 Employers (continued)

Rank	Company	Absolute Growth	Rank	Company	Absolute Growth
301	Sonoco Products Company	1,800	351	Summit Bancorp	1,404
302	Williams-Sonoma, Inc.	1,800	352	AmeriData Technologies, Inc.	1,400
303	Public Storage, Inc.	1,792	353	Avon Products, Inc.	1,400
304	La-Z-Boy Chair Company	1,779	354	ENSERCH Corporation	1,400
305	Community Care of America, Inc.	1,778	355	Steelcase Inc.	1,400
306	Ameritech Corporation	1,751	356	Summit Care Corporation	1,400
307	K-III Communications Corp.	1,750	357	Turner Industries, Ltd.	1,400
308	Huffy Corporation	1,723	358	The Warnaco Group, Inc.	1,400
309	The Williams Companies, Inc.	1,719	359	Hudson Foods, Inc.	1,392
310	CSS Industries, Inc.	1,710	360	Kansas City Southern Industries, Inc.	1,383
311	Aztar Corporation	1,700	361	Lam Research Corporation	1,374
312	Health Management Associates	1,700	362	Ross Stores, Inc.	1,361
313	Heritage Media Corporation	1,700	363	Ernst Home Center, Inc.	1,350
314	Illinois Tool Works Inc.	1,700	364	Primark Corporation	1,342
315	Johnstown America Industries	1,650	365	Molex Incorporated	1,333
316	Florida Progress Corporation	1,645	366	Associates First Capital Corp.	1,329
317	Cisco Systems, Inc.	1,643	367	The Duriron Company, Inc.	1,325
318	Boise Cascade Office Products	1,637	368	Herman Miller, Inc.	1,324
319	Penn Mutual Life Insurance Co.	1,622	369	Rock Bottom Restaurants, Inc.	1,321
320	Brookshire Grocery Company	1,600	370	Heilig-Meyers Co.	1,320
321	Fleming Companies, Inc.	1,600	371	WMS Industries Inc.	1,301
322	Wang Laboratories, Inc.	1,600	372	Bed Bath & Beyond Inc.	1,300
323	Oakwood Homes Corporation	1,595	373	Bristol-Myers Squibb Company	1,300
324	The Pep Boys	1,591	374	Computer Associates International, Inc.	1,300
325	Spaghetti Warehouse, Inc.	1,590	375	The Continuum Company, Inc.	1,300
226	Kemet Corporation	1,586	376	International Data Group	1,300
327	Fritz Companies, Inc.	1,582	377	Lane Industries, Inc.	1,300
328	Whitman Corporation	1,570	378	The Manitowoc Company, Inc.	1,300
329	Showboat, Inc.	1,559	379	Rural/Metro Corporation	1,300
330	Ithaca Holdings, Inc.	1,550	380	Sanifill, Inc.	1,300
331	UAL Corporation	1,510	381	SUPERVALU Inc.	1,300
332	Intuit Inc.	1,504	382	Thomas & Betts Corporation	1,300
333	Air Products and Chemicals, Inc.	1,500	383	Yellow Corporation	1,300
334	Boyd Gaming Corporation	1,500	384	Deluxe Corporation	1,286
335	Colin Service Systems, Inc.	1,500	385	PureTec Corporation	1,283
336	Energy Ventures, Inc.	1,500	386	Borg-Warner Automotive, Inc.	1,270
337	Haworth, Inc.	1,500	387	QUALCOMM Incorporated	1,267
338	The Interpublic Group of Companies, Inc.	1,500	388	Newmont Gold Company	1,265
339	Taylor Corporation	1,500	389	Newmont Mining Corporation	1,265
340	Station Casinos, Inc.	1,470	390	Pediatric Services of America, Inc.	1,265
341	Jordan Industries, Inc.	1,450	391	Sisters of St. Joseph Health System	1,265
342	Pilgrim's Pride Corporation	1,450	392	Mercantile Bancorporation Inc.	1,262
343	Arch Communications Group, Inc.	1,448	393	Value City Department Stores, Inc.	1,258
344	Citation Corporation	1,438	394	Uno Restaurant Corporation	1,256
345	Synovus Financial Corp.	1,427	395	Lincoln National Corporation	1,255
346	Mountasia Entertainment International, Inc.	1,420	396	Envirotest Systems Corp.	1,252
347	Hoffmann-La Roche, Inc.	1,419	397	Barefoot Inc.	1,250
348	Morgan Stanley Group Inc.	1,412	398	Cadbury Beverages Inc.	1,250
349	Ryder System, Inc.	1,408	399	Acxiom Corporation	1,248
350	Intelligent Electronics, Inc.	1,407	400	Wyman-Gordon Company	1,247

Top 500 Companies by One-Year Absolute Employee Growth in Hoover's Top 2,500 Employers (continued)

Rank	Company	Absolute Growth	Rank	Company	Absolute Growth
401	Barnett Banks, Inc.	1,246	451	Southern Pacific Rail Corporation	1,079
402	CSX Corporation	1,218	452	Consolidated Papers, Inc.	1,078
403	McClatchy Newspapers, Inc.	1,217	453	Atmel Corporation	1,071
404	State Farm Mutual Automobile Insurance Company	1,217	454	Rhodes, Inc.	1,071
405	Sun Microsystems, Inc.	1,216	455	Service Corporation International	1,068
406	Genuine Parts Company	1,215	456	General Re Corporation	1,066
407	Boise Cascade Corporation	1,202	457	Nextel Communications, Incorporated	1,066
408	American Greetings Corporation	1,200	458	Park-Ohio Industries, Inc.	1,066
409	Ashland Inc.	1,200	459	Casino America, Inc.	1,062
410	Coram Healthcare Corporation	1,200	460	Western Digital Corporation	1,054
411	Dames & Moore, Inc.	1,200	461	Lauriat's, Inc.	1,050
412	The Dial Corp	1,200	462	Kuhlman Corporation	1,049
413	Edison Brothers Stores, Inc.	1,200	463	Smith Environmental Technologies	1,043
414	Levi Strauss Associates Inc.	1,200	464	Supercuts, Inc.	1,043
415	Mercantile Stores Company, Inc.	1,200	465	SyQuest Technology, Inc.	1,042
416	NPC International, Inc.	1,200	466	Telephone and Data Systems	1,041
417	Snap-on Incorporated	1,200	467	Ramsay Health Care, Inc.	1,037
418	Sybron International Corporation	1,200	468	Sylvan Learning Systems, Inc.	1,031
419	Teradyne, Inc.	1,200	469	Wisconsin Energy Corporation	1,022
420	United Stationers Inc.	1,200	470	Scholastic Corporation	1,021
421	Watson Wyatt Worldwide	1,200	471	G&K Services, Inc.	1,012
422	General Nutrition Companies	1,197	472	Renters Choice, Inc.	1,012
423	Books-A-Million, Inc.	1,180	473	Informix Corporation	1,007
424	Allergan, Inc.	1,175	474	USFreightways Corporation	1,003
425	Navistar International Corp.	1,169	475	AlliedSignal Inc.	1,000
426	SCI Systems, Inc.	1,158	476	American Protective Services	1,000
427	American Management Systems	1,150	477	Avnet, Inc.	1,000
428	Claire's Stores, Inc.	1,150	478	Beverly Enterprises, Inc.	1,000
429	Geriatric & Medical Companies	1,150	479	The Bombay Company, Inc.	1,000
430	Jabil Circuit, Inc.	1,145	480	Boscov's Department Stores	1,000
431	Cintas	1,143	481	BT Office Products International	1,000
432	Mobile Telecommunication Technologies Corp.	1,125	482	CompuServe Corporation	1,000
433	Flying J Inc.	1,121	483	Cox Enterprises, Inc.	1,000
434	The First American Financial	1,116	484	DiMon, Inc.	1,000
435	Rubbermaid Incorporated	1,115	485	Eaton Corporation	1,000
436	Ruddick Corporation	1,110	486	Electronic Data Systems Corp.	1,000
437	Silgan Holdings Inc.	1,110	487	Federal-Mogul Corporation	1,000
438	Nortek, Inc.	1,106	488	General Electric Company	1,000
439	Retirement Care Associates, Inc.	1,104	489	The Golub Corporation	1,000
440	Agway Inc.	1,100	490	The Grand Union Company	1,000
441	Airgas, Inc.	1,100	491	ITT Hartford Group, Inc.	1,000
442	Allmerica Financial Corporation	1,100	492	Jitney-Jungle Stores of America	1,000
443	Children's Discovery Centers	1,100	493	Koch Industries, Inc.	1,000
444	Consolidated Freightways, Inc.	1,100	494	Levy Restaurants	1,000
445	Hormel Foods Corporation	1,100	495	Liberty Mutual Group	1,000
446	Regal Cinemas, Inc.	1,100	496	Musicland Stores Corporation	1,000
447	Vishay Intertechnology, Inc.	1,100	496	Nobel Education Dynamics, Inc.	1,000
448	Petco Animal Supplies, Inc.	1,099	497	Pacific Gas & Electric	1,000
449	Family Bargain Corporation	1,081	498	Packard Bell Electronics, Inc.	1,000
450	Harman International Industries	1,080	499	Pathmark Stores, Inc.	1,000
			500	Quality Food Centers, Inc.	1,000

Note: These rates may have resulted from acquisitions or internal growth.

Top 500 Companies by One-Year Percentage Employee Growth in Hoover's Top 2,500 Employers

Rank	Company	Percentage of Growth	Rank	Company	Percentage of Growth
1	SoftNet Systems, Inc.	1,653.3	51	Hollywood Entertainment Corporation	178.8
2	Colonial Commercial Corp.	1,575.0	52	NAL Financial Group	177.8
3	Crown Casino Corporation	1,540.9	53	Starwave Corporation	176.3
4	Power Computing Corporation	1,400.0	54	FORE Systems, Inc.	173.7
5	Republic Industries, Inc.	927.6	55	Acclaim Entertainment, Inc.	171.2
6	Reunion Industries Inc.	927.5	56	Hollinger International, Inc.	170.1
7	Ride, Inc.	720.5	57	Modern Medical Modalities Corporation	169.7
8	Manufactured Home Communities, Inc.	666.7	58	PriCellular Corporation	169.2
9	MaxServ, Inc.	650.0	59	Quarterdeck Corporation	168.7
10	Netscape Communications Corp.	610.8	60	Digital Generation Systems, Inc.	167.7
11	Assisted Living Concepts, Inc.	573.1	61	Ascend Communications, Inc.	164.3
12	Infoseek Corporation	545.5	62	The Great American Backrub Store, Inc.	161.3
13	Thermo Remediation Inc.	524.3	63	Nellcor Puritan Bennett Inc.	159.4
14	Smith Environmental Technologies Corporation	480.6	64	Universal Automotive Industries	159.1
15	Mothers Work, Inc.	426.7	65	Chiron Corporation	158.4
16	Video Update, Inc.	407.4	66	7th Level, Inc.	157.0
17	Vector Aeromotive Corp.	405.9	67	Datum Inc.	156.9
18	MedCath Incorporated	399.0	68	Bugaboo Creek Steak House, Inc.	156.1
19	PSINet, Inc.	384.5	69	La-Man Corporation	155.0
20	American Biltrite Inc.	372.5	70	Avitar, Inc.	152.2
21	America Online, Inc.	370.8	71	General Acceptance Corporation	152.1
22	Tristar Corporation	368.5	72	SEACOR Holdings, Inc.	151.6
23	Polyphase Corporation	364.8	73	Resource Bancshares Mortgage Group Inc.	150.7
24	Electronic Designs Inc.	337.9	74	Alabama National BanCorporation	150.3
25	Grey Advertising Inc.	323.1	75	Copart, Inc.	150.0
26	Rainforest Cafe, Inc.	288.3	76	The Fresh Juice Company, Inc.	150.0
27	Nine West Group Inc.	281.0	77	Interstate Bakeries Corporation	150.0
28	Arch Communications Group	246.7	78	Protosource Corporation	150.0
29	Edify Corporation	246.0	79	Public Storage, Inc.	148.3
30	Mountasia Entertainment International, Inc.	244.8	80	Renters Choice, Inc.	147.1
31	Fronteer Directory Company, Inc.	237.6	81	Bally Entertainment Corporation	146.4
32	Biomerica Inc.	234.8	82	Penn Mutual Life Insurance Co.	146.1
33	NETCOM On-Line Communication Services, Inc.	226.8	83	Mattson Technology, Inc.	145.5
34	Rubio's Restaurants, Inc.	223.7	84	ERD Waste Corp.	143.2
35	SportsLine USA, Inc.	216.0	85	Sequoia Systems, Inc.	142.1
36	Hungarian Telephone and Cable.	213.3	86	Advanced NMR Systems, Inc.	139.3
37	Trend-Lines, Inc.	213.3	87	Activision, Inc.	139.2
38	VISTA Information Solutions, Inc.	208.8	88	Scangraphics, Inc.	139.1
39	Corporate Express, Inc.	206.7	89	Rocky Mountain Chocolate Factory, Inc.	137.9
40	EXCEL Communications, Inc.	200.0	90	Discovery Communications, Inc.	137.5
41	Technitrol, Inc.	196.1	91	Robotic Vision Systems, Inc.	135.9
42	EmCare Holdings Inc.	192.3	92	JB Oxford Holdings, Inc.	135.6
43	Lauriat's, Inc.	190.9	93	Osicom Technologies, Inc.	133.9
44	Med/Waste, Inc.	188.2	94	The Panda Project, Inc.	131.7
45	SA Telecommunications, Inc.	184.5	95	U.S. Robotics Corporation	130.7
46	Wired Ventures, Inc.	184.0	96	4Front Software International, Inc.	130.3
47	Telegroup Inc.	183.7	97	International CableTel, Inc.	129.6
48	Boston Scientific Corporation	181.9	98	Boardwalk Casino, Inc.	128.6
49	Heartland Wireless Communications, Inc.	181.1	99	Richey Electronics, Inc.	127.4
50	PureTec Corporation	178.9	100	Happiness Express Inc.	127.3

Top 500 Companies by One-Year Percentage Employee Growth in Hoover's Top 2,500 Employers (continued)

Rank	Company	Percentage of Growth	Rank	Company	Percentage of Growth
101	Williams Controls, Inc.	127.3	151	Corrections Corporation of America	100.0
102	Alpharel, Inc.	127.1	152	First Merchants Acceptance Corp.	100.0
103	Crop Growers Corporation	126.8	153	The Maxim Group, Inc.	100.0
104	Air-Cure Technologies, Inc.	126.3	154	Pyramid Breweries Inc.	100.0
105	Measurement Specialties, Inc.	126.3	155	Sanifill, Inc.	100.0
106	Oxford Health Plans, Inc.	126.0	156	REX Stores Corporation	99.0
107	R Corporation	125.7	157	Rent-Way, Inc.	98.4
108	OroAmerica, Inc.	124.7	158	Xpedite Systems, Inc.	98.4
109	Able Telcom Holding Corp.	124.1	159	Cityscape Financial Corporation	98.2
110	ENCON Systems, Inc.	122.5	160	HA-LO Industries, Inc.	98.0
111	Intuit Inc.	122.5	161	Ultrak, Inc.	97.3
112	SubMicron Systems Corporation	121.8	162	Cambridge Technology Partners	97.3
113	Maxxim Medical, Inc.	121.7	163	BCT International, Inc.	97.1
114	Spaghetti Warehouse, Inc.	121.4	164	Mountain Parks Financial Corp.	96.9
115	Intelligent Electronics, Inc.	121.1	165	Sonat Inc.	96.3
116	Pubco Corporation	120.0	166	Tridex Corporation	95.4
117	Allied Digital Technologies Corp.	119.4	167	McAfee Associates, Inc.	95.3
118	Genuardi Super Markets	118.8	168	The Gymboree Corporation	95.1
119	Offshore Logistics, Inc.	117.6	169	Community Medical Transport	94.4
120	Noven Pharmaceuticals, Inc.	115.2	170	U.S. Diagnostic Labs Inc.	94.4
121	Centennial Technologies, Inc.	115.0	171	Allied Healthcare Products, Inc.	94.4
122	Schwegmann Giant Super Markets	114.3	172	Lockheed Martin Corporation	93.9
123	Lexi International, Inc.	114.3	173	Environmental Technologies Corp.	93.3
124	Exogen, Inc.	113.9	174	Marcus Cable Company L.P.	93.2
125	Movie Gallery, Inc.	113.1	175	American Annuity Group, Inc.	93.2
126	Health Management, Inc.	112.9	176	N2K Inc.	92.9
127	Modem Media	112.1	177	Wellsford Residential Property Trust	92.9
128	CFW Communications Company	112.1	178	American Telecasting, Inc.	91.5
129	Nytest Environmental Inc.	111.9	179	Information Resource Engineering	91.5
130	WavePhore, Inc.	111.3	180	Tetra Tech, Inc.	91.5
131	International Tourist Entertainment Corporation	110.3	181	Genesis Health Ventures, Inc.	91.3
132	P-Com, Inc.	110.3	182	Intermedia Communications, Inc.	91.3
133	Semitool, Inc.	109.9	183	Wingate Partners	90.5
134	National TechTeam, Inc.	109.1	184	NextHealth, Inc.	90.2
135	Olympic Financial Ltd.	108.2	185	Avid Technology, Inc.	90.2
136	Soligen Technologies, Inc.	107.4	186	InTime Systems International	88.6
137	Lawson Products, Inc.	106.8	187	Logistix	88.6
138	PeopleSoft, Inc.	106.0	188	Sylvan Learning Systems, Inc.	88.2
139	FirstPlus Financial, Inc.	105.9	189	Iomega Corporation	88.1
140	Amedisys, Inc.	105.5	190	Winstar Communications, Inc.	88.0
141	Brookstone, Inc.	104.8	191	Pacific Rehabilitation & Sports Medicine, Inc.	87.8
142	Eltron International, Inc.	104.8	192	Harveys Casino Resorts	87.5
143	First Alert, Inc.	104.6	193	Kreisler Manufacturing Corp.	87.5
144	Video Sentry Corporation	103.8	194	Natural MicroSystems Corp.	87.0
145	Physician Reliance Network, Inc.	103.8	195	Continental Waste Industries, Inc.	85.9
146	Manatron, Inc.	103.1	196	Supreme International Corp.	85.7
147	Electrosource, Inc.	102.5	197	Viejas Casino and Turf Club	85.7
148	Apple South, Inc.	102.4	198	National Securities Corporation	85.6
149	Iatros Health Network, Inc.	102.2	199	Big Entertainment, Inc.	85.2
150	First Chicago NBD Corporation	100.4	200	Datastream Systems, Inc.	85.1

Top 500 Companies by One-Year Percentage Employee Growth in Hoover's Top 2,500 Employers (continued)

Rank	Company	Percentage of Growth	Rank	Company	Percentage of Growth
201	The AES Corporation	85.0	251	Rimage Corporation	74.0
202	Kuhlman Corporation	84.9	252	Sheridan Healthcare, Inc.	73.9
203	Frontier Corporation	84.8	253	Mobile Telecommunication	
204	Global Village Communication,			Technologies Corp.	73.8
	Incorporated	84.4	254	Stimsonite Corporation	73.6
205	Lindberg Corporation	83.4	255	Owosso Corporation	73.5
206	NetManage, Inc.	83.1	256	Barefoot Inc.	73.5
207	Gretchell Gold Corp.	82.9	257	Rainbow Technologies, Inc.	73.1
208	PRIMESTAR Partners L.P.	82.9	258	RidgeMotors Pontiac/Mize Import	
209	Johnstown America Industries,			Group Inc.	72.9
	Incorporated	82.5	259	The Chase Manhattan Corporation	72.5
210	Cascade Communications Corp.	82.3	260	SoftKey International Inc.	72.2
211	Comcast Corporation	82.1	261	Landry's Seafood Restaurants, Inc.	72.0
212	UGI Corporation	82.0	262	BJ Services Company	71.8
213	ProNet Inc.	81.9	263	Advanced Financial, Inc.	71.8
214	Attachmate Corporation	81.8	264	Whitman Medical Corp.	71.1
215	Motorcar Parts & Accessories, Inc.	81.8	265	First Financial Bancorp, Inc.	71.1
216	Na1Pro BioTherapeutics, Inc.	81.1	266	Vari-L Company, Inc.	70.9
217	EquiMed, Inc.	80.6	267	Gateway 2000, Inc.	70.9
218	Interline Resources Corporation	80.5	268	Wave Technologies International	70.9
219	Consumer Portfolio Services, Inc.	80.3	269	Communications World	
220	Safety Components International	80.2		International, Inc.	70.7
221	Advanced Engineering & Research		270	Galaxy Foods Company	70.0
	Associates, Inc.	80.2	271	VTEL Corporation	69.6
222	Cali Realty Corporation	80.0	272	First Midwest Bancorp, Inc.	69.5
223	Thrifty Oil Co.	80.0	273	Computer Outsourcing Services	69.4
224	Total-Tel USA Communications,		274	Lynch Corporation	69.3
	Incorporated	80.0	275	Books-A-Million, Inc.	69.3
225	Claremont Technology Group, Inc.	79.9	276	Rock Bottom Restaurants, Inc.	69.1
226	CKS Group, Inc.	79.8	277	Brooks Automation, Inc.	68.9
227	Moovies, Inc.	79.8	278	Sunrise Resources, Inc.	68.8
228	Electric Fuel Corporation	79.6	279	Global Resources, Inc.	68.6
229	Lakeland Industries, Inc.	79.0	280	Campo Electronics, Appliances and	
230	VMARK Software, Inc.	78.8		Computers, Inc.	68.5
231	Foundation Health Corporation	78.7	281	Living Centers of America, Inc.	68.5
232	Koo Koo Roo, Inc.	78.6	282	The Manitowoc Company, Inc.	68.4
233	Revco D.S., Inc.	77.8	283	Solectron Corporation	68.2
234	Specialty Teleconstructors, Inc.	77.8	284	Alliance Semiconductor Corp.	68.2
235	CSS Industries, Inc.	77.7	285	Glenayre Technologies, Inc.	68.2
236	Quintiles Transnational Corp.	77.6	286	All American Semiconductor, Inc.	67.9
237	Expert Software, Inc.	77.1	287	Todd Shipyards Corporation	67.9
238	Media Arts Group, Inc.	76.6	288	Acxiom Corporation	67.5
239	SyQuest Technology, Inc.	76.2	289	Wyman-Gordon Company	67.3
240	Horizon Group, Inc.	76.1	290	Cisco Systems, Inc.	67.3
241	TransCor Waste Services, Inc.	76.0	291	Eagle Finance Corp.	67.2
242	Diamond Shamrock, Inc.	75.8	292	Cerprobe Corporation	67.0
243	Jabil Circuit, Inc.	75.5	293	QUALCOMM Incorporated	66.7
244	E-Z Serve Corporation	75.4	294	AmeriData Technologies, Inc.	66.7
245	UICI	75.3	295	Guaranty National Corporation	66.7
246	Mednet MPC Corporation	75.3	296	Inhale Therapeutic Systems	66.7
247	Data Broadcasting Corporation	75.0	297	Nobel Education Dynamics, Inc.	66.7
248	Star Enterprise	75.0	298	PDK Labs Inc.	66.7
249	Sterling Information Group	75.0	299	Pro CD, Inc.	66.7
250	Frontier Airlines, Inc.	74.3	300	Xircom, Inc.	66.7

Top 500 Companies by One-Year Percentage Employee Growth in
Hoover's Top 2,500 Employers (continued)

Rank	Company	Percentage of Growth	Rank	Company	Percentage of Growth
301	Nextel Communications, Inc.	66.6	351	Wolohan Lumber Co.	60.0
302	Compaq Computer Corporation	66.2	352	Centennial Cellular Corp.	59.8
303	Sequana Therapeutics, Inc.	66.2	353	Brightpoint Inc.	59.7
304	Omega Environmental, Inc.	66.2	354	ESS Technology, Inc.	59.6
305	Applebee's International, Inc.	65.5	355	Insituform Technologies, Inc.	59.6
306	Arris Pharmaceutical Corporation	65.4	356	Silicon Valley Group, Inc.	59.5
307	Daktronics, Inc.	65.4	357	SI Diamond Technology, Inc.	59.2
308	Providence Journal Company	65.3	358	Bollinger Industries, Inc.	59.1
309	Casino Resource Corporation	65.2	359	Citation Corporation	58.9
310	Energy Ventures, Inc.	65.2	360	Advanced Technology Materials	58.7
311	CyberOptics Corporation	65.2	361	Werner Enterprises, Inc.	58.5
312	EqualNet Holding Corp.	65.1	362	Doubletree Corporation	58.4
313	American Mobile Satellite Corp.	65.1	363	Thermo Voltek Corp.	58.1
314	Game Financial Corporation	64.5	364	Ben Franklin Retail Stores, Inc.	57.9
315	QuickResponse Services Inc.	64.4	365	Executive TeleCard, Ltd.	57.8
316	LucasArts Entertainment	64.3	366	Royce Laboratories, Inc.	57.8
317	Control Chief Holdings, Inc.	64.0	367	Olympic Steel, Inc.	57.8
318	Navarre Corporation	63.8	368	Family Bargain Corporation	57.8
319	CompDent Corporation	63.7	369	Softdesk, Inc.	57.8
320	Comstock Resources, Inc.	63.6	370	TETRA Technologies, Inc.	57.7
321	First Data Corporation	63.6	371	ScanSource, Inc.	57.6
322	UUNET Technologies, Inc.	63.6	372	Energy BioSystems Corporation	57.4
323	Endosonics Corporation	63.6	373	ATC Communications Group, Inc.	57.4
324	Mecklermedia Corporation	63.3	374	Northwestern Healthcare	57.3
325	Datatrend Services, Inc.	63.2	375	Cabre Corp	57.2
326	Kenneth Cole Productions, Inc.	63.2	376	RWD Technologies, Inc.	57.2
327	Fidelity Federal Bancorp	63.0	377	Beer Across America, Inc.	57.1
328	Lone Star Steakhouse & Saloon	62.9	378	United Video Satellite Group, Inc.	57.1
329	IDEXX Laboratories, Inc.	62.7	379	American Medical Response, Inc.	57.1
330	WMS Industries Inc.	62.5	380	Individual, Inc.	57.0
331	The Todd-AO Corporation	62.5	381	Peak Technologies Group, Inc.	56.9
332	Circon Corporation	62.2	382	Communications Central Inc.	56.9
333	Applied Materials, Inc.	62.2	383	TransAmerican Waste Industries, Incorporated	56.9
334	Norwood Promotional Products	61.7	384	BREED Technologies, Inc.	56.3
335	Lam Research Corporation	61.7	385	Fisher Scientific International Inc.	56.3
336	The Aegis Consumer Funding Group, Inc.	61.5	386	Atmel Corporation	56.2
337	Park-Ohio Industries, Inc.	61.5	387	FTP Software, Inc.	56.1
338	CAI Wireless Systems, Inc.	61.5	388	ETS International, Inc.	55.7
339	McCrory Corporation	61.4	389	U S WEST Media Group	55.7
340	Jack Henry & Associates, Inc.	61.2	390	Alpha Hospitality Corporation	55.6
341	Photronics, Inc.	60.9	391	Grant Geophysical, Inc.	55.4
342	Hugoton Energy Corporation	60.9	392	Arkansas Best Corporation	55.4
343	Summit Care Corporation	60.9	393	Renaissance Solutions, Inc.	55.3
344	EPIC Design Technology, Inc.	60.8	394	Kenwin Shops, Inc.	55.2
345	CellStar Corporation	60.6	395	VisionTek Inc.	55.2
346	CNA Financial Corporation	60.3	396	GaSonics International Corp.	55.0
347	Microtek Medical, Inc.	60.1	397	Capstone Pharmacy Services, Inc.	54.9
348	Granite Broadcasting Corporation	60.0	398	Funco, Inc.	54.9
349	H. E. Butt Grocery Company	60.0	399	Micros-to-Mainframes, Inc.	54.8
350	Sinclair Oil Corporation	60.0	400	Travel Store Inc.	54.8

Top 500 Companies by One-Year Percentage Employee Growth in Hoover's Top 2,500 Employers (continued)

Rank	Company	Percentage of Growth	Rank	Company	Percentage of Growth
401	Grist Mill Co.	54.8	451	HCIA Inc.	51.2
402	Tenet Healthcare Corporation	54.6	452	Mustang Software, Inc.	51.2
403	AMREP Corporation	54.5	453	Macromedia, Inc.	51.1
404	Petco Animal Supplies, Inc.	54.5	454	Orbit Semiconductor, Inc.	51.1
405	National Media Corporation	54.5	455	Molten Metal Technology, Inc.	51.1
406	Technology Solutions Company	54.4	456	Perclose, Inc.	50.8
407	Credit Acceptance Corporation	54.4	457	Tseng Labs, Inc.	50.8
408	Pinnacle Micro, Inc.	54.2	458	Schnuck Markets Inc.	50.8
409	Graff Pay-Per-View Inc.	54.0	459	BE Aerospace, Inc.	50.8
410	Microwave Power Devices, Inc.	54.0	460	Value Health, Inc.	50.8
411	EA Industries, Inc.	53.9	461	S3 Incorporated	50.7
412	International Management Group	53.8	462	R & B, Inc.	50.7
413	Eastern Utilities Associates	53.4	463	Retirement Care Associates, Inc.	50.4
414	Nabors Industries, Inc.	53.3	464	Ambassador Apartments, Inc.	50.2
415	Pediatric Services of America, Inc.	53.1	465	Allied Products Corporation	50.0
416	Ariel Corporation	53.1	466	Aon Corporation	50.0
417	WFS Financial Inc.	53.0	467	ASARCO Incorporated	50.0
418	Cox Communications, Inc.	53.0	468	Coram Healthcare Corporation	50.0
419	Parametric Technology Corp.	53.0	469	Furniture Brands International	50.0
420	ParkerVision, Inc.	52.9	470	Joseph Webb Foods Inc.	50.0
421	Home State Holdings, Inc.	52.9	471	Lexmark International Group, Inc.	50.0
422	Kulicke and Soffa Industries, Inc.	52.9	472	Lukens Medical Corporation	50.0
423	Columbia/HCA Healthcare Corp.	52.9	473	Sigma Plastics Group	50.0
424	Open Environment Corporation	52.9	474	Stratasys, Inc.	50.0
425	Specialty Retail Group, Inc.	52.6	475	SystemSoft Corporation	50.0
426	The TJX Companies, Inc.	52.6	476	Torotel, Inc.	50.0
427	Symantec Corporation	52.6	477	NIKE, Inc.	49.9
428	Storage Trust Realty	52.6	478	Essex Corporation	49.7
429	Boise Cascade Office Products Corporation	52.5	479	Health Management Systems, Inc.	49.6
430	Outback Steakhouse, Inc.	52.4	480	Knight Transportation, Inc.	49.5
431	American HealthCare Providers	52.4	481	Nichols Research Corporation	49.3
432	Ag-Chem Equipment Co., Inc.	52.3	482	The Thaxton Group, Inc.	49.2
433	CIBER, Inc.	52.1	483	FSI International, Inc.	49.2
434	Zoom Telephonics, Inc.	52.1	484	INSO Corporation	49.2
435	Spyglass, Inc.	52.1	485	Mariner Health Group, Inc.	49.1
436	Pomeroy Computer Resources	52.1	486	UCI Medical Affiliates, Inc.	49.0
437	Meadowbrook Rehabilitation Group, Inc	52.1	487	Central and South West Corp.	49.0
438	Diagnostic Health Services, Inc.	52.0	488	Proffitt's, Inc.	48.9
439	ITT Corporation	52.0	489	Gander Mountain, Inc.	48.8
440	Staples, Inc.	51.9	490	Central Hudson Gas & Electric Corporation	48.8
441	Research Medical, Inc.	51.9	491	Burlington Northern Santa Fe Corporation	48.7
442	The Greenbrier Companies, Inc.	51.6	492	Envirotest Systems Corp.	48.6
443	Aspen Technology, Inc.	51.6	493	Shuffle Master, Inc.	48.6
444	The Sports Club Company, Inc.	51.5	494	Landmark Graphics Corporation	48.5
445	The Duriron Company, Inc.	51.5	495	Danka Business Systems PLC	48.3
446	Midland Financial Group, Inc.	51.4	496	Gulf South Medical Supply, Inc.	48.3
447	Greenwich Air Services, Inc.	51.4	497	Micron Technology, Inc.	48.3
448	IntegraMed America, Inc.	51.3	498	Asyst Technologies, Inc.	48.3
449	RF Power Products, Inc.	51.3	499	Pacific Sunwear of California, Inc.	48.1
450	Irvine Sensors Corporation	51.3	500	STERIS Corporation	48.1

Note: These rates may have resulted from acquisitions or internal growth.

Inc.'s 100 Fastest-Growing Small Public Companies

Rank	Company	Sales Growth (% increase) 1991–95	1995 Revenues ($ thou.)	Business Description
1	AmeriData Technologies	135,647	1,500,000	Computers - systems integration, networking services & technical support
2	NetManage	29,278	125,446	Computers - internetworking software & tools
3	Information Storage Devices	18,766	55,467	Electrical components - integrated circuits
4	Excel Technology	17,466	43,914	Lasers - products & systems for scientific, industrial & medicinal fields
5	Silicon Storage Technology	12,062	39,528	Computers - memory devices for components such as CD-ROM drives
6	PerSeptive Biosystems	9,982	89,429	Medical instruments - products & systems for biomolecules
7	S3	9,627	316,309	Computers - graphics accelerator systems
8	Palomar Medical Technologies	9,173	21,792	Lasers - pulsed dye & diode medical lasers; multilayered circuit boards
9	Education Alternatives	9,008	213,582	Consulting - integrated public & private school management
10	Grand Casinos	8,742	372,866	Gambling resorts & casinos
11	Alantec	8,143	53,330	Computers - intelligent switching hubs & LAN products
12	Alliance Semiconductor	8,118	119,327	Electrical components - high-speed SRAM & DRAM semiconductors
13	Mercury Interactive	7,274	39,450	Computers - testing & quality assurance software
14	TheraTx	6,898	329,521	Nursing homes
15	SQA	5,931	12,845	Computers - automated testing & quality management software
16	American Telecasting	5,280	47,501	Cable TV - wireless cable TV (#1 in US)
17	ThrustMaster	4,891	19,415	Computers - game simulation equipment
18	Citrix Systems	4,740	14,568	Computers - multiuser application server products for Windows
19	Advanced NMR Systems	4,475	14,822	Medical instruments - magnetic resonance imaging equipment
20	Logic Works	4,446	30,688	Computers - database design & business-process modeling software
21	PairGain Technologies	4,441	107,224	Telecommunications equipment - high-speed digital line technology
22	Incomnet	4,431	86,000	Computers - hardware & software; telephone services marketing
23	Grow Biz International	4,319	100,213	Franchisors - stores that sell, buy, trade & consign used & new goods
24	I-Flow	4,144	10,143	Medical instruments - compact, portable infusion pumps
25	Standish Care	4,076	8,436	Nursing homes

Inc.'s 100 Fastest-Growing Small Public Companies (continued)

Rank	Company	Sales Growth (% increase) 1991–95	1995 Revenues ($ thou.)	Business Description
26	National Surgery Centers	4,002	53,165	Medical services - multispecialty ambulatory surgery centers
27	FPA Medical Management	3,886	52,692	Medical practice management - health care management services
28	LaserSight	3,785	25,988	Lasers - ophthalmologic laser systems; laser treatment center
29	U.S. Physical Therapy	3,734	24,924	Health care - outpatient physical & occupational therapy
30	Lone Star Steakhouse & Saloon	3,593	340,857	Retail - steakhouse restaurants
31	Orion Network Systems	3,341	22,300	Telecommunications - international satellite communications systems
32	Funco	3,090	80,365	Retail - used video games (FuncoLand)
33	Boston Market	2,944	159,479	Retail - restaurant operators & franchisors (Boston Market)
34	Isolyser	2,815	75,414	Medical products - products for patient care, occupational safety
35	Hollywood Entertainment	2,782	149,400	Retail - video rental superstores
36	On Technology	2,771	44,120	Computers - networking software for heterogeneous networks
37	ATS Medical	2,736	9,301	Medical instruments - open-pivot bileaflet heart valve
38	Creative Computers	2,724	420,900	Retail - mail-order sales of Macintosh products (MacMall)
39	Scopus Technology	2,673	15,250	Computers - customer-support software
40	Manhattan Bagel	2,656	19,154	Franchisors - bagel bakeries, delicatessens & rotisserie chicken
41	TechForce	2,646	49,232	Computers - integrated network support
42	Mednet, MPC	2,646	115,423	Medical practice management - pharmacy card plan processing & services
43	Objective Systems Integrators	2,641	36,011	Computers - client/server software for network operations
44	Cidco	2,622	193,668	Telecommunications equipment - caller identification equipment
45	American Oncology Resources	2,572	99,174	Medical practice management - oncology practice management
46	Network Peripherals	2,525	47,144	Computers - local area network management hardware & software
47	Firefox Communications	2,461	19,768	Computers - server-based connectivity & communications software
48	MetaTools	2,364	16,731	Computers - graphics (Kai's Power Tools)
49	Pete's Brewing	2,270	59,176	Beverages - specialty beers (Pete's Wicked Ale)
50	Hometown Buffet	2,240	152,399	Retail - restaurants

Inc.'s 100 Fastest-Growing Small Public Companies (continued)

Rank	Company	Sales Growth (% increase) 1991–95	1995 Revenues ($ thou.)	Business Description
51	President Casinos	2,239	160,350	Gambling resorts & casinos - riverboat & dockside casinos
52	Executive TeleCard	2,203	27,083	Telecommunications services - telephone charge card
53	Media Arts Group	2,181	52,772	Housewares - collectible, gift & art products & home decor products
54	C-Cube Microsystems	2,162	124,602	Electrical components - video-compression processor chips & software
55	Molten Metal Technology	2,154	44,181	Industrial processing - catalytic breakdown of waste
56	USA Waste Services	2,113	457,099	Waste management - solid waste management
57	SanDisk	2,035	62,839	Electronics - flash memory data storage products
58	Midcom Communications	2,017	200,000	Telecommunications services - long-distance services
59	Biosys	1,998	22,999	Chemicals - bioinsecticides
60	Opal	1,978	44,736	Electronics - inspection systems for integrated circuit manufacturing
61	T-Netix	1,941	27,754	Telecommunications services - call processing services
62	Physician Computer Network	1,890	41,805	Computers - physician practice-management software
63	Plasma & Materials Technologies	1,875	21,290	Machinery - systems for the semiconductor & thin film industries
64	Uncle B's Bakery	1,869	15,319	Food - fresh bagels sold in supermarkets
65	Software Artistry	1,856	25,628	Computers - customer support software (Expert Advisor)
66	Smart Modular Technologies	1,842	274,592	Computers - memory devices for PCs & workstations; modems
67	Oxford Health Plans	1,802	1,765,367	Health maintenance organization
68	UUNet Technologies	1,797	94,461	Computers - Internet access services
69	U.S. Alcohol Testing of America	1,796	8,437	Medical instruments - blood-alcohol measuring instruments
70	CellPro	1,771	8,196	Medical products - biotechnology processes & equipment
71	CommNet Cellular	1,731	89,844	Telecommunications equipment - cellular telephone systems
72	Opta Food Ingredients	1,712	7,067	Food - ingredients for improving nutritional content & taste of food
73	USA Detergents	1,711	104,878	Soap & cleaning preparations - cleaning products & fabric softener
74	Ventritex	1,706	126,922	Medical products - implanted defibrillators (Cadence)
75	HyperMedia Communications	1,690	9,754	Publishing - multimedia-related periodicals, books & newsletters

Rank	Company	Sales Growth (% increase) 1991–95	1995 Revenues ($ thou.)	Business Description
76	Microtel Franchise & Development	1,653	7,294	Hotels & motels - franchisor of economy, limited-service lodging facilities
77	Avant!	1,638	38,004	Computers - integrated circuit design automation software
78	Mackie Designs	1,583	63,919	Electronics - audio mixers
79	Spyglass	1,569	10,350	Computers - software (Mosaic)
80	Transworld Home HealthCare	1,564	71,587	Health care - respiratory therapy & home medical equipment
81	MRV Communications	1,533	39,202	Electrical components - diodes, fiber-optic systems & Ethernet hubs
82	Racotek	1,523	6,088	Telecommunications equipment
83	Hart Brewing	1,518	23,419	Beverages - specialty beers
84	Sun Healthcare Group	1,509	1,135,508	Nursing homes & subacute care facilities
85	Paradigm Technology	1,496	51,923	Electrical components - static random-access memory (SRAM) chips
86	Industrial Services of America	1,476	30,248	Waste management - integrated solid waste handling & equipment sales
87	United Waste Systems	1,468	211,790	Waste management - nonhazardous solid waste management services
88	MFS Communications	1,467	583,194	Telecommunications services - special access & private-line services
89	First Cash	1,464	32,184	Financial - pawn shops
90	Cheyenne Software	1,461	127,927	Computers - local & wide area network software products
91	Modern Medical Modalities	1,415	10,435	Leasing - MRI & computerized axial tomography equipment
92	Pyxis	1,409	202,887	Medical products - medication & supply management & control equipment
93	Ramtron International	1,383	28,900	Electrical components -semiconductor memory devices
94	Alkermes	1,373	13,903	Drugs - delivery systems & products to treat central nervous system
95	Xata	1,346	7,130	Electrical products - onboard information systems for trucking industry
96	ReSound	1,267	107,330	Medical products - hearing aids
97	OnTrak Systems	1,262	26,024	Electrical components - semiconductor equipment
98	Identix	1,260	27,014	Electronics - biometric personal identification & verification systems
99	Top Source Technologies	1,257	18,969	Automotive & trucking - automotive technologies; oil analysis laboratories
100	Mikohn Gaming	1,247	77,797	Gambling equipment - computerized systems for gaming machines

Source: *Inc.*; May 1996

Business Week's 100 Hot Growth Companies

		3-YEAR AVERAGE GROWTH			
Rank	Company	Sales (%)	Profits (%)	Return on Capital (%)	Business Description
1	Remedy	160.5	272.9	43.4	Computers - help desk & support automation software
2	Eltron International	182.5	179.6	49.9	Computers - bar-code label printers, software & related accessories
3	Logic Works	175.7	153.1	42.9	Computers - database design & business-process modeling software
4	APAC TeleServices	107.7	123.2	51.7	Business services - outsourced telephone-based sales & marketing
5	Datastream Systems	78.7	165.5	48.3	Computers - Windows-based maintenance management software
6	UniComp	82.7	206.6	39.1	Computers - systems installation & services; public-address system sales
7	Retirement Care Associates	313.9	196.9	32.5	Nursing homes & retirement centers
8	OnTrak Systems	101.2	228.1	33.4	Electrical components - semiconductor equipment
9	Logan's Roadhouse	78.0	92.9	70.1	Retail - restaurants
10	Opal	82.3	861.5	27.8	Electronics - inspection systems for integrated circuit manufacturing
11	HPR	44.2	140.4	40.9	Computers - clinical database software for health care providers
12	Symetrics Industries	92.2	98.5	32.1	Electronics - data-processing equipment for missiles & aircraft modems
13	Movie Gallery	173.0	157.1	27.6	Retail - videocassette & video game sales & rental
14	GaSonics International	51.6	172.6	30.9	Machinery - equipment used in semiconductor manufacturing
15	ACT Manufacturing	69.0	47.1	55.0	Electrical components - electronic interconnection assemblies
16	USA Detergents	71.2	206.7	27.3	Soap & cleaning preparations - cleaning products & fabric softener
17	PMT Services	42.8	104.5	42.4	Business services - marketing & servicing of credit card systems
18	Astea International	44.5	214.8	29.4	Computers - inventory tracking, order entry & requisitioning software
19	Chad Therapeutics	48.9	58.5	46.2	Medical products - respiratory care & oxygen delivery systems
20	General Employment Enterprises	19.2	318.4	37.3	Personnel - temporary, long-term & permanent staff placement
21	Cambridge Technology Partners	89.6	113.0	27.1	Computers - information-technology consulting & software development

Business Week's 100 Hot Growth Companies (continued)

Rank	Company	3-YEAR AVERAGE GROWTH Sales (%)	Profits (%)	Return on Capital (%)	Business Description
22	Wireless Telecom Group	65.3	98.2	29.1	Electronics - custom & standard noise sources & test equipment
23	Moovies	88.3	59.3	30.8	Retail - video specialty stores
24	MedCath	70.5	282.7	22.4	Medical services - heart-care hospital; cardiology & cardiovascular services
25	Scientific Technologies	41.2	67.5	40.6	Instruments - electrical & electronic industrial controls
26	ESS Technology	80.7	48.2	32.1	Electrical components - integrated semiconductor audio solutions
27	Rock Bottom Restaurants	57.6	35.8	38.7	Retail - restaurants featuring micro-brewed & specialty beer
28	Kenneth Cole Productions	38.8	67.3	39.2	Shoes & related apparel (Kenneth Cole, Unlisted); retail stores
29	Cybex Computer Products	42.9	73.7	33.9	Computers - keyboard, video monitor & mouse switch & extension products
30	Sterling Healthcare Group	43.3	55.9	36.3	Personnel - physician contract-management support services
31	Anchor Gaming	81.8	52.5	28.5	Gambling resorts & casinos - resorts & gaming machines
32	Parlux Fragrances	30.2	270.5	27.0	Cosmetics & toiletries - fragrances & beauty products
33	Align-Rite International	25.0	93.0	35.4	Electrical components - photomasks used to produce integrated circuits
34	INSO	71.9	31.8	30.3	Computers - proofing, reference & information management software
35	Encad	69.4	73.8	26.4	Computers - large-format ink-jet color printers & plotters
36	Diodes	46.5	133.4	25.3	Electrical components - discrete semiconductor products
37	Helix Technology	34.6	96.2	30.0	Instruments - cryogenic & vacuum technology
38	Nobility Homes	45.4	161.6	24.0	Building - manufactured homes
39	Computer Management & Sciences	34.5	107.7	28.6	Computers - information technology software-development services
40	Cerprobe	45.7	59.7	28.9	Electronics - semiconductor test equipment
41	Fusion Systems	50.3	122.7	23.8	Machinery - ultraviolet curing systems
42	The UniMark Group	58.1	472.2	18.2	Food - processed chilled & canned fruits
43	Image Entertainment	17.4	50.7	41.4	Leisure & recreational products - video programming for discs, CDs

| Rank | Company | 3-YEAR AVERAGE GROWTH | | | Business Description |
		Sales (%)	Profits (%)	Return on Capital (%)	
44	NetManage	193.0	200.3	15.3	Computers - internetworking software & tools
45	Unison Software	22.2	132.7	27.9	Computers - network management software
46	Colonial Data Technologies	98.3	240.9	15.6	Telecommunications equipment - caller ID products
47	Storage Computer	132.7	349.5	11.5	Computers - semiconductor memories
48	Atria Software	173.6	170.7	15.9	Computers - software that manages software development (ClearCase)
49	Perceptron	42.9	78.7	26.2	Machinery - machine vision systems for industrial applications
50	Gulf South Medical Supply	49.5	79.3	23.2	Medical & dental supplies - distribution to long-term care providers
51	Hirsch International	29.2	48.3	32.3	Wholesale distribution - computerized embroidery machines
52	Safeskin	54.7	40.0	26.9	Medical & dental supplies - hypoallergenic disposable latex gloves
53	Fresh America	27.4	53.2	31.6	Food - wholesale fruits & vegetables to Sam's Wholesale Clubs
54	TSX	35.2	1728.2	18.8	Electronics - cable TV system operation equipment
55	Taitron Components	49.3	99.0	20.8	Electronics - distribution of transistors & other discrete semiconductors
56	RF Power Products	46.3	148.3	20.0	Electrical products - radio frequency power systems
57	Reflectone	18.3	32.5	37.5	Electronics - flight simulators, military training systems
58	Brooks Automation	61.3	136.5	18.2	Machinery - central wafer handling systems, modules & software
59	VERITAS Software	59.4	187.4	16.8	Computers - open-system software for data management
60	American List	23.1	29.9	35.5	Business services - mailing lists of children & students
61	Applied Voice Technology	31.1	112.3	24.1	Computers - telephone, fax & e-mail software products
62	Computer Telephone	33.4	132.2	22.9	Telecommunications services - discounted calling plans, other services
63	EPIC Design Technology	109.4	28.1	21.8	Computers - simulation & analysis software for integrated circuit design
64	Security Dynamics Technologies	62.6	99.7	18.4	Computers - security & access software

Rank	Company	3-YEAR AVERAGE GROWTH			Business Description
		Sales (%)	Profits (%)	Return on Capital (%)	
65	Data Systems & Software	93.3	82.2	17.3	Computers - consulting services; semiconductor manufacturing
66	Eastbay	35.7	28.1	28.6	Retail - mail-order sales of apparel & licensed & private-label products
67	Coherent Communications Systems	35.6	180.4	18.4	Telecommunications equipment - echo canceller, network products
68	Euphonix	46.5	37.8	24.3	Electronics - digitally controlled audio mixing consoles & components
69	Conso Products	38.1	51.5	25.7	Textiles - decorative trimmings for the home furnishings industry
70	Lafayette Industries	46.7	184.1	15.9	Furniture - display racks, showcases, cabinets & wall display units
71	Macromedia	67.7	171.5	14.8	Computers - multimedia authoring software tools
72	Catalina Marketing	23.2	38.6	28.8	Business services - point-of-scan electronic marketing products & services
73	Miller Industries	60.2	85.1	18.1	Automotive manufacturing - tow truck & vehicle carriers
74	CIBER	70.6	88.6	16.8	Computers - system analysis, design & maintenance, consulting & training
75	Global Village Communication	83.5	75.5	16.3	Computers - data modems & fax cards
76	Educational Development	44.3	71.8	20.4	Wholesale distribution - instructional children's books & materials
77	SOS Staffing Services	27.8	55.9	25.4	Personnel - temporary staffing services
78	Cutter & Buck	34.2	201.8	16.3	Apparel - men's sportswear
79	STERIS	49.6	71.9	18.2	Medical products - sterilizers for surgical equipment
80	Panatech Research & Development	33.1	73.1	21.1	Machinery - precision high-pressure airless paint-spraying equipment
81	CyberOptics	51.2	132.8	15.1	Machinery - process-control & measurement systems
82	Micrel,	47.7	140.2	15.1	Electrical components - analog integrated circuits
83	SafetyTek	33.3	34.7	24.4	Instruments - sensor-based instruments
84	Project Software & Development	23.7	86.3	21.0	Computers - maintenance applications & management systems
85	First Team Sports	44.6	67.7	18.5	Leisure & recreational products - in-line roller skates & accessories

Business Week's 100 Hot Growth Companies (continued)

| Rank | Company | 3-YEAR AVERAGE GROWTH | | | Business Description |
		Sales (%)	Profits (%)	Return on Capital (%)	
86	ATC Environmental	38.2	123.9	17.0	Pollution control equipment & services - environmental consulting
87	Timberline Software	18.6	75.9	21.4	Computers - accounting & financial management software
88	TECHNE	30.0	46.7	23.3	Biomedical & genetic products - research reagents and kits
89	Gentex	39.3	53.1	20.1	Automotive & trucking - rearview mirrors; residential smoke detectors
90	Cognex	52.9	54.6	17.3	Machinery - computerized quality-control systems
91	Ballantyne of Omaha	28.2	52.0	22.5	Electrical products - movie projection equipment & spotlights (#1 in US)
92	Penn National Gaming	16.8	85.1	20.8	Leisure & recreational services - race track & off-track betting facilities
93	Lo-Jack	31.7	193.2	15.1	Protection - automobile tracking devices
94	Right Management Consultants	28.3	80.0	19.6	Consulting - outplacement services
95	Centennial Technologies	41.7	40.8	20.2	Computers - PC cards (memory & data/fax); laser printer font cartridges
96	Fair, Isaac	38.4	51.6	20.1	Business services - data management systems & services
97	Innovex	12.8	117.0	18.7	Computers - lead-wire assemblies for heads of hard disk drives
98	Abatix Environmental	34.1	141.8	15.7	Protection - safety equipment & supplies
99	Urban Outfitters	31.0	43.9	21.8	Retail - apparel, shoes, accessories, household & gift merchandise
100	Knight Transportation	45.6	63.8	17.1	Transportation - short- to medium-haul trucking services

Source: *Business Week*; May 27, 1996

The 50 Largest Companies on
Inc.'s 500 Fastest-Growing Private Companies List

Rank	Company	1994 Sales ($ thou.)	Sales Growth 1990–94 (% increase)	Business Description
1	Furst Group	92,202	42,389	Telecommunications services - long-distance telephone services
2	Telegroup	70,062	25,753	Telecommunications services - long-distance telephone services
3	DPR Construction	174,765	25,302	Building - commercial high-tech & offices
4	Axion	126,369	25,023	Medical services - disease management services
5	International Textiles/Rug Barn	64,881	24,291	Manufactures & distributes decorative home products
6	Premier Ambulatory Systems	34,660	15,443	Hospitals - ambulatory surgery centers
7	Matrix Telecom	59,449	14,543	Telecommunications services - long-distance telephone services
8	United Vision Group	28,009	13,238	Housewares - wood-inlay gifts & furniture & fresh cut flowers
9	KPR Sports International	26,593	11,879	Distributes discontinued athletic shoes to retailers; manufactures footwear
10	American Ophthalmic	21,006	9,625	Medical practice management - eye clinics
11	Simplified Employment Services	21,779	9,410	Personnel - provides employee leasing services
12	TriNet Employer Group	44,771	8,363	Business services - human resources services, including payroll & benefits
13	Simple Technology	98,681	7,794	Computers - memory upgrades & PC cards
14	Information Technology Solutions	50,695	7,784	Provides data processing, engineering & other professional services
15	Oasis Imaging Products	16,073	7,482	Distributes supplies for remanufacturing of laser-printer cartridges
16	Reply	42,255	6,523	Computers - provides upgrades & enhancements for computer systems
17	Benchmarq Microelectronics	23,027	6,517	Electrical components - mixed-signal integrated circuits & modules
18	Born Information Services Group	13,115	6,425	Computers - information systems consulting services
19	Diamond Key Homes	45,562	6,228	Building - homes
20	Guiltless Gourmet	20,046	6,204	Food - low-fat snack foods
21	Logic Works	13,302	6,058	Computers - database design & business-process modeling software
22	Holland Group	27,745	5,905	Personnel - employment & human resources consulting services
23	Biosite Diagnostics	16,320	5,771	Medical products - antibody-based diagnostic test devices
24	Healthcare Recoveries	14,675	5,396	Insurance - insurance-subrogation services
25	PageMart	109,833	5,201	Telecommunications services - wireless messaging services

The 50 Largest Companies on
Inc.'s 500 Fastest-Growing Private Companies List (continued)

Rank	Company	1994 Sales ($ thou.)	Sales Growth 1990–94 (% increase)	Business Description
26	Hub Group Distribution Services	11,612	4,927	Transportation - logistics management services
27	Tivoli Systems	26,878	4,859	Computers - systems management software
28	Secor International	49,657	4,684	Engineering - environmental engineering & consulting services
29	Storybook Heirlooms	26,990	4,436	Retail - dress & casual apparel catalog for girls & their mothers
30	Select Comfort	29,359	4,302	Furniture - air sleep systems
31	Health Tech Industries	18,994	4,112	Medical products - pharmaceuticals & medical supplies distribution
32	NIE International	13,452	3,952	Retail - computer systems & parts distribution
33	Megabyte International	10,318	3,721	Retail - memory hardware distribution
34	Mac USA	46,645	3,714	Computers - peripheral equipment & software
35	Sprint Staffing	22,952	3,663	Personnel - temporary employment services
36	ShowCase	10,018	3,195	Computers - client/server software
37	Counter Technology	10,128	3,157	Telecommunications services - security management & systems design
38	Advanced Technical Resources	13,484	3,088	Personnel - temporary employment services
39	Calsouth	33,841	3,025	Building - single-family homes
40	Optical Laser	10,937	3,007	Wholesale distribution - optical storage products
41	GB Tech	20,028	2,930	Engineering - engineering, science & computer services
42	PRT Corp. of America	13,876	2,910	Computers - software planning, training & development services
43	Sendai Media Group	27,325	2,906	Publishing - computer & video-game magazines; online forum
44	Hall Kinion & Associates	14,326	2,897	Provides high-technology staffing
45	Levenger	40,725	2,845	Retail - mail-order accessories for reading
46	Vektron International	14,359	2,842	Retail - mail-order computers & peripheral components
47	Engineered Endeavors	6,748	2,809	Wireless telecommunications products
48	Working Assets Funding Service	59,991	2,775	Telecommunications services - donation-linked long distance services
49	SunDisk	35,378	2,774	Computers - flash memory storage cards
50	Insync Systems	16,403	2,773	Engineering, manufacturing & testing services

Source: *Inc. 500*; 1995

America's 100 Most Admired Companies

Rank	Company	Rank	Company	Rank	Company
1	Coca-Cola	36	Norwest	71	Xerox
2	Proctor & Gamble	37	Capital Cities/ABC	72	Eli Lilly
3	Rubbermaid	38	Kimberly-Clark	73	Turner Broadcasting
4	Johnson & Johnson	39	Southwest Airlines	74	RR Donnelley & Sons
5	Intel	40	Charles Schwab	75	Leggett & Platt
6	Merck	41	Columbia/HCA Healthcare	76	Nordstrom
7	Microsoft	42	Exxon	77	Union Pacific
8	Mirage Resorts	43	Illinois Tool Works	78	Banc One
9	Hewlett-Packard	44	SBC Communications	79	Martin Marietta
10	Motorola	45	AT&T	80	Schering-Plough
11	Minnesota Mining & Mfg.	46	Sysco	81	Southern
12	Pfizer	47	Alcoa	82	Tribune
13	Walt Disney	48	AlliedSignal	83	Tenet HealthCare
14	McDonald's	49	Mobil	84	Wendy's International
15	Gillette	50	Norfolk Southern	85	Williams
16	Levi Strauss Associates	51	Wal-Mart Stores	86	Armstrong World
17	Berkshire Hathaway	52	Deere	87	Compaq Computer
18	Home Depot	53	Abbott Laboratories	88	Ford Motor
19	Promus	54	Emerson Electric	89	Texas Instruments
20	Boeing	55	CUC International	90	Anheuser-Busch
21	Marriott International	56	Cardinal Health	91	Federal Express
22	Enron	57	Clorox	92	Walgreen
23	Albertson's	58	Dow Chemical	93	Lockheed
24	PepsiCo	59	Dow Jones	94	Unifi
25	Du Pont	60	Fluor	95	Sun Microsystems
26	United Parcel Service	61	Nucor	96	M.A. Hanna
27	Corning	62	Host Marriott	97	Readers Digest Assoc.
28	J.P. Morgan	63	Caterpillar	98	NationsBank
29	United HealthCare	64	Viacom	99	FPL Group
30	Intl. Flavors & Fragrances	65	American Intl. Group	100	Gannett
31	General Electric	66	Citicorp		
32	Publix Super Markets	67	General Mills		
33	Goodyear Tire & Rubber	68	Oracle Systems		
34	Shell Oil	69	Sara Lee		
35	Merrill Lynch	70	Amoco		

Source: *FORTUNE*; March 4, 1996

Companies Providing Best Environment for Lesbian and Gay Employees

Company	City	Company	City
Apple Computer	Cupertino, CA	Lotus Development Corp.	Cambridge, MA
Ben & Jerry's Homemade	Waterbury, VT	MCA Inc.	University City, CA
The Boston Globe	Boston, MA	Pacific Gas & Electric Co.	San Francisco, CA
Charles Schwab and Co.	San Francisco, CA	Quark Inc.	Denver, CO
Federal National Mortgage		Viacom International	New York, NY
Association (Fannie Mae)	Washington, DC	Ziff-Davis Publishing	New York, NY
Levi Strauss & Co.	San Francisco, CA		

Source: *Cracking the Corporate Closet: The 200 Best (and Worst) Companies To Work For, Buy From And Invest In If You're Gay Or Lesbian — And Even If You Aren't,* by Daniel B. Baker, Sean O'Brien Strub, and Bill Henning, New York, Harper Business, 1995.

The 100 Best Companies to Work For

Company	City	Company	City
Acipco	Birmingham, AL	Lowe's	North Wilkesboro, NC
Advanced Micro Devices	Sunnyvale, CA	Lyondell Petrochemical	Houston
Alagasco	Birmingham, AL	Marquette Electronics	Milwaukee
Anheuser-Busch	St. Louis	Mary Kay Cosmetics	Dallas
Apogee Enterprises	Minneapolis	McCormick	Hunt Valley, MD
Armstrong	Lancaster, PA	Merck	Whitehouse Station, NJ
Avis	Garden City, NY	Methodist Hospital	Houston
Baptist Hospital of Miami	Miami	Microsoft	Redmond, WA
BE&K	Birmingham, AL	Herman Miller	Zeeland, MI
Ben & Jerry's Homemade	Waterbury, VT	3M	St. Paul
Beth Israel Hospital Boston*	Boston	Moog	East Aurora, NY
Leo Burnett	Chicago	J.P. Morgan	New York
Chaparral Steel	Midlothian, TX	Morrison & Foerster	San Francisco
Compaq Computer	Houston	Motorola	Schaumburg, IL
Cooper Tire	Findlay, OH	Nissan Motor Manufacturing	Smyrna, TN
Corning	Corning, NY	Nordstrom	Seattle
Cray Research	Eagan, MN	Northwestern Mutual Life	Milwaukee
Cummins Engine	Columbus, IN	Odetics	Anaheim
Dayton Hudson	Minneapolis	Patagonia	Ventura, CA
John Deere	Moline, IL	J. C. Penney	Plano, TX
Delta Air Lines*	Atlanta	Physio-Control	Redmond, WA
Donnelly*	Holland, MI	Pitney Bowes	Stamford, CT
Du Pont	Wilmington, DE	Polaroid	Cambridge, MA
A. G. Edwards	St. Louis	Preston Trucking	Preston, MD
Erie Insurance	Erie, PA	Procter & Gamble	Cincinnati
Federal Express*	Memphis	Publix Super Markets*	Lakeland, FL
Fel-Pro*	Skokie, IL	Quad/Graphics	Pewaukee, WI
First Federal Bank of California	Santa Monica	Reader's Digest	Pleasantville, NY
H. B. Fuller	St. Paul, MN	REI	Seattle
General Mills	Minneapolis	Rosenbluth International*	Philadelphia
Goldman Sachs	New York	SAS Institute	Cary, NC
W. L. Gore & Associates	Newark, DE	J. M. Smucker	Orrville, OH
Great Plains Software	Fargo, ND	Southwest Airlines*	Dallas
Hallmark Cards*	Kansas City, MO	Springfield ReManufacturing	Springfield, MO
Haworth	Holland, MI	Springs	Fort Mill, SC
Hershey Foods	Hershey, PA	Steelcase	Grand Rapids
Hewitt Associates	Lincolnshire, IL	Syntex	Palo Alto, CA
Hewlett-Packard	Palo Alto, CA	Tandem	Cupertino, CA
Honda of America Manufacturing	Marysville, OH	TDIndustries	Dallas
IBM	Armonk, NY	Tennant	Minneapolis
Inland Steel	Chicago	UNUM	Portland, ME
Intel	Santa Clara, CA	USAA*	San Antonio
Johnson & Johnson	New Brunswick, NJ	U S West	Englewood, CO
SC Johnson Wax	Racine, WI	Valassis Communications	Livonia, MI
Kellogg	Battle Creek, MI	Viking Freight System	San Jose
Knight-Ridder	Miami	Wal-Mart	Bentonville, AR
Lands' End	Dodgeville, WI	Wegmans	Rochester, NY
Lincoln Electric	Cleveland	Weyerhaeuser	Tacoma, WA
Los Angeles Dodgers	Los Angeles	Worthington Industries	Columbus, OH
Lotus Development	Cambridge, MA	Xerox	Stamford, CT

Source: Levering, Robert, and Milton Moskowitz. *The 100 Best Companies to Work For in America.*
New York: Doubleday, 1993.
* Indicates one of Top Ten

Top 20 Woman-Owned Businesses

Rank	Company	Owner	1995 Sales ($ mil.)
1	Ingram Industries	Martha Ingram	11,000
2	TLC Beatrice	Loida Nicolas Lewis	2,100
3	Raley's	Joyce Raley Teel	1,840
4	Roll International	Lynda Resnick	1,460
5	Little Caesar Enterprises	Marian Ilitch	1,160
6	Axel Johnson Group	Antonia Axson Johnson	940
7	Warnaco Group	Linda Wachner	916
8	Minyard Food Stores	Liz Minyard, Gretchen Minyard Williams	875
9	Mark III Industries	Sally McClain	605
10	Printpack	Gay Love	570
11	Donna Karan	Donna Karan	550
12	Jockey International	Donna Wolf Steigerwaldt	450
13	Copley Press	Helen Copley	390
14	Troy Motors	Irma Elder	389
15	Owen Healthcare	Dian Graves Owen	384
16	Jenny Craig International	Jenny Craig	336
17	ASI	Christine Liang	326
18	I-Net	Kavelle Bajaj	320
19	Chas. Levy	Barbara Levy Kipper	314
20	Tootsie Roll Industries	Ellen Gordon	313

Source: *Working Woman*; May 1996

Top 20 Hispanic-Owned Businesses

Rank	Company	1995 Sales ($ mil.)
1	Burt Automotive Network	596.3
2	Goya Foods Inc.	560.0
3	Troy Ford Inc.	389.3
4	Ancira Enterprises Inc.	346.0
5	de la Cruz Cos.	302.6
6	AJ Contracting Co. Inc.	260.0
7	Sedano's Supermarkets	257.1
8	International Bancshares Corp.	244.9
9	Vincam Group Inc.	239.4
10	CTA Incorporated	217.0
11	MasTec Inc.	175.0
12	United Poultry Corp.	170.2
13	Capital Bancorp	155.4
14	Lopez Foods Inc.	154.0
15	Precision Trading Corp.	153.0
16	Lloyd A. Wise Cos.	152.7
17	Mexican Industries in Michigan	151.0
18	Coex Coffee International Inc.	146.3
19	Rosendin Electric Inc.	140.0
20	Colsa Corp.	129.3

Source: *Hispanic Business*; June 1996

Top 20 Black-Owned Businesses

Rank	Company	1995 Sales ($ mil.)
1	TLC Beatrice International	2,100.0
2	Johnson Publishing Co. Inc.	316.2
3	Philadelphia Coca-Cola Bottling	315.0
4	H.J. Russell & Co.	172.8
5	Pulsar Data Systems Inc.	165.1
6	Uniworld Group Inc.	133.7
7	Burrell Communications Group	127.9
8	The Anderson-Dubose Co.	119.5
9	Granite Broadcasting Corp.	119.5
10	BET Holdings Inc.	115.0
11	Mays Chemical Co. Inc.	107.0
12	Envirotest Systems Corp.	104.8
13	The Bing Group	101.0
14	RMS Technologies Inc.	95.0
15	Soft Sheen Products Inc.	92.8
16	Midwest Stamping Inc.	90.2
17	Sylvest Management Systems Corp.	84.0
18	Essence Communications Inc.	80.1
19	Thacker Engineering Inc.	76.8
20	Wesley Industries Inc.	75.7

Source: *Black Enterprise*; June 1996

Top 2,500 Employers

ADTRAN, INC.

901 Explorer Blvd.
Huntsville, AL 35806-2807
Chm, Pres & CEO: Mark C. Smith
VP Fin & Admin: Irwin O. Goldstein
Employees: 737

Phone: 205-971-8000
Fax: 205-971-8699

Jobs Added Last Year: 203 (+38.0%)

Telecommunications equipment - high-speed digital-communications products

ALABAMA NATIONAL BANCORPORATION

1927 First Ave. North
Birmingham, AL 35203
Chm & CEO: John H. Holcomb III
No central personnel officer
Employees: 408

Phone: 205-583-3654

Jobs Added Last Year: 245 (+150.3%)

Banks - Southeast

AMERICAN BUILDINGS COMPANY

State Docks Rd.
Eufaula, AL 36072
Pres & CEO: Robert T. Ammerman
Dir HR: Bill O'Neill
Employees: 1,600

Phone: 334-687-2032
Fax: 334-687-7156

Jobs Added Last Year: 200 (+14.3%)

Building products - prefabricated metal building systems for industrial, commercial & institutional markets

AMSOUTH BANCORPORATION

1900 Fifth Ave. North
Birmingham, AL 35203
Pres & CEO: C. Dowd Ritter
EVP & HR Dir: David B. Edmonds
Employees: 5,182

Phone: 205-320-7151
Fax: 205-581-7755

Jobs Cut Last Year: 415 (-7.4%)

Banks - Southeast

BE&K INC.

2000 International Park Dr.
Birmingham, AL 35243
Chm & CEO: Theodore C. Kennedy
Dir HR: Marshall Johnson
Employees: 7,303

Phone: 205-969-3600
Fax: 205-972-6300

Jobs Added Last Year: 386 (+5.6%)

Construction - engineering & maintenance

BIG B, INC.

2600 Morgan Rd.
Bessemer, AL 35023
Chm & CEO: Anthony J. Bruno
VP HR: Eugene A. Beckmann
Employees: 6,300

Phone: 205-424-3421
Fax: 205-425-3525

Jobs Added Last Year: 600 (+10.5%)

Retail - drugstores (383 units)

BOOKS-A-MILLION, INC.

402 Industrial Ln.
Birmingham, AL 35211
Pres & CEO: Clyde B. Anderson
Dir HR: Christine Sanders
Employees: 2,883

Phone: 205-942-3737
Fax: 205-945-1772

Jobs Added Last Year: 1,180 (+69.3%)

Retail - book superstores in the southeast US

BRUNO'S, INC.

800 Lakeshore Pkwy., PO Box 2486
Birmingham, AL 35201-2486
Chm & CEO: William J. Bolton
VP HR: Richard H. Marty
Employees: 25,600

Phone: 205-940-9400
Fax: 205-940-9534

Jobs Cut Last Year: 1,620 (-6.0%)

Retail - supermarkets (Food World, Piggly Wiggly, Food Fair, Foodmax & Bruno's)

CITATION CORPORATION

2 Office Park Circle, Ste. 204
Birmingham, AL 35223
Chm & CEO: T. Morris Hackney
Dir HR: Tom Surtees
Employees: 3,879

Phone: 205-871-5731
Fax: 205-870-8211

Jobs Added Last Year: 1,438 (+58.9%)

Metal products - precision ductile gray & high-alloy iron, steel & aluminum castings for the automotive, light & heavy truck, electrical, railroad, pump, valve, fittings & waterworks markets

THE COLONIAL BANCGROUP, INC.

One Commerce St. Phone: 334-240-5000
Montgomery, AL 36104 Fax: 334-240-5345
Chm, Pres & CEO: Robert E. Lowder
Personnel Dir: Andrea McCain
Employees: 1,751

Jobs Added Last Year: 338 (+23.9%)

Banks - Southeast

MOVIE GALLERY, INC.

739 W. Main St. Phone: 334-677-2108
Dothan, AL 36301 Fax: 334-677-1169
Chm & CEO: Joe T. Malugen
Dir HR: Jim Pongonis
Employees: 4,600

Jobs Added Last Year: 2,441 (+113.1%)

Retail - videocassette & video game sales & rental

DELCHAMPS, INC.

305 Delchamps Dr. Phone: 334-433-0431
Mobile, AL 36602 Fax: 334-433-0437
Chm, Pres & CEO: David W. Morrow
VP Personnel: Thomas R. Trebesh
Employees: 8,397

Jobs Added Last Year: 247 (+3.0%)

Retail - supermarkets

NICHOLS RESEARCH CORPORATION

4040 S. Memorial Pkwy. Phone: 205-883-1140
Huntsville, AL 35802-1326 Fax: 205-880-0367
Chm & CEO: Chris H. Horgen
Dir HR: Scott Parker
Employees: 1,336

Jobs Added Last Year: 441 (+49.3%)

Engineering - information & computer technology & R&D services for the US Department of Defense

HEALTHSOUTH CORPORATION

2 Perimeter Park South Phone: 205-967-7116
Birmingham, AL 35243 Fax: 205-969-4719
Chm & CEO: Richard M. Scrushy
Group VP HR: Brandon O. Hale
Employees: 26,427

Jobs Added Last Year: 8,004 (+43.4%)

Hospitals - health care centers & clinics throughout the US

REGIONS FINANCIAL CORPORATION

417 N. 20th St., PO Box 10247 Phone: 205-326-7100
Birmingham, AL 35202-0247 Fax: 205-326-7571
Chm & CEO: J. Stanley Mackin
SVP HR & Regional Personnel Dir: David Herring
Employees: 6,273

Jobs Added Last Year: 266 (+4.4%)

Banks - Southeast

INTERGRAPH CORPORATION

One Industrial Park Phone: 205-730-2000
Huntsville, AL 35894-0001 Fax: 205-730-7898
Chm & CEO: James W. Meadlock
VP Corp HR: Milford B. French
Employees: 8,400

Jobs Cut Last Year: 800 (-8.7%)

Computers - CAD/CAM/CAE software, computer graphics systems & industry-specific software, works stations & servers

RUBY TUESDAY, INC.

4721 Morrison Dr. Phone: 334-344-3000
Mobile, AL 36609 Fax: 334-344-3066
Chm & CEO: Samuel E. Beall III
SVP HR: Ronald Vilord
Employees: 36,000

Jobs Added Last Year: 3,000 (+9.1%)

Retail - restaurants (367 units: Ruby Tuesday, Mozzarella's Cafe, Tia's)

KINDERCARE LEARNING CENTERS

2400 Presidents Dr. Phone: 334-277-5090
Montgomery, AL 36116 Fax: 334-270-0080
Chm & CEO: Sandra W. Scarr
VP HR: Jerry B. Hill
Employees: 21,000

Jobs Cut Last Year: 500 (-2.3%)

Schools - child care & preschool educational services (#1 in US)

RUSSELL CORPORATION

One Lee St. Phone: 205-329-4000
Alexander City, AL 35010-0272 Fax: 205-329-5346
Chm, Pres & CEO: John C. Adams
Corp VP HR: William P. Dickson Jr.
Employees: 17,766

Jobs Added Last Year: 995 (+5.9%)

Apparel - athletic uniforms, sweat pants & T-shirts

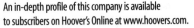 An in-depth profile of this company is available
to subscribers on Hoover's Online at www.hoovers.com.

65

SCI SYSTEMS, INC.

2101 W. Clinton Ave. Phone: 205-882-4800
Huntsville, AL 35805 Fax: 205-882-4804
Chm & CEO: Olin B. King
VP Personnel: Francis X. Henry
Employees: 13,185
Jobs Added Last Year: 1,158 (+9.6%)

Electrical components - electronic circuitry, systems, subsystems
& other assemblies; aerospace & defense products

SONAT INC.

AmSouth-Sonat Tower Phone: 205-325-3800
Birmingham, AL 35203 Fax: 205-325-7490
Chm, Pres & CEO: Ronald L. Kuehn Jr.
VP HR & Sec: Beverley T. Krannich
Employees: 3,750
Jobs Added Last Year: 1,840 (+96.3%)

Oil & gas - production & pipeline

SOUTHERN ENERGY HOMES, INC.

Hwy. 41 North Phone: 205-747-8589
Addison, AL 35540 Fax: 205-747-2963
Pres & CEO: Wendell L. Batchelor
Dir HR: Ron Bland
Employees: 2,338
Jobs Added Last Year: 565 (+31.9%)

Building - manufactured homes sold in the southern US

SOUTHTRUST CORPORATION

420 N. 20th St. Phone: 205-254-5509
Birmingham, AL 35203 Fax: 205-254-5404
Chm & CEO: Wallace D. Malone Jr.
SVP HR: Charles D. Whitfield Jr.
Employees: 7,400
Jobs Added Last Year: 100 (+1.4%)

Banks - Southeast

TORCHMARK CORPORATION

2001 Third Ave. South Phone: 205-325-4200
Birmingham, AL 35233 Fax: 205-325-2908
Chm & CEO: Ronald K. Richey
Dir Personnel: George Thompson
Employees: 5,736
Jobs Cut Last Year: 534 (-8.5%)

Diversified operations - life & health insurance; financial services
including mutual funds & institutional investment; commercial
real estate; oil & gas well operation

THE UNIVERSITY OF ALABAMA

701 20th St. South, Ste. 1070 Phone: 205-934-4636
Birmingham, AL 35294 Fax: 205-975-8505
Chancellor: Philip E. Austin
VP Admin & HR: John H. Walker
Employees: 16,000
Jobs Added Last Year: —

University

VULCAN MATERIALS COMPANY

One Metroplex Dr. Phone: 205-877-3000
Birmingham, AL 35209 Fax: 205-877-3094
Chm & CEO: Herbert A. Sklenar
SVP HR: R. Morrieson Lord
Employees: 6,918
Jobs Added Last Year: 165 (+2.4%)

Construction - aggregates (#1 in US), primarily crushed stone;
industrial & specialty chemicals, including chlorine & caustic soda
& potash; process aids for the pulp & paper & textile industries

ALLIED WASTE INDUSTRIES, INC.

7201 E. Camelback Rd., Ste. 375 Phone: 602-423-2946
Scottsdale, AZ 85251 Fax: 602-423-9424
Chm & CEO: Roger A. Ramsey
Dir HR: Tony Grasso
Employees: 1,440
Jobs Added Last Year: 315 (+28.0%)

Waste management - collection, transfer, recycling & disposal of
nonhazardous waste for residential, commercial & municipal customers

AMERICA WEST AIRLINES, INC.

4000 Sky Harbor Blvd. Phone: 602-693-0800
Phoenix, AZ 85034 Fax: 602-693-5546
Chm, Pres & CEO: William A. Franke
Dir HR: Michael A. Vescuso
Employees: 8,712
Jobs Cut Last Year: 2,003 (-18.7%)

Transportation - airline

APOLLO GROUP, INC.

4615 E. Elwood St.
Phoenix, AZ 85040
Chm & Pres : John G. Sperling
Dir HR: Kathryn Zuber
Employees: 4,315

Phone: 602-966-5394
Fax: 602-968-1159

Jobs Added Last Year: 873 (+25.4%)

Schools - higher-education programs for working adults; Online Campus, college courses on the Internet

AZTAR CORPORATION

2390 E. Camelback Rd., Ste. 400
Phoenix, AZ 85016-3452
Chm, Pres & CEO: Paul E. Rubeli
VP Admin & Sec: Nelson W. Armstrong Jr.
Employees: 9,900

Phone: 602-381-4100
Fax: 602-381-4107

Jobs Added Last Year: 1,700 (+20.7%)

Gambling resorts & casinos in Atlantic City & Las Vegas & Laughlin, NV; riverboat casinos in Caruthersville, MO & Evansville, IN

CERPROBE CORPORATION

600 S. Rockford Dr.
Tempe, AZ 85281
Pres & CEO: C. Zane Close
HR Mgr: Grady Brown
Employees: 299

Phone: 602-967-7885
Fax: 602-967-7758

Jobs Added Last Year: 120 (+67.0%)

Electronics - semiconductor test equipment

THE CIRCLE K CORPORATION

3003 N. Central Ave., Ste. 1600
Phoenix, AZ 85072
Pres & CEO: Robert J. Lavinia
VP HR: Wanda M. Williams
Employees: 20,566

Phone: 602-530-5001
Fax: 602-530-5278

Jobs Cut Last Year: 434 (-2.1%)

Retail - convenience stores (more than 2,500 units)

CSK AUTO, INC.

645 E. Missouri Ave.
Phoenix, AZ 85012
Co-Chm & CEO: Jules Trump
Dir HR: Cindi Heu
Employees: 8,200

Phone: 602-265-9200
Fax: 602-266-4144

Jobs Added Last Year: —

Auto parts - parts & accessories, maintenance items & accessories (Checker Auto Parts, Schuck's Auto Supply, Kragen Auto Parts: 569 stores)

DEL WEBB CORPORATION

6001 N. 24th St.
Phoenix, AZ 85016
Chm & CEO: Philip J. Dion
VP HR: M. Lynn Schuttenberg
Employees: 1,800

Phone: 602-808-8000
Fax: 602-808-8097

Jobs Added Last Year: 400 (+28.6%)

Real estate development - retirement communities (Sun City)

THE DIAL CORP

Dial Tower
Phoenix, AZ 85077
Chm & CEO: John W. Teets
VP HR: Bernie Welle
Employees: 30,100

Phone: 602-207-4000
Fax: 602-207-5473

Jobs Added Last Year: 1,200 (+4.2%)

Diversified operations - in-flight catering; exhibition management (#1 in US); money-order processing (name changed to Viad Corp.)

DOUBLETREE CORPORATION

410 N. 44th St., Ste. 700
Phoenix, AZ 85008
Pres & CEO: Richard M. Kelleher
SVP HR: Ann Rhodes
Employees: 16,400

Phone: 602-220-6666
Fax: 602-220-6602

Jobs Added Last Year: 6,045 (+58.4%)

Hotels & motels - franchisor of DoubleTree & Guest Quarters Suites

ENVIROTEST SYSTEMS CORP.

2525 E. Camelback Rd., Ste. 1150
Phoenix, AZ 85016
Chm: Chester C. Davenport
VP HR: Lucy Nelson
Employees: 3,828

Phone: 602-912-1100
Fax: 602-912-1105

Jobs Added Last Year: 1,252 (+48.6%)

Pollution control equipment & services - auto emissions testing programs for states & municipalities

GATEWAY DATA SCIENCES CORPORATION

3410 E. University Dr., Ste. 100
Phoenix, AZ 85034
Chm & Pres: Michael M. Gordon
VP Fin: Vickie B. Jarvis
Employees: 96

Phone: 602-968-7000
Fax: 602-437-8230

Jobs Added Last Year: 23 (+31.5%)

Computers - software products & customer support services

 An in-depth profile of this company is available to subscribers on Hoover's Online at www.hoovers.com.

67

KNIGHT TRANSPORTATION, INC.

5601 W. Buckeye Rd.
Phoenix, AZ 85043
CEO & Sec: Kevin P. Knight
Dir HR: Tim Kohl
Employees: 492

Phone: 602-269-2000
Fax: 602-269-8409

Jobs Added Last Year: 163 (+49.5%)

Transportation - short- to medium-haul trucking services

MEADOW VALLEY CORPORATION

4411 S. 40th St., Ste. D11
Phoenix, AZ 85040
Pres & CEO: Bradley E. Larson
Safety Dir & Dir HR: Norman Watkins
Employees: 333

Phone: 602-437-5400
Fax: 602-437-1681

Jobs Added Last Year: 107 (+47.3%)

Construction - heavy

MICROAGE, INC.

2400 S. Microage Way
Tempe, AZ 85282-1896
Chm & CEO: Jeffrey D. McKeever
VP HR & Admin: Alan R. Lyons
Employees: 2,088

Phone: 602-804-2000
Fax: 602-966-7339

Jobs Added Last Year: 359 (+20.8%)

Retail - wholesale computer hardware & software (COMPAQ, Hewlett-Packard, IBM, Apple); direct sales of computer equipment & services to large corporate accounts

NATIONAL HEALTH ENHANCEMENT SYSTEMS, INC.

3200 N. Central Ave., Ste. 1750
Phoenix, AZ 85012
Pres & CEO: Gregory J. Petras
Dir Administrative Svcs: Laurinda Bess
Employees: 160

Phone: 602-230-7575
Fax: 602-274-6158

Jobs Added Last Year: 45 (+39.1%)

Computers - health-care-related software

NEXTHEALTH, INC.

16600 N. Lago del Oro Pkwy.
Tucson, AZ 85739
Pres & CEO: John M. Schmitz
Dir HR: Colleen Van Ampting
Employees: 390

Phone: 520-792-5800
Fax: 520-792-2916

Jobs Added Last Year: 185 (+90.2%)

Medical services - psychological treatment programs

PETSMART, INC.

10000 N. 31st Ave., Ste. C100
Phoenix, AZ 85051
Pres & CEO: Mark S. Hansen
VP HR & Training: Peter G. Kanton
Employees: 11,000

Phone: 602-944-7070
Fax: 602-395-6502

Jobs Added Last Year: 3,100 (+39.2%)

Retail - pet supply superstores (#1 in US)

Career Mosaic — http://www.careermosaic.com/

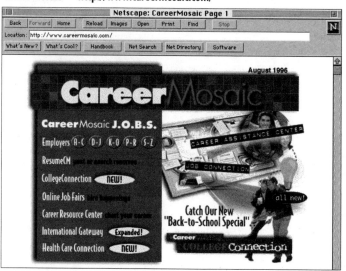

PHELPS DODGE CORPORATION

2600 N. Central Ave.
Phoenix, AZ 85004-3089
Chm, Pres & CEO: Douglas C. Yearley
VP HR: John C. Replogle
Employees: 15,343

Phone: 602-234-8100
Fax: 602-234-8337

Jobs Cut Last Year: 155 (-1.0%)

Mining - copper, gold, silver, molybdenum, copper & lead; chemical & sulfuric acid production; engineered products (Columbian Chemicals)

PINNACLE WEST CAPITAL CORP.

400 E. Van Buren St., Ste. 700
Phoenix, AZ 85004
Chm & Pres: Richard Snell
Dir HR: Connie Rightmar
Employees: 7,335

Phone: 602-379-2500
Fax: 602-379-2545

Jobs Cut Last Year: 105 (-1.4%)

Utility - electric power (Arizona Public Service Company); real estate development

RURAL/METRO CORPORATION

8401 E. Indian School Rd.
Scottsdale, AZ 85251
CEO: Warren Rustand
VP HR: Tracy Bannon
Employees: 5,200

Phone: 602-994-3886
Fax: 602-481-3260

Jobs Added Last Year: 1,300 (+33.3%)

Medical services - emergency & general-transport ambulance services, fire-protection services & other safety related services

SHAMROCK FOODS COMPANY INC.

2228 North Black Canyon Hwy.
Phoenix, AZ 85009
CEO: Norman P. McClelland
Dir HR: Bonnie Taylor
Employees: 1,783

Phone: 602-272-6721
Fax: 602-233-2791

Jobs Added Last Year: 283 (+18.9%)

Food - distribution, dairy products

UNISON HEALTHCARE CORPORATION

7272 East Indian School Rd., Ste. 214
Scottsdale, AZ 85251
Pres & CEO: Jerry M. Walker
VP HR: Amy Duncan
Employees: 2,270

Phone: 602-423-1954
Fax: 602-423-1929

Jobs Added Last Year: 356 (+18.6%)

Health care - long-term & specialty health care services, nursing care, rehabilition therapy & respiratory therapy to subacute patients

WAVEPHORE, INC.

2601 W. Broadway
Tempe, AZ 85282
Chm, Pres & CEO: David E. Deeds
Dir HR: Carol Jacobson
Employees: 112

Phone: 602-438-8700
Fax: 602-438-8890

Jobs Added Last Year: 59 (+111.3%)

Telecommunications equipment - data-transmission encoders & decoders that use broadcast TV transmission routes

ACXIOM CORPORATION

301 Industrial Blvd.
Conway, AR 72032
Chm, Pres & CEO: Charles D. Morgan Jr.
Dir HR: Cindy Childers
Employees: 3,098

Phone: 501-336-1000
Fax: 501-336-3913

Jobs Added Last Year: 1,248 (+67.5%)

Business services - mailing lists, integration list processing & related software; mail-order automation software, data products & data warehousing; CD-ROM telephone directories (ProCD)

ALLTEL CORPORATION

One Allied Dr.
Little Rock, AR 72202
Chm, Pres & CEO: Joe T. Ford
VP HR: John L. Comparin
Employees: 15,698

Phone: 501-661-8000
Fax: 501-661-8487

Jobs Cut Last Year: 635 (-3.9%)

Utility - local & long-distance telephone service; data processing management; cellular phone service

AMERICAN FREIGHTWAYS CORP.

2200 Forward Dr.
Harrison, AR 72601
Chm, Pres & CEO: F. Sheridan Garrison
VP HR: Steve McMath
Employees: 8,867

Phone: 501-741-9000
Fax: 501-741-3003

Jobs Added Last Year: 2,361 (+36.3%)

Transportation - less-than-truckload freight

ARKANSAS BEST CORPORATION

3801 Old Greenwood Rd.   Phone: 501-785-6000
Fort Smith, AR 72903   Fax: 501-785-6004
Pres & CEO: Robert A. Young III
Dir HR: Joe Davis
Employees: 18,459

Jobs Added Last Year: 6,583 (+55.4%)

Transportation - less-than-truckload shipments of general commodities; truck tire retreading & new truck tire sales

BEVERLY ENTERPRISES, INC.

1200 S. Waldron Rd., Ste. 155   Phone: 501-452-6712
Fort Smith, AR 72903   Fax: 501-452-5131
Chm & CEO: David R. Banks
VP HR: Carol C. Johansen
Employees: 83,000

Jobs Added Last Year: 1,000 (+1.2%)

Nursing homes - nursing home chain (#1 in US)

CANNON EXPRESS, INC.

1457 E. Robinson, PO Box 364   Phone: 501-751-9209
Springdale, AR 72764   Fax: 501-750-4826
Chm & CEO: Dean G. Cannon
VP Fin & Admin: Duane Washington
Employees: 896

Jobs Added Last Year: 244 (+37.4%)

Transportation - irregular route, truckload carrier

DILLARD DEPARTMENT STORES, INC.

1600 Cantrell Rd.   Phone: 501-376-5200
Little Rock, AR 72201   Fax: 501-376-5917
Chm & CEO: William Dillard
Dir Personnel: Joyce Wisner
Employees: 40,312

Jobs Added Last Year: 2,480 (+6.6%)

Retail - major department stores

HUDSON FOODS, INC.

1225 Hudson Rd.   Phone: 501-636-1100
Rogers, AR 72756   Fax: 501-631-5192
Chm & CEO: James T. Hudson
Dir Corp HR: Larry Landrith
Employees: 10,303

Jobs Added Last Year: 1,392 (+15.6%)

Food - chicken, turkey, beef & pork products

J.B. HUNT TRANSPORT SERVICES, INC.

615 J.B. Hunt Corporate Dr.   Phone: 501-820-0000
Lowell, AR 72745   Fax: 501-820-8395
Pres & CEO: Kirk Thompson
EVP HR & Risk Mgmt: Stephen L. Palmer
Employees: 12,020

Jobs Added Last Year: 183 (+1.5%)

Transportation - truck, rail & flatbed transport; terminal maintenance

P.A.M. TRANSPORTATION SERVICES, INC.

Hwy. 412 West, PO Box 188   Phone: 501-361-9111
Tontitown, AR 72770   Fax: 501-361-5335
Pres & CEO: Robert W. Weaver
Dir Office Personnel: Linda Scott
Employees: 1,192

Jobs Added Last Year: 293 (+32.6%)

Transportation - irregular route, common & contract trucking services

TYSON FOODS, INC.

2210 W. Oaklawn Dr.   Phone: 501-290-4000
Springdale, AR 72762-6999   Fax: 501-290-4061
Chm & CEO: Leland E. Tollett
SVP HR: William P. Jaycox
Employees: 64,000

Jobs Added Last Year: 8,200 (+14.7%)

Food - poultry, beef & pork products

WAL-MART STORES, INC.

702 SW 8th St.   Phone: 501-273-4000
Bentonville, AR 72716-8611   Fax: 501-273-1917
Pres & CEO: David D. Glass
SVP People Div: Coleman Peterson
Employees: 675,000

Jobs Added Last Year: 53,000 (+8.5%)

Retail - discount & variety (Wal-Mart, Sams); food distribution (McLane Co.); music, video & book distribution (Western Merchandising)

3COM CORPORATION

5400 Bayfront Plaza, PO Box 58145
Santa Clara, CA 95052-8145
Chm, Pres & CEO: Eric A. Benhamou
Dir HR: Susan Gellen
Employees: 3,072

Phone: 408-764-5000
Fax: 408-764-5001

Jobs Added Last Year: 766 (+33.2%)

Computers - local-area network (LAN) routers, hubs, remote access-servers, switches & adapters

ABM INDUSTRIES INCORPORATED

50 Fremont St., 26th Fl.
San Francisco, CA 94105-2230
CEO: William W. Steele
VP & Dir HR: Donna M. Dell
Employees: 45,000

Phone: 415-597-4500
Fax: 415-597-7160

Jobs Added Last Year: 3,000 (+7.1%)

Building - janitorial services & equipment

ACCESS HEALTH, INC.

11020 White Rock Rd.
Rancho Cordova, CA 95670
Chm & CEO: Kenneth B. Plumlee
HR Dir: Gina Dickey
Employees: 342

Phone: 916-851-4000
Fax: 916-852-3890

Jobs Added Last Year: 71 (+26.2%)

Medical practice management - medical information services (Ask-A-Nurse, Cancer HelpLink)

ACTIVISION, INC.

11601 Wilshire Blvd.
Los Angeles, CA 90025
Chm & CEO: Robert A. Kotick
Dir HR: Dara Hyde
Employees: 189

Phone: 310-473-9200
Fax: 310-479-4005

Jobs Added Last Year: 110 (+139.2%)

Computers - interactive software (Pitfall!, Shanghai) & multi-game CD-ROMs (Power Hits)

ADAPTEC, INC.

691 S. Milpitas Blvd.
Milpitas, CA 95035
Pres & CEO: F. Grant Saviers
VP Admin: Daniel W. Bowman
Employees: 2,211

Phone: 408-945-8600
Fax: 408-262-2533

Jobs Added Last Year: 514 (+30.3%)

Computers - small computer system interface (SCSI) hardware & software

ADOBE SYSTEMS INCORPORATED

1585 Charleston Rd.
Mountain View, CA 94043-1225
Chm & CEO: John E. Warnock
HR Dir: Rebecca Guerra
Employees: 2,319

Phone: 415-961-4400
Fax: 415-961-3769

Jobs Added Last Year: 735 (+46.4%)

Computers - font (PostScript) & desktop publishing (PageMaker) software

ADVANCED MICRO DEVICES, INC.

One AMD Place
Sunnyvale, CA 94088-3453
Chm & CEO: W. J. Sanders III
SVP HR: Stanley Winvick
Employees: 12,730

Phone: 408-732-2400
Fax: 408-982-6164

Jobs Added Last Year: 937 (+7.9%)

Electrical components - microprocessors, flash memories, programmable logic devices, integrated circuits & networking devices

ADVENTIST HEALTH

2100 Douglas Blvd.
Roseville, CA 95661
Pres: Frank F. Dupper
Dir HR: Roger Ashley
Employees: 9,725

Phone: 916-781-2000
Fax: 916-783-9909

Jobs Added Last Year: 77 (+0.8%)

Hospitals

AECOM TECHNOLOGY CORPORATION

3250 Wilshire Blvd.
Los Angeles, CA 90010
Chm, Pres & CEO: Richard Newman
Mgr HR: Ann Berty
Employees: 5,000

Phone: 213-381-3612
Fax: 213-388-2165

Jobs Added Last Year: 500 (+11.1%)

Building - architectural & construction management services

AIRSENSORS, INC.

16804 Gridley Place
Cerritos, CA 90703
Pres & CEO: Robert M. Stemmler
Dir HR & Public Affairs: Mark Rodriguez
Employees: 350

Phone: 310-860-6666
Fax: 310-809-1240

Jobs Added Last Year: 75 (+27.3%)

Automotive equipment - fuel management systems & components, including carburetors, converters or regulators, fuel lock-offs, repair kits & replacement parts

 An in-depth profile of this company is available to subscribers on Hoover's Online at www.hoovers.com.

71

AIRTOUCH COMMUNICATIONS, INC.

One California St., 17th Fl. Phone: 415-658-2000
San Francisco, CA 94111 Fax: 415-658-2034
Chm & CEO: Sam Ginn
VP HR: Dwight Jasmann
Employees: 6,650

Jobs Added Last Year: 2,150 (+47.8%)

Telecommunications services - cellular telephone services

ALLERGAN, INC.

2525 Dupont Dr. Phone: 714-752-4500
Irvine, CA 92715-1599 Fax: 714-246-4217
Chm, Pres & CEO: William C. Shepherd
Corp VP HR: Richard J. Hilles
Employees: 6,078

Jobs Added Last Year: 1,175 (+24.0%)

Medical products - specialty therapeutic products for eye & skin care

ALLIANCE SEMICONDUCTOR CORP.

3099 N. First St. Phone: 408-383-4900
San Jose, CA 95134-2006 Fax: 408-383-4999
Chm, Pres & CEO: N. Damodar Reddy
Dir HR: Peggy Maxfield
Employees: 74

Jobs Added Last Year: 30 (+68.2%)

Electrical components - high-speed SRAM & DRAM memory semiconductors

ALPHAREL, INC.

9339 Carroll Park Dr. Phone: 619-625-3000
San Diego, CA 92121 Fax: 619-546-7671
Pres & CEO: Stephen P. Gardner
HR Administrator: Amy Fager
Employees: 193

Jobs Added Last Year: 108 (+127.1%)

Computers - document management software & automation systems

ALTERA CORPORATION

2610 Orchard Pkwy. Phone: 408-894-7000
San Jose, CA 95134-2020 Fax: 408-428-0463
Chm, Pres & CEO: Rodney Smith
VP HR: John K. Fitzhenry
Employees: 881

Jobs Added Last Year: 214 (+32.1%)

Electrical components - programmable logic devices (Flex 8000) & software tools

AMDAHL CORPORATION

1250 E. Arques Ave. Phone: 408-746-6000
Sunnyvale, CA 94088-3470 Fax: 408-773-0833
Pres & CEO: E. Joseph Zemke
SVP HR & Corp Svcs: Anthony M. Pozos
Employees: 8,200

Jobs Added Last Year: 2,600 (+46.4%)

Computers - software for client/server applications & business processes; information technology services; mainframes & storage devices; open systems hardware & software

AMERICAN GOLF CORPORATION

1633 26th St. Phone: 310-315-4200
Santa Monica, CA 90404 Fax: 310-829-4132
CEO & CFO: David Price
Dir HR: Riz Quiliza
Employees: 10,344

Jobs Added Last Year: 344 (+3.4%)

Real estate operations - management of more than 200 private, resort & public golf courses in the US & the UK

AMERICAN PROTECTIVE SERVICES, INC.

7770 Pardee Ln. Phone: 510-568-0276
Oakland, CA 94621-1454 Fax: 510-430-1130
Pres & CEO: Dwight S. Pedersen
SVP Admin: Thomas A. Sutak
Employees: 16,000

Jobs Added Last Year: 1,000 (+6.7%)

Protection - contract security guard services

AMERICAN RESTAURANT GROUP, INC.

450 Newport Center Dr. Phone: 714-721-8000
Newport Beach, CA 92660 Fax: 714-721-8426
Chm & CEO: Anwar S. Soliman
Dir HR: Stephanie Ennis
Employees: 15,000

Jobs Added Last Year: 400 (+2.7%)

Retail - casual dining restaurants (Black Angus, Grandy's, Spoons)

AMGEN INC.

1840 Dehavilland Dr. Phone: 805-447-1000
Thousand Oaks, CA 91320-1789 Fax: 805-447-1985
Chm & CEO: Gordon M. Binder
VP HR: Edward Garnett
Employees: 4,046

Jobs Added Last Year: 500 (+14.1%)

Biomedical & genetic products - therapeutic agents that aid the development of blood cells (Epogen, Neupogen)

APL, LTD.

1111 Broadway   Phone: 510-272-8000
Oakland, CA 94607   Fax: 510-272-7941
Pres & CEO : Timothy J. Rhein
VP HR: Mike Maher
Employees: 5,174
Jobs Added Last Year: 149 (+3.0%)

Transportation - container shipping

APPLIED MAGNETICS CORPORATION

75 Robin Hill Rd.   Phone: 805-683-5353
Goleta, CA 93117   Fax: 805-967-8227
Chm, Pres, CEO & CFO: Craig D. Crisman
Dir HR: David Swanson
Employees: 5,500
Jobs Cut Last Year: 31 (-0.6%)

Computers - magnetic recording heads for rigid disk drives

APPLE COMPUTER, INC.

One Infinite Loop   Phone: 408-996-1010
Cupertino, CA 95014   Fax: 408-974-2113
Chm, CTO & CEO: Gilbert F. Amelio
SVP HR: Kevin J. Sullivan
Employees: 17,615
Jobs Added Last Year: 3,023 (+20.7%)

Computers - personal computers, printers & peripheral products

APPLIED MATERIALS, INC.

3050 Bowers Ave.   Phone: 408-727-5555
Santa Clara, CA 95054-3299   Fax: 408-748-9943
Chm & CEO: James C. Morgan
VP Global HR: Rosemary T. Elliott
Employees: 10,537
Jobs Added Last Year: 4,040 (+62.2%)

Machinery - semiconductor manufacturing equipment (#1 worldwide)

APPLIED DIGITAL ACCESS, INC.

9855 Scranton Rd.   Phone: 619-623-2200
San Diego, CA 92121   Fax: 619-623-2208
Pres & CEO: Peter P. Savage
Dir Benefits for HR: Nancy Davis
Employees: 136
Jobs Added Last Year: 29 (+27.1%)

Telecommunications equipment - network test & performance monitoring systems

ARRIS PHARMACEUTICAL CORPORATION

385 Oyster Point Blvd., Ste. 3   Phone: 415-737-8600
South San Francisco, CA 94080   Fax: 415-737-8590
Pres & CEO: John P. Walker
Dir HR: J. Phillip Cunningham
Employees: 129
Jobs Added Last Year: 51 (+65.4%)

Drugs - synthetic small-molecule therapeutics

Planet Jobs — http://www.phillynews.com/programs/ads/SUNHLP

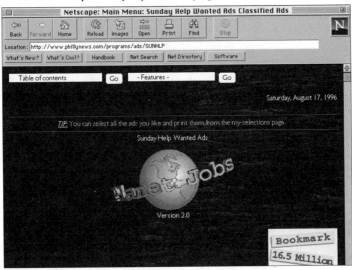

 An in-depth profile of this company is available
to subscribers on Hoover's Online at www.hoovers.com.

73

ASCEND COMMUNICATIONS, INC.

1275 Harbor Bay Pkwy.
Alameda, CA 94502
Pres & CEO: Mory Ejabat
Mgr HR & Investor Relations: Paula Cook
Employees: 304
Phone: 510-769-6001
Fax: 510-814-2300

Jobs Added Last Year: 189 (+164.3%)

Computers - WAN access products

AST RESEARCH, INC.

16215 Alton Pkwy.
Irvine, CA 92619-7005
Pres & CEO: Ian W. Diery
Dir HR: Candice Byrne
Employees: 6,595
Phone: 714-727-4141
Fax: 714-727-8584

Jobs Cut Last Year: 382 (-5.5%)

Computers - personal computers, notebooks, memory expansion boards, graphic adapters & color monitors

ASYST TECHNOLOGIES, INC.

48761 Kato Rd.
Fremont, CA 94538
Chm & CEO: Mihir Parikh
Dir HR: Deborah A. Partridge
Employees: 212
Phone: 510-661-5000
Fax: 510-661-5166

Jobs Added Last Year: 69 (+48.3%)

Filtration products - minienvironment systems designed to reduce contamination in cleanrooms for semiconductor manufacturing

ATLANTIC RICHFIELD COMPANY

515 S. Flower St.
Los Angeles, CA 90071-2256
Chm, Pres & CEO: Mike R. Bowlin
VP HR: John H. Kelly
Employees: 22,000
Phone: 213-486-3511
Fax: 213-486-2063

Jobs Cut Last Year: 1,200 (-5.2%)

Oil & gas - US integrated

ATMEL CORPORATION

2325 Orchard Pkwy.
San Jose, CA 95131
Chm, Pres & CEO: George Perlegos
Dir HR: Valerie Menager
Employees: 2,978
Phone: 408-441-0311
Fax: 408-436-4200

Jobs Added Last Year: 1,071 (+56.2%)

Electrical components - high-performance semiconductors using CMOS technology

AURA SYSTEMS, INC.

2335 Alaska Ave.
El Segundo, CA 90245
CEO: Ziv "Harry" Kurtzman
Dir HR: Rachel G. Choppin
Employees: 325
Phone: 310-643-5300
Fax: 310-643-8719

Jobs Added Last Year: 75 (+30.0%)

Engineering - R&D services, primarily for the defense & aerospace industries; audio reinforcement; communications; interactive media

AUTHENTIC FITNESS CORPORATION

6040 Bandini Blvd.
Commerce, CA 90040
Chm & CEO: Linda J. Wachner
VP HR & Admin: David Grundman
Employees: 1,915
Phone: 213-726-1262
Fax: 213-720-1806

Jobs Added Last Year: 565 (+41.9%)

Apparel - swimwear, swim accessories, skiwear & fitness apparel (Speedo, Catalina, White Stag, Edelweiss)

AVANT! CORPORATION

1208 E. Arques Ave.
Sunnyvale, CA 94086
Chm, Pres & CEO: Gerald C. Hsu
Dir HR: Bella D'Mar Shimun
Employees: 206
Phone: 408-738-8881
Fax: 408-738-0244

Jobs Added Last Year: 63 (+44.1%)

Computers - integrated circuit design automation software (ArcCell, ArcGate)

AVERY DENNISON CORPORATION

150 N. Orange Grove Blvd.
Pasadena, CA 91103
Chm & CEO: Charles D. Miller
VP HR: Susan B. Garelli
Employees: 15,500
Phone: 818-304-2000
Fax: 818-792-7312

Jobs Added Last Year: 100 (+0.6%)

Office & art materials - pressure-sensitive adhesives, 3-ring notebooks, indexing materials, stamp pads & business forms

BANKAMERICA CORPORATION

Bank of America Ctr.
San Francisco, CA 94104
Pres & CEO: David A. Coulter
VC & Personnel Relations Officer: Kathleen J. Burke
Employees: 79,916
Phone: 415-622-3530
Fax: 415-622-7915

Jobs Cut Last Year: 18,640 (-18.9%)

Banks - money center

BAY NETWORKS, INC.

4401 Great America Pkwy.
Santa Clara, CA 95054
Pres & CEO: Andrew K. Ludwick
VP HR: David M. Lietzke
Employees: 3,840

Phone: 408-988-2400
Fax: 408-988-5525

Jobs Added Last Year: 840 (+28.0%)

Computers - internetworking equipment, LAN hub products & management systems (merger of Wellfleet Communications & Synoptics Communications)

BECHTEL GROUP, INC.

50 Beale St.
San Francisco, CA 94105-1895
Chm & CEO: Riley P. Bechtel Jr.
SVP & Mgr HR: Granville Bowie
Employees: 29,000

Phone: 415-768-1234
Fax: 415-768-0263

Jobs Cut Last Year: 200 (-0.7%)

Construction - engineering & environmental services

BECKMAN INSTRUMENTS, INC.

2500 Harbor Blvd.
Fullerton, CA 92634-3100
Chm & CEO: Louis T. Rosso
VP HR: Fidencio M. Mares
Employees: 5,700

Phone: 714-871-4848
Fax: 714-773-8283

Jobs Cut Last Year: 500 (-8.1%)

Instruments - biological laboratory research instrument systems & test kits

BERGEN BRUNSWIG CORPORATION

4000 Metropolitan Dr.
Orange, CA 92668-3510
Chm & CEO: Robert E. Martini
EVP HR: Carol E. Scherman
Employees: 4,770

Phone: 714-385-4000
Fax: 714-385-1442

Jobs Added Last Year: 527 (+12.4%)

Drugs & sundries - wholesale distribution to institutional & retail outlets

BIG 5 SPORTING GOODS

2525 E. El Segundo Blvd.
El Segundo, CA 90245
Chm & CEO: Robert Miller
VP HR: Jeff Fraley
Employees: 4,460

Phone: 310-536-0611
Fax: 310-297-7570

Jobs Added Last Year: 672 (+17.7%)

Retail - full-line sporting goods stores

BIOMAGNETIC TECHNOLOGIES, INC.

9727 Pacific Heights Blvd.
San Diego, CA 92121-3719
Chm, Pres & CEO: James V. Schumacher
Dir HR: Debbie Nowakowski
Employees: 95

Phone: 619-453-6300
Fax: 619-453-4913

Jobs Added Last Year: 20 (+26.7%)

Medical instruments - magnetic source imaging systems

BIOMERICA INC.

1533 Monrovia Ave.
Newport Beach, CA 92663
Pres & Treas: Joseph H. Irani
Dir HR: Janet Moore
Employees: 77

Phone: 714-645-2111
Fax: 714-722-6674

Jobs Added Last Year: 54 (+234.8%)

Medical products - immunodiagnostic products, including blood tests for gastritis & peptic ulcers, tests to detect early heart attacks & at-home tests to detect blood in the stool

BIOSITE DIAGNOSTICS INC.

11030 Roselle St.
San Diego, CA 92121
Pres & CEO: Kim Blickenstaff
Personnel Mgr: Laura Weatherford
Employees: 145

Phone: 619-455-4808
Fax: 619-455-4815

Jobs Added Last Year: 39 (+36.8%)

Medical products - antibody-based diagnostic test devices, including a disposable urine drug test that detects 7 commonly abused drugs (Triage)

BOYDS WHEELS, INC.

8380 Cerritos Ave.
Stanton, CA 90680
Chm & CEO: Boyd Coddington
Dir HR: Blanca O'Brien
Employees: 252

Phone: 714-952-4038
Fax: 714-952-9623

Jobs Added Last Year: 53 (+26.6%)

Auto parts - retail sales & distribution of high-quality aluminum auto wheels, motorcycle wheels, steering wheels, billet aluminum accessories & car-care products

BRODERBUND SOFTWARE, INC.

500 Redwood Blvd.
Novato, CA 94948-6121
Chm & CEO: Douglas G. Carlston
Dir HR: Patsy Murphy
Employees: 563

Phone: 415-382-4400
Fax: 415-382-4582

Jobs Added Last Year: 125 (+28.5%)

Computers - educational & game software & CD-ROMs (Carmen Sandiego, Myst, Print Shop)

 An in-depth profile of this company is available to subscribers on Hoover's Online at www.hoovers.com.

75

CADENCE DESIGN SYSTEMS, INC.

555 River Oaks Pkwy.   Phone: 408-943-1234
San Jose, CA 95134   Fax: 408-943-0513
Pres & CEO: Joseph B. Costello
SVP HR: Scott W. Sherwood
Employees: 3,028
Jobs Added Last Year: 579 (+23.6%)

Computers - electronic design automation software (Allegro, Synergy, Verilog-XL)

CALIFORNIA AMPLIFIER, INC.

460 Calle San Pablo   Phone: 805-987-9000
Camarillo, CA 93012   Fax: 805-987-2655
Chm & CEO: Ira Coron
HR Mgr: Jackie Sheehan
Employees: 441
Jobs Added Last Year: 99 (+28.9%)

Telecommunications equipment - microwave TV distribution systems, wireless cable television & satellite television

CALIFORNIA MICRO DEVICES CORP.

215 Topaz St.   Phone: 408-263-3214
Milpitas, CA 95035-5430 Fax: 408-263-7846
Pres & CEO: Jeffrey C. Kalb
Mgr HR: Zareen Mohta
Employees: 297
Jobs Added Last Year: 68 (+29.7%)

Electrical components - semiconductor ICs, thin-film passive components & mixed analog/digital products

CALIFORNIA MICROWAVE, INC.

555 Twin Dolphin Dr.   Phone: 415-596-9000
Redwood, CA 94065   Fax: 415-596-6600
Chm, Pres & CEO: Philip F. Otto
Dir HR Employment: Ginger Washburn
Employees: 2,382
Jobs Added Last Year: 495 (+26.2%)

Telecommunications equipment - satellite earth stations, microwave radios for wireless communications & electronic intelligence systems

CALIFORNIA PIZZA KITCHEN, INC.

1640 S. Sepulveda Blvd. Phone: 310-575-3000
Los Angeles, CA 90025   Fax: 310-575-5731
Co-Chm: R. Rosenfield
Dir HR: Don FitzGerald
Employees: 5,300
Jobs Added Last Year: 300 (+6.0%)

Retail - national restaurant chain

CALIFORNIA STATE UNIVERSITY

400 Golden Shore, Ste. 330   Phone: 310-985-2740
Long Beach, CA 90802-4275   Fax: 310-985-2035
Chancellor: Barry Munitz
Vice Chancellor HR & Ops: June M. Cooper
Employees: 18,454
Jobs Added Last Year: —

Public university system with 22 campuses

CATHOLIC HEALTHCARE WEST

1700 Montgomery St., Ste. 300 Phone: 415-397-9000
San Francisco, CA 94111   Fax: 415-397-1823
Pres & CEO: Richard J. Kramer
Dir HR: Lawrence Kren
Employees: 20,000
Jobs Added Last Year: 2,382 (+13.5%)

Hospitals - 23 Catholic and community hospitals in Arizona, California & Nevada

CHAD THERAPEUTICS, INC.

9445 De Soto Ave.   Phone: 818-882-0883
Chatsworth, CA 91311   Fax: 818-882-1809
Chm & CEO: Charles R. Adams
HR Mgr: Barbara Muskin
Employees: 70
Jobs Added Last Year: 21 (+42.9%)

Medical products - respiratory care & oxygen delivery systems for home & hospital patients needing supplemental oxygen

THE CHALONE WINE GROUP, LTD.

621 Airpark Rd.   Phone: 707-254-4200
Napa, CA 94558   Fax: 707-254-4201
Pres & CEO: W. Philip Woodward
Dir HR & Investor Relations: Debbie Emery
Employees: 85
Jobs Added Last Year: 18 (+26.9%)

Beverages - wine

THE CHARLES SCHWAB CORP.

101 Montgomery St.   Phone: 415-627-7000
San Francisco, CA 94104 Fax: 415-627-8538
Chm & CEO: Charles R. Schwab
EVP HR: Luis E. Valencia
Employees: 9,200
Jobs Added Last Year: 2,700 (+41.5%)

Financial - brokerage & related investment services

CHART HOUSE ENTERPRISES, INC.

115 S. Acacia Ave.
Solana Beach, CA 92075-1803
Pres: Harry F. Roberts
Dir HR: Rob Wieana
Employees: 6,600

Phone: 619-755-8281
Fax: 619-481-0693

Jobs Cut Last Year: 800 (-10.8%)

Retail - restaurants (Chart House, Islands); wholesale bakery
(Paradise Bakeries)

THE CHEESECAKE FACTORY INC.

26950 Agoura Rd.
Calabasas Hills, CA 91301
Chm, Pres & CEO: David Overton
Dir HR: Jennifer Jackson
Employees: 3,100

Phone: 818-880-9323
Fax: 818-880-6501

Jobs Added Last Year: 600 (+24.0%)

Retail - restaurants & bakeries

CHEVRON CORPORATION

225 Bush St.
San Francisco, CA 94104
Chm & CEO: Kenneth T. Derr
VP HR & Environmental Affairs: Ronald C. Kiskis
Employees: 43,019

Phone: 415-894-7700
Fax: 415-894-0348

Jobs Cut Last Year: 2,739 (-6.0%)

Oil & gas - international integrated

CHILDREN'S DISCOVERY CENTERS OF AMERICA, INC.

851 Irwin St., Ste. 200
San Raphael, CA 94901-3343
Chm & CEO: Richard A. Niglio
VP HR: Paulette Barry
Employees: 4,700

Phone: 415-257-4200
Fax: 415-459-1374

Jobs Added Last Year: 1,100 (+30.6%)

Schools - preschool & child care

CHIRON CORPORATION

4560 Horton St.
Emeryville, CA 94608-2916
Pres & CEO: Edward E. Penhoet
VP HR: Barbara Kerr
Employees: 6,894

Phone: 510-655-8730
Fax: 510-655-9910

Jobs Added Last Year: 4,226 (+158.4%)

Biomedical & genetic products - anticancer treatments, vaccines
& diagnostics; ophthalmic surgical products

CHOLESTECH CORPORATION

3347 Investment Blvd.
Hayward, CA 94545-3808
Pres & CEO: Warren E. Pinckert II
No central personnel officer
Employees: 79

Phone: 510-732-7200
Fax: 510-732-7227

Jobs Added Last Year: 17 (+27.4%)

Medical products - diagnostic analyzers that provide, from a single drop of whole blood & in less than 5 minutes, immediate
feedback of lipid & glucose levels

CIRCON CORPORATION

6500 Hollister Ave.
Santa Barbara, CA 93117-3019
Chm, Pres & CEO: Richard A. Auhll
VP HR: Jon St. Clair
Employees: 1,236

Phone: 805-685-5100
Fax: 805-968-8174

Jobs Added Last Year: 474 (+62.2%)

Medical instruments - endoscopes & electrosurgery equipment

CIRRUS LOGIC, INC.

3100 W. Warren Ave.
Fremont, CA 94538
Pres & CEO: Michael L. Hackworth
VP HR: William H. Bennett
Employees: 3,151

Phone: 510-623-8300
Fax: 510-226-2240

Jobs Added Last Year: 820 (+35.2%)

Electrical components - semiconductors for hard drive & graphics
controllers, accelerators & modems

CISCO SYSTEMS, INC.

170 W. Tasman Dr.
San Jose, CA 95134-1706
Pres & CEO: John T. Chambers
VP HR: Barbara Beck
Employees: 4,086

Phone: 408-526-4000
Fax: 408-526-4100

Jobs Added Last Year: 1,643 (+67.3%)

Computers - multiprotocol routers & software

CITY NATIONAL CORPORATION

400 N. Roxbury Dr.
Beverly Hills, CA 90210
VC & CEO: Russell Goldsmith
No central personnel officer
Employees: 1,500

Phone: 310-888-6000
Fax: 310-888-6643

Jobs Added Last Year: 268 (+21.8%)

Banks - West

 An in-depth profile of this company is available
to subscribers on Hoover's Online at www.hoovers.com.

CKE RESTAURANTS, INC.

1200 N. Harbor Blvd., PO Box 4349   Phone: 714-774-5796
Anaheim, CA 92801   Fax: 714-778-7183
Chm & CEO: William P. Foley II
Dir HR: Victoria Straschil
Employees: 11,100
Jobs Cut Last Year: 225 (-2.0%)

Retail - restaurants (Carl's Jr., Boston Chicken franchisee)

COHU, INC.

5755 Kearny Villa Rd.   Phone: 619-277-6700
San Diego, CA 92123-1170   Fax: 619-277-0221
Pres & CEO: Charles A. Schwan
Mgr HR: Linda Jacobson
Employees: 900
Jobs Added Last Year: 193 (+27.3%)

Machinery - semiconductor manufacturing equipment

CKS GROUP, INC.

10441 Bandley Dr.   Phone: 408-366-5100
Cupertino, CA 95014   Fax: 408-366-5120
Chm, Pres & CEO: Mark D. Kvamme
HR Mgr: Sharon Fitzsimmons
Employees: 187
Jobs Added Last Year: 83 (+79.8%)

Business services - marketing services, including strategic & corporate positioning, corporate identity & product branding, new media, packaging, collateral systems & advertising

COMPUTER MARKETPLACE, INC.

1490 Railroad St.   Phone: 909-735-2102
Corona, CA 91720   Fax: 909-735-5717
Pres & CEO: L. Wayne Kiley
Dir HR: Jackie Mahoney
Employees: 113
Jobs Added Last Year: 23 (+25.6%)

Retail - wholesale new & used computer equipment

CMD TECHNOLOGY, INC.

One Vanderbilt   Phone: 714-454-0800
Irvine, CA 92718   Fax: 714-455-1656
Pres: Simon Huang
Dir HR: Cheryl Bagra
Employees: 187
Jobs Added Last Year: 41 (+28.1%)

Computers - computer data storage & data input/output solutions, including SCSI adapters, IDE controllers, RAID devices & storage servers for PCs & mainframes

COMPUTER SCIENCES CORPORATION

2100 E. Grand Ave.   Phone: 310-615-0311
El Segundo, CA 90245   Fax: 310-322-9805
Pres & CEO: Van B. Honeycutt
VP HR: L. Scott Sharpe
Employees: 33,850
Jobs Added Last Year: 950 (+2.9%)

Consulting - information technology consulting, systems integration & outsourcing

Adams Online — http://www.adamsonline.com/

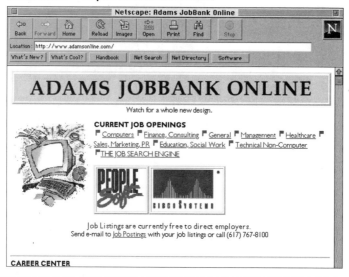

CONSOLIDATED FREIGHTWAYS, INC.

3240 Hillview Ave.   Phone: 415-494-2900
Palo Alto, CA 94304   Fax: 415-813-0160
Chm, Pres & CEO: Donald E. Moffitt
VP HR: James M. Tracey
Employees: 41,600
Jobs Added Last Year: 1,100 (+2.7%)

Transportation - nationwide (CF Motor Freight) & regional (Con-Way) trucking services; air freight (Emery); contract logistics (Menlo)

CONSUMER PORTFOLIO SERVICES, INC.

2 Ada, Ste. 100   Phone: 714-753-6800
Irvine, CA 92718   Fax: 714-753-6805
Pres & CEO: Charles E. Bradley Jr.
VP Personnel: Dottie Warren
Employees: 119
Jobs Added Last Year: 53 (+80.3%)

Financial - purchase, sale & service of automobile installment sales contracts

COPART, INC.

5500 E. Second St.   Phone: 707-748-5000
Benicia, CA 94510   Fax: 707-748-5088
CEO: Willis J. Johnson
Dir HR: Gale DeMartini
Employees: 750
Jobs Added Last Year: 450 (+150.0%)

Business services - processing & auction of salvaged vehicles, primarily for insurance companies

CORNERSTONE IMAGING, INC.

1710 Fortune Dr.   Phone: 408-435-8900
San Jose, CA 95131   Fax: 408-435-8998
Pres & CEO: Thomas T. van Overbeek
HR Mgr: Denise Wescott
Employees: 220
Jobs Added Last Year: 58 (+35.8%)

Computers - document image processing (DIP) display subsystems (#1 worldwide)

CRAIG CORPORATION

550 S. Hope St., Ste. 1825   Phone: 213-239-0555
Los Angeles, CA 90071   Fax: 213-239-0548
Pres: S. Craig Tompkins
Office Mgr: Annabel Robles
Employees: 8,543
Jobs Added Last Year: 543 (+6.8%)

Retail - supermarkets; movie theaters

CREATIVE COMPUTERS, INC.

2645 Maricopa St.   Phone: 310-787-4500
Torrance, CA 90503   Fax: 310-222-5800
Chm, Pres & CEO: Frank Khulusi
Personnel Administrator: Kathy Ressler
Employees: 743
Jobs Added Last Year: 207 (+38.6%)

Retail - mail-order sales of Apple Macintosh hardware, software & peripheral products (MacMall)

CREDENCE SYSTEMS CORPORATION

3500 W. Warren Ave.   Phone: 510-657-7400
Fremont, CA 94538   Fax: 510-623-2560
Pres & CEO: Elwood H. Spedden
No central personnel officer
Employees: 499
Jobs Added Last Year: 144 (+40.6%)

Electronics - automatic semiconductor test equipment

CROWLEY MARITIME CORPORATION

155 Grand Ave.   Phone: 510-251-7500
Oakland, CA 94612   Fax: 510-251-7625
Chm, Pres & CEO: Thomas B. Crowley Jr.
EVP: William A. Pennella
Employees: 5,000
Jobs Added Last Year: 0

Transportation - marine towing & cargo handling

CUBIC CORPORATION

9333 Balboa Ave., PO Box 85587   Phone: 619-277-6780
San Diego, CA 92186-5587   Fax: 619-277-9329
Chm, Pres & CEO: Walter J. Zable
VP HR: Bernie A. Kulchin
Employees: 3,300
Jobs Added Last Year: 650 (+24.5%)

Electronics - military range instrumentation & training systems, communications, surveillance & avionics systems; revenue collection equipment, ticket vending machines & passenger gates

CYPRESS SEMICONDUCTOR CORP.

3901 N. First St.   Phone: 408-943-2600
San Jose, CA 95134-1599   Fax: 408-943-2796
Pres & CEO: T. J. Rodgers
VP HR: Joyce Sziebert
Employees: 1,859
Jobs Added Last Year: 436 (+30.6%)

Electrical components - semiconductors, including logic devices, SRAM & multichip modules, primarily for mainframes & workstations

 An in-depth profile of this company is available to subscribers on Hoover's Online at www.hoovers.com.

DAMES & MOORE, INC.

911 Wilshire Blvd., Ste. 700
Los Angeles, CA 90017
Pres & CEO: Arthur C. Darrow
Chief of Staff: Alan P. Krusi
Employees: 5,300

Phone: 213-683-1560
Fax: 213-628-0015

Jobs Added Last Year: 1,200 (+29.3%)

Engineering - full-service engineering, environmental, construction management & litigation support services

DEL TACO, INC.

1800 W. Katella Ave.
Orange, CA 92667
CEO: Kevin K. Moriarty
Dir HR: Sheryl Wirt
Employees: 8,600

Phone: 714-744-4334
Fax: 714-289-4227

Jobs Added Last Year: 200 (+2.4%)

Retail - fast-food restaurants

DATUM INC.

1363 S. State College Blvd.
Anaheim, CA 92806-5790
Pres & Chm: Louis B. Horwitz
Dir HR: Laurie Pedroza
Employees: 537

Phone: 714-533-8772
Fax: 714-533-6345

Jobs Added Last Year: 328 (+156.9%)

Electronics - precision frequency & timing instrumentation products

DFS GROUP, LTD.

655 Montgomery St.
San Francisco, CA 94111
Chm & CEO: Myron E. Ullman
VP HR Strategy: Peggy Tate
Employees: 10,000

Phone: 415-397-4400
Fax: 415-397-6958

Jobs Cut Last Year: 3,500 (-25.9%)

Retail - duty-free luxury goods stores in airports

DAVIDSON & ASSOCIATES, INC.

19840 Pioneer Ave.
Torrance, CA 90503
Chm & CEO: Robert M. Davidson
Dir HR: Lonna Lynn
Employees: 679

Phone: 310-793-0600
Fax: 310-793-0601

Jobs Added Last Year: 141 (+26.2%)

Computers - educational & entertainment software (Math Blaster, Kid CAD, Zoo Keeper)

DHL WORLDWIDE EXPRESS

333 Twin Dolphin Dr.
Redwood City, CA 94065
Chm, Pres & CEO: Patrick Foley
SVP HR: Gary Sellers
Employees: 40,000

Phone: 415-593-7474
Fax: 415-593-1689

Jobs Added Last Year: 5,000 (+14.3%)

Transportation - air express

DAY RUNNER, INC.

15295 Alton Pkwy.
Irvine, CA 92718
Chm & CEO: Mark A. Vidovich
VP HR: Lee R. Coffey
Employees: 801

Phone: 714-680-3500
Fax: 714-680-0542

Jobs Added Last Year: 203 (+33.9%)

Paper - personal organizers, diaries & assignment books

DIAMOND ENTERTAINMENT CORPORATION

3961 Miraloma Ave.
Anaheim, CA 92806
Chm, CEO & Sec: James K. T. Lu
No central personnel officer
Employees: 114

Phone: 714-693-3399
Fax: 714-693-3339

Jobs Added Last Year: 28 (+32.6%)

Business services - video product duplicating, manufacturing, packaging & distribution

DEL MONTE FOODS COMPANY

One Market Plaza
San Francisco, CA 94105
Co-Chm & Co-CEO: Brian Haycox
VP Corp Personnel: Mark J. Buxton
Employees: 12,500

Phone: 415-247-3000
Fax: 415-247-3565

Jobs Added Last Year: 0

Food - canned

DIGITAL GENERATION SYSTEMS, INC.

875 Battery St.
San Francisco, CA 94111
Pres & CEO: Henry W. Donaldson
No central personnel officer
Employees: 83

Phone: 415-276-6600
Fax: 415-276-6601

Jobs Added Last Year: 52 (+167.7%)

Telecommunications services - multimedia network that provides electronic delivery & related services to the broadcast industry by linking content providers to radio & TV stations

DMX INC.

11400 W. Olympic Blvd., Ste. 1100
Los Angeles, CA 90064-1507
Chm & CEO: Jerold H. Rubinstein
HR Coordinator: Tracy Fujimoto
Employees: 145

Phone: 310-444-1744
Fax: 310-444-1717

Jobs Added Last Year: 45 (+45.0%)

Music publishing - commercial-free cable audio programming

DOLE FOOD COMPANY, INC.

31365 Oak Crest Dr.
Westlake Village, CA 91361
Chm & CEO: David H. Murdock
VP HR: George R. Horne
Employees: 43,000

Phone: 818-879-6600
Fax: 818-879-6618

Jobs Cut Last Year: 3,000 (-6.5%)

Food - fruits, vegetables, nuts & related products & commercial & residential real estate development

DREYER'S GRAND ICE CREAM, INC.

5929 College Ave.
Oakland, CA 94618
Chm & CEO: T. Gary Rogers
No central personnel officer
Employees: 2,500

Phone: 510-652-8187
Fax: 510-601-4592

Jobs Added Last Year: 438 (+21.2%)

Food - premium ice cream & frozen dessert products (Dreyer's, Edy's)

DURA PHARMACEUTICALS, INC.

5880 Pacific Center Blvd.
San Diego, CA 92121-4204
Pres & CEO: Cam L. Garner
Personnel Mgr: Yolanda Jackson
Employees: 300

Phone: 619-457-2553
Fax: 619-457-2555

Jobs Added Last Year: 82 (+37.6%)

Drugs - respiratory health drugs; pulmonary dry powder drug delivery system (Dryhaler)

EARLE M. JORGENSEN HOLDING CO.,INC.

3050 E. Birch St.
Brea, CA 92621
Pres & CEO: Neven C. Hulsey
VP Admin & HR: Steven Wild
Employees: 2,800

Phone: 714-579-8823
Fax: 714-577-3784

Jobs Added Last Year: 239 (+9.3%)

Steel - production; aluminum product distribution

EDELBROCK CORPORATION

2700 California St.
Torrance, CA 90503
Chm, Pres & CEO: O. Victor Edelbrock
Dir HR: Jackie Langlais
Employees: 463

Phone: 310-781-2222
Fax: 310-782-3828

Jobs Added Last Year: 110 (+31.2%)

Automotive & trucking - intake manifolds, carburetors, camshafts, cylinder heads, exhaust systems & other components for cars & motorcycles

EDIFY CORPORATION

2840 San Tomas Expwy.
Santa Clara, CA 95051
Pres & CEO: Jeffrey M. Crowe
VP HR: Patricia A. Tomlinson
Employees: 173

Phone: 408-982-2000
Fax: 408-982-0777

Jobs Added Last Year: 123 (+246.0%)

Computers - software (Electronic Workforce) that allows companies to communicate with their customers & employees through voice mail, fax, email & the World Wide Web

EDISON INTERNATIONAL

2244 Walnut Grove Ave.
Rosemead, CA 91770
Chm & CEO: John E. Bryson
VP HR: Emiko Banfield
Employees: 16,434

Phone: 818-302-1212
Fax: 818-302-2517

Jobs Cut Last Year: 640 (-3.7%)

Utility - electric power (Southern California Edison)

EL CAMINO RESOURCES, LTD.

21051 Warner Center Ln.
Woodland Hills, CA 91364
Pres & CEO: David Harmon
Mgr Corp Svcs: Jo Glascock
Employees: 430

Phone: 818-226-6600
Fax: 818-226-6787

Jobs Added Last Year: 90 (+26.5%)

Retail - new & used computer equipment

ELECTRONIC ARTS INC.

1450 Fashion Island Blvd.
San Mateo, CA 94404-2064
Chm, Pres & CEO: Lawrence F. Probst III
SVP, CFO & Chief Admin Officer: E. Stanton McKee Jr.
Employees: 1,500

Phone: 415-571-7171
Fax: 415-571-6375

Jobs Added Last Year: 328 (+28.0%)

Computers - interactive entertainment software & video-game players

 An in-depth profile of this company is available to subscribers on Hoover's Online at www.hoovers.com.

ELTRON INTERNATIONAL, INC.

41 Moreland Rd. Phone: 805-579-1800
Simi Valley, CA 93065 Fax: 805-579-1808
Chm, Pres & CEO: Donald K. Skinner
Dir HR: Bobby Stocking
Employees: 213

Jobs Added Last Year: 109 (+104.8%)

Computers - bar-code label printers, software & related accessories

ENDOSONICS CORPORATION

6616 Owens Dr. Phone: 510-734-0464
Pleasanton, CA 94588 Fax: 510-734-0465
Pres & CEO: Reinhard J. Warnking
VP Fin & CFO: Donald D. Huffman
Employees: 247

Jobs Added Last Year: 96 (+63.6%)

Medical instruments - intravascular imaging systems, balloon angioplasty catheters & ultrasound imaging & site-specific drug delivery catheters

EPIC DESIGN TECHNOLOGY, INC.

310 N. Mary Ave. Phone: 408-733-8080
Sunnyvale, CA 94086 Fax: 408-988-8324
Chm & CEO: Sang S. Wang
Dir HR: Angela Wanninger
Employees: 127

Jobs Added Last Year: 48 (+60.8%)

Computers - simulation & analysis software for integrated circuit design (PathMill, PowerMill, RailMill, TimeMill, Vertue)

ESS TECHNOLOGY, INC.

46107 Landing Pkwy. Phone: 510-226-1088
Fremont, CA 94538 Fax: 510-226-8868
Chm, Pres & CEO: Fred S. L. Chan
HR Mgr: Steve Gonia
Employees: 158

Jobs Added Last Year: 59 (+59.6%)

Electrical components - integrated mixed signal semiconductor audio solutions (AudioDrive) for multimedia desktop & notebook computer manufacturers

EXAR CORPORATION

48720 Kato Rd. Phone: 408-434-6400
Fremont, CA 94539 Fax: 408-943-8245
Pres & CEO: George D. Wells
Dir HR: Gene Robles
Employees: 500

Jobs Added Last Year: 148 (+42.0%)

Electrical components - analog & mixed-signal ICs & related ASICs

EXCEL REALTY TRUST, INC.

16955 Via Del Campo, Ste. 110 Phone: 619-485-9400
San Diego, CA 92127 Fax: 619-485-8530
Chm, Pres & CEO: Gary B. Sabin
Dir HR: R. B. Muir
Employees: 53

Jobs Added Last Year: 15 (+39.5%)

Real estate investment trust - neighborhood & regional shopping centers

FAMILY RESTAURANTS, INC.

18831 Von Karman Ave. Phone: 714-757-7900
Irvine, CA 92715 Fax: 714-757-7984
Pres & CEO: Kevin S. Relyea
VP HR : Ken Gowen
Employees: 42,500

Jobs Cut Last Year: 9,200 (-17.8%)

Retail - family-oriented (Carrows, Charley Brown's) & Mexican (Chi-Chi's, El Torito, Casa Gallardo) restaurants

FEDCO, INC.

9300 Santa Fe Springs Rd. Phone: 310-946-2511
Santa Fe Springs, CA 90670 Fax: 310-903-3428
Pres & CEO: Edward Butterworth
HR Dir: Sandy Camou
Employees: 5,610

Jobs Added Last Year: 110 (+2.0%)

Retail - membership department stores

FHP INTERNATIONAL CORPORATION

Lake Center Campus Phone: 714-963-7233
Santa Ana, CA 92799 Fax: 714-825-6630
VC, Pres & CEO: Westcott W. Price III
Corp Dir Employment: James Wade
Employees: 13,000

Jobs Cut Last Year: 1,000 (-7.1%)

Health maintenance organization - managed health care services & sales of indemnity health, group life & workers' compensation insurance

THE FIRST AMERICAN FINANCIAL CORP.

114 E. Fifth St. Phone: 714-558-3211
Santa Ana, CA 92701-4699 Fax: 714-541-6372
Pres & CEO: Parker S. Kennedy
Dir HR: Lane Heslington
Employees: 10,149

Jobs Added Last Year: 1,116 (+12.4%)

Financial - title insurance & search (#2 in US), real estate tax monitoring, credit reporting & home warranty services

FIRST INTERSTATE BANCORP

633 W. Fifth St.
Los Angeles, CA 90071
Chm & CEO: William E. B. Siart
EVP HR: Lillian R. Gorman
Employees: 27,200

Phone: 213-614-3001
Fax: 213-614-3741

Jobs Added Last Year: 200 (+0.7%)

Banks - money center

FLUOR CORPORATION

3333 Michelson Dr.
Irvine, CA 92730
Chm & CEO: Leslie G. McCraw
VP HR & Admin: Charles J. Bradley Jr.
Employees: 41,678

Phone: 714-975-2000
Fax: 714-975-5271

Jobs Added Last Year: 1,871 (+4.7%)

Construction - engineering, construction, maintenance & related services (Fluor Daniel)

FIRST SOURCE INTERNATIONAL INC.

7 Journey
Aliso Viejo, CA 92656
Pres: Douglas Dreier
HR Mgr: Stacy George
Employees: 75

Phone: 714-448-7750
Fax: 714-448-7774

Jobs Added Last Year: 15 (+25.0%)

Retail - mail-order sales of computer peripherals, including monitors & mice

FOODMAKER, INC.

9330 Balboa Ave.
San Diego, CA 92123
Pres & CEO: Robert J. Nugent
VP HR & Strategic Planning: Carlo Cetti
Employees: 25,785

Phone: 619-571-2121
Fax: 619-571-2101

Jobs Cut Last Year: 385 (-1.5%)

Retail - fast-food restaurants (over 1,250 units: Jack In The Box)

FLEETWOOD ENTERPRISES, INC.

3125 Myers St., PO Box 7638
Riverside, CA 92513-7638
Chm & CEO: John C. Crean
VP Admin & HR: Robert W. Graham
Employees: 18,000

Phone: 909-351-3500
Fax: 909-351-3690

Jobs Added Last Year: 2,000 (+12.5%)

Bulding - RVs, travel trailers (#1 in US) & manufactured housing

FORTE SOFTWARE, INC.

1800 Harrison St.
Oakland, CA 94612
Chm, Pres & CEO: Martin J. Sprinzen
Administrator: Karen Yoneda
Employees: 221

Phone: 510-869-3400
Fax: 510-869-3480

Jobs Added Last Year: 47 (+27.0%)

Computers - software application & management tools for client/server applications

Edge — http://www.web-xpress.com/india/edge/

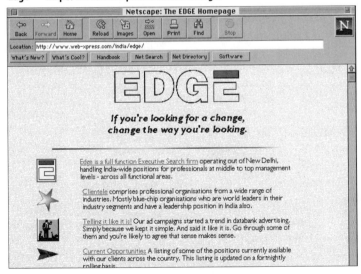

An in-depth profile of this company is available
to subscribers on Hoover's Online at www.hoovers.com.

83

FOSTER POULTRY FARMS INC.

1000 Davis St.
Livingston, CA 95334
Pres & CEO: Robert A. Fox
Dir Personnel: Tim Walsh
Employees: 9,000

Phone: 209-394-7901
Fax: 209-394-6342

Jobs Added Last Year: 2,400 (+36.4%)

Food - poultry processing

FOUNDATION HEALTH CORPORATION

3400 Data Dr.
Rancho Cordova, CA 95670
Chm, Pres & CEO: Daniel D. Crowley
SVP HR: Dan Smithson
Employees: 8,896

Phone: 916-631-5000
Fax: 916-631-5149

Jobs Added Last Year: 3,918 (+78.7%)

Health maintenance organization

FRANKLIN RESOURCES, INC.

777 Mariners Island Blvd.
San Mateo, CA 94404
Pres & CEO: Charles B. Johnson
VP HR: Donna Ikeda
Employees: 4,500

Phone: 415-312-3000
Fax: 415-378-5755

Jobs Added Last Year: 400 (+9.8%)

Financial - investment management & servicing for the Franklin/Templeton group of funds

FRD ACQUISITION CO.

18831 Von Karman Ave.
Irvine, CA 92715
Pres: Mark L. Shipman
VP HR: Beth L. Libhart
Employees: 16,500

Phone: 714-757-7900
Fax: 714-757-7929

Jobs Added Last Year: —

Retail - family-style restaurants (Coco's, Carrow's, jojos, Jeremiah's, Bob's: 348 restaurants), primarily in California

FREEDOM COMMUNICATIONS, INC.

17666 Fitch Ave.
Irvine, CA 92714
Pres: James N. Rosse
VP HR: Mark Ernst
Employees: 5,500

Phone: 714-553-9292
Fax: 714-474-4943

Jobs Cut Last Year: 1,300 (-19.1%)

Publishing - daily (25, including the Orange County Register) & weekly newspapers (34); TV stations (5) & a cable network; magazines (Latin Trade, World Trade, P.O.V.)

FRESENIUS USA, INC.

2637 Shadelands Dr.
Walnut Creek, CA 94598
Pres, CEO & COO: Ben J. Lipps
Dir HR: Dick Grobin
Employees: 1,600

Phone: 510-295-0200
Fax: 510-988-1900

Jobs Added Last Year: 200 (+14.3%)

Medical products - dialysis equipment

FRESH CHOICE, INC.

2901 Tasman Dr., Ste. 109
Santa Clara, CA 95054-1169
Pres & CEO: Robert Ferngren
Dir HR: Lori Stewart
Employees: 2,400

Phone: 408-986-8661
Fax: 408-986-8334

Jobs Added Last Year: 200 (+9.1%)

Retail - self-service salad bar restaurants

FRITZ COMPANIES, INC.

706 Mission St., Ste. 900
San Francisco, CA 94103
Chm, Pres & CEO: Lynn C. Fritz
Dir HR: Steve Enna
Employees: 6,550

Phone: 415-904-8661
Fax: 415-904-8661

Jobs Added Last Year: 1,582 (+31.8%)

Transportation - customs brokerage & freight forwarding

FURON COMPANY

29982 Ivy Glenn Dr.
Laguna Niguel, CA 92667
Chm & CEO: J. Michael Hagan
VP HR: Kevin G. Krogmeier
Employees: 2,483

Phone: 714-831-5350
Fax: 714-363-6275

Jobs Added Last Year: 266 (+12.0%)

Rubber & plastic products - polymer-based industrial parts

THE GAP, INC.

One Harrison St.
San Francisco, CA 94105
Pres & CEO: Millard S. Drexler
SVP HR: Adrienne M. Johns
Employees: 60,000

Phone: 415-952-4400
Fax: 415-589-6833

Jobs Added Last Year: 5,000 (+9.1%)

Retail - apparel & shoes (Gap, GapKids, Banana Republic, Old Navy)

GASONICS INTERNATIONAL CORP.

2730 Junction Ave.
San Jose, CA 95134-1909
Pres & CEO: Dave Toole
Dir HR: Robert Mearns
Employees: 476

Phone: 408-944-0212
Fax: 408-473-9509

Jobs Added Last Year: 169 (+55.0%)

Machinery - photoresist removal equipment used in semiconductor manufacturing

GENERAL MAGIC, INC.

420 N. Mary Ave.
Sunnyvale, CA 94086
Chm & CEO: Marc Porat
VP HR: Stephen Hams
Employees: 208

Phone: 408-774-4000
Fax: 408-774-4010

Jobs Added Last Year: 47 (+29.2%)

Computers - communications software (Telescript) for hand-held computers

GLOBAL RESOURCES, INC.

43445 Business Park Dr., Ste. 113
Temecula, CA 92590
Pres, CEO & CFO: Perry T. Massie
Acctg Mgr: Ralph Denney
Employees: 59

Phone: 909-699-4749
Fax: 909-699-4062

Jobs Added Last Year: 24 (+68.6%)

Leisure & recreational services - recreational gold panning expeditions to several company-operated mining properties; resort operations

GLOBAL VILLAGE COMMUNICATION

1144 E. Arques Ave.
Sunnyvale, CA 94086-4602
Pres & CEO: Neil Selvin
Mgr HR: Mary Cravalho
Employees: 225

Phone: 408-523-1000
Fax: 408-523-2407

Jobs Added Last Year: 103 (+84.4%)

Computers - data modems & fax cards for Macintosh, Windows, OS/2 & DOS computers

THE GOOD GUYS, INC.

7000 Marina Blvd.
Brisbane, CA 94005-1840
Pres & CEO: Robert A. Gunst
VP HR: Geradette M. Vaz
Employees: 4,000

Phone: 415-615-5000
Fax: 415-615-6287

Jobs Added Last Year: 358 (+9.8%)

Retail - consumer electronics

GOTTSCHALKS INC.

7 River Park Place East
Fresno, CA 93720
Chm & CEO: Joseph W. Levy
Dir HR: Marci Woolsen
Employees: 5,181

Phone: 209-434-8000
Fax: 209-434-4804

Jobs Cut Last Year: 196 (-3.6%)

Retail - regional department stores

GRANITE CONSTRUCTION INCORPORATED

585 W. Beach St.
Watsonville, CA 95076-5125
Pres & CEO: David H. Watts
VP & Dir HR: Michael L. Thomas
Employees: 3,322

Phone: 408-724-1011
Fax: 408-722-9657

Jobs Added Last Year: 666 (+25.1%)

Construction - highways, dams, tunnels, mass transit systems

GREAT WESTERN FINANCIAL CORP.

9200 Oakdale Ave.
Chatsworth, CA 91311-6519
Pres & CEO: John F. Maher
SVP HR: Patricia A. Benninger
Employees: 14,393

Phone: 818-775-3411
Fax: 818-775-3434

Jobs Cut Last Year: 1,251 (-8.0%)

Financial - savings & loans

GTI CORPORATION

9715 Business Park Ave.
San Diego, CA 92131-1642
Pres & CEO: Albert J. Hugo-Martinez
Acting Mgr HR: Lynn Wylie
Employees: 8,075

Phone: 619-537-2500
Fax: 619-537-2525

Jobs Cut Last Year: 1,279 (-13.7%)

Electrical components - magnetic-based sigal-processing & power components & subsystems

THE GYMBOREE CORPORATION

700 Airport Blvd., Ste. 200
Burlingame, CA 94010-1912
Pres & CEO: Nancy J. Pedot
VP HR: Nancy Hauge
Employees: 6,000

Phone: 415-579-0600
Fax: 415-579-1733

Jobs Added Last Year: 2,924 (+95.1%)

Retail - children's apparel & toys

 An in-depth profile of this company is available to subscribers on Hoover's Online at www.hoovers.com.

85

HARMONY HOLDINGS, INC.

6806 Lexington Ave.   Phone: 213-960-1400
Hollywood, CA 90038   Fax: 213-960-1415
Pres, CEO & Sec: Gary Horowitz
Dir HR: Maggie Adams
Employees: 108
Jobs Added Last Year: 28 (+35.0%)

TV programming & production - TV commercials

HEWLETT-PACKARD COMPANY

3000 Hanover St.   Phone: 415-857-1501
Palo Alto, CA 94304   Fax: 415-857-7299
Chm, Pres & CEO: Lewis E. Platt
SVP Personnel: F. E. Peterson
Employees: 102,300
Jobs Added Last Year: 3,900 (+4.0%)

Computers - PCs, laser printers (LaserJet), test equipment & information storage products, including the digital audio tape; medical products, including cardiac ultrasound machines

H.F. AHMANSON & COMPANY

4900 Rivergrade Rd.   Phone: 818-960-6311
Irwindale, CA 91706   Fax: 818-814-7389
Chm & CEO: Charles R. Rinehart
First VP HR: Merrill S. Wall
Employees: 9,344
Jobs Cut Last Year: 515 (-5.2%)

Financial - savings & loans, residential real estate mortgage loans, mortgage-backed securities & investment securities operations

HILTON HOTELS CORPORATION

9336 Civic Center Dr.   Phone: 310-278-4321
Beverly Hills, CA 90210   Fax: 310-205-4599
Pres & CEO: Stephen F. Bollenbach
SVP Labor Relations & Personnel Admin: James M. Anderson
Employees: 48,000
Jobs Added Last Year: 4,000 (+9.1%)

Hotels & motels - international chain of hotels & resorts (Waldorf-Astoria, Hilton Hawaiian Village) & casinos (Flamingo Hilton, Las Vegas Hilton)

HOMETOWN BUFFET INC.

9171 Town Centre Dr., Ste. 575   Phone: 619-546-9096
San Diego, CA 92122   Fax: 619-546-0179
Pres & CEO: C. Dennis Scott
VP HR: K. Michael Schrader
Employees: 7,400
Jobs Added Last Year: 2,400 (+48.0%)

Retail - restaurants

HUGHES ELECTRONICS CORP.

7200 Hughes Terrace, PO Box 80028   Phone: 310-568-7200
Los Angeles, CA 90080-0028   Fax: 310-568-6390
Chm & CEO: C. Michael Armstrong
SVP HR: Ted G. Westerman
Employees: 84,000
Jobs Added Last Year: 6,900 (+8.9%)

Electronics - defense & automotive electronics & telecommunications satellites

HUGHES MARKETS, INC.

14005 Live Oak Ave.   Phone: 818-856-6580
Irwindale, CA 91706   Fax: 818-856-6020
Pres & CEO: Fred McLaren
VP HR: David McMahon
Employees: 5,000
Jobs Added Last Year: 100 (+2.0%)

Retail - supermarkets

ICN PHARMACEUTICALS, INC.

3300 Hyland Ave.   Phone: 714-545-0100
Costa Mesa, CA 92626   Fax: 714-556-0131
Chm, Pres & CEO: Milan Panic
SVP HR: Jack Sholl
Employees: 7,880
Jobs Added Last Year: 2,040 (+34.9%)

Drugs - psychiatric, dermatological & cardiovascular pharmaceuticals & diagnostic & nutritional products

IHOP CORP.

525 N. Brand Blvd.   Phone: 818-240-6055
Glendale, CA 91203-1903   Fax: 818-240-0270
Chm, Pres & CEO: Richard K. Herzer
VP HR: Naomi K. Shively
Employees: 2,440
Jobs Added Last Year: 265 (+12.2%)

Retail - restaurants (International House of Pancakes)

INFORMATION STORAGE DEVICES, INC.

2045 Hamilton Ave.   Phone: 408-369-2400
San Jose, CA 95125   Fax: 408-369-2422
Pres & CEO: David L. Angel
No central personnel officer
Employees: 122
Jobs Added Last Year: 39 (+47.0%)

Electrical components - integrated circuits used for recording & playing back human voices in greeting cards, games, building security systems & cellular phones

INFORMIX CORPORATION

4100 Bohannon Dr.
Menlo Park, CA 94025
Chm, Pres & CEO: Phillip E. White
VP HR: Ira H. Dorf
Employees: 3,219

Phone: 415-926-6300
Fax: 415-926-6564

Jobs Added Last Year: 1,007 (+45.5%)

Computers - UNIX database management software

INFOSEEK CORPORATION

2620 Augustine Dr., Ste. 250
Santa Clara, CA 95054
Pres & CEO: Robert E. L. Johnson III
VP Admin: Victoria J. Blakeslee
Employees: 71

Phone: 408-567-2700
Fax: 408-986-1889

Jobs Added Last Year: 60 (+545.5%)

Computers - World Wide Web search service (Infoseek Guide), database access services (Infoseek Professional) & individual information interface (Personal Newswire)

INGRAM MICRO INC.

1600 E. St. Andrew Place
Santa Ana, CA 92705
Acting CEO: John R. Ingram
SVP HR: David M. Finley
Employees: 7,604

Phone: 714-566-1000
Fax: 714-566-7733

Jobs Added Last Year: —

Retail - PC wholesaler (#1 in US)

INHALE THERAPEUTIC SYSTEMS

1001 E. Meadow Circle
Palo Alto, CA 94303
Pres & CEO: Robert B. Chess
Dir HR: Gail Maloof
Employees: 55

Phone: 415-354-0700
Fax: 415-354-0701

Jobs Added Last Year: 22 (+66.7%)

Biomedical & genetic products - pulmonary drug delivery system

INTEGRATED DEVICE TECHNOLOGY

2975 Stender Way
Santa Clara, CA 95054
Pres & CEO: Leonard C. Perham
VP HR: Thomas B. Wroblewski
Employees: 3,828

Phone: 408-727-6116
Fax: 408-492-8674

Jobs Added Last Year: 863 (+29.1%)

Electrical components - high performance ICs in CMOS & BiCMOS technologies for SRAM components, specialty memory products & logic circuit & RISC microprocessors & subsystems

INTEGRATED SYSTEMS, INC.

201 Moffett Park Drive
Sunnyvale, CA 94089
Pres & CEO: David P. St. Charles
VP HR & Ops: Janice Waterman
Employees: 416

Phone: 408-980-1500
Fax: 408-980-0400

Jobs Added Last Year: 102 (+32.5%)

Computers - CAE/CASE software & software for embedded controllers in household & industrial products

INTEL CORPORATION

2200 Mission College Blvd.
Santa Clara, CA 95052-8119
Pres & CEO: Andrew S. Grove
VP & Dir HR: Kirby A. Dyess
Employees: 41,600

Phone: 408-765-8080
Fax: 408-765-1402

Jobs Added Last Year: 9,000 (+27.6%)

Electrical components - microprocessors, chipsets & motherboards; semiconductors, including flash memory & control chips; supercomputers

INTERACTIVE GROUP, INC.

5095 Murphy Canyon Rd.
San Diego, CA 92123
Chm, Pres & CEO: Robert C. Vernon
Dir HR: Doug Fulkerson
Employees: 292

Phone: 619-560-8525
Fax: 619-565-8750

Jobs Added Last Year: 91 (+45.3%)

Computers - manufacturers' make-to-order & make-to-stock support software (INFOFLO, Intrepid)

INTERLINK ELECTRONICS

546 Flynn Rd.
Camarillo, CA 93012
Chm, Pres & CEO: E. Michael Thoben III
HR Dir: Cynthia Batastini
Employees: 85

Phone: 805-484-8855
Fax: 805-484-8988

Jobs Added Last Year: 17 (+25.0%)

Instruments - pressure-sensitive sensors & controls for the computer, consumer electronics, aerospace, automotive, industrial control & measurement & biomedical industries

INTERNATIONAL RECTIFIER CORP.

233 Kansas St.
El Segundo, CA 90245
CEO: Derek B. Lidow
Dir HR: Dennis Marchand
Employees: 3,310

Phone: 310-322-3331
Fax: 310-322-3332

Jobs Added Last Year: 310 (+10.3%)

Electrical components - power-regulating semiconductors for power conversion

 An in-depth profile of this company is available to subscribers on Hoover's Online at www.hoovers.com.

87

INTERNATIONAL REMOTE IMAGING SYSTEMS INC.

9162 Eton Ave. Phone: 818-709-1244
Chatsworth, CA 91311 Fax: 818-700-9661
Chm, Pres, CEO & CFO: Fred H. Deindoerfer
No central personnel officer
Employees: 83

Jobs Added Last Year: 18 (+27.7%)

Medical instruments - automated urinalysis workstation (Yellow IRIS), urine test strips (CHEMSTRIP/IRIStrip) & refractometers

INTUIT INC.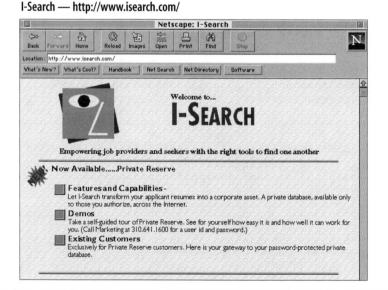

155 Linfield Ave. Phone: 415-322-0573
Menlo Park, CA 94025 Fax: 415-329-2788
Pres & CEO: William V. Campbell
VP HR: Michael A. Ahearn
Employees: 2,732

Jobs Added Last Year: 1,504 (+122.5%)

Computers - personal finance (Quicken), tax preparation (MacInTax, TurboTax) & related electronic software

IRVINE SENSORS CORPORATION

3001 Redhill Ave., Bldg. 3 Phone: 714-549-8211
Costa Mesa, CA 92626 Fax: 714-557-1260
Pres & CEO: Kenneth T. Lian
HR Dir: David Greenhut
Employees: 115

Jobs Added Last Year: 39 (+51.3%)

Electrical components - microchip-stacking technology to increase the operating speed of computer systems

JACOBS ENGINEERING GROUP INC.

251 S. Lake Ave. Phone: 818-449-2171
Pasadena, CA 91101-3063 Fax: 818-578-6893
Pres & CEO: Noel G. Watson
Dir Corp HR: William Gebhardt
Employees: 7,600

Jobs Added Last Year: 660 (+9.5%)

Construction - engineering, design, consulting, construction, construction management services & process plant maintenance for industrial & government clients in the US, the UK & Ireland

JB OXFORD HOLDINGS, INC.

9665 Wilshire Blvd., Ste. 300 Phone: 310-777-8888
Beverly Hills, CA 90212 Fax: 310-247-0970
Pres & CEO: Stephen Rubenstein
Personnel Mgr: Neilja Harewood
Employees: 245

Jobs Added Last Year: 141 (+135.6%)

Financial - securities brokerage & specialized computer products marketing

JENNY CRAIG, INC.

445 Marine View Ave., Ste. 300 Phone: 619-259-7000
Del Mar, CA 92014 Fax: 619-259-2812
Pres & CEO: C. Joseph LaBonte
VP Corp Comm & HR: Jan Strode
Employees: 4,800

Jobs Added Last Year: 520 (+12.1%)

Retail - weight-control centers; portion- & calorie-controlled food products

I-Search — http://www.isearch.com/

JOSEPH WEBB FOODS INC.

1201 Park Center Dr.
Vista, CA 92083
Pres: Allan Motter
HR Mgr: Lori Lansford
Employees: 225

Phone: 619-599-6200
Fax: 619-598-9310

Jobs Added Last Year: 75 (+50.0%)

Wholesale distribution - food

K2 INC.

4900 S. Eastern Ave., Ste. 200
Los Angeles, CA 90040
Pres & CEO: Richard M. Rodstein
Dir Emp Benefits: Michelle Lee
Employees: 4,600

Phone: 213-724-2800
Fax: 213-724-0470

Jobs Added Last Year: 900 (+24.3%)

Leisure & recreational products - skis (K2, Olin), fishing tackle, life vests, wet suits, outdoor apparel & bicycles; swimming pool construction

KAISER FOUNDATION HEALTH PLAN

One Kaiser Plaza
Oakland, CA 94612
Chm & CEO: David M. Lawrence
SVP Strategic Dev & HR: James B. Williams
Employees: 75,000

Phone: 510-271-5934
Fax: 510-271-5917

Jobs Cut Last Year: 9,845 (-11.6%)

Health maintenance organization

KINKO'S, INC.

255 W. Stanley Ave.
Ventura, CA 93002-8000
Pres: Daniel R. Frederickson
VP Dev: Adrianna Foss
Employees: 19,000

Phone: 805-652-4000
Fax: 805-652-4347

Jobs Added Last Year: —

Business services - document production & business communications services (more than 800 units worldwide); electronic document distribution & production (Kinkonet)

KLA INSTRUMENTS CORPORATION

160 Rio Robles, PO Box 49055
San Jose, CA 95161-9055
Chm & CEO: Kenneth Levy
VP HR: Virginia J. DeMars
Employees: 1,654

Phone: 408-468-4200
Fax: 408-434-4266

Jobs Added Last Year: 519 (+45.7%)

Machinery - yield-management & process-monitoring systems for semiconductor manufacturing

KNOTT'S BERRY FARM

8039 Beach Blvd.
Buena Park, CA 90620-9985
Pres & CEO: Terry E. Van Gorder
No central personnel officer
Employees: 6,300

Phone: 714-827-1776
Fax: 714-220-5150

Jobs Added Last Year: 300 (+5.0%)

Diversified operations - amusement parks; restaurants; food manufacturing

KOMAG, INCORPORATED

275 S. Hillview Dr.
Milpitas, CA 95035
Pres & CEO: Stephen C. Johnson
VP HR: Kathryn A. McGann
Employees: 2,915

Phone: 408-946-2300
Fax: 408-946-1126

Jobs Added Last Year: 280 (+10.6%)

Computers - thin-film magnetic media on rigid disk platters for hard-disk drives (#1 worldwide)

KOO KOO ROO, INC.

11075 Santa Monica Blvd., Ste. 225
Los Angeles, CA 90025
Chm & CEO: Kenneth Berg
VC: Donna S. Guido
Employees: 500

Phone: 310-479-2080

Jobs Added Last Year: 220 (+78.6%)

Retail - casual dining restaurants featuring roasted chicken & turkey

LAM RESEARCH CORPORATION

4650 Cushing Pkwy.
Fremont, CA 94538
Chm & CEO: Roger D. Emerick
SVP Fin & CFO: Henk J. Evenhuis
Employees: 3,600

Phone: 510-659-0200
Fax: 510-572-6454

Jobs Added Last Year: 1,374 (+61.7%)

Machinery - semiconductor processing equipment (AutoEtch, Rainbow, TCP) for the fabrication of integrated circuits

LEVI STRAUSS ASSOCIATES INC.

1155 Battery St.
San Francisco, CA 94111-1230
Chm & CEO: Robert D. Haas
SVP HR: Donna J. Goya
Employees: 37,700

Phone: 415-544-6000
Fax: 415-544-3939

Jobs Added Last Year: 1,200 (+3.3%)

Apparel

 An in-depth profile of this company is available to subscribers on Hoover's Online at www.hoovers.com.

89

LEXI INTERNATIONAL, INC.

1645 N. Vine St., Ste. 400
Los Angeles, CA 90028
Pres : Robin Richards
VP: Steve Hemmert
Employees: 1,500

Phone: 213-467-3334
Fax: 213-848-5500

Jobs Added Last Year: 800 (+114.3%)

Business - telemarketing & database marketing

LINEAR TECHNOLOGY CORPORATION

1630 McCarthy Blvd.
Milpitas, CA 95035-7487
Pres & CEO: Robert H. Swanson Jr.
Mgr HR: Steve Marcey
Employees: 1,350

Phone: 408-432-1900
Fax: 408-434-0507

Jobs Added Last Year: 346 (+34.5%)

Electrical components - standard linear integrated circuits for telecommunications equipment, notebook & desktop computers, video & multimedia & computer peripherals

LITTON INDUSTRIES, INC.

21240 Burbank Blvd.
Woodland Hills, CA 91367-6675
Chm, Pres & CEO: John M. Leonis
VP Industrial Relations: Mathias J. Diederich
Employees: 29,100

Phone: 818-598-5000
Fax: 818-598-5940

Jobs Added Last Year: 100 (+0.3%)

Diversified operations - defense electronics; military shipbuilding

LOGICON, INC.

3701 Skypark Dr.
Torrance, CA 90505-4794
Pres & CEO: John R. Woodhull
Dir HR: Judie Keller
Employees: 4,986

Phone: 310-373-0220
Fax: 310-373-0844

Jobs Added Last Year: 472 (+10.5%)

Electronics - military weapons systems, training & simulations systems & command, control, communications & intelligence systems

LOGISTIX

48021 Warm Springs Blvd.
Fremont, CA 94539
Pres & CEO: Stephen Weinstein
VP Fin: Frank Schneider
Employees: 611

Phone: 510-656-8000
Fax: 510-438-9486

Jobs Added Last Year: 287 (+88.6%)

Computers - supply-based services for computers & software

LONGS DRUG STORES CORPORATION

141 N. Civic Dr., PO Box 5222
Walnut Creek, CA 94596
Chm & CEO: Robert M. Long
VP Personnel: Les C. Anderson
Employees: 16,000

Phone: 510-937-1170
Fax: 510-210-6886

Jobs Added Last Year: 400 (+2.6%)

Retail - drugstores in the western US

LOS ANGELES COUNTY DEPARTMENT OF HEALTHCARE SERVICES

313 N. Figueroa
Los Angeles, CA 90012
Dir: Robert Gates
No central personnel officer
Employees: 28,000

Phone: 213-250-8055
Fax: 213-240-7771

Jobs Added Last Year: —

Hospitals - not-for-profit system serving Los Angeles County

LOST ARROW, INC.

259 W. Santa Clara St.
Ventura, CA 93001
Pres: Yvon Chouinard
Dir HR: Terri Wolfe
Employees: 700

Phone: 805-643-8616
Fax: 805-643-7551

Jobs Added Last Year: 180 (+34.6%)

Retail - outdoor apparel & equipment (Patagonia), primarily mail order

LUCASARTS ENTERTAINMENT CO.

PO Box 10307
San Rafael, CA 94912
Pres: Jack Sorensen
HR Mgr: Karen Chelini
Employees: 230

Phone: 415-472-3400
Fax: 415-662-2460

Jobs Added Last Year: 90 (+64.3%)

Computers - film production & interactive games software (The Dig, Rebel Assault II, Full Throttle, Indiana Jones)

MAC FRUGAL'S BARGAINS - CLOSE-OUTS INC.

2430 E. Del Amo Blvd.
Dominguez, CA 90220-6306
Chm, Pres & CEO: Philip L. Carter
VP HR: Frank C. Bianchi
Employees: 7,325

Phone: 310-537-9220
Fax: 310-632-4477

Jobs Cut Last Year: 852 (-10.4%)

Retail - close-out merchandise purchased below regular wholesale & sold below normal retail (278 units)

CALIFORNIA

MACROMEDIA, INC.

600 Townsend St.
San Francisco, CA 94103-4945
Pres & CEO: John C."Bud" Colligan
Dir HR: Denise Minaberry
Employees: 396
Phone: 415-252-2000
Fax: 415-626-0554

Jobs Added Last Year: 134 (+51.1%)

Computers - multimedia authoring software tools (Director, FreeHand, MacroModel, Action!, Authorware Professional)

MATTEL, INC.

333 Continental Blvd.
El Segundo, CA 90245-5012
Chm & CEO: John W. Amerman
SVP HR & Admin: E. Joseph McKay
Employees: 25,000
Phone: 310-252-2000
Fax: 310-252-4423

Jobs Added Last Year: 3,000 (+13.6%)

Toys - dolls, games, action figures & activity toys

MATTSON TECHNOLOGY, INC.

3550 W. Warren Ave.
Fremont, CA 94538
Pres & CEO: Brad Mattson
Dir HR: Sowji Reddy
Employees: 270
Phone: 510-657-5900
Fax: 510-657-0165

Jobs Added Last Year: 160 (+145.5%)

Machinery - semiconductor manufacturing equipment

MAXIM INTEGRATED PRODUCTS, INC.

120 San Gabriel Dr.
Sunnyvale, CA 94086
Chm, Pres & CEO: John F."Jack" Gifford
VP & CFO: Michael J. Byrd
Employees: 1,552
Phone: 408-737-7600
Fax: 408-737-7194

Jobs Added Last Year: 324 (+26.4%)

Electrical components - analog integrated circuits

MAXIS, INC.

2121 N. California Blvd., Ste. 600
Walnut Creek, CA 94596-3572
Chm & CEO: Jeffrey B. Braun
VP HR: Deborah L. Gross
Employees: 210
Phone: 510-254-9700
Fax: 510-253-3736

Jobs Added Last Year: 60 (+40.0%)

Computers - entertainment & educational software (SimCity, SimCity 2000, SimTown)

MCA INC.

100 Universal City Plaza
Universal City, CA 91608
Chm & CEO: Frank J. Biondi Jr.
Dir HR: Ken Khars
Employees: 13,564
Phone: 818-777-1000
Fax: 818-733-1402

Jobs Added Last Year: —

Motion pictures & services - film & music production & distribution

MCAFEE ASSOCIATES, INC.

2710 Walsh Ave., Ste. 200
Santa Clara, CA 95054
Pres & CEO: William L. Larson
Controller, Sec & Chief Acctg Officer: Robert J. Schwei
Employees: 250
Phone: 408-988-3832
Fax: 408-970-9727

Jobs Added Last Year: 122 (+95.3%)

Computers - anti-virus software distributed through electronic online bulletin board services; utility software including LAN management software (Saber LAN Workstation)

MCCLATCHY NEWSPAPERS, INC.

2100 Q St.
Sacramento, CA 95816
Pres & CEO: Gary Pruitt
VP HR: Peter M. CaJacob
Employees: 7,464
Phone: 916-321-1846
Fax: 916-321-1996

Jobs Added Last Year: 1,217 (+19.5%)

Publishing - newspapers (The Sacramento Bee) & online legal-news service

MCKESSON CORPORATION

McKesson Plaza, One Post St.
San Francisco, CA 94104
Chm & CEO: Alan J. Seelenfreund
VP HR & Admin: William A. Armstrong
Employees: 11,300
Phone: 415-983-8300
Fax: 415-983-7160

Jobs Cut Last Year: 900 (-7.4%)

Drugs & sundries - wholesale distribution to chain & independent drugstores; service merchandising; bottled water; Armor All

MEADOWBROOK REHABILITATION GROUP, INC.

2200 Powell St., Ste. 800, PO Box 8506
Emeryville, CA 94608
Chm, Pres & CEO: Harvey Wm. Glasser
Dir HR: Dennis Gregory
Employees: 555
Phone: 510-420-0900
Fax: 510-547-4323

Jobs Added Last Year: 190 (+52.1%)

Health care - comprehensive inpatient & outpatient rehabilitation services for patients with neurologic diseases

 An in-depth profile of this company is available to subscribers on Hoover's Online at www.hoovers.com.

MEASUREX CORPORATION

One Results Way
Cupertino, CA 95014-5991
Chm & CEO: David A. Bossen
VP HR: Phillip E. Peterson
Employees: 2,360

Phone: 408-255-1500
Fax: 408-864-7570

Jobs Added Last Year: 270 (+12.9%)

Instruments - sensor-based information & control systems used in computer-integrated manufacturing applications

MEDIA ARTS GROUP, INC.

10 Almaden Blvd., 9th Fl.
San Jose, CA 95113
Chm, Pres & CEO: Kenneth E. Raasch
Corp Sec: Susan C. Edstrom
Employees: 1,024

Phone: 408-947-4680
Fax: 408-947-4642

Jobs Added Last Year: 444 (+76.6%)

Housewares - collectible, gift & art products, lithographs, miniature cottages & other figurines & home decor products

MERCURY INTERACTIVE CORPORATION

470 Potrero Ave.
Sunnyvale, CA 95086
Chm & CEO: Aryeh Finegold
Dir HR: Betty Hardonag
Employees: 296

Phone: 408-523-9900
Fax: 408-523-9911

Jobs Added Last Year: 84 (+39.6%)

Computers - testing & quality assurance software

METATOOLS, INC.

6303 Carpinteria Ave.
Carpinteria, CA 93013
Chm & CEO: John J. Wilczak
Staff Attorney: Kari Zeni
Employees: 100

Phone: 805-566-6200
Fax: 805-566-6385

Jobs Added Last Year: 20 (+25.0%)

Computers - graphics (Kai's Power Tools)

MICROSEMI CORPORATION

2830 S. Fairview St.
Santa Ana, CA 92704
Chm, Pres & CEO: Philip Frey Jr.
VP HR: James M. Thomas
Employees: 2,309

Phone: 714-979-8220
Fax: 714-557-5989

Jobs Added Last Year: 302 (+15.0%)

Electrical components - power semiconductors, surface mount & custom diode assemblies, transistors & silicon controlled rectifiers

MONTGOMERY WATSON, INC.

300 N. Lake Ave., Ste. 1200
Pasadena, CA 91101
Pres & CEO: Murli Tolaney
Corp HR Mgr: Gary Melillo
Employees: 3,300

Phone: 818-796-9141
Fax: 818-568-6619

Jobs Added Last Year: 200 (+6.5%)

Environmental engineering, construction & technology services & management

MOTORCAR PARTS & ACCESSORIES

2727 Maricopa St.
Torrance, CA 90503
Chm & CEO: Mel Marks
HR Operator: Angie Castillo
Employees: 400

Phone: 310-212-7910
Fax: 310-212-7581

Jobs Added Last Year: 180 (+81.8%)

Automotive & trucking - replacement alternators & starters for imported cars & light trucks

MTS INC.

2500 Del Monte St., Bldg. C
West Sacramento, CA 95691
Pres & CEO: Russell M. Solomon
Payroll & HR Mgr: Shauna Pompei
Employees: 7,600

Phone: 916-373-2500
Fax: 916-373-2535

Jobs Added Last Year: 900 (+13.4%)

Retail - records, books & videos (Tower Records)

MUSTANG SOFTWARE, INC.

6200 Lake Ming Rd.
Bakersfield, CA 93306
Chm, Pres & CEO: James A. Harrer
Dir HR: Lynn Wright
Employees: 65

Phone: 805-873-2500
Fax: 805-873-2599

Jobs Added Last Year: 22 (+51.2%)

Computers - e-mail exchange, file transfer & fax software (Wildcat! BBS, QmodemPro, Off-Line Xpress)

MYLEX CORPORATION

34551 Ardenwood Blvd.
Fremont, CA 94555
Pres & CEO: Albert E. Montross
VP HR: Joe Schmidt
Employees: 193

Phone: 510-796-6100
Fax: 510-745-7654

Jobs Added Last Year: 55 (+39.9%)

Computers - data-storage devices & computer-system boards

NATIONAL SEMICONDUCTOR CORP.

2900 Semiconductor Dr., PO Box 58090
Santa Clara, CA 95052-8090
CEO: Brian Halla
VP HR: Robert G. MacLean
Employees: 22,400

Phone: 408-721-5000
Fax: 408-739-9803

Jobs Added Last Year: 100 (+0.4%)

Electrical components - analog & digital semiconductors, memory products, embedded microprocessors & specialized security microchips

NATIONAL TECHNICAL SYSTEMS, INC.

24007 Ventura Blvd.
Calabasas, CA 91302
Pres: Jack Lin
Dir HR: Linda Freeman
Employees: 432

Phone: 818-591-0776
Fax: 818-591-0899

Jobs Added Last Year: 110 (+34.2%)

Engineering - technical, contract labor, quality registration & environmental services

NATURAL WONDERS, INC.

4209 Technology Dr.
Fremont, CA 94538
Pres & CEO: Kathleen M. Chatfield
Dir Personnel: Karen Daley
Employees: 2,308

Phone: 510-252-9600
Fax: 510-252-6791

Jobs Added Last Year: 233 (+11.2%)

Retail - educational & scientific products

NELLCOR PURITAN BENNETT INC.

4280 Hacienda Dr.
Pleasanton, CA 94588
Pres & CEO: C. Raymond Larkin Jr.
EVP HR, Gen Counsel & Sec: Laureen DeBuono
Employees: 4,400

Phone: 510-463-4000
Fax: 510-463-4450

Jobs Added Last Year: 2,704 (+159.4%)

Medical products - patient monitoring & diagnostic products, measurement instruments & therapeutic products

NETCOM ON-LINE COMMUNICATION SERVICES, INC.

3031 Tisch Way, 2nd Fl.
San Jose, CA 95128
Chm & CEO: David W. Garrison
HR Mgr: Irene Meister
Employees: 500

Phone: 408-556-3233
Fax: 408-556-3250

Jobs Added Last Year: 347 (+226.8%)

Computers - Internet connectivity software (NetCruiser)

NETMANAGE, INC.

10725 N. De Anza Blvd.
Cupertino, CA 95014
Chm, Pres & CEO: Zvi Alon
Dir HR: Pat Roboostoff
Employees: 650

Phone: 408-973-7171
Fax: 408-257-6405

Jobs Added Last Year: 295 (+83.1%)

Computers - internetworking software & tools (Internet Chameleon, ECCO)

The Monster Board — http://www1.monster.com:80/

 An in-depth profile of this company is available to subscribers on Hoover's Online at www.hoovers.com.

93

NETSCAPE COMMUNICATIONS CORP.

501 E. Middlefield Rd.
Mountain View, CA 94043
Pres & CEO: James L. Barksdale
VP HR: Kandis Malefyt
Employees: 725

Jobs Added Last Year: 623 (+610.8%)

Computers - Internet navigation software (Netscape Navigator), Website server software & transaction security software

Phone: 415-254-1900
Fax: 415-528-4125

NETWORK GENERAL CORPORATION

4200 Bohannon Dr.
Menlo Park, CA 94025
Pres & CEO: Leslie G. Denend
Dir HR: Sally Takemoto
Employees: 721

Jobs Added Last Year: 149 (+26.0%)

Computers - local area network analysis software

Phone: 415-473-2000
Fax: 415-321-0855

NEW UNITED MOTOR MANUFACTURING, INC.

45500 Fremont Blvd.
Fremont, CA 94538-6326
Pres & CEO: Iwao Itoh
VP HR: D. William Childs
Employees: 4,700

Jobs Added Last Year: 200 (+4.4%)

Automotive manufacturing (joint venture between General Motors & Toyota)

Phone: 510-498-5500
Fax: 510-770-4010

NEWHALL LAND AND FARMING COMPANY

23823 Valencia Blvd.
Valencia, CA 91355
Chm & CEO: Thomas L. Lee
Dir Emp Relations: Mike Whaling
Employees: 11,000

Jobs Added Last Year: —

Real estate development - master-planned communities

Phone: 805-255-4000
Fax: 805-255-3960

NORTHROP GRUMMAN CORP.

1840 Century Park East
Los Angeles, CA 90067-2199
Chm, Pres & CEO: Kent Kresa
Corp VP & Chief HR & Administrative Officer: Marvin Elkin
Employees: 37,000

Jobs Cut Last Year: 4,000 (-9.8%)

Aerospace - surveillance & attack aircraft, equipment & electronic systems

Phone: 310-553-6262
Fax: 310-553-2076

NTN COMMUNICATIONS, INC.

5966 La Place Ct.
Carlsbad, CA 92008
Chm & CEO: Patrick J. Downs
HR Dir: Genice Eichert
Employees: 275

Jobs Added Last Year: 65 (+31.0%)

TV production & programming - interactive subscription-based TV network (NTN Network)

Phone: 619-438-7400
Fax: 619-438-7470

OAK TECHNOLOGY, INC.

139 Kifer Ct.
Sunnyvale, CA 94086
Chm, Pres & CEO: David D. Tsang
VP HR: Malinda Law
Employees: 291

Jobs Added Last Year: 77 (+36.0%)

Computers - multimedia semiconductors, CD-ROM controllers & MPEG video decoders for use in optical-storage, compression, imaging, video, & PC audio applications

Phone: 408-737-0888
Fax: 408-737-3838

OCCIDENTAL PETROLEUM CORP.

10889 Wilshire Blvd.
Los Angeles, CA 90024
Chm & CEO: Ray R. Irani
EVP HR: Richard W. Hallock
Employees: 17,280

Jobs Cut Last Year: 2,380 (-12.1%)

Oil & gas - exploration, production & transmission

Phone: 310-208-8800
Fax: 310-824-2372

OCTEL COMMUNICATIONS CORP.

1001 Murphy Ranch Rd.
Milpitas, CA 95035-7912
Chm, Pres & CEO: Robert Cohn
VP HR: John Viera
Employees: 2,700

Jobs Added Last Year: 307 (+12.8%)

Telecommunications equipment - voice information processing systems

Phone: 408-321-2000
Fax: 408-321-6978

OPAL, INC.

2903 Bunker Hill Ln., Ste. 103
Santa Clara, CA 95054
Pres & CEO: Rafi Yizhar
HR Mgr: Laura Higbie
Employees: 224

Jobs Added Last Year: 53 (+31.0%)

Electronics - inspection systems for the integrated circuit manufacturing process

Phone: 408-727-6060
Fax: 408-727-6332

ORACLE CORPORATION

500 Oracle Pkwy.
Redwood City, CA 94065
Phone: 415-506-7000
Fax: 415-506-7200
Chm, Pres & CEO: Lawrence J. Ellison
SVP HR: Phillip E. Wilson
Employees: 16,882

Jobs Added Last Year: 4,824 (+40.0%)

Computers - database management systems software (#1 world-wide), network products & productivity tools

ORBIT SEMICONDUCTOR, INC.

169 Java Dr.
Sunnyvale, CA 94089
Phone: 408-744-1800
Fax: 408-747-1263
Chm, Pres & CEO: Gary P. Kennedy
HR Mgr: Dana Myers
Employees: 278

Jobs Added Last Year: 94 (+51.1%)

Electrical components - semiconductors; software for integrated circuit development, production scheduling & inventory control (Encore!)

ORCHARD SUPPLY HARDWARE STORES CORPORATION

6450 Via Del Oro
San Jose, CA 95119
Phone: 408-281-3500
Fax: 408-629-7174
Pres & CEO: Maynard Jenkins
VP HR: Carolyn J. McInnes
Employees: 4,980

Jobs Added Last Year: 390 (+8.5%)

Building products - retail hardware supplies in California (60 units)

OROAMERICA, INC.

443 N. Varney St.
Burbank, CA 91502
Phone: 818-848-5555
Fax: 818-846-4921
Chm, Pres & CEO: Guy Benhamou
Dir HR: Eva Slaughter
Employees: 820

Jobs Added Last Year: 455 (+124.7%)

Precious metals & jewelry - 14-karat gold jewelry manufacturing & distribution

ORTEL CORPORATION

2015 W. Chestnut St.
Alhambra, CA 91803-1542
Phone: 818-281-3636
Fax: 818-281-1007
Pres & CEO: Wim H. J. Selders
Dir HR: Kim Congdon
Employees: 361

Jobs Added Last Year: 82 (+29.4%)

Fiber optics

OSICOM TECHNOLOGIES, INC.

2800 28th St., Ste. 100
Santa Monica, CA 90405
Phone: 310-828-7496
Fax: 310-828-7567
Chm & CEO: Sharon G. Chadha
Mgr: Mary Cochrane
Employees: 138

Jobs Added Last Year: 79 (+133.9%)

Telecommunications equipment - broadband telecommunications networking equipment

PACIFIC BANK, N.A.

351 California St.
San Francisco, CA 94104
Phone: 415-576-2700
Fax: 415-291-9953
Pres & CEO: Michael T. Zan
VP HR: Jill Staten
Employees: 306

Jobs Added Last Year: 76 (+33.0%)

Banks - West

PACIFIC ENTERPRISES

555 W. Fifth St., Ste 2900
Los Angeles, CA 90031-1011
Phone: 213-895-5000
Fax: 213-629-1225
Chm & CEO: Willis B. Wood Jr.
VP HR: G. Joyce Roland
Employees: 7,860

Jobs Cut Last Year: 624 (-7.4%)

Utility - gas distribution (#1 in US: Southern California Gas)

PACIFIC GAS AND ELECTRIC CO.

77 Beale St.
San Francisco, CA 94177
Phone: 415-973-7000
Fax: 415-543-7830
Chm & CEO: Stanley T. Skinner
VP HR: G. Brent Stanley
Employees: 22,000

Jobs Added Last Year: 1,000 (+4.8%)

Utility - electric power & natural gas

PACIFIC MUTUAL LIFE INSURANCE CO.

700 Newport Center Dr.
Newport Beach, CA 92660-9030
Phone: 714-640-3011
Fax: 714-640-7614
Chm & CEO: Thomas C. Sutton
VP HR: Edgar R. Lehman
Employees: 2,700

Jobs Added Last Year: 300 (+12.5%)

Insurance - life & health; annuities, pension investments & group employee benefits

An in-depth profile of this company is available to subscribers on Hoover's Online at www.hoovers.com.

95

PACIFIC SCIENTIFIC COMPANY

620 Newport Center Dr., Ste. 700   Phone: 714-720-1714
Newport Beach, CA 92660   Fax: 714-720-1083
Pres & CEO: Edgar S. Brower
Corp Dir HR: Thomas I. Griffith
Employees: 2,360

Jobs Added Last Year: 512 (+27.7%)

Electronics - meters, controls & safety devices; dimmable fluorescent lighting system that fits regular incandescent lamps (Solium)

PACIFIC SUNWEAR OF CALIFORNIA, INC.

5037 E. Hunter Ave.   Phone: 714-693-8066
Anaheim, CA 92807-6001   Fax: 714-693-8165
Chm, Pres & CEO: Michael W. Rayden
Dir HR: Ryanne Heffernan
Employees: 1,560

Jobs Added Last Year: 507 (+48.1%)

Retail - casual apparel & accessories

PACIFIC TELESIS GROUP

130 Kearny St.   Phone: 415-394-3000
San Francisco, CA 94108   Fax: 415-394-3312
Chm, Pres & CEO: Philip J. Quigley
EVP HR: Jim R. Moberg
Employees: 48,062

Jobs Cut Last Year: 3,528 (-6.8%)

Utility - telephone

PACIFICARE HEALTH SYSTEMS, INC.

5995 Plaza Dr.   Phone: 714-952-1121
Cypress, CA 90630-5028   Fax: 714-220-3725
Pres & CEO: Alan R. Hoops
SVP Corp HR: Wanda Lee
Employees: 4,438

Jobs Added Last Year: 582 (+15.1%)

Health maintenance organization

PACKARD BELL ELECTRONICS, INC.

One Packard Bell Way   Phone: 916-388-0101
Sacramento, CA 95828-0903   Fax: 916-388-1109
Chm, Pres & CEO: Beny Alagem
Dir HR: Karen Schmidt
Employees: 5,000

Jobs Added Last Year: 1,000 (+25.0%)

Computers - PCs

PARACELSUS HEALTHCARE CORPORATION

155 N. Lake Ave., Ste. 1100   Phone: 818-792-8600
Pasadena, CA 91101   Fax: 818-792-8590
VC & CEO: R. J. Messenger
Asst VP HR: Claire Page
Employees: 9,300

Jobs Added Last Year: —

Health care - operation of acute care (18 locations) & specialty hospitals that offer rehabilitative medicine, substance abuse, psychiatric & AIDS treatment in 7 US states

PARCPLACE-DIGITALK, INC.

999 E. Arques Ave.   Phone: 408-481-9090
Sunnyvale, CA 94086-4593   Fax: 408-481-9095
Pres & CEO: William P. Lyons
Mgr HR: Nancy Hill
Employees: 230

Jobs Added Last Year: 53 (+29.9%)

Computers - object-oriented software development tools

THE PARSONS CORPORATION

100 W. Walnut St.   Phone: 818-440-2000
Pasadena, CA 91124   Fax: 818-440-2630
Pres & CEO: James F. McNulty
Dir HR: Graydon Thayer
Employees: 10,000

Jobs Added Last Year: 500 (+5.3%)

Construction - heavy

P-COM, INC.

3175 S. Winchester Blvd.   Phone: 408-866-3666
Campbell, CA 95008   Fax: 408-866-3655
Chm & CEO: George P. Roberts
CFO & VP Fin: Michael J. Sophie
Employees: 164

Jobs Added Last Year: 86 (+110.3%)

Telecommunications equipment - millimeter-wave radio systems for use in wireless networks

PEOPLESOFT, INC.

4440 Rosewood Dr.   Phone: 510-225-3000
Pleasanton, CA 94588   Fax: 510-225-3100
Chm, Pres & CEO: David A. Duffield
VP HR: Steve Zarate
Employees: 1,341

Jobs Added Last Year: 690 (+106.0%)

Computers - human resource & financial administration client/server software, including accounting, benefits adminstration, financial systems, ledger, payroll & project costing software

PERCLOSE, INC.

199 Jefferson Dr.
Menlo Park, CA 94025-1114
Pres & CEO: Henry A. Plain Jr.
Dir HR: Bart Beasley
Employees: 89

Phone: 415-473-3100
Fax: 415-473-3110

Jobs Added Last Year: 30 (+50.8%)

Medical products - minimally invasive systems that surgically close arterial access sites in catherization procedures such as angioplasty & angiography

PETCO ANIMAL SUPPLIES, INC.

9151 Rehco Rd.
San Diego, CA 92121-2270
Chm, Pres & CEO: Brian K. Devine
VP HR: Jan Mitchell
Employees: 3,115

Phone: 619-453-7845
Fax: 619-453-6585

Jobs Added Last Year: 1,099 (+54.5%)

Retail - pet supplies & food (219 stores, including 113 super-stores)

PHARMINGEN

10975 Torreyana Rd.
San Diego, CA 92121-1111
Pres & CEO: Ernest Huang
Dir HR: Nancy Huang
Employees: 178

Phone: 619-677-7737
Fax: 619-677-7749

Jobs Added Last Year: 51 (+40.2%)

Biomedical & genetic products - reagents for biotechnology research, including monoclonal antibodies

PHYSICIANS CLINICAL LABORATORY

2495 Natomas Park Dr., Ste. 600
Sacramento, CA 95833
Pres & CEO: Nathan L. Headley
VP HR: Timothy H. McGeachy
Employees: 1,449

Phone: 916-648-3500
Fax: 916-444-7680

Jobs Added Last Year: 399 (+38.0%)

Medical services - clinical laboratory testing with special expertise in microbiology, virology & immunology

PIA MERCHANDISING SERVICES, INC.

PO Box 19777
Irvine, CA 92713
Chm & CEO: Clinton E. Owens
SVP HR: Mark J. Hallsman
Employees: 1,585

Phone: 714-476-2200
Fax: 714-474-3510

Jobs Added Last Year: 399 (+33.6%)

Business services - in-store merchandising & sales services

PINKERTON'S, INC.

15910 Ventura Blvd., Ste. 900
Encino, CA 91436-2810
Pres & CEO: Denis R. Brown
VP HR: Gary J. Hasenbank
Employees: 47,000

Phone: 818-380-8800
Fax: 800-984-4100

Jobs Added Last Year: 2,000 (+4.4%)

Protection - security guard services, personnel background checks, surveillance, special & undercover investigations, security consulting & personnel screening

PINNACLE MICRO, INC.

19 Technology Dr.
Irvine, CA 92718
Chm, Pres & CEO: Lawrence Goelman
Dir HR: Chuck McGee
Employees: 185

Phone: 714-789-3000
Fax: 714-789-3150

Jobs Added Last Year: 65 (+54.2%)

Computers - optical storage drive peripherals for general data storage

PINNACLE SYSTEMS, INC.

870 W. Maude Ave.
Sunnyvale, CA 94086
Pres & CEO: Mark L. Sanders
Dir HR: Terry Wilson
Employees: 71

Phone: 408-720-9669
Fax: 408-720-9674

Jobs Added Last Year: 23 (+47.9%)

Video equipment - post-production tools for high quality real time video processing

POTLATCH CORPORATION

One Maritime Plaza
San Francisco, CA 94111
Chm & CEO: John M. Richards
VP Emp Relations: Barbara M. Failing
Employees: 6,600

Phone: 415-576-8800
Fax: 415-576-8840

Jobs Cut Last Year: 300 (-4.3%)

Paper & paper products - printing paper, bathroom tissue, paper towels & napkins; dimensional lumber, plywood, oriented strand board & hardwood flooring

PREMISYS COMMUNICATIONS, INC.

48664 Milmont Dr.
Fremont, CA 94538
Pres & CEO: Raymond C. Lin
Dir HR: Ann Mazzini
Employees: 117

Phone: 510-353-7600
Fax: 510-353-7601

Jobs Added Last Year: 29 (+33.0%)

Telecommunications equipment - integrated multiple access products for telecommunications providers

 An in-depth profile of this company is available to subscribers on Hoover's Online at www.hoovers.com.

PROTOSOURCE CORPORATION

2580 W. Shaw
Fresno, CA 93711
Chm, Pres & CEO: Charles T. Howard
Office Mgr & Bookkeeper: Amy DeFendis
Employees: 55

Phone: 209-448-8040
Fax: 209-448-8050

Jobs Added Last Year: 33 (+150.0%)

Computers - agri-business accounting, product tracking & billing system software

PROXIM INC.

295 N. Bernado Ave.
Mountain View, CA 94043
Chm, Pres & CEO: David C. King
Exec Asst: Terri Clymo
Employees: 103

Phone: 415-960-1630
Fax: 415-964-5181

Jobs Added Last Year: 27 (+35.5%)

Telecommunications equipment - wireless data communications products for mobile users

PROXIMA CORPORATION

9440 Carroll Park Dr.
San Diego, CA 92121-2298
Pres & CEO: John E. Rehfeld
VP HR: Frank J. Drdek
Employees: 703

Phone: 619-457-5500
Fax: 619-457-9647

Jobs Added Last Year: 172 (+32.4%)

Video equipment - LCD projection equipment

PUBLIC STORAGE, INC.

600 N. Brand Blvd.
Glendale, CA 91203
Chm & CEO: B. Wayne Hughes
Personnel Mgr: Deanna Dunec
Employees: 3,000

Phone: 818-244-8080
Fax: 818-241-0627

Jobs Added Last Year: 1,792 (+148.3%)

Real estate investment trust - self-storage properties

QUALCOMM INCORPORATED

6455 Lusk Blvd.
San Diego, CA 92121-2779
Chm & CEO: Irwin M. Jacobs
VP HR: Daniel L. Sullivan
Employees: 3,167

Phone: 619-587-1121
Fax: 619-658-2501

Jobs Added Last Year: 1,267 (+66.7%)

Telecommunications equipment - two-way mobile satellite communication & tracking systems; code division multiple access (CDMA) & other advanced communications systems

QUANTUM CORPORATION

500 McCarthy Blvd.
Milpitas, CA 95035
Pres & CEO: Michael A. Brown
VP HR: Deborah E. Barber
Employees: 7,036

Phone: 408-894-4000
Fax: 408-894-3218

Jobs Cut Last Year: 229 (-3.2%)

Computers - disk drives (#1 in US: ProDrive, Empire, Go-Drive, Daytona)

Career Magazine — http://www.careermag.com/careermag/

QUARTERDECK CORPORATION

13160 Mindanao Way
Marina del Rey, CA 90292-9705
Pres & CEO: Gaston Bastiaens
Dir HR: Teresa Hammond
Employees: 532

Phone: 310-309-3700
Fax: 310-309-4218

Jobs Added Last Year: 334 (+168.7%)

Computers - multitasking, windowing & memory management software; software erasing utility program (Clean-Sweep); telecommunications & Internet applications & systems

QUICKRESPONSE SERVICES INC.

1400 Marina Way South
Richmond, CA 94804
Pres & CEO: Tania Amochaev
Dir HR: Jack R. Elliott
Employees: 120

Phone: 510-215-5000
Fax: 510-215-3983

Jobs Added Last Year: 47 (+64.4%)

Business services - electronic data interchange & product-information database

RAINBOW TECHNOLOGIES, INC.

50 Technology Dr.
Irvine, CA 92718-
Chm, Pres & CEO: Walter W. Straub
Mgr HR: Karen Brown
Employees: 270

Phone: 714-450-7300
Fax: 714-450-7450

Jobs Added Last Year: 114 (+73.1%)

Computers - software-protection products (NetSentinel, SentinelEve3, SentinelSuperPro)

RALEY'S INC.

500 W. Capitol Ave.
West Sacramento, CA 95605
Pres & CEO: Charles L. Collings
VP HR: Sam McPherson
Employees: 7,500

Phone: 916-373-3333
Fax: 916-444-3733

Jobs Added Last Year: 350 (+4.9%)

Retail - supermarkets & drugstores

RAYCHEM CORPORATION

300 Constitution Dr.
Menlo Park, CA 94025-1164
Chm, Pres & CEO: Richard A. Kashnow
VP HR: Stephen A. Balogh
Employees: 9,496

Phone: 415-361-4180
Fax: 415-361-2108

Jobs Cut Last Year: 1,273 (-11.8%)

Telecommunications equipment - telephone & cable TV cable connectors, closures & accessories; fiber optic distribution systems for voice, video & data to communications networks

READ-RITE CORPORATION

345 Los Coches St.
Milpitas, CA 95035
Chm & CEO: Cyril J. Yansouni
VP HR: Sherry F. McVicar
Employees: 23,074

Phone: 408-262-6700
Fax: 408-956-3205

Jobs Added Last Year: 4,602 (+24.9%)

Computers - thin-film magnetic read-write heads for hard disks (#1 worldwide); headstack assemblies & heads for tape drives

REGENCY HEALTH SERVICES, INC.

2742 Dow Ave.
Tustin, CA 92680-7245
Pres & CEO: Richard K. Matros
VP HR: Steve Ronilo
Employees: 10,000

Phone: 714-544-4443
Fax: 714-544-8803

Jobs Added Last Year: 0

Nursing homes

RICHEY ELECTRONICS, INC.

7441 Lincoln Way, Ste. 100
Garden Grove, CA 92641
Chm, Pres & CEO: William C. Cacciatore
HR Administrator: Patti Comaselli
Employees: 1,080

Phone: 714-898-8288
Fax: 714-373-1239

Jobs Added Last Year: 605 (+127.4%)

Electronics - distribution of interconnect, electromechanical & passive electronic components

ROCKET SCIENCE GAMES INC.

139 Townsend St., Ste. 100
San Francisco, CA 94107
Pres & CEO: Steven Blank
HR Mgr: Debbie Kerlin
Employees: 65

Phone: 415-442-5000
Fax: 415-442-5001

Jobs Added Last Year: 20 (+44.4%)

Computers - CD-ROM games (Loadstar, Cadillacs & Dinosaurs); CD-ROM speed acceleration technology

ROCKWELL INTERNATIONAL CORP.

2201 Seal Beach Blvd.
Seal Beach, CA 90740-8250
Chm & CEO: Donald R. Beall
SVP Organization & HR: Robert H. Murphy
Employees: 82,671

Phone: 310-797-3311
Fax: 310-797-5690

Jobs Added Last Year: 10,780 (+15.0%)

Aerospace - spacecraft-propulsion systems; axles & brakes for passenger & heavy-duty vehicles; avionics, defense electronics for weapons, communication & guidance systems

ROLL INTERNATIONAL CORPORATION

12233 W. Olympic Blvd., Ste. 380
Los Angeles, CA 90064
Co-Chm, Pres & CEO: Stewart A. Resnick
No central personnel officer
Employees: 7,700

Phone: 310-442-5700
Fax: 310-207-1557

Jobs Added Last Year: 200 (+2.7%)

Retail - mail-order & direct flowers (Teleflora) & collectibles
(Franklin Mint); commercial real estate; school bus transportation

ROSS STORES, INC.

8333 Central Ave.
Newark, CA 94560-3433
CEO: Michael Balmuth
SVP HR: Stephen F. Joyce
Employees: 11,935

Phone: 510-505-4400
Fax: 510-505-4169

Jobs Added Last Year: 1,361 (+12.9%)

Retail - discount apparel & shoes

ROTONICS MANUFACTURING INC.

17022 S. Figueroa St.
Gardena, CA 90248
Chm, Pres & CEO: Sherman McKinniss
Admin Asst: Dawn Whitney
Employees: 480

Phone: 310-538-4932
Fax: 310-516-6838

Jobs Added Last Year: 102 (+27.0%)

Rubber & plastic products - molded products for agricultural &
industrial use, polyethylene tanks, fittings & accessories

RUBIO'S RESTAURANTS, INC.

5151 Shoreham Place, Ste. 260
San Diego, CA 92122
CEO: Ralph Rubio
Personnel Mgr: Julie Epp
Employees: 450

Phone: 619-452-1770
Fax: 619-452-0181

Jobs Added Last Year: 311 (+223.7%)

Retail - fish taco restaurants

S3 INCORPORATED

2770 San Tomas Expwy.
Santa Clara, CA 95051-0968
Pres & CEO: Terry N. Holdt
VP HR: Cecilia A. Hayes
Employees: 217

Phone: 408-980-5400
Fax: 408-980-5444

Jobs Added Last Year: 73 (+50.7%)

Computers - graphics accelerator systems (S3 Vision/VA,
Vision964) & video MPEG accelerators

SABA PETROLEUM COMPANY

17512 Von Karman Ave.
Irvine, CA 92714
Chm, Pres & CEO: Ilyas Chaudhary
No central personnel officer
Employees: 66

Phone: 714-724-1112
Fax: 714-724-1555

Jobs Added Last Year: 20 (+43.5%)

Oil & gas - US exploration & production

SAFEGUARD HEALTH ENTERPRISES, INC.

505 N. Euclid St., Ste. 200
Anaheim, CA 92801
Chm, Pres & CEO: Steven J. Baileys
HR Dir: Debra Hill
Employees: 558

Phone: 714-778-1005
Fax: 714-758-4383

Jobs Added Last Year: 126 (+29.2%)

Medical practice management - managed dental-care plans;
indemnity dental insurance

SAFETY COMPONENTS INT'L, INC.

3190 Pullman St.
Costa Mesa, CA 92626
Chm, Pres & CEO: Robert A. Zummo
Dir HR: Eva Rodriguez
Employees: 975

Phone: 714-662-7756
Fax: 714-662-7649

Jobs Added Last Year: 434 (+80.2%)

Automotive & trucking - passenger-side air bags for Ford, Jaguar,
Lexus, Lincoln, Mazda, Mercury & Toyota models; projectiles &
metal components for tactical & training ammunition

SAFEWAY INC.

5918 Stoneridge Mall Rd.
Pleasanton, CA 94588-3229
Pres & CEO: Steven A. Burd
EVP Labor Relations, HR, Law & Public Affairs: Kenneth W. Oder
Employees: 114,000

Phone: 510-467-3000
Fax: 510-467-3323

Jobs Added Last Year: 4,000 (+3.6%)

Retail - 1059 supermarkets

SANGSTAT MEDICAL CORPORATION

1505 Adams Dr.
Menlo Park, CA 94025-2267
Chm & CEO: Philippe Pouletty
No central personnel officer
Employees: 66

Phone: 415-328-0300
Fax: 415-328-8892

Jobs Added Last Year: 14 (+26.9%)

Medical instruments - therapeutic & monitoring products for
organ transplants

SASCO ELECTRIC COMPANY

12900 Alondra Blvd.   Phone: 310-926-0900
Cerritos, CA 90703   Fax: 310-926-1399
Chm & CEO: Larry Smead
No central personnel officer
Employees: 1,725
Jobs Added Last Year: 435 (+33.7%)

Construction - electrical contracting; data cable installation for data, fire alarm, video, voice, systems & control

SAVE MART SUPERMARKETS

1800 Standiford Ave.   Phone: 209-577-1600
Modesto, CA 95350   Fax: 209-577-3857
Chm & CEO: Robert M. Piccinini
Dir HR & Law: Mike Silveira
Employees: 5,864
Jobs Cut Last Year: 198 (-3.3%)

Retail - supermarkets

SCIENCE APPLICATIONS INTL. CORP.

10260 Campus Point Dr.   Phone: 619-546-6000
San Diego, CA 92121   Fax: 619-546-6634
Chm & CEO: J. Robert Beyster
Corp VP: Bernard Theule
Employees: 20,500
Jobs Added Last Year: 2,700 (+15.2%)

Engineering - R&D services, systems integration

SCRIPPSHEALTH

4275 Campus Point Ct.   Phone: 619-678-7000
San Diego, CA 92121   Fax: 619-678-6558
Pres & CEO: Ames Early
SVP Administrative Svcs: Janet Colson
Employees: 9,596
Jobs Cut Last Year: 104 (-1.1%)

Hospitals - not-for-profit system serving the San Diego area, including 6 hospitals, 15 clinics & 2 skilled nursing facilities

SEAGATE TECHNOLOGY, INC.

920 Disc Dr.   Phone: 408-438-6550
Scotts Valley, CA 95066   Fax: 408-438-6172
Chm, Pres & CEO: Alan F. Shugart
VP HR: Annette Surtees
Employees: 53,000
Jobs Added Last Year: 10,000 (+23.3%)

Computers - rigid magnetic disk drives & other computer memory components (#1 worldwide), including flash memory storage products

SEQUANA THERAPEUTICS, INC.

11099 N. Torrey Pines Rd., Ste. 160   Phone: 619-452-6550
La Jolla, CA 92037   Fax: 619-452-4378
Pres & CEO: Kevin J. Kinsella
Dir HR: Anita Matheson
Employees: 113
Jobs Added Last Year: 45 (+66.2%)

Biomedical & genetic products - positional cloning technology used to discover & characterize genes that cause or predispose individuals to common diseases

SIGMA CIRCUITS, INC.

393 Mathew St.   Phone: 408-727-9169
Santa Clara, CA 95050   Fax: 408-727-0319
CEO: B. Kevin Kelly
Mgr HR: Lee Ann Vriend
Employees: 500
Jobs Added Last Year: 125 (+33.3%)

Electrical components - printed circuit boards, back-plane assemblies, subassemblies & flexible circuits

SILICON GRAPHICS, INC.

2011 N. Shoreline Blvd., PO Box 7311   Phone: 415-960-1980
Mountain View, CA 94039-7311   Fax: 415-390-6220
Chm & CEO: Edward R. McCracken
VP HR: Kirk Froggatt
Employees: 6,300
Jobs Added Last Year: 1,943 (+44.6%)

Computers - graphics hardware & software, interactive 3D graphics, digital media & multiprocessing

SILICON VALLEY GROUP, INC.

2240 Ringwood Ave.   Phone: 408-434-0500
San Jose, CA 95131   Fax: 408-434-0216
Chm & CEO: Papken S. Der Torossian
VP HR: Tom Zippiroli
Employees: 2,653
Jobs Added Last Year: 990 (+59.5%)

Machinery - semiconductor manufacturing equipment

THE SIRENA APPAREL GROUP, INC.

10333 Vacco St.   Phone: 818-442-6680
South El Monte, CA 91733   Fax: 818-442-2280
Pres & CEO: Douglas Arbetman
Personnel Dir: Cari Firmat
Employees: 258
Jobs Added Last Year: 64 (+33.0%)

Apparel - women's swimsuits & resort wear (A Line, Anne Klein, Rose Marie Reid, WearAbouts)

SIZZLER INTERNATIONAL, INC.

12655 W. Jefferson Blvd. Phone: 310-827-2300
Los Angeles, CA 90066 Fax: 310-822-5786
Pres & CEO: Kevin W. Perkins
VP HR & Training: Leon E. Clancy Jr.
Employees: 14,600
Jobs Cut Last Year: 1,400 (-8.8%)

Retail - restaurants (Buffalo Ranch, KFC, Sizzler)

SMART MODULAR TECHNOLOGIES, INC.

4305 Cushing Pkwy. Phone: 510-623-1231
Fremont, CA 94538 Fax: 510-623-1434
Chm, Pres & CEO: Ajay Shah
No central personnel officer
Employees: 354
Jobs Added Last Year: 96 (+37.2%)

Computers - memory devices for PCs & workstations; modems

SOLA INTERNATIONAL INC.

2420 Sand Hill Rd., Ste. 200 Phone: 415-324-6868
Menlo Park, CA 94025 Fax: 415-324-6870
Pres & CEO: John E. Heine
VP HR: Stephen J. Lee
Employees: 5,800
Jobs Added Last Year: 300 (+5.5%)

Medical products - plastic & glass eyeglass lenses

SOLECTRON CORPORATION

777 Gibraltar Dr. Phone: 408-957-8500
Milpitas, CA 95035 Fax: 408-956-6075
Pres & CEO: Koichi Nishimura
VP HR: Thomas Morelli
Employees: 11,049
Jobs Added Last Year: 4,481 (+68.2%)

Electrical components - printed circuit boards & other electrical products

SOLIGEN TECHNOLOGIES, INC.

19408 Londelius St. Phone: 818-718-1221
Northridge, CA 91324 Fax: 818-718-0760
Chm, Pres & CEO: Yehoram Uziel
Dir HR: Randi Peled
Employees: 56
Jobs Added Last Year: 29 (+107.4%)

Machinery - direct shell production casting (DSPC), traditional casting & machining equipment used in production of metal parts & tooling from computer-aided design (CAD) files

SONIC SOLUTIONS

101 Rowland Way Phone: 415-893-8000
Novato, CA 94945 Fax: 415-893-8008
Pres & CEO: Robert J. Doris
No central personnel officer
Employees: 75
Jobs Added Last Year: 21 (+38.9%)

Computers - digital audio workstations for professional applications

SOUTHERN PACIFIC RAIL CORP.

Southern Pacific Bldg., One Market Plaza Phone: 415-541-1000
San Francisco, CA 94105 Fax: 415-541-1033
Pres & CEO: Jerry R. Davis
VP HR: Judy Holm
Employees: 19,089
Jobs Added Last Year: 1,079 (+6.0%)

Transportation - freight rail

SOUTHLAND MICRO SYSTEMS INC.

11 Musick Phone: 714-380-1958
Irvine, CA 92718 Fax: 714-380-0995
Pres: John Meehan
Dir HR: Connie Cole
Employees: 125
Jobs Added Last Year: 25 (+25.0%)

Computers - memory products

SPELLING ENTERTAINMENT GROUP

5700 Wilshire Blvd. Phone: 213-965-5700
Los Angeles, CA 90036-3659 Fax: 213-965-6984
VC: Aaron Spelling
VP HR: Cheryl Wingard
Employees: 900
Jobs Added Last Year: 200 (+28.6%)

TV production & programming - series (Beverly Hills 90210, Melrose Place), miniseries & movies-for-TV; interactive video games & feature films; music & merchandising rights licensing

THE SPORTS CLUB COMPANY, INC.

11100 Santa Monica Blvd., Ste. 300 Phone: 310-479-5200
Los Angeles, CA 90025 Fax: 310-479-8350
Chm, Pres & CEO: D. Michael Talla
Dir HR: Rashmi Patel
Employees: 1,500
Jobs Added Last Year: 510 (+51.5%)

Leisure & recreational services - sports & fitness clubs

STANFORD HEALTH SERVICES

300 Pasteur Dr.
Stanford, CA 94305-5250
Pres & CEO: Peter Van Etten
Dir HR Mgmt: Felix R. Barthelemy
Employees: 5,422
Phone: 415-723-4000
Fax: 415-723-8163

Jobs Added Last Year: 527 (+10.8%)

Hospital

STATER BROS. HOLDINGS INC.

21700 Barton Rd.
Colton, CA 92324
Chm, Pres & CEO: Jack H. Brown
Group SVP HR: Donald Baker
Employees: 9,800
Phone: 909-783-5000
Fax: 909-783-3930

Jobs Cut Last Year: 200 (-2.0%)

Retail - supermarkets

STANFORD UNIVERSITY

857 Serra St.
Stanford, CA 94305-6200
Pres: Gerhard Casper
VP HR: Barbara Butterfield
Employees: 14,030
Phone: 415-723-2300
Fax: 415-725-0247

Jobs Added Last Year: 30 (+0.2%)

Schools

SUMMIT CARE CORPORATION

2600 W. Magnolia Blvd.
Burbank, CA 91505
Chm, Pres & CEO: William C. Scott
Mgr Payroll Svcs: Jo Gatti
Employees: 3,700
Phone: 818-841-8750
Fax: 818-841-5847

Jobs Added Last Year: 1,400 (+60.9%)

Nursing homes - nursing-care facilities & retirement centers

STARPRESS, INC.

425 Market St., 5th Fl.
San Francisco, CA 94105
CEO: Douglas D. Cole
Dir HR: Jill Lewis
Employees: 100
Phone: 415-778-3100
Fax: 415-495-5407

Jobs Added Last Year: 21 (+26.6%)

Computers - CD-ROM & floppy software products, primarily those focusing on health, infotainment, personal productivity & travel, for homes, schools & small businesses

SUN MICROSYSTEMS, INC.

2550 Garcia Ave.
Mountain View, CA 94043-1100
Chm, Pres & CEO: Scott G. McNealy
VP HR: Kenneth M. Alvares
Employees: 14,498
Phone: 415-960-1300
Fax: 415-969-9131

Jobs Added Last Year: 1,216 (+9.2%)

Computers - UNIX-based workstations (#1 worldwide), Internet servers & operating & productivity software

Laran Communications — http://www.web-ads.com/index.html

SUNAMERICA, INC.

One SunAmerica Ctr., 36-07 Century City   Phone: 310-772-6000
Los Angeles, CA 90067-6022   Fax: 310-772-6565
Chm, Pres & CEO: Eli Broad
VP Organization Planning & Dev: Darlene Chandler
Employees: 1,300

Jobs Added Last Year: 300 (+30.0%)

Financial - diversified services, specializing in preretirement savings

SUNRISE MEDICAL INC.

2382 Faraday Ave., Ste. 200   Phone: 619-930-1500
Carlsbad, CA 92008   Fax: 619-930-1575
Chm & CEO: Richard H. Chandler
VP HR: Roberta C. Baade
Employees: 4,054

Jobs Added Last Year: 468 (+13.1%)

Medical & dental supplies - wheelchairs, walkers, crutches & special beds for nursing homes; in-home treatment aids for breathing disorders

SUPERCUTS, INC.

550 California St.   Phone: 415-693-4700
San Francisco, CA 94104   Fax: 415-693-4949
Pres & CEO: Steve Price
HR Mgr: Cathy Knudsen
Employees: 5,007

Jobs Added Last Year: 1,043 (+26.3%)

Retail - hair salons in 39 states & Puerto Rico

SUTTER HEALTH

One Capitol Mall   Phone: 916-733-3000
Sacramento, CA 95814   Fax: 916-554-6611
Pres & CEO: Van R. Johnson
Dir HR: Jim Rude
Employees: 14,000

Jobs Added Last Year: 0

Hospitals - nonprofit system serving northern California (Auburn Faith Community Hospital, Delta Memorial Hospital, Novato Community Hospital, Sutter Memorial Hospital)

SYMANTEC CORPORATION

10201 Torre Ave.   Phone: 408-253-9600
Cupertino, CA 95014-2132   Fax: 408-253-3446
Pres & CEO: Gordon E. Eubanks Jr.
Dir HR: Greg Martin
Employees: 2,200

Jobs Added Last Year: 758 (+52.6%)

Computers - information management, productivity-enhancement & development software (Norton Utilities)

SYNOPSYS, INC.

700 E. Middlefield Rd.   Phone: 415-962-5000
Mountain View, CA 94043-4033   Fax: 415-965-8637
Pres & CEO: Aart J. de Geus
SVP HR & Facilities: Sally A. DeStefano
Employees: 1,388

Jobs Added Last Year: 366 (+35.8%)

Computers - electronic design automation & logic simulation software

SYQUEST TECHNOLOGY, INC.

47071 Bayside Pkwy.   Phone: 510-226-4000
Fremont, CA 94538   Fax: 510-226-4100
Pres, CEO & COO: Edwin L. Harper
VP HR: Robert E. Lyon
Employees: 2,409

Jobs Added Last Year: 1,042 (+76.2%)

Computers - removable hard-disk cartridges & drives

TANDEM COMPUTERS INC.

19333 Vallco Pkwy.   Phone: 408-285-6000
Cupertino, CA 95014-2599   Fax: 408-285-0035
Pres & CEO: Roel Pieper
VP HR: Philip Johnson
Employees: 8,380

Jobs Cut Last Year: 86 (-1.0%)

Computers - available, open & parallel processing computer systems, client/server solutions & enterprise networks

TARGET THERAPEUTICS, INC.

47201 Lakeview Blvd.   Phone: 510-440-7700
Fremont, CA 94538   Fax: 510-440-7780
Pres & CEO: Gary R. Bang
VP HR: John Meyer
Employees: 402

Jobs Added Last Year: 85 (+26.8%)

Medical products - disposable micro-catheters, guidewires, micro-coils & angioplasty products used in treating vascular diseases of the brain

TCSI CORPORATION

2121 Allston Way   Phone: 510-649-3700
Berkeley, CA 94704-1301   Fax: 510-649-3500
Pres & CEO: Roger A. Strauch
Dir HR: Dennis Heller
Employees: 288

Jobs Added Last Year: 68 (+30.9%)

Computers - object-oriented telecommunications software for monitoring networks, rerouting traffic & integrating different telecom services more efficiently

TECTRIX FITNESS EQUIPMENT, INC.

68 Fairbanks
Irvine, CA 92718
CEO: Mike Sweeney
VP HR: Doug Plante
Employees: 83

Phone: 714-380-8082
Fax: 714-380-8710

Jobs Added Last Year: 18 (+27.7%)

Leisure & recreational equipment - virtual reality exercise bikes, providing imaginary trails

TELEDYNE, INC.

2049 Century Park East
Los Angeles, CA 90067-3101
Chm & CEO: William P. Rutledge
VP HR: Craig A. Saline
Employees: 18,000

Phone: 310-551-4306
Fax: 310-551-4366

Jobs Added Last Year: 0

Diversified operations - aviation electronic components, propulsion systems & instruments; superalloys & specialty steels; nitrogen gas systems; pool equipment & oral health products

TENERA, INC.

One Market, Spear Tower, Ste. 1850
San Francisco, CA 94105-1018
Chm & CEO: Michael D. Thomas
VP HR: Brad Gettis
Employees: 238

Phone: 415-536-4744
Fax: 415-536-4714

Jobs Added Last Year: 68 (+40.0%)

Computers - integrated management & software services for electric utilities, government agencies & large transporation corporations

TENET HEALTHCARE CORPORATION

3820 State Street
Santa Barbara, CA 93105
Chm & CEO: Jeffrey C. Barbakow
SVP HR: Alan R. Ewalt
Employees: 60,000

Phone: 805-563-7000
Fax: 805-563-7070

Jobs Added Last Year: 21,200 (+54.6%)

Hospitals - long-term care facilities, physical rehabilitation hospitals & psychiatric facilities

TETRA TECH, INC.

670 N. Rosemead Blvd.
Pasadena, CA 91107
Chm, Pres & CEO: Li-San Hwang
Corp Sec: Richard Lemmon
Employees: 1,706

Phone: 818-449-6400
Fax: 818-351-1188

Jobs Added Last Year: 815 (+91.5%)

Pollution control equipment & services - engineering & consulting services, including facilities, resource & waste management

THERMOTREX CORPORATION

9550 Distribution Ave.
San Diego, CA 92121
Pres & CEO: Firooz Rufeh
Dir HR: Allen Wolski
Employees: 916

Phone: 619-578-5885
Fax: 619-578-1419

Jobs Added Last Year: 243 (+36.1%)

Medical instruments - imaging & needle-biopsy systems for the early detection of breast cancer; general-purpose & specialty X-ray equipment

THOMPSON PBE, INC.

4553 Glencoe Ave., Ste. 200
Marina del Rey, CA 90292
Chm, CEO & Sec: D. Hunt Ramsbottom Jr.
Dir HR: Paula Strauss
Employees: 875

Phone: 310-306-7112
Fax: 310-306-7313

Jobs Added Last Year: 175 (+25.0%)

Auto parts - aftermarket distribution of automotive paint & related supplies to the automotive collision repair industry (#1 in US)

THRIFTY OIL CO.

10000 Lakewood Blvd.
Downey, CA 90240
Pres: Ted Orden
Dir HR: Beverly Brooks
Employees: 1,800

Phone: 310-923-9876
Fax: 310-869-9739

Jobs Added Last Year: 800 (+80.0%)

Oil refining & marketing; convenience stores

THE TIMES MIRROR COMPANY

Times Mirror Square
Los Angeles, CA 90053
Chm, Pres & CEO: Mark H. Willes
SVP HR: James R. Simpson
Employees: 21,877

Phone: 213-237-3700
Fax: 213-237-3800

Jobs Cut Last Year: 5,025 (-18.7%)

Publishing - newspapers (Los Angeles Times), magazines & books

TIMES MIRROR PROFESSIONAL INFO.

Times Mirror Square
Los Angeles, CA 90053
Chm, Pres & CEO, The Times Mirror Co.: Mark H. Willes
VP HR, The Times Mirror Co.: James R. Simpson
Employees: 24,500

Phone: 213-237-3700
Fax: 213-237-3800

Jobs Added Last Year: 185 (+0.8%)

Publishing - educational books (CRC Press, Jeppesen Sanderson, Mosby-Year Book); professional training programs

 An in-depth profile of this company is available
to subscribers on Hoover's Online at www.hoovers.com.

105

THE TODD-AO CORPORATION

1135 N. Mansfield Ave.
Hollywood, CA 90038
Co-Chm & Co-CEO: Robert A. Naify
Dir HR: Kate Reck
Employees: 390

Phone: 213-465-2579
Fax: 213-465-1231

Jobs Added Last Year: 150 (+62.5%)

Motion pictures & services - postproduction sound services &
special visual effects for the film & TV industries

TOUCHSTONE SOFTWARE CORPORATION

2124 Main St.
Huntington Beach, CA 92648
Pres & CEO: C. Shannon Jenkins
Mgr HR: Shan Dabiri
Employees: 53

Phone: 714-969-7746
Fax: 714-960-1886

Jobs Added Last Year: 14 (+35.9%)

Computers - PC utility software (CheckIt)

TRANSAMERICA CORPORATION

600 Montgomery St., 23rd Fl.
San Francisco, CA 94111
Chm & CEO: Frank C. Herringer
VP HR: Rona Pehrson
Employees: 10,400

Phone: 415-983-4000
Fax: 415-983-4234

Jobs Cut Last Year: 400 (-3.7%)

Diversified operations - life insurance; consumer & commercial
lending; leasing; real estate services

TRAVEL STORE INC.

11601 Wilshire Blvd.
Los Angeles, CA 96025
Pres & CEO: Wido Schaefer
No central personnel officer
Employees: 96

Phone: 310-575-5540
Fax: 310-575-5541

Jobs Added Last Year: 34 (+54.8%)

Travel - agency

TREASURE CHEST ADVERTISING COMPANY

511 W. Citrus Edge
Glendora, CA 91740
Pres : Donald Roland
VP HR: Michael Houser
Employees: 4,200

Phone: 818-914-3981
Fax: 818-852-3056

Jobs Added Last Year: 200 (+5.0%)

Printing - commercial web offset printing

TRIDENT MICROSYSTEMS, INC.

189 N. Bernardo Ave.
Mountain View, CA 94043-5203
Chm, Pres & CEO: Frank C. Lin
Dir HR: Sandra Cancela
Employees: 210

Phone: 415-691-9211
Fax: 415-691-9260

Jobs Added Last Year: 63 (+42.9%)

Computers - integrated circuit graphics & multimedia products
for IBM-compatible PCs, including graphical user interface accelerators, graphics controllers & video processors

TYLAN GENERAL, INC.

9577 Chesapeake Dr.
San Diego, CA 92123
Chm, Pres & CEO: David J. Ferran
VP HR & Info Systems: Michal A. Chick
Employees: 437

Phone: 619-571-1222
Fax: 619-576-1703

Jobs Added Last Year: 100 (+29.7%)

Machinery - semiconductor manufacturing equipment

UNIHEALTH

3400 Riverside Dr.
Burbank, CA 91505
Pres & CEO: Terry O. Hartshorn
VP HR: Barbara Cook
Employees: 13,000

Phone: 818-238-6000
Fax: 818-238-7687

Jobs Added Last Year: 0

Hospitals - not-for-profit health care system

UNIONBANCAL CORPORATION

350 California St.
San Francisco, CA 94104-1476
Pres & CEO: Kanetaka Yoshida
SVP HR: Roger Crawford
Employees: 7,230

Phone: 415-705-7000
Fax: 415-445-0425

Jobs Added Last Year: 307 (+4.4%)

Banks - West

UNITED STATES FILTER CORPORATION

40-004 Cook St.
Palm Desert, CA 92211
Chm, Pres & CEO: Richard J. Heckmann
SVP Admin: Gerald E. Rogers
Employees: 3,000

Phone: 619-340-0098
Fax: 619-341-9368

Jobs Added Last Year: 953 (+46.6%)

Filtration products - customized & pre-engineered systems &
equipment for water purification & wastewater treatment

UNIVERSITY OF CALIFORNIA

300 Lakeside Dr., 22nd Fl. Phone: 510-987-0700
Oakland, CA 94612-3550 Fax: 510-987-0894
Pres: Richard Atkinson
Dir Personnel: Alice Gregory
Employees: 133,000
Jobs Added Last Year: 36 (+0.0%)

Public university

UNIVERSITY OF SOUTHERN CALIF.

3620 S. Vermont Ave. Phone: 213-740-2311
Los Angeles, CA 90089 Fax: 213-740-0662
Pres: Steven B. Sample
Dir Personnel: James Ball
Employees: 17,000
Jobs Added Last Year: 0

Public university

UNOCAL CORPORATION

2141 Rosecrans Ave., Ste. 4000 Phone: 310-726-7600
El Segundo, CA 90245 Fax: 310-726-7817
Chm & CEO: Roger C. Beach
VP HR: David A. Demont
Employees: 12,509
Jobs Cut Last Year: 618 (-4.7%)

Oil & gas - US integrated

URS CORPORATION

100 California St., Ste. 500 Phone: 415-774-2700
San Francisco, CA 94111-4529 Fax: 415-398-1904
Pres & CEO: Martin M. Koffel
Dir HR: Barbara Gay
Employees: 1,300
Jobs Added Last Year: 200 (+18.2%)

Engineering - planning, design & program- & construction-management services

US FACILITIES CORPORATION

650 Town Center Dr., Ste. 1600 Phone: 714-549-1600
Costa Mesa, CA 92626 Fax: 714-241-0181
Chm, Pres & CEO: David L. Cargile
VP HR: Patricia S. Boisseranc
Employees: 191
Jobs Added Last Year: 41 (+27.3%)

Insurance - medical stop-loss policies

U.S. HOME & GARDEN INC.

655 Montgomery St. Phone: 415-616-8111
San Francisco, CA 94111 Fax: 415-616-8110
Chm, Pres, CEO & Treas: Robert L. Kassel
Dir HR: Lynda G. Gustafson
Employees: 64
Jobs Added Last Year: 13 (+25.5%)

Chemicals - consumer lawn & garden care products (WeedBlock, Easy Feeder, Tree Wrap) & agricultural products

VANSTAR CORPORATION

5964 W. Las Positas Blvd. Phone: 510-734-4000
Pleasanton, CA 94588 Fax: 510-734-4802
Chm & CEO: William Y. Tauscher
VP HR: Judith Marshall
Employees: 4,300
Jobs Added Last Year: 800 (+22.9%)

Computers - customized, integrated solutions for PC network infrastructures, primarily for Fortune 1000 companies & other large enterprises

THE VANTIVE CORPORATION

2455 Augustine Dr. Phone: 408-982-5700
Santa Clara, CA 95054 Fax: 408-982-5710
Pres & CEO: John R. Luongo
Dir HR: Holly Rail
Employees: 139
Jobs Added Last Year: 36 (+35.0%)

Computers - customer interaction applications software

VARIAN ASSOCIATES, INC.

3050 Hansen Way Phone: 415-493-4000
Palo Alto, CA 94304-1000 Fax: 415-493-0307
Chm & CEO: J. Tracy O'Rourke
VP HR: Ernest M. Felago
Employees: 6,900
Jobs Cut Last Year: 1,200 (-14.8%)

Machinery - semiconductor manufacturing equipment; radiation equipment for cancer therapy & industrial inspections; analytical instruments, electron tubes, vacuum equipment & leak detectors

VERIFONE, INC.

3 Lagoon Dr., Ste. 400 Phone: 415-591-6500
Redwood City, CA 94065-1561 Fax: 415-598-5504
Chm, Pres & CEO: Hatim A. Tyabji
VP HR: Katherine B. Beall
Employees: 2,471
Jobs Added Last Year: 539 (+27.9%)

Telecommunications equipment - transaction automation systems used to authorize financial transaction

 An in-depth profile of this company is available to subscribers on Hoover's Online at www.hoovers.com.

VIDEONICS, INC.

1370 Dell Ave.   Phone: 408-866-8300
Campbell, CA 95008   Fax: 408-866-4859
Chm, Pres & CEO: Michael L. D'Addio
Dir HR: Maryellen Deveine
Employees: 115

Jobs Added Last Year: 26 (+29.2%)

Video equipment - digital video post-production equipment

VIEJAS CASINO AND TURF CLUB

5000 Willows Rd.   Phone: 619-445-5400
Alpine, CA 91901   Fax: 619-445-1987
Gen Mgr: Mario Esquerra
HR Dir: Al Prudente
Employees: 1,300

Jobs Added Last Year: 600 (+85.7%)

Gambling resorts & casinos - gaming club & bingo hall

VIKING OFFICE PRODUCTS, INC.

13809 S. Figueroa St.   Phone: 213-321-4493
Los Angeles, CA 90061-1000   Fax: 310-324-2396
Chm, Pres & CEO: Irwin Helford
VP Admin & Sec: Stephen R. Kroll
Employees: 1,926

Jobs Added Last Year: 351 (+22.3%)

Retail - mail-order & direct sales of office products

VISTA INFORMATION SOLUTIONS, INC.

5060 Shoreham Place   Phone: 619-450-6100
San Diego, CA 92122   Fax: 619-450-6195
Pres & CEO: Thomas R. Gay
Dir HR: Frankie Campe
Employees: 176

Jobs Added Last Year: 119 (+208.8%)

Business services - geodemographic data files, marketing software & custom mapping services

VLSI TECHNOLOGY, INC.

1109 McKay Dr.   Phone: 408-434-3100
San Jose, CA 95131   Fax: 408-263-2511
Chm, Pres & CEO: Alfred J. Stein
VP HR: Eugene E. Tange
Employees: 3,000

Jobs Added Last Year: 272 (+10.0%)

Electrical components - specialized semiconductors; ASICs, ASSPs, microprocessors & data security & software development tools for chip designers

THE VONS COMPANIES, INC.

618 Michillinda Ave.   Phone: 818-821-7000
Arcadia, CA 91007-6300   Fax: 818-821-7933
Chm & CEO: Lawrence A. Del Santo
SVP HR: Dick W. Gonzales
Employees: 30,000

Jobs Added Last Year: 2,000 (+7.1%)

Retail - supermarkets (Vons, Pavilions, EXPO, Williams Bros., Tianguis); milk processing facility, ice cream plant, bakery & distribution operations

Friedland & Marcus — http://www.careermotiv8.com/

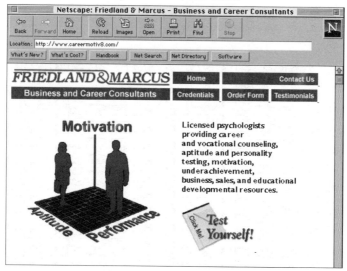

THE WALT DISNEY COMPANY

500 S. Buena Vista St. Phone: 818-560-1000
Burbank, CA 91521 Fax: 818-560-1930
Chm & CEO: Michael D. Eisner
SVP HR: William J. Wilkinson
Employees: 71,000
Jobs Added Last Year: 6,000 (+9.2%)

Leisure & recreational services - theme parks & resorts (Disney World), movies (Touchstone Pictures), radio & TV (Capital Cities/ABC), cable TV (Disney Channel, ESPN) & book publishing

WATSON PHARMACEUTICALS, INC.

311 Bonnie Circle Phone: 909-270-1400
Corona, CA 91720-1724 Fax: 909-270-1096
Chm & CEO: Allen F. Chao
VP HR: George Leisher
Employees: 554
Jobs Added Last Year: 175 (+46.2%)

Drugs - generic, off-patent medications & advanced drug delivery systems to enhance the therapeutic benefits of pharmaceutical compounds

WELLS FARGO & COMPANY

420 Montgomery St. Phone: 415-477-1000
San Francisco, CA 94163 Fax: 415-677-9075
Chm & CEO: Paul Hazen
Personnel Dir: Patricia R. Callahan
Employees: 19,520
Jobs Cut Last Year: 78 (-0.4%)

Banks - consumer banking services, including ATMs (Wells Fargo Express) & 24-hour telephone banking

WESTCORP

23 Pasteur Rd. Phone: 714-727-1000
Irvine, CA 92718-3804 Fax: 714-727-2313
Chm, Pres & CEO: Ernest S. Rady
Personnel Mgr: Denise Cooke
Employees: 1,688
Jobs Added Last Year: 524 (+45.0%)

Financial - savings & loans

WESTERN ATLAS INC.

360 N. Crescent Dr. Phone: 310-888-2500
Beverly Hills, CA 90210-4867 Fax: 310-888-2848
Chm & CEO: Alton J. Brann
Dir HR: Jim Robertson
Employees: 13,900
Jobs Cut Last Year: 300 (-2.1%)

Oil & gas - seismic surveys, well-logging & software development; industrial automation systems, including manufacturing, data collection & machining systems

WESTERN DIGITAL CORPORATION

8105 Irvine Center Dr. Phone: 714-932-5000
Irvine, CA 92718 Fax: 714-932-6096
Chm, Pres & CEO: Charles A. Haggerty
VP HR: Scott T. Hughes
Employees: 7,647
Jobs Added Last Year: 1,054 (+16.0%)

Computers - hard-disk drives, graphics chip sets & add-in cards for enhanced video graphics

WFS FINANCIAL INC.

16485 Laguna Canyon Rd. Phone: 714-753-3000
Irvine, CA 92713-9762 Fax: 714-727-2313
Chm & CEO: Ernest S. Rady
HR Supervisor: Denise Cooke
Employees: 1,108
Jobs Added Last Year: 384 (+53.0%)

Financial - auto loans

WILLIAMS-SONOMA, INC.

100 N. Point St. Phone: 415-421-7900
San Francisco, CA 94133 Fax: 415-983-9887
Chm & CEO: W. Howard Lester
VP HR: Claudia Abrams
Employees: 8,700
Jobs Added Last Year: 1,800 (+26.1%)

Retail - cookware & housewares; home furnishings (Pottery Barn), gardening equipment (Gardener's Eden), storage (Hold Everything) & bed & bath (Chambers) retail/catalog operations

WILSHIRE TECHNOLOGIES, INC.

5441 Avenida Encinas, Ste. A Phone: 619-929-7200
Carlsbad, CA 92008 Fax: 619-929-6949
Pres & CEO: Stephen P. Scibelli Jr.
Mgr Personnel: Christine Murphy
Employees: 52
Jobs Added Last Year: 12 (+30.0%)

Medical & dental supplies - swabs, wipes & other disposable clean-room products used to help reduce contamination

WIRED VENTURES, INC.

520 Third St., 4th Fl. Phone: 415-222-6200
San Francisco, CA 94107-1815 Fax: 415-222-6209
Chm & CEO: Louis Rossetto
No central personnel officer
Employees: 284
Jobs Added Last Year: 184 (+184.0%)

Publishing - magazine (Wired); WWW site (HotWired Internet)

 An in-depth profile of this company is available to subscribers on Hoover's Online at www.hoovers.com.

109

XILINX, INC.

2100 Logic Dr.
San Jose, CA 95124-3400
CEO: Willem P. "Wim" Roelandts
VP HR: Ray F. Madorin
Employees: 868

Phone: 408-559-7778
Fax: 408-559-7114

Jobs Added Last Year: 179 (+26.0%)

Electrical components - field-programmable gate array
semiconductors

XIRCOM, INC.

2300 Corporate Center Dr.
Thousand Oaks, CA 91320-1420
Pres & CEO: Dirk I. Gates
Dir HR: Ken Bauer
Employees: 500

Phone: 805-376-9300
Fax: 805-376-9311

Jobs Added Last Year: 200 (+66.7%)

Computers - network hardware, parallel port & PC LAN adapters,
multifunction PC card modems

THE YUCAIPA COMPANIES

10000 Santa Monica Blvd., 5th Fl.
Los Angeles, CA 90067
CEO: Ronald W. Burkle
VP HR: Don Ropele
Employees: 21,230

Phone: 310-789-7200
Fax: 310-884-2600

Jobs Added Last Year: 6,213 (+41.4%)

Retail - supermarkets (Alpha Beta, Bell, Cala, Dominick's, Falley,
Omni, Ralphs, Smitty's)

4FRONT SOFTWARE INTERNATIONAL, INC.

5650 Greenwood Plaza Blvd., Ste. 107
Englewood, CO 80111
Chm & CEO: Anil Doshi
No central personnel officer
Employees: 175

Phone: 303-721-7341
Fax: 303-220-1818

Jobs Added Last Year: 99 (+130.3%)

Computers - software & hardware sales, consulting, service &
support, specializing in systems integration

ADOLPH COORS COMPANY

12th at Ford
Golden, CO 80401
VP: Peter H. Coors
SVP HR: Robert W. Ehret
Employees: 6,200

Phone: 303-279-6565
Fax: 303-277-6564

Jobs Cut Last Year: 100 (-1.6%)

Beverages - beer (Coors, George Killian's, Keystone, Zima)

AMERICAN COIN MERCHANDISING, INC.

4870 Sterling Dr.
Boulder, CO 80301
Chm, Pres & CEO: Jerome M. Lapin
VP & CFO: W. John Cash
Employees: 164

Phone: 303-444-2559
Fax: 303-443-2264

Jobs Added Last Year: 40 (+32.3%)

Leisure & recreational services - ownership & operation of coin-
operated skill-crane machines that dispense stuffed animals,
watches & other items (d/b/a Sugarloaf Creations, Inc.)

AMERICAN MEDICAL RESPONSE, INC.

2821 S. Parker Rd., 10th Fl.
Aurora, CO 80014
Pres & CEO: Paul T. Shirley
VP HR: Terry Gleason
Employees: 11,000

Phone: 303-614-8500
Fax: 303-614-8519

Jobs Added Last Year: 3,998 (+57.1%)

Medical services - ambulance services

AMERICAN TELECASTING, INC.

4065 N. Sinton Rd., Ste. 201
Colorado Springs, CO 80907
Pres & CEO: Robert D. Hostetler
Dir HR: Sam Walker
Employees: 860

Phone: 719-632-5544
Fax: 719-632-5549

Jobs Added Last Year: 411 (+91.5%)

Cable TV - wireless cable TV (#1 in US)

AMRION, INC.

6565 Odell Place
Boulder, CO 80301-3330
Chm, Pres & CEO: Mark S. J. Crossen
Dir HR: Merilee Peterson
Employees: 275

Phone: 303-530-2525
Fax: 303-530-2592

Jobs Added Last Year: 75 (+37.5%)

Retail - mail-order vitamins & nutritional products

ATLAS AIR, INC.

538 Commons Dr.   Phone: 303-526-5050
Golden, CO 80401   Fax: 303-526-5051
Chm, Pres & CEO: Michael A. Chowdry
Dir HR: Betty Kwong
Employees: 435
Jobs Added Last Year: 89 (+25.7%)

Transportation - air freight

CANYON RESOURCES CORPORATION

14142 Denver West Pkwy., Ste. 250   Phone: 303-278-8464
Golden, CO 80401   Fax: 303-279-3772
Chm, Pres & CEO: Richard H. De Voto
Mgr Corp Comm & Admin: Tere McDowell
Employees: 114
Jobs Added Last Year: 35 (+44.3%)

Mining - gold & minerals

CH2M HILL COMPANIES, LTD.

6060 S. Willow Dr.   Phone: 303-771-0900
Denver, CO 80111   Fax: 303-220-5106
Pres & CEO: Ralph R. Peterson
VP HR: Fred Berry
Employees: 6,876
Jobs Added Last Year: 317 (+4.8%)

Engineering design & consulting

CIBER, INC.

5251 DTC Pkwy., Ste. 1400   Phone: 303-220-0100
Englewood, CO 80011-2742   Fax: 303-220-7100
Chm, CEO & Sec: Bob G. Stevenson
Office Mgr: Dana Harr
Employees: 1,532
Jobs Added Last Year: 525 (+52.1%)

Computers - system analysis, design & maintenance, specialized
on-site consulting services & technical education & training

COMMUNICATIONS WORLD INTL.

6025 S. Quebec St., Ste. 300   Phone: 303-721-8200
Englewood, CO 80111   Fax: 303-721-8299
Pres & CEO: Richard D. Olson
Dir HR: Shawn Rogers
Employees: 70
Jobs Added Last Year: 29 (+70.7%)

Telecommunications - telephone services & equipment

CORAM HEALTHCARE CORPORATION

1125 17th St.   Phone: 303-292-4973
Denver, CO 80202   Fax: 714-955-8769
Pres & CEO: Donald J. Amaral
VP HR: Vito Ponzio
Employees: 3,600
Jobs Added Last Year: 1,200 (+50.0%)

Health care - home infusion therapy services

CORPORATE EXPRESS, INC.

325 Interlocken Pkwy.   Phone: 303-373-2800
Broomfield, CO 80021   Fax: 303-438-5181
Chm & CEO: Jirka Rysavy
Dir HR: Richard W. Hediger
Employees: 12,413
Jobs Added Last Year: 8,366 (+206.7%)

Retail - mail-order office equipment & supplies

CYPRUS AMAX MINERALS COMPANY

9100 E. Mineral Circle   Phone: 303-643-5000
Englewood, CO 80112   Fax: 303-643-5049
Chm, Pres & CEO: Milton H. Ward
Dir Organizational Svcs: Chris Crowl
Employees: 9,700
Jobs Added Last Year: 200 (+2.1%)

Mining - gold, lithium, copper & molybdenum (#1 worldwide);
coal mining & production (#2 in US)

ECHO BAY MINES LTD.

6400 S. Fiddlers Green Circle, Ste. 1000   Phone: 303-714-8600
Englewood, CO 80111-4957   Fax: 303-714-8999
Pres & CEO: Richard C. Kraus
VP HR: Steven A. Conte
Employees: 1,987
Jobs Added Last Year: 216 (+12.2%)

Mining - gold & silver

FRONTIER AIRLINES, INC.

12015 E. 46th Ave.   Phone: 303-371-7400
Denver, CO 80239   Fax: 303-371-7007
Pres, CEO & CFO: Samuel D. Addoms
Dir HR & Properties: John D. Hershner
Employees: 528
Jobs Added Last Year: 225 (+74.3%)

Transportation - airline

 An in-depth profile of this company is available
to subscribers on Hoover's Online at www.hoovers.com.

111

GRETCHELL GOLD CORP.

5460 S. Quebec St., Ste. 240   Phone: 303-771-9000
Englewood, CO 80111   Fax: 303-771-1075
CEO: Charles M. McAuley
VP HR: Donald O. Miller
Employees: 300
Jobs Added Last Year: 136 (+82.9%)
Mining - gold

GRIFFIS/BLESSING INC.

102 N. Cascade, 5th Fl.   Phone: 719-520-1234
Colorado Springs, CO 80903   Fax: 719-520-1204
CEO: Buck Blessing
CFO: Gary Winegar
Employees: 70
Jobs Added Last Year: 15 (+27.3%)

Real estate operations - real estate management, investment & development

GUARANTY NATIONAL CORPORATION

9800 S. Meridian Blvd.   Phone: 303-754-8400
Englewood, CO 80112   Fax: 303-790-7136
Pres & CEO: Roger B. Ware
Dir HR: Kim Bryant
Employees: 1,000
Jobs Added Last Year: 400 (+66.7%)

Insurance - nonstandard property & casualty

J.D. EDWARDS & COMPANY

8055 E. Tufts Ave.   Phone: 303-488-4000
Denver, CO 80237   Fax: 303-488-4678
Pres & CEO: C. E. McVaney
Dir HR: Greg Dixon
Employees: 2,310
Jobs Added Last Year: 678 (+41.5%)

Computers - business development software

JONES COMMUNICATIONS, INC.

9697 E. Mineral Ave., PO Box 3309   Phone: 303-792-3111
Englewood, CO 80155-3309   Fax: 303-790-0533
Chm & CEO: Glenn R. Jones
Group VP HR: Raymond L. Vigil
Employees: 3,480
Jobs Added Last Year: 630 (+22.1%)

Cable TV - acquisition, development & operation of cable TV systems; programming & data encryption service

LIFE PARTNERS GROUP, INC.

7887 E. Belleview Ave.   Phone: 303-779-1111
Englewood, CO 80111   Fax: 303-796-7576
Chm & CEO: John H. Massey
VP HR: Stacy Klein
Employees: 730
Jobs Added Last Year: 190 (+35.2%)

Insurance - life (Massachusetts General Life Insurance, Philadelphia Life Insurance)

LORONIX INFORMATION SYSTEMS, INC.

820 Airport Rd.   Phone: 970-259-6161
Durango, CO 81301   Fax: 970-259-9399
Pres & CEO: M. Dean Gilliam
Dir HR: Lolita Powers
Employees: 70
Jobs Added Last Year: 16 (+29.6%)

Computers - digital identification & video image management systems software for access control, security, retail point-of-sale, human resource management & other control systems

MAIL-WELL, INC.

23 Inverness Way   Phone: 303-790-8023
Englewood, CO 80112   Fax: 303-397-7400
Chm & CEO: Gerald F. Mahoney
Dir HR: Rich Davidson
Employees: 5,644
Jobs Added Last Year: 0

Paper - envelopes (#1 in North America); commercial printing for advertising literature, high-end catalogs & annual reports

MEDIANEWS GROUP, INC.

1560 Broadway, Ste. 1450   Phone: 303-837-0886
Denver, CO 80202   Fax: 303-894-9327
VC, Pres & CEO: William D. Singleton
VP HR: Nick Lebra
Employees: 4,500
Jobs Added Last Year: 200 (+4.7%)

Publishing - daily & weekly newspapers (76, including the Denver Post)

MONACO FINANCE INC.

370 17th St., Ste. 5060   Phone: 303-592-9411
Denver, CO 80202   Fax: 303-592-4872
Chm, Pres & CEO: Morris Ginsburg
Dir HR: Dave Wood
Employees: 167
Jobs Added Last Year: 46 (+38.0%)

Financial - alternative-financing programs for purchasers of used vehicles who do not qualify for traditional sources of financing

MOUNTAIN PARKS FINANCIAL CORP.

6565 E. Evans Ave.   Phone: 303-758-7474
Denver, CO 80224   Fax: 303-758-8915
Chm, Pres & CEO: Dennis M. Mathisen
Ops Officer: Rebecca Kopec
Employees: 315
Jobs Added Last Year: 155 (+96.9%)

Banks - West

NAPRO BIOTHERAPEUTICS, INC.

6304 Spine Rd., Unit A   Phone: 303-530-3891
Boulder, CO 80301   Fax: 303-530-1298
Pres & CEO: Sterling K. Ainsworth
HR Mgr: Amy Owens
Employees: 67
Jobs Added Last Year: 30 (+81.1%)

Biomedical & genetic products - cancer-fighting pharmaceuticals from yew trees

NEWMONT GOLD COMPANY

1700 Lincoln St.   Phone: 303-863-7414
Denver, CO 80203   Fax: 303-837-5837
Chm, Pres & CEO: Ronald C. Cambre
Dir HR: Lou Lazo
Employees: 4,100
Jobs Added Last Year: 1,265 (+44.6%)

Mining - gold & silver

NEWMONT MINING CORPORATION

1700 Lincoln St.   Phone: 303-863-7414
Denver, CO 80203   Fax: 303-837-6034
Chm, Pres & CEO: Ronald C. Cambre
VP HR: Steve A. Conte
Employees: 4,100
Jobs Added Last Year: 1,265 (+44.6%)

Mining - gold & silver

ROCK BOTTOM RESTAURANTS, INC.

1050 Walnut Steet, Ste. 402   Phone: 303-417-4000
Boulder, CO 80302   Fax: 303-417-4198
CEO: Thomas A. Moxcey
Dir HR: Emily Rusnak
Employees: 3,233
Jobs Added Last Year: 1,321 (+69.1%)

Retail - restaurants featuring microbrewed & specialty beer (Rock Bottom, Old Chicago)

ROCKY MOUNTAIN CHOCOLATE FACTORY

265 Turner Dr.   Phone: 970-259-0554
Durango, CO 81301   Fax: 970-247-9593
Chm, Pres & Treas: Franklin E. Crail
Dir HR: Cathy Junkerman
Employees: 402
Jobs Added Last Year: 233 (+137.9%)

Food - gourmet chocolates & other confectionery products

4 Work — http://4work.com/

An in-depth profile of this company is available to subscribers on Hoover's Online at www.hoovers.com.

113

SCHULLER CORPORATION

717 17th St.   Phone: 303-978-2000
Denver, CO 80202   Fax: 303-978-2363
Pres & CEO: W. Thomas Stephens
SVP HR & Purchasing: Ron L. Hammons
Employees: 7,500

Jobs Cut Last Year: 6,100 (-44.9%)

Building products - paperboard & packaging products,
engineered products

STORAGE TECHNOLOGY CORP.

2270 S. 88th St.   Phone: 303-673-5151
Louisville, CO 80028-4309   Fax: 303-673-2296
Chm, Pres & CEO: David E. Weiss
VP HR: Laurie Dodd
Employees: 10,000

Jobs Cut Last Year: 300 (-2.9%)

Computers - information storage & retrieval systems &
networking products

TCI COMMUNICATIONS, INC.

5619 DTC Pkwy.   Phone: 303-267-5500
Englewood, CO 80111-3000   Fax: 303-779-1228
Pres & CEO: Brendan R. Clouston
No central personnel officer
Employees: 32,500

Jobs Added Last Year: 500 (+1.6%)

Cable TV - #1 system in the US; cable programming services

TELEPHONE EXPRESS

1155 Kelly Johnson Blvd., Ste. 400   Phone: 719-592-1250
Colorado Springs, CO 80920   Fax: 719-592-1201
Pres: Mary Beazley
Dir HR: Lorelee Bauer
Employees: 250

Jobs Added Last Year: 50 (+25.0%)

Telecommunications services - long-distance telephone services

T-NETIX, INC.

6675 S. Kenton St.   Phone: 303-790-9111
Englewood, CO 80111   Fax: 303-790-9540
Chm & CEO: Thomas J. Huzjak
VP HR: Katja Christiansen
Employees: 251

Jobs Added Last Year: 66 (+35.7%)

Telecommunications services - call processing services, including
fraud detection & prevention, customized billing & caller &
personal identification

TOTAL PETROLEUM (NORTH AMERICA) LTD.

TOTAL Tower, 900 19th St.   Phone: 303-291-2000
Denver, CO 80202   Fax: 303-291-2104
Pres & CEO: C. Gary Jones
VP Personnel & Industrial Relations: H. Scott Topham
Employees: 6,400

Jobs Added Last Year: —

Oil refining & marketing

UNION BANKSHARES, LTD.

1825 Lawrence St., Ste. 444   Phone: 303-298-5352
Denver, CO 80202   Fax: 303-298-5380
Chm & CEO: Charles R. Harrison
No central personnel officer
Employees: 94

Jobs Added Last Year: 24 (+34.3%)

Banks - West (Union Bank & Trust)

UNITED ARTISTS THEATRE CIRCUIT, INC.

9110 E. Nichols Ave., Ste. 200   Phone: 303-792-3600
Englewood, CO 80112   Fax: 303-790-8907
Chm & CEO: Stewart Blair
Dir HR: Elizabeth Moravak
Employees: 11,100

Jobs Added Last Year: 600 (+5.7%)

Motion pictures & services - theaters (420 units)

U S WEST COMMUNICATIONS GROUP

7800 E. Orchard Rd.   Phone: 303-793-6500
Englewood, CO 80111   Fax: 303-793-6654
Pres & CEO: Solomon D. Trujillo
EVP Public Policy & Acting Chief HR Officer: James H. Stever
Employees: 61,047

Jobs Cut Last Year: 458 (-0.7%)

Utility - telephone; long distance services

U S WEST MEDIA GROUP

7800 E. Orchard Rd., Ste. 290   Phone: 303-793-6500
Englewood, CO 80111   Fax: 303-793-6309
Pres & CEO: Charles M. Lillis
Dir HR: Patty A. Klinge
Employees: 16,000

Jobs Added Last Year: 5,721 (+55.7%)

Publishing - directories (Yellow Pages) & marketing services;
domestic & international cable & wireless networks; interactive
multimedia services

VARI-L COMPANY, INC.

11101 E. 51st Ave.
Denver, CO 80239
Pres, CEO & CFO: David G. Sherman
Dir Personnel: Robert Neu
Employees: 229

Phone: 303-371-1560
Fax: 303-371-0845

Jobs Added Last Year: 95 (+70.9%)

Telecommunications equipment - radio frequency & microwave signal processing components for wireless telecommunications

VICORP RESTAURANTS, INC.

400 W. 48th Ave., PO Box 16601
Denver, CO 80216
Pres & Co-CEO: J. Michael Jenkins
SVP HR: Patricia M. Luzier
Employees: 13,500

Phone: 303-296-2121
Fax: 303-297-8637

Jobs Cut Last Year: 900 (-6.3%)

Retail - family-style restaurants (Bakers Square, Village Inn)

CONNECTICUT

ADVANCED TECHNOLOGY MATERIALS, INC.

7 Commerce Dr.
Danbury, CT 06810-4169
Chm, Pres & CEO: Eugene G. Banucci
Mgr HR: Phyllis Banucci
Employees: 173

Phone: 203-794-1100
Fax: 203-792-8040

Jobs Added Last Year: 64 (+58.7%)

Electrical components - diamond & silicon carbide semiconductors; thin-film precursors

ADVO, INC.

One Univac Ln., PO Box 755
Windsor, CT 06095-0755
Chm & CEO: Robert Kamerschen
SVP HR: J. Thomas Van Berkem
Employees: 5,200

Phone: 860-285-6100
Fax: 860-285-6393

Jobs Cut Last Year: 100 (-1.9%)

Business services - direct marketing

AETNA INC.

151 Farmington Ave.
Hartford, CT 06156
Chm, Pres & CEO: Ronald E. Compton
SVP HR: Mary Ann Champlin
Employees: 40,200

Phone: 860-273-0123
Fax: 860-275-2677

Jobs Cut Last Year: 700 (-1.7%)

Insurance - multiline

AIR EXPRESS INTERNATIONAL CORP.

120 Tokeneke Rd.
Darien, CT 06820
Pres & CEO: Guenter Rohrmann
Dir Personnel: Billie Raisides
Employees: 5,522

Phone: 203-655-7900
Fax: 203-655-5779

Jobs Added Last Year: 739 (+15.5%)

Transportation - air & sea freight

AMERICAN BRANDS, INC.

1700 E. Putnam Ave.
Old Greenwich, CT 06870-0811
Chm & CEO: Thomas C. Hays
SVP & Chief Admin Officer: Steven C. Mendenhall
Employees: 27,700

Phone: 203-698-5000
Fax: 203-637-2580

Jobs Cut Last Year: 7,120 (-20.4%)

Diversified operations - tobacco (Benson & Hedges) & liquor (Gilbey's, Jim Beam, Windsor Canadian); office products (ACCO, Swingline); golfing equipment (Titleist); locks (Master Lock)

AMERIDATA TECHNOLOGIES, INC.

700 Canal St.
Stamford, CT 06902
Co-Chm & Co-Pres: Gerald A. Poch
Dir HR: Sharon Burglund
Employees: 3,500

Phone: 203-357-1464
Fax: 203-357-1531

Jobs Added Last Year: 1,400 (+66.7%)

Computers - systems integration, networking services, technical support, maintenance, rental & other services

AMES DEPARTMENT STORES, INC.

2418 Main St.
Rocky Hill, CT 06067
Pres & CEO: Joseph R. Ettore
SVP HR : Richard L. Carter
Employees: 22,000

Phone: 860-257-2000
Fax: 860-257-2198

Jobs Cut Last Year: 200 (-0.9%)

Retail - discount regional department stores in the northeast, mid-Atlantic & Midwest

 An in-depth profile of this company is available to subscribers on Hoover's Online at www.hoovers.com.

115

AMPHENOL CORPORATION

358 Hall Ave.
Wallingford, CT 06492-7530
Pres & CEO: Martin H. Loeffler
Dir HR: William Hough Jr.
Employees: 5,459

Phone: 203-265-8900
Fax: 203-265-8793

Jobs Added Last Year: 169 (+3.2%)

Electrical connectors - cabling systems

AVITAR, INC.

556 Washington Ave., Ste. 202
North Haven, CT 06473
CEO: Douglas W. Scott
Controller, CFO & Sec: Jay C. Leatherman
Employees: 58

Phone: 203-234-7737
Fax: 203-234-0199

Jobs Added Last Year: 35 (+152.2%)

Health maintenance organization

BLYTH INDUSTRIES, INC.

100 Field Point Rd.
Greenwich, CT 06830-6442
Chm, Pres & CEO: Robert B. Goergen
VP HR: Erik Sprotte
Employees: 2,000

Phone: 203-661-1926
Fax: 203-661-1969

Jobs Added Last Year: 600 (+42.9%)

Housewares - scented candles, outdoor citronella candles & pot pourri products

CADBURY BEVERAGES INC.

6 High Ridge Park, PO Box 3800
Stamford, CT 06905-0800
Pres: John Brock
VP HR: John Soi
Employees: 7,730

Phone: 203-329-0911
Fax: 203-968-7854

Jobs Added Last Year: 1,250 (+19.3%)

Beverages - soft drinks (Schweppes, Canada Dry, Dr Pepper, 7-Up, I.B.C., Crush, Sunkist, Mott's, A&W Root Beer); confectionery

THE CALDOR CORPORATION

20 Glover Ave.
Norwalk, CT 06856-5620
Chm & CEO: Don R. Clarke
EVP HR & Merch. Distribution & Replenishment: Dennis M. Lee
Employees: 24,000

Phone: 203-846-1641
Fax: 203-849-2019

Jobs Added Last Year: 0

Retail - discount branded & private-label merchandise, including housewares, electronics, furniture, toys, apparel, shoes, jewelry & cosmetics

CENTENNIAL CELLULAR CORP.

50 Locust Ave.
New Canaan, CT 06840
Chm & CEO: Bernard P. Gallagher
VP HR: Geoff Broom
Employees: 540

Phone: 203-972-2000
Fax: 203-966-9228

Jobs Added Last Year: 202 (+59.8%)

Telecommunications services - cellular telephone systems

CHAMPION INTERNATIONAL CORP.

One Champion Plaza
Stamford, CT 06921
Chm & CEO: Andrew C. Sigler
SVP Organizational Dev & HR: Mark V. Childers
Employees: 24,129

Phone: 203-358-7000
Fax: 203-358-6444

Jobs Cut Last Year: 486 (-2.0%)

Paper & paper products - papers for business communications, commercial printing, publications & newspapers; pulp, plywood, lumber & timberland operations

CITIZENS UTILITIES COMPANY

High Ridge Park, PO Box 3801
Stamford, CT 06905-1390
Chm, CEO & CFO: Leonard Tow
VP Corp HR: Alessandro V. Ross
Employees: 4,760

Phone: 203-329-8800
Fax: 203-322-7186

Jobs Added Last Year: 466 (+10.9%)

Utility - telephone; natural gas transmission & electric distribution services

COLONIAL DATA TECHNOLOGIES CORP.

80 Pickett District Rd.
New Milford, CT 06776
Chm, Pres & CEO: Robert J. Schock
Mgr HR: Kimberly Schock
Employees: 174

Phone: 860-355-3178
Fax: 860-354-2803

Jobs Added Last Year: 55 (+46.2%)

Telecommunications equipment - caller ID products

CRANE CO.

100 First Stamford Place
Stamford, CT 06902
Chm & CEO: Robert S. Evans
VP HR: Richard B. Phillips
Employees: 10,000

Phone: 203-363-7300
Fax: 203-363-7295

Jobs Cut Last Year: 700 (-6.5%)

Diversified operations - aerospace & defense products & millwork

CUC INTERNATIONAL INC.

707 Summer St. Phone: 203-324-9261
Stamford, CT 06901 Fax: 203-348-4528
Chm & CEO: Walter A. Forbes
VP HR: Fran Johnson
Employees: 11,000

Jobs Added Last Year: 3,000 (+37.5%)

Retail - membership-based shopping, travel, dining & other services by mail order, phone & online network (Comp-U-Card); educational & game software (Davidson Associates, Sierra On-Line)

THE DUN & BRADSTREET CORP.

187 Danbury Rd. Phone: 203-834-4200
Wilton, CT 06897 Fax: 203-834-4201
Chm & CEO: Robert E. Weissman
VP HR: Michael Connors
Employees: 49,500

Jobs Added Last Year: 2,500 (+5.3%)

Business services - marketing (A. C. Nielsen), audience measurement, risk management (Dun & Bradstreet Information Services, Moody's), software & directory information services

DURACELL INTERNATIONAL INC.

Berkshire Corporate Park Phone: 203-796-4000
Bethel, CT 06801 Fax: 203-796-4187
Chm & CEO: Charles R. Perrin
SVP HR: Nancy A. Reardon
Employees: 8,100

Jobs Added Last Year: 400 (+5.2%)

Electrical products - alkaline batteries (#1 worldwide: Duracell)

ECHLIN INC.

100 Double Beach Rd. Phone: 203-481-5751
Branford, CT 06405 Fax: 203-481-6485
Chm & CEO: Frederick J. Mancheski
VP HR: Milton J. Makoski
Employees: 23,400

Jobs Added Last Year: 2,800 (+13.6%)

Automotive & trucking - brake, engine, power transmission & steering & suspension parts

EIS INTERNATIONAL, INC.

1351 Washington Blvd., 5th Fl. Phone: 203-351-4800
Stamford, CT 06902 Fax: 203-961-8632
Chm & CEO: Joseph J. Porfeli
Dir HR: Jo Lovell
Employees: 438

Jobs Added Last Year: 141 (+47.5%)

Telecommunications equipment - inbound & outbound call-processing systems primarily for the telemarketing industry

EMCOR GROUP, INC.

101 Merritt Seven Corporate Park, 7th Fl. Phone: 203-849-7800
Norwalk, CT 06851-1060 Fax: 203-849-7820
Chm, Pres & CEO: Frank T. MacInnis
VP HR: Jim Murphy
Employees: 12,000

Jobs Cut Last Year: 2,000 (-14.3%)

Diversified operations - electrical & HVAC contracting; water supply

ETHAN ALLEN INTERIORS INC.

Ethan Allen Dr. Phone: 203-743-8000
Danbury, CT 06811 Fax: 203-743-8298
Chm, Pres & CEO: M. Farooq Kathwari
Personnel Dir: Charles J. Farfaglia
Employees: 6,048

Jobs Added Last Year: 164 (+2.8%)

Retail - wood furnishings, upholstered products & home furnishing accessories

EXECUTIVE RISK INC.

82 Hopmeadow St. Phone: 860-408-2000
Simsbury, CT 06070-7683 Fax: 860-408-2002
Chm & CEO: L. A. Vander Putten
Dir HR: Margaret A. Reynolds
Employees: 225

Jobs Added Last Year: 45 (+25.0%)

Insurance - corporate directors & officers liability policies that protect executives against shareholder lawsuits

FIRST BRANDS CORPORATION

83 Wooster Heights Rd., Bldg. 301 Phone: 203-731-2300
PO Box 1911 Fax: 203-731-2518
Danbury, CT 06813-1911
Pres & CEO: William V. Stephenson
VP HR: Ronald F. Dainton
Employees: 4,200

Jobs Added Last Year: 500 (+13.5%)

Diversified operations - plastic wrap & bags; cat litter; automotive products; waxes, polishes & cleaners

GARTNER GROUP, INC.

56 Top Gallant Rd. Phone: 203-964-0096
Stamford, CT 06904-2212 Fax: 203-316-1100
Chm, Pres & CEO: Manuel A. Fernandez
SVP HR: Lindon Smith
Employees: 1,175

Jobs Added Last Year: 263 (+28.8%)

Business services - subscription-based research & analysis services

 An in-depth profile of this company is available to subscribers on Hoover's Online at www.hoovers.com.

GENERAL ELECTRIC COMPANY

3135 Easton Tpke.   Phone: 203-373-2211
Fairfield, CT 06431-0001   Fax: 203-373-2071
Chm & CEO: John F. Welch Jr.
SVP HR: William J. Conaty
Employees: 222,000

Jobs Added Last Year: 1,000 (+0.5%)

Diversified operations - financing (GE Capital); aircraft engines; locomotives; appliances; broadcasting (NBC); power systems; plastics; power generation; lighting; medical systems; insurance

GENERAL HOST CORPORATION

One Station Place   Phone: 203-357-9900
Stamford, CT 06902   Fax: 203-564-2084
Chm, Pres & CEO: Harris J. Ashton
VP HR: Carol Cox
Employees: 8,031

Jobs Added Last Year: 0

Retail - lawn & garden products, crafts & Christmas merchandise

GENERAL RE CORPORATION

695 E. Main St.   Phone: 203-328-5000
Stamford, CT 06901   Fax: 203-328-5329
Chm & CEO: Ronald E. Ferguson
VP HR: Theron S. Hoffman Jr.
Employees: 3,426

Jobs Added Last Year: 1,066 (+45.2%)

Insurance - property & casualty reinsurance

GENERAL SIGNAL CORPORATION

One High Ridge Park   Phone: 203-329-4100
Stamford, CT 06904   Fax: 203-329-4223
Chm & CEO: Michael D. Lockhart
SVP HR: Elizabeth D. Conklyn
Employees: 12,900

Jobs Added Last Year: 700 (+5.7%)

Instruments - industrial valves that control & isolate gases, liquids & dry solids; uninterruptible power systems; industrial technology, including WAN switching systems

GERBER SCIENTIFIC, INC.

83 Gerber Rd. West   Phone: 860-644-1551
South Windsor, CT 06074   Fax: 860-643-7039
Chm & Pres: H. Joseph Gerber
Personnel Dir: Anthony R. Pagliuco
Employees: 1,700

Jobs Added Last Year: 200 (+13.3%)

Industrial automation & robotics - CAD/CAM systems

GTE CORPORATION

One Stamford Forum   Phone: 203-965-2000
Stamford, CT 06904   Fax: 203-965-2277
Chm & CEO: Charles R. Lee
SVP HR & Admin: J. Randall MacDonald
Employees: 106,000

Jobs Cut Last Year: 5,000 (-4.5%)

Utility - telephone; cellular communications, information services & in-flight telephone service (Airfone)

Lizard Jobs — http://www.sky.net/~genuinel/lizjobs.html

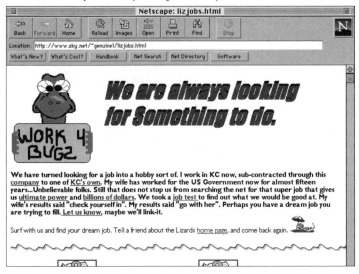

THE HARTFORD STEAM BOILER INSPECTION AND INSURANCE CO.

One State St.
Hartford, CT 06102-5024
Pres & CEO: Gordon W. Kreh
Asst VP HR: Susan W. Ahrens
Employees: 4,400

Phone: 860-722-1866
Fax: 860-722-5106

Jobs Added Last Year: 340 (+8.4%)

Insurance - boiler & industrial-machinery insurance; equipment inspection, safety certification & loss-prevention engineering

HUBBELL INC.

584 Derby Milford Rd.
Orange, CT 06477-4024
Chm, Pres & CEO: G. J. Ratcliffe
Dir HR: George Zurman
Employees: 7,410

Phone: 203-799-4100
Fax: 203-799-4254

Jobs Added Last Year: 5 (+0.1%)

Electrical products - electrical wiring devices & industrial controls

HYPERION SOFTWARE CORPORATION

900 Long Ridge Rd.
Stamford, CT 06902-1247
Chm & CEO: James A. Perakis
Dir HR: Paul Avalone
Employees: 846

Phone: 203-703-3000
Fax: 203-595-8500

Jobs Added Last Year: 266 (+45.9%)

Computers - enterprise-level financial-management software for client/server environments

ITT HARTFORD GROUP, INC.

Hartford Plaza, 690 Asylum Ave.
Hartford, CT 06115-1900
Chm, Pres & CEO: Donald R. Frahm
SVP HR: Helen G. Goodman
Employees: 21,000

Phone: 860-547-5000
Fax: 860-547-2680

Jobs Added Last Year: 1,000 (+5.0%)

Insurance - personal, commercial, specialty & reinsurance property-casualty coverage; individual life policies & annuities; employee benefits & asset management services

KAMAN CORPORATION

Blue Hills Ave.
Bloomfield, CT 06002
Chm, Pres & CEO: Charles H. Kaman
VP HR: Candace A. Clark
Employees: 5,400

Phone: 860-243-7100
Fax: 860-243-6365

Jobs Added Last Year: 161 (+3.1%)

Aerospace - commercial & military helicopters; artificial intelligence systems for all branches of the Armed Forces

LEXMARK INTL. GROUP, INC.

55 Railroad Ave.
Greenwich, CT 06836
Chm, Pres & CEO: Marvin L. Mann
VP HR & Info Programs: A. Richard Murphy
Employees: 7,500

Phone: 203-629-6700
Fax: 203-629-6725

Jobs Added Last Year: 2,500 (+50.0%)

Computers - keyboards, laser & inkjet printers, notebook computers, electric typewriters & associated consumable supplies for the office & home markets

LYNCH CORPORATION

8 Sound Shore Dr., Ste. 290
Greenwich, CT 06830
Chm & CEO: Mario J. Gabelli
VP Admin, Gen Counsel & Sec: Robert Hurwich
Employees: 1,986

Phone: 203-629-3333
Fax: 203-629-3718

Jobs Added Last Year: 813 (+69.3%)

Diversified operations - transportation of manufactured housing & RVs; glass-forming machines; packaging machines; telecommunications services; TV stations

MACDERMID, INCORPORATED

245 Freight St.
Waterbury, CT 06702-0671
Pres & CEO: Daniel H. Leever
Dir HR: Myrna Hill
Employees: 1,083

Phone: 203-575-5700
Fax: 203-575-5630

Jobs Added Last Year: 255 (+30.8%)

Chemicals - specialty chemicals & systems for the chemical treatment, surface preparation & finishing of metals, plastics & other materials

MARINER HEALTH GROUP, INC.

125 Eugene O'Neill Dr.
New London, CT 06320
Chm, Pres & CEO: Arthur W. Stratton Jr.
Dir HR: Joan Wiegers
Employees: 8,200

Phone: 860-701-2000
Fax: 860-701-2140

Jobs Added Last Year: 2,700 (+49.1%)

Medical services - subacute health-care services

MECKLERMEDIA CORPORATION

20 Ketchum St.
Westport, CT 06880
Chm, Pres & CEO: Alan M. Meckler
Emp Benefits Coordinator: Susan Breslin
Employees: 80

Phone: 203-226-6967
Fax: 203-454-5840

Jobs Added Last Year: 31 (+63.3%)

Publishing - magazines (Internet World, Web Developer), books & newspapers (Web Week); trade shows & seminars

 An in-depth profile of this company is available to subscribers on Hoover's Online at www.hoovers.com.

119

MICRO WAREHOUSE, INC.

535 Connecticut Ave.
Norwalk, CT 06854
Chm, Pres & CEO: Peter Godfrey
VP HR: Michael J. Kurtz
Employees: 3,000

Phone: 203-899-4000
Fax: 203-899-4203

Jobs Added Last Year: 700 (+30.4%)

Retail - mail-order sales of peripheral equipment & software (MacWAREHOUSE, MicroWAREHOUSE)

MODEM MEDIA

228 Saugatuck Ave.
Westport, CT 06880
Founding & Mng Partner: Gerald M. O'Connell
Dir HR: Marilyn Fidler
Employees: 70

Phone: 203-341-5200
Fax: 203-341-5260

Jobs Added Last Year: 37 (+112.1%)

Advertising agency specializing in developing corporate web sites (AT&T, Zima)

NATIONAL RE CORPORATION

777 Long Ridge Rd., PO Box 10167
Stamford, CT 06904-2167
Chm, Pres & CEO: William D. Warren
SVP Admin & Personnel: William J. Hunt
Employees: 330

Phone: 203-329-7700
Fax: 203-329-5220

Jobs Added Last Year: 67 (+25.5%)

Insurance - property & casualty reinsurance

NINE WEST GROUP INC.

9 W. Broad St.
Stamford, CT 06902
Co-Chm & Pres: Vincent Camuto
HR Mgr: Debra Trautman
Employees: 15,320

Phone: 203-324-7567
Fax: 203-328-3550

Jobs Added Last Year: 11,299 (+281.0%)

Shoes & related apparel - women's shoes (Nine West, 9 & Co., Calico, Enzo Angiolini)

OLIN CORPORATION

501 Merritt 7, PO Box 4500
Norwalk, CT 06856-4500
Pres & CEO: Donald W. Griffin
VP HR: Peter C. Kosche
Employees: 13,000

Phone: 203-750-3000
Fax: 203-750-3292

Jobs Added Last Year: 200 (+1.6%)

Diversified operations - chemicals; defense products & ammunition; metals; sporting ammunition (Winchester)

OXFORD HEALTH PLANS, INC.

800 Connecticut Ave.
Norwalk, CT 06854
Chm & CEO: Stephen F. Wiggins
VP HR: Jeanne D. Wisniewski
Employees: 4,000

Phone: 203-852-1442
Fax: 203-851-2464

Jobs Added Last Year: 2,230 (+126.0%)

Health maintenance organization

PERKIN-ELMER CORPORATION

761 Main Ave.
Norwalk, CT 06859-0001
Chm, Pres & CEO: Tony L. White
VP HR: Michael J. McPartland
Employees: 5,890

Phone: 203-762-1000
Fax: 203-762-6000

Jobs Cut Last Year: 64 (-1.1%)

Instruments - chemical-analysis & -measurement instrumentation for environmental, agricultural & pharmaceutical use; thermal sprays & equipment

PHYSICIANS HEALTH SERVICES, INC.

120 Hawley Ln.
Trumbull, CT 06611
Pres & CEO: Michael E. Herbert
SVP & Chief Admin Officer: Regina M. Campbell
Employees: 707

Phone: 203-381-6400
Fax: 203-381-6690

Jobs Added Last Year: 220 (+45.2%)

Health maintenance organization

PITNEY BOWES INC.

One Elmcroft Rd.
Stamford, CT 06926-0700
Chm: George B. Harvey
VP Personnel: Johnna G. Torsone
Employees: 27,723

Phone: 203-356-5000
Fax: 203-351-6835

Jobs Cut Last Year: 5,069 (-15.5%)

Office equipment & supplies - mailing & copier systems & facsimile machines

PITTSTON BRINKS GROUP

100 First Stamford Place, PO Box 120070
Stamford, CT 06912-0070
CEO: Michael Dan
VP HR & Admin: Frank T. Lennon
Employees: 8,300

Phone: 203-978-5200
Fax: 203-978-5315

Jobs Cut Last Year: 6,500 (-43.9%)

Protection - residential & commercial burglary, fire & medical alarm systems (Brink's Home Security, Inc.); armored transportation, ATM servicing & other related services (Brink's, Inc.)

PITTSTON BURLINGTON GROUP

100 First Stamford Place   Phone: 203-978-5200
Stamford, CT 06912   Fax: 203-978-5315
Chm: Joseph C. Farrell
Chief Admin Officer: Frank T. Lennon
Employees: 6,500

Jobs Added Last Year: 200 (+3.2%)

Transportation - air freight & logistics management (Burlington Air Express Inc.), providing customized air freight, ocean forwarding & distribution services to industrial customers worldwide

PRAXAIR, INC.

39 Old Ridgebury Rd.   Phone: 203-837-2000
Danbury, CT 06810-5113   Fax: 203-837-2731
Chm & CEO: H. William Lichtenberger
VP HR: Barbara R. Harris
Employees: 18,222

Jobs Added Last Year: 442 (+2.5%)

Chemicals - #1 supplier of atmospheric & process gases in North & South America; high-performance surface coatings & related services, materials & systems

RAYONIER INC.

1177 Summer St.   Phone: 203-348-7000
Stamford, CT 06905-5529   Fax: 203-964-4335
Chm & CEO: Ronald M. Gross
VP Corp Relations: Jay A. Fredericksen
Employees: 2,900

Jobs Added Last Year: 200 (+7.4%)

Building products - lumber & plywood; specialty pulp products

RAYONIER TIMBERLANDS, L.P.

1177 Summer St.   Phone: 203-348-7000
Stamford, CT 06905-5529   Fax: 203-964-4333
Chm, Pres & CEO: Ronald M. Gross
HR Dir: Ann Sheppard
Employees: 2,900

Jobs Added Last Year: 200 (+7.4%)

Business services - timberland management

SILGAN HOLDINGS INC.

4 Landmark Sq.   Phone: 203-975-7110
Stamford, CT 06901   Fax: 203-975-7902
Chm & Co-CEO: R. Philip Silver
Dir HR: Sharon Budds
Employees: 5,110

Jobs Added Last Year: 1,110 (+27.8%)

Containers - plastic, steel & aluminum

SOUTHERN NEW ENGLAND TELECOMMUNICATIONS CORPORATION

227 Church St.   Phone: 203-771-5200
New Haven, CT 06510   Fax: 203-498-1143
Chm & CEO: Daniel J. Miglio
VP HR: Jean LaVecchia
Employees: 9,070

Jobs Cut Last Year: 727 (-7.4%)

Utility - telephone

SPECIALTY RETAIL GROUP, INC.

1720 Post Road East, Ste. 112   Phone: 203-256-4380
Westport, CT 06880   Fax: 203-256-4375
Chm: Kevin R. Greene
CFO: Steven Glass
Employees: 87

Jobs Added Last Year: 30 (+52.6%)

Retail - specialty educational & developmental toys (Building Blocks); real estate services

THE STANLEY WORKS

1000 Stanley Dr.   Phone: 860-225-5111
New Britain, CT 06053   Fax: 860-827-3895
Chm & CEO: Richard H. Ayers
VP HR: Barbara W. Bennett
Employees: 19,784

Jobs Cut Last Year: 216 (-1.1%)

Tools - hand-held, power & industrial tools; hardware; locks; door systems

STARTER CORPORATION

370 James St.   Phone: 203-781-4000
New Haven, CT 06513   Fax: 203-777-8820
Chm & CEO: David A. Beckerman
Dir HR: Juli Wilhelm
Employees: 1,000

Jobs Added Last Year: 200 (+25.0%)

Apparel

TENNECO INC.

1275 King St.   Phone: 203-863-1000
Greenwich, CT 06831   Fax: 203-863-1134
Chm & CEO: Dana G. Mead
SVP HR: Barry R. Schuman
Employees: 60,000

Jobs Added Last Year: 5,000 (+9.1%)

Diversified operations - auto parts; natural gas transportation & marketing (Tenneco Energy); packaging (Tenneco Packaging); ship design, construction & repair (Newport News Shipbuilding)

TEREX CORPORATION

500 Post Rd. East, Ste. 320
Westport, CT 06880
Pres, CEO & COO: Ronald M. DeFeo
VP HR: Steve Hooper
Employees: 3,600

Phone: 203-222-7170
Fax: 203-222-7976

Jobs Added Last Year: 750 (+26.3%)

Machinery - heavy-duty construction, mining, material-handling & maintenance equipment

TOSCO CORPORATION

72 Cummings Point Rd.
Stamford, CT 06902
Chm, Pres & CEO: Thomas D. O'Malley
VP HR: Wanda Williams
Employees: 4,024

Phone: 203-977-1000
Fax: 203-964-3187

Jobs Added Last Year: 411 (+11.4%)

Oil refining & marketing

TRIDEX CORPORATION

61 Wilton Rd.
Westport, CT 06880
Chm, Pres & CEO: Seth M. Lukash
VP HR: Thomas F. Curtin Jr.
Employees: 422

Phone: 203-226-1144
Fax: 203-226-8806

Jobs Added Last Year: 206 (+95.4%)

Computers - specialty printers, printer mechanisms & data processing terminals

UNION CARBIDE CORPORATION

39 Old Ridgebury Rd.
Danbury, CT 06817-0001
Chm, Pres & CEO: William H. Joyce
VP HR: Malcolm A. Kessinger
Employees: 11,521

Phone: 203-794-2000
Fax: 203-794-4336

Jobs Cut Last Year: 483 (-4.0%)

Chemicals - commodity chemicals such as polyethylene & ethylene glycol

UNIROYAL CHEMICAL CORPORATION

Benson Rd.
Middlebury, CT 06749
Chm, Pres & CEO: Robert J. Mazaika
VP HR: Neil A. Melore
Employees: 2,970

Phone: 203-573-2000
Fax: 203-573-3077

Jobs Added Last Year: 240 (+8.8%)

Chemicals - specialty elastomers, rubber chemicals, crop protection chemicals & additives for the plastics & lubricants industries

UNITED STATES SURGICAL CORP.

150 Glover Ave.
Norwalk, CT 06856
Chm, Pres & CEO: Leon C. Hirsch
Senior Dir HR: David A. Renker
Employees: 6,000

Phone: 203-845-1000
Fax: 203-845-4478

Jobs Added Last Year: 78 (+1.3%)

Medical products - surgical wound management products, including sutures, stapling products & other wound closure products

UNITED TECHNOLOGIES CORP.

One Financial Plaza
Hartford, CT 06101
Pres & CEO: George David
SVP HR & Organization: William L. Bucknall Jr.
Employees: 170,600

Phone: 860-728-7000
Fax: 860-728-7979

Jobs Cut Last Year: 900 (-0.5%)

Diversified operations - elevators (Otis); HVAC equipment (Carrier); electrical auto parts; jet engines (Pratt & Whitney) & military & commercial helicopters (Hamilton Standard, Sikorsky)

UNITED WASTE SYSTEMS, INC.

4 Greenwich Office Park
Greenwich, CT 06830
Chm & CEO: Bradley S. Jacobs
Dir HR: Anna Petersen
Employees: 1,507

Phone: 203-622-3131
Fax: 203-622-6080

Jobs Added Last Year: 289 (+23.7%)

Waste management - solid waste management services

UST INC.

100 W. Putnam Ave.
Greenwich, CT 06830
Chm, Pres & CEO: Vincent A. Gierer Jr.
SVP HR: Richard Kohlberger
Employees: 4,082

Phone: 203-661-1100
Fax: 203-622-3626

Jobs Added Last Year: 265 (+6.9%)

Tobacco - smokeless tobacco products (Copenhagen, Skoal); wine (Stimson Lane, Chateau Ste. Michelle, Columbia Crest); home video distribution

VALUE HEALTH, INC.

22 Waterville Rd.
Avon, CT 06001
Chm, Pres & CEO: Robert E. Patricelli
Office Mgr: Myra Davis
Employees: 6,332

Phone: 860-678-3400
Fax: 860-678-3449

Jobs Added Last Year: 2,132 (+50.8%)

Medical practice management - pharmacy & mental-health-care benefit programs & health-care information services

WITCO CORPORATION

One American Ln.
Greenwich, CT 06831-2559
Chm, Pres & CEO: Gary Cook
VP HR: John Bondur
Employees: 8,161

Phone: 203-552-2000
Fax: 203-552-2870

Jobs Added Last Year: 206 (+2.6%)

Chemicals - specialty chemical & petroleum additives & intermediates

W. R. BERKLEY CORPORATION

165 Mason St., PO Box 2518
Greenwich, CT 06836-2518
Chm, Pres & CEO: William R. Berkley
Asst VP HR: Joseph M. Pennachio
Employees: 2,982

Phone: 203-629-2880
Fax: 203-629-3492

Jobs Added Last Year: 375 (+14.4%)

Insurance - property & casualty, fire, commercial multiperil, inland marine, general liability & automotive insurance

XEROX CORPORATION

800 Long Ridge Rd.
Stamford, CT 06904
Chm & CEO: Paul A. Allaire
VP HR & Quality: Hector J. Motroni
Employees: 85,200

Phone: 203-968-3000
Fax: 203-968-4559

Jobs Cut Last Year: 2,400 (-2.7%)

Office equipment & supplies - document-processing products, including black & white copiers, ink-jet & electrostatic printers, fax products, scanners & PC & workstation software

YALE UNIVERSITY

451 College St.
New Haven, CT 06520
Pres: Richard C. Levin
Assoc VP Admin: Peter Vallone
Employees: 10,000

Phone: 203-432-4771
Fax: 203-432-7891

Jobs Added Last Year: —

Private university offering 60 undergraduate & 61 graduate degree programs

AMERICA SERVICE GROUP INC.

Two Penns Way, Ste. 200
New Castle, DE 19720
Pres & CEO: Scott L. Mercy
VP HR: Anne Novak
Employees: 1,858

Phone: 302-322-8200
Fax: 302-322-0960

Jobs Added Last Year: 359 (+23.9%)

Health care - on-site health programs & outpatient care for correctional facilities & other government agencies

Yahoo — http://www.yahoo.com/Business_and_Economy/Employment

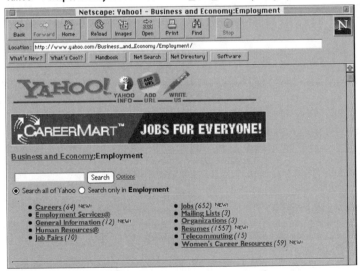

BENEFICIAL CORPORATION

301 N. Walnut St.   Phone: 302-425-2500
Wilmington, DE 19801   Fax: 302-425-2518
Chm & CEO: Finn M. W. Caspersen
Dir HR: Calvin Christopher
Employees: 9,000

Jobs Added Last Year: 500 (+5.9%)

Financial - consumer-finance insurance, credit insurance & other financial services

CABRE CORP

1209 Orange St.   Phone: 302-658-7581
Wilmington, DE 19801   Fax: 302-658-5459
Pres & CEO: Gary W. Havener
No central personnel officer
Employees: 228

Jobs Added Last Year: 83 (+57.2%)

Telecommunications equipment - antenna systems, towers & communications accessories for the US government (Antenna Products Corp.); audio speaker systems (Audile, Inc.)

THE COLUMBIA GAS SYSTEM, INC.

20 Montchanin Rd.   Phone: 302-429-5000
Wilmington, DE 19807-0020   Fax: 302-429-5730
Chm & Pres: O. G. Richard III
VP HR: Dennis P. Geran
Employees: 9,981

Jobs Cut Last Year: 619 (-5.8%)

Utility - natural gas distribution

CONSOL ENERGY INC.

300 Delaware Ave., Ste. 567   Phone: 412-831-4000
Wilmington, DE 19801-1622   Fax: 412-831-4151
Pres & CEO: William G. Karis
VP HR: B. V. Hyler
Employees: 8,743

Jobs Cut Last Year: 996 (-10.2%)

Coal

E. I. DU PONT DE NEMOURS AND CO.

1007 Market St.   Phone: 302-774-1000
Wilmington, DE 19898   Fax: 302-774-7321
Pres & CEO: John A. Krol
VP HR: Daniel W. Burger Jr.
Employees: 105,000

Jobs Cut Last Year: 2,000 (-1.9%)

Diversified operations - oil (Conoco); specialty fibers (Lycra), chemicals & polymers (Teflon); herbicides; plastic films (Mylar); medical products; printing & publishing products

HERCULES INCORPORATED

Hercules Plaza, 1313 N. Market St.   Phone: 302-594-5000
Wilmington, DE 19894-0001   Fax: 302-594-7032
Pres & CEO: R. Keith Elliott
VP HR: Edward V. Carrington
Employees: 7,892

Jobs Cut Last Year: 4,097 (-34.2%)

Chemicals - specialty products, including rosin & hydrocarbon resins for adhesives, polymers for disposable diapers & latex paints & natural gums for food & beverages

MBNA CORPORATION

1100 King St.   Phone: 302-453-9930
Wilmington, DE 19801   Fax: 302-456-2280
Chm & CEO: Alfred Lerner
EVP HR: Ken Pizer
Employees: 13,000

Jobs Added Last Year: 4,000 (+44.4%)

Financial - issuance of premium & standard credit cards (VISA, MasterCard) marketed primarily through membership associations & financial institutions; consumer loans & deposit services

ROLLINS ENVIRONMENTAL SERVICES

One Rollins Plaza, PO Box 2349   Phone: 302-426-2784
Wilmington, DE 19899-2349   Fax: 302-426-2909
Chm & CEO: John W. Rollins
Dir HR: Dave Desch
Employees: 1,855

Jobs Added Last Year: 560 (+43.2%)

Waste management - transportation, treatment & disposal of industrial chemical waste by incineration & other methods; waste processing, recycling & repackaging facilities

ROLLINS TRUCK LEASING CORP.

One Rollins Plaza, PO Box 1791   Phone: 302-426-2700
Wilmington, DE 19899   Fax: 302-426-3599
Chm & CEO: John W. Rollins
Pres & COO: John W. Rollins Jr.
Employees: 3,129

Jobs Added Last Year: 205 (+7.0%)

Leasing - tractors, trailers & trucks

W. L. GORE & ASSOCIATES INC.

555 Papermill Rd.   Phone: 302-738-4880
Newark, DE 19711   Fax: 302-738-7710
Pres & CEO: Robert W. Gore
Mgr Personnel: Barbara Debnam
Employees: 5,860

Jobs Added Last Year: 160 (+2.8%)

Diversified operations - fabrics, electronics, industrial & medical products

DISTRICT OF COLUMBIA

AMERICAN RED CROSS

431 18th St. NW
Washington, DC 20006-5310
Acting Pres: Gene Dyson
VP HR: James E. Thomas III
Employees: 31,000
Phone: 202-737-8300
Fax: 202-639-3711

Jobs Cut Last Year: 1,169 (-3.6%)

Not-for-profit organization providing relief services for victims of natural & man-made disasters

CAPSTAR HOTEL INVESTORS, INC.

1010 Wisconsin Ave. NW
Washington, DC 20007
Chm, Pres & CEO: Paul W. Whetsell
SVP HR: Woody Montgomery
Employees: 5,325
Phone: 202-965-4455
Fax: 202-965-0478

Jobs Added Last Year: —

Hotels & motels - investment in & management of full-service hotels (48 locations) in the US

DANAHER CORPORATION

1250 24th St. NW, Ste. 800
Washington, DC 20037
Pres & CEO: George M. Sherman
VP HR: Dennis Longo
Employees: 10,500
Phone: 202-828-0850
Fax: 202-828-0860

Jobs Added Last Year: 540 (+5.4%)

Tools - hand-held & custom-designed; process & environmental controls; parts for auto & diesel truck engines & wheel-service equipment; environmental controls

FEDERAL PRISON INDUSTRIES, INC.

320 First St. NW
Washington, DC 20534
CEO: Kathleen Hawk
Asst Dir HR: Ron Thompson
Employees: 17,000
Phone: 202-508-8440

Jobs Added Last Year: 800 (+4.9%)

Diversified operations - clothing, furniture, stainless steel counters & signs, electronic wiring & cables produced by prison labor for federal agencies

GEICO CORPORATION

One GEICO Plaza
Washington, DC 20076
Pres & CEO: Olza M. Nicely
Group VP HR: David Schindler
Employees: 8,278
Phone: 301-986-3000
Fax: 301-986-2851

Jobs Added Last Year: 127 (+1.6%)

Insurance - property & casualty

THE GEORGE WASHINGTON UNIVERSITY

2121 I St. NW, 8th Fl.
Washington, DC 20037
Pres: Stephen J. Trachtenberg
Dir HR: Jim Clifford
Employees: 11,000
Phone: 202-994-1000
Fax: 202-994-0654

Jobs Added Last Year: —

University

GEORGETOWN UNIVERSITY INC.

37th & O St. NW
Washington, DC 20057
Pres: Leo J. O'Donovan
Dir HR: Eileen Frenrich
Employees: 12,100
Phone: 202-687-5055
Fax: 202-687-3608

Jobs Added Last Year: —

University

HARMAN INTERNATIONAL IND.

1101 Pennsylvania Ave. NW, Ste. 1010
Washington, DC 20004
Chm & CEO: Sidney Harman
VP HR: Frederick R. Philpott
Employees: 7,929
Phone: 202-393-1101
Fax: 202-393-3064

Jobs Added Last Year: 1,080 (+15.8%)

Audio & video products - audio products for professional, consumer & automotive original equipment manufacturers

MCI COMMUNICATIONS CORP.

1801 Pennsylvania Ave. NW
Washington, DC 20006
Chm & CEO: Bert C. Roberts Jr.
SVP & Chief HR Officer: William D. Wooten
Employees: 50,367
Phone: 202-872-1600
Fax: 202-887-3140

Jobs Added Last Year: 9,367 (+22.8%)

Telecommunications services - long distance service (#2 in US); messaging & Internet services

MEDLANTIC HEALTHCARE GROUP

100 Irving St. NW   Phone: 202-877-7800
Washington, DC 20010   Fax: 202-877-5542
CEO: John P. McDaniel
VP HR: Linda Hitchcock
Employees: 6,500

Jobs Added Last Year: —

Hospitals - network serving the Washington, DC area
(8 hospitals: Washington Hospital Center, National Rehabilitation
Hospital)

NATIONAL RAILROAD PASSENGER CORPORATION

60 Massachusetts Ave. NE   Phone: 202-906-3860
Washington, DC 20002   Fax: 202-906-3865
Chm & CEO: Thomas M. Downs
VP HR & Labor Relations: Dennis Wright
Employees: 24,100

Jobs Added Last Year: 100 (+0.4%)

Transportation - rail (Amtrak)

POTOMAC ELECTRIC POWER COMPANY

1900 Pennsylvania Ave. NW   Phone: 202-872-2456
Washington, DC 20068   Fax: 202-331-6874
Chm & CEO: Edward F. Mitchell
VP HR: Anthony S. Macerollo
Employees: 5,100

Jobs Added Last Year: 237 (+4.9%)

Utility - electric power

SMITHSONIAN INSTITUTION

1000 Jefferson Dr. SW   Phone: 202-357-2700
Washington, DC 20560   Fax: 202-786-2515
Sec: I. Michael Heyman
Acting Dir HR: Susan G. Roehmer
Employees: 6,600

Jobs Cut Last Year: 71 (-1.1%)

Museum

SOFTWARE PUBLISHERS ASSN.

1730 M St. NW, Ste. 700   Phone: 202-452-1600
Washington, DC 20036-4510   Fax: 202-223-8756
Pres: Ken Wasch
HR Mgr: Joan Luedtkey
Employees: 65

Jobs Added Last Year: 15 (+30.0%)

Computers - not-for-profit trade association of publishers,
developers, distributors, retailers & consultants for the computer
software industry

UNITED STATES POSTAL SERVICE

475 L'Enfant Plaza SW   Phone: 202-268-2000
Washington, DC 20260-0010   Fax: 202-268-2392
CEO & Postmaster Gen: Marvin H. Runyon
VP HR: Gail G. Sonnenberg
Employees: 753,384

Jobs Added Last Year: 24,440 (+3.4%)

Transportation - mail delivery

U.S. OFFICE PRODUCTS COMPANY

1440 New York Ave., Ste. 310   Phone: 202-628-9500
Washington , DC 20005   Fax: 202-628-9509
Chm & CEO: Jonathon J. Ledecky
Asst VP HR: Donna Glover
Employees: 1,017

Jobs Added Last Year: 253 (+33.1%)

Wholesale distribution - office products

THE WASHINGTON POST COMPANY

1150 15th St. NW   Phone: 202-334-6000
Washington, DC 20071   Fax: 202-334-1031
Chm & CEO: Donald E. Graham
VP HR: Beverly R. Keil
Employees: 7,010

Jobs Added Last Year: 210 (+3.1%)

Publishing - newspapers & magazines (Newsweek); TV
broadcasting; training centers (Stanley H. Kaplan)

WATSON WYATT WORLDWIDE

601 13th St. NW, Ste. 1000   Phone: 202-508-4600
Washington, DC 20005   Fax: 202-508-4688
Pres & CEO: A. W. "Pete" Smith Jr.
Dir HR: Ralph Christenson
Employees: 4,700

Jobs Added Last Year: 1,200 (+34.3%)

Consulting - specializing in human services, health care & risk
management

FLORIDA

ABLE TELCOM HOLDING CORP.

1601 Forum Place, Ste. 1110
West Palm Beach, FL 33637
Pres & CEO: William J. Mercurio
Dir HR: Daniel L. Osborne
Employees: 930

Phone: 561-688-0400
Fax: 561-688-0455

Jobs Added Last Year: 515 (+124.1%)

Telecommunications services - installation & maintenance services for Latin American & domestic telephone companies; highway signs & traffic control products

ABR INFORMATION SERVICES, INC.

34125 US Hwy. 19 North
Palm Harbor, FL 34684-2116
Chm, Pres & CEO: James E. MacDougald
VP HR: Suzanne MacDougald
Employees: 302

Phone: 813-785-2819
Fax: 813-785-4306

Jobs Added Last Year: 66 (+28.0%)

Medical practice management - health-care benefits administration, information & compliance services

ALAMO RENT A CAR, INC.

110 SE Sixth St.
Fort Lauderdale, FL 33301
VC & CEO: D. Keith Cobb
Exec Dir HR Dev: Connie Hoffmann
Employees: 7,000

Phone: 954-522-0000
Fax: 954-468-2162

Jobs Added Last Year: 0

Leasing - auto rental

ALL AMERICAN SEMICONDUCTOR, INC.

16115 NW 52nd Ave.
Miami, FL 33014
Chm & CEO: Paul Goldberg
HR Mgr: Denise Topfer
Employees: 571

Phone: 305-621-8282
Fax: 305-620-7831

Jobs Added Last Year: 231 (+67.9%)

Electrical components - wholesale semiconductors

AMERICAN BANKERS INSURANCE GROUP

11222 Quail Roost Dr.
Miami, FL 33157-6596
VC, Pres & CEO: Gerald N. Gaston
SVP, ABLAC Subsidiary: Phil Sharkey
Employees: 2,498

Phone: 305-253-2244
Fax: 305-252-6987

Jobs Added Last Year: 398 (+19.0%)

Insurance - life, unemployment, accident, health & homeowners

A+ NETWORK, INC.

40 S. Palafox St.
Pensacola, FL 32501
Pres & CEO: Charles A. Emling III
Dir HR: Earl Posey
Employees: 1,264

Phone: 904-432-4555
Fax: 904-432-0308

Jobs Added Last Year: 365 (+40.6%)

Telecommunications services - wireless mobile communications (paging) & telemessaging services in small & medium-sized markets in the southeastern US

BARNETT BANKS, INC.

50 N. Laura St.
Jacksonville, FL 32202-3638
Chm & CEO: Charles E. Rice
Chief HR Exec: Paul T. Kerins
Employees: 20,175

Phone: 904-791-7720
Fax: 904-791-7166

Jobs Added Last Year: 1,246 (+6.6%)

Banks - Southeast

BCT INTERNATIONAL, INC.

3000 NE 30th Place, 5th Fl.
Fort Lauderdale, FL 33306-1957
Chm & CEO: William A. Wilkerson
HR Mgr: Joann Gandalfo
Employees: 136

Phone: 954-563-1224
Fax: 954-565-0742

Jobs Added Last Year: 67 (+97.1%)

Printing - business cards & personalized products (#1 wholesale printing chain worldwide); trade thermography

BE AEROSPACE, INC.

1400 Corporate Center Way
Wellington, FL 33414
VC & CEO: Robert J. Khoury
Dir HR: Larry Spence
Employees: 2,714

Phone: 561-791-5000
Fax: 561-791-7900

Jobs Added Last Year: 914 (+50.8%)

Aerospace - aircraft cabin interior products (#1 worldwide), including seating, entertainment & service systems, galley structures & food & beverage preparation & storage equipment

BIG ENTERTAINMENT, INC.

2255 Glades Rd., Ste. 237 W.
Boca Raton, FL 33431-7383
Chm & CEO: Mitchell Rubenstein
Dir HR: Beth Krumper
Employees: 150

Phone: 561-998-8000
Fax: 561-998-2974

Jobs Added Last Year: 69 (+85.2%)

Publishing - science fiction comic books; online comics

 An in-depth profile of this company is available to subscribers on Hoover's Online at www.hoovers.com.

127

BLOCKBUSTER ENTERTAINMENT

One Blockbuster Plaza, 200 S. Andrews Ave. Phone: 954-832-3000
Fort Lauderdale, FL 33301-1860   Fax: 954-832-4086
Chm & CEO: William R. Fields
Dir HR: H. Scott Barrett
Employees: 45,000
Jobs Added Last Year: 4,600 (+11.4%)

Retail - video rentals; TV & film production (Spelling, Republic Pictures); software development (Virgin Interactive); children's entertainment (50.1% of Discovery Zone)

BREED TECHNOLOGIES, INC.

5300 Old Tampa Hwy.   Phone: 941-668-6000
Lakeland, FL 33807-3050   Fax: 941-668-6007
Chm & CEO: Allen K. Breed
SVP HR: Thomas T. O'Conner
Employees: 5,000
Jobs Added Last Year: 1,800 (+56.3%)

Automotive & trucking - air bags & crash sensors

CARNIVAL CORPORATION

Carnival Place, 3655 NW 87th Ave.   Phone: 305-599-2600
Miami, FL 33178-2428   Fax: 305-471-4700
Chm & CEO: M. Micky Arison
Dir HR: Susan S. Herrmann
Employees: 15,280
Jobs Cut Last Year: 1,970 (-11.4%)

Travel services - multiple-night cruise line

CHECKERS DRIVE-IN RESTAURANTS

600 Cleveland St., 8th Fl.   Phone: 813-441-3500
Clearwater, FL 34615   Fax: 813-443-7047
Pres & CEO: Albert J. DiMarco Jr.
VP HR: Anthony L. Austin
Employees: 6,676
Jobs Cut Last Year: 1,371 (-17.0%)

Retail - drive-through fast-food restaurants

CLAIRE'S STORES, INC.

3 SW 129th Ave.   Phone: 954-433-3900
Pembroke Pines, FL 33027   Fax: 954-433-3999
Chm, Pres & CEO: Rowland Schaefer
Exec Dir HR: Tina Perkins
Employees: 6,650
Jobs Added Last Year: 1,150 (+20.9%)

Retail - women's fashion accessories (Claire's Boutiques, Topkapi, Dara Michelle)

CLINICORP, INC.

1601 Belvedere Rd., Ste. 500 East   Phone: 561-684-2225
West Palm Beach, FL 33406   Fax: 561-689-2225
Pres & COO: Gerard A. Herlihy
No central personnel officer
Employees: 160
Jobs Added Last Year: 44 (+37.9%)

Medical practice management - chiropractic & integrated health care clinics

Career.com — http://www.career.com/

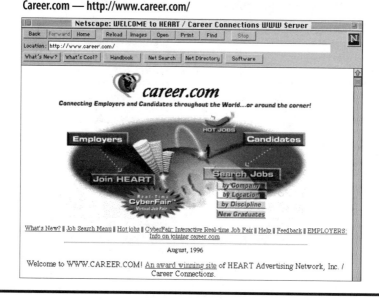

COMMUNITY CARE OF AMERICA, INC.

3050 N. Horseshoe Dr., Ste. 260
Naples, FL 33942
Pres & CEO: Gary W. Singleton
Dir HR: Bonnie Severs
Employees: 5,638

Phone: 941-435-0085
Fax: 941-435-0087

Jobs Added Last Year: 1,778 (+46.1%)

Medical practice management - local health care network development in medically underserved rural communities

COULTER CORPORATION

11800 SW 147th Ave.
Miami, FL 33196
Chm: Wallace Coulter
Dir HR: James Ring
Employees: 5,000

Phone: 305-380-3800
Fax: 305-380-8312

Jobs Added Last Year: 0

Medical products - medical equipment & electronic equipment

DANKA BUSINESS SYSTEMS PLC

11201 Danka Circle North
St. Petersburg, FL 33716
CEO: Daniel M. Doyle
VP HR: Cindy Durning
Employees: 10,500

Phone: 813-576-6003
Fax: 813-579-8521

Jobs Added Last Year: 3,420 (+48.3%)

Office equipment - photocopiers, facsimile equipment & related services, parts & supplies (Konica, Minolta, Sharp, Canon)

DARDEN RESTAURANTS, INC.

5900 Lake Ellenor Dr.
Orlando, FL 32809
Chm & CEO: Joe R. Lee
SVP Personnel: Frank E. Ruble
Employees: 124,730

Phone: 407-245-4000
Fax: 407-245-5135

Jobs Added Last Year: 9,212 (+8.0%)

Retail - casual dining restaurants (#1 worldwide: Olive Garden, Red Lobster)

DISCOUNT AUTO PARTS, INC.

4900 Frontage Rd. South
Lakeland, FL 33801
Pres & CEO: Peter J. Fontaine
Dir HR: Bobbie Bricker
Employees: 2,825

Phone: 941-687-9226
Fax: 941-284-2063

Jobs Added Last Year: 653 (+30.1%)

Auto parts - retail automotive replacement parts, maintenance items & accessories

ECKERD CORPORATION

8333 Bryan Dairy Rd.
Largo, FL 34647
Pres, CEO & COO: Francis A. Newman
EVP Admin & Sec: James M. Santo
Employees: 44,600

Phone: 813-399-6000
Fax: 813-399-6409

Jobs Added Last Year: 1,900 (+4.4%)

Retail - drugstores & photofinishing services

EXPERT SOFTWARE, INC.

800 Douglas Rd., Ste. 750
Coral Gables, FL 33134-3128
CEO & Sec: Kenneth P. Currier
Dir HR: Sara Johnson
Employees: 147

Phone: 305-567-9990
Fax: 305-443-0786

Jobs Added Last Year: 64 (+77.1%)

Computers - personal, business productivity & hobbyist software (Home Design 3D, Diet, Forms, Casino)

FLORIDA PROGRESS CORPORATION

Barnett Tower, One Progress Plaza
St. Petersburg, FL 33701-8028
Chm & CEO: Jack B. Critchfield
Dir HR: Patricia Blizzard
Employees: 7,174

Phone: 813-824-6400
Fax: 813-824-6751

Jobs Added Last Year: 1,645 (+29.8%)

Utility - electric power; coal mining & transportation; life insurance (Mid-Continent)

FPL GROUP, INC.

700 Universe Blvd.
Juno Beach, FL 33408
Chm, Pres & CEO: James L. Broadhead
VP HR: Lawrence J. Kelleher
Employees: 11,400

Phone: 561-694-4000
Fax: 561-694-6385

Jobs Cut Last Year: 735 (-6.1%)

Utility - electric power; cable TV services; citrus groves

GALAXY FOODS COMPANY

2441 Viscount Row
Orlando, FL 32809
Chm, Pres & CEO: Angelo S. Morini
HR Mgr: Chris Carlile
Employees: 51

Phone: 407-855-5500
Fax: 407-855-7485

Jobs Added Last Year: 21 (+70.0%)

Food - cholesterol- & lactose-free cheese substitutes & cheese-related products

An in-depth profile of this company is available to subscribers on Hoover's Online at www.hoovers.com.

129

GOLDFIELD CORPORATION

100 Rialto Place, Ste. 500
Melbourne, FL 32901
Chm, Pres & CEO: John H. Sottile
No central personnel officer
Employees: 118

Phone: 407-724-1700
Fax: 407-724-1703

Jobs Added Last Year: 29 (+32.6%)

Construction - electrical facilities for utilities & industrial clients; mineral & metal mines

GREENWICH AIR SERVICES, INC.

4590 NW 36th St., PO Box 522187
Miami, FL 33152
Chm & CEO: Eugene P. Conese
VP HR: William Skelley
Employees: 1,196

Phone: 305-526-7000
Fax: 305-526-7005

Jobs Added Last Year: 406 (+51.4%)

Transportation - airplane engine repair & rebuilding services

HARRIS CORPORATION

1025 W. NASA Blvd.
Melbourne, FL 32919
Chm, Pres & CEO: Phillip W. Farmer
VP HR: Nick E. Heldreth
Employees: 26,600

Phone: 407-727-9100
Fax: 407-727-9344

Jobs Cut Last Year: 1,600 (-5.7%)

Diversified operations - telecommunications equipment; semiconductors; electronic systems; office equipment

HARVARD INDUSTRIES, INC.

2502 N. Rocky Point Dr., Ste. 960
Tampa, FL 33607-1421
Chm, Pres & CEO: Vincent J. Naimoli
VP HR: James Luci
Employees: 6,515

Phone: 813-288-5000
Fax: 813-281-0851

Jobs Added Last Year: 896 (+15.9%)

Diversified operations - automotive parts; aerospace fasteners; furniture

HEALTH MANAGEMENT ASSOCIATES

5811 Pelican Bay Blvd., Ste. 500
Naples, FL 33963-2710
Chm, Pres & CEO: William J. Schoen
Dir HR: Fred Prow
Employees: 7,000

Phone: 941-598-3131
Fax: 941-597-5794

Jobs Added Last Year: 1,700 (+32.1%)

Hospitals - acute care hospitals

HEALTHPLAN SERVICES CORPORATION

3501 Frontage Rd.
Tampa, FL 33607
Pres & CEO: James K. Murray Jr.
Personnel Supervisor: Renee Renton
Employees: 940

Phone: 813-289-1000
Fax: 813-289-7937

Jobs Added Last Year: 233 (+33.0%)

Medical practice management - managed-health-care services

HUGHES SUPPLY, INC.

20 N. Orange Ave., Ste. 200
Orlando, FL 32801
CEO: David H. Hughes
HR Mgr: Jon Rago
Employees: 3,350

Phone: 407-841-4755
Fax: 407-648-4606

Jobs Added Last Year: 550 (+19.6%)

Building products - wholesale construction, electrical & mechanical products

INTERMEDIA COMMUNICATIONS, INC.

3625 Queen Palm Dr.
Tampa, FL 33619
Chm, Pres & CEO: David C. Ruberg
SVP HR: Robert A. Ruh
Employees: 287

Phone: 813-621-0011
Fax: 813-620-3195

Jobs Added Last Year: 137 (+91.3%)

Telecommunications services - alternative access local telephone services

INTERNATIONAL ASSETS HOLDING CORPORATION

201 W. Canton Ave., Ste. 100
Winter Park, FL 32789
Chm & CEO: Diego J. Veitia
Ops Mgr: Sheri Cuff
Employees: 72

Phone: 407-629-1400
Fax: 407-629-2470

Jobs Added Last Year: 20 (+38.5%)

Financial - securities brokerage firm

INTIME SYSTEMS INTERNATIONAL, INC.

1655 Palm Beach Blvd., Ste. 200
West Palm Beach, FL 33401
Pres & CEO: William E. Berry
HR Dir: Lynn Bentley
Employees: 83

Phone: 561-478-0022
Fax: 561-689-4759

Jobs Added Last Year: 39 (+88.6%)

Computers - time- & attendance-management software; consulting services

IVAX CORPORATION

4400 Biscayne Blvd.
Miami, FL 33137-3227
Chm & CEO: Phillip Frost
Dir HR: Marsha Buckner
Employees: 7,893
Jobs Cut Last Year: 292 (-3.6%)

Phone: 305-575-6000
Fax: 305-575-6298

Medical products - diagnostic devices, personal-care products & pharmaceuticals

JABIL CIRCUIT, INC.

10800 Roosevelt Blvd.
St. Petersburg, FL 33716
Chm & CEO: William D. Morean
Dir HR: Fred McCoy
Employees: 2,661
Jobs Added Last Year: 1,145 (+75.5%)

Phone: 813-577-9749
Fax: 813-579-8529

Electrical components - electronic circuit boards & systems for OEMs in the international PC, computer peripheral, communications & automotive markets

KIMMINS CORPORATION

1501 Second Ave.
Tampa, FL 33605
Pres: Francis M. Williams
No central personnel officer
Employees: 1,000
Jobs Added Last Year: 275 (+37.9%)

Phone: 813-248-3878
Fax: 813-247-0180

Waste management - asbestos abatement, solid waste management & environmental contracting services

KNIGHT-RIDDER, INC.

One Herald Plaza
Miami, FL 33132-1693
Chm & CEO: P. Anthony Ridder
VP HR: Mary Jean Connors
Employees: 22,800
Jobs Added Last Year: 1,800 (+8.6%)

Phone: 305-376-3800
Fax: 305-376-3828

Publishing - newspapers (28, including the Philadelphia Inquirer); electronic news-retrieval & information services & financial information services

KREISLER MANUFACTURING CORPORATION

5960 Central Ave., Ste. H
St. Petersburg, FL 33707
Chm, Pres & CFO: Edward L. Stern
VP HR: Edward A. Stern
Employees: 75
Jobs Added Last Year: 35 (+87.5%)

Phone: 813-347-1144
Fax: 813-347-1155

Aerospace - fuel manifolds & air, oil & de-icer lines

LA-MAN CORPORATION

2180 W. State Route 434
Longwood, FL 32779
Pres & CEO: J. William Brandner
VP, Treas & CFO: Otto J. Nicols
Employees: 153
Jobs Added Last Year: 93 (+155.0%)

Phone: 407-865-5995
Fax: 407-865-7740

Products which reduce or eliminate water or condensate problems in compressed air lines

LEVITZ FURNITURE INCORPORATED

6111 Broken Sound Pkwy. NW
Boca Raton, FL 33487-2799
Chm & CEO: Michael Bozic
VP HR: Nicholas S. Masullo
Employees: 6,757
Jobs Added Last Year: 481 (+7.7%)

Phone: 561-994-6006
Fax: 561-998-5615

Retail - home furnishings

LINCARE HOLDINGS INC.

19337 US 19 North, Ste. 500
Clearwater, FL 34624
Pres & CEO: James T. Kelly
Dir Emp Relations: Byron R. Krogen
Employees: 2,200
Jobs Added Last Year: 400 (+22.2%)

Phone: 813-530-7700
Fax: 813-532-9692

Medical services - respiratory therapy services

MED/WASTE, INC.

3890 N.W. 132nd St., Ste. K
Opa Locka, FL 33054
Pres & CEO: Daniel A. Stauber
Office Mgr: Barbara Ferrino
Employees: 98
Jobs Added Last Year: 64 (+188.2%)

Phone: 305-688-3931
Fax: 305-688-0661

Waste management - medical waste management & disposal

MIAMI SUBS CORPORATION

6300 NW 31st Ave.
Fort Lauderdale, FL 33309
Chm, Pres & CEO: Thomas J. Russo
Dir HR: R. Steve Sparling
Employees: 863
Jobs Added Last Year: 270 (+45.5%)

Phone: 954-973-0000
Fax: 954-973-7616

Retail - restaurants

 An in-depth profile of this company is available to subscribers on Hoover's Online at www.hoovers.com.

131

NABI

5800 Park of Commerce Blvd. NW
Boca Raton, FL 33487
Chm & CEO: David J. Gury
Dir HR: Bill Vandervalk
Employees: 2,073

Phone: 561-989-5800
Fax: 561-989-5801

Jobs Added Last Year: 385 (+22.8%)

Biomedical & genetic products - plasma & plasma-based products for diagnostic & therapeutic applications

NAL FINANCIAL GROUP

500 Cypress Creek Rd. West, Ste. 590
Fort Lauderdale, FL 33309
Chm & CEO: Robert R. Bartolini
Dir HR: Donna Lea
Employees: 200

Phone: 954-938-8200
Fax: 305-938-8209

Jobs Added Last Year: 128 (+177.8%)

Financial - prime & sub-prime auto & consumer loans & leases

NOVEN PHARMACEUTICALS, INC.

11960 SW 144th St.
Miami, FL 33186
Chm & Pres: Steven Sablotsky
Mgr HR: Leona Bodie
Employees: 226

Phone: 305-253-5099
Fax: 305-251-1887

Jobs Added Last Year: 121 (+115.2%)

Medical products - transdermal drug-delivery systems

OFFICE DEPOT, INC.

2200 Old Germantown Rd.
Delray Beach, FL 33445
Chm, Pres, CEO & COO: David I. Fuente
EVP HR: F. Terry Bean
Employees: 31,000

Phone: 561-278-4800
Fax: 561-265-4403

Jobs Added Last Year: 5,000 (+19.2%)

Retail - office equipment & supplies

OUTBACK STEAKHOUSE, INC.

550 N. Reo St., Ste. 200
Tampa, FL 33609
Chm & CEO: Chris T. Sullivan
VP Training & Dev: Trudy I. Cooper
Employees: 16,000

Phone: 813-282-1225
Fax: 813-282-1209

Jobs Added Last Year: 5,500 (+52.4%)

Retail - restaurants (Outback Steakhouse, Carrabba's Italian Grill)

PALMER WIRELESS, INC.

12800 University Dr., Ste. 500
Fort Myers, FL 33907-5337
Pres & CEO: William J. Ryan
VP HR: Donna Gapen
Employees: 521

Phone: 941-433-4350
Fax: 941-433-8213

Jobs Added Last Year: 126 (+31.9%)

Telecommunications equipment - cellular telephone systems & services in the southeastern US

THE PANDA PROJECT, INC.

5201 Congress Ave., Ste. C-100
Boca Raton, FL 33487
Chm, Pres & CEO: Stanford W. Crane Jr.
Office Mgr: Diane Charpentier
Employees: 139

Phone: 561-994-2300
Fax: 561-994-0191

Jobs Added Last Year: 79 (+131.7%)

Electrical components - chip packages which house & protect semiconductor components (Spider Pack)

PARKERVISION, INC.

8493 Baymeadows Way
Jacksonville, FL 32256
Chm, Pres & CEO: Jeffrey Parker
No central personnel officer
Employees: 78

Phone: 904-737-1367
Fax: 904-731-0958

Jobs Added Last Year: 27 (+52.9%)

Video equipment - automated video camera control system (CameraMan)

PHOTRONICS, INC.

1061 E. Indiantown Rd.
Jupiter, FL 33477
Chm & CEO: Constantine S. Macricostas
SVP, Gen Counsel & Sec: Jeffrey P. Moonan
Employees: 684

Phone: 561-747-4163
Fax: 561-747-1432

Jobs Added Last Year: 259 (+60.9%)

Electrical components - photomasks (quartz plates) used to manufacture semiconductor wafers

PLANET HOLLYWOOD INTERNATIONAL, INC.

7380 Sand Lake Rd., Ste. 600
Orlando, FL 32819
Pres: Robert Earl
Dir HR: Lissa Bobet
Employees: 6,500

Phone: 407-363-7827
Fax: 407-363-4862

Jobs Added Last Year: —

Retail - theme restaurants (Planet Hollywood, Official All-Star Cafe)

PUBLIX SUPER MARKETS, INC.

1936 George Jenkins Blvd.
Lakeland, FL 33801-3760
Chm & CEO: Howard M. Jenkins
VP HR: James H. Rhodes
Employees: 95,000

Phone: 941-688-1188
Fax: 941-284-5532

Jobs Added Last Year: 5,000 (+5.6%)

Retail - supermarkets in Florida, Georgia & South Carolina
(over 500 units)

PUEBLO XTRA INTERNATIONAL, INC.

1300 NW 22nd Ave.
Pompano Beach, FL 33069
Pres & CEO: William T. Keon III
Dir HR & Dir Emp Benefits: Ron Ochsenwald
Employees: 11,000

Phone: 954-977-2500
Fax: 954-979-5770

Jobs Added Last Year: 400 (+3.8%)

Retail - supermarkets in Florida & Puerto Rico

REPUBLIC INDUSTRIES, INC.

200 E. Las Olas Blvd., Ste. 1400
Fort Lauderdale, FL 33301
Chm & CEO: H. Wayne Huizenga
Dir Admin: Philip Troskey
Employees: 4,090

Phone: 954-761-8333
Fax: 954-779-3884

Jobs Added Last Year: 3,692 (+927.6%)

Waste management - solid waste disposal, collection & recycling;
electronic security systems for commercial & residential use; used
car sales (AutoNation USA)

ROYCE LABORATORIES, INC.

5350 NW 165th St.
Miami, FL 33014
Chm & CEO: Patrick J. McEnany
HR Mgr: Paula Mayo
Employees: 131

Phone: 305-624-1500
Fax: 305-621-8416

Jobs Added Last Year: 48 (+57.8%)

Drugs - generic

RYDER SYSTEM, INC.

3600 NW 82nd Ave.
Miami, FL 33166
Chm, Pres & CEO: M. Anthony Burns
EVP HR & Admin: Thomas E. McKinnon
Employees: 44,503

Phone: 305-593-3726
Fax: 305-593-3336

Jobs Added Last Year: 1,408 (+3.3%)

Leasing - trucks, tractors & trailers; logistics services; student
transportation; automobile & light truck transportation

ST. JOE CORP.

1650 Prudential Dr., Ste. 400
Jacksonville, FL 32207
Pres: Robert E. Nedley
VP Admin: Edward Brownlie
Employees: 5,000

Phone: 904-396-6600
Fax: 904-396-4042

Jobs Added Last Year: 100 (+2.0%)

Real estate operations - Florida's largest private property owner

Recruiters Online Network — http://www.ipa.com/

An in-depth profile of this company is available
to subscribers on Hoover's Online at www.hoovers.com.

133

SAMSONITE CORPORATION

40301 Fisher Island Dr.   Phone: 305-532-2426
Fisher Island, FL 33109   Fax: 305-532-2789
Chm, Pres & CEO: Richard R. Nicolosi
VP HR: Kim Henry
Employees: 7,100
Jobs Added Last Year: 600 (+9.2%)

Diversified operations - luggage (American Tourister, Lark, Samsonite), water treatment (Culligan) & apparel (McGregor, Fashion 500)

SENSORMATIC ELECTRONICS CORP.

500 NW 12th Ave.   Phone: 954-420-2000
Deerfield Beach, FL 33442   Fax: 954-420-2593
Chm & CEO: Ronald G. Assaf
Dir HR: Larry Smith
Employees: 7,500
Jobs Added Last Year: 2,000 (+36.4%)

Protection - electronic article-surveillance products & systems for retail & industrial applications

SHERIDAN HEALTHCARE, INC.

4651 Sheridan St., Ste. 400   Phone: 954-987-5822
Hollywood, FL 33021   Fax: 954-983-4531
Chm, Pres & CEO: Mitchell Eisenberg
Dir HR: Karen Winselman
Employees: 600
Jobs Added Last Year: 255 (+73.9%)

Medical practice management

SPORTSLINE USA, INC.

6340 NW Fifth Way   Phone: 954-351-2120
Fort Lauderdale, FL 33309   Fax: 954-351-9175
Chm, Pres & CEO: Michael Levy
Dir HR: Gary van Arsdale
Employees: 79
Jobs Added Last Year: 54 (+216.0%)

Computers - online interactive sports information service

STEIN MART, INC.

1200 Riverplace Blvd.   Phone: 904-346-1500
Jacksonville, FL 32207   Fax: 904-346-1280
Chm & CEO: Jay Stein
SVP HR: D. Hunt Hawkins
Employees: 6,300
Jobs Added Last Year: 1,000 (+18.9%)

Retail - apparel & shoes

SUNBEAM CORPORATION

2100 New River Center, 200 E. Las Olas Blvd. Phone: 954-767-2100
Fort Lauderdale, FL 33301   Fax: 954-767-2107
Chm & CEO: Albert J. Dunlap
EVP HR: James D. Wilson
Employees: 12,000
Jobs Added Last Year: 0

Appliances - warming blankets, bath scales, blood-pressure monitors, small kitchen appliances; outdoor furniture

SUPREME INTERNATIONAL CORPORATION

7945 NW 48th St.   Phone: 305-592-2830
Miami, FL 33166   Fax: 305-594-2307
Chm & CEO: George Feldenkreis
Dir HR: Juan L. Pujol
Employees: 260
Jobs Added Last Year: 120 (+85.7%)

Apparel - men's & boys' sportswear, primarily sport shirts (Natural Issue, Corsa, Monte Carlo, Career Club) & dress pants (Feldini, Natural Issue)

TECH DATA CORPORATION

5350 Tech Data Dr.   Phone: 813-539-7429
Clearwater, FL 34620-3134   Fax: 813-538-7050
Chm & CEO: Steven A. Raymund
VP HR: Lawrence W. Hamilton
Employees: 2,625
Jobs Added Last Year: 360 (+15.9%)

Retail - wholesale networking, mass storage, peripherals, hardware & software products for value-added resellers & computer retailers in the US, Canada, Latin America & the Caribbean

TECHFORCE CORPORATION

15950 Bay Vista Dr.   Phone: 813-532-3600
Clearwater, FL 34620   Fax: 813-532-3980
CEO: John A. Koehler
Dir HR: Lynn Henderson
Employees: 441
Jobs Added Last Year: 107 (+32.0%)

Computers - integrated network support

TECO ENERGY, INC.

TECO Plaza, 702 N. Franklin St.   Phone: 813-228-4111
Tampa, FL 33602   Fax: 813-228-1670
Chm, Pres & CEO: Timothy L. Guzzle
VP HR: Roger A. Dunn
Employees: 9,401
Jobs Added Last Year: 595 (+6.8%)

Utility - electric power

THERMO REMEDIATION INC.

1964 S. Orange Blossom Trail
Apopka, FL 32703
Chm & CEO: John P. Appleton
Dir HR: Fred Florio
Employees: 718

Phone: 617-622-1000
Fax: 617-622-1207

Jobs Added Last Year: 603 (+524.3%)

Pollution control equipment & services - soil-remediati
on services

TPI ENTERPRISES, INC.

777 S. Flagler Dr., Phillips Point East Tower, Ste. 909   Phone: 561-835-8888
West Palm Beach, FL 33401   Fax: 561-835-4982
Pres & CEO: J. Gary Sharp
Dir HR: Julie Collins
Employees: 9,870

Jobs Cut Last Year: 430 (-4.2%)

Retail - family-style (Shoney's: 187 franchises) & seafood
restaurants (Captain D's: 69 franchises)

TRANSCOR WASTE SERVICES, INC.

1502 Second Ave. East
Tampa, FL 33605
Chm & Pres : Francis M. Williams
No central personnel officer
Employees: 440

Phone: 813-248-3878
Fax: 813-247-0198

Jobs Added Last Year: 190 (+76.0%)

Waste management - solid waste disposal

TRANSMEDIA NETWORK INC.

11900 Biscayne Blvd.
North Miami, FL 33181
Chm, Pres & CEO: Melvin Chasen
VP Ops: Kathryn Ferara
Employees: 119

Phone: 305-892-3300
Fax: 305-892-3317

Jobs Added Last Year: 27 (+29.3%)

Business services - private restaurant charge card (The
Restaurant Card)

TUPPERWARE CORPORATION

14901 S. Orange Blossom Trail
Orlando, FL 32837
Chm & CEO: Warren L. Batts
SVP HR: Carol A. Kiryluk
Employees: 6,600

Phone: 407-826-5050
Fax: 407-826-8829

Jobs Added Last Year: —

Housewares - food storage containers & other consumer
products

THE UNIVERSITY OF FLORIDA

226 Tigert Hall
Gainesville, FL 32611
Pres: John V. Lombardi
Dir HR: Jack Hidler
Employees: 21,500

Phone: 352-392-3261
Fax: 352-392-6278

Jobs Added Last Year: —

University

U.S. DIAGNOSTIC LABS INC.

777 S. Flagler Dr., Ste. 1104 West
West Palm Beach, FL 33401
Pres: Robert D. Burke
HR Mgr: Elise Nulman
Employees: 350

Phone: 407-832-0006
Fax: 407-833-8391

Jobs Added Last Year: 170 (+94.4%)

Medical services - diagnostic-imaging facilities & clinical
laboratories

VECTOR AEROMOTIVE CORP.

7601 Centurion Pkwy.
Jacksonville, FL 32256
Pres & CEO: D. Peter Rose
CFO & Treas: Dario Navarro
Employees: 86

Phone: 904-645-0505
Fax: 904-646-5947

Jobs Added Last Year: 69 (+405.9%)

Automotive manufacturing - sports cars (Vector W2, Vector
W2-A, Avtech SC)

VIDEO JUKEBOX NETWORK, INC.

1221 Collins Ave.
Miami Beach, FL 33139
Pres & CEO: Alan R. McGlade
CFO & Chief Administrative Officer: Luann M. Hoffman
Employees: 108

Phone: 305-674-5000
Fax: 305-674-4900

Jobs Added Last Year: 29 (+36.7%)

TV production & programming - interactive music-video TV
programming (The Box)

WACKENHUT CORPORATION

4200 Wackenhut Dr.
Palm Beach Gardens, FL 33140-4243
Chm & CEO: George R. Wackenhut
VP HR: Sandra Nusbaum
Employees: 39,000

Phone: 561-622-5656
Fax: 561-691-6736

Jobs Added Last Year: —

Protection - security guard services, correctional facilities
management, integrated security programs, job corps facilities
management & nuclear power plant security

An in-depth profile of this company is available
to subscribers on Hoover's Online at www.hoovers.com.

135

WALTER INDUSTRIES, INC.

1500 N. Dale Mabry Hwy., PO Box 31601   Phone: 813-871-4811
Tampa, FL 33631-3601   Fax: 813-871-4430
Chm & CEO: Kenneth E. Hyatt
VP HR & PR: David L. Townsend
Employees: 7,900
Jobs Added Last Year: 200 (+2.6%)

Diversified operations – home building & financing, natural resources & industrial manufacturing

WINDMERE CORPORATION

5980 Miami Lakes Dr.   Phone: 305-362-2611
Miami Lakes, FL 33014   Fax: 305-364-0635
Chm, Pres & CEO: David M. Friedson
Dir HR: David Warren
Employees: 10,250
Jobs Cut Last Year: 1,810 (-15.0%)

Appliances - personal care products (Durable Electrical Metal Factory) including can openers, fans, hair dryers, curling irons (Hot 'n Steamy, Mirror Go Lightly, Jumbo Curl, Clothes Shaver)

WINN-DIXIE STORES, INC.

5050 Edgewood Ct.   Phone: 904-783-5000
Jacksonville, FL 32254-3699   Fax: 904-783-5294
Chm & CEO: A. Dano Davis
VP & Dir Assoc Relations & HR: L. H. May
Employees: 123,000
Jobs Added Last Year: 11,000 (+9.8%)

Retail - supermarkets

WORLD ACCESS INC.

4501 Vineland Rd.   Phone: 407-843-7031
Orlando, FL 32811-7375   Fax: 407-841-0942
Chm & CEO: Steven A. Odom
HR Mgr: DeAna Mullins-Gudino
Employees: 235
Jobs Added Last Year: 52 (+28.4%)

Telecommunications services - circuit board repair, pay telephone refurbishment & electronic manufacturing services such as design & testing of circuit board assemblies & subsystems

AGCO CORPORATION

4830 River Green Pkwy.   Phone: 770-813-9200
Duluth, GA 30136   Fax: 770-813-6118
Chm, Pres & CEO: Robert J. Ratliff
Dir HR: John Broadwell
Employees: 5,548
Jobs Cut Last Year: 241 (-4.2%)

Machinery - farm, including combines, hay tools, tractors & implements

ALUMAX INC.

5655 Peachtree Pkwy.   Phone: 770-246-6600
Norcross, GA 30092-2812   Fax: 770-246-6756
Chm & CEO: Allen Born
VP HR & Admin: Gary D. McDowell
Employees: 14,000
Jobs Added Last Year: 0

Mining - aluminum

AMERICAN BUSINESS PRODUCTS, INC.

2100 Riveredge Pkwy., Ste. 1200   Phone: 770-953-8300
Atlanta, GA 30328   Fax: 770-952-2343
Pres & CEO: Robert W. Gundeck
No central personnel officer
Employees: 4,452
Jobs Added Last Year: 300 (+7.2%)

Paper - business forms, special mailers, file folders, labels, brochures & envelopes

AMERICAN CANCER SOCIETY, INC.

1599 Clifton Rd. NE   Phone: 404-329-7250
Atlanta, GA 30329-4251   Fax: 404-325-0230
CEO: John R. Seffrin
Natl VP HR: Aurelia C. Stanley
Employees: 4,656
Jobs Added Last Year: 556 (+13.6%)

Charitable organization

AMERICAN FAMILY RESTAURANTS, INC.

300 Northwoods Pkwy., Ste. 235   Phone: 770-729-1300
Norcross, GA 30071   Fax: 770-729-0772
Chm, Pres & CEO: Jeffrey D. Miller
Dir HR: Don Kirkham
Employees: 4,650
Jobs Added Last Year: 450 (+10.7%)

Retail - restaurants (Denny's, Ruby's Country Store & Bar-B-Q)

APPLE SOUTH, INC.

Hancock at Washington
Madison, GA 30650
Chm & CEO: Thomas E. DuPree Jr.
SVP HR & Sec: John G. McLeod Jr.
Employees: 17,000

Phone: 706-342-4552
Fax: 706-342-4057

Jobs Added Last Year: 8,600 (+102.4%)

Retail - restaurants (Applebee's, Hardees, Gianni's Little Italy, Tomato Rumba's)

AUTOMOBILE PROTECTION CORP. - APCO

15 Dunwoody Park Dr., Ste. 100
Atlanta, GA 30338
Pres & CEO: Larry I. Dorfman
Dir HR: Ramona Benson
Employees: 86

Phone: 770-394-7070
Fax: 770-394-2919

Jobs Added Last Year: 26 (+43.3%)

Business services - 3rd-party administrative services, car insurance services & software to car dealers & banks

BEAULIEU OF AMERICA, INC.

PO Box 4539
Dalton, GA 30719
Pres & CEO: Carl Bouckaert
Dir HR: Joel Deason
Employees: 6,500

Phone: 706-278-6666
Fax: 706-278-7941

Jobs Added Last Year: 0

Textiles - carpet (#1 privately held carpet company worldwide)

BEAZER HOMES USA, INC.

5775 Peachtree Dunwoody Rd., Ste. C-550
Atlanta, GA 30342
Pres & CEO: Ian J. McCarthy
Benefits Mgr: Jennifer Jones
Employees: 912

Phone: 404-250-3420
Fax: 404-250-3428

Jobs Added Last Year: 202 (+28.5%)

Building - single-family houses in the Southeast & Southwest

BELLSOUTH CORPORATION

1155 Peachtree St. NE
Atlanta, GA 30309-3610
Chm, Pres & CEO: John L. Clendenin
EVP Corp Rel: H. C. "Buddy" Henry Jr.
Employees: 87,600

Phone: 404-249-2000
Fax: 404-249-5599

Jobs Cut Last Year: 4,500 (-4.9%)

Utility - telephone

CARMIKE CINEMAS, INC.

1301 First Ave.
Columbus, GA 31901-2109
Pres & CEO: Michael W. Patrick
HR Dir: Sadie Harper
Employees: 10,082

Phone: 706-576-3400
Fax: 706-576-3471

Jobs Added Last Year: 2,022 (+25.1%)

Motion pictures & services - theaters

THE COCA-COLA COMPANY

One Coca-Cola Plaza
Atlanta, GA 30313
Chm & CEO: Roberto C. Goizueta
VP HR: Michael W. Walters
Employees: 32,000

Phone: 404-676-2121
Fax: 404-676-6792

Jobs Cut Last Year: 1,000 (-3.0%)

Beverages - soft drinks, fruit juices & other beverages (Coca-Cola, Sprite, Fanta, Fruitopia, POWERaDE, Minute Maid Juices To Go, Nestea)

COCA-COLA ENTERPRISES INC.

2500 Windy Ridge Pkwy.
Atlanta, GA 30339
VC & CEO: Summerfield K. Johnston Jr.
VP HR: Jarratt H. Jones
Employees: 33,000

Phone: 770-989-3000
Fax: 770-989-3788

Jobs Added Last Year: 3,000 (+10.0%)

Beverages - bottling (#1 worldwide) of carbonated soft drinks (Coca-Cola, Sprite, Fanta), sparkling waters, juice drinks (Minute Maid, Fruitopia), isotonics & teas (Nestea)

COMMUNICATIONS CENTRAL INC.

1150 Northmeadow Pkwy., Ste. 118
Roswell, GA 30076
Pres & CEO: Rodger L. Johnson
Dir HR: Peggy Walsh
Employees: 251

Phone: 770-442-7300
Fax: 770-442-7319

Jobs Added Last Year: 91 (+56.9%)

Telecommunications equipment - public & inmate facility payphones (#2 in the US); long-distance services

COMPDENT CORPORATION

8800 Roswell Rd., Ste. 244
Atlanta, GA 30350
Chm, Pres & CEO: David R. Klock
Dir HR: Karen R. Mitchell
Employees: 280

Phone: 770-998-8936
Fax: 770-998-6871

Jobs Added Last Year: 109 (+63.7%)

Medical practice management - managed dental care services

 An in-depth profile of this company is available to subscribers on Hoover's Online at www.hoovers.com.

137

COTTON STATES LIFE INSURANCE CO.

244 Perimeter Ctr. Pkwy. NE, PO Box 105303 Phone: 770-391-8600
Atlanta, GA 30348-5303 Fax: 770-391-8820
Pres & CEO: J. Ridley Howard
VP HR: Wendy M. Chamblee
Employees: 184

Jobs Added Last Year: 43 (+30.5%)

Insurance - life, accident & health

COX COMMUNICATIONS, INC.

1400 Lake Hearn Dr. Phone: 404-843-5000
Atlanta, GA 30319 Fax: 404-843-5975
Pres & CEO: James O. Robbins
Dir HR: Marybeth Lemer
Employees: 6,695

Jobs Added Last Year: 2,320 (+53.0%)

Cable TV - US cable TV systems; investments in The Discovery
Channel, TLC, E! Entertainment; international cable TV (UK Gold);
programming; telecommunications operations

COX ENTERPRISES, INC.

1400 Lake Hearn Dr. Phone: 404-843-5000
Atlanta, GA 30319 Fax: 404-843-5142
Chm & CEO: James Cox Kennedy
VP HR: Marybeth H. Leamer
Employees: 38,000

Jobs Added Last Year: 1,000 (+2.7%)

Publishing - newspapers (Atlanta Journal-Constitution, Austin
American-Statesman, Palm Beach Post); TV & radio broadcasting;
cable TV (75% ownership of Cox Communications); auto auctions

CRAWFORD & COMPANY

5620 Glenridge Dr. NE Phone: 404-256-0830
Atlanta, GA 30342 Fax: 404-847-4025
Chm, Pres & CEO: Dennis A. Smith
SVP HR: Gerald N. Cox
Employees: 7,854

Jobs Cut Last Year: 42 (-0.5%)

Medical practice management - claims administration, health
care management & risk management services for insurance
companies & government agencies

DELTA AIR LINES, INC.

Hartsfield Atlanta International Airport Phone: 404-715-2600
Atlanta, GA 30320-6001 Fax: 404-765-2233
Chm, Pres & CEO: Ronald W. Allen
VP Personnel : Robert G. Adams
Employees: 59,717

Jobs Cut Last Year: 11,695 (-16.4%)

Transportation - airline

DICKENS DATA SYSTEMS, INC.

1175 Northmeadow Pkwy., Ste. 150 Phone: 770-475-8860
Roswell, GA 30076 Fax: 770-442-7950
CEO: Gordon Dickens
Mgr HR: Nancy Anheir
Employees: 130

Jobs Added Last Year: 34 (+35.4%)

Computers - UNIX products for IBM RS/6000 & PS/2

Career Mart — http://www.careermart.com/

EMORY UNIVERSITY INC.

1380 Oxford Rd. NE
Atlanta, GA 30322
Pres: William M. Chace
Assoc VP HR: Alice Miller
Employees: 16,000
Jobs Added Last Year: —

University

Phone: 404-727-6123
Fax: 404-727-3750

EQUIFAX INC.

1600 Peachtree St. NW
Atlanta, GA 30309
Pres & CEO: Daniel W. McGlaughlin
SVP : Donald F. Wash
Employees: 14,200
Jobs Added Last Year: 0

Phone: 404-885-8000
Fax: 404-888-8682

Business services - credit reporting, market research & insurance support services

EQUIMED, INC.

3754 LaVista Rd.
Tucker, GA 30084-5637
Pres & CEO: Larry W. Pearson
VP HR: Edward Russell
Employees: 576
Jobs Added Last Year: 257 (+80.6%)

Phone: 404-320-6211
Fax: 404-320-0023

Medical services - eye-care & eye-surgery services

FLOWERS INDUSTRIES, INC.

US Hwy 19, PO Box 1338
Thomasville, GA 31799-1338
Chm & CEO: Amos R. McMullian
Dir HR: B. Scott Rich
Employees: 7,500
Jobs Cut Last Year: 700 (-8.5%)

Phone: 912-226-9110
Fax: 912-226-9231

Food - specialty branded foods, breads (Nature's Own, Cobblestone), snacks, vegetable & convenience food products

GENUINE PARTS COMPANY

2999 Circle 75 Pkwy.
Atlanta, GA 30339
Chm & CEO: Larry L. Prince
SVP HR: Ed Van Stedum
Employees: 22,500
Jobs Added Last Year: 1,215 (+5.7%)

Phone: 770-953-1700
Fax: 770-956-2212

Auto parts - distribution of replacement parts for automobiles, trucks & industrial equipment; office products

GEORGIA-PACIFIC CORPORATION

Georgia-Pacific Ctr., 133 Peachtree St. NE
Atlanta, GA 30303
Chm & CEO: Alston D. Correll
SVP HR: Gerard R. Brandt
Employees: 47,500
Jobs Added Last Year: 500 (+1.1%)

Phone: 404-652-4000
Fax: 404-521-4422

Building products - plywood, strand board, dimensional lumber & gypsum wallboard; pulp, paper & paper products

GOLD KIST INC.

244 Perimeter Center Pkwy.
Atlanta, GA 30346
CEO: Gaylord O. Coan
VP HR: W. Andy Epperson
Employees: 15,700
Jobs Added Last Year: —

Phone: 770-393-5000
Fax: 770-393-5061

Food - poultry & pork products

GOLDEN POULTRY COMPANY, INC.

244 Perimeter Center Pkwy. NE,
PO Box 2210
Atlanta, GA 30301
CEO: John Bekkers
VP HR: Andy Epperson
Employees: 5,097
Jobs Added Last Year: 532 (+11.7%)

Phone: 770-393-5000
Fax: 770-393-5421

Food - poultry products

GRANCARE, INC.

One Ravinia Dr., Ste. 1500
Atlanta, GA 30346
Chm, Pres & CEO: Gene E. Burleson
VP & Dir HR: Mark H. Rubenstein
Employees: 16,000
Jobs Added Last Year: 4,600 (+40.4%)

Phone: 770-393-0199
Fax: 770-393-8054

Nursing homes; routine & specialty medical & rehabilitative services; pharmacy services

GRAPHIC INDUSTRIES, INC.

2155 Monroe Dr. NE
Atlanta, GA 30324
Chm & CEO: Mark C. Pope III
No central personnel officer
Employees: 3,379
Jobs Added Last Year: 418 (+14.1%)

Phone: 404-874-3327
Fax: 404-874-7589

Printing - financial & corporate printing, reprographic services, commercial printing, direct mail printing & other graphic communications

 An in-depth profile of this company is available to subscribers on Hoover's Online at www.hoovers.com.

139

GREENFIELD INDUSTRIES, INC.

470 Old Evans Rd.
Evans, GA 30809
Pres & CEO: Paul W. Jones
VP HR: Roger B. Farley
Employees: 4,350

Phone: 706-863-7708
Fax: 706-860-8559

Jobs Added Last Year: 525 (+13.7%)

Machine tools & related products - rotary cutting tools

THE HOME DEPOT, INC.

2727 Paces Ferry Rd.
Atlanta, GA 30339-4089
Chm & CEO: Bernard Marcus
SVP HR: Stephen R. Messana
Employees: 80,000

Phone: 770-433-8211
Fax: 770-431-2707

Jobs Added Last Year: 12,700 (+18.9%)

Retail - home improvement, building materials & garden
supplies

HOUSECALL MEDICAL RESOURCES, INC.

1000 Abernathy Rd., Bldg. 400, Ste. 1825
Atlanta, GA 30328
Pres & CEO: George D. Shaunnessy
Dir HR: John Eckmond
Employees: 5,500

Phone: 770-379-9000
Fax: 770-395-9891

Jobs Added Last Year: —

Medical services - home health care services

IMAGE INDUSTRIES, INC.

1112 Georgia Hwy. 140, PO Box 5555
Armuchee, GA 30105
Pres & CEO: H. Stanley Padgett
Corp Controller: Michael W. Zima
Employees: 1,419

Phone: 706-235-8444
Fax: 706-235-0386

Jobs Added Last Year: 409 (+40.5%)

Recycling - plastic; carpet manufacturing

JOHN H. HARLAND COMPANY

2939 Miller Rd.
Decatur, GA 30035
Pres & CEO: Robert J. Amman
VP & Dir HR: Arlene Bates
Employees: 7,000

Phone: 770-981-9460
Fax: 770-593-5200

Jobs Added Last Year: 0

Paper - business forms, checks, banking forms & related
documents

KENWIN SHOPS, INC.

4747 Granite Dr.
Tucker, GA 30084
Pres & Asst Treas: Robert Schwartz
No central personnel officer
Employees: 447

Phone: 770-938-0451
Fax: 770-938-4631

Jobs Added Last Year: 159 (+55.2%)

Retail - women's & children's apparel

KUHLMAN CORPORATION

One Skidaway Village Walk, Ste. 201
Savannah, GA 31411
Chm & CEO: Robert S. Jepson Jr.
HR & Benefits Administrator: Betty Spaulding
Employees: 2,284

Phone: 912-598-7809
Fax: 912-598-0737

Jobs Added Last Year: 1,049 (+84.9%)

Electrical products - transformers for use in electrical distribution
systems & wire & cable

MAGELLAN HEALTH SERVICES, INC.

3414 Peachtree Rd. NE, Ste. 1400
Atlanta, GA 30326
Chm, Pres & CEO: E. Mac Crawford
VP Administrative Svcs: C. Clark Wingfield Jr.
Employees: 12,900

Phone: 404-841-9200
Fax: 404-841-5793

Jobs Cut Last Year: 600 (-4.4%)

Hospitals - psychiatric hospitals & mental health care facilities

THE MAXIM GROUP, INC.

210 Town Park Dr.
Kennesaw, GA 30144
Pres & CEO : A. J. Nassar
Dir HR: Larry Van Etten
Employees: 600

Phone: 770-590-9369
Fax: 770-590-8141

Jobs Added Last Year: 300 (+100.0%)

Franchisors - retail floor-covering dealers (Kinnaird and Francke
Interiors)

MEDAPHIS CORPORATION

2700 Cumberland Pkwy., Ste. 300
Atlanta, GA 30339
Chm, Pres & CEO: Randolph G. Brown
VP Corp Svcs: Denis Cortese
Employees: 10,000

Phone: 770-319-3300
Fax: 770-957-0670

Jobs Added Last Year: 2,000 (+25.0%)

Medical practice management - medical accounts-receivable
management services; information technology services
(BSG Corporation)

MOHAWK INDUSTRIES, INC.

160 S. Industrial Blvd.
Calhoun, GA 30701
Chm & CEO: David L. Kolb
Dir HR: Jerry Melton
Employees: 11,450

Phone: 706-629-7721
Fax: 706-625-4576

Jobs Cut Last Year: 3,615 (-24.0%)

Textiles - woven & tufted carpet & rugs for residential & commercial use (#2 in US)

MORRIS COMMUNICATIONS CORPORATION

PO Box 1928
Augusta, GA 30903
Chm & CEO: William S. Morris III
Dir HR: Bill Beauchamp
Employees: 5,400

Phone: 706-724-0851
Fax: 706-722-7125

Jobs Added Last Year: 260 (+5.1%)

Publishing - newspapers (32 dailies) & magazines; radio & TV broadcasting; outdoor advertising; computer services

MORRISON FRESH COOKING, INC.

4893 Riverdale Rd., Ste. 260
Atlanta, GA 30337
CEO: Ronnie L. Tatum
VP HR: Scears Lee III
Employees: 8,700

Phone: 334-344-3000
Fax: 334-344-3066

Jobs Added Last Year: —

Retail - home-style cafeteria restaurants (177 units)

MOUNTASIA ENTERTAINMENT INTERNATIONAL, INC.

5895 Windward Pkwy., Ste. 220
Alpharetta, GA 30202-4128
Chm, Pres & CEO: L. Scott Demerau
HR Dir: Jalayne Markey
Employees: 2,000

Phone: 770-442-6640
Fax: 770-442-6644

Jobs Added Last Year: 1,420 (+244.8%)

Leisure & recreational services - facilities that include miniature golf, underground caves, go-karts, game rooms & batting cages

NATIONAL SERVICE INDUSTRIES, INC.

1420 Peachtree St. NE
Atlanta, GA 30309-3002
Chm & CEO: James S. Balloun
Staff VP HR: F. Andrew Logue
Employees: 21,100

Phone: 404-853-1000
Fax: 404-853-1015

Jobs Cut Last Year: 900 (-4.1%)

Diversified operations - textile rental; chemicals; lighting equipment; envelope & insulation service

NEW WORLD COMMUNICATIONS GROUP INC.

3200 Windy Hill Rd., Ste. 1100-West
Atlanta, GA 30339
CEO: William C. Bevins
Dir Personnel: Jim Gorman
Employees: 2,700

Phone: 770-955-0045
Fax: 770-563-9600

Jobs Added Last Year: 400 (+17.4%)

Broadcasting - TV (7 NBC affiliates & one Fox affiliate); TV programming & distribution; film & TV library

OXFORD INDUSTRIES, INC.

222 Piedmont Ave., NE
Atlanta, GA 30308
Chm, Pres & CEO: J. Hicks Lanier
VP HR: J. Herbert Kraft
Employees: 8,577

Phone: 404-659-2424
Fax: 404-653-1545

Jobs Cut Last Year: 754 (-8.1%)

Apparel - shirts, slacks & sportswear for men, women & children

PEDIATRIC SERVICES OF AMERICA

3159 Campus Dr.
Norcross, GA 30071-1042
Chm, Pres & CEO: Joseph D. Sansone
Dir HR: Paula Holcomb
Employees: 3,647

Phone: 770-441-1580
Fax: 770-729-0316

Jobs Added Last Year: 1,265 (+53.1%)

Health care - pediatric home health care services, home nursing & respiratory & infusion therapy

RACETRAC PETROLEUM, INC.

300 Technology Ct.
Smyrna, GA 30082
Chm & CEO: Carl E. Bolch Jr.
VP HR: Bob Stier
Employees: 2,700

Phone: 770-431-7600
Fax: 770-431-7612

Jobs Added Last Year: 400 (+17.4%)

Oil refining & marketing; convenience stores

RETIREMENT CARE ASSOCIATES, INC.

6000 Lake Forrest Dr., Ste. 200
Atlanta, GA 30328
Pres : Chris Brogdon
Dir HR: George Hunt
Employees: 3,296

Phone: 404-255-7500
Fax: 404-843-9677

Jobs Added Last Year: 1,104 (+50.4%)

Nursing homes & retirement centers

 An in-depth profile of this company is available to subscribers on Hoover's Online at www.hoovers.com.

141

RHODES, INC.

4370 Peachtree Rd. NE
Atlanta, GA 30319
Chm & CEO: Irwin L. Lowenstein
SVP Training & HR: Jack A. Hurst
Employees: 3,761

Phone: 404-264-4600
Fax: 404-264-4796

Jobs Added Last Year: 1,071 (+39.8%)

Retail - home furnishings

ROADMASTER INDUSTRIES, INC.

250 Spring St. NW, Ste. 3-S
Atlanta, GA 30303
CEO: Henry Fong
EVP Admin & Treas: Charles Sanders
Employees: 5,700

Phone: 404-586-9000
Fax: 404-586-3319

Jobs Cut Last Year: 100 (-1.7%)

Leisure & recreational products - bicycles & fitness equipment, including stationary aerobic equipment & multistation weight systems; tricycles, wagons, sleds (Flexible Flyer) & swing sets

ROCK-TENN COMPANY

504 Thrasher St., PO Box 4098
Norcross, GA 30091
Chm & CEO: Bradley Currey Jr.
VP Risk Mgmt & Admin: Brad Newman
Employees: 6,001

Phone: 770-448-2193
Fax: 770-263-4483

Jobs Added Last Year: 73 (+1.2%)

Paper & paper products - recycled paperboard, packaging products & laminated paperboard products

ROLLINS, INC.

2170 Piedmont Rd. NE
Atlanta, GA 30324
Pres & CEO: R. Randall Rollins
Asst VP HR: Kathleen Mayton
Employees: 8,956

Phone: 404-888-2000
Fax: 404-888-2662

Jobs Added Last Year: 182 (+2.1%)

Diversified - pest control, plantscaping (Orkin); electronic security systems (Rollins)

SCIENTIFIC-ATLANTA, INC.

One Technology Pkwy. South
Norcross, GA 30092-2967
Pres & CEO: James F. McDonald
SVP HR: Brian C. Koenig
Employees: 4,700

Phone: 770-903-5000
Fax: 770-903-4617

Jobs Added Last Year: 700 (+17.5%)

Telecommunications equipment - earth station satellite antennas, receiver, transmitters & cable TV distribution amplifiers; signal-measurement & -monitoring equipment

SHAW INDUSTRIES, INC.

616 East Walnut Ave.
Dalton, GA 30720
Chm & CEO: Robert E. Shaw
Dir HR: Larry Oakley
Employees: 25,000

Phone: 706-278-3812
Fax: 706-275-1040

Jobs Added Last Year: 400 (+1.6%)

Textiles - nylon carpet

THE SOUTHERN COMPANY

270 Peachtree St.
Atlanta, GA 30303
Chm, Pres & CEO: A. W. Dahlberg
VP HR: C. Alan Martin
Employees: 31,882

Phone: 770-393-0650
Fax: 770-668-2674

Jobs Added Last Year: 4,056 (+14.6%)

Utility - electric power

SOUTHWIRE COMPANY, INC.

One Southwire Dr.
Carrollton, GA 30119
Chm & CEO: Roy Richards Jr.
VP HR: William Hearnburg
Employees: 5,200

Phone: 770-832-4242
Fax: 770-832-4929

Jobs Added Last Year: 200 (+4.0%)

Wire & cable products, metal fabricating & rods

SUNTRUST BANKS, INC.

303 Peachtree St. NE
Atlanta, GA 30308
Chm & CEO: James B. Williams
SVP HR: Carolyn Cartwright
Employees: 19,415

Phone: 404-588-7711
Fax: 404-827-6001

Jobs Added Last Year: 15 (+0.1%)

Banks - Southeast

SYNOVUS FINANCIAL CORP.

One Arsenal Place, 901 Front Ave., Ste. 301
Columbus, GA 31901
Chm : James H. Blanchard
Dir HR: Helen Johnson
Employees: 6,727

Phone: 706-649-2387
Fax: 706-649-2479

Jobs Added Last Year: 1,427 (+26.9%)

Banks - Southeast

THERATX, INCORPORATED

400 Northridge Rd., Ste. 400
Atlanta, GA 30350
Pres & CEO: John A. Bardis
Dir HR: Jerry N. Gross
Employees: 4,278

Phone: 770-518-9449
Fax: 770-641-0483

Jobs Added Last Year: 226 (+5.6%)

Nursing homes

TOTAL SYSTEM SERVICES, INC.

1200 Sixth Ave.
Columbus, GA 31902-1755
Chm & CEO: Richard W. Ussery
SVP & Dir HR: Elizabeth R. James
Employees: 2,269

Phone: 706-649-2310
Fax: 706-649-2342

Jobs Added Last Year: 266 (+13.3%)

Financial - credit, debit & private-label card processing services &
other data processing (THE TOTAL SYSTEM)

TRISM, INC.

1425 Franklin Rd.
Marietta, GA 30067
Chm & CEO: James M. Revie
Sec, Gen Counsel & VP HR: Mike May
Employees: 2,910

Phone: 770-427-4231

Jobs Added Last Year: 281 (+10.7%)

Transportation - specialty trucking

TURNER BROADCASTING SYSTEM

One CNN Ctr., 100 International Blvd.
Atlanta, GA 30303
Chm & Pres: Robert E. Ted Turner III
VP Admin: William M. Shaw
Employees: 7,000

Phone: 404-827-1700
Fax: 404-827-2437

Jobs Added Last Year: 1,000 (+16.7%)

Broadcasting - cable TV (CNN, TNT, Cartoon Network); pro sports
teams (Atlanta Braves & Hawks); movies(Castle Rock, New Line);
World Championship Wrestling; film library

UNITED PARCEL SERVICE OF AMERICA

55 Glenlake Pkwy. NE
Atlanta, GA 30328
Chm & CEO: Kent C. Nelson
SVP: Lea Soupata
Employees: 332,000

Phone: 770-828-6000
Fax: 770-828-6593

Jobs Added Last Year: 12,000 (+3.8%)

Transportation - air & ground package delivery

WEEKS CORPORATION

4497 Park Dr.
Norcross, GA 30093
Chm & CEO: A. Ray Weeks Jr.
Dir HR: Linda Billings
Employees: 223

Phone: 770-923-4076
Fax: 770-717-3310

Jobs Added Last Year: 53 (+31.2%)

Real estate investment trust - industrial buildings & parks in
Atlanta

WESTPOINT STEVENS INC.

507 W. 10th St.
West Point, GA 31833
Chm & CEO: Holcombe T. Green Jr.
VP HR: Foy F. Fisher
Employees: 17,500

Phone: 706-645-4000
Fax: 706-645-4068

Jobs Added Last Year: 150 (+0.9%)

Textiles - home furnishings

XCELLENET, INC.

5 Concourse Pkwy., Ste. 850
Atlanta, GA 30328
Chm & CEO: Dennis M. Crumpler
VP HR: Joel A. Miller
Employees: 250

Phone: 770-804-8100
Fax: 770-804-8102

Jobs Added Last Year: 72 (+40.4%)

Computers - client/server system development software for
remote & mobile business transactions (RemoteWare)

SCHULER HOMES, INC.

848 Fort Street Mall, 4th Fl.
Honolulu, HI 96813
Chm, Pres & CEO: James K. Schuler
Personnel Dir: Joanne Halsey
Employees: 87

Phone: 808-521-5661
Fax: 808-538-1476

Jobs Added Last Year: 19 (+27.9%)

Building - single-family homes, condominiums & townhouses in
Hawaii

 An in-depth profile of this company is available
to subscribers on Hoover's Online at www.hoovers.com.

ALBERTSON'S, INC.

250 Parkcenter Blvd.
Boise, ID 83706
Chm & CEO: Gary G. Michael
SVP HR: Steven D. Young
Employees: 80,000

Phone: 208-385-6200
Fax: 208-385-6349

Jobs Added Last Year: 4,000 (+5.3%)

Retail - 766 supermarkets in 19 western, midwestern & southern US states

BOISE CASCADE CORPORATION

1111 W. Jefferson St.
Boise, ID 83728-0001
Chm & CEO: George J. Harad
SVP HR & Corp Relations: Alice E. Hennessey
Employees: 17,820

Phone: 208-384-6161
Fax: 208-384-7298

Jobs Added Last Year: 1,202 (+7.2%)

Paper & paper products - uncoated free sheets, coated papers, containerboard & corrugated containers, newsprint & market pulp

J.R. SIMPLOT COMPANY

999 Main St., Ste. 1300
Boise, ID 83702
Pres & CEO: Stephen A. Beebe
VP HR: Ted Roper
Employees: 10,000

Phone: 208-336-2110
Fax: 208-389-7515

Jobs Added Last Year: 0

Diversified operations - food processing (french fries for McDonalds), fertilizer & livestock

MICRON TECHNOLOGY, INC.

8000 S. Federal Way
Boise, ID 83707-0006
Chm, Pres & CEO: Steve Appleton
Dir HR: Susan Metzger
Employees: 8,080

Phone: 208-368-4000
Fax: 208-368-4435

Jobs Added Last Year: 2,630 (+48.3%)

Electrical components - integrated circuit memory chips (DRAM, SRAM), complex printed circuit boards & complete PCs

ABBOTT LABORATORIES

100 Abbott Park Rd.
Abbott Park, IL 60064-3500
Chm & CEO: Duane L. Burnham
SVP HR: Ellen M. Walvoord
Employees: 50,241

Phone: 847-937-6100
Fax: 847-937-1511

Jobs Added Last Year: 777 (+1.6%)

Drugs - pharmaceuticals & nutritional products (Similac, Pedialyte, Ensure); hospital & laboratory products; diagnostic products, including immuno-assay testing; pesticides

A.C. NIELSEN CO.

150 N. Martingale Rd.
Schaumburg, IL 60173
Chm & CEO: Nicholas L. Trivisonno
VC: Michael P. Connors
Employees: 17,000

Phone: 847-498-6300
Fax: 847-498-7286

Jobs Added Last Year: —

Business services - marketing of retail measurement services, modeling & analytical services

ACE HARDWARE CORPORATION

2200 Kensington Ct.
Oak Brook, IL 60521
Pres: Dave Hodnik
VP HR: Fred J. Neer
Employees: 3,917

Phone: 708-990-6600
Fax: 708-573-4894

Jobs Added Last Year: 253 (+6.9%)

Building products - member-owned hardware wholesale cooperative

ADVOCATE HEALTH CARE

2025 Windsor Dr.
Oak Brook, IL 60521
Pres & CEO: Richard R. Risk
SVP HR: Ben Grigaliunas
Employees: 21,145

Phone: 708-572-9393
Fax: 708-990-5025

Jobs Added Last Year: 745 (+3.7%)

Hospitals - not-for-profit system serving the Chicagoland area (Christ Hospital & Medical Center, Lutheran General Hospital, Ravenswood Hospital Medical Center, Good Samaritan Hospital)

AGI, INC.

1950 N. Ruby St.   Phone: 708-344-9100
Melrose Park, IL 60160   Fax: 708-344-9113
CEO: Richard Block
Dir HR: Marie Renteria
Employees: 525

Jobs Added Last Year: 125 (+31.3%)

Containers - full-service packaging for the entertainment, cosmetics & toiletries, multimedia & food industries

AKZO NOBEL INC.

300 S. Riverside Plaza   Phone: 312-906-7500
Chicago, IL 60606   Fax: 312-906-7680
Pres & CEO: Piet Provo Kluit
Chief HR Officer: Dan Barker
Employees: 11,720

Jobs Added Last Year: 120 (+1.0%)

Diversified operations - adhesives & paints; pulp & paper chemicals, salt; lasers

ALBERTO-CULVER COMPANY

2525 Armitage Ave.   Phone: 708-450-3000
Melrose Park, IL 60160-1163   Fax: 708-450-3354
Pres & CEO: Howard B. Bernick
VP HR, Alberto-Culver USA: Douglas E. Meneely
Employees: 9,900

Jobs Added Last Year: 600 (+6.5%)

Cosmetics & toiletries - hair care products (Alberto VO5, Bold Hold, Consort, Alberto Balsam); cash-and-carry beauty supply stores (#1 worldwide: Sally Beauty Supply)

ALLEGIANCE CORPORATION

One Baxter Pkwy.   Phone: 847-948-2000
Deerfield, IL 60015   Fax: 847-948-3948
Chm & CEO: Lester B. Knight
VP HR: Robert B. DeBaun
Employees: 22,000

Jobs Added Last Year: —

Medical practice management - health care products & cost management services for hospitals & other health care providers (#1 in US)

ALLIANT FOODSERVICE INC.

One Parkway Dr. North   Phone: 847-405-8500
Deerfield, IL 60015   Fax: 847-405-8980
Pres & CEO: James A. Miller
VP HR: George Arseneau
Employees: 8,800

Jobs Added Last Year: 0

Food - exclusive distributor of Kraft products

ALLIED PRODUCTS CORPORATION

10 S. Riverside Plaza   Phone: 312-454-1020
Chicago, IL 60606   Fax: 312-454-1511
Chm, Pres & CEO: Richard A. Drexler
No central personnel officer
Employees: 2,400

Jobs Added Last Year: 800 (+50.0%)

Diversified operations - farm equipment, tool & die equipment & insulation, chemicals & plastics

College Grad Job Hunter — http://www.collegegrad.com

THE ALLSTATE CORPORATION

Allstate Plaza, 2775 Sanders Rd.
Northbrook, IL 60062-6127
Chm & CEO: Jerry D. Choate
SVP HR: Joan M. Crockett
Employees: 44,300
Phone: 847-402-5000
Fax: 847-402-0045

Jobs Cut Last Year: 2,000 (-4.3%)

Insurance - property & casualty (#2 in US)

AMOCO CORPORATION

200 E. Randolph Dr.
Chicago, IL 60601-7125
Chm & CEO: H. Laurance Fuller
SVP HR: R. Wayne Anderson
Employees: 42,689
Phone: 312-856-6111
Fax: 312-856-2460

Jobs Cut Last Year: 516 (-1.2%)

Oil & gas - US integrated

AMBASSADOR APARTMENTS, INC.

77 W. Wacker Dr., 40th Fl., Ste. 4040
Chicago, IL 60601
CEO: David M. Glickman
Dir HR: Margaret Shontz
Employees: 425
Phone: 312-917-1600
Fax: 312-782-5867

Jobs Added Last Year: 142 (+50.2%)

Real estate investment trust - apartment properties, primarily in Arizona, Illinois & Texas

AMSTED INDUSTRIES INCORPORATED

205 N. Michigan Ave., 44th Fl.
Chicago, IL 60601
Pres & CEO: Gordon R. Lohman
Dir HR: Gary B. Montgomery
Employees: 9,300
Phone: 312-645-1700
Fax: 312-819-8425

Jobs Added Last Year: 300 (+3.3%)

Machinery - railroad & industrial equipment, building products

AMERICAN HEALTHCARE PROVIDERS, INC.

4801 Southwick Dr.
Matteson, IL 60443
Pres: Asif A. Sayeed
Mgr HR: Bill Sparks
Employees: 259
Phone: 708-503-5000
Fax: 708-508-5001

Jobs Added Last Year: 89 (+52.4%)

Managed health care services

ANDERSEN CONSULTING

100 S. Wacker Dr., Ste. 1070
Chicago, IL 60606
Chm: George T. Shaheen
No central personnel officer
Employees: 38,000
Phone: 312-507-2900
Fax: 312-507-7965

Jobs Added Last Year: 6,000 (+18.8%)

Consulting - management & technology consulting services

AMERIKING, INC.

2215 Enterprise Dr., Ste. 1502
Westchester, IL 60154
Chm, CEO & Managing Owner: Lawrence E. Jaro
VP HR: Scott E. Vasatka
Employees: 6,031
Phone: 708-947-2150
Fax: 708-947-2160

Jobs Added Last Year: —

Retail - independent restaurant franchisee (Burger King) in the midwestern US

ANDERSEN WORLDWIDE

69 W. Washington St.
Chicago, IL 60602-3094
Chm, CEO & Mng Partner: Lawrence A. Weinbach
Mng Partner: Peter Pesce
Employees: 82,121
Phone: 312-580-0069
Fax: 312-507-2548

Jobs Added Last Year: 9,399 (+12.9%)

Business services - accounting & technical consulting

AMERITECH CORPORATION

30 S. Wacker Dr.
Chicago, IL 60606
Chm, Pres & CEO: Richard C. Notebaert
SVP HR: Walter M. Oliver
Employees: 65,345
Phone: 312-750-5000
Fax: 312-207-8136

Jobs Added Last Year: 1,751 (+2.8%)

Telecommunications services - telephone & cellular communications, security monitoring, online shopping (MusicNet, Peapod), distance learning & library management system services

ANDREW CORPORATION

10500 W. 153rd St.
Orland Park, IL 60462
Chm, Pres & CEO: Floyd L. English
No central personnel officer
Employees: 3,345
Phone: 708-349-3300
Fax: 708-349-5943

Jobs Added Last Year: 421 (+14.4%)

Telecommunications equipment - coaxial cables, microwave antennas for point-to-point communication systems & other special purpose antennas

ANIXTER INTERNATIONAL INC.

2 N. Riverside Plaza, Ste. 1900   Phone: 312-902-1515
Chicago, IL 60606   Fax: 312-902-1573
Pres & CEO: Rod F. Dammeyer
VP HR: Alan Drizd
Employees: 5,100
Jobs Added Last Year: 900 (+21.4%)

Electrical products - wiring systems for voice, data & video networks

AON CORPORATION

123 N. Wacker Dr.   Phone: 312-701-3000
Chicago, IL 60606   Fax: 312-701-3100
Chm, Pres & CEO: Patrick G. Ryan
Dir HR: Virginia Schooley
Employees: 27,000
Jobs Added Last Year: 9,000 (+50.0%)

Insurance - accident & health, property & casualty

APAC TELESERVICES, INC.

One Parkway North Ctr., Ste. 510   Phone: 847-945-0055
Deerfield, IL 60015   Fax: 847-374-3215
Chm, Pres & CEO: Theodore G. Schwartz
Corp VP HR: Victor Preisser
Employees: 6,500
Jobs Cut Last Year: 500 (-7.1%)

Business services - outsourced telephone-based sales, marketing & customer-management services

ARCHER-DANIELS-MIDLAND CO.

4666 Faries Pkwy., PO Box 1470   Phone: 217-424-5200
Decatur, IL 62525   Fax: 217-424-5839
Chm & CEO: Dwayne O. Andreas
Personnel Mgr: Sheila Watts-Mannweiler
Employees: 14,833
Jobs Cut Last Year: 1,180 (-7.4%)

Agricultural operations - procuring, transporting, storing, processing & merchandising of agricultural commodities & products

ARTHUR J. GALLAGHER & CO.

2 Pierce Place   Phone: 708-773-3800
Itasca, IL 60143-3141   Fax: 708-285-4000
Pres & CEO: J. Patrick Gallagher Jr.
VP HR: Bette Brinkerhoff
Employees: 3,700
Jobs Added Last Year: 400 (+12.1%)

Insurance - brokerage & related services

BAKER & MCKENZIE

One Prudential Plaza, 130 E. Randolph Dr.   Phone: 312-861-8800
Chicago, IL 60601   Fax: 312-861-8823
Chm: John C. Klotsche
Dir HR: Mary Weis
Employees: 5,248
Jobs Added Last Year: 134 (+2.6%)

Law firm

BALLY ENTERTAINMENT CORP.

8700 W. Bryn Mawr Ave.   Phone: 312-399-1300
Chicago, IL 60631   Fax: 312-693-2982
Chm, Pres & CEO: Arthur M. Goldberg
VP HR: Harold Morgan
Employees: 27,600
Jobs Added Last Year: 16,400 (+146.4%)

Gambling resorts & casinos in Atlantic City (Bally's Park Place, The Grand), Las Vegas (Bally's Las Vegas) & New Orleans (Bally's New Orleans)

BALLY TOTAL FITNESS HOLDING CORP.

8700 W. Bryn Mawr Ave.   Phone: 312-380-3000
Chicago, IL 60631   Fax: 312-693-2982
Chm & CEO: Arthur M. Goldberg
SVP HR: Harold Morgan
Employees: 14,400
Jobs Added Last Year: 500 (+3.6%)

Leisure & recreational services - fitness centers in the US & Canada (#1 in US)

BAXTER INTERNATIONAL INC.

One Baxter Pkwy.   Phone: 847-948-2000
Deerfield, IL 60015   Fax: 847-948-3948
Chm & CEO: Vernon R. Loucks Jr.
SVP HR: Herbert E. Walker
Employees: 56,580
Jobs Added Last Year: 3,080 (+5.8%)

Medical products - hospital & health care products & services, including renal therapy, biotechnology operations, heart valves, catheters & intravenous solutions

BEER ACROSS AMERICA, INC.

55 Albrecht Dr.   Phone: 847-604-8008
Lake Bluff, IL 60044   Fax: 847-604-8820
Pres: Louis Amoroso
Dir HR: Karen O'Connell
Employees: 110
Jobs Added Last Year: 40 (+57.1%)

Beverages - beer-, wine- & coffee-of-the-month mail-order clubs (Beer Across America, International Wine Cellars, CoffeeQuest)

 An in-depth profile of this company is available to subscribers on Hoover's Online at www.hoovers.com.

147

BELL & HOWELL COMPANY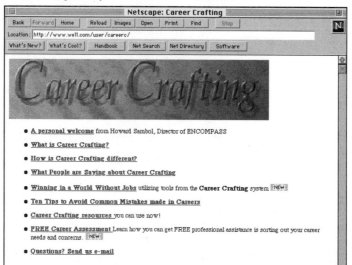

5215 Old Orchard Rd.　　Phone: 847-470-7660
Skokie, IL 60077-1076　　Fax: 847-470-9825
Chm & CEO: William J. White
VP HR: Maria T. Rubly
Employees: 5,966

Jobs Added Last Year: 175 (+3.0%)

Diversified operations - access to periodicals & scholarly papers in electronic & microfilm formats (UMI) & to technical reference information; high-volume commercial mail processing systems

BEN FRANKLIN RETAIL STORES, INC.

500 E. North Ave.　　Phone: 708-462-6100
Carol Stream, IL 60188-2168　　Fax: 708-462-6243
CEO: Bob Kendig
VP HR: Michele Benoit
Employees: 1,974

Jobs Added Last Year: 724 (+57.9%)

Retail - discount & variety

BIGSBY & KRUTHERS COMPANIES

57 W. Grand Ave., Ste. 700　　Phone: 312-644-5668
Chicago, IL 60610　　Fax: 312-644-0404
CEO: Gene Silverberg
No central personnel officer
Employees: 260

Jobs Added Last Year: 66 (+34.0%)

Retail - apparel for big & tall men (Bigsby & Kruthers) & neckware (Knot Shops)

BLUE CROSS AND BLUE SHIELD ASSOCIATION

676 N. St. Clair St.　　Phone: 312-440-6000
Chicago, IL 60611　　Fax: 312-440-6609
Pres & CEO: Patrick A. Hays
VP & Chief Admin Officer: Kris Kurschner
Employees: 146,000

Jobs Cut Last Year: 352 (-0.2%)

Insurance - prepaid health care plans

BODINE ELECTRIC COMPANY

2500 W. Bradley Place　　Phone: 312-478-3515
Chicago, IL 60618　　Fax: 312-478-3146
Pres: John R. Bodine
HR Mgr: Denise Taylor
Employees: 718

Jobs Added Last Year: 193 (+36.8%)

Machinery - fractional horsepower AC & DC motors & controls

BOISE CASCADE OFFICE PRODUCTS CORPORATION

800 W. Bryn Mawr Ave.　　Phone: 708-773-5000
Itasca, IL 60143　　Fax: 708-773-3607
Pres & CEO: Peter G. Danis Jr.
Dir Personnel: John Love
Employees: 4,757

Jobs Added Last Year: 1,637 (+52.5%)

Retail - direct mail sales of office supplies & furniture

Career Crafting — http://www.well.com/user/careerc/

BORG-WARNER AUTOMOTIVE, INC.

200 S. Michigan Ave. Phone: 312-322-8500
Chicago, IL 60604 Fax: 312-322-8849
Chm, Pres & CEO: John F. Fiedler
VP HR: Geraldine Kinsella
Employees: 8,600
Jobs Added Last Year: 1,270 (+17.3%)

Automotive & trucking - components & systems

BORG-WARNER SECURITY CORP.

200 S. Michigan Ave. Phone: 312-322-8500
Chicago, IL 60604 Fax: 312-322-8849
Chm & CEO: J. Joe Adorjan
SVP HR: John D. O'Brien
Employees: 96,974
Jobs Added Last Year: 5,276 (+5.8%)

Protection - guard, alarm, armored transportation & courier
security services

BRUNSWICK CORPORATION

One N. Field Ct. Phone: 847-735-4700
Lake Forest, IL 60045-4811 Fax: 847-735-4765
Chm & CEO: Peter N. Larson
VP & Chief HR Officer: Kenneth B. Zeigler
Employees: 20,900
Jobs Added Last Year: 100 (+0.5%)

Leisure & recreational products - sporting goods, boat motors &
bowling centers

BT OFFICE PRODUCTS INTL.

2150 E. Lake Cook Rd., Ste. 590 Phone: 847-793-7500
Buffalo Grove, IL 60089 Fax: 847-808-3011
Pres & CEO: Rudolf A. J. Huyzer
Office Mgr: Rhonda Barnes
Employees: 5,000
Jobs Added Last Year: 1,000 (+25.0%)

Office equipment & supplies - distribution of office products

BUDGET RENT A CAR CORPORATION

4225 Naperville Rd. Phone: 708-955-1900
Lisle, IL 60532 Fax: 708-955-7799
Pres & CEO: William N. Plamondon
VP HR: David Finley
Employees: 8,000
Jobs Cut Last Year: 700 (-8.0%)

Leasing - car & truck rental

CAREMARK INTERNATIONAL INC.

2215 Sanders Rd., Ste. 400 Phone: 847-559-4700
Northbrook, IL 60062 Fax: 847-559-4792
Chm & CEO: C. A. Lance Piccolo
VP HR: Kent J. DeLucenay
Employees: 11,000
Jobs Added Last Year: 1,850 (+20.2%)

Health care - alternative-site patient care

CATERPILLAR INC.

100 NE Adams St. Phone: 309-675-1000
Peoria, IL 61629 Fax: 309-675-1182
Chm & CEO: Donald V. Fites
VP HR: Wayne M. Zimmerman
Employees: 54,352
Jobs Added Last Year: 366 (+0.7%)

Machinery - construction, mining & agricultural machinery, for
building highways, dams, water systems, offices & housing devel-
opments; engines for trucks, boats & agricultural equipment

CDW COMPUTER CENTERS, INC.

1020 E. Lake Cook Rd. Phone: 847-465-6000
Buffalo Grove, IL 60089 Fax: 847-465-6800
Chm, CEO, Sec & Treas: Michael P. Krasny
VP HR: Mary C. Gerlits
Employees: 536
Jobs Added Last Year: 146 (+37.4%)

Retail - computers, peripherals & software

CELEX GROUP, INC.

919 Springer Dr. Phone: 708-953-8440
Lombard, IL 60148 Fax: 708-953-1353
Chm & CEO: Arnold M. "Mac" Anderson
Dir Personnel: Linda Sondgeroth
Employees: 516
Jobs Added Last Year: 128 (+33.0%)

Retail - direct sales of motivational & gift products (Successories)

CHAS. LEVY COMPANIES

1200 N. North Branch Phone: 312-440-4400
Chicago, IL 60622 Fax: 312-440-4434
Pres & CEO: Carol G. Kloster
VP HR: Jim Crawford
Employees: 2,234
Jobs Added Last Year: 234 (+11.7%)

Wholesale distribution - books & magazines

 An in-depth profile of this company is available
to subscribers on Hoover's Online at www.hoovers.com.

THE CHERRY CORPORATION

3600 Sunset Ave. Phone: 847-662-9200
Waukegan, IL 60087-3298 Fax: 847-360-3508
Chm, Pres & CEO: Peter B. Cherry
Dir HR: Nancy Guarascio
Employees: 4,399

Jobs Added Last Year: 413 (+10.4%)

Electrical components - switches, keyboards, keyboard switches, gas-discharge displays, electronic automotive products, linear integrated circuits & electronic automotive products

CNA FINANCIAL CORPORATION

CNA Plaza Phone: 312-822-5000
Chicago, IL 60685 Fax: 312-822-6419
CEO: Laurence A. Tisch
SVP HR: Floyd E. Brady
Employees: 25,000

Jobs Added Last Year: 9,400 (+60.3%)

Insurance - property, casualty, life, health & accident

COMARK, INC.

444 Scott Dr. Phone: 708-924-6670
Bloomingdale , IL 60108 Fax: 708-924-6790
Pres: Chuck Rolande
Dir HR: Chris Schuver
Employees: 605

Jobs Added Last Year: 133 (+28.2%)

Retail - software, computer & peripherals

DEAN FOODS COMPANY

3600 N. River Rd. Phone: 312-625-6200
Franklin Park, IL 60131 Fax: 708-928-8621
Chm & CEO: Howard M. Dean
Dir HR: Jerry Berger
Employees: 11,800

Jobs Cut Last Year: 300 (-2.5%)

Food - dairy & specialty food products

DEERE & COMPANY

John Deere Rd. Phone: 309-765-8000
Moline, IL 61265-8098 Fax: 309-765-4956
Chm & CEO: Hans W. Becherer
SVP Eng, Tech & HR: Michael S. Plunkett
Employees: 33,400

Jobs Cut Last Year: 852 (-2.5%)

Machinery - agricultural (#1 worldwide) & heavy equipment; home gardening equipment

DEVRY INC.

One Tower Ln. Phone: 708-571-7700
Oakbrook Terrace, IL 60181-4624 Fax: 708-571-0317
Chm & CEO: Dennis J. Keller
Dir HR: Carl A. Weinstein
Employees: 3,770

Jobs Added Last Year: 495 (+15.1%)

Schools - trade (DeVry Institutes), corporate training (Corporate Educational Services) & business (Keller School of Management)

DUCHOSSOIS ENTERPRISES, INC.

845 N. Larch Ave. Phone: 708-279-3600
Elmhurst, IL 60126 Fax: 708-530-6091
Pres & CEO: Richard L. Duchossois
HR Mgr: Lyn Fleichhacker
Employees: 8,000

Jobs Added Last Year: 0

Diversified operations - transportation; horse racetrack (Arlington International Racecourse); defense; consumer products

EAGLE FINANCE CORP.

1425 Tri-State Pkwy. Phone: 847-855-7150
Gurnee, IL 60031 Fax: 847-855-7225
Chm, Pres & CEO: Charles F. Wonderlic
Dir HR: Charles F. Wonderlic Jr.
Employees: 219

Jobs Added Last Year: 88 (+67.2%)

Financial - purchase & service of auto sales contracts & direct consumer loans

EAGLE FOOD CENTERS, INC.

Rte. 67 & Knoxville Rd. Phone: 309-787-7700
Milan, IL 61264 Fax: 309-787-7893
Pres & CEO: Robert J. Kelly
VP HR: Randy P. Smith
Employees: 7,511

Jobs Cut Last Year: 830 (-10.0%)

Retail - supermarkets

ED MINIAT, INC.

945 W. 38th St. Phone: 312-927-9200
Chicago, IL 60609 Fax: 312-927-8839
Pres: Ronald M. Miniat
Personnel Mgr: Danielle Gutelius
Employees: 300

Jobs Added Last Year: 87 (+40.8%)

Food - processed meats; cooking oils

ELCO INDUSTRIES, INC.

1111 Samuelson Rd.
Rockford, IL 61125-7009
Pres & CEO: John C. Lutz
Personnel Mgr: Mike Muskievicz
Employees: 2,180
Jobs Added Last Year: 209 (+10.6%)

Metal products - fasteners

EVEREN CAPITAL CORP.

77 W. Wacker Dr.
Chicago, IL 60601
Chm & CEO: James R. Boris
HR Mgr Employment Div: Jennifer DiBiase
Employees: 3,350
Jobs Added Last Year: 510 (+18.0%)

Financial - brokerage, securities & investment banking services to corporate & municipal clients

FALCON BUILDING PRODUCTS, INC.

2 N. Riverside Plaza, Ste. 1100
Chicago, IL 60606
Pres & CEO: William K. Hall
No central personnel officer
Employees: 3,650
Jobs Added Last Year: 250 (+7.4%)

Building products - air distribution products, bathroom fixtures (Mansfield) & air compressors

FEDERAL SIGNAL CORPORATION

1415 W. 22nd St., Ste. 1100
Oak Brook, IL 60521-9945
Chm, Pres & CEO: Joseph J. Ross
No central personnel officer
Employees: 5,989
Jobs Added Last Year: 746 (+14.2%)

Diversified operations - emergency vehicles; cutting tools; communications equipment; neon signs

FELLOWES MANUFACTURING COMPANY

1789 Norwood Ave.
Itasca, IL 60143
Pres & COO: James Fellowes
Dir HR: D'Arcy Didier
Employees: 1,461
Jobs Added Last Year: 203 (+16.1%)

Office equipment - file cabinets & other document storage products; portable paper shredders

FIRST ALERT, INC.

Phone: 815-397-5151
Fax: 815-395-8270

3901 Liberty Street Rd.
Aurora, IL 60504-2495
Chm, Pres & CEO: Malcolm Candlish
Mgr HR: Lisa Reynolds
Employees: 4,287
Jobs Added Last Year: 2,192 (+104.6%)

Phone: 708-851-7330
Fax: 708-851-1331

Protection - home-safety devices, including smoke & carbon monoxide detectors

FIRST CHICAGO NBD CORPORATION

One First National Plaza
Chicago, IL 60670
Pres & CEO: Verne G. Istock
EVP HR : Timothy P. Moen
Employees: 35,328
Jobs Added Last Year: 17,698 (+100.4%)

Phone: 312-732-4000
Fax: 312-407-5498

Banks - Midwest

FIRST FINANCIAL BANCORP, INC.

121 E. Locust St.
Belvidere, IL 61008-3688
Pres: Steven C. Derr
Ops Mgr: Pat McCoy
Employees: 65
Jobs Added Last Year: 27 (+71.1%)

Phone: 815-544-3167
Fax: 815-544-0802

Banks - Midwest

FIRST MERCHANTS ACCEPTANCE CORP.

570 Lake Cook Rd., Ste. 126
Deerfield, IL 60015
Pres & CEO: Mitchell C. Kahn
VP Ops: Brian Hausmann
Employees: 200
Jobs Added Last Year: 100 (+100.0%)

Phone: 847-948-9300
Fax: 847-948-9303

Financial - purchase & service of dealer-originated retail installment contracts on used automotbiles

FIRST MIDWEST BANCORP, INC.

300 Park Blvd., Ste. 405
Itasca, IL 60143-0459
Pres & CEO: Robert P. O'Meara
HR Dir: Phillip E. Glotfelty
Employees: 2,192
Jobs Added Last Year: 899 (+69.5%)

Phone: 708-875-7450
Fax: 708-778-4070

Banks - Midwest

Phone: 312-574-6000
Fax: 312-574-8966

Phone: 312-906-9700
Fax: 312-454-0614

Phone: 708-954-2000
Fax: 708-954-2030

Phone: 708-893-1600
Fax: 708-893-9777

 An in-depth profile of this company is available to subscribers on Hoover's Online at www.hoovers.com.

151

FMC CORPORATION

200 E. Randolph Dr.   Phone: 312-861-6000
Chicago, IL 60601   Fax: 312-861-5913
Chm & CEO: Robert N. Burt
VP HR: Michael W. Murray
Employees: 22,164

Jobs Added Last Year: 820 (+3.8%)

Diversified operations - chemicals, defense systems, machinery, equipment & precious metals

FOLLETT CORPORATION

2233 West St.   Phone: 708-583-2000
River Grove, IL 60171-1895   Fax: 708-452-9347
Pres & CEO: P. Richard Steve Litzsinger
VP & Sec: Richard Waichler
Employees: 7,500

Jobs Added Last Year: 300 (+4.2%)

Diversified operations - college bookstores; software; publishing

FRANCISCAN SISTERS HEALTH CARE CORP.

9223 W. St. Francis Rd.   Phone: 815-469-4888
Frankfort, IL 60432   Fax: 815-469-4864
Pres: Jerry Pearson
VP HR: John Landstrom
Employees: 5,750

Jobs Added Last Year: —

Hospitals - not-for-profit system comprised of 4 hospitals, 2 nursing homes, 25 clinics & a college of nursing

FRUIT OF THE LOOM, INC.

5000 Sears Tower, 233 S. Wacker Dr.   Phone: 312-876-1724
Chicago, IL 60606   Fax: 312-993-1749
Chm & CEO: William Farley
VP Admin: Burgess D. Ridge
Employees: 33,300

Jobs Cut Last Year: 4,100 (-11.0%)

Apparel - underwear & activewear (Fruit of the Loom, BVD, John Henry), licensed sports apparel & casual & jeanswear (Gitano)

GATX CORPORATION

500 W. Monroe St.   Phone: 312-621-6200
Chicago, IL 60661-3676   Fax: 312-621-6646
Chm, Pres & CEO: Ronald H. Zech
VP HR: William L. Chambers
Employees: 5,100

Jobs Cut Last Year: 700 (-12.1%)

Transportation - railroad tank car & freight car leasing; tank storage terminals, pipelines & related facilities

GENERAL INSTRUMENT CORP.

8770 W. Bryn Mawr Ave., Ste. 1300   Phone: 312-695-1000
Chicago, IL 60631   Fax: 312-695-1001
Chm, Pres, CEO & COO: Richard S. Friedland
VP HR: Clark E. Tucker
Employees: 12,300

Jobs Added Last Year: 0

Telecommunications equipment - cable- & satellite-TV supplies, including interactive cable converters, wireless systems, satellite-TV encryption systems & fiber-optic cables

HA-LO INDUSTRIES, INC.

5980 Touhy Ave.   Phone: 847-647-2300
Niles, IL 60714   Fax: 847-647-5999
Chm, Pres & CEO: Lou Weisbach
HR Mgr: Sabina Filipovic
Employees: 400

Jobs Added Last Year: 198 (+98.0%)

Business services - premium advertising products & corporate event planning

HARTMARX CORPORATION

101 N. Wacker Dr.   Phone: 312-372-6300
Chicago, IL 60606   Fax: 312-444-2710
Chm & CEO: Elbert O. Hand
Mgr Emp Relations: Lorraine Dickson
Employees: 8,200

Jobs Cut Last Year: 2,800 (-25.5%)

Apparel - men's suits, sportcoats & slacks (Hart Schaffner & Marx, Sansabelt, Austin Reed, Pierre Cardin), golfwear (Jack Nicklaus) & women's career apparel (KM by Krizia)

HEWITT ASSOCIATES LLC

100 Half Day Rd.   Phone: 847-295-5000
Lincolnshire, IL 60069   Fax: 847-295-7634
CEO: Dale L. Gifford
Dir HR: David Wille
Employees: 5,357

Jobs Added Last Year: 864 (+19.2%)

Consulting - specializing in human resources

HINSDALE FINANCIAL CORPORATION

One Grant Sq.   Phone: 708-323-1776
Hinsdale, IL 60521   Fax: 708-323-0052
Pres & CEO: Kenne P. Bristol
SVP HR: Margaret W. Perfetto
Employees: 337

Jobs Added Last Year: 80 (+31.1%)

Banks - Midwest

HOLLINGER INTERNATIONAL, INC.

401 N. Wabash Ave., Ste. 740   Phone: 312-321-2299
Chicago, IL 60611   Fax: 312-321-0629
Chm & CEO: Conrad M. Black
Dir HR: Roland McBride
Employees: 19,500

Jobs Added Last Year: 12,280 (+170.1%)

Publishing - newspapers in Australia, Canada, the US & the UK
(137, including the Chicago Sun-Times, The Jerusalem Post, The
Daily Telegraph: publicly traded subsidiary of Hollinger Inc.)

HOSTMARK MANAGEMENT GROUP, INC.

1600 Golf Rd., Ste. 800   Phone: 847-439-8500
Rolling Meadows, IL 60008   Fax: 847-439-8755
Chm & CEO: C. A. Cataldo
Dir HR: Christine Miller
Employees: 6,100

Jobs Added Last Year: 0

Real estate development - hotels & restaurants management &
development

HOUSEHOLD INTERNATIONAL, INC.

2700 Sanders Rd.   Phone: 847-564-5000
Prospect Heights, IL 60070   Fax: 847-205-7490
Chm & CEO: William F. Aldinger
SVP HR: Colin P. Kelly
Employees: 13,000

Jobs Cut Last Year: 2,500 (-16.1%)

Financial - consumer & home equity loans; private-label
credit cards

HYATT CORPORATION

200 W. Madison St.   Phone: 312-750-1234
Chicago, IL 60606   Fax: 312-750-8550
Chm & CEO: Jay A. Pritzker
SVP Planning & HR: Larry Deans
Employees: 47,000

Jobs Cut Last Year: 5,275 (-10.1%)

Hotels

IDEX CORPORATION

630 Dundee Rd., Ste. 400   Phone: 847-498-7070
Northbrook, IL 60062   Fax: 847-498-3940
Chm, Pres & CEO: Donald N. Boyce
VP HR: Jerry N. Derck
Employees: 3,233

Jobs Added Last Year: 233 (+7.8%)

Machinery - fluid-handling & industrial equipment

IGA, INC.

8725 W. Higgins Rd.   Phone: 312-693-4520
Chicago, IL 60631-2773   Fax: 312-693-1271
Chm & CEO: Thomas S. Haggai
VP Fin & MIS: James Anderson
Employees: 128,000

Jobs Cut Last Year: 2,000 (-1.5%)

Retail - cooperative alliance of 3,600 independent supermarkets
with operations in 49 states, Australia, Canada, China, Japan,
Korea, Papua New Guinea & the West Indies

Career Internetworking — http://www.careerkey.com/

An in-depth profile of this company is available
to subscribers on Hoover's Online at www.hoovers.com.

153

ILLINOIS SUPERCONDUCTOR CORP.

451 Kingston Ct. Phone: 847-391-9400
Mount Prospect, IL 60056 Fax: 847-299-9609
Pres & CEO: Ora E. Smith
HR Specialist: Beth Kubow
Employees: 50

Jobs Added Last Year: 13 (+35.1%)

Telecommunications equipment - wireless products, including cellular phone filters

ILLINOIS TOOL WORKS INC.

3600 W. Lake Ave. Phone: 847-724-7500
Glenview, IL 60025-5811 Fax: 847-657-4261
Chm, Pres & CEO: W. James Farrell
SVP HR: John Karpan
Employees: 21,200

Jobs Added Last Year: 1,700 (+8.7%)

Metal products - industrial components, including fasteners & switches; welding & finishing equipment; adhesives & polymers; consumer packaging

IMC GLOBAL INC.

2100 Sanders Rd. Phone: 847-272-9200
Northbrook, IL 60062-6146 Fax: 847-205-4805
Chm & CEO: Wendell F. Bueche
SVP HR: B. Russell Lockridge
Employees: 6,800

Jobs Added Last Year: 300 (+4.6%)

Fertilizers - crop nutrients for the international agricultural community; mining & processing of potash

INFLO HOLDINGS CORPORATION

One Hollow Tree Ln. Phone: 708-833-2900
Elmhurst, IL 60126 Fax: 708-530-8773
CEO: Sam K. Reed
VP Personnel: Dennis P. Christensen
Employees: 9,000

Jobs Added Last Year: —

Food - cookies & crackers (Keebler)

INLAND STEEL INDUSTRIES, INC.

30 W. Monroe St. Phone: 312-346-0300
Chicago, IL 60603 Fax: 312-899-3197
Chm, Pres & CEO: Robert J. Darnall
VP HR: Judd R. Cool
Employees: 15,400

Jobs Cut Last Year: 100 (-0.6%)

Steel - carbon & high-strength low-alloy steel products

JEWEL FOOD STORES, INC.

1955 W. North Ave. Phone: 708-531-6000
Melrose Park, IL 60160 Fax: 708-531-6001
Gen Mgr: Edward J. McManus
Dir HR: Ed Buron
Employees: 29,000

Jobs Added Last Year: —

Retail - supermarkets

JMB REALTY CORPORATION

900 N. Michigan Ave. Phone: 312-440-4800
Chicago, IL 60611 Fax: 312-915-2310
Pres & CEO: Neil Bluhm
Dir HR: Gail Silvers
Employees: 12,500

Jobs Added Last Year: 0

Real estate operations & management (owns 405 of Urban Shopping Centers)

JOHNSTOWN AMERICA INDUSTRIES, INC.

980 N. Michigan Ave., Ste. 1000 Phone: 312-280-8844
Chicago, IL 60611 Fax: 312-280-4820
Pres & CEO: Thomas M. Begel
Office Mgr & Asst to CEO: Gail Marshall
Employees: 3,650

Jobs Added Last Year: 1,650 (+82.5%)

Transportation - railroad freight cars

JORDAN INDUSTRIES, INC.

1751 Lake Cook Rd. Phone: 847-945-5591
Deerfield, IL 60015 Fax: 847-945-5698
Chm & CEO: John W. Jordan
No central personnel officer
Employees: 5,350

Jobs Added Last Year: 1,450 (+37.2%)

Diversified operations - safety reflectors; torque converters & hydraulic pumps; missile handling products; electric motors; precision gear & gear box products; home health care products

KEMPER NATIONAL INSURANCE COMPANIES

One Kemper Dr. Phone: 847-320-2000
Long Grove, IL 60049-0001 Fax: 847-320-2494
COO: Alfred K. Kenyon
VP HR: Robert L. Davis
Employees: 8,837

Jobs Added Last Year: 542 (+6.5%)

Insurance - property & casualty

LANE INDUSTRIES, INC.

1200 Shermer Rd.   Phone: 847-498-6789
Northbrook, IL 60062   Fax: 847-498-2104
Chm, Pres & CEO: William N. Lane III
Mgr HR: Linda Datz
Employees: 8,300
Jobs Added Last Year: 1,300 (+18.6%)

Diversified operations - business machines & supplies; ranching; lodging; broadcasting

LAWSON PRODUCTS, INC.

1666 E. Touhy Ave.   Phone: 847-827-9666
Des Plaines, IL 60018   Fax: 847-827-8277
Chm & CEO: Bernard Kalish
VP HR: James J. Smith
Employees: 1,675
Jobs Added Last Year: 865 (+106.8%)

Metal products - distribution of expendable maintenance, repair & replacement products

LETTUCE ENTERTAIN YOU

5419 N. Sheridan Rd.   Phone: 312-878-7340
Chicago, IL 60640   Fax: 312-878-7667
Pres & CEO: Richard Melman
VP HR: Susan Southgate-Fox
Employees: 4,500
Jobs Added Last Year: 900 (+25.0%)

Retail - theme restaurants (Ed Debevics, Shaw's Crab House, The Pump Room, R.J. Grunt's, Scoozi!, Hat Dance, Mity Nice Grill, Un Grand Cafe)

LEVY RESTAURANTS

980 N. Michigan Ave., 4th Fl.   Phone: 312-664-8200
Chicago, IL 60611   Fax: 312-280-2739
CEO: Lawrence F. Levy
VP HR: Margie Mintz
Employees: 4,500
Jobs Added Last Year: 1,000 (+28.6%)

Retail - restaurants (D.B. Kaplan's, Dos Hermanos) & food concessions (Arlington Park, Comiskey Park, Disney World, McCormick Place, Wrigley Field)

LINDBERG CORPORATION

6133 N. River Rd., Ste. 700   Phone: 847-823-2021
Rosemont, IL 60018   Fax: 847-823-0795
Pres & CEO: George H. Bodeen
VP & Mgr HR: Jerome R. Sullivan
Employees: 1,119
Jobs Added Last Year: 509 (+83.4%)

Metal processing & fabrication - heat-treating processes to improve mechanical properties, durability & wear resistance of metal

LOYOLA UNIVERSITY OF CHICAGO

820 N. Michigan Ave.   Phone: 312-915-6000
Chicago, IL 60611   Fax: 312-915-6449
Pres & CEO: John J. Piderit
Dir HR: Mimi Winter
Employees: 9,556
Jobs Added Last Year: —

Jesuit-run Catholic university offering 50 undergraduate degree programs & 49 graduate degree programs

MACLEAN-FOGG COMPANY

1000 Allanson Rd.   Phone: 847-566-0010
Mundelein, IL 60060   Fax: 847-566-0026
Pres & CEO: Barry L. MacLean
Dir HR: Vince Piat
Employees: 1,500
Jobs Added Last Year: 300 (+25.0%)

Metal processing & fabrication - components for the automotive, power utility & telecommunications industries

MANUFACTURED HOME COMMUNITIES

2 N. Riverside Plaza   Phone: 312-454-0100
Chicago, IL 60606   Fax: 312-474-0205
Chm & CEO: Samuel Zell
Gen Counsel: Ellen Kelleher
Employees: 4,600
Jobs Added Last Year: 4,000 (+666.7%)

Real estate investment trust - manufactured-housing communities

THE MARMON GROUP, INC.

225 W. Washington St.   Phone: 312-372-9500
Chicago, IL 60606   Fax: 312-845-5305
Pres & CEO: Robert A. Pritzker
Personnel Dir: George Frese
Employees: 28,000
Jobs Added Last Year: 0

Diversified operations - industrial materials; international marketing, sales & distribution services (Getz Bros. & Co. Inc.); automobile products; medical products

MCDONALD'S CORPORATION

McDonald's Plaza   Phone: 708-575-3000
Oak Brook, IL 60521   Fax: 708-575-3392
Chm & CEO: Michael R. Quinlan
SVP : Stanley R. Stein
Employees: 212,000
Jobs Added Last Year: 29,000 (+15.8%)

Retail - fast-food restaurants

An in-depth profile of this company is available to subscribers on Hoover's Online at www.hoovers.com.

155

MEDLINE INDUSTRIES, INC.

1200 Town Line Rd. Phone: 847-949-5500
Mundelein, IL 60060 Fax: 847-949-2109
Chm & CEO: James S. Mills
VP Emp Svcs: Heidi Dinter
Employees: 2,200
Jobs Added Last Year: 200 (+10.0%)

Medical supplies, including clothing & linens, shoe covers, surgical instruments, admission kits, catheters, irrigation trays, walkers, wheelchairs & furniture

MERCURY FINANCE COMPANY

40 Skokie Blvd., Ste. 200 Phone: 847-564-3720
Northbrook, IL 60062 Fax: 847-564-3758
Pres & CEO: John N. Brincat
Dir HR: Robert Lutgen
Employees: 1,800
Jobs Added Last Year: 300 (+20.0%)

Financial - consumer loans & credit insurance

METAMOR TECHNOLOGIES LTD

One N. Franklin, Ste. 1500 Phone: 312-638-2667
Chicago, IL 60606 Fax: 312-251-2998
Pres: Irv Shapiro
HR Mgr: Marcie Newman
Employees: 176
Jobs Added Last Year: 46 (+35.4%)

Computers - systems integration

METHODE ELECTRONICS, INC.

7444 W. Wilson Ave. Phone: 708-867-9600
Chicago, IL 60656 Fax: 708-867-9130
Pres: William T. Jensen
Dir HR: Louise Moyana
Employees: 3,000
Jobs Added Last Year: 500 (+20.0%)

Electronic components - connectors, controls, printed circuits & distribution systems

MMI COMPANIES, INC.

540 Lake Cook Rd. Phone: 847-940-7550
Deerfield, IL 60015-5290 Fax: 847-374-1332
Chm & CEO: B. Frederick Becker
VP HR: Merrilee Hepler
Employees: 500
Jobs Added Last Year: 100 (+25.0%)

Insurance - medical malpractice insurance & specialized clinical risk management services

MOLEX INCORPORATED

2222 Wellington Ct. Phone: 708-969-4550
Lisle, IL 60532 Fax: 708-969-1352
Chm & CEO: Frederick A. Krehbiel
Corp VP HR: Kathi M. Regas
Employees: 9,500
Jobs Added Last Year: 1,333 (+16.3%)

Electrical connectors - electrical & fiber optic connectors; switches & application tooling for the computer, business equipment, enterainment, automotive & telecommunications industries

MONTGOMERY WARD HOLDING

One Montgomery Ward Plaza Phone: 312-467-2000
Chicago, IL 60671-0042 Fax: 312-467-3975
Chm & CEO: Bernard F. Brennan
EVP HR: Robert A. Kasenter
Employees: 55,000
Jobs Cut Last Year: 3,600 (-6.1%)

Retail - major department stores

MORTON INTERNATIONAL, INC.

Morton Int'l. Bldg., 100 N. Riverside Plaza Phone: 312-807-2000
Chicago, IL 60606-1596 Fax: 312-807-2241
Chm & CEO: S. Jay Stewart
VP HR: Christopher K. Julsrud
Employees: 13,800
Jobs Added Last Year: 700 (+5.3%)

Chemicals - adhesives, coatings & specialty products; salt; automobile airbags

MOTOROLA, INC.

1303 E. Algonquin Rd. Phone: 847-576-5000
Schaumburg, IL 60196 Fax: 847-576-8003
VC & CEO: Gary L. Tooker
SVP & Dir HR: Glenn A. Gienko
Employees: 142,000
Jobs Added Last Year: 10,000 (+7.6%)

Electrical products - wireless communications products (#1 worldwide: cellular telephone, paging & two-way radio) & electronic equipment, systems & components

NALCO CHEMICAL COMPANY

One Nalco Center Phone: 708-305-1000
Naperville, IL 60563-1198 Fax: 708-305-2900
Chm & CEO: Edward J. Mooney
SVP HR: James F. Lambe
Employees: 6,081
Jobs Added Last Year: 146 (+2.5%)

Chemicals - industrial specialty chemicals & services for cooling systems & boilers, metalworking, papermaking, water treatment & petroleum- & mineral-refining operation

NATIONAL COUNCIL OF YOUNG MEN'S CHRISTIAN ASSOCIATIONS OF THE UNITED STATES OF AMERICA

101 N. Wacker Dr., Ste. 1400
Phone: 312-977-0031
Chicago, IL 60606
Fax: 312-977-9063
Natl Exec Dir: David Mercer
Dir HR: Wyley Moore
Employees: 20,000
Jobs Added Last Year: 0

Leisure & recreational services - athletic facilities

NAVISTAR INTERNATIONAL CORP.

455 N. Cityfront Plaza Dr.
Phone: 312-836-2000
Chicago, IL 60611
Fax: 312-836-2192
Chm, Pres & CEO: John R. Horne
SVP Emp Relations & Admin: John M. Sheahin
Employees: 16,079
Jobs Added Last Year: 1,169 (+7.8%)

Automotive manufacturing - medium & heavy diesel trucks

NEWELL CO.

29 E. Stephenson St.
Phone: 815-235-4171
Freeport, IL 61032-0943
Fax: 815-233-8060
VC & CEO: William P. Sovey
VP Personnel Relations: William K. Doppstadt
Employees: 23,000
Jobs Added Last Year: 3,000 (+15.0%)

Diversified operations - hardware, housewares, office & industrial products

NORTHERN TRUST CORPORATION

50 S. La Salle St.
Phone: 312-630-6000
Chicago, IL 60675
Fax: 312-630-1512
Chm & CEO: William A. Osborn
SVP HR: William Setterstrom
Employees: 6,259
Jobs Cut Last Year: 349 (-5.3%)

Banks - Midwest

NORTHWESTERN HEALTHCARE

980 N. Michigan Ave., Ste. 1500
Phone: 312-335-6000
Chicago, IL 60611
Fax: 312-335-6020
Pres & CEO: Bruce E. Spivey
No central personnel officer
Employees: 16,427
Jobs Added Last Year: 5,982 (+57.3%)

Hospitals - system serving the Chicago area (member institutions include The Children's Memorial Medical Center, Evanston Hospital Corporation, Northwestern Memorial Hospital)

NORTHWESTERN UNIVERSITY

633 Clark St.
Phone: 847-491-3741
Evanston, IL 60208-1117
Fax: 847-491-2376
Pres: Henry S. Bienen
Assoc VP HR: Guy E. Miller
Employees: 5,800
Jobs Added Last Year: 150 (+2.7%)

Private, non-denominational university offering 95 undergraduate & 74 graduate degree programs

OLD REPUBLIC INTERNATIONAL CORP.

307 N. Michigan Ave.
Phone: 312-346-8100
Chicago, IL 60601
Fax: 312-726-0309
Chm, Pres & CEO: A. C. Zucaro
Dir Personnel: Charles Strizak
Employees: 5,460
Jobs Added Last Year: 60 (+1.1%)

Insurance - property & liability, title, mortgage-guaranty, life & disability

OUTBOARD MARINE CORPORATION

100 SeaHorse Dr.
Phone: 847-689-6200
Waukegan, IL 60085
Fax: 847-689-5555
Chm, Pres & CEO: Harry W. Bowman
VP HR: Richard H. Medland
Employees: 8,900
Jobs Added Last Year: 428 (+5.1%)

Leisure & recreational products - powerboats (Chris-Craft) & marine motors (Johnson, Evinrude)

PAMPERED CHEF LTD.

350 S. Rte. 53
Phone: 708-261-8900
Addison, IL 60101
Fax: 708-261-8586
Pres: Dorris Christopher
Pres: Dorris Christopher
Employees: 20,550
Jobs Added Last Year: 150 (+0.7%)

Retail - direct sales of gourmet kitchen & cooking supplies

PIONEER FINANCIAL SERVICES, INC.

1750 E. Golf Rd.
Phone: 847-995-0400
Schaumburg, IL 60173
Fax: 847-413-7264
Chm & CEO: Peter W. Nauert
Dir HR: Beverly Long
Employees: 1,800
Jobs Added Last Year: 230 (+14.6%)

Insurance - accident & health

 An in-depth profile of this company is available to subscribers on Hoover's Online at www.hoovers.com.

157

PITTWAY CORPORATION

200 S. Wacker Dr., Ste. 700
Chicago, IL 60606-5802
Pres & CEO: King Harris
No central personnel officer
Employees: 6,000

Phone: 312-831-1070
Fax: 312-831-0808

Jobs Added Last Year: 600 (+11.1%)

Diversified operations - burglar & fire alarms (Ademco Security); trade magazine publishing (Penton); real estate

PREMARK INTERNATIONAL, INC.

1717 Deerfield Rd.
Deerfield, IL 60015
Pres & CEO: James M. Ringler
SVP HR: James C. Coleman
Employees: 24,300

Phone: 847-405-6000
Fax: 847-405-6013

Jobs Added Last Year: 300 (+1.3%)

Diversified operations - commercial foodservice equipment (Hobart); flooring (Florida Tile); electrical appliances (West Bend) such as bread makers & fitness equipment

THE QUAKER OATS COMPANY

Quaker Tower, 321 N. Clark St.
Chicago, IL 60610-4714
Chm, Pres & CEO: William D. Smithburg
SVP HR: Douglas J. Ralston
Employees: 17,000

Phone: 312-222-7111
Fax: 312-222-8532

Jobs Cut Last Year: 3,000 (-15.0%)

Food - cereals, beverages (Ardmore Farms, Gatorade, Snapple) & other food products (Adria pasta, Rice-A-Roni)

RAND MCNALLY & COMPANY

8255 N. Central Park Ave.
Skokie, IL 60076-2970
Chm & CEO: Andrew McNally IV
VP HR & Gen Counsel: Kurt D. Steele
Employees: 4,650

Phone: 847-329-8100
Fax: 847-673-0539

Jobs Added Last Year: 450 (+10.7%)

Publishing - maps, atlases & other geographic information books, including travel CD-ROMs (TripMaker); tickets & baggage tags; labels, tags & cards for automated systems; computer services

RESTAURANT CO.

One Pierce Place, Ste. 100E
Itasca, IL 60143-2615
Chm & CEO: Donald Smith
VP HR: Jeanne Scott
Employees: 40,000

Phone: 708-250-0471
Fax: 708-250-0382

Jobs Added Last Year: 5,000 (+14.3%)

Retail - restaurants (Perkins, Friendly's Ice Cream)

RIDGEMOTORS PONTIAC/MIZE IMPORT GROUP INC.

1509 River Rd.
Des Plaines, IL 60018
Dealer Principal: Kevin Mize
Dir HR: Sue Bursonia
Employees: 121

Phone: 847-824-3141
Fax: 847-824-7638

Jobs Added Last Year: 51 (+72.9%)

Retail - new & used cars

Career Ladders — http://www.careerladders.com/

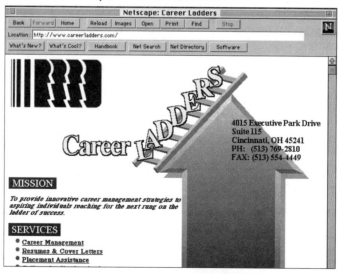

RLI CORP.

9025 N. Lindbergh Dr.
Peoria, IL 61615
Pres: G. D. Stephens
VP HR: M. E. Quine
Employees: 570

Phone: 309-692-1000
Fax: 309-692-1068

Jobs Added Last Year: 144 (+33.8%)

Insurance - property & casualty (Mt. Hawley Insurance Co., Replacement Lens Inc., RLI Aviation, RLI Insurance Ltd.); extended-service ophthalmic programs; office automation sofware

R. R. DONNELLEY & SONS COMPANY

77 W. Wacker Dr.
Chicago, IL 60601-1696
Chm & CEO: John R. Walter
SVP HR: Ann Weiser
Employees: 41,000

Phone: 312-326-8000
Fax: 312-326-8543

Jobs Added Last Year: 4,500 (+12.3%)

Printing - telephone books, magazines, mail-order catalogs & hard- & softcover books; information services, including database management & electronic media production; mailing list services

RUSH-PRESBYTERIAN-ST. LUKE'S MEDICAL CENTER

1653 W. Congress Pkwy.
Chicago, IL 60612
Pres & CEO: Leon M. Henikoff
Asst VP HR: Thomas Ferguson
Employees: 8,324

Phone: 312-942-5000
Fax: 312-942-5581

Jobs Cut Last Year: 187 (-2.2%)

Hospitals - not-for-profit system comprised of 8 hospitals in the Chicago area

RYKOFF-SEXTON, INC.

1050 Warrenville Rd.
Lisle, IL 60532
Pres & CEO: Mark Van Stekelenburg
SVP HR & Gen Counsel: Robert J. Harter Jr.
Employees: 5,400

Phone: 708-964-1414
Fax: 708-971-6327

Jobs Added Last Year: 70 (+1.3%)

Food - wholesale to restaurants, industrial cafeterias, health care facilities, hotels, schools & colleges

SAFETY-KLEEN CORP.

1000 N. Randall Rd.
Elgin, IL 60123
Pres & CEO: John G. Johnson Jr.
SVP HR: Robert J. Burian
Employees: 6,700

Phone: 847-697-8460
Fax: 847-468-8555

Jobs Added Last Year: 100 (+1.5%)

Pollution control equipment & services - liquid-waste management, parts-cleaning services & related products

SARA LEE CORPORATION

3 First National Plaza
Chicago, IL 60602-4260
Chm & CEO: John H. Bryan
SVP HR: Gary C. Grom
Employees: 149,100

Phone: 312-726-2600
Fax: 312-726-3712

Jobs Added Last Year: 3,200 (+2.2%)

Diversified operations - foods & coffee; hosiery (Hanes, L'eggs); shoe care (Kiwi) & leather goods (Coach)

SEARS, ROEBUCK AND CO.

3333 Beverly Rd.
Hoffman Estates, IL 60179
Chm & CEO: Arthur C. Martinez
EVP Admin: Anthony J. Rucci
Employees: 275,000

Phone: 847-286-2500
Fax: 800-427-3049

Jobs Cut Last Year: 85,570 (-23.7%)

Retail - major department stores

SERTA INC.

325 Spring Lake Dr.
Itasca, IL 60143
Pres & CEO: Edward F. Lilly
No central personnel officer
Employees: 2,500

Phone: 708-285-9300

Jobs Added Last Year: 500 (+25.0%)

Furniture - mattresses & box springs

SERVICEMASTER LTD PARTNERSHIP

One ServiceMaster Way
Downers Grove, IL 60515-9969
Pres & CEO: Carlos H. Cantu
VP People Mgmt: Debra Kass
Employees: 34,000

Phone: 708-271-1300
Fax: 708-271-5753

Jobs Added Last Year: 0

Building - custodial & pest control services (Terminix International, TruGreen-ChemLawn, American Home Shield)

SIGMATRON INTERNATIONAL, INC.

2201 Landmeier Rd.
Elk Grove Village, IL 60007
Pres & CEO: Gary R. Fairhead
Personnel Mgr: Nancy Geiser
Employees: 917

Phone: 847-956-8000
Fax: 847-956-8082

Jobs Added Last Year: 214 (+30.4%)

Electrical components - printed circuit boards & turnkey electronic products

 An in-depth profile of this company is available to subscribers on Hoover's Online at www.hoovers.com.

159

SOFTNET SYSTEMS, INC.

717 Forest Ave.   Phone: 847-793-2000
Lake Forest, IL 60045   Fax: 847-793-2005
Pres & CEO: John Jellinek
Office Mgr: Emily Harder
Employees: 263

Jobs Added Last Year: 248 (+1,653.3%)

Computers - imaging processing systems for hospital documents; telecommunication products

SPECIALTY FOODS CORPORATION

520 Lake Cook Rd., Ste. 520   Phone: 847-267-3000
Deerfield, IL 60015-4927   Fax: 847-267-0015
Pres & CEO: Paul J. Liska
VP HR: John D. Reisenberg
Employees: 14,000

Jobs Added Last Year: 100 (+0.7%)

Food - cheese, baked goods, prepared meats, pickles & chips

SPIEGEL, INC.

3500 Lacey Rd.   Phone: 708-986-8800
Downers Grove, IL 60515-5432   Fax: 708-769-3101
VC, Pres & CEO: John J. Shea
SVP HR: Harold S. Dahlstrand
Employees: 13,600

Jobs Added Last Year: 2,496 (+22.5%)

Retail - mail-order sales of apparel, household furnishing & general merchandise; outdoorwear stores (Eddie Bauer)

SPYGLASS, INC.

Naperville Corporate Ctr.,   Phone: 708-505-1010
1230 E. Diehl Rd., Ste. 304   Fax: 708-505-4944
Naperville, IL 60563
Pres & CEO: Douglas P. Colbeth
HR Coordinator: Roberta Hewerdine
Employees: 73

Jobs Added Last Year: 25 (+52.1%)

Computers - software (Mosaic) for the World Wide Web

SQUARE D COMPANY

1415 S. Roselle Rd.   Phone: 847-397-2600
Palatine, IL 60067   Fax: 847-397-8814
Chm & CEO: Didier Pineau-Valencienne
VP HR: Charles L. Hite
Employees: 16,500

Jobs Cut Last Year: 2,000 (-10.8%)

Electrical distribution equipment & industrial controls

STATE FARM MUTUAL AUTOMOBILE INSURANCE COMPANY

One State Farm Plaza   Phone: 309-766-2311
Bloomington, IL 61710   Fax: 309-766-6169
Chm, Pres & CEO: Edward B. Rust Jr.
VP Personnel: John P. Coffey
Employees: 71,437

Jobs Added Last Year: 1,217 (+1.7%)

Insurance - multiline & misc.

STIMSONITE CORPORATION

7524 N. Natchez Ave.   Phone: 847-647-7717
Niles, IL 60714   Fax: 847-647-8503
Pres : Jay R. Taylor
VP HR: Michael A. Cherwin
Employees: 460

Jobs Added Last Year: 195 (+73.6%)

Rubber & plastic products - reflective highway safety products

STONE CONTAINER CORPORATION

150 N. Michigan Ave.   Phone: 312-346-6600
Chicago, IL 60601-7568   Fax: 312-649-4294
Chm, Pres & CEO: Roger W. Stone
VP HR & Benefits Admin: Gayle M. Sparapani
Employees: 25,900

Jobs Cut Last Year: 3,200 (-11.0%)

Paper & paper products - newsprint, groundwood paper, kraft paper bags, containerboard & corrugated containers, boxboard & folding cartons & market pulp; lumber, plywood & veneer

SUNDSTRAND CORPORATION

4949 Harrison Ave.   Phone: 815-226-6000
Rockford, IL 61108   Fax: 815-226-2699
Pres & CEO: Robert H. Jenkins
VP Personnel & PR: Gary Hedges
Employees: 9,200

Jobs Added Last Year: 0

Aerospace - components & subsystems, electric power systems, mechanical & fluid systems, torpedo propulsion & constant speed drives; industrial components

SWEETHEART HOLDINGS, INC.

7575 S. Kostner Ave.   Phone: 312-767-3300
Chicago, IL 60652   Fax: 312-838-2226
Pres & CEO: William F. McLaughlin
VP HR: James Mullen
Employees: 8,600

Jobs Added Last Year: 0

Plastic & paper disposable food service & packaging products, including cups, plates & flatware

SYSTEM SOFTWARE ASSOCIATES, INC.

500 W. Madison St., 32nd Fl.
Chicago, IL 60661
Chm & CEO: Roger E. Covey
Dir HR: Marc Ugol
Employees: 2,000

Phone: 312-258-6000
Fax: 312-474-7500

Jobs Added Last Year: 210 (+11.7%)

Computers - business-application, maintenance-management, CASE & electronic-data-interchange software

TECHNOLOGY SOLUTIONS COMPANY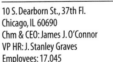

205 N. Michigan Ave., Ste. 1500
Chicago, IL 60601
Pres & CEO: John T. Kohler
Dir HR: Debbie Steele
Employees: 423

Phone: 312-861-9600
Fax: 312-861-9601

Jobs Added Last Year: 149 (+54.4%)

Computers - consulting & systems integration services

TELEPHONE AND DATA SYSTEMS, INC.

30 N. LaSalle St., Ste. 4000
Chicago, IL 60602-2587
Chm, Pres & CEO: LeRoy T. Carlson Jr.
VP HR: C. Theodore Herbert
Employees: 6,363

Phone: 312-630-1900
Fax: 312-630-1908

Jobs Added Last Year: 1,041 (+19.6%)

Utility - telephone; cellular telephone services; radio paging

TELLABS, INC.

4951 Indiana Ave.
Lisle, IL 60532
Pres & CEO: Michael J. Birck
Dir HR: Dan Stolle
Employees: 2,800

Phone: 708-969-8800
Fax: 708-512-8202

Jobs Added Last Year: 215 (+8.3%)

Telecommunications equipment - signal-processing & access-control equipment

TRIBUNE COMPANY

435 N. Michigan Ave.
Chicago, IL 60611
Chm, Pres & CEO: John W. Madigan
SVP Admin: John T. Sloan
Employees: 10,500

Phone: 312-222-9100
Fax: 312-222-9205

Jobs Added Last Year: 0

Publishing - newspapers (Chicago Tribune); radio & TV broadcasting (WGN); newsprint operations; book publishing (Contemporary, NTC); professional baseball team (Chicago Cubs)

TRUE NORTH COMMUNICATIONS INC.

101 E. Erie St.
Chicago, IL 60611-2897
Chm & CEO: Bruce Mason
VP & Mgr HR: Doris Radcliffe
Employees: 4,369

Phone: 312-751-7227
Fax: 312-751-3501

Jobs Added Last Year: 440 (+11.2%)

Advertising - direct marketing, public relations & sales promotions services

TUTHILL CORPORATION

908 N. Elm St.
Hinsdale, IL 60521
Pres: James Tuthill Jr.
Dir HR: Sandy Millray
Employees: 2,300

Phone: 708-655-2266
Fax: 708-655-2297

Jobs Added Last Year: 300 (+15.0%)

Industrial processing - engineered industrial products & components

UAL CORPORATION

1200 E. Algonquin Rd.
Elk Grove Township, IL 60007
Chm & CEO: Gerald Greenwald
SVP People: Paul G. George
Employees: 79,410

Phone: 847-700-4000
Fax: 847-700-5229

Jobs Added Last Year: 1,510 (+1.9%)

Transportation - airline (United Airlines)

UNICOM CORPORATION

10 S. Dearborn St., 37th Fl.
Chicago, IL 60690
Chm & CEO: James J. O'Connor
VP HR: J. Stanley Graves
Employees: 17,045

Phone: 312-394-7399
Fax: 312-394-7251

Jobs Cut Last Year: 1,415 (-7.7%)

Utility - electric power

UNITED STATES CELLULAR CORP.

8410 W. Bryn Mawr, Ste. 700
Chicago, IL 60631
Pres & CEO: H. Donald Nelson
VP HR: Douglas S. Arnold
Employees: 3,175

Phone: 312-399-8900
Fax: 312-399-8936

Jobs Added Last Year: 925 (+41.1%)

Telecommunications services - cellular telephone services

 An in-depth profile of this company is available to subscribers on Hoover's Online at www.hoovers.com.

161

UNITED STATIONERS INC.

2200 E. Golf Rd.　　　　　Phone: 847-699-5000
Des Plaines, IL 60016-1267　　Fax: 847-699-8046
Chm & CEO: Joel D. Spungin
VP HR: Robert H. Cornell
Employees: 4,800

Jobs Added Last Year: 1,200 (+33.3%)

Office equipment & supplies - wholesale supplies, furniture, computer products, facilities management supplies & business presentation products

UNITRIN, INC.

One E. Wacker Dr.　　　　Phone: 312-661-4500
Chicago, IL 60601　　　　Fax: 312-661-4690
Pres & CEO: Richard C. Vie
Dir HR: Ken Oehler
Employees: 7,600

Jobs Added Last Year: 311 (+4.3%)

Insurance - life, health, property & casualty; consumer finance services

UNIVERSAL AUTOMOTIVE INDUSTRIES, INC.

3350 N. Kedzie　　　　　Phone: 312-478-2323
Chicago, IL 60618-5722　　Fax: 312-478-2610
Chm, Pres & CEO: Yehuda Tzur
HR Mgr: Martha Cvkota
Employees: 285

Jobs Added Last Year: 175 (+159.1%)

Auto parts - wholesale aftermarket replacement parts for domestic & imported cars, vans & light trucks; brake rotors (UBP Universal Brake Parts)

THE UNIVERSITY OF CHICAGO

5801 S. Ellis Ave.　　　　Phone: 312-702-1234
Chicago, IL 60637　　　　Fax: 312-702-0353
Pres: Hugo F. Sonnenschein
VP HR & Support Svcs: JoAnn Shaw
Employees: 10,954

Jobs Added Last Year: —

Private, non-denominational university offering 50 undergraduate degree programs & 91 graduate degree programs; hospitals (The University of Chicago Hospitals)

THE UNIVERSITY OF ILLINOIS

346 Henry Admin. Bldg.　　Phone: 217-333-2464
Urbana, IL 61801　　　　Fax: 217-244-5821
Pres: James J. Stukel
Vice Chancellor HR & Admin: Charles Colbert
Employees: 20,000

Jobs Added Last Year: —

University

U.S. ROBOTICS CORPORATION

8100 N. McCormick Blvd.　　Phone: 847-982-5010
Skokie, IL 60076-2999　　　Fax: 847-933-5551
Chm, Pres & CEO: Casey G. Cowell
VP HR: Elizabeth S. Ryan
Employees: 3,347

Jobs Added Last Year: 1,896 (+130.7%)

Computers - modems, wide- & local-area network hubs (Courier, Megahertz, Sportster, Total Control, WorldPort) & Ethernet adapter cards

USFREIGHTWAYS CORPORATION

9700 Higgins Rd., Ste. 570　　Phone: 847-696-0200
Rosemont, IL 60018　　　　Fax: 847-696-2080
Pres & CEO: John Campbell Carruth
Exec Sec & Office Mgr: Rosemary Maziarka
Employees: 13,187

Jobs Added Last Year: 1,003 (+8.2%)

Transportation - less-than-truckload general commodities carrier

USG CORPORATION

125 S. Franklin St.　　　　Phone: 312-606-4000
Chicago, IL 60606-4678　　Fax: 312-606-4093
Pres & CEO: William C. Foote
VP HR & Ops: S. Gary Snodgrass
Employees: 12,400

Jobs Added Last Year: 100 (+0.8%)

Building products - gypsum wallboard, joint compound, cement board & ceiling products; acoustical tile & insulation

VELSICOL CHEMICAL CORPORATION

10400 W. Higgins Rd., Ste. 600　Phone: 847-298-9000
Rosemont, IL 60018　　　　Fax: 847-298-9015
CEO: Arthur R. Sigel
Dir HR: Donna Jennings
Employees: 750

Jobs Added Last Year: 150 (+25.0%)

Chemicals - cyclic intermediates, plasticizers & pesticides

VISIONTEK INC.

1175 Lakeside Dr.　　　　Phone: 847-360-7500
Gurnee, IL 60031　　　　Fax: 847-360-7401
CEO: Mark Polinsky
Dir HR: Michele Feldman
Employees: 270

Jobs Added Last Year: 96 (+55.2%)

Computers - PC & printer memory upgrades

WALGREEN CO.

200 Wilmot Rd. Phone: 847-940-2500
Deerfield, IL 60015 Fax: 847-940-2804
Chm & CEO: Charles R. Walgreen III
SVP HR: John A. Rubino
Employees: 68,000

Jobs Added Last Year: 6,100 (+9.9%)

Retail - drugstores (2,132 units)

WALLACE COMPUTER SERVICES, INC.

4600 W. Roosevelt Rd. Phone: 708-449-8600
Hillside, IL 60162 Fax: 708-449-1161
Pres & CEO: Robert J. Cronin
Dir HR: Barry L. White
Employees: 3,765

Jobs Added Last Year: 235 (+6.7%)

Printing - business forms, industrial & consumer catalogs, directories & price lists; pressure-sensitive labels & other office supplies

WHITMAN CORPORATION

3501 Algonquin Rd. Phone: 847-818-5000
Rolling Meadows, IL 60008 Fax: 847-818-5045
Chm & CEO: Bruce S. Chelberg
SVP HR: Lawrence J. Pilon
Employees: 16,841

Jobs Added Last Year: 1,570 (+10.3%)

Diversified operations - soft drink bottling (Pepsi General); auto service (Midas); refrigeration equipment

WM. WRIGLEY JR. COMPANY

410 N. Michigan Ave. Phone: 312-644-2121
Chicago, IL 60611 Fax: 312-644-0097
Pres & CEO: William Wrigley
VP Personnel: David E. Boxell
Employees: 7,300

Jobs Added Last Year: 300 (+4.3%)

Food - gum (Big Red, Doublemint, Extra, Freedent, Juicy Fruit, Spearmint, Winterfresh, Hubba Bubba)

WISCONSIN CENTRAL TRANSPORTATION CORP.

6250 N. River Rd., Ste. 9000 Phone: 847-318-4600
Rosemont, IL 60018 Fax: 847-318-4618
Pres & CEO: Edward A. Burkhardt
Asst VP HR: David French
Employees: 2,002

Jobs Added Last Year: 298 (+17.5%)

Transportation - regional railroad (#1 in US: Wisconsin Central Ltd., Fox Valley & Western Ltd., WCL Railcars, Inc.)

WMS INDUSTRIES INC.

3401 N. California Ave. Phone: 312-961-1111
Chicago, IL 60618 Fax: 312-961-1090
Pres, CEO & COO: Neil D. Nicastro
Dir HR: Michael Sirchio
Employees: 3,381

Jobs Added Last Year: 1,301 (+62.5%)

Leisure & recreational products - pinball & video games (Mortal Kombat); gambling equipment

1st Impressions — http://www.1st-imp.com/goldmine.html

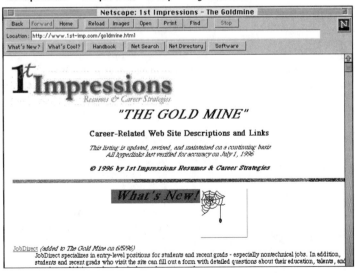

An in-depth profile of this company is available to subscribers on Hoover's Online at www.hoovers.com.

163

WMX TECHNOLOGIES, INC.

3003 Butterfield Rd.
Oak Brook, IL 60521
Pres, CEO & COO: Phillip B. Rooney
SVP HR & Comm: D. P. Payne
Employees: 73,200

Phone: 708-572-8800
Fax: 708-572-0757

Jobs Cut Last Year: 1,200 (-1.6%)

Pollution control equipment & services - waste collection, disposal & recycling; trash-to-energy power plant operations; water treatment facilities; environmental engineering & consulting

W.W. GRAINGER, INC.

455 Knightsbridge Pkwy.
Lincolnshire, IL 60069-3620
Pres & CEO: Richard L. Keyser
VP HR: Gary J. Goberville
Employees: 11,853

Phone: 847-793-9030

Jobs Added Last Year: 510 (+4.5%)

Wholesale distribution - industrial equipment & supplies

ZEBRA TECHNOLOGIES CORP.

333 Corporate Woods Pkwy.
Vernon Hills, IL 60061-3109
Chm & CEO: Edward L. Kaplan
Dir HR: Ellen Barnes
Employees: 627

Phone: 847-634-6700
Fax: 847-634-1830

Jobs Added Last Year: 126 (+25.1%)

Optical character recognition - bar code printers & related equipment

ZENITH ELECTRONICS CORPORATION

1000 Milwaukee Ave.
Glenview, IL 60025-2493
Interim Pres & CEO: Peter S. Willmott
VP HR: Dennis Winkleman
Employees: 18,100

Phone: 847-391-7000
Fax: 847-391-7291

Jobs Cut Last Year: 4,400 (-19.6%)

Audio & video home products - TVs, including high-definition, large-screen & projection models; VCRs; remote controls; analog & digital set-top cable boxes, cable systems & cable modems

AMBANC CORP.

302 Main St.
Vincennes, IN 47591-0438
Chm, Pres & CEO: Robert G. Watson
Dir HR: Richard A. Fox
Employees: 309

Phone: 812-885-6418
Fax: 812-885-6433

Jobs Added Last Year: 77 (+33.2%)

Banks - Midwest

AMTRAN, INC.

7337 W. Washington St.
Indianapolis, IN 46231
Chm & CEO: J. George Mikelsons
VP HR: Richard W. Meyer Jr.
Employees: 4,830

Phone: 317-247-4000
Fax: 317-240-7091

Jobs Added Last Year: 830 (+20.8%)

Travel services - travel club & travel agencies; chartered & scheduled airline services

ANTHEM INC.

120 Monument Circle
Indianapolis, IN 46204
Chm, Pres & CEO: L. Ben Lytle
SVP & Chief HR Officer: Daniel W. Kendall
Employees: 16,290

Phone: 317-488-6000
Fax: 317-488-6028

Jobs Added Last Year: 3,490 (+27.3%)

Insurance - life

ARVIN INDUSTRIES, INC.

One Noblitt Plaza, PO Box 3000
Columbus, IN 47202-3000
Pres: V. William Hunth
VP HR: Raymond P. Mack
Employees: 12,071

Phone: 812-379-3000
Fax: 812-379-3688

Jobs Cut Last Year: 2,764 (-18.6%)

Automotive & trucking - original equipment, automotive replacement parts & technology

BALL CORPORATION

345 S. High St.
Muncie, IN 47305-2326
Pres & CEO: George A. Sissel
VP HR: David A. Westerlund
Employees: 7,424

Phone: 317-747-6100
Fax: 317-747-6850

Jobs Cut Last Year: 5,435 (-42.3%)

Glass products - food & beverage packaging products; aerospace & communication systems & professional services

BIOMET, INC.

Airport Industrial Park, PO Box 587
Warsaw, IN 46581-0587
Pres & CEO: Dane A. Miller
VP HR: Darlene K. Whaley
Employees: 1,882

Phone: 219-267-6639
Fax: 219-267-8137

Jobs Added Last Year: 520 (+38.2%)

Medical instruments - orthopedic implant systems

BRIGHTPOINT INC.

6402 Corporate Dr.
Indianapolis, IN 46278
Chm, Pres & CEO: Robert J. Laikin
HR Mgr: Donna Smith
Employees: 115

Phone: 317-297-6100
Fax: 317-387-5493

Jobs Added Last Year: 43 (+59.7%)

Wholesale distribution - cellular telephones & related equipment

CENTRAL NEWSPAPERS, INC.

135 N. Pennsylvania St., Ste. 1200
Indianapolis, IN 46204-2400
Pres & CEO: Louis A. Weil III
No central personnel officer
Employees: 5,188

Phone: 317-231-9200
Fax: 317-231-9208

Jobs Added Last Year: 158 (+3.1%)

Publishing - newspapers (Indianapolis Star, Phoenix Gazette, Arizona Republic)

CNB BANCSHARES, INC.

20 NW Third St.
Evansville, IN 47739-0001
Pres & CEO: James J. Giancola
SVP HR: John M. Oberhelman
Employees: 1,817

Phone: 812-464-3400
Fax: 812-464-3551

Jobs Added Last Year: 320 (+21.4%)

Banks - Midwest

COACHMEN INDUSTRIES, INC.

601 E. Beardsley Ave.
Elkhart, IN 46514
Chm & CEO: Thomas H. Corson
VP Personnel: James R. Frahm
Employees: 3,443

Phone: 219-262-0123
Fax: 219-262-8823

Jobs Added Last Year: 656 (+23.5%)

Building - mobile homes & RVs

CONSOLIDATED PRODUCTS, INC.

500 Century Bldg., 36 S. Pennsylvania St.
Indianapolis, IN 46204
Pres & CEO: Alan B. Gilman
VP HR: John P. Hawes
Employees: 9,500

Phone: 317-633-4100
Fax: 317-633-4105

Jobs Added Last Year: 1,800 (+23.4%)

Retail - restaurants (Steak n Shake, Colorado Steakhouse)

CUMMINS ENGINE COMPANY, INC.

500 Jackson St.
Columbus, IN 47201
Chm & CEO: James A. Henderson
VP HR: Brenda S. Pitts
Employees: 24,300

Phone: 812-377-5000
Fax: 812-377-3334

Jobs Cut Last Year: 1,300 (-5.1%)

Engines - diesel & gasoline engines for commercial vehicles & agricultural & industrial uses

ELI LILLY AND COMPANY

Lilly Corporate Ctr.
Indianapolis, IN 46285
Chm & CEO: Randall L. Tobias
VP HR: Pedro P. Granadillo
Employees: 26,800

Phone: 317-276-2000
Fax: 317-276-2095

Jobs Added Last Year: 1,900 (+7.6%)

Drugs - nervous-system agents (Prozac), intestinal drugs (Axid) & animal health products (Tylan); pharmacy management, claims processing & adjudication; communications networks

EMMIS BROADCASTING CORPORATION

950 N. Meridian St., Ste. 1200
Indianapolis, IN 46204
Chm & CEO: Jeffrey H. Smulyan
Dir HR: Carolyn Herald
Employees: 402

Phone: 317-266-0100
Fax: 317-631-3750

Jobs Added Last Year: 88 (+28.0%)

Broadcasting - radio (one AM & 6 FM stations); magazine publishing

ESSEX GROUP INC.

1601 Wall St.
Fort Wayne, IN 46802
Pres & CEO: Stanley C. Craft
VP HR: Dominick Lucenta
Employees: 4,102

Phone: 219-461-4000
Fax: 219-461-4150

Jobs Added Last Year: 252 (+6.5%)

Wire & cable products & electrical insulation

 An in-depth profile of this company is available to subscribers on Hoover's Online at www.hoovers.com.

165

FIDELITY FEDERAL BANCORP

18 NW Fourth St., PO Box 1347   Phone: 812-424-0921
Evansville, IN 47706-1347   Fax: 800-280-3292
Chm & CEO: Bruce A. Cordingley
Asst VP HR: Deborah H. Gorman
Employees: 119
Jobs Added Last Year: 46 (+63.0%)

Banks - Midwest

THE FINISH LINE, INC.

3308 N. Mitthoeffer Rd.   Phone: 317-899-1022
Indianapolis, IN 46236   Fax: 317-899-0237
Chm, Pres & CEO: Alan H. Cohen
VP Fin & CFO: Steven J. Schneider
Employees: 2,900
Jobs Added Last Year: 615 (+26.9%)

Retail - men's, women's & children's brand-name athletic & leisure footwear, activewear & accessories

GENERAL ACCEPTANCE CORPORATION

5015 W. State Rd. 46   Phone: 812-876-3555
Bloomington, IN 47404   Fax: 812-876-6191
Chm, Pres & CEO: Malvin L. Algood
Personnel Mgr: Rus Algood
Employees: 300
Jobs Added Last Year: 181 (+152.1%)

Financial - purchase & service of installment sales contracts secured by used automobiles

GREAT LAKES CHEMICAL CORPORATION

One Great Lakes Blvd.   Phone: 317-497-6100
West Lafayette, IN 47906-0200   Fax: 317-497-6316
Pres & CEO: Robert B. McDonald
Dir HR: J. Michael Roberts
Employees: 8,000
Jobs Added Last Year: —

Chemicals - specialty chemicals & allied products, including petroleum additives, water treatment chemicals & flame retardants

GUIDANT CORPORATION

111 Monument Circle, 29th Fl.   Phone: 317-971-2000
Indianapolis, IN 46204-5129   Fax: 317-971-2040
Pres & CEO: Ronald W. Dollens
VP HR & Bus Dev: James A. Baumgardt
Employees: 4,980
Jobs Added Last Year: 473 (+10.5%)

Medical products - cardiac rhythm management & coronary artery disease intervention products (spinoff of Eli Lilly & Co.)

HILLENBRAND INDUSTRIES, INC.

700 State Rte. 46 East   Phone: 812-934-7000
Batesville, IN 47006-9166   Fax: 812-934-7364
Pres & CEO: W. August "Gus" Hillenbrand
VP HR: James G. Thorne
Employees: 9,800
Jobs Cut Last Year: 200 (-2.0%)

Diversified operations - hospital beds; caskets (Batesville) & funeral-planning insurance; security locks (Medeco)

HOLY CROSS HEALTH SYSTEM

3606 E. Jefferson Blvd.   Phone: 219-233-8558
South Bend, IN 46615   Fax: 219-233-8891
Chm: Edward Osborn
VP HR: Dave Dickerson
Employees: 16,856
Jobs Added Last Year: —

Hospitals

INDIANA UNIVERSITY

212 Bryan Hall   Phone: 812-855-4004
Bloomington, IN 47405   Fax: 812-855-5678
Pres: Myles Brand
Dir HR: Maurice Smith
Employees: 17,000
Jobs Added Last Year: —

University

IRWIN FINANCIAL CORPORATION

500 Washington St.   Phone: 812-376-1020
Columbus, IN 47201   Fax: 812-376-1709
Pres: John A. Nash
VP & HR Dir: Carrie Houston
Employees: 1,790
Jobs Added Last Year: 522 (+41.2%)

Financial - mortgage banking, investment & financial counseling, venture-capital services & credit insurance

KIMBALL INTERNATIONAL, INC.

1600 Royal St.   Phone: 812-482-1600
Jasper, IN 47549-1001   Fax: 812-482-8012
Pres & CEO: Douglas A. Habig
VP HR: Randall L. Catt
Employees: 8,675
Jobs Added Last Year: 212 (+2.5%)

Furniture - office furniture & cabinets; grand pianos

LINCOLN NATIONAL CORPORATION

200 E. Berry St.   Phone: 219-455-2000
Fort Wayne, IN 46802-2706   Fax: 219-455-1590
Chm & CEO: Ian M. Rolland
SVP & Dir HR: George E. Davis
Employees: 10,250
Jobs Added Last Year: 1,255 (+14.0%)

Insurance - life & health reinsurance (#1 worldwide) & property, casualty & life insurance

MARSH SUPERMARKETS, INC.

9800 Crosspoint Blvd.   Phone: 317-594-2100
Indianapolis, IN 46256-3350   Fax: 317-594-2704
Chm, Pres & CEO: Don E. Marsh
VP HR: Bruce A. Bain
Employees: 12,400
Jobs Added Last Year: 800 (+6.9%)

Retail - supermarkets (Marsh, LoBill Foods) & convenience stores (Village Pantry)

AG SERVICES OF AMERICA, INC.

2302 W. First St., Thunder Ridge Ct.   Phone: 319-277-0261
Cedar Falls, IA 50613   Fax: 319-277-0144
Pres & CEO: Henry C. Jungling Jr.
Dir HR: Robert Boelman
Employees: 79
Jobs Added Last Year: 17 (+27.4%)

Agricultural operations - supply of farm inputs, including seed, fertilizer, chemicals, crop insurance & cash advances for rent, fuel & irrigation to farmers primarily in the central US

NATIONAL STEEL CORPORATION

4100 Edison Lakes Pkwy.   Phone: 219-273-7000
Mishawaka, IN 46545-3440   Fax: 219-273-7869
Pres, CEO & COO: V. John Goodwin
SVP Admin & Corp Sec: David A. Pryzbylski
Employees: 9,474
Jobs Cut Last Year: 237 (-2.4%)

Steel - production

CASEY'S GENERAL STORES, INC.

One Convenience Blvd.   Phone: 515-965-6100
Ankeny, IA 50021-8045   Fax: 515-965-6160
Chm & CEO: Donald F. Lamberti
Dir HR: Bill Walljaster
Employees: 8,035
Jobs Added Last Year: 762 (+10.5%)

Retail - convenience stores

STANT CORPORATION

425 Commerce Dr.   Phone: 317-962-6655
Richmond, IN 47374-2646   Fax: 317-962-6866
Pres & CEO: David R. Paridy
SVP HR: W. Thomas Margetts
Employees: 7,600
Jobs Cut Last Year: 500 (-6.2%)

Automotive & trucking - gas caps, radiator caps, thermostats, wiper blades & other parts

GREAT LAKES AVIATION LTD.

1965 330th St.   Phone: 712-262-1000
Spencer, IA 51301-9211   Fax: 712-262-1001
Pres & CEO: Douglas G. Voss
HR Mgr: Penny Bretl
Employees: 1,090
Jobs Added Last Year: 237 (+27.8%)

Transportation - regional airline

WABASH NATIONAL CORPORATION

1000 Sagamore Pkwy. S.   Phone: 317-448-1591
Lafayette, IN 47905   Fax: 317-447-9405
Chm, Pres & CEO: Donald J. Ehrlich
VP HR: Charles E. Fish
Employees: 3,454
Jobs Added Last Year: 491 (+16.6%)

Automotive & trucking - intermodal, standard & customized truck trailers, dry freight vans, refrigerated trailers & bimodal vehicles

HON INDUSTRIES INC.

414 E. Third St., PO Box 1109   Phone: 319-264-7400
Muscatine, IA 52761-7109   Fax: 319-264-7217
Pres & CEO: Jack D. Michaels
VP HR: Daniel G. DePuydt
Employees: 5,933
Jobs Cut Last Year: 198 (-3.2%)

Furniture - metal & wood office furniture; homebuilding products

HY-VEE FOOD STORES, INC.

1801 Osceola Ave.   Phone: 515-774-2121
Chariton, IA 50049   Fax: 515-774-7211
Chm & CEO: Ronald D. Pearson
Mgr HR: Jerry Willis
Employees: 10,956

Jobs Added Last Year: 764 (+7.5%)

Retail - supermarkets, drug & convenience stores

LEE ENTERPRISES, INCORPORATED

400 Putnam Bldg., 215 N. Main St.   Phone: 319-383-2100
Davenport, IA 52801-1924   Fax: 319-323-9609
Pres & CEO: Richard D. Gottlieb
VP HR: Floyd Whellan
Employees: 5,600

Jobs Added Last Year: 900 (+19.1%)

Publishing - newspapers; network-affiliated TV stations; graphic
arts products for the newspaper industry

MAYTAG CORPORATION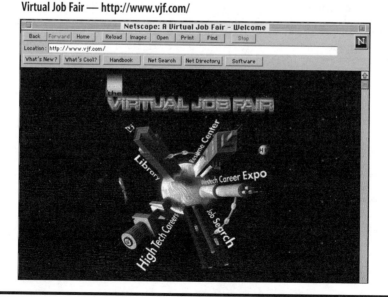

403 W. Fourth St. North   Phone: 515-792-8000
Newton, IA 50208   Fax: 515-791-6209
Chm & CEO: Leonard A. Hadley
VP HR: Jon O. Nicholas
Employees: 16,595

Jobs Cut Last Year: 3,177 (-16.1%)

Appliances - dishwashers, refrigerators, cooking appliances &
laundry equipment (Maytag, Jenn-Air, Admiral, Magic Chef);
vacuum cleaners (Hoover); vending equipment (Dixie-Narco)

MEREDITH CORPORATION

1716 Locust St.   Phone: 515-284-3000
Des Moines, IA 50309-3023   Fax: 515-284-2700
Chm & CEO: Jack D. Rehm
Corp Mgr Emp Svcs: Denise Rock
Employees: 2,400

Jobs Added Last Year: 206 (+9.4%)

Publishing - magazines (Better Homes & Gardens, Ladies' Home
Journal) & books; TV stations

MIDAMERICAN ENERGY COMPANY

666 Grand Ave.   Phone: 515-242-4300
Des Moines, IA 50309   Fax: 515-281-2217
Pres : Stanley J. Bright
VP HR & Info Tech: David J. Levy
Employees: 3,602

Jobs Added Last Year: 594 (+19.7%)

Utility - electric power & natural gas

PACE HEALTH MANAGEMENT SYSTEMS

1025 Ashworth Rd., Ste. 420   Phone: 515-222-1717
West Des Moines, IA 50265   Fax: 515-222-1716
CEO: Mark J. Emkjer
No central personnel officer
Employees: 50

Jobs Added Last Year: 14 (+38.9%)

Computers - point-of-care clinical software that automates the
recording, retrieval & management of patient care information

Virtual Job Fair — http://www.vjf.com/

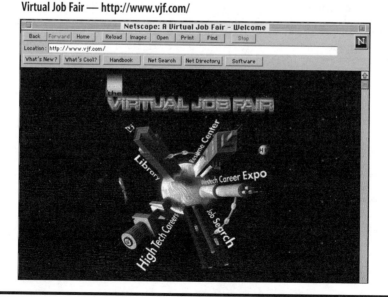

THE PRINCIPAL FINANCIAL GROUP

711 High St.
Des Moines, IA 50392-0001
Chm, Pres & CEO: David J. Drury
VP HR: Tom Gaard
Employees: 16,500

Phone: 515-247-5111
Fax: 515-246-5475

Jobs Added Last Year: 225 (+1.4%)

Insurance - life

TELEGROUP INC.

505 N. Third St.
Fairfield, IA 52556
Pres: Clifford Rees
Dir HR: John Smilek
Employees: 400

Phone: 515-472-5000
Fax: 515-472-4747

Jobs Added Last Year: 259 (+183.7%)

Telecommunications services - domestic & international long-distance telephone services

TERRA INDUSTRIES INC.

600 Fourth St., PO Box 6000
Sioux City, IA 51102-6000
Pres & CEO: Burton M. Joyce
VP HR: John S. Burchfield
Employees: 3,500

Phone: 712-277-1340
Fax: 712-277-1340

Jobs Added Last Year: 300 (+9.4%)

Agricultural operations - fertilizers, crop protection products & seed; agricultural chemicals

THE UNIVERSITY OF IOWA

105 Jessup Hall
Iowa City, IA 52242
Pres: Hunter R. Rawlings III
Dir Personnel: Marvin Lynch
Employees: 23,000

Phone: 319-335-0062
Fax: 319-335-2951

Jobs Added Last Year: —

University

ADVANCED FINANCIAL, INC.

5425 Martindale
Shawnee, KS 66218
Chm & Pres: Norman L. Peterson
Dir HR: Kathleen J. Keller
Employees: 122

Phone: 913-441-1160
Fax: 913-441-8992

Jobs Added Last Year: 51 (+71.8%)

Financial - mortgages & related services

APPLEBEE'S INTERNATIONAL, INC.

4551 W. 107th St., Ste. 100
Overland Park, KS 66207
Chm & CEO: Abe J. Gustin Jr.
Dir HR: Roz Mallet
Employees: 14,400

Phone: 913-967-4000
Fax: 913-967-8108

Jobs Added Last Year: 5,700 (+65.5%)

Retail - casual dining restaurants (Applebee's Neighborhood Grill & Bar, Rio Bravo Cantina)

ATCHISON CASTING CORPORATION

400 S. 4th St.
Atchison, KS 66002-0188
Chm, Pres & CEO: Hugh H. Aiken
VP HR: Gene N. Brackin
Employees: 1,760

Phone: 913-367-2121
Fax: 913-367-2155

Jobs Added Last Year: 424 (+31.7%)

Steel - iron & steel castings

BRITE VOICE SYSTEMS, INC.

7309 E. 21st St.
Wichita, KS 67206-1083
Chm, Pres & CEO: Stanley G. Brannan
Dir HR: Tamila Phillips
Employees: 582

Phone: 316-652-6500
Fax: 316-652-6800

Jobs Added Last Year: 152 (+35.3%)

Telecommunications equipment - voice processing systems

DUCKWALL-ALCO STORES, INC.

401 Cottage St.
Abilene, KS 67410-0129
Chm & Pres: Glen L. Shank
VP Personnel: Dennis P. Alesio
Employees: 3,500

Phone: 913-263-3350
Fax: 913-263-7531

Jobs Added Last Year: 500 (+16.7%)

Retail - discount (ALCO)

 An in-depth profile of this company is available
to subscribers on Hoover's Online at www.hoovers.com.

169

HUGOTON ENERGY CORPORATION

301 N. Main, Ste. 1900
Wichita, KS 67202
Phone: 316-262-1522
Fax: 316-269-6870
Chm, Pres & CEO: Floyd C. Wilson
EVP & CFO: W. Mark Womble
Employees: 111
Jobs Added Last Year: 42 (+60.9%)
Oil & gas - US exploration & production

KOCH INDUSTRIES, INC.

4111 E. 37th St. North
Wichita, KS 67220-3203
Phone: 316-828-5500
Fax: 316-828-5739
Chm & CEO: Charles G. Koch
Dir HR: Paul Wheeler
Employees: 13,000
Jobs Added Last Year: 1,000 (+8.3%)
Oil & gas - US integrated; chemicals; minerals; agriculture

LONE STAR STEAKHOUSE & SALOON

224 E. Douglas, Ste. 700
Wichita, KS 67202-3415
Phone: 316-264-8899
Fax: 316-264-2926
Chm, Pres & CEO: Jamie B. Coulter
VP Personnel Dev: Jeffrey M. Johnson
Employees: 14,500
Jobs Added Last Year: 5,600 (+62.9%)
Retail - steakhouse restaurants

NPC INTERNATIONAL, INC.

720 W. 20th St.
Pittsburg, KS 66762
Phone: 316-231-3390
Fax: 316-231-1188
Chm & CEO: O. Gene Bicknell
Dir HR & Legal Counsel: Jan Villamarie
Employees: 11,500
Jobs Added Last Year: 1,200 (+11.7%)
Retail - restaurants (Tony Roma's, Skipper's, Pizza Hut)

OTR EXPRESS INC.

804 N. Meadowbrook Dr.
Olathe, KS 66062
Phone: 913-829-1616
Fax: 913-829-0622
Pres: William P. Ward
VP Compensation & Benefits: Janice K. Ward
Employees: 574
Jobs Added Last Year: 124 (+27.6%)
Transportation - irregular-route trucking services

PAYLESS SHOESOURCE, INC.

3231 E. 6th Street
Topeka, KS 66607-2207
Phone: 913-233-5171
Fax: 913-295-6220
Chm & CEO: Steven J. Douglass
SVP HR: Jed L. Norden
Employees: 24,000
Jobs Added Last Year: —
Retail - discount footwear (#1 US self-service family shoe store chain)

SEABOARD CORPORATION

9000 W. 67th St.
Shawnee Mission, KS 66202
Phone: 913-676-8800
Fax: 913-676-8872
Pres: H. Harry Bresky
Dir HR: Doug Schult
Employees: 12,873
Jobs Added Last Year: 2,617 (+25.5%)
Food - poultry, pork & lamb products, flour & baked goods, fruits, vegetables & shrimp

SPRINT CORPORATION

2330 Shawnee Mission Pkwy.
Westwood, KS 66205
Phone: 913-624-3000
Fax: 913-624-3281
Chm & CEO: William T. Esrey
SVP HR: I. Benjamin Watson
Employees: 48,265
Jobs Cut Last Year: 561 (-1.1%)
Telecommunications services - long-distance (#3 in US) & local service; directory publishing (Yellow Pages); voice & data services (Global One) & equipment; wireless communications services

YELLOW CORPORATION

10777 Barkley Ave.
Overland Park, KS 66211
Phone: 913-696-6100
Fax: 913-344-4872
Chm, Pres & CEO: A. Maurice Myers
Dir Emp Benefits: Harold Marshall
Employees: 34,700
Jobs Added Last Year: 1,300 (+3.9%)
Transportation - trucking services (Yellow Freight System) & related customer information systems

ASHLAND INC.

1000 Ashland Dr.   Phone: 606-329-3333
Russell, KY 41169   Fax: 606-329-5274
Chm & CEO: John R. Hall
Administrative VP HR: Philip W. Block
Employees: 32,800
Jobs Added Last Year: 1,200 (+3.8%)

Oil & gas - integrated; construction services

BROWN-FORMAN CORPORATION

850 Dixie Hwy.   Phone: 502-585-1100
Louisville, KY 40210   Fax: 502-774-7876
Pres & CEO: Owsley Brown II
SVP & Exec Dir HR & Info Svcs: Russell C. Buzby
Employees: 7,300
Jobs Added Last Year: 200 (+2.8%)

Beverages - spirits (Jack Daniels, Early Times, Southern Comfort)
& wine; consumer durables (Lenox china, luggage & leather
accessories)

CHURCHILL DOWNS INCORPORATED

700 Central Ave.   Phone: 502-636-4400
Louisville, KY 40208   Fax: 502-636-4407
Pres & CEO: Thomas H. Meeker
VP HR: Jeanne Reeves
Employees: 2,500
Jobs Added Last Year: 400 (+19.0%)

Leisure & recreational services - thoroughbred horse racing,
including the Kentucky Derby; pari-mutuel wagering

HUMANA INC.

The Humana Bldg., 500 W. Main St.   Phone: 502-580-1000
Louisville, KY 40202   Fax: 502-580-3424
Chm & CEO: David A. Jones
VP HR: Robert A. Horrar
Employees: 16,800
Jobs Added Last Year: 4,800 (+40.0%)

Health maintenance organization - managed care health plans,
including preferred provider organizations & administrative
services-only plans

LG&E ENERGY CORP.

220 Main St., PO Box 32030   Phone: 502-627-2000
Louisville, KY 40232   Fax: 502-627-2023
Chm, Pres & CEO: Roger W. Hale
EVP & Chief Admin Officer: Steve R. Wood
Employees: 3,767
Jobs Added Last Year: 796 (+26.8%)

Utility - electric power & natural gas

LONG JOHN SILVER'S RESTAURANTS, INC.

101 Jerrico Dr.   Phone: 606-263-6000
Lexington, KY 40579   Fax: 606-263-6680
Pres & CEO: Clyde E. Culp
VP HR: Wayne Hougland
Employees: 18,000
Jobs Cut Last Year: 100 (-0.6%)

Retail - seafood restaurants

NATIONAL PROCESSING, INC.

1231 Durrett Ln.   Phone: 502-364-2000
Louisville, KY 40285-0001   Fax: 502-364-2362
Pres & CEO: Tony G. Holcombe
Dir HR: Marsh Lindhelm
Employees: 5,564
Jobs Added Last Year: —

Business services - check & card transaction processing for mer-
chants & other businesses; administrative & financial outsourcing; ticket processing for providers of travel-related services

PAPA JOHN'S INTERNATIONAL, INC.

11492 Bluegrass Pkwy., Ste. 175   Phone: 502-266-5200
Louisville, KY 40299-2370   Fax: 502-266-2925
Chm & CEO: John H. Schnatter
VP HR: Carol A. Trask
Employees: 4,000
Jobs Added Last Year: 201 (+5.3%)

Retail - pizza restaurants & delivery services (878 units)

POMEROY COMPUTER RESOURCES, INC.

1840 Airport Exchange Blvd., Ste. 240   Phone: 606-282-7111
Erlanger, KY 41018   Fax: 606-283-8281
Chm, Pres & CEO: David B. Pomeroy
Dir HR: Kim Garner
Employees: 441
Jobs Added Last Year: 151 (+52.1%)

Retail - value-added reseller of PCs & peripherals

PROVIDIAN CORPORATION

Providian Ctr., 400 W. Market St.   Phone: 502-560-2000
Louisville, KY 40202   Fax: 502-560-3975
Chm & CEO: Irving W. Bailey II
SVP Admin: Lawrence Pitterman
Employees: 8,600
Jobs Cut Last Year: 385 (-4.3%)

Insurance - life, accident, health & property & casualty

 An in-depth profile of this company is available
to subscribers on Hoover's Online at www.hoovers.com.

171

RALLY'S HAMBURGERS, INC.

10002 Shelbyville Rd., Ste. 150
Louisville, KY 40223
Pres & CEO: Donald E. Doyle
VP Admin: Butch Dulaney
Employees: 6,550

Phone: 502-245-8900
Fax: 502-245-7407

Jobs Added Last Year: —

Retail - double drive-through hamburger restaurants

RES-CARE, INC.

10140 Linn Station Rd.
Louisville, KY 40223
Pres & CEO: Ronald G. Geary
VP HR: Diana L. Fornear
Employees: 5,200

Phone: 502-394-2100
Fax: 502-394-2206

Jobs Added Last Year: 0

Schools - residential, training & support services for the physically & mentally disabled; Job Corps vocational training centers

THE UNIVERSITY OF KENTUCKY

111 Administration Bldg.
Lexington, KY 40506
Pres: Charles T. Wethington Jr.
Dir HR: James Webb
Employees: 12,021

Phone: 606-257-9000
Fax: 606-257-4000

Jobs Added Last Year: —

University

LOUISIANA

AMEDISYS, INC.

3029 S. Sherwood Forest Blvd., Ste. 300
Baton Rouge, LA 70816
CEO: William F. Borne
HR Mgr: Cindy Doll
Employees: 413

Phone: 504-292-2031
Fax: 504-292-8163

Jobs Added Last Year: 212 (+105.5%)

Health care - home health care & supplemental staffing

AVONDALE INDUSTRIES, INC.

5100 River Rd.
Avondale, LA 70094
Chm, Pres & CEO: Albert L. Bossier Jr.
VP HR: Ernie Griffin
Employees: 5,300

Phone: 504-436-2121
Fax: 504-436-5584

Jobs Cut Last Year: 900 (-14.5%)

Boat building - military & commercial ships

BAYOU STEEL CORPORATION

River Rd., PO Box 5000
LaPlace, LA 70069-1156
Chm & CEO: Howard M. Meyers
VP HR: Henry S. Vasquez
Employees: 545

Phone: 504-652-4900
Fax: 504-652-8950

Jobs Added Last Year: 117 (+27.3%)

Steel - beams, billets, reinforcing bar & other products from scrap metal

CAMPO ELECTRONICS, APPLIANCES AND COMPUTERS, INC.

109 Northpark Blvd., 5th Fl.
Covington, LA 70433
Chm, Pres & CEO: Anthony P. Campo
Dir HR: Bonnie Kinerd
Employees: 1,500

Phone: 504-867-5000
Fax: 504-867-5001

Jobs Added Last Year: 610 (+68.5%)

Retail - consumer electronics, major appliances & home office products

ENTERGY CORPORATION

639 Loyola Ave.
New Orleans, LA 70113
Chm & CEO: Edwin Lupberger
Mgr Emp Relations: Joseph Hotard
Employees: 13,521

Phone: 504-529-5262
Fax: 504-569-4001

Jobs Cut Last Year: 2,516 (-15.7%)

Utility - electric power

FREEPORT-MCMORAN INC.

1615 Poydras St.
New Orleans, LA 70112
Pres & CEO: Rene L. Latiolais
Dir HR: Robert Gettys
Employees: 7,913

Phone: 504-582-4000
Fax: 504-582-1847

Jobs Added Last Year: —

Mining - gold, silver & copper

J. RAY MCDERMOTT SA

1450 Poydras St. Phone: 504-587-5300
New Orleans, LA 70112-6050 Fax: 504-587-6153
Chm & CEO: Robert E. Howson
Dir HR: Lou Sannino
Employees: 10,400
Jobs Added Last Year: 200 (+2.0%)
Construction - offshore platforms & pipelines

RAMSAY HEALTH CARE, INC.

639 Loyola Ave., Ste. 1700 Phone: 504-525-2505
New Orleans, LA 70113 Fax: 504-585-0505
CEO: Gregory H. Browne
Dir HR: Shannon Dishiara
Employees: 3,310
Jobs Added Last Year: 1,037 (+45.6%)
Medical services - psychiatric & chemical dependency
evaluations & inpatient, outpatient, partial-hospitalization &
residential-treatment programs

LOUISIANA STATE UNIVERSITY SYSTEM

3810 W. Lakeshore Dr. Phone: 504-388-6935
Baton Rouge, LA 70808 Fax: 504-388-5524
Chancellor: William E. Davis
Dir HR: Sharyon Lipscomb
Employees: 22,000
Jobs Added Last Year: —
University

SCHWEGMANN GIANT SUPER MARKETS

PO Box 26099 Phone: 504-947-9921
New Orleans, LA 92121 Fax: 504-942-5407
Chm, Pres & CEO: John F. Schwegmann
Dir HR: Lee Janies
Employees: 4,961
Jobs Added Last Year: 2,646 (+114.3%)
Retail - supermarkets

MCDERMOTT INTERNATIONAL, INC.

1450 Poydras St. Phone: 504-587-5400
New Orleans, LA 70112-6050 Fax: 504-587-6153
Chm & CEO: Robert E. Howson
Dir HR: L. J. Sannino
Employees: 25,400
Jobs Added Last Year: 200 (+0.8%)
Machinery - power-generation equipment & offshore-industrial
facilities

STEWART ENTERPRISES, INC.

110 Veterans Memorial Blvd. Phone: 504-837-5880
Metairie, LA 70005 Fax: 504-849-2307
VC & CEO: Joseph P. Henican III
Dir Personnel & Admin: Edward L. Baucom
Employees: 6,600
Jobs Added Last Year: 400 (+6.5%)
Funeral services & related - funeral homes, cemeteries &
crematories (#3 in the US)

OFFSHORE LOGISTICS, INC.

224 Rue de Jean, PO Box 5-C Phone: 318-233-1221
Lafayette, LA 70505 Fax: 318-235-6678
Chm, Pres & CEO: James B. Clement
Personnel Mgr: Robert Mosley
Employees: 1,347
Jobs Added Last Year: 728 (+117.6%)
Transportation - charter helicopter service for the petroleum
industry

TIDEWATER INC.

1440 Canal St. Phone: 504-568-1010
New Orleans, LA 70112 Fax: 504-566-4582
Chm, Pres & CEO: William C. O'Malley
VP & Gen Counsel: Cliffe Laborde
Employees: 7,300
Jobs Added Last Year: 430 (+6.3%)
Oil & gas - offshore drilling support services, air-compression
equipment & services & ship repair services

PICCADILLY CAFETERIAS, INC.

3232 Sherwood Forest Blvd., PO Box 2467 Phone: 504-293-9440
Baton Rouge, LA 70821 Fax: 504-296-8370
Pres & CEO: Ronald A. LaBorde
EVP HR & Gen Mgr: Joseph S. Polito
Employees: 7,600
Jobs Added Last Year: 300 (+4.1%)
Retail - cafeterias

TURNER INDUSTRIES, LTD.

8687 United Plaza Blvd., Ste. 500 Phone: 504-922-5050
Baton Rouge, LA 70809 Fax: 504-922-5055
Chm: Bert S. Turner
EVP: Thomas H. Turner
Employees: 8,100
Jobs Added Last Year: 1,400 (+20.9%)
Construction - industrial construction & maintenance, including
pipe fabrication & environmental services

 An in-depth profile of this company is available
to subscribers on Hoover's Online at www.hoovers.com.

173

L.L. BEAN, INC.

Casco St.
Freeport, ME 04033
Pres & CEO: Leon A. Gorman
VP HR: Bob Peixotto
Employees: 3,800

Phone: 207-865-4761
Fax: 207-865-6738

Jobs Added Last Year: 300 (+8.6%)

Retail - mail order outdoor sporting goods & clothing

HANNAFORD BROS. CO.

145 Pleasant Hill Rd.
Scarborough, ME 04074
Pres & CEO: Hugh G. Farrington
SVP HR: Michael J. Strout
Employees: 20,400

Phone: 207-883-2911
Fax: 207-885-3165

Jobs Added Last Year: 3,900 (+23.6%)

Retail - supermarkets (Shop 'n Save, Hannaford, Wilson's)

UNUM CORPORATION

2211 Congress St.
Portland, ME 04122
Chm, Pres & CEO: James F. Orr III
SVP HR: Eileen C. Farrar
Employees: 6,900

Phone: 207-770-2211
Fax: 207-770-6933

Jobs Cut Last Year: 300 (-4.2%)

Insurance - life, disability, health & dental; annnuities & long-term-care insurance

IDEXX LABORATORIES, INC.

One IDEXX Dr.
Westbrook, ME 04092
Chm & CEO: David E. Shaw
Dir HR: Debra Coyman
Employees: 802

Phone: 207-856-0300
Fax: 207-856-0346

Jobs Added Last Year: 309 (+62.7%)

Biomedical & genetic products - biodetection systems that test for disease in animals, food & the environment

Get A Job — http://www.getajob.com/

BALTIMORE GAS AND ELECTRIC CO.

39 W. Lexington St.
Baltimore, MD 21201
Chm & CEO: Christian H. Poindexter
VP Mgmt Svcs: John Files
Employees: 9,279

Phone: 410-234-5000
Fax: 410-234-5126

Jobs Added Last Year: 279 (+3.1%)

Utility - electric power & natural gas

THE BLACK & DECKER CORPORATION

701 E. Joppa Rd.
Towson, MD 21286
Chm, Pres & CEO: Nolan D. Archibald
VP HR: Leonard A. Strom
Employees: 29,300

Phone: 410-716-3900
Fax: 410-716-2933

Jobs Cut Last Year: 6,500 (-18.2%)

Tools - electric power tools & related accessories; lawn & garden tools; door security hardware; small appliances, including hand-held vacuums, irons & food processors; plumbing products

CAPITOL MULTIMEDIA, INC.

7315 Wisconsin St., Ste. 800-E
Bethesda, MD 20814
Pres & CEO: Robert I. Bogin
No central personnel officer
Employees: 160

Phone: 301-907-7000
Fax: 301-907-7000

Jobs Added Last Year: 37 (+30.1%)

Computers - educational interactive consumer software & business applications focusing on the children's market within the CD-ROM interactive software industry

CAPSTONE PHARMACY SERVICES, INC.

2930 Washington Blvd.
Baltimore, MD 21230
Pres & CEO: R. Dirk Allison
Dir HR: Kim Bolford
Employees: 601

Phone: 410-646-7373
Fax: 410-646-4396

Jobs Added Last Year: 213 (+54.9%)

Medical services

CLARK ENTERPRISES, INC.

7500 Old Georgetown Rd.
Bethesda, MD 20814
Chm & CEO: A. James Clark
Dir Compensation & Benefits: Andrea Danko-Koenig
Employees: 5,000

Phone: 301-657-7100
Fax: 301-657-7263

Jobs Added Last Year: 0

Diversified operations - construction (Clark Construction Group); communications; real estate

THE COSMETIC CENTER

8839 Greenwood Place
Savage, MD 20763
Pres, CEO & COO: Ben S. Kovalsky
No central personnel officer
Employees: 1,720

Phone: 301-497-6800
Fax: 301-497-6632

Jobs Added Last Year: 330 (+23.7%)

Retail - brand-name cosmetics, fragrances, beauty aids & related items

DAVCO RESTAURANTS, INC.

1657 Crofton Blvd.
Crofton, MD 21114
Chm, Pres & CEO: Ronald D. Kirstien
SVP HR: Richard H. Borchers
Employees: 7,700

Phone: 410-721-3770
Fax: 410-793-0754

Jobs Added Last Year: 700 (+10.0%)

Retail - fast-food restaurants (215 Wendy's restaurants: #1 franchisee worldwide)

DISCOVERY COMMUNICATIONS, INC.

7700 Wisconsin Ave.
Bethesda, MD 20814
Chm & CEO: John Hendricks
Dir HR: Pandit Wright
Employees: 500

Phone: 301-986-1999
Fax: 301-986-1889

Jobs Added Last Year: 100 (+25.0%)

Broadcasting - science & education cable TV programming (Discovery Channel, Learning Channel); nature- & science-themed retail stores

ESSEX CORPORATION

9150 Guilford Rd.
Columbia, MD 21046
Chm, Pres & CEO: Harry Letaw Jr.
Dir HR: Dorothy DeShazo
Employees: 262

Phone: 301-953-7797
Fax: 301-953-7880

Jobs Added Last Year: 87 (+49.7%)

Diversified operations - professional & support services; security & special warfare programs; maintenance, logistics & information technology; aerospace simulators

FCNB CORP

7200 FCNB Court
Frederick, MD 21703
Pres & CEO: A. Patrick Linton
VP HR: David Esworthy
Employees: 305

Phone: 301-662-2191
Fax: 301-698-6141

Jobs Added Last Year: 74 (+32.0%)

Banks - Northeast

 An in-depth profile of this company is available to subscribers on Hoover's Online at www.hoovers.com.

175

FUSION SYSTEMS CORPORATION

7600 Standish Place
Rockville, MD 20855-2798
Pres & CEO: Leslie S. Levine
Dir HR: Carol Barnes
Employees: 593

Phone: 301-251-0300
Fax: 301-279-0578

Jobs Added Last Year: 137 (+30.0%)

Machinery - ultraviolet curing systems used in semiconductor manufacturing equipment & printing & coating applications

GIANT FOOD INC.

6300 Sheriff Rd.
Landover, MD 20785
Pres & CEO: Pete L. Manos
SVP Labor Relations & Personnel: Roger D. Olson
Employees: 25,600

Phone: 301-341-4100
Fax: 301-341-4804

Jobs Added Last Year: 600 (+2.4%)

Retail - supermarkets

GOODWILL INDUSTRIES INTL.

9200 Wisconsin Ave.
Bethesda, MD 20814
Pres & CEO: David M. Cooney
Dir HR: Doug Werber
Employees: 130,000

Phone: 301-530-6500
Fax: 301-530-1516

Jobs Added Last Year: —

Charitable organization

GROUP 1 SOFTWARE, INC.

4200 Parliament Place, Ste. 600
Lanham, MD 20706-1844
Chm & CEO: Robert S. Bowen
Dir HR: Trent Lutz
Employees: 227

Phone: 301-731-2300
Fax: 301-731-0360

Jobs Added Last Year: 56 (+32.7%)

Computers - mailing list/list management software

HCIA INC.

300 E. Lombard St.
Baltimore, MD 21202
Chm, Pres & CEO: George D. Pillari
Dir HR: John Robison
Employees: 502

Phone: 410-332-7532
Fax: 410-576-9429

Jobs Added Last Year: 170 (+51.2%)

Medical practice management - integrated clinical- & financial-information systems & products

HECHINGER COMPANY

3500 Pennsy Dr.
Landover, MD 20785-1691
Chm, Pres & CEO: John W. Hechinger Jr.
SVP HR: Carol A. Stevens
Employees: 20,000

Phone: 301-341-1000
Fax: 301-341-0980

Jobs Added Last Year: 0

Building products - retail home improvement & garden centers (Home Quarters Warehouse, Inc. & Hechinger Stores Company)

HOST MARRIOTT SERVICES CORPORATION

10400 Fernwood Rd.
Bethesda, MD 20817
Pres & CEO: William W. McCarten
No central personnel officer
Employees: 22,400

Phone: 301-380-7000

Jobs Added Last Year: 400 (+1.8%)

Hotels & motels - full-service hotels & resorts; food & gift concession areas; merchandise stores at arenas & tourist attractions

IGEN, INC.

16020 Industrial Dr.
Gaithersburg, MD 20877
Chm & CEO: Samuel J. Wohlstadter
VP HR: Kathy Dickerson
Employees: 119

Phone: 301-984-8000
Fax: 301-230-0158

Jobs Added Last Year: 33 (+38.4%)

Medical instruments - diagnostic systems utilizing proprietary technology (ORIGEN) based on electrochemiluminescence for immunoassays, nucleic acid probes & clinical chemistry tests

INFORMATION RESOURCE ENGINEERING

8029 Corporate Dr.
Baltimore, MD 21236
Chm, Pres & CEO: Anthony A. Caputo
VP Fin & Admin, Sec & Treas: David A. Skalitzky
Employees: 90

Phone: 410-931-7500
Fax: 410-931-7524

Jobs Added Last Year: 43 (+91.5%)

Computers - data transmission security software using encryption technology

INTEGRATED HEALTH SERVICES, INC.

10065 Red Run Blvd.
Owings Mills, MD 21117
Chm & CEO: Robert N. Elkins
VP HR: Jan Zdanis
Employees: 23,000

Phone: 410-998-8400
Fax: 410-998-8714

Jobs Added Last Year: 1,800 (+8.5%)

Medical services - subacute & postacute health care services

JOHNS HOPKINS HEALTH SYSTEM

600 N. Wolfe St.
Baltimore, MD 21287
CEO: James A. Block
Dir HR: Bonnie Alterwitz
Employees: 10,936
Jobs Added Last Year: —

Phone: 410-955-5000
Fax: 410-955-6575

Hospitals; research facilities

THE JOHNS HOPKINS UNIVERSITY INC.

3400 N. Charles St.
Baltimore, MD 21218
Pres: William Richardson
Acting VP HR: Edgar Roulhac
Employees: 18,000
Jobs Added Last Year: —

Phone: 410-516-8000
Fax: 410-516-8900

University

JP FOODSERVICE, INC.

9830 Patuxent Woods Dr.
Columbia, MD 21046
Chm & CEO: James L. Miller
VP HR: Dan Berliant
Employees: 2,500
Jobs Added Last Year: 400 (+19.0%)

Phone: 410-312-7110
Fax: 410-312-7591

Food - wholesale to restaurants

LEGG MASON, INC.

111 S. Calvert St., PO Box 1476
Baltimore, MD 21203-1476
Chm, Pres & CEO: Raymond A. Mason
VP HR: Gail Reichard
Employees: 3,200
Jobs Added Last Year: 300 (+10.3%)

Phone: 410-539-0000
Fax: 410-539-4096

Financial - investment management of individual & institutional mutual funds; investment banking for corporations & municipalities; insurance & annuities; commercial mortgage banking

LOCKHEED MARTIN CORPORATION

6801 Rockledge Dr.
Bethesda, MD 20817-1877
CEO: Norman R. Augustine
VP HR: Robert B. Corlett
Employees: 160,000
Jobs Added Last Year: 77,500 (+93.9%)

Phone: 301-897-6000
Fax: 301-897-6704

Aerospace - spacecraft, space & strategic missiles, launch vehicles; aeronautics; information & technology services; electronics; energy systems

MANOR CARE, INC.

10750 Columbia Pike
Silver Spring, MD 20901
Chm, Pres & CEO: Stewart Bainum Jr.
SVP HR: Charles A. Shields
Employees: 31,000
Jobs Added Last Year: 5,500 (+21.6%)

Phone: 301-681-9400
Fax: 301-905-4062

Nursing homes; hotel/motel franchisor (Clarion, Comfort, Econo Lodge, Friendship, Quality, Rodeway, Sleep Inns); institutional pharmacies (Vitalink)

MANUGISTICS GROUP, INC.

2115 E. Jefferson St.
Rockville, MD 20852-4999
Chm, Pres & CEO: William M. Gibson
Dir HR: Carl Di Pietro
Employees: 499
Jobs Added Last Year: 102 (+25.7%)

Phone: 301-984-5000
Fax: 301-984-5017

Computers - supply chain management software to monitor & control manufacturing operations

MARRIOTT INTERNATIONAL, INC.

10400 Fernwood Rd.
Bethesda, MD 20817
Chm, Pres & CEO: J. W. Marriott Jr.
SVP HR: Clifford J. Ehrlich
Employees: 179,400
Jobs Added Last Year: 15,960 (+9.8%)

Phone: 301-380-3000
Fax: 301-380-5067

Hotels & motels; food- & facilities-management services

MCCORMICK & COMPANY, INC.

18 Loveton Circle
Sparks, MD 21152-6000
Chm & CEO: Charles P. "Buzz" McCormick Jr.
VP HR: Karen D. Weatherholtz
Employees: 8,900
Jobs Added Last Year: 0

Phone: 410-771-7301
Fax: 410-771-7462

Food - spices, seasonings & flavorings; plastic packaging

MICRO-INTEGRATION CORP.

One Science Park
Frostburg, MD 21532
Chm, Pres & CEO: John A. Parsons
Dir HR: Kathy Snyder
Employees: 87
Jobs Added Last Year: 27 (+45.0%)

Phone: 301-689-0800
Fax: 301-689-0808

Computers - communications links, terminal emulation, application programming interfaces & client/server applications & development tools

 An in-depth profile of this company is available to subscribers on Hoover's Online at www.hoovers.com.

177

MICROS SYSTEMS, INC.

12000 Baltimore Ave.
Beltsville, MD 20705-1291
Pres & CEO: A. L. Giannopoulous
Mgr HR: Cathy Rensel
Employees: 653

Phone: 301-210-6000
Fax: 301-210-3334

Jobs Added Last Year: 203 (+45.1%)

Computers - point-of-sale computer systems for hospitality providers

MID ATLANTIC MEDICAL SERVICES, INC.

4 Taft Ct.
Rockville, MD 20850
Chm, Pres & CEO: George T. Jochum
Senior Dir HR: Gloria Stem
Employees: 2,374

Phone: 301-294-5140
Fax: 301-762-1430

Jobs Added Last Year: 349 (+17.2%)

Health maintenance organization

ORION NETWORK SYSTEMS, INC.

2440 Research Blvd., Ste. 400
Rockville, MD 20850
Pres & CEO: W. Neil Bauer
VP HR: Stanley Cooper
Employees: 145

Phone: 301-258-8101
Fax: 301-258-8119

Jobs Added Last Year: 31 (+27.2%)

Telecommunications - international satellite communications systems (Orion 1)

PEAK TECHNOLOGIES GROUP, INC.

9200 Berger Rd.
Columbia, MD 21046
Chm, Pres & CEO: Nicholas R. H. Toms
Dir HR: Mike Bush
Employees: 813

Phone: 410-312-6000
Fax: 410-312-6065

Jobs Added Last Year: 295 (+56.9%)

Optical character recognition - industrial bar code systems

PERDUE FARMS INCORPORATED

Old Ocean City Rd., PO Box 1537
Salisbury, MD 21802
Chm & CEO: James A. Perdue
VP HR: Tom Moyers
Employees: 18,600

Phone: 410-543-3000
Fax: 410-543-3874

Jobs Added Last Year: 0

Food - poultry processing

PHH CORPORATION

11333 McCormick Rd.
Hunt Valley, MD 21031-1000
Chm, Pres & CEO: Robert D. Kunisch
VP HR & Quality, Gen Counsel & Asst Sec: Samuel H. Wright
Employees: 5,000

Phone: 410-771-3600
Fax: 410-771-1123

Jobs Added Last Year: 70 (+1.4%)

Business services - integrated management services, expense-management programs & mortgage-banking services; vehicle management & leasing programs; employee relocation services

Online Career Center — http://www.occ.com/occ/

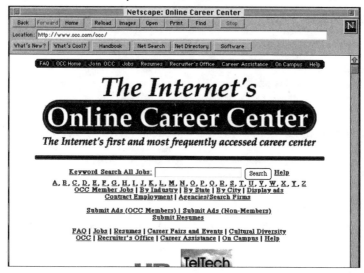

THE ROUSE COMPANY

10275 Little Patuxent Pkwy.
Columbia, MD 21044
Pres & CEO: Anthony W. Deering
VP & Dir Personnel & Administrative Svcs: William D. Boden
Employees: 5,085

Phone: 410-992-6000
Fax: 410-992-6363

Jobs Added Last Year: 390 (+8.3%)

Real estate operations - regional malls (Baltimore's Harborplace, Boston's Faneuil Hall Marketplace, New York's South Street Seaport)

RWD TECHNOLOGIES, INC.

10480 Little Patuxent Pkwy.
Park View, Ste. 1200
Columbia, MD 21044-3530
Chm & CEO: Robert W. Deutsch
Dir Admin & Personnel: Jan P. Keller
Employees: 522

Phone: 410-730-4377
Fax: 410-964-0039

Jobs Added Last Year: 190 (+57.2%)

Computers - training & documentation services, performance support & manufacturing production systems

SYLVAN LEARNING SYSTEMS, INC.

9135 Guilford Rd.
Columbia, MD 21046
Chm & CEO: R. Christopher Hoehn-Saric
Dir HR: Leslie Muller
Employees: 2,200

Phone: 410-880-0889
Fax: 410-880-8717

Jobs Added Last Year: 1,031 (+88.2%)

Schools - franchised tutoring centers

TESSCO TECHNOLOGIES INC.

34 Loveton Circle
Sparks, MD 21152-5100
Chm, Pres & CEO: Robert B. Barnhill Jr.
People Dev: Lynne Tucey
Employees: 178

Phone: 410-472-7000
Fax: 410-472-7575

Jobs Added Last Year: 37 (+26.2%)

Wholesale distribution - wireless-communication products

UNC INCORPORATED

175 Admiral Cochrane Dr.
Annapolis, MD 21401-7394
Chm, Pres, CEO & COO: Dan A. Colussy
VP HR: Gerald J. Knapp
Employees: 5,730

Phone: 410-266-7333
Fax: 410-266-5706

Jobs Added Last Year: 320 (+5.9%)

Aerospace - turbine-engine components & assemblies; overhaul of aircraft & industrial gas turbine engines & aircraft accessories; maintenance & training, repair & logistical contract services

THE UNIVERSITY OF MARYLAND SYSTEM

3300 Metzerott Rd.
Adelphi, MD 20783
Chancellor: Donald N. Langenberg
Dir HR: Karen Farber
Employees: 25,690

Phone: 301-445-1905
Fax: 301-445-2761

Jobs Added Last Year: —

University

USF&G CORPORATION

100 Light St.
Baltimore, MD 21202
Chm, Pres & CEO: Norman P. Blake Jr.
SVP HR & Gen Counsel: John A. MacColl
Employees: 6,200

Phone: 410-547-3000
Fax: 410-625-5682

Jobs Cut Last Year: 100 (-1.6%)

Insurance - property, casualty & life; management consulting & asset management

YOUTH SERVICES INTERNATIONAL

2 Park Center Ct., Ste. 200
Owings Mills, MD 21117
Chm & CEO: W. James Hindman
SVP HR: Louis F. Hejl Jr.
Employees: 1,560

Phone: 410-356-8600
Fax: 410-356-8634

Jobs Added Last Year: 488 (+45.5%)

Protection - treatment programs for troubled & at-risk youth

ACT MANUFACTURING, INC.

108 Forest Ave.
Hudson, MA 01749
Chm, Pres & CEO: John A. Pino
Dir HR: Dodie Cavazza
Employees: 655

Phone: 508-562-1200
Fax: 508-568-1904

Jobs Added Last Year: 145 (+28.4%)

Electrical components - electronic interconnection assemblies

ADAMS MEDIA CORPORATION

260 Center St. Phone: 617-767-8100
Holbrook, MA 02343 Fax: 617-767-0994
Pres: Bob Adams
VP Fin & Admin: Allan B. Tatel
Employees: 75

Jobs Added Last Year: 15 (+25.0%)

Publishing - books, software & online service for job hunters (Adams JobBank, Adams Resume & Cover Letters)

ADDISON-WESLEY LONGMAN/PENGUIN

One Jacob Way Phone: 617-944-3700
Reading, MA 01867 Fax: 617-944-9338
CEO, Addison-Wesley: J. Larry Jones
VP & Dir HR, Addison-Wesley: George Goldberg
Employees: 7,310

Jobs Added Last Year: 110 (+1.5%)

Publishing - educational, general-interest & professional books & software; audiotapes & children's books

ADVANCED DEPOSITION TECHNOLOGIES

580 Myles Standish Industrial Park Phone: 508-823-0707
Taunton, MA 02780 Fax: 508-823-4434
Chm, Pres, CEO & Treas: Glen Walters
No central personnel officer
Employees: 53

Jobs Added Last Year: 12 (+29.3%)

Chemicals - thin-metal coatings for microwave food packaging, capacitors, electronic security devices, electrostatic protective materials & solar films

ADVANCED NMR SYSTEMS, INC.

46 Jonspin Rd. Phone: 508-657-8876
Wilmington, MA 01887-1019 Fax: 508-658-5381
Chm, CEO & Treas: Jack Nelson
VP HR: Elaine McCarthy
Employees: 201

Jobs Added Last Year: 117 (+139.3%)

Medical instruments - magnetic resonance imaging equipment (InstaScan)

AFFILIATED COMMUNITY BANCORP, INC.

716 Main St. Phone: 617-894-6810
Waltham, MA 02154
Pres & CEO: Timothy J. Hansberry
Dir HR: Pat Valley
Employees: 162

Jobs Added Last Year: 42 (+35.0%)

Banks - Northeast (Lexington Savings Bank, Federal Savings Bank)

ALLMERICA FINANCIAL CORP.

440 Lincoln St. Phone: 508-855-1000
Worcester, MA 01653 Fax: 508-853-6332
Pres & CEO: John F. O'Brien
VP Corp Svcs: Bruce C. Anderson
Employees: 7,800

Jobs Added Last Year: 1,100 (+16.4%)

Insurance - life, property & casualty & employee benefit & institutional services

AMERICAN BILTRITE INC.

57 River St. Phone: 617-237-6655
Wellesley Hills, MA 02181 Fax: 617-237-6880
Chm & CEO: Roger S. Marcus
VP Fin & CFO: Gilbert K. Gailius
Employees: 2,835

Jobs Added Last Year: 2,235 (+372.5%)

Building products - resilient floor tile products; rubber-studded tile products; footwear products; adhesive-coated pressure-sensitive papers & films, sensitive tapes & adhesive products

ANALOG DEVICES, INC.

One Technology Way Phone: 617-329-4700
Norwood, MA 02062-9106 Fax: 617-326-8703
Chm & CEO: Ray Stata
VP HR: Ross Brown
Employees: 6,000

Jobs Added Last Year: 600 (+11.1%)

Electrical components - linear, mixed-signal & digital integrated circuits, for OEMs in the communications, computer, instrumentation, military/aerospace & consumer electronics industries

APPLIED SCIENCE AND TECHNOLOGY

35 Cabot Rd. Phone: 617-933-5560
Woburn, MA 01801-1053 Fax: 617-933-0750
Chm, Pres & CEO: Richard S. Post
CFO & SVP Fin: John M. Tarrh
Employees: 120

Jobs Added Last Year: 27 (+29.0%)

Machinery - semiconductor manufacturing equipment

ARCH COMMUNICATIONS GROUP, INC.

1800 W. Park Dr., Ste. 250 Phone: 508-898-0962
Westborough, MA 01581 Fax: 508-366-0846
Pres & CEO: C. Edward Baker Jr.
HR Mgr: Carol Burns
Employees: 2,035

Jobs Added Last Year: 1,448 (+246.7%)

Telecommunications services - paging services (#3 in the US)

ASECO CORPORATION

500 Donald Lynch Blvd.
Marlboro, MA 01752
Chm, Pres & CEO: Carl S. Archer Jr.
HR Mgr: Frank Coen
Employees: 126

Phone: 508-481-8896
Fax: 508-481-0369

Jobs Added Last Year: 26 (+26.0%)

Electronics - semiconductor test handlers

ASPEN TECHNOLOGY, INC.

10 Canal Park
Cambridge, MA 02141
Chm & CEO: Lawrence B. Evans
Dir HR: Ann McDonald
Employees: 417

Phone: 617-577-0100
Fax: 617-577-0722

Jobs Added Last Year: 142 (+51.6%)

Computers - CAE software products for the chemicals, petroleum, pharmaceuticals, metals & minerals, food & consumer products, pulp & paper & electric power industries

AVID TECHNOLOGY, INC.

One Park West
Tewksbury, MA 01876
Chm & CEO: William J. Miller
VP HR: Judith M. Oppenheim
Employees: 1,476

Phone: 508-640-6789
Fax: 508-640-1366

Jobs Added Last Year: 700 (+90.2%)

Computers - digital, nonlinear film-, video- & audio-editing systems

BANKBOSTON CORPORATION

100 Federal St.
Boston, MA 02110
Chm, Pres & CEO: Charles K. Gifford
Exec Dir HR: Helen G. Drinan
Employees: 17,881

Phone: 617-434-2200
Fax: 617-434-7547

Jobs Cut Last Year: 474 (-2.6%)

Banks - Northeast

BBN CORPORATION

150 Cambridge Park Dr.
Cambridge, MA 02140
Chm, Pres & CEO: George H. Conrades
VP HR: Steven Heinrich
Employees: 2,000

Phone: 617-873-2000
Fax: 617-873-5011

Jobs Added Last Year: 306 (+18.1%)

Computers - internetworking services & products, collaborative systems & acoustic technologies, data analysis & process optimization software products; Internet access services (BBN Planet)

BIG Y FOODS INC.

280 Chestnut St.
Springfield, MA 01102
CEO & SVP: Donald H. D'Amour
Dir Personnel: Donald Trella
Employees: 3,940

Phone: 413-784-0600
Fax: 413-732-8475

Jobs Added Last Year: 635 (+19.2%)

Retail - supermarkets

BOSTON SCIENTIFIC CORPORATION

One Boston Scientific Place
Natick, MA 01760-1537
Chm & CEO: Peter M. Nicholas
VP HR: Jamie Rubin
Employees: 8,000

Phone: 508-650-8000
Fax: 508-650-8939

Jobs Added Last Year: 5,162 (+181.9%)

Medical instruments - catheters & other devices used in reduced-incision surgical procedures

BOSTON TECHNOLOGY, INC.

100 Quannapowitt Pkwy.
Wakefield, MA 01880
Pres & CEO: John C. W. Taylor
SVP Admin & Gen Counsel: A. K. Wnorowski
Employees: 559

Phone: 617-246-9000
Fax: 617-246-4510

Jobs Added Last Year: 140 (+33.4%)

Telecommunications equipment - voice messaging system (CO ACCESS)

BOSTON UNIVERSITY

147 Bay State Rd.
Boston, MA 02215
Pres: John Westling
Dir HR: Manuel Monteiro
Employees: 15,000

Phone: 617-353-2000
Fax: 617-353-2053

Jobs Added Last Year: —

University

BRADLEES, INC.

One Bradlees Circle
Braintree, MA 02184
Chm & CEO: Mark A. Cohen
SVP HR: Randall E. Dickerson
Employees: 16,000

Phone: 617-380-3000
Fax: 617-380-5915

Jobs Added Last Year: 2,000 (+14.3%)

Retail - discount regional department stores

 An in-depth profile of this company is available to subscribers on Hoover's Online at www.hoovers.com.

BROOKS AUTOMATION, INC.

15 Elizabeth Dr.
Chelmsford, MA 01824
Pres: Robert J. Therrien
HR Administrator: Barbara Chouinard
Employees: 255

Phone: 508-262-2400
Fax: 508-262-2500

Jobs Added Last Year: 104 (+68.9%)

Machinery - central wafer handling systems & modules, including vacuum transfer robots, vacuum cassette elevator load locks, vacuum alignment & thermal conditioning modules

BROOKTROUT TECHNOLOGY, INC.

410 First Ave.
Needham, MA 02194-2722
Pres: Eric R. Giler
HR Mgr: Lisbeth Mag
Employees: 93

Phone: 617-449-4100
Fax: 617-449-9009

Jobs Added Last Year: 24 (+34.8%)

Telecommunications equipment - facsimile & voice processing systems including multichannel fax boards & fax-on-demand retrieval technology

BTU INTERNATIONAL, INC.

23 Esquire Rd.
North Billerica, MA 01862-2596
Chm, Pres & CEO: Paul J. van der Wansem
Dir HR: Donald Masson
Employees: 406

Phone: 508-667-4111
Fax: 508-667-9068

Jobs Added Last Year: 84 (+26.1%)

Electrical components - thermal-processing equipment & related controls for electronics & power generation industries; solder-reflow furnaces for circuit board surface-mount applications

CAMBRIDGE SOUNDWORKS, INC.

311 Needham St.
Newton, MA 02164
Pres & CEO: Thomas J. DeVesto
Mgr HR: Avery Casper-Filbin
Employees: 289

Phone: 617-332-5936
Fax: 617-332-9229

Jobs Added Last Year: 77 (+36.3%)

Audio & video home products - stereo & home theater speakers & computer multimedia systems

CAMBRIDGE TECHNOLOGY PARTNERS

304 Vassar St.
Cambridge, MA 02139
Pres & CEO: James K. Sims
SVP HR: Susan J. Loker
Employees: 1,077

Phone: 617-374-9800
Fax: 617-374-8300

Jobs Added Last Year: 531 (+97.3%)

Computers - information-technology consulting & software-development services

CASCADE COMMUNICATIONS CORP.

5 Carlisle Rd.
Westford, MA 01886
Pres & CEO: Daniel E. Smith
Dir HR: Mary Cogan
Employees: 423

Phone: 508-692-2600
Fax: 508-692-9214

Jobs Added Last Year: 191 (+82.3%)

Computers - wide area network switches & network-interface modules

CENTENNIAL TECHNOLOGIES, INC.

37 Manning Rd.
Billerica, MA 01821
Chm & CEO: Emanuel Pinez
Personnel Mgr: Patty O'Neil
Employees: 86

Phone: 508-670-0646
Fax: 508-670-9025

Jobs Added Last Year: 46 (+115.0%)

Computers - PC cards (memory & data/fax) for products in industrial & commercial applications; laser printer font cartridges

CML GROUP, INC.

524 Main St.
Acton, MA 01720
Chm & CEO: Charles M. Leighton
No central personnel officer
Employees: 6,800

Phone: 508-264-4155
Fax: 508-264-4073

Jobs Cut Last Year: 6 (-0.1%)

Retail - apparel (Britches), exercise equipment (NordicTrack) & gardening equipment (Smith & Hawken)

COGNEX CORPORATION

One Vision Dr.
Natick, MA 01760
Chm, Pres & CEO: Robert J. Shillman
HR Mgr: Jo Ann Woodyard
Employees: 307

Phone: 508-650-3000
Fax: 508-650-3333

Jobs Added Last Year: 87 (+39.5%)

Machinery - computerized quality-control systems

COMPUTER TELEPHONE CORP.

360 Second Ave.
Waltham, MA 02154-1104
Chm, Pres & CEO: Robert J. Fabbricatore
Dir HR: Sandi Crespi
Employees: 228

Phone: 617-466-8080
Fax: 617-466-1306

Jobs Added Last Year: 50 (+28.1%)

Telecommunications services - discounted telephone calling plans, 800-number services, data transport services & long-distance service

CONTINENTAL CABLEVISION, INC.

The Pilot House, Lewis Wharf   Phone: 617-742-9500
Boston, MA 02110   Fax: 617-742-0530
Chm & CEO: Amos B. Hostetter Jr.
SVP HR: H. Clare Muhm
Employees: 9,200

Jobs Added Last Year: 200 (+2.2%)

Cable TV (#3 in US)

CRA MANAGED CARE, INC.

312 Union Wharf   Phone: 617-367-2163
Boston, MA 02109   Fax: 617-367-8519
Pres, CEO & COO: Donald J. Larson
Asst Treas: Martha Kuppens
Employees: 2,125

Jobs Added Last Year: 225 (+11.8%)

Business services - field case management & specialized cost
containment services designed to reduce workers' compensation
costs

CUMBERLAND FARMS INC.

777 Dedham St.   Phone: 617-828-4900
Canton, MA 02021   Fax: 617-828-5246
Pres: Lily H. Bentas
VP HR: Foster G. Macrides
Employees: 7,200

Jobs Cut Last Year: 300 (-4.0%)

Retail - convenience stores; gas distribution

DAKA INTERNATIONAL, INC.

One Corporate Place, 55 Ferncroft Rd.   Phone: 508-774-9115
Danvers, MA 01923-4001   Fax: 508-774-1334
Chm & CEO: William H. Baumhauer
SVP HR: Louis A. Kaucic
Employees: 13,100

Jobs Added Last Year: 400 (+3.1%)

Retail - restaurants (Fuddruckers, Champps Americana); contract
food service

DATA GENERAL CORPORATION

4400 Computer Dr.   Phone: 508-898-5000
Westboro, MA 01580   Fax: 508-898-4003
Pres & CEO: Ronald L. Skates
VP HR: Jonathan W. Lane
Employees: 5,000

Jobs Cut Last Year: 800 (-13.8%)

Computers - servers & workstations (AViiON), storage systems
(CLARiiON), PCs & hardware & software support & maintenance
services

DATA TRANSLATION, INC.

100 Locke Dr.   Phone: 508-481-3700
Marlborough, MA 01752-1192   Fax: 508-481-8620
Chm, Pres & CEO: Alfred A. Molinari Jr.
HR Representative: Hillary Barrett
Employees: 347

Jobs Added Last Year: 76 (+28.0%)

Computers - digital editing (Media 100), data acquisition &
imaging products

PeopleBank — http://www.peoplebank.com

An in-depth profile of this company is available
to subscribers on Hoover's Online at www.hoovers.com.

183

DATATREND SERVICES, INC.

1515 Washington St.   Phone: 617-848-6700
Braintree, MA 02184   Fax: 617-691-1300
Pres, CEO & CFO: Mark A. Hanson
Controller: Richard Donahue
Employees: 62

Jobs Added Last Year: 24 (+63.2%)

Retail - microcomputers, peripheral components & accessories

DIGITAL EQUIPMENT CORPORATION

111 Powdermill Rd.   Phone: 508-493-5111
Maynard, MA 01754-1499   Fax: 508-493-8780
Chm, Pres & CEO: Robert B. Palmer
VP Worldwide HR: Savino "Sid" R. Ferrales
Employees: 61,700

Jobs Cut Last Year: 16,100 (-20.7%)

Computers - PCs, workstations & servers, peripherals & software products

EASTERN UTILITIES ASSOCIATES

One Liberty Sq.   Phone: 617-357-9590
Boston, MA 02109   Fax: 617-357-7320
Chm & CEO: Donald G. Pardus
Mgr HR: Victor Tremblay
Employees: 1,775

Jobs Added Last Year: 618 (+53.4%)

Utility - electric power

ELCOM INTERNATIONAL, INC.

10 Oceana Way   Phone: 617-551-3380
Norwood, MA 02062   Fax: 617-762-1540
Chm & CEO: Robert J. Crowell
Dir HR: Mary Palengo
Employees: 802

Jobs Added Last Year: 172 (+27.3%)

Computers - interactive electronic commerce software systems

ELECTRONIC DESIGNS INC.

One Research Dr.   Phone: 508-366-5151
Westborough, MA 01581   Fax: 508-836-4850
Chm & CEO: Donald F. McGuinness
Dir HR: Sally Baronian
Employees: 127

Jobs Added Last Year: 98 (+337.9%)

Electrical components - semiconductor memory circuits & flat panel display products; industrial applications for synthetic diamond films & coatings

EMC CORPORATION

171 South St.   Phone: 508-435-1000
Hopkinton, MA 01748-9103   Fax: 508-497-6961
Pres & CEO: Michael C. Ruettgers
VP HR: Brian P. O'Connell
Employees: 4,100

Jobs Added Last Year: 725 (+21.5%)

Computers - computer storage & retrieval products

ENCON SYSTEMS, INC.

86 South St.   Phone: 508-435-7700
Hopkinton, MA 01748   Fax: 508-435-7744
Interim CEO & Pres: Robert Wexler
Office Mgr: Kathleen Popielarczyk
Employees: 178

Jobs Added Last Year: 98 (+122.5%)

Building - energy-management services for commercial & industrial clients

ERGO SCIENCE CORPORATION

Charlestown Navy Yard, 4th Fl., 100 1st Ave. Phone: 617-241-6800
Charlestown, MA 02129-2051   Fax: 617-241-8822
Pres & CEO: J. Warren Huff
CFO & VP Admin: Alan T. Barber
Employees: 62

Jobs Added Last Year: 13 (+26.5%)

Biomedical & genetic products - development of novel treatments for metabolic & immune system disorders

ESC MEDICAL SYSTEMS LTD.

100 Crescent Rd.   Phone: 617-444-8446
Needham, MA 02194   Fax: 617-444-8812
Pres & CEO: Shimon Eckhouse
Office & Convention Mgr: Liliana Bachrach
Employees: 55

Jobs Added Last Year: 13 (+31.0%)

Medical instruments - devices that use intense pulsed light technology for noninvasive treatment of varicose veins & other benign vascular lesions

FLEET FINANCIAL GROUP, INC.

One Federal St.   Phone: 617-292-2000
Boston, MA 02110-2010   Fax: 617-423-5224
Chm, Pres & CEO: J. Terrence Murray
SVP HR: Anne Szostak
Employees: 30,800

Jobs Added Last Year: 9,300 (+43.3%)

Banks - Northeast

FMR CORP.

82 Devonshire St.
Boston, MA 02109
Chm & CEO: Edward "Ned" C. Johnson III
SVP Admin: David C. Weinstein
Employees: 18,000

Phone: 617-570-7000
Fax: 617-476-6345

Jobs Added Last Year: 3,400 (+23.3%)

Financial - mutual fund management & discount brokerage (Fidelity Investments); magazine publishing (Worth); community newspapers; limo service

FTP SOFTWARE, INC.

2 High St.
North Andover, MA 01845
Chm & CEO: David H. Zirkle
VP HR: Charlotte H. Evans
Employees: 740

Phone: 508-685-4000
Fax: 508-794-4488

Jobs Added Last Year: 266 (+56.1%)

Computers - internetworking software (PC/TCP)

FURMAN LUMBER, INC.

32 Manning Rd.
Billerica, MA 01821
CEO: Barry Kronick
Dir HR: Bill Perry
Employees: 5,400

Phone: 508-670-3800
Fax: 508-670-3998

Jobs Added Last Year: —

Building products - wholesale lumber & building materials

GC COMPANIES, INC.

27 Boylston St.
Chestnut Hill, MA 02167
Chm & CEO: Richard A. Smith
VP HR: Daniel Stravinski
Employees: 7,400

Phone: 617-277-4320
Fax: 617-278-5397

Jobs Added Last Year: 50 (+0.7%)

Motion pictures & services - theaters (General Cinema)

GENOME THERAPEUTICS CORPORATION

100 Beaver St.
Waltham, MA 02154
Chm, Pres & CEO: Robert J. Hennessey
VP, Treas & CFO: Fenel M. Eloi
Employees: 105

Phone: 617-893-5007
Fax: 617-893-8277

Jobs Added Last Year: 25 (+31.3%)

Biomedical & genetic products - genetic pharmaceuticals used to identify gene targets that can be used to develop therapeutic, vaccine & diagnostic products

GENSYM CORPORATION

125 Cambridge Park Dr., 5th Fl.
Cambridge, MA 02140
Chm, CEO, Treas & Sec: Lowell B. Hawkinson
Mgr HR: Louise Callahan
Employees: 226

Phone: 617-547-2500
Fax: 617-547-1962

Jobs Added Last Year: 55 (+32.2%)

Computers - intelligent real-time software (G2) that can reach conclusions, provide advice & take actions

GENZYME CORPORATION

One Kendall Sq.
Cambridge, MA 02139-1562
Chm, Pres & CEO: Henri A. Termeer
SVP HR: John V. Heffernan
Employees: 2,286

Phone: 617-252-7500
Fax: 617-252-7600

Jobs Added Last Year: 265 (+13.1%)

Biomedical & genetic products - diversified human health care; therapeutics; diagnostic services & products; pharmaceuticals & fine chemicals; tissue repair

THE GILLETTE COMPANY

Prudential Tower Bldg.
Boston, MA 02199
Chm & CEO: Alfred M. Zeien
SVP Personnel & Admin: Robert E. DiCenso
Employees: 33,500

Phone: 617-421-7000
Fax: 617-421-7123

Jobs Added Last Year: 700 (+2.1%)

Cosmetics & toiletries - shaving blades, razors, preparations & electric shavers (Braun); writing instruments (Parker, Paper Mate, Waterman); toothbrushes (Oral-B) & oral care appliances

GROUND ROUND RESTAURANTS, INC.

35 Braintree Hill Office Park
Braintree, MA 02184
Chm, Pres & CEO: Daniel R. Scoggin
Dir HR: Gerry Leneweaver
Employees: 9,400

Phone: 617-380-3100
Fax: 617-380-3168

Jobs Added Last Year: 0

Retail - casual dining restaurants in 23 states

HARCOURT GENERAL, INC.

27 Boylston St.
Chestnut Hill, MA 02167
Pres, CEO & COO: Robert J. Tarr Jr.
VP HR: Gerald T. Hughes
Employees: 15,219

Phone: 617-232-8200
Fax: 617-278-5397

Jobs Cut Last Year: 211 (-1.4%)

Diversified operations - publishing (Harcourt Brace; Holt, Rinehart & Winston; Academic Press); specialty retailing (Neiman Marcus, Bergdorf Goodman)

An in-depth profile of this company is available to subscribers on Hoover's Online at www.hoovers.com.

HILLS STORES COMPANY

15 Dan Rd.
Canton, MA 02021
Pres & CEO: E. Jackson Smailes
VP HR: Larry Miller
Employees: 17,900

Phone: 617-821-1000
Fax: 617-821-4379

Jobs Cut Last Year: 1,600 (-8.2%)

Retail - discount regional department stores

HOUGHTON MIFFLIN COMPANY

222 Berkeley St.
Boston, MA 02116-3764
Chm, Pres & CEO: Nader F. Darehshori
SVP HR: Margaret M. Doherty
Employees: 2,350

Phone: 617-351-5000
Fax: 617-351-1105

Jobs Added Last Year: 351 (+17.6%)

Publishing - textbooks, educational & testing materials, reference works & fiction & nonfiction books

INDIVIDUAL, INC.

8 New England Executive Park West
Burlington, MA 01803
Chm: Andy Devereaux
Dir HR: Linda Schofield
Employees: 157

Phone: 617-273-6000
Fax: 617-273-6060

Jobs Added Last Year: 57 (+57.0%)

Computers - enterprisewide news service (First! for Notes) & agent-based news service (First! for Mosaic)

INSO CORPORATION

31 St. James Ave.
Boston, MA 02116-4101
Pres & CEO: Steven R. Vana-Paxhia
Dir HR: Judith Tavano-Finkle
Employees: 176

Phone: 617-753-6500
Fax: 617-753-6666

Jobs Added Last Year: 58 (+49.2%)

Computers - proofing, reference & information management software (IntelliScope)

INTERNATIONAL DATA GROUP

One Exeter Plaza, 15th Fl.
Boston, MA 02116
Chm & CEO: Patrick J. McGovern
VP HR: Martha Stephens
Employees: 8,500

Phone: 617-534-1200
Fax: 617-262-2300

Jobs Added Last Year: 1,300 (+18.1%)

Publishing - computer magazines (PC World, Publish, ComputerWorld); market research & trade shows

J. BAKER, INC.

555 Turnpike St.
Canton, MA 02021
Pres & CEO: Jerry M. Socol
First SVP & Dir HR: Virginia M. Pitts
Employees: 11,579

Phone: 617-828-9300
Fax: 617-828-2357

Jobs Cut Last Year: 3,075 (-21.0%)

Retail - shoe concessions in department stores

JOHN HANCOCK MUTUAL LIFE INSURANCE COMPANY

PO Box 111
Boston, MA 02117
Chm & CEO: Stephen L. Brown
VP Corp HR: A. Page Palmer
Employees: 15,000

Phone: 617-572-6000
Fax: 617-572-6451

Jobs Cut Last Year: 1,000 (-6.3%)

Insurance - life

KEANE, INC.

10 City Sq.
Boston, MA 02129-3798
Pres & CEO: John F. Keane
VP HR: Edward C. Sugrue
Employees: 5,338

Phone: 617-241-9200
Fax: 617-241-9507

Jobs Added Last Year: 798 (+17.6%)

Computers - software design, integration & management services for corporations & health care facilities

LAURIAT'S, INC.

10 Pequot Way
Canton, MA 02021
Pres & CEO: Daniel Gurr
Dir HR: Richard Markiewicz
Employees: 1,600

Phone: 617-821-0071
Fax: 617-821-0167

Jobs Added Last Year: 1,050 (+190.9%)

Retail - bookstores in the Northeast (Encore Books, Lauriat's Booksellers, Royal Discount Bookstores, Book Corner)

LIBERTY MUTUAL GROUP

175 Berkeley St.
Boston, MA 02117
Chm & CEO: Gary L. Countryman
Dir HR: Julie Baumgartner
Employees: 23,000

Phone: 617-357-9500
Fax: 617-350-7648

Jobs Added Last Year: 1,000 (+4.5%)

Insurance - multiline & employee benefits services

LIFELINE SYSTEMS, INC.

640 Memorial Dr.
Cambridge, MA 02139
Pres & CEO: Ronald Feinstein
VP HR: Heather E. Edelman
Employees: 342

Phone: 617-679-1000
Fax: 617-923-1384

Jobs Added Last Year: 72 (+26.7%)

Medical products - emergency-response equipment & monitoring services

THE L.S. STARRETT COMPANY

121 Crescent St.
Athol, MA 01331-1915
Chm & CEO: Douglas R. Starrett
Personnel Dir: Joel Shaughnessy
Employees: 2,834

Phone: 508-249-3551
Fax: 508-249-8495

Jobs Added Last Year: 271 (+10.6%)

Tools - hand held measuring tools, including micrometers, steel rules & combination squares; precision instruments

MASSACHUSETTS INSTITUTE OF TECHNOLOGY

77 Massachusetts Ave.
Cambridge, MA 02139
Pres & CEO: Charles M. Vest
VP & Dir Personnel: Joan Rice
Employees: 10,000

Phone: 617-253-1000
Fax: 617-253-8000

Jobs Added Last Year: —

University

MASSACHUSETTS MUTUAL LIFE INSURANCE COMPANY

1295 State St.
Springfield, MA 01111-0001
Pres & CEO: Thomas B. Wheeler
SVP Corp HR: Susan A. Alfano
Employees: 9,395

Phone: 413-788-8411
Fax: 413-744-8889

Jobs Added Last Year: 346 (+3.8%)

Insurance - life

MICRION CORPORATION

One Corporation Way
Peabody, MA 01960-7990
Pres & CEO: Nicholas Economou
Dir HR: Sheryl Cheny
Employees: 148

Phone: 508-531-6464
Fax: 508-531-9648

Jobs Added Last Year: 35 (+31.0%)

Electronics - focused-ion-beam systems that locate problems during semiconductor production

MICROCOM, INC.

500 River Ridge Dr.
Norwood, MA 02062-5028
Pres & CEO: Roland D. Pampel
HR Mgr: Bill Cashman
Employees: 405

Phone: 617-551-1000
Fax: 617-551-1968

Jobs Added Last Year: 92 (+29.4%)

Computers - modems, communication software & remote inter-networking products

MICROTOUCH SYSTEMS, INC.

300 Griffin Brook Park Dr.
Methuen, MA 01844-1873
Pres & CEO: Wes Davis
Mgr HR: Annemarie Bell
Employees: 478

Phone: 508-659-9000
Fax: 508-659-9100

Jobs Added Last Year: 101 (+26.8%)

Computers - touch-screen monitors (#1 worldwide: TruePoint Kiosk Monitor)

MILLIPORE CORPORATION

80 Ashby Rd.
Bedford, MA 01730-2271
Chm, Pres & CEO: C. William Zadel
VP HR: Glenda Burkhart
Employees: 3,338

Phone: 617-275-9200
Fax: 617-533-3301

Jobs Added Last Year: 221 (+7.1%)

Filtration products - membrane filters

MOLTEN METAL TECHNOLOGY, INC.

51 Sawyer Rd.
Waltham, MA 02154
Chm, Pres & CEO: William M. Haney III
VP HR: Katharyn F. Santoro
Employees: 284

Phone: 617-487-9700
Fax: 617-487-7870

Jobs Added Last Year: 96 (+51.1%)

Industrial processing - catalytic breakdown of hazardous & nonhazardous waste

NATURAL MICROSYSTEMS CORPORATION

8 Erie Dr.
Natick, MA 01760
Pres & CEO: Robert Schechter
HR Mgr: Christine Wheeler
Employees: 129

Phone: 508-650-1300
Fax: 508-650-1352

Jobs Added Last Year: 60 (+87.0%)

Computers - integrated hardware & software products used to develop link PCs & public telephone networks

 An in-depth profile of this company is available to subscribers on Hoover's Online at www.hoovers.com.

187

THE NEIMAN MARCUS GROUP, INC.

27 Boylston St.
Chestnut Hill, MA 02167
Pres, CEO & COO: Robert J. Tarr Jr.
VP HR: Gerald T. Hughes
Employees: 10,000

Phone: 617-232-0760
Fax: 617-739-1395

Jobs Cut Last Year: 5,400 (-35.1%)

Retail - major department stores (Nieman Marcus, Bergdorf Goodman); mail order (NM Direct)

NORTHEAST UTILITIES

174 Brush Hill Ave.
West Springfield, MA 01090-0010
Chm, Pres & CEO: Bernard M. Fox
SVP HR & Administrative Svcs: Cheryl W. Grise
Employees: 9,051

Phone: 413-785-5871
Fax: 860-665-5092

Jobs Cut Last Year: 344 (-3.7%)

Utility - electric power

NUMBER NINE VISUAL TECHNOLOGY CORP.

18 Hartwell Ave.
Lexington, MA 02173
Pres & CEO: Andrew Najda
No central personnel officer
Employees: 144

Phone: 617-674-0009
Fax: 617-674-2919

Jobs Added Last Year: 29 (+25.2%)

Computer - video- & graphic-accelerator subsystems, chips & software

OPEN ENVIRONMENT CORPORATION

25 Travis St.
Boston, MA 02134
Pres & CEO: Nathan P. Morton
VP HR: Juanita Duserick
Employees: 214

Phone: 617-562-0900
Fax: 617-562-5942

Jobs Added Last Year: 74 (+52.9%)

Computers - client/server software development tools

PARAMETRIC TECHNOLOGY CORP.

128 Technology Dr.
Waltham, MA 02154
Chm & CEO: Steven C. Walske
Dir HR: Carl Ockerbloom
Employees: 1,960

Phone: 617-398-5000
Fax: 617-398-6000

Jobs Added Last Year: 679 (+53.0%)

Computers - computer-aided design, manufacturing & engineering software (Pro/ENGINEER)

PICTURETEL CORPORATION

222 Rosewood Dr.
Danvers, MA 01923
Chm, Pres & CEO: Norman E. Gaut
VP HR: Lawrence M. Bornstein
Employees: 1,182

Phone: 508-762-5000
Fax: 508-762-5245

Jobs Added Last Year: 257 (+27.8%)

Telecommunications equipment - videoconferencing systems using standard telephone lines

Med Search America — http://www.medsearch.com/

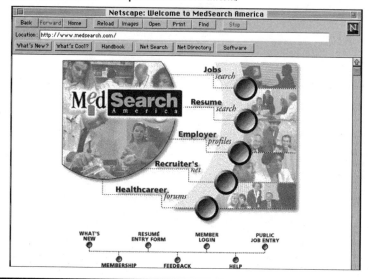

POLAROID CORPORATION

549 Technology Sq.
Cambridge, MA 02139
Chm & CEO: Gary T. DiCamillo
VP HR: Joseph G. Parham Jr.
Employees: 11,662

Phone: 617-386-2000
Fax: 617-386-3118

Jobs Cut Last Year: 442 (-3.7%)

Photographic equipment & supplies - instant cameras & film; medical imaging systems

PRIMARK CORPORATION

1000 Winter St., Ste. 4300N
Waltham, MA 02154
Chm, Pres & CEO: Joseph E. Kasputys
Mgr HR: Diane Robesen
Employees: 5,131

Phone: 617-466-6611
Fax: 617-890-6187

Jobs Added Last Year: 1,342 (+35.4%)

Computers - financial information services (Datastream, Disclosure); weather imaging systems & software (WSI); aircraft maintenance

PRO CD, INC.

222 Rosewood Dr.
Danvers, MA 01923
Pres & CEO: James Bryant
Dir HR: Deirdre Purple
Employees: 100

Phone: 508-750-0000
Fax: 508-750-0020

Jobs Added Last Year: 40 (+66.7%)

Publishing - telephone directories (Select Phone) on CD-ROM

RAYTHEON COMPANY

141 Spring St.
Lexington, MA 01273
Chm & CEO: Dennis J. Picard
VP HR: Gail Philip Anderson
Employees: 73,200

Phone: 617-862-6600
Fax: 617-860-2172

Jobs Added Last Year: 13,000 (+21.6%)

Diversified operations - defense electronics, energy & environmental products, corporate jets (Beech, Hawker & King Air) & appliances (Amana & Speed Queen)

REEBOK INTERNATIONAL LTD.

100 Technology Center Dr.
Stoughton, MA 02072
Chm, Pres & CEO: Paul B. Fireman
SVP Law , HR & Admin: John B. Douglas III
Employees: 6,700

Phone: 617-341-5000
Fax: 617-341-7402

Jobs Added Last Year: 200 (+3.1%)

Shoes & related apparel - athletic, dress & casual footwear & apparel (Reebok, Weebok, The Pump, Boks, Avia, Rockport, Tinley)

RENAISSANCE SOLUTIONS, INC.

55 Old Bedford Rd.
Lincoln, MA 01773
Pres & CEO: David P. Norton
VP HR: Timothy Riley
Employees: 118

Phone: 617-259-8833
Fax: 617-259-0565

Jobs Added Last Year: 42 (+55.3%)

Consulting - management consulting & client/server systems integration services

SECURITY DYNAMICS TECHNOLOGIES, INC.

One Alewife Ctr.
Cambridge, MA 02140
Chm, Pres & CEO: Charles R. Stuckey Jr.
Mgr HR: Chris Gundling
Employees: 162

Phone: 617-547-7820
Fax: 617-354-8836

Jobs Added Last Year: 37 (+29.6%)

Computers - security & access software (SecurID Card, ACE-Server)

SEQUOIA SYSTEMS, INC.

400 Nickerson Rd.
Marlborough, MA 01752
Pres & CEO: J. Michael Stewart
Dir HR: Don Colanton
Employees: 443

Phone: 508-480-0800
Fax: 508-481-8740

Jobs Added Last Year: 260 (+142.1%)

Computers - fault-tolerant PCs used primarily for online transaction processing

SOFTKEY INTERNATIONAL INC.

One Athenaeum St.
Cambridge, MA 02142
Chm & CEO: Michael J. Perik
VP HR: Mary De Saint Croix
Employees: 775

Phone: 617-494-1200
Fax: 617-225-0318

Jobs Added Last Year: 325 (+72.2%)

Computers - word processing, education & entertainment software (The Trail Family, The Mathkeys Family, The GeoGraph Family)

SPECTRAN CORPORATION

50 Hall Rd.
Sturbridge, MA 01566
Pres & CEO: Glenn E. Moore
HR Supervisor: Sue Jowett
Employees: 300

Phone: 508-347-2261
Fax: 508-347-2747

Jobs Added Last Year: 76 (+33.9%)

Fiber optics - multimode optical fiber for data communications & single-mode fiber for telecommunications

STAPLES, INC.

One Research Dr.
Westboro, MA 01581
Chm & CEO: Thomas G. Stemberg
Dir HR: Cathy Wells
Employees: 22,132

Phone: 508-370-8500
Fax: 508-370-8989

Jobs Added Last Year: 7,566 (+51.9%)

Retail - discount office equipment & supplies

STATE STREET BOSTON CORPORATION

225 Franklin St.
Boston, MA 02110
Chm & CEO: Marshall N. Carter
SVP HR: Trevor Lukes
Employees: 11,324

Phone: 617-786-3000
Fax: 617-654-3386

Jobs Added Last Year: 197 (+1.8%)

Banks - Northeast

STREAM INTERNATIONAL INC.

105 Rosemont Rd.
Westmont, MA 02090
CEO: Rory J. Cowan
Dir HR: LeeAnn Raso
Employees: 7,000

Phone: 617-751-1000
Fax: 617-751-7751

Jobs Added Last Year: —

Computers - software upgrades & training to corporations;
software & manual production for software manufacturers

SUMMIT TECHNOLOGY INC.

21 Hickory Dr.
Waltham, MA 02154
Chm & CEO: David F. Muller
Mgr HR: Candice Cohen
Employees: 290

Phone: 617-890-1234
Fax: 617-890-0313

Jobs Added Last Year: 79 (+37.4%)

Lasers - ophthalmic laser systems to correct nearsightedness &
other refractive vision disorders; mail order contact lens
replacement service (#1 in US: Lens Express)

SYSTEMSOFT CORPORATION

2 Vision Dr.
Natick, MA 01760-2059
Chm, Pres & CEO: Robert F. Angelo
Dir HR: Randi Nichols
Employees: 138

Phone: 508-651-0088
Fax: 508-651-8188

Jobs Added Last Year: 46 (+50.0%)

Computers - PCMCIA software for laptops, notebooks &
subnotebooks

TERADYNE, INC.

321 Harrison Ave.
Boston, MA 02118
Chm & CEO: Alexander V. d'Arbeloff
Corp Dir Personnel: James Dawson
Employees: 5,200

Phone: 617-482-2700
Fax: 617-422-2910

Jobs Added Last Year: 1,200 (+30.0%)

Electronics - semiconductor, circuit board & telecommunications
test equipment & backplane connection systems

THERMO ELECTRON CORPORATION

81 Wyman St.
Waltham, MA 02254-9046
Chm, Pres & CEO: George N. Hatsopoulos
Dir HR: Fred Florio
Employees: 14,400

Phone: 617-622-1000
Fax: 617-622-1123

Jobs Added Last Year: 4,166 (+40.7%)

Diversified operations - analytical & monitoring instruments; biomedical products; paper-recycling & papermaking equipment;
alternative energy power systems; industrial process equipment

THERMO TERRATECH INC.

81 Wyman Street
Waltham, MA 02254-9046
Pres & CEO: John P. Appleton
Dir HR: Fred Florio
Employees: 2,367

Phone: 617-622-1000
Fax: 617-622-1207

Jobs Added Last Year: 758 (+47.1%)

Pollution control equipment & services - specialized environmental services, including soil & water remediation, waste industrial
fluids reclamation & nuclear radiation safety

THERMO VOLTEK CORP.

470 Wildwood St.
Woburn, MA 01888-1578
Chm, Pres & CEO: John W. Wood Jr.
Dir HR: Fred Florio
Employees: 245

Phone: 617-622-1000
Fax: 617-622-1207

Jobs Added Last Year: 90 (+58.1%)

Electronics - electromagnetic interference test equipment

THE TJX COMPANIES, INC.

770 Cochituate Rd.
Framingham, MA 01701
Pres & CEO: Bernard Cammarata
VP Human Svcs: Mark O. Jacobson
Employees: 58,000

Phone: 508-390-1000
Fax: 508-390-3635

Jobs Added Last Year: 20,000 (+52.6%)

Retail - apparel (T.J. Maxx, Chadwick's of Boston, HomeGoods,
Marshalls, Winners Apparel Ltd.)

TREND-LINES, INC.

135 American Legion Hwy.
Revere, MA 02151
Pres & CEO: Stanley D. Black
VP HR: Kathleen A. Harris
Employees: 802

Phone: 617-853-0900
Fax: 617-853-0066

Jobs Added Last Year: 546 (+213.3%)

Retail - woodworking tools (Woodworkers Warehouse) & golf products (Golf Day)

UNIFIRST CORPORATION

68 Jonspin Rd.
Wilmington, MA 01887-1086
VC, Pres & CEO: Ronald D. Croatti
Dir HR: Brett Bouchard
Employees: 6,000

Phone: 508-658-8888
Fax: 508-657-5663

Jobs Added Last Year: 500 (+9.1%)

Linen supply & related - industrial garment rental

UNITED ASSET MANAGEMENT CORP.

One International Place
Boston, MA 02110
Pres & CEO: Norton H. Reamer
EVP & CFO: William H. Park
Employees: 2,171

Phone: 617-330-8900
Fax: 617-330-1133

Jobs Added Last Year: 296 (+15.8%)

Financial - investment management for corporate, public & union pension funds, mutual funds, endowments, foundations & individuals

UNO RESTAURANT CORPORATION

100 Charles Park Rd.
West Roxbury, MA 02132
Chm & CEO: Aaron D. Spencer
SVP HR & Training: Thomas W. Gathers
Employees: 5,815

Phone: 617-323-9200
Fax: 617-323-4252

Jobs Added Last Year: 1,256 (+27.5%)

Retail - pizza restaurants (Pizzeria Uno Restaurant & Bar) specializing in Chicago-style deep-dish pizza

VIDEOSERVER, INC.

63 Third Ave.
Burlington, MA 01803
Pres & CEO: Robert L. Castle
Dir HR: Carol Raymond
Employees: 133

Phone: 617-229-2000
Fax: 617-505-2101

Jobs Added Last Year: 35 (+35.7%)

Computers - networking equipment & associated software for multimedia conferencing over wide area networks (Multimedia Conference Servers)

VMARK SOFTWARE, INC.

50 Washington St.
Westboro, MA 01581-1021
Chm, Pres & CEO: Robert M. Morrill
Dir HR: Sally N. Burke
Employees: 456

Phone: 508-366-3888
Fax: 508-366-3669

Jobs Added Last Year: 201 (+78.8%)

Computers - database management systems (UniVerse) & related UNIX software for the client/server business solutions market

WABAN INC.

One Mercer Rd.
Natick, MA 01760
Pres & CEO: Herbert J. Zarkin
Asst VP & Dir HR: Thomas Davis III
Employees: 19,000

Phone: 508-651-6500
Fax: 508-651-6623

Jobs Added Last Year: 1,000 (+5.6%)

Retail - discount warehouse (BJ's Wholesale) & home improvement (Homebase, HomeClub)

WANG LABORATORIES, INC.

600 Technology Park Dr.
Billerica, MA 01821-4130
Chm & CEO: Joseph M. Tucci
EVP, CFO & Acting HR: Franklyn A. Caine
Employees: 6,900

Phone: 508-967-5000
Fax: 508-967-0436

Jobs Added Last Year: 1,600 (+30.2%)

Computers - workflow, imaging, document management & related software applications for client/server open systems; integration & support services for office networks worldwide

WYMAN-GORDON COMPANY

244 Worcester St.
North Grafton, MA 01536-8001
Pres & CEO: David P. Gruber
Dir HR: G. L. Robertson
Employees: 3,100

Phone: 508-839-4441
Fax: 508-839-7500

Jobs Added Last Year: 1,247 (+67.3%)

Aerospace - components for jet turbine & gas turbine engines & airframes for the commercial & defense aerospace markets

ZOOM TELEPHONICS, INC.

207 South St.
Boston, MA 02111
Chm, Pres & CEO: Frank B. Manning
Dir HR: Marty Levin
Employees: 251

Phone: 617-423-1072
Fax: 617-338-5015

Jobs Added Last Year: 86 (+52.1%)

Computers - data & fax modems, speed dialers (Hotshot) & voice/data processors

 An in-depth profile of this company is available to subscribers on Hoover's Online at www.hoovers.com.

BLUE CROSS BLUE SHIELD OF MICHIGAN

600 Lafayette Blvd.
Detroit, MI 48226
Pres & CEO: Richard E. Whitmer
SVP HR: George Francis
Employees: 6,500

Phone: 313-225-9000
Fax: 313-225-5629

Jobs Added Last Year: —

Insurance - health, hospital & medical service plans

ALLIED DIGITAL TECHNOLOGIES

7375 Woodward Ave.
Detroit, MI 48202-3145
Co-Chm: William H. Smith
Dir HR: Larry Henry
Employees: 1,490

Phone: 313-871-2222
Fax: 313-871-4120

Jobs Added Last Year: 811 (+119.4%)

Business services - CD, audio- & videocassette duplication services

BORDERS GROUP, INC.

500 E. Washington St.
Ann Arbor, MI 48104
Chm & CEO: Robert F. DiRomualdo
VP HR: Richard L. Flanagan
Employees: 20,000

Phone: 313-913-1100
Fax: 313-913-1965

Jobs Added Last Year: 3,300 (+19.8%)

Retail - mall book stores (#1 in US: Walden Books), superstores (#2 in US: Borders) & retail music stores (Planet Music)

AMERICAN AXLE & MANUFACTURING, INC.

1840 Holbrook Ave.
Detroit, MI 48212-3488
Pres & CEO: Richard Dauch
VP Corp HR: Bob Mathis
Employees: 8,500

Phone: 313-974-2000
Fax: 313-974-3090

Jobs Added Last Year: 150 (+1.8%)

Automotive driveline system, chassis component & forged product supplier

CHRYSLER CORPORATION

1000 Chrysler Dr.
Auburn Hills, MI 48326-2766
Chm & CEO: Robert J. Eaton
VP Corp Personnel: Kathleen M. Oswald
Employees: 126,000

Phone: 810-576-5741
Fax: 810-956-3747

Jobs Added Last Year: 5,000 (+4.1%)

Automotive manufacturing - cars & trucks (Chrysler, Plymouth, Jeep Cherokee, Dodge, Eagle)

AMWAY CORPORATION

7575 Fulton St. East
Ada, MI 49355-0001
Pres: Richard M. DeVos Jr.
VP Worldwide HR: Gary Carraway
Employees: 13,000

Phone: 616-787-6000
Fax: 616-787-6177

Jobs Added Last Year: 500 (+4.0%)

Retail - multitier seller of household, personal care, health & fitness products

CITIZENS BANKING CORPORATION

328 S. Saginaw St.
Flint, MI 48502
Pres & CEO: Robert J. Vitito
SVP: Marilyn A. Allor
Employees: 1,907

Phone: 810-766-7500
Fax: 810-766-6948

Jobs Added Last Year: 303 (+18.9%)

Financial - savings & loans

ARBOR DRUGS, INC.

3331 W. Big Beaver Rd.
Troy, MI 48084
Chm, Pres & CEO: Eugene Applebaum
VP HR: Ronald F. Haase
Employees: 5,700

Phone: 810-643-9420
Fax: 810-637-1636

Jobs Added Last Year: 500 (+9.6%)

Retail - drugstores (167 units)

CMS ENERGY CORPORATION

330 Town Center Dr., Ste. 1100
Dearborn, MI 48126
Chm & CEO: William T. McCormick Jr.
Exec Dir HR: John F. Drake
Employees: 10,072

Phone: 313-436-9261
Fax: 313-436-9225

Jobs Added Last Year: 100 (+1.0%)

Utility - electric power & natural gas; oil & gas exploration; natural gas pipelines

COMERICA INCORPORATED

500 Woodward Ave.
Detroit, MI 48226
Chm & CEO: Eugene A. Miller
EVP & Dir HR: Richard A. Collister
Employees: 13,500

Phone: 313-370-5000
Fax: 313-965-4648

Jobs Added Last Year: 2 (+0.0%)

Banks - Midwest

COMPUWARE CORPORATION

31440 Northwestern Hwy.
Farmington Hills, MI 48334-2564
Chm & CEO: Peter Karmanos Jr.
SVP HR: W. James Prowse
Employees: 4,105

Phone: 810-737-7300
Fax: 810-737-1822

Jobs Added Last Year: 784 (+23.6%)

Computers - system software; data processing services

CREDIT ACCEPTANCE CORPORATION

25505 W. Twelve Mile Rd., Ste. 3000
Southfield, MI 48034-8339
Chm & CEO: Donald A. Foss
Independent Personnel Consultant: Harry E. Craig
Employees: 406

Phone: 810-353-2700
Fax: 810-353-9776

Jobs Added Last Year: 143 (+54.4%)

Financial - funding, receivables management, collection, sales training & related products & services for auto dealers that sell used vehicles to consumers with substandard credit ratings

DETROIT DIESEL CORPORATION

13400 Outer Dr. West
Detroit, MI 48239-4001
Pres: Ludvik F. Koci
SVP Admin: Paul Walters
Employees: 6,250

Phone: 313-592-5000
Fax: 313-592-7580

Jobs Added Last Year: 850 (+15.7%)

Engines - heavy-duty diesel & alternative fuel engines & engine parts for the transportation, construction, industrial, marine & military industries

THE DETROIT MEDICAL CENTER

4201 St. Antoine Blvd.
Detroit, MI 48201
Pres & CEO: David J. Campbell
VP HR: Dan Zuhlke
Employees: 10,000

Phone: 313-745-5192
Fax: 313-993-0438

Jobs Added Last Year: —

Hospitals

DOMINO'S PIZZA, INC.

30 Frank Lloyd Wright Dr., PO Box 997
Ann Arbor, MI 48106-0997
Founder, CEO & Pres: Thomas S. Monaghan
Dir HR: Ron Woodman
Employees: 125,000

Phone: 313-930-3030
Fax: 313-668-4614

Jobs Added Last Year: 10,000 (+8.7%)

Retail - pizza delivery & carryout (over 5,200 stores)

NationJob Network — http://www.nationjob.com/

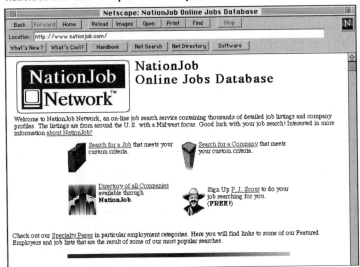

DOUGLAS & LOMASON COMPANY

24600 Hollywood Ct.
Farmington Hills, MI 48335-1671
Chm, Pres & CEO: Harry A. Lomason II
VP HR: Ollie V. Cheatham
Employees: 5,900

Phone: 810-478-7800
Fax: 810-478-5189

Jobs Cut Last Year: 139 (-2.3%)

Automotive & trucking - original equipment

THE DOW CHEMICAL COMPANY

2030 Dow Ctr.
Midland, MI 48674
Pres & CEO: William S. Stavropoulos
VP HR: Lawrence J. Washington Jr.
Employees: 39,537

Phone: 517-636-1000
Fax: 517-636-1830

Jobs Cut Last Year: 14,193 (-26.4%)

Chemicals - thermoplastics, thermosets & fabricated products; consumer, pharmaceutical & agricultural products

DOW CORNING CORPORATION

2200 W. Salzburg Rd.
Midland, MI 48686-0994
Chm & CEO: Richard A. Hazleton
Dir HR: Gifford Brown
Employees: 8,400

Phone: 517-496-4000
Fax: 517-496-4511

Jobs Added Last Year: 100 (+1.2%)

Chemicals - silicone products, including nipples for baby bottles, sealants for the construction industry, capsules for drugs & needle lubricants for medical use

DTE ENERGY COMPANY

2000 Second Ave.
Detroit, MI 48226-1279
Chm & CEO: John E. Lobbia
VP HR: Haven E. Cockerham
Employees: 8,340

Phone: 313-235-8000
Fax: 313-235-9828

Jobs Cut Last Year: 154 (-1.8%)

Utility - electric power

EXIDE CORPORATION

1400 N. Woodward Ave.
Bloomfield Hills, MI 48304
Chm, Pres & CEO: Arthur M. Hawkins
EVP HR: Jack J. Sosiak
Employees: 11,712

Phone: 810-258-0080
Fax: 810-258-0080

Jobs Added Last Year: 712 (+6.5%)

Automotive & trucking - starting, lighting & ignition batteries; lead acid batteries (#1 in North America)

FEDERAL-MOGUL CORPORATION

26555 Northwestern Hwy.
Southfield, MI 48034
Chm & CEO: Dennis J. Gormley
VP HR: James M. Eastman
Employees: 17,200

Phone: 810-354-7700
Fax: 810-354-8950

Jobs Added Last Year: 1,000 (+6.2%)

Automotive & trucking - replacement parts; light- & heavy-duty trucks; farm & construction vehicles

FINISHMASTER, INC.

4259 40th St. SE
Kentwood, MI 49512
Pres & CEO: Ronald P. White
Dir HR: Bob Pruim
Employees: 461

Phone: 616-949-7604
Fax: 616-949-7279

Jobs Added Last Year: 107 (+30.2%)

Auto parts - wholesale paints, coatings & paint-related accessories

FIRST OF AMERICA BANK CORPORATION

211 S. Rose St.
Kalamazoo, MI 49007-5264
Chm & CEO: Richard F. Chormann
SVP HR: Richard Washburn
Employees: 13,330

Phone: 616-376-9000
Fax: 616-376-8224

Jobs Cut Last Year: 160 (-1.2%)

Banks - Midwest

FORD MOTOR COMPANY

The American Rd.
Dearborn, MI 48121-1899
Chm, Pres & CEO: Alexander J. Trotman
VP HR: Robert O. Kramer
Employees: 346,990

Phone: 313-322-3000
Fax: 313-390-8929

Jobs Added Last Year: 9,212 (+2.7%)

Automotive manufacturing - cars & trucks (Ford, Lincoln, Mercury, Jaguar); car rental (Hertz); financial services

GENERAL MOTORS CORPORATION

3044 W. Grand Blvd.
Detroit, MI 48202-3091
Chm, Pres & CEO: John F. Smith Jr.
VP Personnel, North American Ops: Gerald A. Knechtel
Employees: 745,000

Phone: 313-556-5000
Fax: 313-556-5108

Jobs Added Last Year: 52,200 (+7.5%)

Automotive manufacturing - cars & trucks (Chevrolet, Buick, Cadillac, Pontiac, Oldsmobile, Saturn); systems & components; international operations (GMIO); financing & insurance (GMAC)

GENTEX CORPORATION

600 N. Centennial St. Phone: 616-772-1800
Zeeland, MI 49464 Fax: 616-772-7348
Chm & CEO: Fred T. Bauer
Dir HR: John Van Haitsma
Employees: 831

Jobs Added Last Year: 170 (+25.7%)

Automotive & trucking - glare-control rearview mirrors; residential smoke detectors

GREAT DANE HOLDINGS INC.

2016 N. Pitcher St. Phone: 616-343-6121
Kalamazoo, MI 49007 Fax: 616-343-2244
Pres & CEO: David R. Markin
VP HR: Marcia Koestner
Employees: 5,750

Jobs Cut Last Year: 34 (-0.6%)

Diversified operations - Yellow Cab (Chicago); insurance and maintenance operations for taxis; truck trailer manufacturing; stamped metal parts for autos

GUARDIAN INDUSTRIES CORP.

2300 Harmon Rd. Phone: 810-340-1800
Auburn Hills, MI 48326-1714 Fax: 810-340-9988
Pres & CEO: William Davidson
Dir Personnel: Kenneth Battjes
Employees: 8,100

Jobs Added Last Year: 100 (+1.3%)

Glass products - flat glass, fiberglass insulation, plastics

HANDLEMAN COMPANY

500 Kirts Blvd. Phone: 810-362-4400
Troy, MI 48084-4142 Fax: 810-362-3615
Pres & CEO: Stephen Strome
VP HR: Rodger Apple
Employees: 4,147

Jobs Added Last Year: 405 (+10.8%)

Wholesale distribution - music audiocassettes & CDs, videos, books & personal computer software

HAWORTH, INC.

One Haworth Ctr. Phone: 616-393-3000
Holland, MI 49423 Fax: 616-393-1570
Chm & CEO: Richard G. Haworth
VP HR: Randy Evans
Employees: 8,900

Jobs Added Last Year: 1,500 (+20.3%)

Furniture - office

HENRY FORD HEALTH SYSTEM

1 Ford Place Phone: 313-876-2600
Detroit, MI 48202 Fax: 313-876-8451
Pres & CEO: Gail L. Warden
Corp VP HR: Dennis Dowdell Jr.
Employees: 17,000

Jobs Added Last Year: —

Hospitals - not-for-profit system with 9 hospitals, 35 ambulatory care centers & 6 emergency facilities serving Michigan (Henry Ford Hospital, Henry Ford Cottage Hospital)

HERMAN MILLER, INC.

855 E. Main Ave., PO Box 302 Phone: 616-654-3300
Zeeland, MI 49464-0302 Fax: 616-654-3632
Pres & CEO: Michael A. Volkema
VP People: Craig Schrotenboer
Employees: 7,264

Jobs Added Last Year: 1,324 (+22.3%)

Furniture - office & institutional furniture

HORIZON GROUP, INC.

1050 W. Western Ave. Phone: 616-728-5170
Muskegon, MI 49441 Fax: 616-726-4722
Chm, Pres & CEO: Jeffrey A. Kerr
Dir HR: Cristal McWilliams
Employees: 493

Jobs Added Last Year: 213 (+76.1%)

Real estate investment trust - factory outlet malls

JPE, INC.

900 Victors Way, Ste. 140 Phone: 313-662-2323
Ann Arbor, MI 48108 Fax: 313-662-0133
Chm & CEO: John Psarouthakis
No central personnel officer
Employees: 880

Jobs Added Last Year: 198 (+29.0%)

Automotive & trucking - spring-related & undercarriage parts, hydraulic brake parts & fuel system products

KELLOGG COMPANY

One Kellogg Sq. Phone: 616-961-2000
Battle Creek, MI 49016-3599 Fax: 616-961-2871
Chm, Pres & CEO: Arnold G. Langbo
SVP HR: Robert L. Creviston
Employees: 14,487

Jobs Cut Last Year: 1,170 (-7.5%)

Food - cereals (Rice Krispies, Froot Loops) & baked goods (Eggo, Pop-Tarts)

 An in-depth profile of this company is available to subscribers on Hoover's Online at www.hoovers.com.

195

KMART CORPORATION

3100 W. Big Beaver Rd.
Troy, MI 48084
Chm, Pres & CEO: Floyd Hall
EVP HR & Admin: Warren F. Cooper
Employees: 307,000

Phone: 810-643-1000
Fax: 810-643-5249

Jobs Cut Last Year: 41,000 (-11.8%)

Retail - discount stores & home improvement stores (Builders Square)

KYSOR INDUSTRIAL CORPORATION

One Madison Ave.
Cadillac, MI 49601-9785
Chm & CEO: George R. Kempton
Mgr Compensation & Benefits: Kent Rosenau
Employees: 2,500

Phone: 616-779-2200
Fax: 616-775-2661

Jobs Added Last Year: 264 (+11.8%)

Automotive & trucking - truck fuel tanks, engine-performance systems; refrigerated display cases, walk-in coolers & A/C systems

LA-Z-BOY CHAIR COMPANY

1284 N. Telegraph Rd.
Monroe, MI 48162-3390
Chm & Pres: Charles T. Knabusch
VP HR: Louis E. Roussey
Employees: 11,149

Phone: 313-242-1444
Fax: 313-241-4422

Jobs Added Last Year: 1,779 (+19.0%)

Furniture - reclining chairs & other upholstered furniture

LEAR CORPORATION

21557 Telegraph Rd.
Southfield, MI 48034
Chm & CEO: Kenneth L. Way
SVP HR & Corp Relations: Roger A. Jackson
Employees: 35,000

Phone: 810-746-1500
Fax: 810-746-1722

Jobs Added Last Year: 10,960 (+45.6%)

Automotive & trucking - automobile seats (#1 worldwide); car & truck interiors

LITTLE CAESAR ENTERPRISES, INC.

2211 Woodward Ave.
Detroit, MI 48201
Pres & CEO: Michael Ilitch
Dir HR: Darrell Snygg
Employees: 90,000

Phone: 313-983-6000
Fax: 313-983-6494

Jobs Cut Last Year: 5,000 (-5.3%)

Retail - pizza restaurants; sports arenas; professional sports teams

MANATRON, INC.

2970 S. Ninth St.
Kalamazoo, MI 49009
Pres & CEO: Paul R. Sylvester
HR Mgr: Mary Gephart
Employees: 390

Phone: 616-375-5300
Fax: 616-375-9826

Jobs Added Last Year: 198 (+103.1%)

Data collection & systems

MASCO CORPORATION

21001 Van Born Rd.
Taylor, MI 48180
Chm & CEO: Richard A. Manoogian
VP HR: Daniel R. Foley
Employees: 20,500

Phone: 313-274-7400
Fax: 313-374-6666

Jobs Cut Last Year: 30,800 (-60.0%)

Building products - plumbing; faucets (Peerless, Delta), cabinets, hardware; home furnishings; ovens

MASCOTECH, INC.

21001 Van Born Rd.
Taylor, MI 48180
Chm & CEO: Richard A. Manoogian
VP HR: Daniel R. Foley
Employees: 10,800

Phone: 313-274-7405
Fax: 313-374-6666

Jobs Cut Last Year: 1,900 (-15.0%)

Automotive & trucking - powertrain & chassis parts; engineering services to car makers

MEIJER, INC.

2929 Walker Ave. NW
Grand Rapids, MI 49504-9428
Chm: Fred Meijer
SVP Personnel: Windy Ray
Employees: 65,000

Phone: 616-453-6711
Fax: 616-791-2572

Jobs Cut Last Year: 5,000 (-7.1%)

Retail - supermarkets (over 100 units), discount & retail stores

NATIONAL TECHTEAM, INC.

22000 Garrison Ave.
Dearborn, MI 48124-2306
Chm & CEO: William F. Coyro Jr.
Dir HR: Kris Munroe
Employees: 1,056

Phone: 313-277-2277
Fax: 313-277-6409

Jobs Added Last Year: 551 (+109.1%)

Computers - computer support, training, consulting, systems integration & other services

NEOGEN CORPORATION

620 Lesher Place — Phone: 517-372-9200
Lansing, MI 48912-1509 — Fax: 517-372-0108
Pres & CEO: James L. Herbert Jr.
Mgr HR: Christine Stock
Employees: 150
Jobs Added Last Year: 35 (+30.4%)

Medical products - test & diagnostic products for residue- and quality-control for agricultural producers, food processors, laboratories & major pharmaceutical companies

PENSKE CORPORATION

13400 Outer Dr. West — Phone: 313-592-5000
Detroit, MI 48239 — Fax: 313-592-5256
Chm, Pres & CEO: Roger S. Penske
VP Personnel: Robert Carter
Employees: 16,700
Jobs Added Last Year: 5,200 (+45.2%)

Diversified operations - auto dealerships, truck leasing & rental, diesel engine manufacturing (Detroit Diesel)

PERRIGO COMPANY

117 Water St. — Phone: 616-673-8451
Allegan, MI 49010 — Fax: 616-673-7534
Chm, Pres & CEO: Michael J. Jandernoa
VP HR: Mike Stewart
Employees: 4,409
Jobs Added Last Year: 530 (+13.7%)

Cosmetics & toiletries - over-the-counter pharmaceuticals & personal care products (#1 in US) for the store brand market (WalMart, Kmart, CVS, Revco, Kroger, Walgreens, Eckerd)

PULTE CORPORATION

33 Bloomfield Hills Pkwy., Ste. 200 — Phone: 810-647-2750
Bloomfield Hills, MI 48304 — Fax: 810-433-4598
Pres & CEO: Robert K. Burgess
VP HR: Michael O'Brien
Employees: 3,900
Jobs Added Last Year: 500 (+14.7%)

Building - single- & multifamly homes; financial services in the southern & eastern US

R. L. POLK & CO.

1155 Brewery Park Blvd. — Phone: 313-393-0880
Detroit, MI 48207-2697 — Fax: 313-393-2860
Chm & CEO: Stephen R. Polk
SVP HR: Joan Miszak
Employees: 5,000
Jobs Added Last Year: —

Publishing - city & bank directories; direct marketing; automotive statistics

SISTERS OF ST. JOSEPH HEALTH SYSTEM

455 E. Eisenhower Parkway — Phone: 313-741-1700
Ann Arbor, MI 48108 — Fax: 313-741-5796
CEO: John Lore
Dir HR: Peter Kruger
Employees: 15,100
Jobs Added Last Year: 1,265 (+9.1%)

Hospitals

SPX CORPORATION

700 Terrace Point Dr. — Phone: 616-724-5000
Muskegon, MI 49443-3301 — Fax: 616-724-5720
Chm, Pres & CEO: John B. Blystone
VP HR: Stephen A. Lison
Employees: 8,296
Jobs Added Last Year: 96 (+1.2%)

Automotive & trucking - components for repair & maintenance; service tools & equipment

THE STANDARD PRODUCTS CO.

2401 S. Gulley Rd. — Phone: 313-561-1100
Dearborn, MI 48124 — Fax: 313-561-6526
Chm & CEO: James S. Reid Jr.
VP HR: John C. Brandmahl
Employees: 10,308
Jobs Added Last Year: 828 (+8.7%)

Rubber & plastic products - window & door weather-sealing products & plastic trim products for the automotive industry

STEELCASE INC.

901 44th St. SE — Phone: 616-247-2710
Grand Rapids, MI 49508 — Fax: 616-246-9015
Pres & CEO: James P. Hackett
VP HR: Dan Wiljanen
Employees: 19,200
Jobs Added Last Year: 1,400 (+7.9%)

Furniture - office furniture & equipment

STRYKER CORPORATION

2725 Fairfield Rd., PO Box 4085 — Phone: 616-385-2600
Kalamazoo, MI 49003-4085 — Fax: 616-385-1062
Chm, Pres & CEO: John W. Brown
Dir HR: David Huisjen
Employees: 4,629
Jobs Added Last Year: 408 (+9.7%)

Medical instruments - endoscopic systems, orthopedic & spinal implants, powered surgical instruments & medical video camers

 An in-depth profile of this company is available to subscribers on Hoover's Online at www.hoovers.com.

197

TECUMSEH PRODUCTS COMPANY

100 E. Patterson St.
Tecumseh, MI 49286
Pres & CEO: Todd W. Herrick
VP & Corp Dir Industrial Relations & Personnel: Wallace Stubbs
Employees: 15,600
Phone: 517-423-8411
Fax: 517-423-8760

Jobs Added Last Year: —

Engines - gasoline engines, transmission, transaxles & differentials for lawn equipment & RVs; compressors

THORN APPLE VALLEY, INC.

26999 Central Park Blvd., Ste. 300
Southfield, MI 48076
Pres & CEO: Joel Dorfman
EVP Pork & HR: Edward E. Boan
Employees: 3,800
Phone: 810-213-1000
Fax: 810-552-0986

Jobs Added Last Year: 400 (+11.8%)

Food - packaged meat & poultry products & fresh pork

UNITED AMERICAN HEALTHCARE CORPORATION

1155 Brewery Park Blvd.
Detroit, MI 48207
Chm & CEO: Julius V. Combs
Asst VP Corp Admin: Elizabeth Griffin
Employees: 603
Phone: 313-393-0200
Fax: 313-393-7940

Jobs Added Last Year: 147 (+32.2%)

Medical practice management

THE UNIVERSITY OF MICHIGAN

503 Thompson St.
Ann Arbor, MI 48109
Interim Pres: Homer Neal
Exec Dir HR: Jackie McClain
Employees: 38,000
Phone: 313-764-1817
Fax: 313-936-9582

Jobs Added Last Year: —

University

WHIRLPOOL CORPORATION

2000 North M-63
Benton Harbor, MI 49022-2692
Chm & CEO: David R. Whitwam
VP HR & Asst Sec: Ed R. Dunn
Employees: 45,435
Phone: 616-923-5000
Fax: 616-923-5486

Jobs Added Last Year: 6,419 (+16.5%)

Appliances - automatic washers & dryers, built-in ovens, microwave ovens, refrigerators, stoves, air conditioners & mixers (KitchenAid, Kenmore, Sears)

WOLOHAN LUMBER CO.

1740 Midland Rd.
Saginaw, MI 48605
Chm, Pres & CEO: James L. Wolohan
VP HR: William E. Stark
Employees: 2,400
Phone: 517-793-4532
Fax: 517-793-4582

Jobs Added Last Year: 900 (+60.0%)

Building products - retail lumber, building & home improvement supplies

Career Companion — http://www.careercompanion.com/

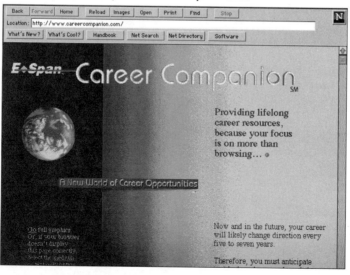

WOLVERINE WORLD WIDE, INC.

9341 Courtland Dr.
Rockford, MI 49351
Phone: 616-866-5500
Fax: 616-866-0257
Chm & CEO: Geoffrey B. Bloom
VP HR: Robert Sedrowski
Employees: 5,586
Jobs Added Last Year: 381 (+7.3%)

Shoes & related apparel - comfort footwear (Hush Puppies)

ADC TELECOMMUNICATIONS, INC.

4900 W. 78th St.
Minneapolis, MN 55435
Phone: 612-938-8080
Fax: 612-946-3292
Chm, Pres & CEO: William J. Cadogan
VP HR: Pamela J. Nichols
Employees: 2,984
Jobs Added Last Year: 340 (+12.9%)

Telecommunications equipment - cable-management, transmission & networking equipment & services

AG-CHEM EQUIPMENT CO., INC.

5720 Smetana Dr., Ste. 100
Minnetonka, MN 55343-9688
Phone: 612-933-9006
Fax: 612-933-7432
Chm, Pres & CEO: Alvin E. McQuinn
Dir HR: James Olson
Employees: 1,569
Jobs Added Last Year: 539 (+52.3%)

Machinery - off-road equipment & implements for agricultural fertilization, application of pesticides & herbicides, industrial waste treatment & other industrial uses

ALLIANT TECHSYSTEMS INC.

600 Second St. NE
Hopkins, MN 55343-8384
Phone: 612-931-6000
Fax: 612-939-5920
Pres & CEO: Richard Schwartz
VP Admin: John Buck
Employees: 7,700
Jobs Cut Last Year: 500 (-6.1%)

Weapons & weapon systems - munitions, marine systems, electronic systems & other defense products

ALLINA HEALTH SYSTEM

5601 Smetana Dr.
Minnetonka, MN 55343
Phone: 612-992-2000
Fax: 612-992-3890
Exec Officer: Gordon M. Sprenger
HR Officer: Mark G. Mishek
Employees: 20,000
Jobs Added Last Year: —

Hospitals - not-for-profit health care delivery system

ANALYSTS INTERNATIONAL CORP.

7615 Metro Blvd.
Minneapolis, MN 55439-3050
Phone: 612-835-5900
Fax: 612-835-4924
Chm & CEO: Frederick W. Lang
No central personnel officer
Employees: 3,170
Jobs Added Last Year: 570 (+21.9%)

Computers - system design & programming services for large corporate clients

ANGEION CORPORATION

3650 Annapolis Lane, Ste. 170
Minneapolis, MN 55447-5434
Phone: 612-550-9388
Fax: 612-550-9487
Chm, Pres & CEO: Whitney A. McFarlin
VP HR: Robert S. Garin
Employees: 81
Jobs Added Last Year: 26 (+47.3%)

Medical products - cardiovascular devices to treat irregular heartbeats

APOGEE ENTERPRISES, INC.

7900 Xerxes Ave. South, Ste. 1800
Minneapolis, MN 55431-1159
Phone: 612-835-1874
Fax: 612-835-3196
Chm & CEO: Donald W. Goldfus
Corp Benefits Mgr: Mary Lehnert
Employees: 6,163
Jobs Cut Last Year: 21 (-0.3%)

Glass products - insulated, tempered & laminated architectural, automotive, security & picture-frame glass

AUDIO KING CORPORATION

3501 S. Hwy. 100
Minneapolis, MN 55416
Phone: 612-920-0505
Fax: 612-920-0940
Pres, CEO & Treas: Henry G. Thorne
No central personnel officer
Employees: 403
Jobs Added Last Year: 120 (+42.4%)

Retail - audio & video equipment (Audio King, Audio Video Environments, Fast Track & Electronics Outlet)

An in-depth profile of this company is available to subscribers on Hoover's Online at www.hoovers.com.

199

BEMIS COMPANY, INC.

222 S. Ninth St., Ste. 2300
Minneapolis, MN 55402-4099
Pres & CEO: John H. Roe
VP HR: Lawrence E. Schwanke
Employees: 8,515

Phone: 612-376-3000
Fax: 612-376-3180

Jobs Added Last Year: 395 (+4.9%)

Containers - flexible packaging, specialty coating & graphics products

BEST BUY CO., INC.

7075 Flying Cloud Dr.
Eden Prairie, MN 55344
Chm & CEO: Richard M. Schulze
VP HR & Gen Counsel: Joseph M. Joyce
Employees: 33,500

Phone: 612-947-2000
Fax: 612-947-2422

Jobs Added Last Year: 8,200 (+32.4%)

Retail - consumer electronics & prerecorded music

BUFFETS, INC.

10260 Viking Dr.
Eden Prairie, MN 55344
Chm & CEO: Roe H. Hatlen
VP Training & HR: Brent P. DeMesquita
Employees: 15,540

Phone: 612-942-9760
Fax: 612-942-9658

Jobs Cut Last Year: 375 (-2.4%)

Retail - restaurants (Old Country Buffet, Country Buffet)

CARGILL, INCORPORATED

15407 McGinty Rd.
Minnetonka, MN 55440-5625
Chm, Pres & CEO: Ernest S. Micek
SVP HR: Everett MacLennan
Employees: 73,300

Phone: 612-742-6000
Fax: 612-742-7393

Jobs Added Last Year: 2,600 (+3.7%)

Food - trading & processing; steel; animal feeds; salt (Leslie); largest US private company

CARLSON COMPANIES, INC.

12755 State Hwy. 55, Carlson Pkwy.
Minneapolis, MN 55441
Chm & CEO: Curtis L. Carlson
VP HR: Terry M. Butorac
Employees: 69,000

Phone: 612-540-5000
Fax: 612-449-2219

Jobs Added Last Year: 6,500 (+10.4%)

Business services - travel, hospitality (Radisson) & restaurants (T.G.I. Friday's)

CERIDIAN CORPORATION

8100 34th Ave. South
Minneapolis, MN 55425
Chm, Pres & CEO: Lawrence Perlman
VP Organizational Resources: Michael Kotten
Employees: 10,200

Phone: 612-853-8100
Fax: 612-853-5300

Jobs Added Last Year: 2,700 (+36.0%)

Data collection & services; payroll & payroll-related services, human resource information & benefit management services; electronic systems for defense agencies

CHILDREN'S BROADCASTING CORP.

724 First Ave. North, 4th Fl.
Minneapolis, MN 55401
Chm & Pres: Christopher T. Dahl
Mgr HR: Amy Lynn
Employees: 210

Phone: 612-338-3300
Fax: 612-338-4318

Jobs Added Last Year: 50 (+31.3%)

Radio production & programming - children's radio programming (music, stories, current events, weather, interactive quizzes & interviews)

CHRONIMED INC.

13911 Ridgedale Dr.
Minnetonka, MN 55305
Chm, Pres & CEO: Maurice R. Taylor II
Dir HR: Dolly Sollie
Employees: 232

Phone: 612-541-0239
Fax: 612-451-4969

Jobs Added Last Year: 48 (+26.1%)

Retail - mail-order distribution of prescription drugs, medical & nutritional products & educational products

CYBEROPTICS CORPORATION

5900 Golden Hills Dr.
Minneapolis, MN 55416
Pres: Steven K. Case
Dir HR: Robin Peterson
Employees: 185

Phone: 612-542-5000
Fax: 612-542-5100

Jobs Added Last Year: 73 (+65.2%)

Machinery - laser- & video-based process-control & measurement systems

DAYTON HUDSON CORPORATION

777 Nicollet Mall
Minneapolis, MN 55402-2055
Chm & CEO: Robert J. Ulrich
SVP Personnel: Edwin H. Wingate
Employees: 214,000

Phone: 612-370-6948
Fax: 612-370-5502

Jobs Added Last Year: 20,000 (+10.3%)

Retail - major department stores (Dayton's, Hudson's, Marshall Field's, Mervyn's); discount stores (Target)

DELUXE CORPORATION

3680 Victoria St. North
Shoreview, MN 55126-2966
Chm, Pres & CEO: John A."Gus" Blanchard III
VP HR: Mike Reeves
Employees: 19,286
Phone: 612-483-4477
Fax: 612-481-4163

Jobs Added Last Year: 1,286 (+7.1%)

Paper - business forms & check printing; electronic funds transfer software

DIAMETRICS MEDICAL, INC.

2658 Patton Rd.
Roseville, MN 55113
Pres & CEO: David T. Giddings
Dir HR: Dennis DeVall
Employees: 218
Phone: 612-639-8035
Fax: 612-639-8549

Jobs Added Last Year: 61 (+38.9%)

Biomedical & genetic products - in vitro blood chemistry testing system that provides immediate diagnostic results

DIGI INTERNATIONAL INC.

6400 Flying Cloud Dr.
Eden Prairie, MN 55344
Pres & CEO: Ervin F. Kamm Jr.
Dir HR: T. Harrison Bryant
Employees: 605
Phone: 612-943-9020
Fax: 612-943-5396

Jobs Added Last Year: 175 (+40.7%)

Computers - communications hardware & software products that deliver connectivity solutions for multiuser environments, LAN & WAN remote access markets & LAN connect markets

DIGI-KEY CORPORATION

701 Brooks Ave. South
Thief River Falls, MN 56701
Chm & CEO: Ronald Stormdahl
VP Admin: Mari Finney
Employees: 533
Phone: 218-681-6674
Fax: 218-681-3380

Jobs Added Last Year: 143 (+36.7%)

Electronics - parts distribution

DONALDSON COMPANY, INC.

1400 W. 94th St., PO Box 1299
Minneapolis, MN 55440
Chm, Pres & CEO: William G. Van Dyke
VP HR: John E. Thames
Employees: 5,038
Phone: 612-887-3131
Fax: 612-887-3155

Jobs Added Last Year: 621 (+14.1%)

Filtration products - hydraulic-fluid, oil & fuel filters, air cleaners, mufflers for heavy equipment, air intake & exhaust filtration systems & filters used in computer hard-disk drives

ECOLAB INC.

Ecolab Ctr.
St. Paul, MN 55102-1390
Pres & CEO: Allan L. Schuman
VP HR: Diana D. Lewis
Employees: 9,000
Phone: 612-293-2233
Fax: 612-225-3059

Jobs Added Last Year: 794 (+9.7%)

Building - maintenance, sanitizing & cleaning products & services for the hospitality, institutional & industrial markets

FALLON MCELLIGOTT, INC.

901 Marquette Ave., Ste. 3200
Minneapolis, MN 55402
Chm: Pat Fallon
Dir Admin: John Forney
Employees: 300
Phone: 612-321-2345
Fax: 612-321-2346

Jobs Added Last Year: 75 (+33.3%)

Advertising

FASTENAL COMPANY

2001 Theurer Blvd.
Winona, MN 55987-1500
Chm & Pres: Robert A. Kierlin
Dir HR: Terry Hanley
Employees: 2,045
Phone: 507-454-5374
Fax: 507-454-6542

Jobs Added Last Year: 452 (+28.4%)

Building products - retail threaded fasteners, power tool & safety supply stores (FastTool: 37 stores)

FINGERHUT COMPANIES, INC.

4400 Baker Rd.
Minnetonka, MN 55343
Chm, Pres & CEO: Theodore Deikel
SVP HR: John D. Buck
Employees: 9,500
Phone: 612-932-3100
Fax: 612-932-3292

Jobs Added Last Year: 500 (+5.6%)

Retail - catalog & TV sales of brand-name & private-label electronics, home textiles, housewares, sporting goods & toys, apparel, jewelry, automotive products & lawn & garden tools

FIRST BANK SYSTEM, INC.

First Bank Plaza, 601 Second Ave. South
Minneapolis, MN 55402-4302
Chm, Pres & CEO: John F. Grundhofer
EVP HR: Robert H. Sayre
Employees: 13,231
Phone: 612-973-1111
Fax: 612-973-2446

Jobs Cut Last Year: 769 (-5.5%)

Banks - Midwest

An in-depth profile of this company is available to subscribers on Hoover's Online at www.hoovers.com.

201

FSI INTERNATIONAL, INC.

322 Lake Hazeltine Dr.
Chaska, MN 55318-1096
Chm, Pres & CEO: Joel A. Elftmann
VP Quality & HR: Timothy D. Krieg
Employees: 968

Phone: 612-448-5440
Fax: 612-448-2825

Jobs Added Last Year: 319 (+49.2%)

Machinery - microlithography, surface-conditioning & chemical-management equipment used in the manufacture of semiconductors

FUNCO, INC.

10120 W. 76th St.
Minneapolis, MN 55344
Chm & CEO: David R. Pomije
VP Retail Ops & HR: Jeffery R. Gatesmith
Employees: 951

Phone: 612-946-8883
Fax: 612-946-7251

Jobs Added Last Year: 337 (+54.9%)

Retail - used video games (FuncoLand)

GAME FINANCIAL CORPORATION

10911 W. Hwy. 55, Ste. 205
Plymouth, MN 55441-6114
Pres & CEO: Gary A. Dachis
Dir HR: Marnie Dachis
Employees: 125

Phone: 612-476-8500
Fax: 612-544-6836

Jobs Added Last Year: 49 (+64.5%)

Financial - funds transfer services to individuals in casinos, including cash advances & check cashing

G&K SERVICES, INC.

505 Waterford Park, Ste. 455
Minneapolis, MN 55441
Chm & CEO: Richard Fink
Dir HR: Lynn Weiss
Employees: 4,978

Phone: 612-546-7440
Fax: 612-546-7872

Jobs Added Last Year: 1,012 (+25.5%)

Linen supply & related - rental & sales of uniforms, floor mats, dust mops & cloths, wiping towels & linen items

GENERAL MILLS, INC.

Number One General Mills Blvd.
Minneapolis, MN 55426
Chm & CEO: Stephen W. Sanger
SVP Personnel: Michael A. Peel
Employees: 9,882

Phone: 612-540-2311
Fax: 612-540-4925

Jobs Cut Last Year: 115,818 (-92.1%)

Food - cereals (Cheerios, Wheaties), snack foods (Bugles, Pop Secret), prepared mixes (Bisquick, Hamburger Helper) & frostings (Betty Crocker)

GRAND CASINOS, INC.

13705 First Ave. North
Minneapolis, MN 55441
Chm & CEO: Lyle Berman
VP HR: Jeffrey Wagner
Employees: 4,500

Phone: 612-449-9092
Fax: 612-449-9353

Jobs Added Last Year: 700 (+18.4%)

Gambling resorts & casinos

GREEN TREE FINANCIAL CORP.

345 St. Peter St., 11th Fl.
St. Paul, MN 55102-1639
Chm & CEO: Lawrence M. Coss
VP HR: Barbara Didrickson
Employees: 2,811

Phone: 612-293-3400
Fax: 612-293-3503

Jobs Added Last Year: 653 (+30.3%)

Financial - mortgages & related services for manufactured homes, home improvements, consumer products & equipment financing

GRIST MILL CO.

21340 Hayes Ave., PO Box 430
Lakeville, MN 55044-0430
Pres & CEO: Glen S. Bolander
HR Dir: Tom Traub
Employees: 650

Phone: 612-469-4981
Fax: 612-469-5550

Jobs Added Last Year: 230 (+54.8%)

Food - fruit snacks, ready-to-eat cereals, candy & granola bars, fruit-filled cereal bars & pie crusts marketed under store brand or private-label names

GROW BIZ INTERNATIONAL, INC.

4200 Dahlberg Dr.
Minneapolis, MN 55422-4837
Pres & CEO: Ronald G. Olson
Dir HR: Patricia Knott
Employees: 293

Phone: 612-520-8500
Fax: 612-520-8410

Jobs Added Last Year: 59 (+25.2%)

Franchisors - sports, toy, computer, CD & clothing stores that sell, buy, trade & consign used & new merchandise

H. B. FULLER COMPANY

2400 Energy Park Dr.
St. Paul, MN 55108
Pres & CEO: Walter Kissling
VP HR: James A. Metts
Employees: 6,400

Phone: 612-645-3401
Fax: 612-645-6936

Jobs Added Last Year: 0

Chemicals - adhesives, sealants, coatings & paints for such industries as packaging, woodworking, automotive, aerospace, graphic arts, appliances, filtration & windows

HEALTH FITNESS PHYSICAL THERAPY, INC.

3500 W. 80th St., Ste. 200
Bloomington, MN 55431
Chm, Pres & CEO: Loren Brink
VP HR & Admin: Tina Oskey
Employees: 475

Phone: 612-831-6830
Fax: 612-831-7264

Jobs Added Last Year: 123 (+34.9%)

Health care - physical therapy clinics; corporate & hospital-based fitness centers

HOLIDAY COMPANIES

4567 W. 80th St.
Bloomington, MN 55437
Chm: Ronald Erickson
Dir HR: Bob Nye
Employees: 5,100

Phone: 612-830-8700
Fax: 612-830-8864

Jobs Added Last Year: 100 (+2.0%)

Retail - convenience stores & grocery wholesaling

HONEYWELL INC.

Honeywell Plaza
Minneapolis, MN 55408-1792
Chm & CEO: Michael R. Bonsignore
VP HR: James T. Porter
Employees: 50,100

Phone: 612-951-1000
Fax: 612-951-0137

Jobs Cut Last Year: 700 (-1.4%)

Diversified operations - industrial & environmental control systems, avionics, HVAC systems

HORMEL FOODS CORPORATION

One Hormel Place
Austin, MN 55912-3680
Chm, Pres & CEO: Joel W. Johnson
VP HR: James A. Jorgenson
Employees: 10,600

Phone: 507-437-5737
Fax: 507-437-5489

Jobs Added Last Year: 1,100 (+11.6%)

Food - luncheon meat (Spam), chili, beef stew (Dinty Moore), hash (Mary Kitchen), bacon (Black Label), ham (Cure 81), franks (Light & Lean 97) & other foods, including salsa

HUTCHINSON TECHNOLOGY INCORPORATED

40 W. Highland Park
Hutchinson, MN 55350
Pres, CEO & COO: Wayne M. Fortun
VP HR: Rebecca A. Albrecht
Employees: 4,858

Phone: 320-587-3797
Fax: 320-587-1892

Jobs Added Last Year: 283 (+6.2%)

Computers - mechanical suspension assembly arms for hard disk drives

IMATION CORP.

One Imation Place
Oakdale, MN 55128
Chm, Pres & CEO: William T. Monahan
No central personnel officer
Employees: 12,000

Phone: 612-704-4000
Fax: 612-704-4200

Jobs Added Last Year: —

Computers - removable magnetic & optical media; color proofing systems (Matchprint); private label film for the amateur photography market; data storage tape cartridges (Travan)

Career Network — http:/sgx.com/hg/

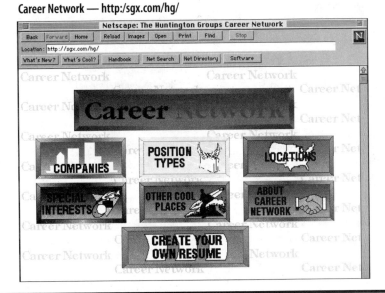

 An in-depth profile of this company is available to subscribers on Hoover's Online at www.hoovers.com.

203

INTERNATIONAL MULTIFOODS CORPORATION

33 S. Sixth St., PO Box 2942
Minneapolis, MN 55402-0942
Chm & CEO: Robert M. Price
VP HR: Robert Maddocks
Employees: 7,115

Phone: 612-340-3300
Fax: 612-340-3338

Jobs Cut Last Year: 380 (-5.1%)

Food - wholesale food distribution through vending machines; bakery & agricultural product production

KAHLER REALTY CORPORATION

20 SW Second Ave.
Rochester, MN 55902
Pres & CEO: Harold W. Milner
VP Corp HR: Simon W. Workman
Employees: 3,400

Phone: 507-285-2700
Fax: 507-285-2772

Jobs Added Last Year: 200 (+6.3%)

Hotels & motels

KINNARD INVESTMENTS, INC.

Kinnard Financial Ctr.,
920 Second Ave. South
Minneapolis, MN 55402
Chm, Pres & CEO: Thomas J. Mulvaney
Dir HR: Debra Best
Employees: 500

Phone: 612-370-2700
Fax: 612-370-2725

Jobs Added Last Year: 100 (+25.0%)

Financial - securities brokerage, trading, investment banking, asset management & related financial services

LAND O'LAKES, INC.

4001 Lexington Ave. North, PO Box 116
Arden Hills, MN 55126
Pres & CEO: John E. Gherty
VP HR: Jack Martin
Employees: 5,185

Phone: 612-481-2222
Fax: 612-481-2022

Jobs Cut Last Year: 315 (-5.7%)

Food - dairy products

LUND INTERNATIONAL HOLDINGS

911 Lund Blvd.
Anoka, MN 55303
Chm: Allan W. Lund
Human Support Mgr: Steve Treichel
Employees: 272

Phone: 612-576-4200
Fax: 612-576-4297

Jobs Added Last Year: 69 (+34.0%)

Automotive & trucking - appearance accessories for light trucks, sport utility vehicles & vans

MAYO FOUNDATION

200 First St. NW
Rochester, MN 55905
CEO: Robert R. Waller
Chm Dept HR: Sharon Gardner
Employees: 25,433

Phone: 507-284-2511
Fax: 507-284-0161

Jobs Added Last Year: 3,577 (+16.4%)

Hospitals - physician-led multi-campus system (including Mayo Medical School, Mayo School of Health-Related Sciences, International Education, Mayo Graduate School)

MEDTRONIC, INC.

7000 Central Ave. NE
Minneapolis, MN 55432-3476
Chm & CEO: William W. George
SVP HR: Janet S. Fiola
Employees: 8,896

Phone: 612-574-4000
Fax: 612-574-4879

Jobs Added Last Year: 187 (+2.1%)

Medical instruments - pacemakers & related cardiovascular products

MERRILL CORPORATION

One Merrill Circle
St. Paul, MN 55108-5267
Pres & CEO: John W. Castro
VP HR: Kathleen A. Larkin
Employees: 2,253

Phone: 612-646-4501
Fax: 612-649-1348

Jobs Added Last Year: 514 (+29.6%)

Printing - transactional documents, catalogs, directories & technical manuals

3M

3M Center
St. Paul, MN 55144-1000
Chm & CEO: Livio D. DeSimone
VP HR: Richard A. Lidstad
Employees: 70,687

Phone: 612-733-1110
Fax: 612-733-9973

Jobs Cut Last Year: 14,479 (-17.0%)

Diversified operations - industrial & consumer products, including tape (Scotch Magic Tape), paper notes (Post-it) & fabric protector (Scotchgard); medical, dental & personal care products

MUSICLAND STORES CORPORATION

10400 Yellow Circle Dr.
Minnetonka, MN 55343
Chm, Pres & CEO: Jack W. Eugster
VP HR: Jay Landauer
Employees: 17,000

Phone: 612-931-8000
Fax: 612-931-8300

Jobs Added Last Year: 1,000 (+6.3%)

Retail - prerecorded music & videocassettes (Musicland, Sam Goody)

NASH FINCH COMPANY

7600 France Ave. South
Minneapolis, MN 55435
Pres & CEO: Alfred N. Flaten
VP HR: Edgar F. Timberlake
Employees: 11,536

Phone: 612-832-0534
Fax: 612-844-1234

Jobs Cut Last Year: 1,554 (-11.9%)

Food - wholesale distribution to supermarkets; retail grocery stores (Econofoods, Sun Mart, Food Folks)

NAVARRE CORPORATION

7400 49th Ave. North
New Hope, MN 55428
Chm, Pres & CEO: Eric H. Paulson
Corp Sec & Dir HR: Marilyn K. Gabbert
Employees: 131

Phone: 612-535-8333
Fax: 612-533-2156

Jobs Added Last Year: 51 (+63.8%)

Wholesale distribution - prerecorded music & PC software

NEW HORIZON KIDS QUEST, INC.

3650 Annapolis Lane, North, Ste. 101
Plymouth, MN 55447
Chm & CEO: William Dunkley
Dir Personnel: Linda Heruth
Employees: 387

Phone: 612-557-1111
Fax: 612-577-9261

Jobs Added Last Year: 107 (+38.2%)

Leisure & recreational services - supervised licensed children's entertainment facilities (Kids Quest Centers) & child care centers (New Horizon Centers)

NORTHERN STATES POWER COMPANY

414 Nicollet Mall
Minneapolis, MN 55401
Chm, Pres & CEO: James J. Howard
VP HR: Cynthia L. Lesher
Employees: 6,829

Phone: 612-330-5500
Fax: 612-330-2900

Jobs Cut Last Year: 841 (-11.0%)

Utility - electric power & natural gas

NORTHWEST AIRLINES CORP.

2700 Lone Oak Pkwy
Eagan, MN 55112-3034
Pres & CEO: John H. Dasburg
SVP Corp Comm, Advertising & HR: Christopher E. Clouser
Employees: 45,000

Phone: 612-726-2111
Fax: 612-727-7617

Jobs Added Last Year: 921 (+2.1%)

Transportation - airline

NORWEST CORPORATION

Norwest Ctr., Sixth & Marquette
Minneapolis, MN 55479
Chm, Pres & CEO: Richard M. Kovacevich
EVP HR: Stephen W. Hansen
Employees: 45,404

Phone: 612-667-1234
Fax: 612-667-7680

Jobs Added Last Year: 6,604 (+17.0%)

Banks - Midwest

OLYMPIC FINANCIAL LTD.

7825 Washington Ave. South
Minneapolis, MN 55439-2435
Chm, Pres & CEO: Jeffrey C. Mack
VP HR: Mary E. West
Employees: 633

Phone: 612-942-9880
Fax: 612-942-0015

Jobs Added Last Year: 329 (+108.2%)

Financial - purchase & service of retail installment contracts for new & used cars

PENTAIR, INC.

1500 County Rd. B2 West, Ste. 400
St. Paul, MN 55113-3105
Chm, Pres & CEO: Winslow H. Buxton
VP HR: Deb S. Knutson
Employees: 9,000

Phone: 612-636-7920
Fax: 612-639-5251

Jobs Cut Last Year: 1,300 (-12.6%)

Diversified operations - woodworking machinery & power tools; electronic enclosures & wireways; automotive-service equipment; sporting ammunition; coated & uncoated printing paper

POLARIS INDUSTRIES INC.

1225 Hwy. 169 North
Minneapolis, MN 55441-5078
Chm & CEO: W. Hall Wendel Jr.
Mgr HR: Mary Zins
Employees: 3,500

Phone: 612-542-0500
Fax: 612-542-0599

Jobs Added Last Year: 650 (+22.8%)

Leisure & recreational products - snowmobiles, all-terrain vehicles & personal watercraft

POSSIS MEDICAL, INC.

9055 Evergreen Blvd. NW
Coon Rapids, MN 55433-8003
Pres & CEO: Robert G. Dutcher
Mgr HR: Betty Anastasia
Employees: 150

Phone: 612-550-1010
Fax: 612-545-5670

Jobs Added Last Year: 41 (+37.6%)

Medical products - thrombectomy systems & coronary bypass & dialysis grafts

 An in-depth profile of this company is available to subscribers on Hoover's Online at www.hoovers.com.

RAINFOREST CAFE, INC.

607 Washington Ave. South, Ste. 204
Minneapolis, MN 55415
Chm & CEO: Lyle Berman
Dir HR: Lori Frazier
Employees: 761

Phone: 612-945-5400
Fax: 612-945-5444

Jobs Added Last Year: 565 (+288.3%)

Retail - tropical themed, environmentally conscious restaurants & retail facilities

REGIS CORPORATION

7201 Metro Blvd.
Edina, MN 55439
Chm & CEO: Myron Kunin
No central personnel officer
Employees: 16,000

Phone: 612-947-7777
Fax: 612-947-7600

Jobs Added Last Year: 500 (+3.2%)

Retail - mall-based hair & beauty salons (1,800 units: Regis Hairstylists, MasterCuts); retail hair care products (Trade Secret)

RELIASTAR FINANCIAL CORP.

20 Washington Ave. South
Minneapolis, MN 55401
Chm & CEO: John G. Turner
VP HR: Adaire C. Peterson
Employees: 2,963

Phone: 612-372-5432
Fax: 612-342-3966

Jobs Added Last Year: 367 (+14.1%)

Insurance - life & health; employee benefit services

RIMAGE CORPORATION

7725 Washington Ave. South
Minneapolis, MN 55439-2423
Pres: David J. Suden
Office Mgr: Renee Dallman
Employees: 268

Phone: 612-944-8144
Fax: 612-944-7808

Jobs Added Last Year: 114 (+74.0%)

Computers - diskette, digital tape & CD-ROM duplication & finishing equipment

THE ST. PAUL COMPANIES, INC.

385 Washington St.
St. Paul, MN 55102
Chm, Pres & CEO: Douglas W. Leatherdale
SVP HR: Greg A. Lee
Employees: 12,300

Phone: 612-310-7911
Fax: 612-221-8294

Jobs Cut Last Year: 600 (-4.7%)

Insurance - property- & professional-liability, workers' compensation, medical-service & business insurance; investment banking & asset management

SCHWAN'S SALES ENTERPRISES, INC.

115 W. College Dr.
Marshall, MN 56258
Pres & CEO: Alfred Schwan
Head of Personnel: Larry Gibbs
Employees: 6,000

Phone: 507-532-3274
Fax: 507-537-8145

Jobs Added Last Year: —

Food - frozen food, including pizza (Tony's, Red Baron)

SHUFFLE MASTER, INC.

10921 Valley View Rd.
Eden Prairie, MN 55344
Pres, CEO & COO: Joseph J. Lahti
HR Mgr: Kris Johnson
Employees: 104

Phone: 612-943-1951
Fax: 612-943-2090

Jobs Added Last Year: 34 (+48.6%)

Gambling equipment & services - automatic card shuffling systems & gaming-related devices

STRATASYS, INC.

14950 Martin Dr.
Eden Prarie, MN 55344-2020
Chm, Pres, CEO, CFO & Treas: S. Scott Crump
HR Administrator: Cari Feik
Employees: 81

Phone: 612-937-3000
Fax: 612-937-0070

Jobs Added Last Year: 27 (+50.0%)

Engineering - rapid prototyping hardware & software that create physical models from CAD workstations

SUMMIT MEDICAL SYSTEMS, INC.

One Carlson Pkwy.
Minneapolis, MN 55447
Pres & CEO: Kevin R. Green
Dir HR: Kathy Pinger
Employees: 150

Phone: 612-473-3250
Fax: 612-473-8534

Jobs Added Last Year: 40 (+36.4%)

Computers - database software for the health care industry

SUNRISE RESOURCES, INC.

5500 Wayzata Blvd., Ste. 725
Golden Valley, MN 55416
Pres: Errol Carlstrom
No central personnel officer
Employees: 54

Phone: 612-593-1904
Fax: 612-513-3299

Jobs Added Last Year: 22 (+68.8%)

Business services - lease financing, marketing & credit services

SUPERVALU INC.

11840 Valley View Rd.
Eden Prairie, MN 55344
Chm, Pres & CEO: Michael W. Wright
SVP HR: Ronald C. Tortelli
Employees: 44,800

Phone: 612-828-4000
Fax: 612-828-8998

Jobs Added Last Year: 1,300 (+3.0%)

Food - wholesale to grocers; supermarkets

TAYLOR CORPORATION

1725 Roecrest Dr.
North Mankato, MN 56003
CEO: Glen Taylor
Personnel Administrator: Marie Eckert
Employees: 8,000

Phone: 507-625-2828
Fax: 507-625-2988

Jobs Added Last Year: 1,500 (+23.1%)

Printing - commercial

UNITED HEALTHCARE CORPORATION

300 Opus Ctr., 9900 Bren Rd. East
Minnetonka, MN 55343
Chm, Pres & CEO: William W. McGuire
VP HR & Administrative Support Svcs: Robert J. Backes
Employees: 9,600

Phone: 612-936-1300
Fax: 612-935-1471

Jobs Added Last Year: 200 (+2.1%)

Health maintenance organization

UNIVERSITY OF MINNESOTA

202 Morrill Hall, 100 Church St. SE
Minneapolis, MN 55445
Pres: Nils Hasselmo
Assoc VP HR: Carol Carrier
Employees: 20,000

Phone: 612-625-5000
Fax: 612-626-1332

Jobs Added Last Year: —

University

VAUGHN COMMUNICATIONS, INC.

5050 W. 78th St.
Minneapolis, MN 55435
Chm, Pres, CEO & Treas: E. David Willette
Personnel Mgr: Liz Pielo
Employees: 673

Phone: 612-832-3200
Fax: 612-832-3147

Jobs Added Last Year: 177 (+35.7%)

Business services - videotape duplication services; gift products & collectibles

VIDEO SENTRY CORPORATION

6365 Carlson Dr.
Eden Prarie, MN 55346
Chm, Pres & CEO: Andrew L. Benson
Dir HR: Richard G. May
Employees: 53

Phone: 612-934-9900
Fax: 612-934-9719

Jobs Added Last Year: 27 (+103.8%)

Protection - closed circuit TV security surveillance system for loss prevention & theft detection in retail & distribution centers

VIDEO UPDATE, INC.

287 E. Sixth St.
St. Paul, MN 55101-1926
Chm & CEO: Daniel A. Potter
Dir HR: Terry Kistling
Employees: 685

Phone: 612-222-0006
Fax: 612-297-6086

Jobs Added Last Year: 550 (+407.4%)

Retail - videocassette, video game & audio book rental super-stores

WEST PUBLISHING CO.

610 Opperman Dr.
Eagan, MN 55123
Chm & CEO: Dwight D. Opperman
VP HR: Timothy J. Blantz
Employees: 7,000

Phone: 612-687-7000
Fax: 612-687-5388

Jobs Added Last Year: 1,000 (+16.7%)

Publishing - law & college textbooks & online services (Westlaw)

CASINO AMERICA, INC.

711 Washington Loop
Biloxi, MS 39530
Chm & CEO: Bernard Goldstein
VP HR & Risk Mgmt : Robert F. Boone
Employees: 3,840

Phone: 601-436-7000
Fax: 601-435-5998

Jobs Added Last Year: 1,062 (+38.2%)

Gambling resorts & casinos - riverboat casinos (Isle of Capri Casino) & dockside gaming in Mississippi & Louisiana

An in-depth profile of this company is available
to subscribers on Hoover's Online at www.hoovers.com.

207

CASINO RESOURCE CORPORATION

1719 Beach Blvd., Ste. 306   Phone: 601-435-1976
Biloxi, MS 39531   Fax: 601-374-5935
Chm & CEO: John J. Pilger
No central personnel officer
Employees: 190

Jobs Added Last Year: 75 (+65.2%)

Real estate operations - timeshare property sales; hotel management

DEPOSIT GUARANTY CORP.

210 E. Capitol St.   Phone: 601-354-8564
Jackson, MS 39201   Fax: 601-354-8192
Chm & CEO: E. B. Robinson Jr.
SVP & Dir HR: Susan S. Cain
Employees: 2,994

Jobs Added Last Year: 381 (+14.6%)

Banks - Southeast

GULF SOUTH MEDICAL SUPPLY, INC.

426 Christine Dr.   Phone: 601-856-5900
Ridgeland, MS 39157   Fax: 601-853-4801
Chm, Pres & CEO: Thomas G. Hixon
Dir HR: Louie Vaughn
Employees: 341

Jobs Added Last Year: 111 (+48.3%)

Medical & dental supplies - exam gloves, bandages, incontinence products & oxygen supplies distribution to nursing homes & other long-term care providers

HANCOCK FABRICS, INC.

3406 W. Main St.   Phone: 601-842-2834
Tupelo, MS 38801   Fax: 601-842-2834
Chm & CEO: Morris O. Jarvis
VP Personnel: David H. Jensen
Employees: 7,000

Jobs Cut Last Year: 100 (-1.4%)

Retail - fabric & notions

JITNEY-JUNGLE STORES OF AMERICA, INC.

453 N. Mill St.   Phone: 601-948-0361
Jackson, MS 39202   Fax: 601-352-0483
Chm, Pres & CEO: W. H. Holman Jr.
SVP HR: Jerry Jones
Employees: 11,000

Jobs Added Last Year: 1,000 (+10.0%)

Retail - supermarkets

MICROTEK MEDICAL, INC.

512 Lehmberg Rd., PO Box 2487   Phone: 601-327-1863
Columbus, MS 39704   Fax: 601-327-5921
Pres & CEO: Kimber L. Vought
Mgr Personnel: Nancy Betts
Employees: 860

Jobs Added Last Year: 323 (+60.1%)

Medical products - infection- & fluid-control products, middle ear prostheses & tympanostomy tubes

Jobtrak — http://www.jobtrak.com/

MOBILE TELECOMMUNICATION TECHNOLOGIES CORP.

200 S. Lamar St.
Jackson, MS 39201
Chm & CEO: John N. Palmer
Dir HR: Bob Pike
Employees: 2,650
Phone: 601-944-1300
Fax: 601-944-7158

Jobs Added Last Year: 1,125 (+73.8%)

Telecommunications services - nationwide & international wireless messaging services (Skytel)

SANDERSON FARMS, INC.

225 N. 13th Ave., PO Box 988
Laurel, MS 39441-0988
Pres & CEO: Joe F. Sanderson Jr.
Dir HR: Jesse Walters
Employees: 5,278
Phone: 601-649-4030
Fax: 601-426-1461

Jobs Added Last Year: 424 (+8.7%)

Food - fresh & frozen chicken (Miss Goldy) & frozen entrees (Sanderson Farms)

WORLDCOM, INC.

515 E. Amite St.
Jackson, MS 39201-2702
Pres & CEO: Bernard J. Ebbers
VP HR & Admin: Dennis Sickle
Employees: 7,500
Phone: 601-360-8600
Fax: 601-974-8350

Jobs Added Last Year: 0

Telecommunications services - long-distance telephone & telecommunications services

A.G. EDWARDS, INC.

One N. Jefferson
St. Louis, MO 63103
Chm, Pres & CEO: Benjamin F. Edwards III
VP & Dir Personnel: Ron Hoenninger
Employees: 11,279
Phone: 314-289-3000
Fax: 314-955-5612

Jobs Added Last Year: 538 (+5.0%)

Financial - investment banking, securities & commodities brokerage & asset management

ALLEGIANT BANCORP, INC.

4323 N. Grand Blvd.
St. Louis, MO 63107
Chm & CEO: Marvin S. Wool
Dir HR: Shelley Teel
Employees: 98
Phone: 314-534-3000
Fax: 314-692-2458

Jobs Added Last Year: 20 (+25.6%)

Banks - Midwest

ALLIED HEALTHCARE PRODUCTS, INC.

1720 Sublette Ave.
St. Louis, MO 63110
Pres & CEO: David V. LaRusso
VP HR & Gen Mgr: James M. MacNee
Employees: 1,048
Phone: 314-771-2400
Fax: 314-771-0650

Jobs Added Last Year: 509 (+94.4%)

Medical products - respiratory therapy equipment, medical gas equipment & emergency medical products for hospitals, postacute care facilities, home health care & trauma care

ANGELICA CORPORATION

424 S. Woods Mill Rd.
Chesterfield, MO 63017-3406
Chm & Pres: Lawrence J. Young
VP HR: John S. Aleman
Employees: 9,700
Phone: 314-854-3800
Fax: 314-854-3890

Jobs Cut Last Year: 100 (-1.0%)

Linen supply & related - health care uniforms & linens & general linen services for casinos, hotels, motels & restaurants

ANHEUSER-BUSCH COMPANIES, INC.

One Busch Place
St. Louis, MO 63118
Chm & Pres: August A. Busch III
VP Corp HR: William L. Rammes
Employees: 45,529
Phone: 314-577-2000
Fax: 314-577-2900

Jobs Added Last Year: 2,907 (+6.8%)

Beverages - beer (#1 brewer worldwide: Budweiser, Michelob); theme parks (Sea World, Busch Gardens)

A. P. GREEN INDUSTRIES, INC.

Green Blvd.
Mexico, MO 65265
Chm, Pres & CEO: Paul F. Hummer II
Dir HR: Ron Bromblett
Employees: 1,966
Phone: 573-473-3626
Fax: 573-473-3330

Jobs Added Last Year: 310 (+18.7%)

Industrial processing - lime products used in steel, aluminum, pulp & paper processing; clay & alumina refractory products

 An in-depth profile of this company is available to subscribers on Hoover's Online at www.hoovers.com.

209

BELDEN INC.

7701 Forsyth Blvd., Ste. 800
St. Louis, MO 63105
Chm, Pres & CEO: C. Baker Cunningham
VP HR: Cathy O. Staples
Employees: 3,800

Phone: 314-854-8000
Fax: 314-854-8001

Jobs Added Last Year: 876 (+30.0%)

Wire & cable products - multiconductor wire, coaxial cable, fiber-optic cable & electrical wire

BERG ELECTRONICS

101 S. Hanley Rd.
St. Louis, MO 63105
CEO: James N. Mills
VP HR: Larry Bacon
Employees: 5,400

Phone: 314-726-1323
Fax: 314-746-2276

Jobs Added Last Year: 700 (+14.9%)

Electrical connectors for computers

BHA GROUP, INC.

8800 E. 63rd St.
Kansas City, MO 64133
Pres & CEO: James E. Lund
HR Dir: Rick Lindquist
Employees: 762

Phone: 816-356-8400
Fax: 816-353-1873

Jobs Added Last Year: 207 (+37.3%)

Pollution control equipment & services - replacement parts & accessories for fabric filter air-pollution control equipment

BJC HEALTH SYSTEM

4444 Forest Park Ave.
St. Louis, MO 63108
Pres & CEO: Fred Brown
VP HR & Organizational Dev: William Behrendt
Employees: 23,000

Phone: 314-286-2000
Fax: 314-362-0708

Jobs Added Last Year: —

Hospitals - integrated health care delivery system serving the St. Louis area

BOATMEN'S BANCSHARES, INC.

One Boatmen's Plaza, 800 Market St.
St. Louis, MO 63101
Chm & CEO: Andrew B. Craig III
SVP HR: Arthur J. Fleischer
Employees: 17,023

Phone: 314-466-6000
Fax: 314-466-4235

Jobs Added Last Year: 2,854 (+20.1%)

Banks - Midwest

BROWN GROUP, INC.

8300 Maryland Ave.
St. Louis, MO 63105
Chm, Pres & CEO: B. A. Bridgewater Jr.
Dir Personnel: Stephen D. Scanlan
Employees: 11,000

Phone: 314-854-4000
Fax: 314-854-4274

Jobs Cut Last Year: 3,500 (-24.1%)

Retail - shoes (Naturalizer, Famous Footwear, Dr. Scholl's)

BUTLER MANUFACTURING COMPANY

BMA Tower, Penn Valley Park,
PO Box 419917
Kansas City, MO 64141-0917
Chm & CEO: Robert H. West
VP Admin: John W. Huey
Employees: 3,966

Phone: 816-968-3000
Fax: 816-968-3279

Jobs Added Last Year: 402 (+11.3%)

Building products - preengineered nonresidential metal buildings

CPI CORP.

1706 Washington Ave.
St. Louis, MO 63103-1790
Chm & CEO: Alyn V. Essman
EVP HR: Fran Scheper
Employees: 15,000

Phone: 314-231-1575
Fax: 314-621-9286

Jobs Cut Last Year: 1,500 (-9.1%)

Retail - preschool portrait photography; posters, prints & frames

DAUGHTERS OF CHARITY NATIONAL HEALTH SYSTEM

4600 Edmundson Rd.
St. Louis, MO 63134
Pres & CEO: Donald A. Brennan
VP HR: David Smith
Employees: 62,300

Phone: 314-253-6700
Fax: 314-253-6714

Jobs Cut Last Year: 5,100 (-7.6%)

Hospitals

DST SYSTEMS, INC.

1055 Broadway
Kansas City, MO 64105
Pres & CEO: Thomas A. McDonnell
VP HR: Joan Horan
Employees: 5,000

Phone: 816-435-1000
Fax: 816-435-8618

Jobs Added Last Year: 0

Computers - information processing & computer software services & products, primarily for mutual funds, insurance providers, banks & other financial services organizations

THE EARTHGRAINS COMPANY

8400 Maryland Ave.   Phone: 314-259-7000
St. Louis, MO 63105
Chm & CEO: Barry H. Beracha
VP HR: Edward J. Wizeman
Employees: 16,200

Jobs Added Last Year: 200 (+1.3%)

Food - fresh-baked goods (#2 in US), including bread (Rainbo, Colonial, Earth Grains, Grant's Farm, IronKids, Essentials) & snack cakes (Break Cake)

EDISON BROTHERS STORES, INC.

501 N. Broadway   Phone: 314-331-6000
St. Louis, MO 63102-2196   Fax: 314-331-7200
Chm, Pres & CEO: Alan D. Miller
EVP HR: Eric A. Freesmeier
Employees: 24,600

Jobs Added Last Year: 1,200 (+5.1%)

Retail - men's clothing (J. Riggins, Jeans West) & women's shoes & clothing

EDWARD D. JONES & CO.

12555 Manchester Rd.   Phone: 314-515-2000
St. Louis, MO 63131   Fax: 314-851-3728
CEO: John W. Bachmann
Dir HR: Bob Pearce
Employees: 10,000

Jobs Added Last Year: 2,582 (+34.8%)

Financial - securities brokerage, real estate

EMERSON ELECTRIC CO.

8000 W. Florissant Ave.   Phone: 314-553-2000
St. Louis, MO 63136   Fax: 314-553-3527
Chm, Pres & CEO: Charles F. Knight
VP HR: C. T. Kelly
Employees: 78,900

Jobs Added Last Year: 5,000 (+6.8%)

Machinery - computer power supplies, meters & HVAC equipment; electric motors, hand-held tools & other electric equipment

ENTERPRISE RENT-A-CAR

600 Corporate Park Dr.   Phone: 314-512-5000
St. Louis, MO 63105   Fax: 314-512-4202
Pres & CEO: Andrew C. Taylor
VP HR: Jerry Spector
Employees: 14,703

Jobs Cut Last Year: 3,797 (-20.5%)

Leasing - car rental

FALCON PRODUCTS, INC.

9387 Dielman Industrial Dr.   Phone: 314-991-9200
St. Louis, MO 63132   Fax: 314-991-9227
Chm & CEO: Franklin A. Jacobs
Dir HR: Chuck Pineau
Employees: 1,743

Jobs Added Last Year: 362 (+26.2%)

Furniture - tables, booths, chairs & sheet metal kitchen equipment

FARMLAND INDUSTRIES, INC.

3315 N. Oak Trafficway   Phone: 816-459-6000
Kansas City, MO 64116   Fax: 816-459-6979
Pres & CEO: Harry D. Cleberg
VP HR: Holly D. McCoy
Employees: 12,700

Jobs Added Last Year: 700 (+5.8%)

Diversified operations - meat packing; petroleum refining

FERRELLGAS PARTNERS, L.P.

One Liberty Plaza   Phone: 816-792-1600
Liberty, MO 64068   Fax: 816-792-7985
Chm & CEO: James E. Ferrell
Dir Emp Svcs: Jim Coyne
Employees: 3,657

Jobs Added Last Year: 566 (+18.3%)

Energy - propane & other natural gas retail operations

FURNITURE BRANDS INTERNATIONAL

101 S. Hanley Rd.   Phone: 314-863-1100
St. Louis, MO 63105-3493 Fax: 314-863-5306
Chm, Pres & CEO : Richard B. Loynd
Ops Dir: Robert Haas
Employees: 20,700

Jobs Added Last Year: 6,900 (+50.0%)

Furniture - residential (#1 in US: Broyhill & Lane, Thomasville Furniture Industries)

GRAYBAR ELECTRIC COMPANY, INC.

34 N. Meramec Ave.   Phone: 314-512-9200
Clayton, MO 63105-3882   Fax: 314-512-9453
Pres & CEO: J. R. Seaton
VP HR: Jack F. Van Pelt
Employees: 6,200

Jobs Added Last Year: 700 (+12.7%)

Electrical products - wholesale

 An in-depth profile of this company is available to subscribers on Hoover's Online at www.hoovers.com.

HALLMARK CARDS, INC.

2501 McGee St. Phone: 816-274-5111
Kansas City, MO 64108 Fax: 816-274-8513
Pres & CEO: Irvine O. Hockaday Jr.
VP HR: Ralph Christensen
Employees: 12,100
Jobs Cut Last Year: 700 (-5.5%)

Greeting cards & related products, including art supplies (Crayola, Magic Marker); TV programming

H&R BLOCK, INC.

4410 Main St. Phone: 816-753-6900
Kansas City, MO 64111 Fax: 816-753-5346
Pres & CEO: Richard H. Brown
Asst VP & Dir HR: Nicki Gustin
Employees: 91,000
Jobs Added Last Year: 8,200 (+9.9%)

Financial - tax preparation; online information network (CompuServe)

HUNTCO INC.

14323 S. Outer Forty, Ste. 600N Phone: 314-878-0155
Town & Country, MO 63017 Fax: 314-878-4537
Chm & CEO: B. D. Hunter
VP & Treas: Tony Verkruyse
Employees: 432
Jobs Added Last Year: 102 (+30.9%)

Steel - flat-rolled carbon steel

INTERSTATE BAKERIES CORPORATION

12 E. Armour Blvd., PO Box 419627 Phone: 816-561-6600
Kansas City, MO 64111 Fax: 816-561-6600
Chm & CEO: Charles A. Sullivan
SVP HR: Russell Baker
Employees: 35,000
Jobs Added Last Year: 21,000 (+150.0%)

Food - bakery products (#1 US wholesale baker: Butternut, Holsum, Merita, Mrs. Karl's, Sweetheart, Hostess, Wonder)

JACK HENRY & ASSOCIATES, INC.

663 Hwy. 60, PO Box 807 Phone: 417-235-6652
Monett, MO 65708 Fax: 417-235-8406
Chm & CEO: Michael E. Henry
Dir HR: Michael R. Wallace
Employees: 295
Jobs Added Last Year: 112 (+61.2%)

Computers - outsourcing & system integration services software for the retail banking industry

JEFFERSON SAVINGS BANCORP, INC.

14915 Manchester Rd. Phone: 314-227-3000
Ballwin, MO 63011 Fax: 314-227-5009
Chm, Pres & CEO: David V. McCay
VP HR: Ellen Stanko
Employees: 210
Jobs Added Last Year: 65 (+44.8%)

Financial - savings & loans

JEFFERSON SMURFIT CORPORATION

Jefferson Smurfit Ctr., 8182 Maryland Ave. Phone: 314-746-1100
St. Louis, MO 63105 Fax: 314-746-1281
CEO: James E. Terrill
VP Personnel & HR: Michael F. Harrington
Employees: 16,200
Jobs Cut Last Year: 400 (-2.4%)

Containers - corrugated shipping containers; containerboard & recycled cylinder board; wastepaper recycling; newsprint mills; house paneling

JOHN Q. HAMMONS HOTELS, INC.

300 John Q. Hammons Pkwy., Ste. 900 Phone: 417-864-6573
Springfield, MO 65806 Fax: 417-864-8900
Chm & CEO: John Q. Hammons
No central personnel officer
Employees: 8,000
Jobs Added Last Year: 2,200 (+37.9%)

Hotels & motels (more than 35 units; Embassy Suites, Holiday Inn)

JONES MEDICAL INDUSTRIES, INC.

1945 Craig Rd. Phone: 314-576-6100
St. Louis, MO 63146 Fax: 314-469-5749
Chm, Pres & CEO: Dennis M. Jones
No central personnel officer
Employees: 334
Jobs Added Last Year: 74 (+28.5%)

Drugs - critical-care pharmaceuticals & vitamin & nutritional products

KANSAS CITY SOUTHERN INDUSTRIES, INC.

114 W. 11th St. Phone: 816-556-0303
Kansas City, MO 64105-1804 Fax: 816-556-0297
Pres & CEO: Landon H. Rowland
VP HR: Hugh Salmons
Employees: 9,600
Jobs Added Last Year: 1,383 (+16.8%)

Transportation - rail; transaction-processing systems; mutual fund management services

KELLWOOD COMPANY

600 Kellwood Pkwy.   Phone: 314-576-3100
Chesterfield, MO 63017   Fax: 314-576-3388
Chm & CEO: William J. McKenna
VP HR: Leon M. McWhite
Employees: 15,750
Jobs Added Last Year: 350 (+2.3%)

Apparel

LEGGETT & PLATT, INCORPORATED

One Leggett Rd.   Phone: 417-358-8131
Carthage, MO 64836   Fax: 417-358-5691
Chm & CEO: Harry M. Cornell Jr.
VP HR: John A. Hale
Employees: 16,600
Jobs Added Last Year: 600 (+3.8%)

Furniture - components for the bedding & home furniture industry

MALLINCKRODT GROUP INC.

7733 Forsyth Blvd.   Phone: 314-854-5200
St. Louis, MO 63105-1820   Fax: 314-854-5380
Chm & CEO: C. Ray Holman
VP HR: Bruce K. Crockett
Employees: 10,300
Jobs Added Last Year: 100 (+1.0%)

Diversified operations - medical devices; human & animal health care products; specialty chemicals

MARITZ INC.

1375 N. Highway Dr.   Phone: 314-827-4000
Fenton, MO 63099   Fax: 314-827-5505
Chm & CEO: William E. Maritz
SVP HR: Terry Goring
Employees: 6,410
Jobs Added Last Year: 330 (+5.4%)

Business services - market research

THE MAY DEPARTMENT STORES CO.

611 Olive St.   Phone: 314-342-6300
St. Louis, MO 63101-1799   Fax: 314-342-4461
Chm & CEO: David C. Farrell
SVP HR: Douglas J. Giles
Employees: 130,000
Jobs Added Last Year: 11,000 (+9.2%)

Retail - major department stores (Lord & Taylor, Foley's, Robinsons-May, Hecht's, Kaufmann's, Filene's) & shoe stores (Famous-Barr, Meier & Frank)

MCDONNELL DOUGLAS CORP.

PO Box 516   Phone: 314-232-0232
St. Louis, MO 63166-0516   Fax: 314-234-7064
Pres & CEO: Harry C. Stonecipher
SVP HR & Quality: Laurie A. Broedling
Employees: 63,612
Jobs Cut Last Year: 2,148 (-3.3%)

Aerospace - military & commercial (#3 worldwide) aircraft; helicopters; missiles; space launch vehicles; financial services

America's Job Bank — http://www.ajb.dni.us/

An in-depth profile of this company is available
to subscribers on Hoover's Online at www.hoovers.com.

213

MEMC ELECTRONIC MATERIALS, INC.

501 Pearl Dr.   Phone: 314-279-5500
St. Peters, MO 63376   Fax: 314-279-5161
CEO: Roger D. McDaniel
Corp VP HR: Huston E. Sherrill
Employees: 6,400

Jobs Added Last Year: 440 (+7.4%)

Electrical components - silicon wafers used in the production of semiconductors

MERCANTILE BANCORPORATION INC.

PO Box 524   Phone: 314-425-2525
St. Louis, MO 63166-0524   Fax: 314-425-1286
Chm, Pres & CEO: Thomas H. Jacobsen
EVP HR: Jon Pierce
Employees: 6,918

Jobs Added Last Year: 1,262 (+22.3%)

Banks - Midwest

MONSANTO COMPANY

800 N. Lindbergh Blvd.   Phone: 314-694-1000
St. Louis, MO 63167   Fax: 314-694-6572
Chm & CEO: Robert B. Shapiro
VP HR: Teresa E. McCaslin
Employees: 28,514

Jobs Cut Last Year: 840 (-2.9%)

Chemicals - fat substitute, herbicides, industrial chemicals, pharmaceuticals

O'REILLY AUTOMOTIVE, INC.

233 S. Patterson   Phone: 417-862-6708
Springfield, MO 65802   Fax: 417-869-8903
Pres & CEO: David E. O'Reilly
Dir HR: Steve Pope
Employees: 2,623

Jobs Added Last Year: 542 (+26.0%)

Auto parts - automotive aftermarket parts, tools, supplies, equipment & accessories for do-it-yourself customers, professional mechanics & service technicians

PAYLESS CASHWAYS, INC.

2 Pershing Sq., 2300 Main St.   Phone: 816-234-6000
Kansas City, MO 64108   Fax: 816-234-6361
Chm & CEO: David Stanley
SVP HR: E. J. Holland Jr.
Employees: 18,100

Jobs Cut Last Year: 300 (-1.6%)

Building products - retail building materials & home-improvement products

RALCORP HOLDINGS, INC.

800 Market St., PO Box 618   Phone: 314-877-7095
St. Louis, MO 63188-0618   Fax: 314-877-7666
Pres & Co-CEO: Richard A. Pearce
VP HR: Jack Owazarczak
Employees: 7,200

Jobs Added Last Year: 100 (+1.4%)

Food - cereal (Cookie Crisp), baby food (Beech-Nut) & crackers (Bremner) & cookies; coupon redemption services; ski resorts (Keystone, Breckenridge)

RALSTON PURINA COMPANY

Checkerboard Sq.   Phone: 314-982-1000
St. Louis, MO 63164-0001   Fax: 314-982-2134
Chm, Pres & Co-CEO: William P. Stiritz
VP & Dir Admin: Charles Sommer
Employees: 31,837

Jobs Cut Last Year: 202 (-0.6%)

Diversified operations - pet food (Purina Dog Chow, Purina Cat Chow); batteries (Eveready, Energizer); animal feed; food additives

REHABCARE GROUP, INC.

7733 Forsyth Blvd., Ste. 1700   Phone: 314-863-7422
St. Louis, MO 63105   Fax: 314-863-0769
Pres & CEO: James M. Usdan
SVP HR: Stephen J. Toth
Employees: 1,595

Jobs Added Last Year: 357 (+28.8%)

Medical services - medical rehabilitation programs & therapy services in acute-care hospitals, skilled nursing units & outpatient facilities

SCHNUCK MARKETS INC.

11420 Lackland Rd.   Phone: 314-994-9900
St. Louis, MO 63146   Fax: 314-994-4465
Chm & CEO: Craig D. Schnuck
VP HR: William Jones
Employees: 12,000

Jobs Added Last Year: 4,042 (+50.8%)

Retail - supermarkets

SIGMA-ALDRICH CORPORATION

3050 Spruce St.   Phone: 314-771-5765
St. Louis, MO 63103   Fax: 314-534-2674
Pres & CEO: Tom Cori
VP HR: Terry Colvin
Employees: 5,682

Jobs Added Last Year: 148 (+2.7%)

Chemicals - biochemicals, radiolabeled chemicals, diagnostic reagents & related products; metal products used in routing & supporting electrical, mechanical & telecommunications services

SISTERS OF MERCY HEALTH SYSTEM-ST. LOUIS

2039 N. Geyer Rd. Phone: 314-965-6100
St. Louis, MO 63131 Fax: 314-965-9182
CEO: Mary R. Rocklage
Dir HR: Diane Carter
Employees: 24,000
Jobs Added Last Year: 7,100 (+42.0%)
Hospitals

SSM HEALTH CARE SYSTEM INC.

477 N. Lindbergh Blvd. Phone: 314-994-7800
St. Louis, MO 63141 Fax: 314-994-7900
CEO: Sister Mary Jean Ryan
SVP HR: Steven Barney
Employees: 19,000
Jobs Added Last Year: —
Hospitals

STORAGE TRUST REALTY

2407 Rangeline Phone: 573-499-4799
Columbia, MO 65202 Fax: 573-442-5554
CEO: Michael G. Burnam
Dir HR: Bill Fuller
Employees: 357
Jobs Added Last Year: 123 (+52.6%)
Real estate investment trust - self-storage facilities

TOROTEL, INC.

13402 S. 71 Hwy. Phone: 816-761-6314
Grandview, MO 64030 Fax: 816-763-2278
Chm, Pres & CEO: Dale H. Sizemore Jr.
HR Mgr: Cindy K. Dark
Employees: 150
Jobs Added Last Year: 50 (+50.0%)
Electrical products - magnetic components, transformers, inductors, reactors, chokes & toroidal coils; power supplies for the computer & telecommunication markets

TRANS WORLD AIRLINES, INC.

One City Centre, 515 N. 6th Street Phone: 314-589-3000
St. Louis, MO 63101 Fax: 314-589-3129
Pres & CEO: Jeffrey H. Erickson
SVP Emp Relations: Charles J. Thibaudeau
Employees: 23,628
Jobs Added Last Year: 828 (+3.6%)
Transportation - airline

UNION ELECTRIC COMPANY

1901 Chouteau Ave. Phone: 314-621-3222
St. Louis, MO 63103 Fax: 314-992-6693
Pres & CEO: Charles W. Mueller
VP HR: Jean Hannis
Employees: 6,190
Jobs Cut Last Year: 76 (-1.2%)
Utility - electric power & natural gas

UNITOG COMPANY

101 W. 11th St. Phone: 816-474-7000
Kansas City, MO 64105 Fax: 816-842-2303
Chm, Pres & CEO: Randolph K. Rolf
SVP HR: John W. Hall
Employees: 4,105
Jobs Added Last Year: 880 (+27.3%)
Linen supply & related - uniform rental services

THE UNIVERSITY OF MISSOURI SYSTEM

321 University Hall Phone: 573-882-6211
Columbia, MO 65211 Fax: 573-882-2721
Pres: George A. Russell
Assoc VP HR: R. Kenneth Hutchinson
Employees: 18,997
Jobs Cut Last Year: 1,961 (-9.4%)
University

VENTURE STORES, INC.

2001 E. Terra Ln. Phone: 314-281-5500
O'Fallon, MO 63366-0110 Fax: 314-281-6000
Chm, Pres & CEO: Robert N. Wildrick
SVP HR: Robert B. Hensley
Employees: 15,000
Jobs Cut Last Year: 2,000 (-11.8%)
Retail - discount & variety

WASHINGTON UNIVERSITY

1 Brookings Dr. Phone: 314-935-5000
St. Louis, MO 63130 Fax: 314-935-5146
Chancellor: Mark S. Wrighton
Vice Chancellor HR: Gloria White
Employees: 7,100
Jobs Added Last Year: 46 (+0.7%)
University

An in-depth profile of this company is available to subscribers on Hoover's Online at www.hoovers.com.

215

WAVE TECHNOLOGIES INT'L.

10845 Olive Blvd., Ste. 250
St. Louis, MO 63141
Phone: 314-995-5767
Fax: 314-995-3894
Chm, Pres & CEO: Kenneth W. Kousky
Dir HR: Diane Kisker
Employees: 217

Jobs Added Last Year: 90 (+70.9%)

Computers - training & instructional services & products related to local & wide area networks, telecommunications systems, advanced operating systems & the Internet

MONTANA

CROP GROWERS CORPORATION

201 Crop Growers Dr.
Great Falls, MT 59401
Phone: 406-452-8101
Fax: 406-771-0838
Acting CEO: Larry Martinez
Dir HR: Lori Hardy
Employees: 517

Jobs Added Last Year: 289 (+126.8%)

Insurance - multiperil crop, private crop hail & other peril insurance

SEMITOOL, INC.

655 W. Reserve Dr.
Kalispell, MT 59901
Phone: 406-752-2107
Fax: 406-752-5522
Chm, Pres & CEO: Raymon F. Thompson
Personnel Mgr: Vicki Billmayer
Employees: 1,098

Jobs Added Last Year: 575 (+109.9%)

Machinery - batch & single substrate spray chemical processing tools, thermal processing equipment & wafer-carrier cleaning systems used in the fabrication of semiconductors

NEBRASKA

AMERICAN BUSINESS INFORMATION

5711 S. 86th Circle
Omaha, NE 68127
Phone: 402-593-4500
Fax: 402-331-1505
Chm & CEO: Vinod Gupta
Dir HR: Jeff Bauman
Employees: 870

Jobs Added Last Year: 238 (+37.7%)

Business services - business-to-business marketing information in the form of mailing labels, printed directories, computer diskettes & CD-ROMs

BERKSHIRE HATHAWAY INC.

1440 Kiewit Plaza
Omaha, NE 68131
Phone: 402-346-1400
Fax: 402-346-3375
Chm & CEO: Warren E. Buffett
Sec: Forrest N. Krutter
Employees: 24,000

Jobs Added Last Year: 2,000 (+9.1%)

Diversified operations - insurance, investment; candy (See's); home furnishings; publishing (World Book); cleaning systems (Kirby)

THE BUCKLE, INC.

2407 W. 24th St.
Kearney, NE 68847
Phone: 308-236-8491
Fax: 308-236-4493
Chm & CEO: Daniel J. Hirschfeld
No central personnel officer
Employees: 3,000

Jobs Added Last Year: 400 (+15.4%)

Retail - apparel & shoes

CONAGRA, INC.

One ConAgra Dr.
Omaha, NE 68102-5001
Phone: 402-595-4000
Fax: 402-595-4595
Chm & CEO: Philip B. Fletcher
SVP HR: Gerald B. Vernon
Employees: 90,871

Jobs Added Last Year: 3,871 (+4.4%)

Food - packaged food & meat products; farm supplies & clothing stores (Country General Stores); sewing supplies (Dyno Merchandise) & stores (Northwest Fabrics and Crafts)

IBP, INC.

515 IBP Ave.
Dakota City, NE 68731
Phone: 402-494-2061
Fax: 402-241-2068
Chm & CEO: Robert L. Peterson
VP HR: Kenneth J. Kimbro
Employees: 34,000

Jobs Added Last Year: 3,300 (+10.7%)

Food - fresh beef & pork products (#1 worldwide)

INACOM CORP.

10810 Farnam Dr. Phone: 402-392-3900
Omaha, NE 68154 Fax: 402-392-3602
Pres & CEO: Bill L. Fairfield
VP Corp Resources: Larry Fazzini
Employees: 2,196

Jobs Added Last Year: 312 (+16.6%)

Retail - wholesale microcomputer systems, workstations, networking & telecommunications equipment & related products

MFS COMMUNICATIONS COMPANY

3555 Farnam St., Ste. 200 Phone: 402-977-5300
Omaha, NE 68131 Fax: 402-231-3505
Chm & CEO: James Q. Crowe
SVP HR: Michael R. Frank
Employees: 3,500

Jobs Added Last Year: 529 (+17.8%)

Telecommunications services - special access & private-line services; network systems integration & facilities management services

THE MUTUAL OF OMAHA COMPANIES

Mutual of Omaha Plaza Phone: 402-342-7600
Omaha, NE 68175 Fax: 402-978-2775
VC, Pres & CEO: John W. Weekly
EVP HR: Robert B. Bogart
Employees: 7,850

Jobs Cut Last Year: 480 (-5.8%)

Insurance - property & casualty

PAMIDA HOLDINGS CORPORATION

8800 F St. Phone: 402-339-2400
Omaha, NE 68127 Fax: 402-596-7330
Pres & CEO: Steven S. Fishman
VP HR: Paul Kanutson
Employees: 6,100

Jobs Cut Last Year: 1,100 (-15.3%)

Retail - discount & variety

PETER KIEWIT SONS', INC.

1000 Kiewit Plaza Phone: 402-342-2052
Omaha, NE 68131 Fax: 402-271-2829
Chm & Pres: Walter Scott Jr.
VP HR: Brad Chapman
Employees: 14,300

Jobs Added Last Year: 300 (+2.1%)

Construction - heavy; coal mining; telecommunications

THE UNIVERSITY OF NEBRASKA

3835 Holdrege St. Phone: 402-472-2111
Lincoln, NE 68583-0742 Fax: 402-472-2410
Pres: L. Dennis Smith
Dir HR: John Russell
Employees: 15,000

Jobs Added Last Year: —

University

VALMONT INDUSTRIES, INC.

W. Hwy. 275 Phone: 402-359-2201
Valley, NE 68064 Fax: 402-359-2848
Pres & CEO: Mogens C. Bay
VP HR: Tom L. Whalen
Employees: 4,166

Jobs Added Last Year: 412 (+11.0%)

Diversified operations - microcomputer resale, industrial & irrigation products

WERNER ENTERPRISES, INC.

Interstate 80 & Hwy. 50 Phone: 402-895-6640
Omaha, NE 68138-9104 Fax: 402-895-1387
Chm & CEO: Clarence L. Werner
Dir HR: Doug Pedersen
Employees: 5,822

Jobs Added Last Year: 2,148 (+58.5%)

Transportation - truck

AMERCO

1325 Airmotive Way, Ste. 100 Phone: 702-688-6300
Reno, NV 89502-3239 Fax: 702-688-6338
Chm & Pres: Edward J. "Joe" Shoen
VP HR: Henry P. Kelly
Employees: 12,000

Jobs Cut Last Year: 1,500 (-11.1%)

Leasing - trucks & trailers (U-Haul International); insurance (Ponderosa Holdings)

ANCHOR GAMING

815 Pilot Rd., Ste. G
Las Vegas, NV 89119
Chm & CEO: Stanley E. Fulton
Office Mgr: Suzy Delzer
Employees: 736

Phone: 702-896-7568
Fax: 702-896-6221

Jobs Added Last Year: 150 (+25.6%)

Gambling resorts & casinos - resorts in Las Vegas & Colorado;
gaming machines

BOARDWALK CASINO, INC.

3750 Las Vegas Blvd. South
Las Vegas, NV 89109
Chm, Pres & CEO: Norbert W. Jansen
Dir HR: Linda Garner
Employees: 400

Phone: 702-735-2400
Fax: 702-739-7918

Jobs Added Last Year: 225 (+128.6%)

Gambling resorts & casinos - hotel & casino on the Las Vegas
Strip

BOYD GAMING CORPORATION

2950 S. Industrial Rd.
Las Vegas, NV 89109
Chm & CEO: William S. Boyd
VP HR: Catherine A. Shanklin
Employees: 11,500

Phone: 702-792-7200
Fax: 702-792-7266

Jobs Added Last Year: 1,500 (+15.0%)

Gambling resorts & casinos in Las Vegas (Stardust, Sam's Town,
Fremont), Louisiana, Mississippi & Missouri

CIRCUS CIRCUS ENTERPRISES, INC.

2880 Las Vegas Blvd. South
Las Vegas, NV 89109-1120
Chm & CEO: Clyde T. Turner
Corp Dir HR: Kit Turner
Employees: 20,200

Phone: 702-734-0410
Fax: 702-734-2051

Jobs Added Last Year: 1,925 (+10.5%)

Gambling resorts & casinos (Circus Circus, Excalibur, Luxor)

COMMUNITY PSYCHIATRIC CENTERS

6600 W. Charleston Blvd., Ste. 118
Las Vegas, NV 89102
Chm & CEO: Richard L. Conte
VP Admin: Ronald Ooley
Employees: 9,400

Phone: 702-259-3600
Fax: 702-259-3650

Jobs Cut Last Year: 375 (-3.8%)

Hospitals

HARVEYS CASINO RESORTS

Hwy. 50 & Stateline Ave.
Lake Tahoe, NV 89449
Pres & CEO: Charles W. Scharer
VP HR: Tom Evans
Employees: 4,950

Phone: 702-588-2411
Fax: 702-588-6643

Jobs Added Last Year: 2,310 (+87.5%)

Gambling resorts & casinos - hotel/casinos on Lake Tahoe, in
Colorado (Harveys Wagon Wheel) in Las Vegas (Hard Rock Hotel)
& in Council Bluffs, IA (Harveys Kanesville Queen)

Career Path — http://www.careerpath.com/

LADY LUCK GAMING CORPORATION

206 N. Third St.
Las Vegas, NV 89101
Chm & CEO: Andrew H. Tompkins
Dir Personnel: Marge Isom
Employees: 2,850
Phone: 702-477-3000
Fax: 702-477-3003

Jobs Added Last Year: 750 (+35.7%)

Gambling resorts & casinos - dockside, riverboat & land-based casinos

MEDNET MPC CORPORATION

871-C Grier Dr.
Las Vegas, NV 89119
Pres & CEO: M. B. Merryman
No central personnel officer
Employees: 333
Phone: 702-361-3119
Fax: 702-361-2422

Jobs Added Last Year: 143 (+75.3%)

Medical practice management - pharmacy card plan processing & related pharmacy services

MGM GRAND, INC.

3799 Las Vegas Blvd. South
Las Vegas, NV 89109
Chm & CEO: J. Terrence Lanni
SVP HR & Admin: Cynthia K. Murphy
Employees: 6,400
Phone: 702-891-3333
Fax: 702-891-1114

Jobs Cut Last Year: 720 (-10.1%)

Gambling resorts & casinos

MIRAGE RESORTS, INCORPORATED

3400 Las Vegas Blvd. South
Las Vegas, NV 89109
Chm, Pres & CEO: Stephen A. Wynn
VP HR: Arte Nathan
Employees: 14,600
Phone: 702-791-7111
Fax: 702-792-7414

Jobs Cut Last Year: 2,200 (-13.1%)

Gambling resorts & casinos in Las Vegas (Mirage, Treasure Island, Golden Nugget) & Laughlin, NV (Golden Nugget)

RIO HOTEL & CASINO, INC.

3700 W. Flamingo Rd.
Las Vegas, NV 89103
Chm & CEO: Anthony A. Marnell II
Dir HR: Karen Brasier
Employees: 3,075
Phone: 702-252-7733
Fax: 702-252-7633

Jobs Added Last Year: 775 (+33.7%)

Gambling resorts & casinos in Las Vegas

SHOWBOAT, INC.

2800 Fremont St.
Las Vegas, NV 89104
Pres & CEO: J. Kell Houssels III
SVP HR: Paul S. Harris
Employees: 7,675
Phone: 702-385-9141
Fax: 702-385-9163

Jobs Added Last Year: 1,559 (+25.5%)

Gambling resorts & casinos, hotels & bowling centers

SIERRA HEALTH SERVICES, INC.

2724 N. Tenaya Way
Las Vegas, NV 89128
Chm & CEO: Anthony M. Marlon
Exec Dir HR: Dan Tanwater
Employees: 2,300
Phone: 702-242-7000
Fax: 702-242-9711

Jobs Added Last Year: 700 (+43.8%)

Health maintenance organization

STATION CASINOS, INC.

2411 W. Sahara Ave., PO Box 29500
Las Vegas, NV 89126-3300
Chm. Pres & CEO: Frank J. Fertitta III
Dir HR: David Lloyd
Employees: 7,000
Phone: 702-367-2411
Fax: 702-367-2424

Jobs Added Last Year: 1,470 (+26.6%)

Gambling resorts & casinos in Las Vegas (Palace Station Hotel & Casino, Texas Gambling Hall & Hotel) & St. Charles, MO (St. Charles Riverfront Station); vending & payphone services

SWIFT TRANSPORTATION CO., INC.

1455 Hulda Way
Sparks, NV 89431
Chm, Pres & CEO: Jerry C. Moyes
Dir HR: Bruce Taylor
Employees: 5,300
Phone: 702-359-9031
Fax: 702-352-6303

Jobs Added Last Year: 0

Transportation - regional short- to medium-haul truckload carrier

NEW HAMPSHIRE

 An in-depth profile of this company is available
to subscribers on Hoover's Online at www.hoovers.com.

219

BROOKSTONE, INC.

17 Riverside St.
Nashua, NH 03062
Pres, CEO & COO: Michael Anthony
VP HR: Jo-Ann B. Karalus
Employees: 1,522

Phone: 603-594-0260
Fax: 603-577-8005

Jobs Added Last Year: 779 (+104.8%)

Retail - personal care products, garden items, gifts, household items & leisure & recreational products

CABLETRON SYSTEMS, INC.

35 Industrial Way, PO Box 5005
Rochester, NH 03866-5005
Pres & CEO: S. Robert Levine
Dir HR: Linda Pepin
Employees: 5,377

Phone: 603-332-9400
Fax: 603-337-2211

Jobs Added Last Year: 407 (+8.2%)

Computers - local area network hubs

FISHER SCIENTIFIC INTERNATIONAL INC.

Liberty Ln.
Hampton, NH 03842
Pres & CEO: Paul M. Montrone
Mgr Emp Benefits: Sherry Lovdon
Employees: 7,500

Phone: 603-929-2650
Fax: 603-926-0222

Jobs Added Last Year: 2,700 (+56.3%)

Instruments - scientific

HADCO CORPORATION

12A Manor Pkwy.
Salem, NH 03079
Pres & CEO: Andrew E. Lietz
VP HR: Richard P. Saporito
Employees: 2,346

Phone: 603-898-8000
Fax: 603-898-6227

Jobs Added Last Year: 347 (+17.4%)

Electrical components - high-density double-sided & complex multilayer printed circuits & backplane assemblies used in the computer & industrial automation industries

SOFTDESK, INC.

7 Liberty Hill Rd.
Henniker, NH 03242
Chm, Pres, CEO & Treas: David C. Arnold
Dir HR: Robin Pullo
Employees: 273

Phone: 603-428-5000
Fax: 603-428-5325

Jobs Added Last Year: 100 (+57.8%)

Computers - CAD software for professionals in the architecture, engineering & construction industries

STANDEX INTERNATIONAL CORP.

6 Manor Pkwy.
Salem, NH 03079
Pres, CEO & COO: Edward J. Trainor
Dir Industrial Relations & Emp Benefits: James Mettling
Employees: 5,000

Phone: 603-893-9701
Fax: 603-893-7324

Jobs Cut Last Year: 100 (-2.0%)

Food service equipment; educational & religious periodical publishing & printing; automotive parts & systems

THE TIMBERLAND CO.

200 Domain Dr.
Stratham, NH 03885
Chm, Pres & CEO: Sidney W. Swartz
VP HR: Lisa Letizio
Employees: 5,500

Phone: 603-772-9500
Fax: 603-773-1640

Jobs Cut Last Year: 500 (-8.3%)

Shoes & related apparel - hiking boots & boating shoes

TYCO INTERNATIONAL LTD.

One Tyco Park
Exeter, NH 03833-1108
Chm, Pres & CEO: L. Dennis Kozlowski
Dir HR: Daniel Casteel
Employees: 34,000

Phone: 603-778-9700
Fax: 603-778-7700

Jobs Added Last Year: 10,000 (+41.7%)

Diversified operations - sprinkler systems, fire extinguishers, hydrants & hoses; packaging products; electrical components; flow control products; disposable medical products

WPI GROUP, INC.

1155 Elm St.
Manchester, NH 03101
Chm & CEO: Michael H. Foster
VP HR: Karen S. Hebert
Employees: 315

Phone: 603-627-3500
Fax: 603-627-3150

Jobs Added Last Year: 75 (+31.3%)

Electrical components - power-conversion systems & complete power systems

THE AEGIS CONSUMER FUNDING

525 Washington Blvd.
Jersey City, NJ 07310
Phone: 201-418-7300
Fax: 201-418-7393
Chm, Pres & CEO: Angelo R. Appierto
Dir HR: Kate Fitzpatrick
Employees: 210

Jobs Added Last Year: 80 (+61.5%)

Financial - auto loans to individuals with nonprime credit

ALLIEDSIGNAL INC.

101 Columbia Rd.
Morristown, NJ 07962
Phone: 201-455-2000
Fax: 201-455-4807
Chm & CEO: Lawrence A. Bossidy
SVP HR & Comm: Donald J. Redlinger
Employees: 88,500

Jobs Added Last Year: 1,000 (+1.1%)

Diversified operations - aerospace engines, equipment & avionics systems; air brakes & antilock-braking systems for heavy-duty trucks; polymers, fluorine products & specialty chemicals

AMERICAN HOME PRODUCTS CORP.

5 Giralda Farms
Madison, NJ 07940-0874
Phone: 201-660-5000
Fax: 201-660-5771
Chm, Pres & CEO: John R. Stafford
VP HR: Rene R. Lewin
Employees: 64,712

Jobs Cut Last Year: 9,297 (-12.6%)

Drugs - pharmaceuticals (Prempro) & consumer health products (Advil, Anacin, Dristan, Chapstick, Centrum, Orudis); herbicides (Cyanamid) & pesticides; food products (Chef Boyardee, Gulden's)

AMERICAN STANDARD COMPANIES

One Centennial Ave.
Piscataway, NJ 08855-6820
Phone: 908-980-6000
Fax: 908-980-6120
Chm, Pres & CEO: Emmanuel A. Kampouris
VP HR: Adrian B. Deshotel
Employees: 43,000

Jobs Added Last Year: 4,500 (+11.7%)

Building products - bathroom & kitchen fixtures & fittings; air-conditioning systems; auto braking systems

ARIEL CORPORATION

2540 Rte. 130
Cranbury, NJ 08512-3507
Phone: 609-860-2900
Fax: 609-860-1155
Chm, Pres & CEO: Anthony M. Agnello
Mgr HR: Linda Colmenares
Employees: 75

Jobs Added Last Year: 26 (+53.1%)

Computers - semiconductor boards

AUTOMATIC DATA PROCESSING, INC.

One ADP Blvd.
Roseland, NJ 07068-1728
Phone: 201-994-5000
Fax: 201-994-5387
Chm & CEO: Josh S. Weston
VP HR: Michael R. Holmes
Employees: 25,000

Jobs Added Last Year: 3,000 (+13.6%)

Business services - data-processing & distribution services; payroll services; investment quotation services

BASF CORPORATION

3000 Continental Dr. North
Mt. Olive, NJ 07828-1234
Phone: 201-426-2600
Fax: 201-426-2610
Chm, Pres & CEO: J. Dieter Stein
Dir HR: Robert Stein
Employees: 14,000

Jobs Cut Last Year: 445 (-3.1%)

Diversified operations - chemicals, consumer products, dyes & oil & gas

BECTON, DICKINSON AND COMPANY

One Becton Dr.
Franklin Lakes, NJ 07417-1880
Phone: 201-847-6800
Fax: 201-847-6475
Chm, Pres & CEO: Clateo Castellini
VP HR: Andrew Kaslow
Employees: 18,100

Jobs Cut Last Year: 500 (-2.7%)

Medical & dental supplies - IV catheters (Insyte Autoguard), needle holders (Vacutainer) & needle disposal containers; diagnostic equipment, hematology instruments & microbiology systems

BED BATH & BEYOND INC.

715 Morris Ave.
Springfield, NJ 07081
Phone: 201-379-1520
Fax: 201-379-1731
Pres & Co-CEO: Leonard Feinstein
Dir HR: Wayne Sarrow
Employees: 5,400

Jobs Added Last Year: 1,300 (+31.7%)

Retail - bed, bath, kitchen & other household furnishings

BELL COMMUNICATIONS RESEARCH INC.

445 South St.
Morristown, NJ 07960-6438
Phone: 201-740-3000
Fax: 201-740-6877
Pres & CEO: George H. Heilmeier
VP HR: Gwen P. Taylor
Employees: 6,172

Jobs Added Last Year: —

Consulting - engineering & consulting services; applied research; telecommunications & information networking software

 An in-depth profile of this company is available to subscribers on Hoover's Online at www.hoovers.com.

221

THE BISYS GROUP, INC.

150 Clove Rd.　　　　　　Phone: 201-812-8600
Little Falls, NJ 07424　　　Fax: 201-812-1217
Chm & CEO: Lynn J. Mangum
SVP HR: Mark J. Rybarczyk
Employees: 1,500

Jobs Added Last Year: 250 (+20.0%)

Business services - computing, administrative & marketing-support services

BURLINGTON COAT FACTORY WAREHOUSE

1830 Rte. 130 North　　　Phone: 609-387-7800
Burlington, NJ 08016　　　Fax: 609-387-7071
Chm, Pres & CEO: Monroe G. Milstein
HR Mgr: Kyle Gonzales
Employees: 15,000

Jobs Cut Last Year: 2,000 (-11.8%)

Retail - discount apparel, including outerwear, for men, women & children; linens; bath shop items; gifts & accessories

CALI REALTY CORPORATION

11 Commerce Dr.　　　　Phone: 908-272-8000
Cranford, NJ 07016　　　Fax: 908-272-6755
Pres & CEO: Thomas A. Rizk
Office Mgr: Nicholas Mitarotondo
Employees: 90

Jobs Added Last Year: 40 (+80.0%)

Real estate investment trust - office buildings

CAMPBELL SOUP COMPANY

Campbell Place　　　　　Phone: 609-342-4800
Camden, NJ 08103-1799　　Fax: 609-342-3878
Chm, Pres & CEO: David W. Johnson
VP HR: Edward F. Walsh
Employees: 43,781

Jobs Cut Last Year: 597 (-1.3%)

Food - canned soups, salsa (Pace), cookies (Pepperidge Farm), candy (Godiva), meat (Swift-Armour), prepared foods (Franco-American) & pickles (Vlasic)

CHECKPOINT SYSTEMS, INC.

101 Wolf Dr., PO Box 188　　Phone: 609-848-1800
Thorofare, NJ 08086　　　Fax: 609-848-0937
Pres, CEO & COO: Kevin P. Dowd
Personnel Mgr: Joanne Nacucchio
Employees: 2,540

Jobs Added Last Year: 736 (+40.8%)

Protection - electronic security systems for commercial use

THE CHUBB CORPORATION

15 Mountain View Rd.　　Phone: 908-903-2000
Warren, NJ 07061-1615　　Fax: 908-580-2027
Chm, Pres & CEO: Dean R. O'Hare
SVP & Mng Dir HR: Baxter Graham
Employees: 10,000

Jobs Cut Last Year: 1,200 (-10.7%)

Insurance - property, casualty, life & health; commercial & residential real estate development

COMPUTER HORIZONS CORPORATION

49 Old Bloomfield Ave.　　Phone: 201-402-7400
Mountain Lakes, NJ 07046-1495　Fax: 201-402-7988
Chm & Pres: John J. Cassese
Mgr HR: Michelle Friedberg
Employees: 2,511

Jobs Added Last Year: 361 (+16.8%)

Computers - contract programming services

CONTINENTAL WASTE INDUSTRIES, INC.

67 Walnut Ave., Ste. 103　　Phone: 908-396-0018
Clark, NJ 07066　　　　　Fax: 908-396-4381
Pres & CEO: Carlos E. Aguero
No central personnel officer
Employees: 725

Jobs Added Last Year: 335 (+85.9%)

Pollution control equipment & services - nonhazardous landfill disposal, solid waste collection, transfer station operations & recycling

CPC INTERNATIONAL INC.

International Plaza　　　　Phone: 201-894-4000
Englewood Cliffs, NJ 07632-9976　Fax: 201-894-2186
Chm, Pres & CEO: Charles R. Shoemate
VP HR: Richard P. Bergman
Employees: 52,500

Jobs Added Last Year: 10,600 (+25.3%)

Food - soups & sauces (Knorr), pastas, baked goods (Thomas' English muffins, Arnold breads), peanut butter (Skippy), mayonnaise (Hellman's) & corn oil (Mazola)

C. R. BARD, INC.

730 Central Ave.　　　　Phone: 908-277-8000
Murray Hill, NJ 07974　　Fax: 908-277-8240
Chm & CEO: William H. Longfield
VP HR: Hope Greenfield
Employees: 9,400

Jobs Added Last Year: 750 (+8.7%)

Medical & dental supplies - Foley catheters, procedural kits & surgical-drainage & wound-management devices

CYTEC INDUSTRIES INC.

5 Garret Mountain Plaza
West Paterson, NJ 07424-1599
Chm, Pres & CEO: Darryl D. Fry
VP Emp Relations: James W. Hirsch
Employees: 5,200

Phone: 201-357-3319
Fax: 201-357-3088

Jobs Added Last Year: 200 (+4.0%)

Chemicals - specialty chemicals for water treatment & the appliance, automotive & paper industries

EA INDUSTRIES, INC.

185 Monmouth Pkwy.
West Long Branch, NJ 07764-9989
Pres & CEO: Joseph R. Spalliero
Mgr HR: Barbara Evenson
Employees: 514

Phone: 908-229-1100
Fax: 908-571-0583

Jobs Added Last Year: 180 (+53.9%)

Electrical components - integrated-circuit components & assemblies

ENGELHARD CORPORATION

101 Wood Ave.
Iselin, NJ 08830-0770
Chm & CEO: Orin R. Smith
VP HR: William M. Dugle
Employees: 5,075

Phone: 908-205-6000
Fax: 908-632-9253

Jobs Cut Last Year: 755 (-13.0%)

Chemicals - chemical additives used in petroleum products, paints, printing inks & plastics; paper, plastic, paint & coating manufacturing chemicals

ENVIRONMENTAL TECHNOLOGIES CORP.

550 James St.
Lakewood, NJ 08701
Pres & CEO: George Cannan Sr.
COO: Carol Costante
Employees: 87

Phone: 908-370-3400
Fax: 908-370-3088

Jobs Added Last Year: 42 (+93.3%)

Chemicals - refrigerants & refrigerant reclaiming services & equipment

EXOGEN, INC.

10 Constitution Ave., PO Box 6860
Piscataway, NJ 08855
Pres & CEO: Patrick A. McBrayer
Dir HR: Mark McNulty
Employees: 77

Phone: 908-981-0990
Fax: 908-981-0003

Jobs Added Last Year: 41 (+113.9%)

Medical instruments - devices for noninvasive treatment of musculoskeletal injury & disease

FEDDERS CORPORATION

505 Martinsville Rd.
Liberty Corner, NJ 07938
VC, Pres & CEO: Salvatore Giordano Jr.
VP HR: Marlene Bolpe
Employees: 2,000

Phone: 908-604-8686
Fax: 908-604-0715

Jobs Added Last Year: 200 (+11.1%)

Building products - window, through-the-wall & split ductless room air conditioners

All Business Network — http://www.all-biz.com/job.html

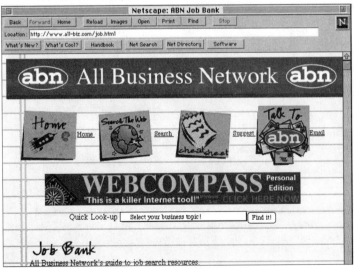

An in-depth profile of this company is available to subscribers on Hoover's Online at www.hoovers.com.

223

FIRST DATA CORPORATION

401 Hackensack Ave.
Hackensack, NJ 07601
Chm & CEO: Henry C. Duques
SVP HR: Donald F. Crowley
Employees: 36,000

Phone: 201-525-4700
Fax: 770-342-0402

Jobs Added Last Year: 14,000 (+63.6%)

Financial - credit card processing, worldwide money transfer (Western Union), merchant & consumer payment, debt collection, accounts receivable management & mutual fund processing

FOOTSTAR, INC.

933 Macarthur Blvd.
Mahwah, NJ 07430
Chm & CEO: J. M. Robinson
Chief HR Officer: Charles Messina
Employees: 12,600

Phone: 201-934-2000

Jobs Added Last Year: —

Retail - leased shoe departments in Kmarts (Meldisco: over 2,500 units); branded athletic shoes & apparel specialty stores (Footaction: over 400 units)

FOSTER WHEELER CORPORATION

Perryville Corporate Park
Clinton, NJ 08809-4000
Chm, Pres & CEO: Richard J. Swift
VP HR & Admin: James E. Schessler
Employees: 12,650

Phone: 908-730-4000
Fax: 908-730-4315

Jobs Added Last Year: 965 (+8.3%)

Construction - industrial facilities; steam generators, nuclear power plant equipment & chemical-processing equipment

FRANKLIN ELECTRONIC PUBLISHERS

One Franklin Plaza
Burlington, NJ 08016
Chm, Pres & CEO: Morton E. David
No central personnel officer
Employees: 271

Phone: 609-261-4800
Fax: 609-261-2984

Jobs Added Last Year: 65 (+31.6%)

Publishing - electronic books (#1 worldwide: Spelling Ace, Med-Spell MED-55, Holy Bible - New International Version)

GAF CORPORATION

1361 Alps Rd.
Wayne, NJ 07470
Chm & CEO: Samuel J. Heyman
SVP HR: Jim Strupp
Employees: 5,400

Phone: 201-628-3000
Fax: 201-628-3311

Jobs Added Last Year: 900 (+20.0%)

Diversified operations - specialty derivative chemicals, mineral products, filter products & advanced materials; asphalt roofing products & accessories; commercial radio broadcasting

GENERAL PUBLIC UTILITIES CORP.

100 Interpace Pkwy.
Parsippany, NJ 07054-1149
Chm, Pres & CEO: James R. Leva
VP HR: Richard Postweiler
Employees: 10,310

Phone: 201-263-6500
Fax: 201-263-6822

Jobs Cut Last Year: 224 (-2.1%)

Utility - electric power

THE GRAND UNION COMPANY

201 Willowbrook Blvd.
Wayne, NJ 07470
Pres & CEO: Joseph J. McCaig
SVP Personnel: Charles Barrett
Employees: 15,000

Phone: 201-890-6000
Fax: 201-890-6671

Jobs Cut Last Year: 1,000 (-6.3%)

Retail - supermarkets (231 units: Grand Union)

THE GREAT ATLANTIC & PACIFIC TEA COMPANY, INC.

2 Paragon Dr.
Montvale, NJ 07645
Chm & CEO: James Wood
SVP HR: H. Nelson "Bud" Lewis
Employees: 89,000

Phone: 201-573-9700
Fax: 201-930-8106

Jobs Cut Last Year: 3,000 (-3.3%)

Retail - supermarkets

GUEST SUPPLY, INC.

720 US Hwy. One
North Brunswick, NJ 08902
Pres & CEO: Clifford W. Stanley
Mgr HR: Joan Constanzo
Employees: 927

Phone: 908-246-3011
Fax: 908-828-2342

Jobs Added Last Year: 221 (+31.3%)

Cosmetics & toiletries - personal care guest amenities (including shampoo, shower caps & sewing kits), housekeeping supplies, room accessories & textiles for the lodging industry

THE HERTZ CORPORATION

225 Brae Blvd.
Park Ridge, NJ 07656-0713
Chm & CEO: Frank A. Olson
Dir Emp Relations: Joann Petraglia
Employees: 19,500

Phone: 201-307-2000
Fax: 201-307-2644

Jobs Added Last Year: 300 (+1.6%)

Leasing - autos & construction equipment; sale of used cars

HFS INCORPORATED

339 Jefferson Rd.　　　　　　Phone: 201-428-9700
Parsippany, NJ 07054　　　　　Fax: 201-428-6057
Chm & CEO: Henry R. Silverman
Dir Compensation & Benefits: Jim LaBella
Employees: 3,000

Jobs Added Last Year: 900 (+42.9%)

Franchisors - hotels & motels (#1 worldwide: Days Inn, Howard Johnson, Park Inn, Ramada, Super 8); real estate brokerages (Century 21, Coldwell Banker); car rental (Avis)

HOFFMANN-LA ROCHE, INC.

340 Kingsland St.　　　　　　Phone: 201-235-5000
Nutley, NJ 07110-1199　　　　Fax: 201-562-2208
Pres & CEO: Patrick J. Zenner
SVP Fin, HR & Admin: Martin F. Spadler
Employees: 26,000

Jobs Added Last Year: 1,419 (+5.8%)

Drugs - vitamins, such as E, C, A & carotenoids; fine chemicals; pharmaceuticals, including Rocephin, Versed, Dormicum, Klonopin, Rivoril, Accutane, Roaccutane & Valium Roche

HOME STATE HOLDINGS, INC.

3 S. Revmont Dr.　　　　　　Phone: 908-935-2600
Shrewsbury, NJ 07702　　　　Fax: 908-935-0156
VC, Pres, CEO & Treas: Robert Abidor
VP HR: Geraldine Dohanyos
Employees: 211

Jobs Added Last Year: 73 (+52.9%)

Insurance - personal & commercial auto insurance

HUNGARIAN TELEPHONE AND CABLE CORP.

227 Rte. 206, Bldg. One, Unit 11　　Phone: 201-927-6560
Flanders, NJ 07836　　　　　　Fax: 201-927-7339
Chm, Pres & CEO: Robert Genova
Controller: Heidi Horvath
Employees: 730

Jobs Added Last Year: 497 (+213.3%)

Telecommunications services

INDUCTOTHERM INDUSTRIES

10 Indel Ave.　　　　　　　Phone: 609-267-9000
Rancocas, NJ 08073　　　　　Fax: 609-267-0497
Chm, Pres & CEO: Henry M. Rowan
VP Admin: David Broddock
Employees: 4,823

Jobs Added Last Year: 439 (+10.0%)

Machinery - general industrial

INGERSOLL-RAND COMPANY

200 Chestnut Ridge Rd.　　　Phone: 201-573-0123
Woodcliff Lake, NJ 07675　　Fax: 201-573-3168
Chm, Pres & CEO: James E. Perrella
VP HR: Donald H. Rice
Employees: 41,133

Jobs Added Last Year: 5,201 (+14.5%)

Machinery - engineered equipment & bearings, locks & tools, air compressors, construction equipment, golf carts, tools & door hardware

INTERFERON SCIENCES, INC.

783 Jersey Ave.　　　　　　Phone: 908-249-3250
New Brunswick, NJ 08901　　Fax: 908-249-6895
CEO: Lawrence M. Gordon
Dir HR: Sarah Walker
Employees: 69

Jobs Added Last Year: 14 (+25.5%)

Drugs - alpha-interferon-based pharmaceuticals

INTERNATIONAL THOROUGHBRED BREEDERS, INC.

PO Box 1232　　　　　　　Phone: 609-488-3838
Cherry Hill, NJ 08034　　　Fax: 609-488-3835
Pres & COO: Arthur Winkler
No central personnel officer
Employees: 801

Jobs Added Last Year: 241 (+43.0%)

Leisure & recreational services - horse racetrack operations & thoroughbred horse breeding & sales

J. M. HUBER CORPORATION

333 Thornall St.　　　　　　Phone: 908-549-8600
Edison, NJ 08818　　　　　　Fax: 908-549-2239
Chm, Pres & CEO: Peter T. Francis
VP HR: Joseph P. Matturro
Employees: 5,100

Jobs Cut Last Year: 63 (-1.2%)

Diversified operations - engineered minerals; chemicals; electronics

JOHNSON & JOHNSON

One Johnson & Johnson Plaza　Phone: 908-524-0400
New Brunswick, NJ 08933　　Fax: 908-524-3300
Chm & CEO: Ralph S. Larsen
VP Admin: Roger S. Fine
Employees: 82,300

Jobs Added Last Year: 800 (+1.0%)

Cosmetics & toiletries - baby shampoo (Johnson's), pain killers (Tylenol), bandages (Band-Aid), toothbrushes (Reach), powder (Shower to Shower) & soap (Neutrogena); clinical diagnostics

 An in-depth profile of this company is available to subscribers on Hoover's Online at www.hoovers.com.

225

LCS INDUSTRIES, INC.

120 Brighton Rd.   Phone: 201-778-5588
Clifton, NJ 07012   Fax: 201-778-6001
Pres & CEO: Arnold J. Scheine
VP Personnel: Monica A. Mahon
Employees: 1,637

Jobs Added Last Year: 525 (+47.2%)

Business services - direct-response, fulfillment & list-marketing services

LECHTERS, INC.

One Cape May St.   Phone: 201-481-1100
Harrison, NJ 07029-9998   Fax: 201-481-5493
Chm, Pres & CEO: Donald Jonas
VP HR: Robert J. Harloe
Employees: 7,416

Jobs Added Last Year: 505 (+7.3%)

Retail - housewares & giftware

THE LIPOSOME COMPANY, INC.

One Research Way   Phone: 609-452-7060
Princeton, NJ 08540   Fax: 609-452-1890
Chm, Pres & CEO: Charles A. Baker
VP HR: George G. Renton
Employees: 297

Jobs Added Last Year: 80 (+36.9%)

Biomedical & genetic products - lipid- & lipsome-based pharmaceuticals for the treatment, prevention & diagnosis of life-threatening illnesses

LUCENT TECHNOLOGIES INC.

600 Mountain Ave.   Phone: 908-582-8500
Murray Hill, NJ 07974-0636   Fax: 908-508-2576
Chm & CEO: Henry B. Schacht
SVP HR: Curt Artis
Employees: 131,000

Jobs Added Last Year: —

Telecommunications equipment - private branch exchanges (PBXs); voice processing systems & messaging systems; video-conferencing systems & maintenance & repair services

MAYFAIR SUPERMARKETS INC.

681 Newark Ave.   Phone: 908-352-6400
Elizabeth, NJ 07208   Fax: 908-352-0103
Chm & Pres: Stanley P. Kaufelt
VP HR: John Kovaleski
Employees: 4,500

Jobs Added Last Year: 300 (+7.1%)

Retail - supermarkets

MEASUREMENT SPECIALTIES, INC.

80 Little Falls Rd.   Phone: 201-808-1819
Fairfield, NJ 07004-1615   Fax: 201-808-1787
Chm, Pres & CEO: Joseph R. Mallon Jr.
Dir HR: Pete Sentowski
Employees: 215

Jobs Added Last Year: 120 (+126.3%)

Instruments - digital electronic measurement devices

MERCK & CO., INC.

One Merck Dr.   Phone: 908-423-1000
Whitehouse Station, NJ 08889-0100   Fax: 908-735-1813
Chm, Pres & CEO: Raymond V. Gilmartin
VP HR: Steven M. Darien
Employees: 45,200

Jobs Cut Last Year: 2,300 (-4.8%)

Drugs - cardiovascular, gastrointestinal (Pepcid), anti-inflammation (Clinoril), antibiotic, neurological, ophthalmic & respiratory treatments; vaccines; animal health & crop protection products

METROMEDIA COMPANY

One Meadowlands Plaza   Phone: 201-531-8000
East Rutherford, NJ 07073   Fax: 201-833-1349
Chm, Pres, CEO & Gen Partner: John W. Kluge
SVP, Sec & Gen Counsel: Arnold L. Wadler
Employees: 20,000

Jobs Added Last Year: 0

Diversified operations - restaurants (Bennigan's, Bonanza, Ponderosa, Steak and Ale); movies (Orion Pictures); telecommunications (WorldCom); kiosks in music stores (Muse Inc.)

M. H. MEYERSON & CO., INC.

30 Montgomery St.   Phone: 201-332-3380
Jersey City, NJ 07302   Fax: 201-332-1562
Chm, CEO & CFO: Martin H. Meyerson
Dir HR: Gene Whitehouse
Employees: 160

Jobs Added Last Year: 40 (+33.3%)

Financial - wholesale trading, correspondent services, retail services & investment banking

MOBILEMEDIA CORPORATION

65 Challenger Rd.   Phone: 201-440-8400
Ridgefield Park, NJ 07660   Fax: 201-440-2889
CEO: Michael K. Lorelli
Dir HR: Tracey Zimmerman
Employees: 1,554

Jobs Added Last Year: 270 (+21.0%)

Telecommunications services - paging & wireless messaging services

MODERN MEDICAL MODALITIES CORPORATION

95 Madison Ave., Ste. 301   Phone: 201-538-9955
Morristown, NJ 07960   Fax: 201-267-7359
Chm & Pres: Roger Findlay
No central personnel officer
Employees: 89

Jobs Added Last Year: 56 (+169.7%)

Leasing - MRI & computerized axial tomography equipment to hospitals & physicians; medical imaging center management

THE MULTICARE COMPANIES, INC.

411 Hackensack Ave.   Phone: 201-488-8818
Hackensack, NJ 07601   Fax: 201-488-2990
Pres & Co-CEO: Daniel E. Straus
VP HR: Ronald G. Clarendon
Employees: 6,980

Jobs Cut Last Year: 20 (-0.3%)

Medical services - skilled-nursing care, Alzheimer's care & related support services

NABISCO HOLDINGS CORP.

7 Campus Dr.   Phone: 201-682-5000
Parsippany, NJ 07054   Fax: 201-969-9178
Chm, Pres & CEO: H. John Greeniaus
EVP HR: C. Michael Sayeau
Employees: 45,000

Jobs Added Last Year: —

Food - cookies (Oreos, Chips Ahoy!), snacks (SnackWells, Ritz, Wheat Thins), condiments (A.1., Grey Poupon) & gum & candy (Bubble Yum, Care-Free, Life Savers, Breath Savers)

NEXTEL COMMUNICATIONS, INC.

201 Rte. 17 North   Phone: 201-438-1400
Rutherford, NJ 07070   Fax: 201-438-5540
Chm & CEO: Daniel Akerson
Dir HR: Lane Foster
Employees: 2,666

Jobs Added Last Year: 1,066 (+66.6%)

Telecommunications services - fleet-dispatch, cellular phone & paging services

NMR OF AMERICA, INC.

430 Mountain Ave.   Phone: 908-665-9400
Murray Hill, NJ 07974-2732   Fax: 908-665-2767
Chm, Pres & CEO: Joseph G. Dasti
Dir HR: Leslie Cohen
Employees: 150

Jobs Added Last Year: 33 (+28.2%)

Medical practice management - diagnostic-imaging system installation & management

NOVADIGM, INC.

One International Blvd., Ste 200   Phone: 201-512-1000
Mahwah, NJ 07495   Fax: 201-512-1452
Chm, Pres & CEO: Albion J. Fitzgerald
No central personnel officer
Employees: 92

Jobs Added Last Year: 22 (+31.4%)

Computers - networking & connectivity system management software

PATHMARK STORES, INC.

301 Blair Rd., PO Box 5301   Phone: 908-499-3000
Woodbridge, NJ 07095-0915   Fax: 908-499-3072
Interim Chm & CEO: John Boyle
VP HR: Maureen McGurl
Employees: 29,000

Jobs Added Last Year: 1,000 (+3.6%)

Retail - supermarkets, drugstores & home improvement centers

PEERLESS TUBE COMPANY

58-76 Locust Ave.   Phone: 201-743-5100
Bloomfield, NJ 07003   Fax: 201-743-6169
Chm & CEO: Frederic Remington Jr.
Treas & VP Fin: Paul Peterik
Employees: 350

Jobs Added Last Year: 90 (+34.6%)

Containers - collapsible metal tubes & seamless extruded aluminum aerosol containers for the pharmaceutical, drug, cosmetic toiletries & household product industries

PLAYERS INTERNATIONAL INC.

1300 Atlantic Ave., Ste. 800 Phone: 609-449-7777
Atlantic City, NJ 08401   Fax: 609-340-8165
Pres & CEO: Howard Goldberg
No central personnel officer
Employees: 2,261

Jobs Added Last Year: 306 (+15.7%)

Gambling resorts & casinos - riverboat casinos in Metropolis, IL & Lake Charles, LA; casino & resort in Mesquite, NV (Players Island Resort Casino & Spa); horseracing track in Paducah, KY

PRIME HOSPITALITY CORP.

700 Rte. 46 East   Phone: 201-882-1010
Fairfield, NJ 07004   Fax: 201-882-8577
Pres & CEO: David A. Simon
SVP HR: Denis W. Driscoll
Employees: 5,500

Jobs Added Last Year: 500 (+10.0%)

Hotels & motels - full- & limited-service hotels (Wellesley Inns & AmeriSuites); Marriott, Radisson, Sheraton, Holiday Inn, Ramada & Howard Johnson licensee

 An in-depth profile of this company is available to subscribers on Hoover's Online at www.hoovers.com.

PRINCETON UNIVERSITY

One Nassau Hall
Princeton, NJ 08544
Pres: Harold T. Shapiro
VP HR: Audrey S. Smith
Employees: 8,500

Phone: 609-258-3000
Fax: 609-258-1294

Jobs Added Last Year: —

University

THE PRUDENTIAL INSURANCE COMPANY OF AMERICA

751 Broad St.
Newark, NJ 07102-3777
Chm & CEO: Arthur F. Ryan
SVP HR: Donald C. Mann
Employees: 100,000

Phone: 201-802-6000
Fax: 201-802-2812

Jobs Added Last Year: 614 (+0.6%)

Insurance - health & life

PUBLIC SERVICE ENTERPRISE GROUP INCORPORATED

80 Park Plaza
Newark, NJ 07101
Chm, Pres & CEO: E. James Ferland
VP HR: Martin P. Mellett
Employees: 11,452

Phone: 201-430-7000
Fax: 201-430-5983

Jobs Cut Last Year: 938 (-7.6%)

Utility - electric power & natural gas

PULLMAN COMPANY

3 Werner Way, Ste. 200
Lebanon, NJ 08833
Chm: Roger Pollazzi
HR Mgr: Michael Farrell
Employees: 6,000

Phone: 908-236-9234
Fax: 908-236-6653

Jobs Added Last Year: —

Automotive & trucking - suspension bushings, high-pressure hoses & fittings, specialty wear-resistant components & multi-purpose storage tanks

PURETEC CORPORATION

65 Railroad Ave.
Ridgefield, NJ 07657
Chm & CEO: Fred W. Broling
VP HR: Joseph T. Bruno
Employees: 2,000

Phone: 201-941-6550
Fax: 201-941-0602

Jobs Added Last Year: 1,283 (+178.9%)

Recycling - plastic, including high-grade recycled PET & PVC for fiber, packaging & compound applications; custom-plastics injection molding; garden hose (#1 worldwide)

RF POWER PRODUCTS, INC.

502 Gibbsboro-Marlton Rd.
Voorhees, NJ 08043
Chm, Pres & CEO: Joseph Stach
Mgr HR: Susan Johnston
Employees: 171

Phone: 609-751-0033
Fax: 609-783-7423

Jobs Added Last Year: 58 (+51.3%)

Electrical products - radio frequency power systems, matching networks & other semiconductor products

CareerSite — http://www.careersite.com

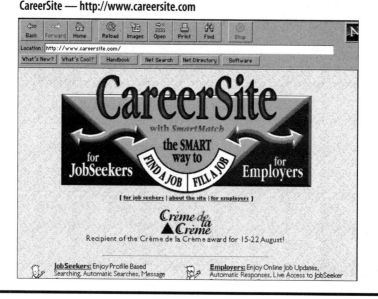

RICKEL HOME CENTERS, INC.

200 Helen St.
South Plainfield, NJ 07080
CEO: Antonio C. Alvarez
Dir HR: Al Hauser
Employees: 5,000

Phone: 908-668-7000
Fax: 908-668-7134

Jobs Cut Last Year: 500 (-9.1%)

Retail - home improvement centers

SCHERING-PLOUGH CORPORATION

One Giralda Farms
Madison, NJ 07940-1000
Chm & CEO: Robert P. Luciano
SVP HR: Gordon C. O'Brien
Employees: 20,100

Phone: 201-822-7000
Fax: 201-822-7048

Jobs Cut Last Year: 1,100 (-5.2%)

Drugs - respiratory, antibiotic & dermatological prescription drugs, consumer health care products (Dr. Scholl's, Coppertone) & animal-health & foot-care products

SEALED AIR CORPORATION

Park 80 Plaza East
Saddle Brook, NJ 07663-5291
Pres & CEO: T. J. Dermot Dunphy
Mgr Emp Benefits: Heidi Calcagno
Employees: 3,940

Phone: 201-791-7600
Fax: 201-703-4205

Jobs Added Last Year: 940 (+31.3%)

Containers - packaging & cushioning materials including padded mailing envelopes (Jiffy) & food packaging products

THE SHERWOOD GROUP, INC.

10 Exchange Place Ctr., 15th Fl.
Jersey City, NJ 07032
CEO: Arthur Kontos
No central personnel officer
Employees: 425

Phone: 212-294-8000
Fax: 212-946-4445

Jobs Added Last Year: 116 (+37.5%)

Financial - wholesale securities brokerage of Nasdaq and small-cap companies & retail deep-discount securities brokerage (National Discount Brokers)

SIGMA PLASTICS GROUP

PO Box 433
Lyndhurst, NJ 07071
Chm & CEO: Alfred Teo
No central personnel officer
Employees: 1,800

Phone: 201-933-6000
Fax: 201-933-6429

Jobs Added Last Year: 600 (+50.0%)

Chemicals - polyethylene bags

SL INDUSTRIES, INC.

520 Fellowship Rd., Ste. 306-C
Mt. Laurel, NJ 08054-3409
Pres & CEO: Owen Farren
No central personnel officer
Employees: 1,639

Phone: 609-727-1500
Fax: 609-727-1683

Jobs Added Last Year: 372 (+29.4%)

Electrical products - electric-power products, aviation spark plugs, lubrication components & metal piping

SUMMIT BANCORP

301 Carnegie Ctr.
Princeton, NJ 08543
Chm & CEO: T. Joseph Semrod
EVP : Alfred M. D'Augusta
Employees: 7,547

Phone: 609-987-3200
Fax: 609-921-9202

Jobs Added Last Year: 1,404 (+22.9%)

Banks - Northeast (United Jersey Bank)

TOTAL-TEL USA COMMUNICATIONS, INC.

150 Clove Rd., Eighth Fl., Box 449
Little Falls, NJ 07424
Pres & CEO: Warren H. Feldman
Dir HR: Karen Singer
Employees: 180

Phone: 201-773-7000
Fax: 201-812-8302

Jobs Added Last Year: 80 (+80.0%)

Telecommunications services - long distance

TOYS "R" US, INC.

461 From Rd.
Paramus, NJ 07652
VC & CEO: Michael Goldstein
SVP HR: Jeffrey S. Wells
Employees: 60,000

Phone: 201-262-7800
Fax: 201-262-7606

Jobs Added Last Year: 2,000 (+3.4%)

Retail - toys & children's clothing

TRANSNET CORPORATION

45 Columbia Rd.
Somerville, NJ 08876-3576
Pres & CEO: Steven J. Wilk
Mgr HR: Susan Wilk
Employees: 131

Phone: 908-253-0500
Fax: 908-253-0600

Jobs Added Last Year: 30 (+29.7%)

Retail - wholesale hardware & software

 An in-depth profile of this company is available to subscribers on Hoover's Online at www.hoovers.com.

229

TRANSTECHNOLOGY CORPORATION

700 Liberty Ave.　　　　　Phone: 908-964-5666
Union, NJ 07083-8198　　　Fax: 908-688-8518
Chm, Pres & CEO: Michael J. Berthelot
Dir HR: Monica Lazorchak
Employees: 1,437

Jobs Added Last Year: 423 (+41.7%)

Metal products - fasteners; helicopter rescue hoists & cargo-hook equipment

UNION CAMP CORPORATION

1600 Valley Rd.　　　　　Phone: 201-628-2000
Wayne, NJ 07470　　　　　Fax: 201-628-2848
Chm & CEO: W. Craig McClelland
SVP HR: Russell W. Boekenheide
Employees: 18,258

Jobs Cut Last Year: 636 (-3.4%)

Paper & paper products - printing papers, kraft paper & paperboard; lumber, plywood & particleboard

UNITED RETAIL GROUP, INC.

365 W. Passaic St.　　　　Phone: 201-845-0880
Rochelle Park, NJ 07662　　Fax: 201-909-2162
Chm, Pres & CEO: Raphael Benaroya
EVP Organizational Dev: Charles R. Wilkerson
Employees: 5,300

Jobs Added Last Year: 900 (+20.5%)

Retail - women's large-size apparel & accessories

U.S. INDUSTRIES, INC.

101 Wood Ave. South　　　Phone: 908-767-0700
Iselin, NJ 08830　　　　　Fax: 908-767-2222
Chm & CEO: David H. Clarke
VP Admin: Dorothy E. Sander
Employees: 18,640

Jobs Cut Last Year: 4,590 (-19.8%)

Diversified operations - whirlpools & spas (Jacuzzi); lighting fixtures; golf clubs (Tommy Armour); cookware (Farberware); automotive components; toys (Ertl); garden tools (Ames); footwear

WARNER-LAMBERT COMPANY

201 Tabor Rd.　　　　　　Phone: 201-540-2000
Morris Plains, NJ 07950-2693　Fax: 201-540-3761
Chm & CEO: Melvin R. Goodes
VP HR: Raymond M. Fino
Employees: 37,000

Jobs Added Last Year: 1,000 (+2.8%)

Drugs - prescription drugs for treating diabetes & cardiovascular disease; consumer, health care & personal care (ept, Listerine, Zantac) products; confectionery products (Chicklets, Dentyne)

WHEATON INC.

1101 Wheaton Ave.　　　　Phone: 609-825-1400
Millville, NJ 08332　　　　Fax: 609-825-8461
Pres & CEO: Robert I. Veghte
VP HR: Thomas Clary
Employees: 6,100

Jobs Added Last Year: 100 (+1.7%)

Glass & plastic containers

WHITMAN MEDICAL CORP.

485 Bldg. E, US Hwy. One South　Phone: 908-636-3640
Iselin, NJ 08830-3005　　　Fax: 908-636-2359
Pres: Randy S. Proto
HR Mgr: Bob Sloop
Employees: 479

Jobs Added Last Year: 199 (+71.1%)

School - sonography & medical diagnostic ultrasound training (#1 in US: Ultrasound Diagnostic School)

XPEDITE SYSTEMS, INC.

446 State Hwy. 35　　　　　Phone: 908-389-3900
Eatontown, NJ 07724　　　　Fax: 908-389-8823
Pres & CEO: Roy B. Andersen Jr.
Admin Mgr: Jayne Droge
Employees: 490

Jobs Added Last Year: 243 (+98.4%)

Business services - fax distribution service (Fax Broadcast); gateway messaging services

FURR'S SUPERMARKETS, INC.

1730 Montano Rd. NW　　　Phone: 505-344-6525
Albuquerque, NM 87107　　　Fax: 505-761-0866
CEO: Jan Friederich
VP HR: Delwyn James
Employees: 6,000

Jobs Added Last Year: —

Retail - supermarkets (64 units) in the Southwest

HORIZON/CMS HEALTHCARE CORP.

6001 Indian School Rd. NE, Ste. 530
Albuquerque, NM 87110
Chm, Pres & CEO: Neal M. Elliott
VP HR: Rodney C. Panyik
Employees: 15,500

Phone: 505-881-4961
Fax: 505-881-5097

Jobs Cut Last Year: 200 (-1.3%)

Nursing homes, subacute care, pharmacy services, rehabilitation
therapies, laboratory services & Alzheimer's care

LUKENS MEDICAL CORPORATION

500 Laser Rd.
Rio Rancho, NM 87124
Chm, Pres & CEO: Robert S. Huffstodt
No central personnel officer
Employees: 99

Phone: 505-892-4118
Fax: 505-891-0479

Jobs Added Last Year: 33 (+50.0%)

Medical products - wound closure products, including suture
products & bonewax

MESA AIR GROUP, INC.

2325 E. 30th St.
Farmington, NM 87401
Chm & CEO: Larry L. Risley
Dir Personnel: Franklin Roberts
Employees: 3,900

Phone: 505-327-0271
Fax: 505-326-4485

Jobs Added Last Year: 400 (+11.4%)

Transportation - airline

SANTA FE PACIFIC GOLD CORPORATION

6200 Uptown Blvd. NE, Ste. 400
Albuquerque, NM 87110
Chm, Pres & CEO: Patrick M. James
Dir HR: Bill Vance
Employees: 1,864

Phone: 505-880-5300
Fax: 505-880-5436

Jobs Added Last Year: 229 (+14.0%)

Mining - gold

SPECIALTY TELECONSTRUCTORS, INC.

12001 State Hwy. 14 North
Cedar Crest, NM 87008
Chm, Pres & CEO: Michael R. Budagher
Dir HR: Bill Wilson
Employees: 80

Phone: 505-281-2197
Fax: 505-281-8652

Jobs Added Last Year: 35 (+77.8%)

Telecommunications equipment - wireless transmitting &
receiving facilities for providers of wireless communication
services

SUN HEALTHCARE GROUP, INC.

5131 Masthead St. NE
Albuquerque, NM 87109
Chm & CEO: Andrew L. Turner
SVP HR: Julie Colins
Employees: 27,100

Phone: 505-821-3355
Fax: 505-822-0747

Jobs Added Last Year: 6,900 (+34.2%)

Nursing homes & subacute care facilities

THERMO INSTRUMENT SYSTEMS INC.

504 Airport Rd.
Santa Fe, NM 87504-2108
Pres & CEO: Arvin H. Smith
HR Administrator: Pauline Varele
Employees: 4,752

Phone: 617-622-1000
Fax: 617-622-1207

Jobs Added Last Year: 786 (+19.8%)

Instruments - analytical, monitoring, process control, imaging,
inspection & measurement instruments for identifying &
analyzing air pollution & for monitoring industrial processes

ACCLAIM ENTERTAINMENT, INC.

One Acclaim Plaza
Glen Cove, NY 11542
Co-Chm & CEO: Gregory E. Fischbach
VP Planning & Ops: John Ma
Employees: 800

Phone: 516-656-5000
Fax: 516-656-2040

Jobs Added Last Year: 505 (+171.2%)

Computers - video games (WWF Raw, NFL Quarterback Club, The
Simpsons), PC CD-ROM games (StarGate, Batman Forever) &
comic books (Ninjak, Bloodshot)

ADVANCE PUBLICATIONS, INC.

950 Fingerboard Rd.
Staten Island, NY 10305
Chm & CEO: Samuel I. "Si" Newhouse Jr.
No central personnel officer
Employees: 19,000

Phone: 718-981-1234
Fax: 718-981-1415

Jobs Added Last Year: 0

Publishing - newspapers, books (Random House) & magazines
(New Yorker, Conde Nast, Allure, Bon Appetit, Bride's, Details,
Gentlemen's Quarterly, Vanity Fair, Vogue); cable TV

 An in-depth profile of this company is available
to subscribers on Hoover's Online at www.hoovers.com.

231

AGWAY INC.

333 Butternut Dr. — Phone: 315-449-6431
DeWitt, NY 13214 — Fax: 315-449-6253
Pres, CEO & Gen Mgr: Donald P. Cardarelli
VP HR: Margaret N. Luttinger
Employees: 9,000

Jobs Added Last Year: 1,100 (+13.9%)

Agricultural cooperative - animal feed, fertilizer, gasoline & other fuel; retail of farm-related products; financial services

ALBANY INTERNATIONAL CORP.

1373 Broadway — Phone: 518-445-2200
Albany, NY 12204 — Fax: 518-445-2265
Pres & CEO: Francis L. McKone
Dir HR: Barry D. Jessee
Employees: 5,658

Jobs Added Last Year: 254 (+4.7%)

Textiles - monofilament belts used in paper manufacturing

ALEXANDER & ALEXANDER SERVICES

1185 Avenue of the Americas — Phone: 212-840-8500
New York, NY 10036 — Fax: 212-444-4559
Chm, Pres & CEO: Frank G. Zarb
SVP HR: Mark J. Schneiderman
Employees: 11,900

Jobs Cut Last Year: 1,400 (-10.5%)

Insurance - brokerage & management consulting

ALLCITY INSURANCE COMPANY

122 Fifth Ave. — Phone: 212-387-3000
New York, NY 10011 — Fax: 212-691-6374
Pres & CEO: Andrew W. Attivissimo
Asst VP HR: James Boylan
Employees: 851

Jobs Added Last Year: 201 (+30.9%)

Insurance - property & casualty

ALLEGHANY CORPORATION

375 Park Ave. — Phone: 212-752-1356
New York, NY 10152 — Fax: 212-759-8149
Pres & CEO: John J. Burns Jr.
No central personnel officer
Employees: 9,462

Jobs Added Last Year: 1,812 (+23.7%)

Financial - title insurance (#1 worldwide: Chicago Title and Trust) & financial services (Underwriters Reinsurance Co.); industrial minerals (World Minerals); heads & steel fastener distribution

ALLEGHENY POWER SYSTEM, INC.

12 E. 49th St. — Phone: 212-752-2121
New York, NY 10017-1028 — Fax: 212-836-4340
Pres & CEO: Alan J. Noia
VP: Richard J. Gagliardi
Employees: 5,750

Jobs Cut Last Year: 311 (-5.1%)

Utility - electric power

ALPHA HOSPITALITY CORPORATION

12 E. 49th St. — Phone: 212-750-3500
New York, NY 10017 — Fax: 212-750-3508
Chm & Co-CEO: Stanley S. Tollman
HR Mgr: Tom Damewood
Employees: 1,030

Jobs Added Last Year: 368 (+55.6%)

Gambling resorts & casinos (Bayou Caddy's Jubilee Casino)

AMERADA HESS CORPORATION

1185 Avenue of the Americas — Phone: 212-997-8500
New York, NY 10036 — Fax: 212-536-8390
Chm & CEO: John B. Hess
SVP HR: Neal Gelfand
Employees: 9,574

Jobs Cut Last Year: 284 (-2.9%)

Oil & gas - US integrated

AMERICAN BANKNOTE CORP.

200 Park Ave. — Phone: 212-557-9100
New York, NY 10106 — Fax: 212-338-0753
Chm & CEO: Morris Weissman
VP HR & Admin: JoAnne O. Martinez
Employees: 2,380

Jobs Added Last Year: 225 (+10.4%)

Printing - counterfeit-resistant documents, including food coupons, social security cards, treasury checks, currency, passports, motor vehicle titles, birth certificates & travelers cheques

AMERICAN EXPRESS COMPANY

World Financial Ctr., 200 Vesey St. — Phone: 212-640-2000
New York, NY 10285 — Fax: 212-619-9802
Chm & CEO: Harvey Golub
EVP Quality & HR: Joseph W. Keilty
Employees: 70,347

Jobs Cut Last Year: 2,065 (-2.9%)

Financial - charge & credit cards, travelers' cheques & other stored value products; financial planning, brokerage services, mutual funds, insurance & other investment products

AMERICAN INTERNATIONAL GROUP

70 Pine St.
New York, NY 10270
Chm & CEO: Maurice R. Greenberg
SVP HR: Axel I. Freudmann
Employees: 34,500

Phone: 212-770-7000
Fax: 212-770-7821

Jobs Added Last Year: 2,500 (+7.8%)

Insurance - property & casualty, marine, life & specialty insurance; financial services

AMERICAN RETAIL GROUP, INC.

1114 Avenue of the Americas
New York, NY 10036
Pres: Roland Brenninkmeyer
VP HR: Tom Elliott
Employees: 17,000

Phone: 212-391-4141
Fax: 212-302-4381

Jobs Added Last Year: 0

Retail - apparel (over 1,200 stores: EMS, Maurices, Miller's Outpost, Modern Woman, Steinbach, Uptons, Women's World)

AMREP CORPORATION

641 Lexington Ave.
New York, NY 10022
Chm: Edward B. Cloues II
Dir HR: Christine Kamer
Employees: 1,700

Phone: 212-541-7300
Fax: 212-705-4740

Jobs Added Last Year: 600 (+54.5%)

Real estate development - single-family houses in Rio Rancho, NM & Denver; publication subscription fulfillment services

ARROW ELECTRONICS, INC.

25 Hub Dr.
Melville, NY 11747
Chm & CEO: Stephen P. Kaufman
VP: Thomas F. Hallam
Employees: 7,000

Phone: 516-391-1300
Fax: 516-391-1640

Jobs Added Last Year: 500 (+7.7%)

Electronics - distribution of semiconductors, computer parts & related equipment (#1 worldwide) to industrial & commercial customers

ASARCO INCORPORATED

180 Maiden Ln.
New York, NY 10038
Chm, Pres & CEO: Richard de J. Osborne
VP HR: David B. Woodbury
Employees: 12,000

Phone: 212-510-2000
Fax: 212-510-1855

Jobs Added Last Year: 4,000 (+50.0%)

Mining - copper, lead, zinc, silver & molybdenum; smelting & refinery operations; specialty chemicals & aggregates

AT&T CORP.

32 Avenue of the Americas
New York, NY 10013-2412
Chm & CEO: Robert E. Allen
EVP HR: Harold W. Burlingame
Employees: 299,300

Phone: 212-387-5400
Fax: 212-841-4715

Jobs Cut Last Year: 5,200 (-1.7%)

Telecommunications services - long-distance (#1 in US), credit card (Universal), cellular (AT&T Wireless Services) & Internet access services (AT&T WorldNet)

CareerNet — http://www.careers.org/

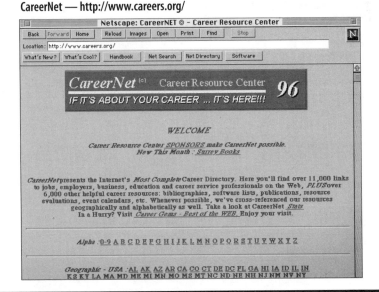

AVIS, INC.

900 Old Country Rd.
Garden City, NY 11530
Chm & CEO: Joseph V. Vittoria
SVP HR & Sec: Donald L. Korn
Employees: 12,800

Phone: 516-222-3000
Fax: 516-222-4381

Jobs Cut Last Year: 1,200 (-8.6%)

Leasing - autos

AVNET, INC.

80 Cutter Mill Rd.
Great Neck, NY 11021-3107
Chm & CEO: Leon Machiz
VP HR: Robert Zierk
Employees: 9,000

Phone: 516-466-7000
Fax: 516-466-1203

Jobs Added Last Year: 1,000 (+12.5%)

Electronics - parts distribution (#2 worldwide) for industrial & military customers; TV & audio equipment manufacturing

AVON PRODUCTS, INC.

9 W. 57th St.
New York, NY 10019-2683
Chm & CEO: James E. Preston
SVP Global HR & Corp Affairs: Marcia L. Worthing
Employees: 31,800

Phone: 212-546-6015
Fax: 212-546-6136

Jobs Added Last Year: 1,400 (+4.6%)

Cosmetics & toiletries - cosmetics, fragrances, gifts, decorative products, apparel, jewelry & accessories

THE BANK OF NEW YORK CO., INC.

48 Wall St.
New York, NY 10286
Chm & CEO: J. Carter Bacot
SVP Personnel: Frank L. Peterson
Employees: 15,810

Phone: 212-495-1784
Fax: 212-495-2546

Jobs Added Last Year: 333 (+2.2%)

Banks - money center

BANKERS TRUST NEW YORK CORP.

280 Park Ave.
New York, NY 10017
Chm & CEO: Frank N. Newman
EVP HR: Mark Bieler
Employees: 14,069

Phone: 212-250-2500
Fax: 212-454-1704

Jobs Cut Last Year: 460 (-3.2%)

Banks - money center

BARNES & NOBLE, INC.

122 Fifth Ave.
New York, NY 10011
Chm & CEO: Leonard Riggio
VP HR: Mike Malone
Employees: 21,400

Phone: 212-633-3300
Fax: 212-675-0413

Jobs Cut Last Year: 2,100 (-8.9%)

Retail - book superstores (#1 in US: Barnes & Noble, Bookstop, Bookstar) & mall stores (B. Dalton, Doubleday, Scribner's)

BAUSCH & LOMB INCORPORATED

One Bausch & Lomb Place
Rochester, NY 14604
Interim Chm & CEO: William H. Waltrip
VP HR: Deborah K. Smith
Employees: 14,000

Phone: 716-338-6000
Fax: 716-338-6007

Jobs Cut Last Year: 400 (-2.8%)

Medical products - pharmaceuticals, contact lenses & optics

THE BEAR STEARNS COMPANIES INC.

245 Park Ave.
New York, NY 10167
Pres & CEO: James E. Cayne
Mng Dir Personnel: Stephen A. Lacoff
Employees: 7,481

Phone: 212-272-2000
Fax: 212-272-8239

Jobs Added Last Year: 160 (+2.2%)

Financial - investment banking & securities trading & brokerage

BIG V SUPERMARKETS INC.

176 N. Main St.
Florida, NY 10921
CEO: Joseph Fisher
VP HR: Don Trella
Employees: 5,000

Phone: 914-651-4411
Fax: 914-651-7048

Jobs Added Last Year: 100 (+2.0%)

Retail - supermarkets

BLIMPIE INTERNATIONAL, INC.

740 Broadway
New York, NY 10003
Chm, Pres & CEO: Anthony P. Conza
Dir HR: Pam Gower
Employees: 73

Phone: 212-673-5900
Fax: 212-995-2566

Jobs Added Last Year: 15 (+25.9%)

Franchisors - restaurants (Blimpie)

BOZELL, JACOBS, KENYON & ECKHARDT

40 W. 23rd St.　　　　　　Phone: 212-727-5000
New York, NY 10010　　　Fax: 212-463-8419
CEO: Charles D. Peebler Jr.
HR Representative: Michael Bruce
Employees: 3,931
Jobs Added Last Year: 833 (+26.9%)

Advertising - full-service global advertising & public relations agency

BRISTOL-MYERS SQUIBB COMPANY

345 Park Ave.　　　　　　Phone: 212-546-4000
New York, NY 10154-0037　Fax: 212-546-4020
Chm, Pres & CEO: Charles A. Heimbold Jr.
SVP HR: Charles G. Tharp
Employees: 49,000
Jobs Added Last Year: 1,300 (+2.7%)

Drugs - prescription pharmaceuticals, medical devices & other health care products; househould chemicals & beauty aids

BUCK CONSULTANTS, INC.

2 Penn Plaza　　　　　　　Phone: 212-330-1000
New York, NY 10121-0047　Fax: 212-695-4184
Pres: Joseph A. LoCicero
Dir HR: William M. Brackley
Employees: 1,840
Jobs Added Last Year: 320 (+21.1%)

Consulting - employee benefits, actuarial & compensation consulting services

BUSH INDUSTRIES, INC.

One Mason Dr.　　　　　　Phone: 716-665-2000
Jamestown, NY 14702-0460　Fax: 716-665-2074
Chm, Pres & CEO: Paul S. Bush
Dir HR: Ernest Artista
Employees: 1,900
Jobs Added Last Year: 200 (+11.8%)

Furniture - home & office ready-to-assemble & assembled furniture (Bush, Eric Morgan by Bush, Case Casard by Bush)

CAI WIRELESS SYSTEMS, INC.

12 Corporate Woods Blvd., Ste. 102　Phone: 518-462-2632
Albany, NY 12211　　　　　　　　Fax: 518-462-3045
Chm, Pres & CEO: Jared E. Abbruzzese
Dir HR: Lynne Parkinson
Employees: 352
Jobs Added Last Year: 134 (+61.5%)

Cable TV - wireless cable system

CANANDAIGUA WINE COMPANY, INC.

116 Buffalo St.　　　　　　Phone: 716-394-7900
Canandaigua, NY 14424　Fax: 716-394-6017
Pres & CEO: Richard Sands
VP HR: Al Kidd
Employees: 2,500
Jobs Added Last Year: 350 (+16.3%)

Beverages - wine (Manischewitz, Almaden, Inglenook, Paul Masson), imported beer distribution (Corona, St. Pauli Girl, Tsingtao) & distilled spirits (Fleischmann, Montezuma)

CAPITAL CITIES/ABC, INC.

77 W. 66th St.　　　　　　Phone: 212-456-7777
New York, NY 10023-6298　Fax: 212-456-6850
Pres & COO: Robert A. Iger
VP & Exec Asst to Chm: William J. Wilkinson
Employees: 20,000
Jobs Cut Last Year: 200 (-1.0%)

Broadcasting - radio & TV; publishing

CARQUEST CORP.

580 White Plains Rd.　　　Phone: 914-332-1515
Tarrytown, NY 10591　　　Fax: 914-332-8504
Pres, CEO & CFO: Daniel Bock
Office Mgr: Nikki Bellizze
Employees: 6,200
Jobs Added Last Year: 200 (+3.3%)

Auto parts - wholesale parts & accessories

CATHOLIC MEDICAL CENTER OF BROOKLYN & QUEENS

88-25 153rd St.　　　　　　Phone: 718-558-6900
Jamaica, NY 11432　　　　Fax: 718-326-2918
Pres & CEO: William D. McGuire
Dir HR: Patrick McEneaey
Employees: 6,700
Jobs Added Last Year: 200 (+3.1%)

Hospitals - not-for-profit system serving Brooklyn & Queens

CELADON GROUP, INC.

888 Seventh Ave.　　　　　Phone: 212-977-4447
New York, NY 10106　　　Fax: 212-315-5281
Chm & CEO: Stephen Russell
Dir HR: Peter Bennet
Employees: 2,040
Jobs Added Last Year: 464 (+29.4%)

Transportation - trucking & freight forwarding, especially long-haul, full truckload service; international air & ocean transportation & customs brokerage services

 An in-depth profile of this company is available to subscribers on Hoover's Online at www.hoovers.com.

235

CELLULAR COMMUNICATIONS, INC.

110 E. 59th St., 26th Fl.　　　Phone: 212-906-8440
New York, NY 10022　　　　　Fax: 212-752-1157
CEO: William B. Ginsberg
HR Supervisor: Beth Wilson
Employees: 2,200
Jobs Added Last Year: 360 (+19.6%)

Telecommunications services - cellular systems in Indiana,
Kentucky, Michigan & Ohio

CELLULAR COMMUNICATIONS OF PUERTO RICO, INC.

110 E. 59th St., 26th Fl.　　　Phone: 212-355-3466
New York, NY 10022　　　　　Fax: 212-752-1157
CEO & Treas: George S. Blumenthal
Dir HR: Carmen Cruz
Employees: 540
Jobs Added Last Year: 160 (+42.1%)

Telecommunications services - cellular & paging systems in the
Commonwealth of Puerto Rico & the US Virgin Islands

CENTRAL HUDSON GAS & ELECTRIC CORPORATION

284 South Ave.　　　　Phone: 914-452-2000
Poughkeepsie, NY 12601-4879　　Fax: 914-486-5894
Chm & CEO: John E. Mack III
VP HR & Admin: Joseph D. DeVirgilio Jr.
Employees: 1,376
Jobs Added Last Year: 451 (+48.8%)

Utility - electric power & natural gas

THE CHASE MANHATTAN CORP.

270 Park Ave., Ste. 220　　　Phone: 212-270-6000
New York, NY 10017-2798　　　Fax: 212-270-2613
Chm & CEO: Walter V. Shipley
EVP HR: John J. Farrell
Employees: 72,695
Jobs Added Last Year: 30,565 (+72.5%)

Banks - money center

CHEYENNE SOFTWARE, INC.

3 Expressway Plaza　　　Phone: 516-484-5110
Roslyn Heights, NY 11577　　Fax: 516-484-7106
Chm, Pres & CEO: ReiJane Huai
Dir HR: Andy Boyland
Employees: 621
Jobs Added Last Year: 191 (+44.4%)

Computers - local & wide area network software products

CHIC BY H.I.S, INC.

1372 Broadway　　　Phone: 212-302-6400
New York, NY 10018　　Fax: 212-819-9172
Chm & CEO: Burton M. Rosenberg
Dir Office Svcs: Thomas Ricca
Employees: 5,000
Jobs Cut Last Year: 125 (-2.4%)

Apparel - denim jeans, casual pants & shorts for women, girls
(Chic), men & boys (H.I.S)

CITICORP

399 Park Ave.　　　Phone: 212-559-4822
New York, NY 10043　　Fax: 212-559-5138
Chm: John S. Reed
Sr HR Officer: Lawrence R. Phillips
Employees: 85,300
Jobs Added Last Year: 2,700 (+3.3%)

Banks - money center

THE CITY UNIVERSITY OF NEW YORK

535 E. 80th St.　　　Phone: 212-794-5555
New York, NY 10021　　Fax: 212-794-5397
Chancellor: W. Ann Reynolds
Dir HR: J. Demby
Employees: 25,800
Jobs Cut Last Year: 2,809 (-9.8%)

Public university offering undergraduate & graduate degree programs in the arts & sciences

CITYSCAPE FINANCIAL CORPORATION

565 Taxter Rd.　　　Phone: 914-592-6677
Elmsford, NY 10523-5200　　Fax: 914-592-7101
Pres & CEO: Robert Grosser
Dir HR: Diane Travis
Employees: 216
Jobs Added Last Year: 107 (+98.2%)

Financial - origination, sales & service of mortgage loans on one
to 4-family residential properties

COLGATE-PALMOLIVE COMPANY

300 Park Ave.　　　Phone: 212-310-2000
New York, NY 10022　　Fax: 212-310-3405
Chm & CEO: Reuben Mark
VP Global HR: Robert J. Joy
Employees: 37,300
Jobs Added Last Year: 4,500 (+13.7%)

Soap & cleaning preparations (Ajax, Fab, Palmolive, Softsoap),
toothpaste (Colgate), personal care products (Mennen) & pet
food (Hill's)

COLIN SERVICE SYSTEMS, INC.

One Brockway Place   Phone: 914-328-0800
White Plains, NY 10601   Fax: 914-328-7849
Pres: Larry H. Colin
Dir HR: Bob Kinsley
Employees: 8,500
Jobs Added Last Year: 1,500 (+21.4%)

Building - housekeeping services

COLONIAL COMMERCIAL CORP.

3601 Hempstead Tpke.   Phone: 516-796-8400
Levittown, NY 11756-1315   Fax: 516-796-8696
Chm & Pres: Bernard Korn
No central personnel officer
Employees: 67
Jobs Added Last Year: 63 (+1,575.0%)

Consulting - consumer accounts receivable consulting services

COLTEC INDUSTRIES INC.

430 Park Ave.   Phone: 212-940-0400
New York, NY 10022-3597   Fax: 212-940-0598
Chm, Pres & CEO: John W. Guffey Jr.
EVP Admin: Laurence H. Polsky
Employees: 9,600
Jobs Cut Last Year: 200 (-2.0%)

Aerospace - systems & components for commercial & military aircraft; engines for naval ships & power plants; automotive fuel, transmission, suspension parts; seals, gaskets & bearings

COLUMBIA UNIVERSITY IN THE CITY OF NEW YORK

Broadway & W. 116th St., 311 Dodge Hall   Phone: 212-854-1754
New York, NY 10027   Fax: 212-678-4817
Pres: George Rupp
VP HR: Robert S. Early
Employees: 16,565
Jobs Added Last Year: 1,926 (+13.2%)

Public university offering 80 undergraduate & 110 graduate degree programs

COMMUNITY BANK SYSTEM, INC.

5790 Widewaters Pkwy.   Phone: 315-445-2282
DeWitt, NY 13214   Fax: 315-445-2997
Pres & CEO: Sanford A. Belden
VP HR: Susan D. Abbott
Employees: 563
Jobs Added Last Year: 123 (+28.0%)

Banks - Northeast

COMMUNITY MEDICAL TRANSPORT, INC.

45 Morris St.   Phone: 914-963-6666
Yonkers, NY 10705   Fax: 914-963-7896
Pres & CEO: Dean L. Sloane
VP Ops & Sec: Craig V. Sloane
Employees: 175
Jobs Added Last Year: 85 (+94.4%)

Medical services - ambulance & specialized medical transport services

COMPUTER ASSOCIATES INTL. INC.

One Computer Associates Plaza   Phone: 516-342-5224
Islandia, NY 11788-7000   Fax: 516-342-5329
Chm & CEO: Charles B. Wang
SVP HR: Lisa Mars
Employees: 8,800
Jobs Added Last Year: 1,300 (+17.3%)

Computers - data processing management & personal finance software

COMPUTER OUTSOURCING SERVICES

360 W. 31st St.   Phone: 212-564-3730
New York, NY 10001   Fax: 212-564-0591
Chm, Pres & CEO: Zach Lonstein
HR Dir: Ronald Green
Employees: 449
Jobs Added Last Year: 184 (+69.4%)

Business services - payroll & data processing services

COMPUTER TASK GROUP, INCORPORATED

800 Delaware Ave.   Phone: 716-882-8000
Buffalo, NY 14209-2094   Fax: 716-887-7246
Chm & CEO: Gale S. Fitzgerald
VP HR & Organizational Dev: Vincent J. Gallenti
Employees: 5,014
Jobs Added Last Year: 498 (+11.0%)

Consulting - information technology services, including staffing & project management

COMVERSE TECHNOLOGY, INC.

170 Crossways Park Dr.   Phone: 516-677-7200
Woodbury, NY 11797   Fax: 516-677-7355
Pres & CEO: Kobi Alexander
Mgr HR: Teri Caperna
Employees: 1,008
Jobs Added Last Year: 286 (+39.6%)

Computers - integrated voice & fax mail systems (TRILOGUE) & data surveillance CD products

 An in-depth profile of this company is available
to subscribers on Hoover's Online at www.hoovers.com.

237

CONSOLIDATED EDISON COMPANY OF NEW YORK, INC.

4 Irving Place
New York, NY 10003
Chm, Pres & CEO: Eugene R. McGrath
VP HR: Edwin Ortiz
Employees: 16,582

Phone: 212-460-4600
Fax: 212-982-7816

Jobs Cut Last Year: 515 (-3.0%)

Utility - electric power & natural gas

CONTINENTAL GRAIN COMPANY

277 Park Ave.
New York, NY 10172-0002
Chm & CEO: Donald L. Staheli
VP HR: Dwight Coffin
Employees: 16,000

Phone: 212-207-5100
Fax: 212-207-5181

Jobs Added Last Year: 0

Food - commodity merchandising & processing

COOPERS & LYBRAND L.L.P.

1251 Avenue of the Americas
New York, NY 10020
Chm & CEO: Nicholas G. Moore
VC HR: Iris D. Goldfein
Employees: 70,500

Phone: 212-536-2000
Fax: 212-536-3145

Jobs Added Last Year: 2,140 (+3.1%)

Business services - accounting, auditing & consulting services

CORNELL UNIVERSITY

Cornell University Campus
Ithaca, NY 14853
Pres: Frank H. Rhodes
Assoc VP HR: Beth Warren
Employees: 9,600

Phone: 607-255-2000
Fax: 607-255-0327

Jobs Added Last Year: —

University

CORNING INCORPORATED

One Riverfront Plaza
Corning, NY 14831-0001
Chm & CEO: Roger G. Ackerman
SVP HR: E. Marie McKee
Employees: 41,000

Phone: 607-974-9000
Fax: 607-974-8551

Jobs Cut Last Year: 2,000 (-4.7%)

Glass products - specialty glass products, oven-proof glassware (Corningware, Pyrex) & crystal (Steuben); sunglasses (Serengeti); laboratory services; antipollution catalytic converters; fiber optics

CULBRO CORPORATION

387 Park Ave. South
New York, NY 10016-8899
Chm, Pres, CEO & COO: Edgar M. Cullman Jr.
Dir HR: Mary Raffaniello
Employees: 2,910

Phone: 212-561-8700
Fax: 212-561-8979

Jobs Added Last Year: 215 (+8.0%)

Diversified operations - cigars (Partagas); disposable lighter distribution; packaging & labeling systems; nursery products; real estate development

Bullseye Job Shop— http://interoz.com/usr/gcbristow/

Netscape: BULLSEYE JOB SHOP

Location: http://interoz.com/usr/gcbristow/

Revised on April 1, 1996 This site is Netscape enhanced!

BULLSEYE JOB SHOP

Press the picture for sound (gunfighter.wav)

Accesses: 0 7 4 3 3

A "ONE-STOP" RESOURCE FOR JOB SEEKERS

The existence of this list is a result of my own job search and, there are many more sites that can be added.

A YAHOO search says there are over 8,000 sites available with jobs, employment opportunities and

CYGNE DESIGNS, INC.

1372 Broadway
New York, NY 10018
Chm & CEO: Bernard M. Manuel
Dir HR: Remy Nicholas
Employees: 5,000

Phone: 212-354-6474
Fax: 212-921-8318

Jobs Added Last Year: 0

Apparel - women's & men's clothing

DEAN WITTER, DISCOVER & CO.

2 World Trade Ctr., 66th Fl.
New York, NY 10048
Chm & CEO: Philip J. Purcell
SVP HR: Michael Cunningham
Employees: 30,779

Phone: 212-392-2222
Fax: 212-392-8405

Jobs Added Last Year: 2,304 (+8.1%)

Financial - securities brokering (Dean Witter, Reynolds), investment banking & credit card issuance (Discover)

DELAWARE NORTH COMPANIES INC.

438 Main St.
Buffalo, NY 14202
Chm & CEO: Jeremy M. Jacobs
VP HR: Marlene Jennings-Galla
Employees: 15,000

Phone: 716-858-5000
Fax: 716-858-5479

Jobs Added Last Year: 0

Diversified operations - food services at airports, parks, stadiums & arenas; pari-mutuel horse & dog tracks, professional hockey team (Boston Bruins); metals & typography

DELOITTE TOUCHE TOHMATSU INTERNATIONAL

1633 Broadway
New York, NY 10019-6754
Chm & CEO: J. Michael Cook
Natl Dir HR: James H. Wall
Employees: 59,000

Phone: 212-492-4000
Fax: 212-492-4154

Jobs Added Last Year: 2,400 (+4.2%)

Business services - accounting & consulting

DIME BANCORP, INC.

589 Fifth Ave.
New York, NY 10017
Chm & CEO: James M. Large Jr.
No central personnel officer
Employees: 2,345

Phone: 212-326-6170
Fax: 212-326-6169

Jobs Added Last Year: 645 (+37.9%)

Financial - savings & loans

DONNA KARAN INTERNATIONAL INC.

550 Seventh Ave.
New York, NY 10018
Chm, CEO & Chief Designer: Donna Karan
No central personnel officer
Employees: 1,570

Phone: 212-789-1500
Fax: 212-789-9410

Jobs Added Last Year: 260 (+19.8%)

Apparel - women's international fashion design house (DKNY, Donna Karan New York); men's (DK Men) & women's (Donna Karan New York) fragrances

DOVER CORPORATION

280 Park Ave.
New York, NY 10017-1292
Pres & CEO: Thomas L. Reece
No central personnel officer
Employees: 25,332

Phone: 212-922-1640
Fax: 212-922-1656

Jobs Added Last Year: 2,340 (+10.2%)

Diversified operations - 70 manufacturing companies (service elevators; laboratory, heat-transfer & food-service equipment; fluid-delivery systems; parking meters & power generators)

DOW JONES & COMPANY, INC.

World Financial Center, 200 Liberty St.
New York, NY 10281
Chm & CEO: Peter R. Kann
VP Emp Relations: James A. Scaduto
Employees: 11,200

Phone: 212-416-2000
Fax: 212-732-8356

Jobs Added Last Year: 935 (+9.1%)

Publishing - newspapers (Barron's, Wall Street Journal), magazines (SmartMoney) & online services (Telerate, Wall Street Journal Interactive Edition); general-interest daily newspapers

THE DRESS BARN, INC.

30 Dunnigan Dr.
Suffern, NY 10901
Chm & CEO: Elliot S. Jaffe
VP HR: David Montieth
Employees: 7,000

Phone: 914-369-4500
Fax: 914-369-4829

Jobs Added Last Year: 600 (+9.4%)

Retail - women's discount specialty apparel stores (Dress Barn, Westport Ltd., Dress Barn Woman, Westport Woman)

THE DYSON-KISSNER-MORAN CORP.

565 Fifth Ave., Rm. 4
New York, NY 10017-2424
Chm & CEO: Robert R. Dyson
Office Mgr: Louise Donahue
Employees: 10,000

Phone: 212-661-4600
Fax: 212-986-7169

Jobs Added Last Year: —

Diversified operations - real estate development; crafts; plumbing & heating; electronics

 An in-depth profile of this company is available to subscribers on Hoover's Online at www.hoovers.com.

EASTMAN KODAK COMPANY

343 State St.
Rochester, NY 14650
Chm, Pres, CEO & COO: George M. C. Fisher
SVP & Dir HR: Michael P. Morley
Employees: 96,600

Phone: 716-724-4000
Fax: 716-724-1089

Jobs Added Last Year: 300 (+0.3%)

Photographic equipment & supplies - film, photographic plates, papers & chemicals, cameras, projectors & processing equipment

ELECTRIC FUEL CORPORATION

885 Third Ave., Ste. 2900
New York, NY 10022
Pres & CEO: Yehuda Harats
No central personnel officer
Employees: 167

Phone: 212-230-2172
Fax: 212-230-2173

Jobs Added Last Year: 74 (+79.6%)

Automotive & trucking - advanced zinc-air batteries for powering electric vehicles; battery refueling systems

EMPIRE BLUE CROSS AND BLUE SHIELD

622 Third Ave.
New York, NY 10017-6758
Pres & CEO: Michael A. Stocker
SVP HR & Svcs: Michael L. Kent
Employees: 6,500

Phone: 212-476-1000
Fax: 212-370-0575

Jobs Added Last Year: —

Insurance - health, hospital & medical service plans

THE EQUITABLE COMPANIES INC.

787 Seventh Ave.
New York, NY 10019
Pres & CEO: Joseph J. Melone
VP HR: John O' Hara
Employees: 13,300

Phone: 212-554-1234
Fax: 212-554-2237

Jobs Cut Last Year: 300 (-2.2%)

Insurance - life & health; financial services (Donaldson, Lufkin & Jenrette, Alliance Capital Management)

ERD WASTE CORP.

356 Veterans Memorial Hwy.
Commack, NY 11725
Chm & CEO: Robert M. Rubin
Controller, CFO & Dir HR: Kathryn Kohsiek
Employees: 107

Phone: 516-543-0606
Fax: 516-543-0678

Jobs Added Last Year: 63 (+143.2%)

Waste management - management & disposal of municipal solid waste, industrial & commercial nonhazardous solid waste & hazardous waste

ERNST & YOUNG LLP

787 Seventh Ave.
New York, NY 10019
Chm: Philip A. Laskaway
VC HR: Robert Center
Employees: 68,452

Phone: 212-773-3000
Fax: 212-773-6350

Jobs Added Last Year: 7,165 (+11.7%)

Business services - accounting & consulting (670 offices in more than 130 countries)

THE ESTEE LAUDER COMPANIES INC.

767 Fifth Ave.
New York, NY 10153
Chm & CEO: Leonard A. Lauder
SVP Corp HR: Andrew J. Cavanaugh
Employees: 9,900

Phone: 212-572-4200
Fax: 212-572-3941

Jobs Cut Last Year: 100 (-1.0%)

Cosmetics & toiletries - skin-care & cosmetic products (Estee Lauder, Clinique, Aramis, Prescriptives, Origins)

EXCEL TECHNOLOGY, INC.

45 Adams Ave.
Hauppauge, NY 11788
Chm, Pres & CEO: J. Donald Hill
Dir HR: Karen Kujawski
Employees: 271

Phone: 516-273-6900
Fax: 516-273-6958

Jobs Added Last Year: 75 (+38.3%)

Lasers - products & systems for scientific, industrial & medicinal fields

EXECUTIVE TELECARD, LTD.

8 Avenue C
Nanuet, NY 10954
Pres & COO: Anthony Balinger
EVP: Robert Schuck
Employees: 131

Phone: 914-627-2060
Fax: 914-627-3631

Jobs Added Last Year: 48 (+57.8%)

Telecommunications services - telephone charge card

THE FAIRCHILD CORPORATION

110 E. 59th St.
New York, NY 10022
Chm, Pres & CEO: Jeffrey J. Steiner
Dir HR: Maureen Rickbeil
Employees: 3,800

Phone: 212-308-6700
Fax: 212-888-5674

Jobs Added Last Year: 300 (+8.6%)

Aerospace - aerospace fasteners; tooling & electronic control systems for the plastic injection molding & die casting industries; telecommunications services & equipment

FAMILY BARGAIN CORPORATION

315 E. 62nd St.   Phone: 212-980-9670
New York, NY 10021   Fax: 212-593-4586
CEO: John A. Selzer
No central personnel officer
Employees: 2,951
Jobs Added Last Year: 1,081 (+57.8%)

Retail - off-price apparel

FAY'S, INCORPORATED

7245 Henry Clay Blvd.   Phone: 315-451-8000
Liverpool, NY 13088   Fax: 315-451-2470
Chm & CEO: Henry A. Panasci Jr.
VP Personnel: Donald R. Bregande
Employees: 9,000
Jobs Added Last Year: 0

Retail - drugstores (272 units); discount auto parts & supply stores; discount office supply

FINLAY ENTERPRISES, INC.

521 Fifth Ave.   Phone: 212-808-2060
New York, NY 10175   Fax: 212-557-3848
Chm, Pres & CEO: David B. Cornstein
VP HR: Joyce Manning
Employees: 6,250
Jobs Added Last Year: 0

Retail - jewelry outlets in department stores in US & France

FLIGHTSAFETY INTERNATIONAL, INC.

Marine Air Terminal, La Guardia Airport   Phone: 718-565-4100
Flushing, NY 11371-1061   Fax: 718-565-4134
Chm & Pres: Albert L. Ueltschi
Corp Dir HR: Thomas W. Riffe
Employees: 2,484
Jobs Added Last Year: 238 (+10.6%)

Schools - technology training using simulators, professional instructors & computer-based systems for corporate, airline, military & government-affiliated operators of aircraft & ships

FOREST LABORATORIES, INC.

909 Third Ave.   Phone: 212-421-7850
New York, NY 10022-4731   Fax: 212-750-9152
Pres & CEO: Howard Solomon
Dir HR: Bernard McGovern
Employees: 1,612
Jobs Added Last Year: 293 (+22.2%)

Drugs - branded & generic forms of both prescription & nonprescription drugs

FRANCISCAN SISTERS OF THE POOR HEALTH SYSTEM, INC.

708 Third Ave., Ste. 200   Phone: 212-818-1987
New York, NY 10017   Fax: 212-808-0096
Pres: Joanne Schuster
Dir HR: June Casterton
Employees: 14,200
Jobs Added Last Year: 200 (+1.4%)

Hospitals - not-for-profit system

THE FRESH JUICE COMPANY, INC.

350 Northern Blvd.   Phone: 516-482-5190
Great Neck, NY 11021   Fax: 516-482-5453
Chm, Pres & CEO: Steven Smith
Treas & CFO: Kathy Siegal
Employees: 50
Jobs Added Last Year: 30 (+150.0%)

Food - wholesale distribution of frozen Florida orange juice, grapefruit juice, apple juice & other noncarbonated beverages (Just Pik't) to grocers

FRONTIER CORPORATION

Frontier Ctr., 180 S. Clinton Ave.   Phone: 716-777-1000
Rochester, NY 14646-0700   Fax: 716-325-4624
Chm, Pres & CEO: Ronald L. Bittner
Pres, Frontier Svcs Group: Janet Sansone
Employees: 7,837
Jobs Added Last Year: 3,597 (+84.8%)

Utility - long-distance & local telephone

GENOVESE DRUG STORES, INC.

80 Marcus Dr.   Phone: 516-420-1900
Melville, NY 11747   Fax: 516-845-8487
Chm & Pres: Leonard Genovese
VP & Dir HR: Sue Crickmore
Employees: 4,700
Jobs Added Last Year: 700 (+17.5%)

Retail - drugstores (121 units)

GLEASON CORPORATION

1000 University Ave., PO Box 22970   Phone: 716-256-8750
Rochester, NY 14692-2970   Fax: 716-461-4092
Chm & Pres: James S. Gleason
VP Admin & HR: John B. Kodweis
Employees: 1,455
Jobs Added Last Year: 376 (+34.8%)

Machine tools & related products - bevel-gear machinery

 An in-depth profile of this company is available to subscribers on Hoover's Online at www.hoovers.com.

241

GLOBAL DIRECTMAIL CORPORATION

22 Harbor Park Dr. Phone: 516-625-1555
Port Washington, NY 11050 Fax: 516-625-0038
Chm & CEO : Richard Leeds
Dir HR: Lillian Berman
Employees: 1,693
Jobs Added Last Year: 204 (+13.7%)

Retail - direct marketing of brand name & private label computer-related products, office products & industrial products (Global, Misco)

THE GOLDMAN SACHS GROUP, L.P.

85 Broad St. Phone: 212-902-1000
New York, NY 10004 Fax: 212-902-1512
Senior Partner & Chm of Mgmt Comm: Jon S. Corzine
Partner, Personnel: Jonathan L. Cohen
Employees: 7,200
Jobs Cut Last Year: 1,800 (-20.0%)

Financial - investment banking & securities brokerage

THE GOLUB CORPORATION

501 Duanesburg Rd. Phone: 518-355-5000
Schenectady, NY 12306 Fax: 518-355-0843
Chm & CEO: Lewis Golub
VP HR: Curt Hopkins
Employees: 9,000
Jobs Added Last Year: 1,000 (+12.5%)

Retail - supermarkets

GOULDS PUMPS, INC.

300 WillowBrook Office Park Phone: 716-387-6600
Fairport, NY 14450-4285 Fax: 716-387-6696
Chm, Pres & CEO: Thomas C. McDermott
VP HR: Mary Ann Lambertsen
Employees: 4,900
Jobs Added Last Year: 700 (+16.7%)

Machinery - centrifugal pumps

GRAFF PAY-PER-VIEW INC.

536 Broadway Phone: 212-941-1434
New York, NY 10012 Fax: 212-941-4746
Chm & CEO: J. Roger Faherty
Dir Office Svcs: Joan Simari
Employees: 154
Jobs Added Last Year: 54 (+54.0%)

Cable TV - adult entertainment channels (Spice, Spice 2); pay-per-view movie channels (Cable Video Store, Theatre Vision)

GRANITE BROADCASTING CORPORATION

767 Third Ave. Phone: 212-826-2530
New York, NY 10017 Fax: 212-826-2858
Chm & CEO: W. Don Cornwell
No central personnel officer
Employees: 944
Jobs Added Last Year: 354 (+60.0%)

Broadcasting - TV (9 network-affiliated stations)

THE GREAT AMERICAN BACKRUB STORE

958 Third Ave. Phone: 212-832-1766
New York, NY 10022 Fax: 212-758-7671
CEO: Terrance C. Murray
Dir HR: Bob Napodano
Employees: 81
Jobs Added Last Year: 50 (+161.3%)

Retail - massages & related products

GREY ADVERTISING INC.

777 Third Ave. Phone: 212-546-2000
New York, NY 10017 Fax: 212-546-1495
Chm, Pres & CEO: Edward H. Meyer
SVP & Dir HR: Kevin Bergin
Employees: 6,000
Jobs Added Last Year: 4,582 (+323.1%)

Advertising - marketing consultation, product publicity, public relations & sales promotion services for clients in such industries as apparel, automobile, beverages, chemicals & computers

GRIFFON CORPORATION

100 Jericho Quadrangle Phone: 516-938-5544
Jericho, NY 11753 Fax: 516-938-5644
Chm & CEO: Harvey R. Blau
Sec: Susan Roland
Employees: 3,600
Jobs Added Last Year: 700 (+24.1%)

Diversified operations - home products; customized plastic films; garage doors & fireplaces

GRYPHON HOLDINGS INC.

30 Wall St. Phone: 212-825-1200
New York, NY 10005-2201 Fax: 212-825-0200
Pres & CEO: Stephen A. Crane
Dir HR: Robert Coffee
Employees: 125
Jobs Added Last Year: 26 (+26.3%)

Insurance - professional liability, earthquake coverage & other specialty property & casualty

THE GUARDIAN LIFE INSURANCE COMPANY OF AMERICA

201 Park Ave. South   Phone: 212-598-8000
New York, NY 10003   Fax: 212-598-8813
Pres & CEO: Joseph Sargent
VP HR & Administrative Support: Douglas C. Kramer
Employees: 7,900

Jobs Added Last Year: 298 (+3.9%)

Insurance - multiline & miscellaneous

HAPPINESS EXPRESS INC.

One Harbor Park Dr.   Phone: 516-484-3700
Port Washington, NY 11050   Fax: 516-484-3750
Chm, Pres & CEO: Joseph A. Sutton
Dir HR: Jessica Datoro
Employees: 50

Jobs Added Last Year: 28 (+127.3%)

Housewares - children's lamps, nightlights, banks & dolls of licensed characters (The Lion King, Barney, Power Rangers)

HARDINGE INC.

One Hardinge Dr.   Phone: 607-734-2281
Elmira, NY 14902-1507   Fax: 607-734-5517
Pres & CEO: Robert E. Agan
VP HR: Doug Tifft
Employees: 1,345

Jobs Added Last Year: 380 (+39.4%)

Machine tools & related products - metal cutting lathes & related tooling & accessories

HARPERCOLLINS PUBLISHERS, INC.

10 E. 53rd St.   Phone: 212-207-7000
New York, NY 10022-5299   Fax: 212-207-7617
Pres & CEO: Anthea Disney
SVP HR: Barbara Hufham
Employees: 6,000

Jobs Cut Last Year: 300 (-4.8%)

Publishing - books, including trade, business, reference & educational (ScottForesman)

HEALTH MANAGEMENT, INC.

4250 Veterans Memorial Hwy.   Phone: 516-981-0034
Holbrook, NY 11741   Fax: 516-981-0522
Pres & CEO: William J. Nicol
Personnel & Human Svcs Dir: Virginia Belloise
Employees: 413

Jobs Added Last Year: 219 (+112.9%)

Medical practice management - comprehensive outpatient drug therapies

HEALTH MANAGEMENT SYSTEMS

401 Park Ave. South   Phone: 212-685-4545
New York, NY 10016   Fax: 212-889-8776
Chm, Pres, CEO & Treas: Paul J. Kerz
VP HR: Lewis D. Levetown
Employees: 630

Jobs Added Last Year: 209 (+49.6%)

Medical practice management - information management & data processing services for hospitals, health care providers & government health services agencies

Information Incorporation Inc. — http://www.informationinc.com/

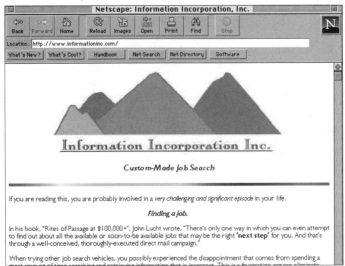

 An in-depth profile of this company is available to subscribers on Hoover's Online at www.hoovers.com.

243

THE HEARST CORPORATION

959 Eighth Ave.   Phone: 212-649-2000
New York, NY 10019   Fax: 212-765-3528
Pres & CEO: Frank A. Bennack Jr.
VP HR, Heart Magazines Div: Kenneth A. Feldman
Employees: 13,500
Jobs Cut Last Year: 500 (-3.6%)

Publishing - magazines, newspapers, books & multimedia; broadcasting & cable TV; comic strip & feature syndication

HIRSCH INTERNATIONAL CORP.

200 Wireless Blvd.   Phone: 516-436-7100
Hauppauge, NY 11788   Fax: 516-436-7054
Chm, Pres & CEO: Henry Arnberg
Dir HR: Susan Lange
Employees: 201
Jobs Added Last Year: 60 (+42.6%)

Wholesale distribution - computerized single- & multihead embroidery machines

HUDSON GENERAL CORPORATION

111 Great Neck Rd.   Phone: 516-487-8610
Great Neck, NY 11022   Fax: 516-487-4855
Chm, Pres & CEO: Jay B. Langner
Dir Insurance & HR: Robert T. Cavaliere
Employees: 3,700
Jobs Added Last Year: 400 (+12.1%)

Transportation - aircraft ground handling, deicing & fueling services; snow removal, cargo warehousing, ramp sweeping & glycol recovery

IEC ELECTRONICS CORP.

105 Norton St.   Phone: 315-331-7742
Newark, NY 14513-1298   Fax: 315-331-3547
Chm, Pres & CEO: Roger E. Main
VP HR: Joe Schadeberg
Employees: 2,456
Jobs Added Last Year: 536 (+27.9%)

Electrical components - printed circuit board assemblies, modems & video enhancement cards

INNODATA CORPORATION

95 Rockwell Place   Phone 718-625-7750
New York, NY 11217   Fax: 718-522-9235
Chm & CEO: Barry Hertz
Ops Mgr: Jack Cohen
Employees: 3,100
Jobs Added Last Year: 680 (+28.1%)

Data collection & systems - data entry & conversion, scanning, indexing & abstracting services

INTEGRAMED AMERICA, INC.

One Manhattanville Rd.   Phone: 914-253-8000
Purchase, NY 10577   Fax: 914-253-8008
Pres & CEO: Gerardo Canet
Dir HR: Rita Gruber
Employees: 171
Jobs Added Last Year: 58 (+51.3%)

Medical services - assisted reproductive technology services

INTERNATIONAL BUSINESS MACHINES CORPORATION

One Old Orchard Rd.   Phone: 914-765-1900
Armonk, NY 10504   Fax: 914-288-1147
Chm & CEO: Louis V. Gerstner Jr.
SVP HR: J. Thomas Bouchard
Employees: 225,347
Jobs Added Last Year: 5,508 (+2.5%)

Computers - mainframes, micros, processors, software & peripherals; IT consulting, systems integration & development services

INTERNATIONAL CABLETEL, INC.

110 E. 59th St., 26th Fl.   Phone: 212-371-3714
New York, NY 10022
Pres & CEO: George S. Blumenthal
Dir HR: Beth Wilson
Employees: 1,550
Jobs Added Last Year: 875 (+129.6%)

Telecommunications services - integrated "last-mile" services (voice, data & video services provided from a distribution network to a customer's premises)

INTERNATIONAL PAPER COMPANY

2 Manhattanville Rd.   Phone: 914-397-1500
Purchase, NY 10577   Fax: 914-397-1928
Chm & CEO: John T. Dillon
SVP HR: Robert M. Byrnes
Employees: 81,500
Jobs Added Last Year: 11,500 (+16.4%)

Paper & paper products - specialty products including business, coated, fine printing, artist & repographic papers & containerboards; pulp & wood products

INTERNATIONAL POST LIMITED

545 Fifth Ave.   Phone: 212-986-6300
New York, NY 10017   Fax: 212-986-1364
Pres & CEO: Martin Irwin
HR Dir: Carla Moxham
Employees: 322
Jobs Added Last Year: 95 (+41.9%)

TV services - film-to-tape transfer, electronic video editing & computer-generated graphics primarily for the TV advertising & program distribution industries

THE INTERPUBLIC GROUP OF COMPANIES, INC.

1271 Avenue of the Americas   Phone: 212-399-8000
New York, NY 10020   Fax: 212-399-8130
Chm, Pres & CEO: Philip H. Geier Jr.
SVP HR: C. Kent Kroeber
Employees: 19,700

Jobs Added Last Year: 1,500 (+8.2%)

Advertising - market research, sales promotion, product development, direct marketing, telemarketing & other related services

INVESTMENT TECHNOLOGY GROUP INC.

900 Third Ave.   Phone: 212-755-6800
New York, NY 10022   Fax: 212-444-6290
Pres & CEO: Raymond L. Killian Jr.
Admin Mgr: Nadia Casiano
Employees: 122

Jobs Added Last Year: 28 (+29.8%)

Financial - automated securities trade execution & analysis services

ITT CORPORATION

1330 Avenue of the Americas   Phone: 212-258-1000
New York, NY 10019   Fax: 212-258-1297
Chm & CEO: Rand V. Araskog
SVP HR: Ralph W. Pausig
Employees: 38,000

Jobs Added Last Year: 13,000 (+52.0%)

Hotels & motels - hotels & casinos (Caesars Palace, Sheraton), sports entertainment & communications & information services

ITT INDUSTRIES, INC.

4 West Red Oak Ln.   Phone: 914-641-2000
White Plains, NY 10604   Fax: 914-696-2950
Chm, Pres & CEO: D. Travis Engen
SVP & Dir HR: James P. Smith Jr.
Employees: 59,000

Jobs Added Last Year: 600 (+1.0%)

Diversified operations - insurance; financing services; telephone-directory publishing; technical schools; hotels & casinos; electronic products for the automotive & defense industries

J. CREW GROUP INC.

625 Sixth Ave.   Phone: 212-886-2500
New York, NY 10011   Fax: 212-886-2666
Chm & CEO: Arthur Cinader
VP HR: Marianne Ruggiero
Employees: 6,600

Jobs Added Last Year: 200 (+3.1%)

Retail - mail order & retail apparel & home furnishings

JOHNSON & HIGGINS

125 Broad St.   Phone: 212-574-7000
New York, NY 10004   Fax: 212-574-7190
Chm, Pres & CEO: David A. Olsen
Mgr HR: James R. Reardon
Employees: 8,750

Jobs Added Last Year: 0

Insurance - risk management consulting & insurance brokerage

J.P. MORGAN & CO. INCORPORATED

60 Wall St.   Phone: 212-483-2323
New York, NY 10260-0060   Fax: 212-648-5193
Chm, Pres & CEO: Douglas A. Warner III
Mng Dir HR: Herbert J. Hefke
Employees: 15,613

Jobs Cut Last Year: 1,442 (-8.5%)

Banks - money center

K-III COMMUNICATIONS CORP.

745 Fifth Ave.   Phone: 212-745-0100
New York, NY 10151   Fax: 212-745-0169
Chm & CEO: William F. Reilly
VP HR: Michaelanne C. Discepolo
Employees: 6,300

Jobs Added Last Year: 1,750 (+38.5%)

Publishing - periodicals (American Baby, Modern Bride, New Woman, New York, Sail, Seventeen, Soap Opera Digest) & books (World Almanac); educational TV programming (Channel One)

KENNETH COLE PRODUCTIONS, INC.

152 W. 57th St.   Phone: 212-265-1500
New York, NY 10019   Fax: 212-265-1662
Pres & CEO: Kenneth D. Cole
Dir HR: Gloria Guerraro
Employees: 465

Jobs Added Last Year: 180 (+63.2%)

Shoes & related apparel (Kenneth Cole, Unlisted); retail stores

KINNEY SYSTEM, INC.

60 Madison Ave.   Phone: 212-889-4444
New York, NY 10010   Fax: 212-889-2053
Chm & CEO: Lewis Katz
Dir HR: Jeffrey Goldmacher
Employees: 2,200

Jobs Added Last Year: 400 (+22.2%)

Transportation - public parking lots

 An in-depth profile of this company is available to subscribers on Hoover's Online at www.hoovers.com.

245

KPMG PEAT MARWICK LLP

767 Fifth Ave.   Phone: 212-909-5000
New York, NY 10153   Fax: 212-909-5299
Chm: Jon C. Madonna
Dir HR: Howard R. Marcus
Employees: 72,000

Jobs Cut Last Year: 4,200 (-5.5%)

Business services - accounting & consulting

LEHMAN BROTHERS HOLDINGS INC.

3 World Financial Ctr.   Phone: 212-526-7000
New York, NY 10285   Fax: 212-526-5952
Chm & CEO: Richard S. Fuld Jr.
Mng Dir HR: Maryanne Rasmussen
Employees: 7,771

Jobs Added Last Year: 821 (+11.8%)

Financial - investment bankers

KRYSTALTECH INTERNATIONAL INC.

555 W. 57th St., Ste. 1750   Phone: 212-261-0400
New York, NY 10017-2925   Fax: 212-262-0414
CEO: Dan Tochner
No central personnel officer
Employees: 55

Jobs Added Last Year: 12 (+27.9%)

Retail - computer parts & peripherals

LIZ CLAIBORNE, INC.

1441 Broadway   Phone: 212-354-4900
New York, NY 10018   Fax: 212-626-3416
Pres & CEO: Paul R. Charron
SVP HR: Jorge L. Figueredo
Employees: 7,400

Jobs Cut Last Year: 600 (-7.5%)

Apparel - women's apparel, accessories, cosmetics & fragrances & men's clothing, cologne & furnishings

LAKELAND INDUSTRIES, INC.

711-2 Koehler Ave.   Phone: 516-981-9700
Ronkonkoma, NY 11779-7410   Fax: 516-981-9751
Pres & Chm: Raymond J. Smith
No central personnel officer
Employees: 222

Jobs Added Last Year: 98 (+79.0%)

Apparel - disposable & limited use suits for toxic waste clean-up teams, fire & heat protective apparel, safety & industrial work gloves & industrial & medical woven cloth garments

LOEWS CORPORATION

667 Madison Ave.   Phone: 212-545-2000
New York, NY 10021-8087   Fax: 212-545-2525
Co-Chm & Co-CEO: Laurence A. Tisch
VP HR: Alan Momeyer
Employees: 34,700

Jobs Added Last Year: 9,300 (+36.6%)

Diversified operations - insurance (CNA); tobacco (Newport); watches & clocks (Bulova); deep water drilling (Diamond Offshore)

LANCIT MEDIA PRODUCTIONS, LTD.

601 W. 50th St.   Phone: 212-977-9100
New York, NY 10019   Fax: 212-477-9164
Chm & CEO: Cecily Truett
Personnel Dir: JoAnn Pezzella
Employees: 60

Jobs Added Last Year: 17 (+39.5%)

TV production & programming - children's TV programming (The Puzzle Place, Backyard Safari); film production

LONG ISLAND LIGHTING COMPANY

175 E. Old Country Rd.   Phone: 516-755-6650
Hicksville, NY 11801   Fax: 516-931-3165
Chm, Pres & CEO: William J. Catacosinos
VP HR: Robert X. Kelleher
Employees: 5,688

Jobs Cut Last Year: 262 (-4.4%)

Utility - electric power & natural gas

LEFRAK ORGANIZATION INC.

97-77 Queens Blvd.   Phone: 718-459-9021
Rego Park, NY 11374   Fax: 718-897-0688
EVP & CEO: Arthur Klein
Dir HR: Cheryl Jensen
Employees: 17,400

Jobs Cut Last Year: 100 (-0.6%)

Real estate development & management; entertainment; oil & gas exploration

LORAL CORPORATION

600 Third Ave.   Phone: 212-697-1105
New York, NY 10016   Fax: 212-661-8988
Chm & CEO: Bernard L. Schwartz
VP Admin: Stephen L. Jackson
Employees: 28,900

Jobs Cut Last Year: 3,700 (-11.3%)

Electronics - advanced electronic systems, components & service for the military, US government & foreign governments

LUNN INDUSTRIES, INC.

One Garvies Point Rd. Phone: 516-671-9000
Glen Cove, NY 11542-2828 Fax: 516-671-9005
Chm & CEO: Alan W. Baldwin
Dir HR: Lana Defelice
Employees: 175

Jobs Added Last Year: 35 (+25.0%)

Metal products - metal bonding, bonding panels, composite
assemblies utilizing honeycomb fiber & resin laminates &
filament wound assemblies

MACANDREWS & FORBES HOLDINGS

35 E. 62nd St. Phone: 212-688-9000
New York, NY 10021 Fax: 212-572-8400
Chm & CEO: Ronald O. Perelman
Dir Facilities: Christine Castari
Employees: 22,800

Jobs Added Last Year: 472 (+2.1%)

Diversified operations - cosmetics (Revlon); banking; publishing
(Marvel Entertainment); outdoor equipment (Coleman); boats
(Boston Whaler); cigars

THE MACMANUS GROUP

1675 Broadway Phone: 212-468-3622
New York, NY 10019 Fax: 212-468-4385
Chm & CEO: Roy J. Bostock
EVP & Dir HR: William L. Clayton
Employees: 6,333

Jobs Cut Last Year: 72 (-1.1%)

Advertising

MAPINFO CORPORATION

One Global View Phone: 518-285-6000
Troy, NY 12180 Fax: 518-285-7060
Pres & CEO: Brian D. Owen
HR Dir: Joseph Clement
Employees: 298

Jobs Added Last Year: 88 (+41.9%)

Computers - desktop mapping software (MapInfo)

MARK IV INDUSTRIES, INC.

One Towne Centre, 501 John James Audubon Pkwy.,
PO Box 810 Phone: 716-689-4972
Amherst, NY 14226-0810 Fax: 716-689-6098
Chm & CEO: Salvatore H. Alfiero
Mgr Welfare Benefits & Corp Office of HR: Christine Werth
Employees: 16,000

Jobs Cut Last Year: 200 (-1.2%)

Diversified operations - transportation; process control equipment; professional audio

MARSH & MCLENNAN COMPANIES

1166 Avenue of the Americas Phone: 212-345-5000
New York, NY 10036 Fax: 212-345-4838
Chm : A. J. C. Smith
SVP HR & Admin: Francis N. Bonsignore
Employees: 25,000

Jobs Cut Last Year: 1,000 (-3.8%)

Insurance - brokerage, consulting & investment management
services

MCCRORY CORPORATION

667 Madison Ave. Phone: 212-735-9500
New York, NY 10021 Fax: 212-735-9450
Chm & CEO: Meshulam Ricklis
SVP HR & Info Tech: Tom Russell
Employees: 11,300

Jobs Added Last Year: 4,300 (+61.4%)

Retail - discount & variety stores

THE MCGRAW-HILL COMPANIES, INC.

1221 Avenue of the Americas Phone: 212-512-2000
New York, NY 10020-1095 Fax: 212-512-4871
Chm & CEO: Joseph L. Dionne
SVP HR: Barbara B. Maddock
Employees: 15,004

Jobs Cut Last Year: 335 (-2.2%)

Publishing - books, periodicals & electronic (Business Week, BYTE,
Standard & Poor's); financial services; radio & TV broadcasting

MCKINSEY & COMPANY

55 E. 52nd St. Phone: 212-446-7000
New York, NY 10022 Fax: 212-688-8575
Mng Dir: Rajat Gupta
Principal & Personnel Dir: Jerome Vascellaro
Employees: 6,050

Jobs Added Last Year: 50 (+0.8%)

Consulting - management

MELVILLE CORPORATION

One Theall Rd. Phone: 914-925-4000
Rye, NY 10580 Fax: 914-925-4026
Chm & CEO: Stanley P. Goldstein
SVP HR: Jerald L. Maurer
Employees: 96,832

Jobs Cut Last Year: 20,582 (-17.5%)

Retail - drugstores (CVS), home furnishings (Linens 'n Things),
apparel (Bob's) & health & beauty aids

MEMORIAL SLOAN-KETTERING CANCER CENTER

633 Third Ave.　　　　　　　Phone: 212-639-3553
New York, NY 10017　　　　　Fax: 212-639-3535
Pres & CEO: Paul A. Marks
VP HR: Michael Browne
Employees: 6,050

Jobs Added Last Year: 16 (+0.3%)

Hospitals - not-for-profit cancer center

MERRILL LYNCH & CO., INC.

World Financial Ctr, 250 Vesey St.　Phone: 212-449-1000
New York, NY 10281-1332　　　　Fax: 212-236-4384
Chm & CEO: Daniel P. Tully
SVP HR: Patrick J. Walsh
Employees: 46,000

Jobs Added Last Year: 2,200 (+5.0%)

Financial - investment, finance & insurance services

METROPOLITAN LIFE INSURANCE CO.

One Madison Ave.　　　　　　Phone: 212-578-2211
New York, NY 10010-3690　　Fax: 212-578-3320
Chm, Pres & CEO: Harry R. Kamen
SVP HR: Anne E. Hayden
Employees: 41,000

Jobs Cut Last Year: 12,000 (-22.6%)

Insurance - life, health, property & casualty

MICROS-TO-MAINFRAMES, INC.

614 Corporate Way　　　　　Phone: 914-268-5000
Valley Cottage, NY 10989　　Fax: 914-268-9695
Co-CEO, VP & Sec: Steven H. Rothman
Dir HR: Dottie Sloaman
Employees: 96

Jobs Added Last Year: 34 (+54.8%)

Computers - systems integration; hardware & software sales

MICROWAVE POWER DEVICES, INC.

49 Wireless Blvd.　　　　　　Phone: 516-231-1400
Hauppauge, NY 11788-3935　Fax: 516-231-4084
Pres & CEO: Edward J. Shubel
Dir HR: Polly Winters
Employees: 385

Jobs Added Last Year: 135 (+54.0%)

Telecommunications equipment - power amplifiers & related subsystems for cellular base stations

MONRO MUFFLER BRAKE, INC.

2340 Brighton-Henrietta Town Line Rd.　Phone: 716-427-2280
Rochester, NY 14623　　　　　　　　　Fax: 716-427-2295
Pres & CEO: Lawrence C. Day
HR Mgr: Gail Ryan
Employees: 1,694

Jobs Added Last Year: 265 (+18.5%)

Consumer products - undercar repair service, located primarily in the northeast US

Blackwell Career Management — http://www.bizxp.com/career/bla00001.html

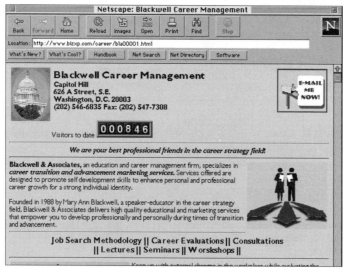

MONTEFIORE MEDICAL CENTER

111 E. 210th St.
New York, NY 10467
Pres: Spencer Foreman
SVP Corp Relations: Donald G. Revelle
Employees: 8,278

Phone: 718-920-4321
Fax: 718-920-6321

Jobs Added Last Year: 55 (+0.7%)

Hospitals - patient care, medical education & research

MORGAN STANLEY GROUP INC.

1585 Broadway
New York, NY 10036
Pres & Mng Dir: John J. Mack
Principal Dev Officer: Elizabeth Lynch
Employees: 9,685

Phone: 212-761-4000
Fax: 212-761-0086

Jobs Added Last Year: 1,412 (+17.1%)

Financial - investment banking, merchant banking, stock brokerage & securities underwriting

MTA NEW YORK CITY TRANSIT

370 Jay St.
New York, NY 11201
Pres: Lawrence G. Reuter
VP HR: Liz H. Lowe
Employees: 44,000

Phone: 718-330-3000
Fax: 718-243-8501

Jobs Added Last Year: 2,914 (+7.1%)

Transportation - buses & subways in the Manhattan, Brooklyn, Bronx, Queens & Staten Island boroughs of New York City

THE MUTUAL LIFE INSURANCE COMPANY OF NEW YORK

1740 Broadway
New York, NY 10019
Chm & CEO: Michael I. Roth
Asst VP Exec Compensation: Catherine Gushue
Employees: 6,385

Phone: 212-708-2000
Fax: 212-708-2056

Jobs Cut Last Year: 15 (-0.2%)

Insurance - individual life & disability; annuities, mutual funds & investment securities

N2K INC.

55 Broad St., 10th Fl.
New York, NY 10004
Chm & CEO: Lawrence L. Rosen
Controller: Rich Harris
Employees: 108

Phone: 212-378-5555
Fax: 212-742-1755

Jobs Added Last Year: 52 (+92.9%)

Computers - entertainment, information & merchandising Web sites (Music Boulevard, Jazz Central Station, Rocktropolis) & sites for individual artists (David Bowie, The Rolling Stones)

NATIONAL BROADCASTING CO. INC.

30 Rockefeller Plaza
New York, NY 10112-0002
Pres & CEO: Robert C. Wright
EVP Emp Relations: Edward L. Scanlon
Employees: 5,000

Phone: 212-664-4444
Fax: 212-664-6193

Jobs Added Last Year: —

Broadcasting - TV network (NBC) serving more than 200 affiliated stations; TV program production; cable TV stations (CNBC, America's Talking, NBC Super Channel; Canal de Noticias NBC)

NAUTICA ENTERPRISES, INC.

40 W. 57th St., 3rd Fl.
New York, NY 10019
Chm, Pres & CEO: Harvey Sanders
Dir HR: Laura Crespo
Employees: 1,000

Phone: 212-541-5990
Fax: 212-956-3373

Jobs Added Last Year: 240 (+31.6%)

Apparel - men's & boys'

NEW YORK CITY HEALTH AND HOSPITALS CORPORATION

125 Worth St.
New York, NY 10025
Acting Pres: Luis Marcos
VP Corp Affairs: Raquel Ayala
Employees: 41,711

Phone: 212-788-3327
Fax: 212-788-3358

Jobs Cut Last Year: 3,289 (-7.3%)

Hospitals - not-for-profit system serving New York City (#1 US municipal hospital system)

NEW YORK LIFE INSURANCE CO.

51 Madison Ave.
New York, NY 10010
Chm & CEO: Harry G. Hohn
EVP HR & Sec: George J. Trapp
Employees: 13,050

Phone: 212-576-7000
Fax: 212-576-8145

Jobs Cut Last Year: 2,484 (-16.0%)

Insurance - life

THE NEW YORK TIMES COMPANY

229 W. 43rd St.
New York, NY 10036
Chm & CEO: Arthur Ochs "Punch" Sulzberger
SVP Broadcasting, Corp Dev & HR: Katharine P. Darrow
Employees: 12,300

Phone: 212-556-1234
Fax: 212-556-4011

Jobs Cut Last Year: 500 (-3.9%)

Publishing - newspapers (The New York Times, The Boston Globe) & magazines (Golf Digest); broadcasting; information services

NEW YORK UNIVERSITY

70 Washington Sq. South
New York, NY 10012
Pres: L. Jay Oliva
No central personnel officer
Employees: 15,400

Phone: 212-998-1212
Fax: 212-995-4040

Jobs Added Last Year: 100 (+0.7%)

Public university offering 160 undergraduate & 155 graduate
degree programs

NIAGARA MOHAWK POWER CORP.

300 Erie Blvd. West
Syracuse, NY 13202
Chm & CEO: William E. Davis
SVP HR: David J. Arrington
Employees: 8,800

Phone: 315-474-1511
Fax: 315-428-5101

Jobs Cut Last Year: 400 (-4.3%)

Utility - electric power & natural gas

NORTON MCNAUGHTON, INC.

463 Seventh Ave.
New York, NY 10018
Chm & CEO: Sanford Greenberg
Mgr HR: Mary Tackmann
Employees: 315

Phone: 212-947-2960
Fax: 212-563-2766

Jobs Added Last Year: 75 (+31.3%)

Apparel - women's career & casual clothing

NU HORIZONS ELECTRONIC CORP.

6000 New Horizons Blvd.
Amityville, NY 11701
Chm & CEO: Irving Lubman
Personnel Mgr: Patty Englert
Employees: 400

Phone: 516-226-6000
Fax: 516-226-5505

Jobs Added Last Year: 93 (+30.3%)

Electronics - distribution of high-technology active & passive
electronic components

NYNEX CORPORATION

1095 Avenue of the Americas
New York, NY 10036
Chm & CEO: Ivan G. Seidenberg
VP HR: Donald J. Sacco
Employees: 65,800

Phone: 212-395-2121
Fax: 212-921-2917

Jobs Added Last Year: 400 (+0.6%)

Utility - telephone; telecommunications, wireless communications, directory publishing & video entertainment & information
services

NYTEST ENVIRONMENTAL INC.

60 Seaview Blvd.
Port Washington, NY 11050
Pres & CEO: John Gaspari
Dir HR: Lori Sanborn
Employees: 178

Phone: 516-625-5500
Fax: 516-625-1274

Jobs Added Last Year: 94 (+111.9%)

Pollution control equipment & services - specialized analytical
services for the accurate measurement of hazardous wastes

OGDEN CORPORATION

Two Pennsylvania Plaza
New York, NY 10121
Chm, Pres & CEO: R. Richard Ablon
Dir HR: Lane Varanello
Employees: 45,000

Phone: 212-868-6100
Fax: 212-868-5714

Jobs Added Last Year: 0

Diversified operations - entertainment services (Grizzly Park);
aviation, including airport facilities & inflight catering; utilities,
including electric & water

OMNICOM GROUP INC.

437 Madison Ave.
New York, NY 10022
Chm & CEO: Bruce Crawford
Dir HR & Benefits: Leslie Chiocco
Employees: 19,400

Phone: 212-415-3600
Fax: 212-415-3530

Jobs Added Last Year: 3,300 (+20.5%)

Advertising (BBDO Worldwide, DDB Needham, TBWA)

ONEIDA LTD.

163 Kenwood Ave.
Oneida, NY 13421-2829
Chm & CEO: William D. Matthews
VP HR: Darwin Johnston
Employees: 5,708

Phone: 315-361-3000
Fax: 315-361-3658

Jobs Added Last Year: 118 (+2.1%)

Housewares - tableware & china; industrial wire

PAINE WEBBER GROUP INC.

1285 Avenue of the Americas
New York, NY 10019-6028
Chm & CEO: Donald B. Marron
Chief Admin Officer: Ronald M. Schwartz
Employees: 15,900

Phone: 212-713-2000
Fax: 212-713-4889

Jobs Cut Last Year: 400 (-2.5%)

Financial - securities brokerage & investment banking & asset
management services

PALL CORPORATION

2200 Northern Blvd.
East Hills, NY 11548-1289
Chm & CEO: Eric Krasnoff
Corp Dir Employment: Geri Schwalb
Employees: 6,500

Phone: 516-484-5400
Fax: 516-484-3529

Jobs Added Last Year: 300 (+4.8%)

Filtration products - filter media & other fluid-clarification equipment

PARK ELECTROCHEMICAL CORP.

5 Dakota Dr.
Lake Success, NY 11042
Pres & Chm: Jerry Shore
No central personnel officer
Employees: 2,240

Phone: 516-354-4100
Fax: 516-354-4128

Jobs Added Last Year: 410 (+22.4%)

Electrical components - advanced laminates & semi-finished circuit boards; bathtub spouts, shower heads & faucet housings; specialty resins for military & telecommunications products

PARSONS & WHITTEMORE, INC.

4 International Dr.
Rye Brook, NY 10573
CEO: George F. Landegger
Mgr HR: Richard Martin
Employees: 2,000

Phone: 914-937-9009
Fax: 914-937-2259

Jobs Added Last Year: 200 (+11.1%)

Diversified operations - pulp & paper, industrial machinery

PAYCHEX, INC.

911 Panorama Trail South
Rochester, NY 14625-0397
Chm, Pres & CEO: B. Thomas Golisano
Dir HR: Rick Girard
Employees: 3,500

Phone: 716-385-6666
Fax: 716-383-3428

Jobs Added Last Year: 400 (+12.9%)

Business services - computerized payroll-processing & payroll-tax-preparation services; human resource products & services

PDK LABS INC.

145 Ricefield Ln.
Hauppauge, NY 11788
Pres, CEO & CFO: Michael B. Krasnoff
No central personnel officer
Employees: 150

Phone: 516-273-2630
Fax: 516-273-1582

Jobs Added Last Year: 60 (+66.7%)

Vitamins & nutritional products - nonprescription pharmaceuticals & vitamins, including caffeine products, pain relievers, decongestants & diet aids; cosmetics

PEERLESS IMPORTERS, INC.

16 Bridgewater St.
New York, NY 11222
Pres: John Magliocco
No central personnel officer
Employees: 1,400

Phone: 718-383-5500
Fax: 718-383-5500

Jobs Added Last Year: 200 (+16.7%)

Beverages - wine & liquor distribution

THE PENN TRAFFIC COMPANY

1200 State Fair Blvd.
Syracuse, NY 13209
Pres & CEO: John T. Dixon
VP HR: Jack Henry
Employees: 27,000

Phone: 315-453-7284
Fax: 315-461-2474

Jobs Cut Last Year: 1,500 (-5.3%)

Retail - supermarkets (Insalaco, P&C, Riverside, Bi-Lo)

PEPSICO, INC.

Phone: 914-253-2000
Fax: 914-253-2070

Purchase, NY 10577-1444
CEO: Roger A. Enrico
SVP Personnel: William R. Bensyl
Employees: 480,000

Jobs Added Last Year: 9,000 (+1.9%)

Beverages - soft drinks (Pepsi-Cola, Mountain Dew, Slice); snack foods (Fritos, Doritos, Cheetos, Ruffles, Lay's); restaurants (KFC, Pizza Hut, Taco Bell)

PFIZER INC.

235 E. 42nd St.
New York, NY 10017-5755
Chm & CEO: William C. Steere Jr.
SVP Emp Resources: William J. Robison
Employees: 43,800

Phone: 212-573-2323
Fax: 212-573-7851

Jobs Added Last Year: 3,000 (+7.4%)

Diversified operations - drugs; surgical, orthopedic & cardiac devices; animal-health products; specialty chemicals & minerals; consumer products

PHARMHOUSE CORPORATION

860 Broadway
New York, NY 10003
Pres, CEO & COO: Kenneth A. Davis
SVP Admin: Joseph Keller
Employees: 2,200

Phone: 212-477-9400
Fax: 212-477-2900

Jobs Added Last Year: 200 (+10.0%)

Retail - deep discount drug & general merchandise

 An in-depth profile of this company is available to subscribers on Hoover's Online at www.hoovers.com.

251

PHILIP MORRIS COMPANIES INC.

120 Park Ave.
New York, NY 10017
Chm & CEO: Geoffrey C. Bible
SVP HR & Admin: Lawrence A. Gates
Employees: 151,000

Phone: 212-880-5000
Fax: 212-878-2167

Jobs Cut Last Year: 14,000 (-8.5%)

Diversified - cigarettes (Marlboro, Benson & Hedges, Virginia Slims); food (Kraft, Jell-O, Oscar Mayer); beverages (Maxwell House, Kool-Aid, Crystal Light); beer (Miller, Icehouse, Red Dog)

PHILLIPS-VAN HEUSEN CORPORATION

1290 Avenue of the Americas
New York, NY 10104-0101
Chm, Pres & CEO: Bruce J. Klatsky
VP HR: Eugene O. Kessler
Employees: 12,900

Phone: 212-541-5200
Fax: 212-468-7064

Jobs Cut Last Year: 900 (-6.5%)

Apparel - men's & women's shirts, sweaters, neckwear, outerwear, footwear & accessories

PHOTOCIRCUITS CORPORATION

31 Sea Cliff Ave.
New York, NY 11542
Pres & CEO: John Endee
Dir HR: Robert Potorski
Employees: 2,400

Phone: 516-674-1000
Fax: 516-674-1383

Jobs Added Last Year: 400 (+20.0%)

Electrical components - printed circuit boards

THE PORT AUTHORITY OF NY AND NJ

One World Trade Center
New York, NY 10048
Exec Dir: George J. Marlin
Dir HR: Louis J. LaCapra
Employees: 9,250

Phone: 212-435-7000
Fax: 212-435-4660

Jobs Added Last Year: 50 (+0.5%)

Diversified operations - airport, rail passenger, bus terminal & marine terminal operations; real estate operations (World Trade Center); cargo handling

PRICELLULAR CORPORATION

45 Rockefeller Plaza
New York, NY 10020
Pres: Robert Price
VP & Corp Sec: Kim I. Pressman
Employees: 350

Phone: 212-459-0800
Fax: 212-245-3058

Jobs Added Last Year: 220 (+169.2%)

Telecommunications services - cellular telephone systems

PRO-FAC COOPERATIVE, INC.

90 Linden Place, PO Box 681
Rochester, NY 14603
Pres & Dir: Bruce R. Fox
VP HR: Lois Warlick-Jarvie
Employees: 4,752

Phone: 716-383-1850
Fax: 716-383-1281

Jobs Added Last Year: 427 (+9.9%)

Food - canned vegetables & fruits

RAINBOW APPAREL COMPANY

1000 Pennsylvania Ave.
New York, NY 11207
CEO: Joseph Chehebar
Dir HR: Louis Laiken
Employees: 8,050

Phone: 718-485-3000
Fax: 718-485-3807

Jobs Added Last Year: 50 (+0.6%)

Retail - women's clothing stores

THE READER'S DIGEST ASSOCIATION

Reader's Digest Rd.
Pleasantville, NY 10570-7000
Chm & CEO: James P. Schadt
SVP HR: Glenda K. Burkhardt
Employees: 6,200

Phone: 914-238-1000
Fax: 914-238-4559

Jobs Cut Last Year: 500 (-7.5%)

Publishing - periodicals (#1 magazine worldwide: Reader's Digest), condensed best-selling & how-to books, videos & CD-ROMs

RELIANCE GROUP HOLDINGS, INC.

55 E. 52nd St.
New York, NY 10055
Chm & CEO: Saul P. Steinberg
VP HR: Joel H. Rothwax
Employees: 9,165

Phone: 212-909-1100
Fax: 212-909-1864

Jobs Cut Last Year: 510 (-5.3%)

Insurance - property & casualty & title

RENCO GROUP INC.

45 Rockefeller Plaza
New York, NY 10111
Pres & CEO: Ira L. Rennert
VP Law: Dennis Sadlowski
Employees: 6,995

Phone: 212-541-6000
Fax: 212-541-6197

Jobs Cut Last Year: 5 (-0.1%)

Diversified operations - steel (WCI Steel); furniture; cages; all terrain vehicles (Hummer)

RESTAURANT ASSOCIATES CORPORATION

120 W. 45th St. Phone: 212-789-8100
New York, NY 10036 Fax: 212-302-8032
Pres & CEO: Nick Valenti
Dir HR: M. Hunt
Employees: 9,000
Jobs Added Last Year: —

Retail - themed restaurants in New York (Cafe Centro, Trattoria), steakhouses in New Jersey & New York (Charlie Brown's) & Mexican restaurants in California (Acapulco)

REVLON, INC.

625 Madison Ave. Phone: 212-527-4000
New York, NY 10022 Fax: 212-525-6946
Chm & CEO: Jerry M. Levin
Dir HR: Ron Dunbar
Employees: 14,000
Jobs Cut Last Year: 300 (-2.1%)

Cosmetics (#2 worldwide)

RICH PRODUCTS CORPORATION

1150 Niagara St. Phone: 716-878-8000
Buffalo, NY 14213 Fax: 716-878-8266
Chm: Robert E. Rich Sr.
VP HR: Brian Townson
Employees: 6,500
Jobs Cut Last Year: 500 (-7.1%)

Diversified operations - soybean-based creamer (Coffee Rich); frozen foods; pro sports (Buffalo Bisons [AAA baseball] and Sabres [hockey]); radio broadcasting

THE RIESE ORGANIZATION

162 W. 34th St. Phone: 212-536-7400
New York, NY 10001 Fax: 212-737-0492
CEO: Dennis Riese
Dir HR: Andrew Johnson
Employees: 5,150
Jobs Added Last Year: 150 (+3.0%)

Retail - fast-food & casual-theme franchised restaurants (TGI Fridays, Houlihan's, Dunkin' Donuts)

RJR NABISCO HOLDINGS CORP.

1301 Avenue of the Americas Phone: 212-258-5600
New York, NY 10019-6013 Fax: 212-969-9173
Chm, Pres & CEO: Steven F. Goldstone
SVP HR & Admin: Gerald I. Angowitz
Employees: 76,000
Jobs Added Last Year: 5,400 (+7.6%)

Tobacco - cigarettes (Camel, Doral, Salem & Winston); food products

ROBOTIC VISION SYSTEMS, INC.

425 Rabro Dr. East Phone: 516-273-9700
Hauppauge, NY 11788 Fax: 516-273-1167
Chm, Pres & CEO: Pat V. Costa
Dir HR: Pat Jennison
Employees: 302
Jobs Added Last Year: 174 (+135.9%)

Industrial automation & robotics - automated 3-dimensional vision-based systems for inspection & measurement

Up Software, Inc. — http://www.upsoftware.com/

An in-depth profile of this company is available to subscribers on Hoover's Online at www.hoovers.com.

253

SAKS HOLDINGS, INC.

12 E. 49th St.
New York, NY 10017
Chm & CEO: Philip B. Miller
EVP HR: Owen Dorsey
Employees: 11,000
Phone: 212-940-4048
Fax: 212-940-4299

Jobs Added Last Year: 800 (+7.8%)

Retail - major department stores (46 units: Saks Fifth Avenue); off-price clearance centers (Off 5th); mail order catalogs (Off 5th, Folio)

SALOMON INC

7 World Trade Center
New York, NY 10048
Chm & CEO: Robert E. Denham
Mng Dir HR: Ed Weihenmayer
Employees: 8,439
Phone: 212-783-7000
Fax: 212-783-2110

Jobs Cut Last Year: 638 (-7.0%)

Financial - investment banking, global securities & commodities trading & oil refining

SBARRO, INC.

763 Larkfield Rd.
Commack, NY 11725
Pres & Treas: Anthony Sbarro
VP HR: James M. O'Shea
Employees: 7,700
Phone: 516-864-0200
Fax: 516-462-9058

Jobs Cut Last Year: 1,400 (-15.4%)

Retail - cafeteria-style pizza & pasta restaurants in airports, malls & universities

SCHLUMBERGER LIMITED

277 Park Ave.
New York, NY 10172-0266
Chm, Pres & CEO: D. Euan Baird
VP Personnel: Pierre E. Bismuth
Employees: 51,000
Phone: 212-350-9400
Fax: 212-350-9564

Jobs Added Last Year: 3,000 (+6.3%)

Oil & gas - production enhancement & monitoring services

SCHOLASTIC CORPORATION

555 Broadway
New York, NY 10012-3999
Chm, Pres & CEO: Richard Robinson
VP HR: Larry V. Holland
Employees: 5,636
Phone: 212-343-6100
Fax: 212-343-6928

Jobs Added Last Year: 1,021 (+22.1%)

Publishing - books (The Baby-Sitters Club, The Magic School Bus) & periodicals; online services for schools (Scholastic Network)

SEQUA CORPORATION

200 Park Ave.
New York, NY 10166
Chm & CEO: Norman E. Alexander
VP HR: Michael F. Robilotto
Employees: 8,700
Phone: 212-986-5500
Fax: 212-370-1969

Jobs Cut Last Year: 500 (-5.4%)

Diversified operations - aerospace, machinery, metal-coating & specialty-chemical products

SHOREWOOD PACKAGING CORP.

277 Park Ave.
New York, NY 10172
Chm & CEO: Paul B. Shore
No central personnel officer
Employees: 2,700
Phone: 212-371-1500
Fax: 212-752-5610

Jobs Added Last Year: 500 (+22.7%)

Paper & paper products - paperboard packaging for the cosmetics, home video, music, software, tobacco, toiletries & general consumer markets

SIMON & SCHUSTER INC.

1230 Avenue of the Americas
New York, NY 10020
Pres & CEO: Jonathon Newcomb
SVP HR: Benjamin Roter
Employees: 10,200
Phone: 212-698-7000
Fax: 212-632-8090

Jobs Added Last Year: 700 (+7.4%)

Publishing - books (#1 worldwide) for the educational (#1 in US), consumer, business, reference & professional markets; online service for consumer books

SOVRAN SELF STORAGE, INC.

5166 Main St.
Williamsville, NY 14221
Pres & CEO: Kenneth F. Myszka
Controller: Steve Palmeri
Employees: 230
Phone: 716-633-1850
Fax: 716-633-1860

Jobs Added Last Year: 71 (+44.7%)

Leasing - enclosed self-storage space in the eastern US for residential & commercial users on a month-to-month rental basis

STARRETT CORPORATION

909 Third Ave.
New York, NY 10022
Pres: Irving Fischer
Dir HR: Evelyn F. Betlesky
Employees: 1,486
Phone: 212-751-3100
Fax: 212-759-7699

Jobs Added Last Year: 386 (+35.1%)

Building - single- & multifamily homes in Florida & Puerto Rico; institutional, office & residential buildings in New York City; mortgage financing

STATE UNIVERSITY OF NEW YORK

State University Plaza　　　Phone: 518-443-5311
Albany, NY 12246　　　　　Fax: 518-443-5322
Interim Chancellor: John W. Ryan
Assoc Vice Chancellor HR: Thomas M. Mannix
Employees: 48,300
Jobs Added Last Year: 106 (+0.2%)

University

STONE & WEBSTER, INCORPORATED

250 W. 34th St.　　　　　Phone: 212-290-7500
New York, NY 10119　　　Fax: 212-290-7507
CEO: H. Kerner
Dir HR: Darlene Lucas
Employees: 5,000
Jobs Added Last Year: 0

Construction - engineering & consulting services; construction & full environmental services for power, industrial, governmental, transportation & civil works projects

TELEPORT COMMUNICATIONS GROUP INC.

One Teleport Dr.　　　　　Phone: 718-355-2000
Staten Island, NY 10311-1011　Fax: 718-355-4876
Chm, Pres, CEO & COO: Robert Annunziata
HR Recruiter: Wayne Balnicki
Employees: 1,499
Jobs Added Last Year: 374 (+33.2%)

Telecommunications services - local services to long-distance carriers & resellers & wireless communications companies

TEXACO INC.

2000 Westchester Ave.　　Phone: 914-253-4000
White Plains, NY 10650　　Fax: 914-253-7753
Chm & CEO: Peter I. Bijur
VP HR: John D. Ambler
Employees: 28,247
Jobs Cut Last Year: 1,466 (-4.9%)

Oil & gas - international integrated

TIFFANY & CO.

727 5th Ave.　　　　　　Phone: 212-755-8000
New York, NY 10022　　　Fax: 212-605-4465
Chm & CEO: William R. Chaney
VP HR: Michael H. Mitchell
Employees: 3,656
Jobs Added Last Year: 350 (+10.6%)

Retail - fine jewelry, timepieces, sterling silverware, china, crystal, stationery, writing instruments, fragrances, leather goods, scarves & ties

TIME WARNER INC.

75 Rockefeller Plaza　　　Phone: 212-484-8000
New York, NY 10019　　　Fax: 212-956-2847
Chm & CEO: Gerald M. Levin
VP Admin: Carolyn McCandless
Employees: 65,500
Jobs Added Last Year: 12,200 (+22.9%)

Publishing - periodicals (Time, Money, People, Sports Illustrated) & books (Warner); movies (Warner Brothers); cable TV (#2 in US); cable programming (HBO, Cinemax); music (Atlantic, Elektra)

TLC BEATRICE INTERNATIONAL HOLDINGS, INC.

9 W. 57th St.　　　　　　Phone: 212-756-8900
New York, NY 10019　　　Fax: 212-888-3093
Chm & CEO: Loida N. Lewis
VP: Rene S. Meilly
Employees: 4,500
Jobs Added Last Year: 200 (+4.7%)

Food - wholesale & retail distribution, grocery product marketing & manufacturing, primarily in Europe

TOLLMAN HUNDLEY HOTELS

100 Summit Lake Dr.　　Phone: 914-747-3636
Valhalla, NY 10595　　　Fax: 914-747-1938
CEO: Monty Hundley
Mgr HR: Tom Damewood
Employees: 7,140
Jobs Added Last Year: 140 (+2.0%)

Hotels & motels

TOWER AIR, INC.

J. F. K. International Airport, Hangar #17　Phone: 718-553-4300
Jamaica, NY 11430-2478　Fax: 718-553-4312
Chm, Pres & CEO: Morris K. Nachtomi
Dir HR: Pamela Marett
Employees: 1,842
Jobs Added Last Year: 475 (+34.7%)

Transportation - scheduled-service & charter-service airline

TOWERS PERRIN

245 Park Ave.　　　　　Phone: 212-309-3400
New York, NY 10167　　　Fax: 212-309-3760
Chm, Pres & CEO: John T. Lynch
Mgr HR: Ken Ranftle
Employees: 5,050
Jobs Added Last Year: 50 (+1.0%)

Consulting & reinsurance

 An in-depth profile of this company is available to subscribers on Hoover's Online at www.hoovers.com.

255

TRAVELERS GROUP INC.

388 Greenwich St.
New York, NY 10013
Chm & CEO: Sanford I. Weill
EVP HR: Barry L. Mannes
Employees: 47,600

Phone: 212-816-8000
Fax: 212-816-8915

Jobs Cut Last Year: 4,400 (-8.5%)

Insurance - property & casualty; retail brokerage (Smith Barney Shearson)

TRIARC COMPANIES, INC.

900 Third Ave.
New York, NY 10022
Chm & CEO: Nelson Peltz
HR Mgr: Maura Buzzard
Employees: 10,275

Phone: 212-230-3000
Fax: 212-230-3023

Jobs Cut Last Year: 975 (-8.7%)

Diversified operations - textiles; soft drink concentrates (Royal Crown Cola); restaurants (Arby's); gas distribution

TRUMP ORGANIZATION

725 Fifth Ave.
New York, NY 10022-2519
Chm: Donald J. Trump
No central personnel officer
Employees: 19,000

Phone: 212-832-2000
Fax: 212-935-0141

Jobs Added Last Year: 0

Diversified operations - hotels (Plaza), casinos (Trump Taj Mahal) & real estate (Trump Tower, Empire State Building)

UIS, INC.

600 Fifth Ave., 27th Fl.
New York, NY 10020
Chm, Pres & CEO: Andrew E. Pietrini
Dir HR: Joseph F. Arrigo
Employees: 8,255

Phone: 212-581-7660
Fax: 212-581-7517

Jobs Added Last Year: 155 (+1.9%)

Diversified - auto parts; candy (Necco wafers)

UNAPIX ENTERTAINMENT, INC.

500 Fifth Ave., 46th Fl.
New York, NY 10110
Pres & CEO: David M. Fox
No central personnel officer
Employees: 55

Phone: 212-575-7070
Fax: 212-575-6869

Jobs Added Last Year: 17 (+44.7%)

Motion pictures & services - licensing of movies, TV programs, home video & educational products

UNIFLEX INC.

383 W. John St.
Hicksville, NY 11802
Chm & CEO: Herbert Barry
VP Fin & Treas: Robert Gugliotta
Employees: 380

Phone: 516-932-2000
Fax: 516-932-3129

Jobs Added Last Year: 100 (+35.7%)

Containers - plastic packaging products

THE UNIVERSITY OF ROCHESTER

Administration Bldg.
Rochester, NY 14627
Pres & CEO: Thomas H. Jackson
Dir Personnel: B. E. Donbaugh
Employees: 11,956

Phone: 716-275-2121
Fax: 716-275-2190

Jobs Added Last Year: 303 (+2.6%)

University

VARITY CORPORATION

672 Delaware Ave.
Buffalo, NY 14209-2202
Chm & CEO: Victor A. Rice
VP Mgmt Resourcing: Arthur A. Rogers
Employees: 9,800

Phone: 716-888-8000
Fax: 716-888-8010

Jobs Cut Last Year: 711 (-6.8%)

Automotive & trucking - antilock braking devices, door-lock components, diesel engines & electromechanical sensors

VIACOM INC.

1515 Broadway
New York, NY 10036
Chm & CEO: Sumner M. Redstone
SVP HR & Admin: William A. Roskin
Employees: 81,700

Phone: 212-258-6000
Fax: 212-258-6354

Jobs Added Last Year: 11,700 (+16.7%)

Diversified operations - information & entertainment operations, including broadcasting, film, cable TV, publishing, video rentals (Blockbuster) & theme parks

THE WARNACO GROUP, INC.

90 Park Ave.
New York, NY 10016
Chm, Pres & CEO: Linda J. Wachner
Dir HR: Lissa Law
Employees: 16,200

Phone: 212-661-1300
Fax: 212-370-0832

Jobs Added Last Year: 1,400 (+9.5%)

Apparel - women's intimate apparel (Warner's, Calvin Klein, Olga, Valentino Intimo) & men's apparel (Chaps by Ralph Lauren, Christian Dior) & accessories (Calvin Klein)

WEGMANS FOOD MARKETS INC.

1500 Brooks Ave.
Rochester, NY 14624
Chm & CEO: Robert B. Wegman
Dir HR: Gerald Pierce
Employees: 15,000
Jobs Cut Last Year: 584 (-3.7%)

Retail - supermarkets

Phone: 716-328-2550
Fax: 716-464-4626

WESTVACO CORPORATION

299 Park Ave.
New York, NY 10171
Chm, Pres & CEO: John A. Luke Jr.
VP HR: Robert J. Furnas
Employees: 13,030
Jobs Cut Last Year: 1,140 (-8.0%)

Phone: 212-688-5000
Fax: 212-318-5050

Paper & paper products - bleached & unbleached paper, paperboard & packaging products; specialty chemicals

WELLSFORD RESIDENTIAL PROPERTY TRUST

610 Fifth Ave., 7th Fl.
New York, NY 10020
Pres & CEO: Edward Lowenthal
HR Mgr: Linda Jarnagin
Employees: 540
Jobs Added Last Year: 260 (+92.9%)

Phone: 212-333-2300
Fax: 212-333-2323

Real estate investment trust - multifamily properties in the Southwest & Pacific Northwest

WESTINGHOUSE/CBS GROUP

51 W. 52nd St.
New York, NY 10019-6188
Pres & CEO: Peter A. Lund
SVP HR: Joan Showalter
Employees: 9,000
Jobs Added Last Year: 2,600 (+40.6%)

Phone: 212-975-4321
Fax: 212-975-8714

Broadcasting - radio & TV

WHX CORPORATION

110 E. 59th St.
New York, NY 10022
Pres: J. L. Wareham
Dir HR: Kathy Beerf
Employees: 5,996
Jobs Added Last Year: —

Phone: 212-355-5200
Fax: 212-355-5336

Steel - production

WILLIAM GREENBERG JR. DESSERTS & CAFES, INC.

533 W. 47th St.
New York, NY 10036
Chm & CEO: Maria M. Marfuggi
Office Mgr: Delia Wallace
Employees: 62
Jobs Added Last Year: 14 (+29.2%)

Phone: 212-586-2826
Fax: 212-586-2418

Food - pastries, cakes, cookies & other desserts; wholesale bakery products for restaurants, hotels & corporate dining facilities

IntelliMatch — http://www.intellimatch.com/

WINSTAR COMMUNICATIONS, INC.

230 Park Ave., 31st Fl., Ste. 3126
New York, NY 10169
Phone: 212-687-7577
Fax: 212-687-1565
Chm & CEO: William J. Rouhana Jr.
EVP & CFO: Fredric E. von Stange
Employees: 173
Jobs Added Last Year: 81 (+88.0%)

Telecommunications services - long-distance services; wireless network

WOOLWORTH CORPORATION

Woolworth Bldg., 233 Broadway
New York, NY 10279-0003
Phone: 212-553-2000
Fax: 212-553-2042
Chm & CEO: Roger N. Farah
SVP HR: John F. Gillespie
Employees: 94,000
Jobs Cut Last Year: 25,000 (-21.0%)

Retail - discount & variety, athletic footwear

WORLD COLOR PRESS, INC.

101 Park Ave., 19th Fl.
New York, NY 10178
Phone: 212-986-2440
Fax: 212-455-9266
Chm, Pres & CEO: Robert G. Burton
EVP, Chief Legal & Administrative Officer & Sec: Jennifer L. Adams
Employees: 8,200
Jobs Added Last Year: 900 (+12.3%)

Printing - consumer magazines & catalogs

W.W. NORTON & COMPANY, INC.

500 Fifth Ave.
New York, NY 10110
Phone: 212-354-5500
Fax: 212-869-0856
Pres: W. Drake McFeely
Personnel Mgr: Lisa Gaeth
Employees: 400
Jobs Added Last Year: 80 (+25.0%)

Publishing - trade, college, professional & medical books

YAR COMMUNICATIONS, INC.

220 Fifth Ave.
New York, NY 10001
Phone: 212-447-4000
Fax: 212-447-4020
CEO: Yuri Radzievsky
No central personnel officer
Employees: 150
Jobs Added Last Year: 30 (+25.0%)

Multicultural advertising & marketing

YOUNG & RUBICAM INC.

285 Madison Ave.
New York, NY 10017-6486
Phone: 212-210-3000
Fax: 212-370-3796
Chm & CEO: Peter A. Georgescu
EVP & Dir People Svcs Worldwide: Robert Wells
Employees: 10,404
Jobs Added Last Year: 472 (+4.8%)

Advertising & communications

NORTH CAROLINA

ALEX LEE INC.

120 Fourth St. SW
Hickory, NC 28602
Phone: 704-323-4424
Fax: 704-323-4435
Chm & CEO: Boyd Lee George
VP HR: Glenn Debiasi
Employees: 5,400
Jobs Added Last Year: —

Food - wholesale

BELK STORES SERVICES, INC.

2801 W. Tyvola Rd.
Charlotte, NC 28217
Phone: 704-357-1000
Fax: 704-357-1876
Chm: John M. Belk
SVP HR: Thomas M. Belk Jr.
Employees: 18,000
Jobs Added Last Year: 0

Retail - regional department stores

BURLINGTON INDUSTRIES, INC.

3330 W. Friendly Ave.
Greensboro, NC 27410
Phone: 910-379-2000
Fax: 910-379-4504
Pres & CEO: George W. Henderson III
VP HR & PR: James M. Guin
Employees: 22,500
Jobs Cut Last Year: 1,300 (-5.5%)

Textiles - worsted fabrics, worsted blend fabrics, knitted fabrics & synthetic yarns

CAROLINA POWER & LIGHT CO.

411 Fayetteville St.
Raleigh, NC 27601
Chm & CEO: Sherwood H. Smith Jr.
SVP HR: Cecil L. Goodnight
Employees: 7,812
Jobs Cut Last Year: 88 (-1.1%)

Phone: 919-546-6111
Fax: 919-546-7678

Utility - electric power

THE CATO CORPORATION

8100 Denmark Rd.
Charlotte, NC 28273-5975
Chm & CEO: Wayland H. Cato Jr.
SVP HR & Asst Sec: Stephen R. Clark
Employees: 6,600
Jobs Added Last Year: 0

Phone: 704-554-8510
Fax: 704-551-7573

Retail - women's apparel (Cato, Cato Fashions, Cato Plus, It's Fashion!)

COLLINS & AIKMAN CORPORATION

701 McCullough Dr.
Charlotte, NC 28262
CEO: Thomas E. Hannah
VP HR: Harold Sunday
Employees: 11,700
Jobs Cut Last Year: 300 (-2.5%)

Phone: 704-548-2382
Fax: 704-548-2360

Textiles - automotive seat covers, upholstery fabrics, wallcoverings & decorative furnishings

CONE MILLS CORPORATION

1201 Maple St.
Greensboro, NC 27405
Pres & CEO: J. Patrick Danahy
VP HR: James S. Butner
Employees: 7,900
Jobs Cut Last Year: 200 (-2.5%)

Phone: 910-379-6220
Fax: 910-379-6287

Textiles - denim, flannel & chamois fabric

DUKE POWER COMPANY

422 S. Church St.
Charlotte, NC 28242-0001
Chm & CEO: William H. Grigg
VP Organization Effectiveness: Christopher C. Rolfe
Employees: 17,121
Jobs Added Last Year: 69 (+0.4%)

Phone: 704-594-0887
Fax: 704-382-3814

Utility - electric power

DUKE UNIVERSITY

Durham, NC 27706
Pres: Nannerl O. Keohane
Dir HR: Bill Ald
Employees: 22,500
Jobs Added Last Year: —

Phone: 919-684-8111
Fax: 919-684-8547

University

EXIDE ELECTRONICS GROUP, INC.

8609 Six Forks Rd.
Raleigh, NC 27615
Pres & CEO: James A. Risher
VP HR: Sally Odle
Employees: 1,700
Jobs Added Last Year: 300 (+21.4%)

Phone: 919-872-3020
Fax: 919-870-3100

Electrical products - uninterruptible power systems (#1 worldwide) & related equipment; power management & facilities-monitoring software to provide backup during power outages

FAMILY DOLLAR STORES, INC.

10401 Old Monroe Rd., PO Box 1017
Matthews, NC 28201-1017
Chm, CEO & Treas: Leon Levine
VP HR: Terry A. Cozort
Employees: 18,500
Jobs Added Last Year: 2,000 (+12.1%)

Phone: 704-847-6961
Fax: 704-847-5534

Retail - self-service discount & variety soft goods

FIELDCREST CANNON, INC.

326 E. Stadium Dr.
Eden, NC 27288
Chm & CEO: James M. Fitzgibbons
VP HR: Richard E. Reece
Employees: 13,160
Jobs Cut Last Year: 766 (-5.5%)

Phone: 910-627-3000
Fax: 910-627-3133

Textiles - bed & bath products, carpets & rugs

FIRST UNION CORPORATION

One First Union Center
Charlotte, NC 28288-0013
Chm & CEO: Edward E. Crutchfield
EVP HR: Don R. Johnson
Employees: 44,536
Jobs Added Last Year: 12,678 (+39.8%)

Phone: 704-374-6565
Fax: 704-374-2140

Banks - Southeast

 An in-depth profile of this company is available to subscribers on Hoover's Online at www.hoovers.com.

259

FOOD LION, INC.

2110 Executive Dr., PO Box 1330
Salisbury, NC 28145-1330
Chm, Pres & CEO: Tom E. Smith
VP HR & Asst Sec: Eugene R. McKinley
Employees: 69,345

Phone: 704-633-8250
Fax: 704-636-5024

Jobs Added Last Year: 4,505 (+6.9%)

Retail - supermarkets

GLENAYRE TECHNOLOGIES, INC.

5935 Carnegie Blvd.
Charlotte, NC 28209
Pres & CEO: Ramon D. Ardizzone
VP HR: Beverly W. Cox
Employees: 1,850

Phone: 704-553-0038
Fax: 212-643-8921

Jobs Added Last Year: 750 (+68.2%)

Telecommunications equipment - switches, transmitters, controls & software used in mobile data transmission, paging & voice-messaging applications

GUILFORD MILLS, INC.

4925 W. Market St.
Greensboro, NC 27407
Chm, Pres, CEO & COO: Charles A. Hayes
VP HR: William R. Houser
Employees: 5,335

Phone: 910-316-4000
Fax: 910-316-4059

Jobs Cut Last Year: 75 (-1.4%)

Textiles - warp-knit fabrics, synthetic yarn, nylon, acetate & polyester; elastomeric & circular knit fabrics for swimwear, dress & sportswear

HIGHWOODS PROPERTIES, INC.

3100 Smoketree Ct., Ste. 700
Raleigh, NC 27604
Pres & CEO: Ronald P. Gibson
Dir HR: Ronald P. Gibson
Employees: 124

Phone: 919-872-4924
Fax: 919-876-2448

Jobs Added Last Year: 39 (+45.9%)

Real estate investment trust - office & warehouse properties

INGLES MARKETS, INCORPORATED

PO Box 6676
Asheville, NC 28816
Chm & CEO: Robert P. Ingle
HR Mgr: Pat Boyd
Employees: 10,010

Phone: 704-669-2941
Fax: 704-669-3667

Jobs Added Last Year: 58 (+0.6%)

Retail - supermarkets

ITHACA HOLDINGS, INC.

PO Box 620
Wilkesboro, NC 28697
Pres & CEO: Jim D. Waller
Dir HR: Steve Propst
Employees: 11,850

Phone: 910-667-5231
Fax: 910-667-6661

Jobs Added Last Year: 1,550 (+15.0%)

Textiles - undergarments & apparel

LABORATORY CORP. OF AMERICA HOLDINGS

1447 York Ct.
Burlington, NC 27215
Pres & CEO: James B. Powell
EVP HR: Robert E. Whalen
Employees: 24,600

Phone: 910-584-5171
Fax: 910-222-1568

Jobs Added Last Year: 4,600 (+23.0%)

Medical services - clinical laboratory services (#1 worldwide) for the diagnosis, monitoring & treatment of disease

LADD FURNITURE, INC.

One Plaza Center, Box HP-3
High Point, NC 27261-1500
Pres & CEO: Fred L. Schuermann Jr.
Dir HR: Keith Gsell
Employees: 6,600

Phone: 910-889-0333
Fax: 910-889-5839

Jobs Cut Last Year: 1,100 (-14.3%)

Furniture - wood, metal & upholstered furniture

LANCE, INC.

8600 S. Boulevard, PO Box 32368
Charlotte, NC 28232
Pres & CEO: P. A. Stroup III
VP Admin: T. B. Horack
Employees: 5,041

Phone: 704-554-1421
Fax: 704-554-5586

Jobs Cut Last Year: 777 (-13.4%)

Food - cookies, cracker & cookie sandwiches, peanuts, potato & corn chips, popcorn, cakes, candies, chewing gum, beef snacks & sausages

LOWE'S COMPANIES, INC.

State Hwy. 268 East (Elkin Hwy.)
North Wilkesboro, NC 28659
Pres & CEO: Leonard G. Herring
VP HR: Perry G. Jennings
Employees: 44,546

Phone: 910-651-4000
Fax: 910-651-4766

Jobs Added Last Year: 6,991 (+18.6%)

Building products - retail home decorating, electronic & construction products

MEDCATH INCORPORATED

7621 Little Ave., Ste. 106
Charlotte, NC 28226
Pres & CEO: Stephen R. Puckett
CFO & Sec: Daniel L. Belongia
Employees: 524

Phone: 704-543-3060
Fax: 704-541-2615

Jobs Added Last Year: 419 (+399.0%)

Medical services - heart-care hospital; cardiology & cardiovascular services for heart specialists

MEDIC COMPUTER SYSTEMS, INC.

8601 Six Forks Rd.
Raleigh, NC 27615-2965
Pres & CEO: John P. McConnell
Mgr HR: Jan Guy
Employees: 952

Phone: 919-847-8102
Fax: 919-846-1555

Jobs Added Last Year: 252 (+36.0%)

Computers - business software for physicians' offices

NATIONSBANK CORPORATION

100 N. Tryon St., 18th Fl.
Charlotte, NC 28255
Chm & CEO: Hugh L. McColl Jr.
HR Mgr: Raichelle Hall
Employees: 58,322

Phone: 704-386-5000
Fax: 704-386-1709

Jobs Cut Last Year: 3,162 (-5.1%)

Banks - money center

NUCOR CORPORATION

2100 Rexford Rd.
Charlotte, NC 28211
Chm: F. Kenneth Iverson
Personnel Svcs Mgr: Jim Coblin
Employees: 6,200

Phone: 704-366-7000
Fax: 704-362-4001

Jobs Added Last Year: 300 (+5.1%)

Steel - hot-rolled, cold-rolled & cold-finished steel products

OAKWOOD HOMES CORPORATION

7800 McCloud Rd.
Greensboro, NC 27409-9634
Pres & CEO: Nicholas J. St. George
SVP HR: Tom Brinkley
Employees: 5,195

Phone: 910-664-2400
Fax: 910-632-3224

Jobs Added Last Year: 1,595 (+44.3%)

Building - manufactured homes

PCA INTERNATIONAL, INC.

815 Matthews-Mint Hill Rd.
Matthews, NC 28105
Pres & CEO: John Grosso
VP HR: Richard Brunson
Employees: 3,300

Phone: 704-847-8011
Fax: 704-847-8010

Jobs Added Last Year: 200 (+6.5%)

Retail - photographic portraits of children, adults & families

QUINTILES TRANSNATIONAL CORP.

4709 Creekstone Dr.
Riverbirch Bldg., Ste. 300
Durham, NC 27703-8411
Chm & CEO: Dennis Gillings
VP HR: Phil Newton
Employees: 2,025

Phone: 919-941-2000
Fax: 919-941-9113

Jobs Added Last Year: 885 (+77.6%)

Medical services - clinical-trial management, preclinical testing & formulation of clinical-trial drugs

REGIONAL ACCEPTANCE CORPORATION

3004 S. Memorial Dr.
Greenville, NC 27834
Pres & CEO: William R. Stallings Sr.
COO: Joe Lacaunota
Employees: 140

Phone: 919-756-2148
Fax: 919-355-3827

Jobs Added Last Year: 40 (+40.0%)

Financial - auto loans & insurance services

ROSE'S STORES, INC.

218 S. Garnett St.
Henderson, NC 27536
Chm, Pres & CEO: R. Edward Anderson
Dir HR: Camilla S. Wheeler
Employees: 8,000

Phone: 919-430-2600
Fax: 919-492-4226

Jobs Cut Last Year: 800 (-9.1%)

Retail - discount general merchandise (113 units)

RUDDICK CORPORATION

2000 Two First Union Center
Charlotte, NC 28282
Pres: John W. Copeland
VP Personnel, Harris Teeter: C. Lavette Teeter Sr.
Employees: 20,200

Phone: 704-372-5404
Fax: 704-372-6409

Jobs Added Last Year: 1,110 (+5.8%)

Diversified operations - supermarkets (Harris Teeter); sewing thread (American & Efrid); business forms & labels (Jordan Graphics, Inc.); venture capital (Ruddick Investment Company)

 An in-depth profile of this company is available to subscribers on Hoover's Online at www.hoovers.com.

261

STANDARD COMMERCIAL CORPORATION

2201 Miller Rd.
Wilson, NC 27893
Pres & CEO: J. Alec G. Murray
HR Mgr: Nancy Haynes
Employees: 2,285

Phone: 919-291-5507
Fax: 919-237-1109

Jobs Added Last Year: 280 (+14.0%)

Tobacco - leaf tobacco processing; wholesale & retail building materials

TRION, INC.

101 McNeill Rd.
Sanford, NC 27331-0760
Pres & CEO: Steven L. Schneider
Dir HR: Michael P. Womble
Employees: 439

Phone: 919-775-2201
Fax: 919-774-8771

Jobs Added Last Year: 123 (+38.9%)

Machinery - indoor air cleaning equipment & equipment to electrostatically distribute thin films of lubricant, corrosion inhibitors & protective coatings to metal strips on high-speed process lines

UNIFI, INC.

7201 W. Friendly Ave.
Greensboro, NC 27410
Pres & CEO: William T. Kretzer
Dir HR: Raymond Hunt
Employees: 6,000

Phone: 910-294-4410
Fax: 910-316-5422

Jobs Added Last Year: —

Textiles - natural & synthetic yarns

UNITED DOMINION INDUSTRIES LIMITED

2300 One First Union Ctr.
Charlotte, NC 28202-6039
Chm & CEO: W. R. Holland
VP HR: Timothy J. Verhagen
Employees: 10,666

Phone: 704-347-6800
Fax: 704-347-6900

Jobs Cut Last Year: 1,334 (-11.1%)

Diversified operations - prefabricated metal buildings; aerospace components; construction; engineering

VANGUARD CELLULAR SYSTEMS, INC.

2002 Pisgah Church Rd., Ste. 300
Greensboro, NC 27455
Pres & CEO: Haynes G. Griffin
VP HR & Quality Dev: Neva J. Reavis
Employees: 1,400

Phone: 910-282-3690
Fax: 910-545-2500

Jobs Added Last Year: 350 (+33.3%)

Telecommunications services - nonwireline cellular telephone services

WACHOVIA CORPORATION

100 N. Main St.
Winston-Salem, NC 27150
Pres & CEO: Leslie M. Baker Jr.
Dir Personnel: Hector McEachern
Employees: 15,996

Phone: 910-770-5000
Fax: 910-732-7021

Jobs Added Last Year: 394 (+2.5%)

Banks - Southeast

Job Web — http://www.jobweb.org/

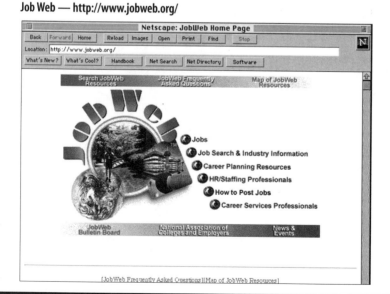

FRONTEER DIRECTORY COMPANY, INC.

216 N. 23rd St.
Bismarck, ND 58501
Pres & CEO: Dennis W. Olsen
HR Mgr: Ione Good
Employees: 287

Phone: 701-258-4970
Fax: 701-258-4258

Jobs Added Last Year: 202 (+237.6%)

Publishing - telephone directories in North & South Dakota, Montana, Idaho, Utah, Wyoming & Minnesota

LUTHERAN HEALTH SYSTEMS

4310 17th Ave. SW
Fargo, ND 58106-7500
Chm & CEO: Steven R. Orr
VP HR: Gerri Twomey
Employees: 13,800

Phone: 701-277-7500
Fax: 701-277-7636

Jobs Added Last Year: 66 (+0.5%)

Hospitals - not-for-profit system with 36 hospitals serving 17 states, primarily in the Northwest & upper Midwest

AK STEEL HOLDING CORPORATION

703 Curtis St.
Middletown, OH 45043
Pres & CEO: Richard Wardrop Jr.
Dir HR: Robert Dorenbusch
Employees: 5,762

Phone: 513-425-5000
Fax: 513-425-2676

Jobs Cut Last Year: 229 (-3.8%)

Steel - low-carbon flat-rolled steel for automotive, appliance, construction & manufacturing markets

AMCAST INDUSTRIAL CORPORATION

7887 Washington Village Dr.
Dayton, OH 45401-0098
Pres & CEO: John H. Shuey
VP HR: William J. Durbin
Employees: 2,400

Phone: 513-291-7000
Fax: 513-291-7005

Jobs Added Last Year: 300 (+14.3%)

Metal processing & fabrication

AMERICAN ANNUITY GROUP, INC.

250 E. Fifth St.
Cincinnati, OH 45202
Chm & CEO: Carl H. Lindner
EVP: Jim Mortensen
Employees: 850

Phone: 513-333-5300
Fax: 513-357-3397

Jobs Added Last Year: 410 (+93.2%)

Insurance - life underwriters

AMERICAN ELECTRIC POWER CO.

One Riverside Plaza
Columbus, OH 43215-2373
Chm, Pres & CEO: E. Linn Draper Jr.
VP HR: Rodney B. Plimpton
Employees: 18,502

Phone: 614-223-1000
Fax: 614-223-1823

Jobs Cut Last Year: 1,158 (-5.9%)

Utility - electric power

AMERICAN FINANCIAL GROUP, INC.

One E. Fourth St.
Cincinnati, OH 45202
Chm: Carl H. Lindner
VP HR: Lawrence Otto
Employees: 9,800

Phone: 513-579-2121
Fax: 513-579-2113

Jobs Cut Last Year: 45,040 (-82.1%)

Insurance - specialty property & casualty; tax-deferred annuities

AMERICAN GREETINGS CORP.

One American Rd.
Cleveland, OH 44144-2398
Chm & CEO: Morry Weiss
SVP HR: Harvey Levin
Employees: 36,800

Phone: 216-252-7300
Fax: 216-252-6777

Jobs Added Last Year: 1,200 (+3.4%)

Greeting cards & gift items

An in-depth profile of this company is available to subscribers on Hoover's Online at www.hoovers.com.

263

AMERILINK CORPORATION

1900 E. Dublin-Granville Rd.
Columbus, OH 43229
Chm, Pres & CEO: Larry R. Linhart
Dir HR: Kelly Lape
Employees: 364

Phone: 614-895-1313
Fax: 614-895-8942

Jobs Added Last Year: 102 (+38.9%)

Telecommunications equipment - cabling systems (NaCom) for the transmission of video, voice & data

BANC ONE CORPORATION

100 E. Broad St.
Columbus, OH 43271-0251
Chm & CEO: John B. McCoy
Chief HR Officer: Michael W. Hager
Employees: 46,900

Phone: 614-248-5944
Fax: 614-882-1068

Jobs Cut Last Year: 1,900 (-3.9%)

Banks - money center

BAREFOOT INC.

450 W. Wilson Bridge Rd.
Worthington, OH 43085
Pres & CEO: Patrick J. Norton
No central personnel officer
Employees: 2,950

Phone: 614-846-1800
Fax: 614-846-5142

Jobs Added Last Year: 1,250 (+73.5%)

Building - lawn care service, tree & shrub care, lawn aeration, liming & seeding

BATTELLE MEMORIAL INSTITUTE

505 King Ave.
Columbus, OH 43201-2693
Pres & CEO: Douglas E. Olesen
SVP HR: Robert W. Smith Jr.
Employees: 7,500

Phone: 614-424-6424
Fax: 614-424-5263

Jobs Cut Last Year: 1,083 (-12.6%)

Engineering - R&D services

BELDEN & BLAKE CORPORATION

5200 Stoneham Rd.
North Canton, OH 44720-1543
Chm & CEO: Henry S. Belden IV
Mgr HR: James C. Ewing
Employees: 576

Phone: 330-499-1660
Fax: 330-497-5463

Jobs Added Last Year: 139 (+31.8%)

Oil & gas - production & pipeline

THE B.F.GOODRICH COMPANY

3925 Embassy Pkwy.
Akron, OH 44333-1799
Chm & CEO: John D. Ong
VP HR: Gary L. Habegger
Employees: 12,287

Phone: 330-374-3985
Fax: 330-374-2333

Jobs Cut Last Year: 1,105 (-8.3%)

Chemicals - specialty plastics, additives, sealants, coatings & adhesives; aerospace operations, maintenance, repair & overhaul services of commercial & general aviation aircraft

BOB EVANS FARMS, INC.

3776 S. High St.
Columbus, OH 43207-0863
Chm, CEO & Sec: Daniel E. Evans
Group VP Admin & HR: James B. Radebaugh
Employees: 28,300

Phone: 614-491-2225
Fax: 614-492-4949

Jobs Added Last Year: 4,500 (+18.9%)

Retail - restaurants; pork sausage & ham products

BORDEN, INC.

180 E. Broad St.
Columbus, OH 43215
Chm & CEO: C. Robert Kidder
SVP HR & Corp Affairs: Randy D. Kautto
Employees: 27,500

Phone: 614-225-4000
Fax: 614-225-3410

Jobs Cut Last Year: 4,800 (-14.9%)

Food - dairy products, pasta (Creamette), pasta sauce (Classico), potato chips (Wise) & snacks (Cracker Jack); glue (Elmer's, Krazy Glue); packaging & industrial products

CALIBER SYSTEM, INC.

3560 W. Market St.
Akron, OH 44333
Chm, Pres & CEO: Daniel J. Sullivan
VP HR: Donald C. Brown
Employees: 25,700

Phone: 330-665-5646
Fax: 330-665-8898

Jobs Cut Last Year: 24,900 (-49.2%)

Transportation - small-package ground delivery, trucking services (Roadway Express) & air freight services

CARDINAL HEALTH, INC.

655 Metro Place South, Ste. 925
Dublin, OH 43017
Pres & CEO: John C. Walter
SVP HR: Carole W. Tomko
Employees: 4,000

Phone: 614-717-5880
Fax: 614-761-8919

Jobs Added Last Year: 500 (+14.3%)

Drugs & sundries - wholesale pharmaceuticals, surgical & hospital supplies, therapeutic plasma & other pharmaceutical, health & beauty care products; drugstores (Medicine Shoppes)

CENTERIOR ENERGY CORPORATION

6200 Oak Tree Blvd.
Independence, OH 44131
Chm, Pres & CEO: Robert J. Farling
Dir HR: John Paganie
Employees: 6,821

Phone: 216-447-3100
Fax: 216-447-3240

Jobs Added Last Year: 54 (+0.8%)

Utility - electric power

CHEMED CORPORATION

2600 Chemed Center, 255 E. Fifth St.
Cincinnati, OH 45202-4726
Chm & CEO: Edward L. Hutton
VP HR: David G. Sparks
Employees: 7,335

Phone: 513-762-6900

Jobs Added Last Year: 733 (+11.1%)

Diversified operations - sanitation & janitorial supplies, sewer maintenance services & medical products

CHIQUITA BRANDS INTERNATIONAL

250 E. Fifth St.
Cincinnati, OH 45202
Chm & CEO: Carl H. Lindner
VP HR: Jean B. Lapointe
Employees: 36,000

Phone: 513-784-8000
Fax: 513-784-8030

Jobs Cut Last Year: 4,000 (-10.0%)

Food - fruits & vegetables, including bananas, apples, citrus, tropical fruit, tomatoes, avocados & eggplant; fruit juices & flavored teas (Chiquita, Ferraro's Earth Juice, Naked Sun Tea)

CINCINNATI BELL INC.

201 E. Fourth St.
Cincinnati, OH 45201
Pres & CEO: John T. LaMacchia
SVP HR & Admin: Thomas A. Cruz
Employees: 15,000

Phone: 513-397-9900
Fax: 513-784-1613

Jobs Cut Last Year: 600 (-3.8%)

Utility - telephone service; billing services to the cellular communications industry (Cincinnati Bell Info. Systems); telephone marketing, research, fulfillment & database services (MATRIXX)

CINCINNATI FINANCIAL CORPORATION

PO Box 145496
Cincinnati, OH 45250-5496
Pres & CEO: Robert B. Morgan
Dir Personnel: Greg Ziegler
Employees: 2,289

Phone: 513-870-2000
Fax: 513-870-2088

Jobs Added Last Year: 239 (+11.7%)

Insurance - property, casualty, life, accident, health & fire

CINCINNATI MILACRON INC.

4701 Marburg Ave.
Cincinnati, OH 45209
Chm & CEO: Daniel J. Meyer
VP HR: Theodore Mauser
Employees: 11,790

Phone: 513-841-8100
Fax: 513-841-8991

Jobs Added Last Year: 3,395 (+40.4%)

Machine tools & related products

CINERGY CORP.

139 E. Fourth St.
Cincinnati, OH 45202
VC, Pres & CEO: James E. Rogers
Mgr HR Strategy: Jerry Liggett
Employees: 8,602

Phone: 513-381-2000
Fax: 513-287-4212

Jobs Cut Last Year: 266 (-3.0%)

Utility - electric power & natural gas

CINTAS CORPORATION

6800 Cintas Blvd., PO Box 625737
Cincinnati, OH 45262-5737
Pres & CEO: Robert J. Kohlhepp
VP HR: Scott D. Farmer
Employees: 9,724

Phone: 513-459-1200
Fax: 513-573-4130

Jobs Added Last Year: 1,143 (+13.3%)

Linen supply & related - uniform rental & sale

CLEVELAND-CLIFFS INC.

1100 Superior Ave.
Cleveland, OH 44114-2589
Chm, Pres & CEO: M. Thomas Moore
VP HR: Richard F. Novak
Employees: 6,224

Phone: 216-694-5700
Fax: 216-694-4880

Jobs Added Last Year: 853 (+15.9%)

Metal processing & fabrication - iron ore processing facilities; aluminum mining

COLE NATIONAL CORPORATION

5915 Landerbrook Dr.
Mayfield Heights, OH 44124
Chm, CEO & CFO: Jeffrey A. Cole
Mgr HR: Ken Braun
Employees: 9,700

Phone: 216-449-4100
Fax: 216-461-3489

Jobs Cut Last Year: 4,700 (-32.6%)

Retail - optical products & services (Cole Vision, Montgomery Ward Vision Center); specialty gifts (Things Remembered); key copying, watch repair, gifts & engraving (Cole Gift Centers)

An in-depth profile of this company is available to subscribers on Hoover's Online at www.hoovers.com.

265

COMPUSERVE CORPORATION

5000 Arlington Centre Blvd.
Columbus, OH 43220
Pres & CEO: Robert J. Massey
VP HR: Judy Reinhard
Employees: 3,500

Phone: 614-457-8600
Fax: 614-457-0348

Jobs Added Last Year: 1,000 (+40.0%)

Computers - online information service & Internet access provider

CONSOLIDATED STORES CORPORATION

300 Phillipi Rd., PO Box 28512
Columbus, OH 43228
Chm & CEO: Michael L. Glazer
SVP HR: Brad Waite
Employees: 21,633

Phone: 614-278-6800
Fax: 614-278-6676

Jobs Added Last Year: 1,934 (+9.8%)

Retail - close-out operations

COOPER TIRE & RUBBER COMPANY

Lima & Western Aves.
Findlay, OH 45840
Chm, Pres & CEO: Patrick W. Rooney
Dir Emp Relations & Dev: Darrell L. Wolfe
Employees: 8,284

Phone: 419-423-1321
Fax: 419-424-4108

Jobs Added Last Year: 412 (+5.2%)

Rubber tires

DANA CORPORATION

4500 Dorr St.
Toledo, OH 43615
Chm & CEO: Southwood J. Morcott
HR Mgr: Rick Aubry
Employees: 45,900

Phone: 419-535-4500
Fax: 419-535-4643

Jobs Added Last Year: 6,400 (+16.2%)

Automotive & trucking - axles, components & systems; driveshafts; frames & structural systems; sealing & filtration products

DIEBOLD, INCORPORATED

5995 Mayfair Rd.
North Canton, OH 44720-8077
Chm, Pres & CEO: Robert W. Mahoney
VP HR: Charles B. Scheurer
Employees: 5,178

Phone: 330-489-4000
Fax: 330-490-4549

Jobs Added Last Year: 447 (+9.4%)

Protection - security products & cameras; automatic teller machine manufacturing; product- & system-maintenance services

D.I.Y. HOME WAREHOUSE, INC.

5811 Canal Rd., Ste.180
Valley View, OH 44125
Pres & CEO: Clifford L. Reynolds
VP HR: Marilyn Hayden
Employees: 1,325

Phone: 216-328-5100
Fax: 216-328-5109

Jobs Added Last Year: 375 (+39.5%)

Building products - retail home repair & remodeling products

DRUG EMPORIUM, INC.

155 Hidden Ravines Dr.
Powell, OH 43065
Chm & CEO: David L. Kriegel
VP Admin: Jane Lagusch
Employees: 5,600

Phone: 614-548-7080
Fax: 614-548-6541

Jobs Cut Last Year: 200 (-3.4%)

Retail - health & beauty aids, OTC medications, prescription drugs, greeting cards, cosmetics & other consumable products

THE DURIRON COMPANY, INC.

3100 Research Blvd.
Dayton, OH 45420
Chm, Pres & CEO: William M. Jordan
HR Mgr: Joseph R. Weil
Employees: 3,900

Phone: 513-476-6100
Fax: 513-476-9162

Jobs Added Last Year: 1,325 (+51.5%)

Machinery - corrosion-resistant fluid movement & control equipment

EATON CORPORATION

Eaton Center
Cleveland, OH 44114-2584
Chm & CEO: Stephen R. Hardis
VP HR: Susan J. Cook
Employees: 52,000

Phone: 216-523-5000
Fax: 216-523-4787

Jobs Added Last Year: 1,000 (+2.0%)

Automotive & trucking - truck transmissions, axles, engine components, hydraulic products & controls

EDWARD J. DEBARTOLO CORP.

7655 Market St.
Youngstown, OH 44513
CEO: Edward J. DeBartolo Sr.
Dir HR: Marie Denise DeBartolo York
Employees: 12,000

Phone: 330-758-7292
Fax: 330-758-3598

Jobs Added Last Year: 0

Real estate development & management; professional footbal team (San Francisco 49ers)

THE ELDER-BEERMAN STORES CORP.

3155 El-Bee Rd.
Dayton, OH 45439
Chm & CEO: Milton E. Hartley
SVP HR: Patricia Gifford
Employees: 9,400
Phone: 513-296-2700
Fax: 513-296-2915

Jobs Added Last Year: 700 (+8.0%)

Retail - regional department stores

THE E.W. SCRIPPS COMPANY

312 Walnut St., Ste. 2800
Cincinnati, OH 45202
Chm, Pres & CEO: William R. Burleigh
SVP Fin & CFO: Daniel J. Castellini
Employees: 6,700
Phone: 513-977-3000
Fax: 513-977-3721

Jobs Cut Last Year: 1,000 (-13.0%)

Publishing - newspapers (23); TV & radio stations & cable TV systems

FABRI-CENTERS OF AMERICA, INC.

5555 Darrow Rd.
Hudson, OH 44236
Chm, Pres & CEO: Alan Rosskamm
SVP HR: Rosalind Thompson
Employees: 17,200
Phone: 216-656-2600
Fax: 216-463-6675

Jobs Cut Last Year: 400 (-2.3%)

Retail - fabric & notions

FEDERATED DEPARTMENT STORES

7 W. Seventh St.
Cincinnati, OH 45202
Chm & CEO: Allen I. Questrom
EVP Legal Svcs & HR: Thomas G. Cody
Employees: 119,100
Phone: 513-579-7000
Fax: 513-579-7555

Jobs Added Last Year: 7,400 (+6.6%)

Retail - major department stores (Bloomingdale's, Macy's, Stern's, Jordan Marsh, Rich's, Goldsmith's, Lazarus, Burdines, Bullock's, Bon Marche)

FERRO CORPORATION

1000 Lakeside Ave.
Cleveland, OH 44144-1183
Chm & CEO: Albert C. Bersticker
Dir HR: Paul Richard
Employees: 6,914
Phone: 216-641-8580
Fax: 216-696-7583

Jobs Added Last Year: 97 (+1.4%)

Paints & allied products - colors, coatings, ceramics, plastics & chemicals

FIFTH THIRD BANCORP

Fifth Third Ctr.
Cincinnati, OH 45263
Pres & CEO: George A. Schaefer Jr.
VP HR: Dan Keefe
Employees: 6,108
Phone: 513-579-5300
Fax: 513-741-8909

Jobs Added Last Year: 464 (+8.2%)

Banks - Midwest

FOREST CITY ENTERPRISES, INC.

10800 Brookpark Rd.
Cleveland, OH 44130
Pres & CEO: Charles A. Ratner
VP HR: Minta A. Monchein
Employees: 3,287
Phone: 216-267-1200
Fax: 216-931-3113

Jobs Added Last Year: 994 (+43.3%)

Real estate development

FRISCH'S RESTAURANTS, INC.

2800 Gilbert Ave.
Cincinnati, OH 45206
Pres & CEO: Craig F. Maier
VP HR: Ronald E. Heineman
Employees: 6,700
Phone: 513-961-2660
Fax: 513-559-5160

Jobs Added Last Year: 400 (+6.3%)

Retail - restaurants & drive-through service (Big Boy)

GENCORP INC.

175 Ghent Rd.
Fairlawn, OH 44333-3300
Chm, Pres & CEO: John B. Yasinsky
VP HR: Samuel W. Harmon
Employees: 11,700
Phone: 330-869-4200
Fax: 330-869-4211

Jobs Cut Last Year: 1,270 (-9.8%)

Diversified operations - molded rubber products for vehicle bodies & window sealing; polymer products; aerospace & defense products (Aerojet); solid & liquid rocket propulsion systems

GLIMCHER REALTY TRUST

20 S. Third St.
Columbus, OH 43215
Pres: David J. Glimcher
HR Coordinator: Pat Peakes
Employees: 140
Phone: 614-621-9000
Fax: 614-621-9311

Jobs Added Last Year: 42 (+42.9%)

Real estate investment trust

THE GOODYEAR TIRE & RUBBER CO.

1144 E. Market St.   Phone: 330-796-2121
Akron, OH 44316-0001   Fax: 330-796-6502
Chm, Pres, COO & CEO: Samir F. Gibara
VP HR & Total Quality Culture: Mike L. Burns
Employees: 88,790

Jobs Cut Last Year: 1,508 (-1.7%)

Rubber products - tires, industrial rubber products & rubber-related chemicals

HEALTH CARE AND RETIREMENT CORPORATION

One SeaGate   Phone: 419-252-5500
Toledo, OH 43604-2616   Fax: 419-252-5510
Chm, Pres & CEO: Paul A. Ormond
VP & Dir HR & Labor Relations: Wade B. O'Brian
Employees: 18,500

Jobs Added Last Year: 2,000 (+12.1%)

Health care - long-term care, skilled nursing & rehabilitative services

HUFFY CORPORATION

225 Byers Rd.   Phone: 513-866-6251
Miamisburg, OH 45342   Fax: 513-865-5470
Chm & CEO: Richard L. Molen
VP HR: George A. Plotner
Employees: 8,144

Jobs Added Last Year: 1,723 (+26.8%)

Leisure & recreational products - bicycles, lawn & garden tools, basketball equipment; inventory services

HUNTINGTON BANCSHARES INC.

One Huntington Ctr., 41 S. High St.   Phone: 614-480-8300
Columbus, OH 43287   Fax: 614-476-5284
Chm & CEO: Frank Wobst
VP & Dir HR: Les Ridout
Employees: 7,551

Jobs Cut Last Year: 601 (-7.4%)

Banks - Midwest

INSILCO CORPORATION

425 Metro Place North, 5th Fl.   Phone: 614-792-0468
Dublin, OH 43017   Fax: 614-791-3197
Chm, Pres & CEO: Robert L. Smialek
VP HR & Asst Sec: Les G. Jacobs
Employees: 5,032

Jobs Added Last Year: 109 (+2.2%)

Diversified operations - metal fabricating; electronics & communications; office supplies (Rolodex)

INTERNATIONAL LOTTERY, INC.

6665 Creek Rd.   Phone: 513-792-7000
Cincinnati, OH 45242   Fax: 513-792-7001
Chm & CEO: Stephen E. Raville
Dir HR: Kathleen Pomeraning
Employees: 74

Jobs Added Last Year: 15 (+25.4%)

Gambling equipment - instant lottery ticket vending machines

E-Span — http://www.espan.com/

INTERNATIONAL MANAGEMENT GROUP

One Erie View Plaza, Ste. 1300
Cleveland, OH 44114
CEO: Mark H. McCormack
VP HR: Dan Lewis
Employees: 2,000

Phone: 216-522-1200
Fax: 216-522-1145

Jobs Added Last Year: 700 (+53.8%)

Business services - sports, business & entertainment management & marketing

INTIMATE BRANDS, INC.

3 Limited Pkwy.
Columbus, OH 43230
Chm & CEO: Leslie H. Wexner
No central personnel officer
Employees: 30,800

Phone: 614-479-7101
Fax: 614-479-7079

Jobs Added Last Year: 8,800 (+40.0%)

Retail - women's intimate apparel (Victoria's Secret) & toiletries (Bath & Body Works)

INVACARE CORPORATION

899 Cleveland St., PO Box 4028
Elyria, OH 44036-2125
Chm, Pres & CEO: A. Malachi Mixon III
VP HR: Richard A. Sayers II
Employees: 3,740

Phone: 216-329-6000
Fax: 216-366-6160

Jobs Added Last Year: 447 (+13.6%)

Medical products - home medical equipment, including manual & motorized wheelchairs, motorized scooters, home care beds & respiratory products & seating & positioning products

JACOR COMMUNICATIONS, INC.

1300 PNC Ctr., 201 E. Fifth St.
Cincinnati, OH 45202
Pres & Co-COO: Randy Michaels
SVP & CFO: Jon M. Berry
Employees: 1,147

Phone: 513-621-1300
Fax: 513-621-0090

Jobs Added Last Year: 303 (+35.9%)

Broadcasting - radio (7 AM & 8 FM stations)

KEYCORP

127 Public Sq.
Cleveland, OH 44114-1306
Pres & CEO: Robert W. Gillespie
EVP Corp HR: Thomas E. Helfrich
Employees: 29,563

Phone: 216-689-3000
Fax: 216-689-0519

Jobs Added Last Year: 352 (+1.2%)

Banks - money center

THE KROGER CO.

1014 Vine St.
Cincinnati, OH 45202
Chm & CEO: Joseph A. Pichler
Group VP Labor Relations & HR: Thomas E. Murphy
Employees: 205,000

Phone: 513-762-4000
Fax: 513-762-4454

Jobs Added Last Year: 5,000 (+2.5%)

Retail - supermarkets

LANCASTER COLONY CORPORATION

37 W. Broad St.
Columbus, OH 43215
Chm & CEO: John B. Gerlach
Corp Counsel: David Segal
Employees: 6,000

Phone: 614-224-7141
Fax: 614-469-8219

Jobs Added Last Year: 400 (+7.1%)

Diversified operations - specialty foods, automotive accessories, glassware & candles

THE LIMITED, INC.

3 Limited Pkwy.
Columbus, OH 43230
Chm, Pres & CEO: Leslie H. Wexner
EVP & Dir HR: Arnold F. Kanarick
Employees: 104,000

Phone: 614-479-7000
Fax: 614-479-7080

Jobs Cut Last Year: 1,600 (-1.5%)

Retail - apparel (Lerner New York, Express, Abercrombie & Fitch)

THE LINCOLN ELECTRIC COMPANY

22801 St. Clair Ave.
Cleveland, OH 44117-1199
Chm & CEO: Donald F. Hastings
VP HR: Ray Vogt
Employees: 6,000

Phone: 216-481-8100
Fax: 216-486-1751

Jobs Added Last Year: 307 (+5.4%)

Machinery - welding & cutting equipment & electric motors

THE LTV CORPORATION

25 W. Prospect Ave.
Cleveland, OH 44115
Chm, Pres & CEO: David H. Hoag
SVP Personnel & Corp Affairs: Frank Filipovitz
Employees: 14,400

Phone: 216-622-5000
Fax: 216-622-4610

Jobs Cut Last Year: 2,100 (-12.7%)

Steel - coated, cold-rolled & hot-rolled sheet & strip & tubular & tin mill products; oil & gas drilling equipment

An in-depth profile of this company is available to subscribers on Hoover's Online at www.hoovers.com.

269

M.A. HANNA COMPANY

200 Public Sq., Ste. 36-5000
Cleveland, OH 44114-2304
Chm & CEO: Martin D. Walker
VP HR: Lani L. Beach
Employees: 5,695

Phone: 216-589-4000
Fax: 216-589-4200

Jobs Cut Last Year: 864 (-13.2%)

Chemicals - plastic & rubber resins, compounds & colorants

MTD PRODUCTS INC.

PO Box 368022
Valley City, OH 44136
Chm & CEO: Curtis E. Moll
VP HR: Mike Murray
Employees: 5,100

Phone: 330-225-2600
Fax: 330-225-0896

Jobs Added Last Year: 100 (+2.0%)

Machinery - outdoor power equipment

MAX & ERMA'S RESTAURANTS, INC.

4849 Evanswood Dr.
Columbus, OH 43229
Chm, Pres & CEO: Todd B. Barnum
VP Mktg & Strategic Dev: Karen A. Brennan
Employees: 2,814

Phone: 614-431-5800
Fax: 614-431-4111

Jobs Added Last Year: 577 (+25.8%)

Retail - casual dining restaurants

NACCO INDUSTRIES, INC.

5875 Landerbrook Dr.
Mayfield Heights, OH 44124-4017
Chm, Pres & CEO: Alfred M. Rankin Jr.
Senior Attorney & Asst Sec: Suzanne Schulze Taylor
Employees: 12,300

Phone: 216-449-9600
Fax: 216-449-9561

Jobs Added Last Year: 2,400 (+24.2%)

Diversified operations - forklifts (Hyster, Yale); small appliances (Hamilton Beach, Proctor-Silex); coal

THE MEAD CORPORATION

Courthouse Plaza NE
Dayton, OH 45463
Chm & CEO: Steven C. Mason
VP HR: Charles J. Mazza
Employees: 15,200

Phone: 513-495-6323
Fax: 513-461-2424

Jobs Cut Last Year: 900 (-5.6%)

Paper & paper products - packaging, school & office products; on-line information services

NATIONAL CITY CORPORATION

1900 E. Ninth St.
Cleveland, OH 44114-3484
Chm & CEO: David A. Daberko
SVP HR: Shelley J. Seifert
Employees: 20,767

Phone: 216-575-2000
Fax: 216-575-3332

Jobs Added Last Year: 466 (+2.3%)

Banks - Midwest

MERCANTILE STORES COMPANY, INC.

9450 Seward Rd.
Fairfield, OH 45014
Chm & CEO: David L. Nichols
VP HR: Louis Ripley
Employees: 31,700

Phone: 513-881-8000
Fax: 513-881-8689

Jobs Added Last Year: 1,200 (+3.9%)

Retail - regional department stores in the midwestern & southern US

NATIONWIDE INSURANCE ENT.

One Nationwide Plaza
Columbus, OH 43215-2220
Chm, Pres & CEO: D. Richard McFerson
VP HR: Susan A. Wolken
Employees: 27,476

Phone: 614-249-7111
Fax: 614-249-9071

Jobs Cut Last Year: 16,524 (-37.6%)

Insurance - multiline (Nationwide, Wausau)

MERCY HEALTH SYSTEM

2335 Grandview Ave.
Cincinnati, OH 45206
CEO: Sister Marjorie Bosse
SVP HR: Ronald J. Baril
Employees: 18,100

Phone: 513-221-2736
Fax: 513-559-3835

Jobs Added Last Year: —

Hospitals

NCR CORP.

1700 S. Patterson Blvd.
Dayton, OH 45479
Chm & CEO: Lars Nyberg
SVP Global HR: Richard H. Evans
Employees: 43,000

Phone: 513-445-5000
Fax: 513-445-1893

Jobs Cut Last Year: 3,250 (-7.0%)

Computers - commercial database systems, automated teller machines, financial processing systems, network management & multiprocessing systems, business forms & vendor support

NUMED HOME HEALTH CARE, INC.

6505 Rockside Rd., Ste. 400
Independence, OH 44131
Chm & CEO: Jay K. Taneja
Chm & CEO: Jay K. Taneja
Employees: 340

Phone: 216-447-6066
Fax: 216-447-0999

Jobs Added Last Year: 105 (+44.7%)

Health care - intermittent home health care & temporary staffing of nursing personnel

OFFICEMAX, INC.

3605 Warrensville Center Rd.
Shaker Heights, OH 44122-5203
Chm, Pres & CEO: Michael Feuer
Divisional VP & HR: Suzanne Forsythe
Employees: 21,171

Phone: 216-921-6900
Fax: 216-491-4040

Jobs Added Last Year: 1,857 (+9.6%)

Retail - high-volume deep-discount office products superstores

THE OHIO STATE UNIVERSITY

190 N. Oval Mall
Columbus, OH 43210
Pres: Gordon Gee
VP HR: Linda Tom
Employees: 27,000

Phone: 614-292-2424
Fax: 614-292-1231

Jobs Added Last Year: —

University

OLYMPIC STEEL, INC.

5080 Richmond Rd.
Bedford Heights, OH 44146
Chm, Pres & CEO: Michael D. Siegal
HR Officer: Jill Little
Employees: 838

Phone: 216-292-3800
Fax: 216-292-3974

Jobs Added Last Year: 307 (+57.8%)

Steel - flat-rolled carbon, stainless & tubular steel products

OM GROUP, INC.

3800 Terminal Tower
Cleveland, OH 44113-2204
Chm & CEO: James P. Mooney
VP HR, Gen Counsel & Sec: Michael J. Scott
Employees: 425

Phone: 216-781-0083
Fax: 216-781-0902

Jobs Added Last Year: 101 (+31.2%)

Chemicals - metal-based specialty products, including custom catalysts, paint & ink additives, bonding agents for steel-belted radial tires, coloring agents, ceramics & glass & powders

OWENS CORNING

Fiberglas Tower
Toledo, OH 43659
Chm & CEO: Glen H. Hiner
SVP HR: Gregory M. Thomson
Employees: 17,300

Phone: 419-248-8000
Fax: 419-248-5337

Jobs Added Last Year: 300 (+1.8%)

Building products - insulation, roofing, windows, patio doors; fiberglass reinforcements & polyester resins

OWENS-ILLINOIS, INC.

One SeaGate
Toledo, OH 43666
Chm & CEO: Joseph H. Lemieux
Dir HR Mgmt: Gary Benjamin
Employees: 30,100

Phone: 419-247-5000
Fax: 419-247-2839

Jobs Added Last Year: 3,400 (+12.7%)

Glass products - containers & bottles; plastic containers & closures, prescription containers & six-pack carriers

PARKER-HANNIFIN CORPORATION

17325 Euclid Ave.
Cleveland, OH 44112
Pres & CEO: Duane E. Collins
VP HR: Daniel T. Garey
Employees: 30,590

Phone: 216-531-3000
Fax: 216-383-9414

Jobs Added Last Year: 3,860 (+14.4%)

Instruments - fluid-power-system components & hydraulic, pneumatic & fuel systems

PARK-OHIO INDUSTRIES, INC.

600 Tower E., 20600 Chagrin Blvd.
Cleveland, OH 44122
Chm & CEO: Edward F. Crawford
Dir HR: Betty Buris
Employees: 2,800

Phone: 216-991-9700
Fax: 216-991-9317

Jobs Added Last Year: 1,066 (+61.5%)

Rubber & plastic products - plastic pails; diesel-engine manufacturing equipment; barbecue grills, lawn spreaders & patio tables

THE PROCTER & GAMBLE COMPANY

One Procter & Gamble Plaza, PO Box 599
Cincinnati, OH 45201-0599
Chm & CEO: John E. Pepper
SVP HR: Benjamin L. Bethell
Employees: 99,200

Phone: 513-983-1100
Fax: 513-983-9369

Jobs Added Last Year: 2,700 (+2.8%)

Soap & cleaning preparations - laundry & cleaning products, personal care products, food & beverages

 An in-depth profile of this company is available
to subscribers on Hoover's Online at www.hoovers.com.

271

THE PROGRESSIVE CORPORATION

6300 Wilson Mills Rd. Phone: 216-461-5000
Mayfield Village, OH 44143 Fax: 216-446-7481
Chm, Pres & CEO: Peter B. Lewis
Chief HR Officer: Tiona M. Thompson
Employees: 8,025
Jobs Added Last Year: 481 (+6.4%)
Insurance - property & casualty, primarily auto insurance

PUBCO CORPORATION

3830 Kelley Ave. Phone: 216-881-5300
Cleveland, OH 44114 Fax: 216-881-8380
Chm, Pres, CEO & CFO : Robert H. Kanner
No central personnel officer
Employees: 220
Jobs Added Last Year: 120 (+120.0%)
Retail - regional department stores (The Kline Companies);
construction products (Allied Construction Products); apparel;
real estate operations

RED ROOF INNS, INC.

4355 Davidson Rd. Phone: 614-876-3200
Hilliard, OH 73026-2491 Fax: 614-771-7838
Chm, Pres & CEO: Francis W. Cash
SVP HR: Walter A. Furnas
Employees: 5,200
Jobs Added Last Year: 700 (+15.6%)
Hotels & motels - limited-service lodging chain

REPUBLIC ENGINEERED STEELS, INC.

410 Oberlin Rd. SW Phone: 216-837-6000
Massillon, OH 44647 Fax: 216-837-6083
Chm, Pres & CEO: Russell Maier
VP HR: Rick Miller
Employees: 4,849
Jobs Added Last Year: 249 (+5.4%)
Steel - engineered bars

REVCO D.S., INC.

1925 Enterprise Pkwy. Phone: 216-425-9811
Twinsburg, OH 44087 Fax: 216-487-6539
Pres & CEO: D. Dwayne Hoven
SVP HR: Douglas W. Coffey
Employees: 32,000
Jobs Added Last Year: 14,000 (+77.8%)
Retail - drugstores (#2 in US with over 2,100 units)

REX STORES CORPORATION

2875 Needmore Rd. Phone: 513-276-3931
Dayton, OH 45414 Fax: 513-276-8643
Chm & CEO: Stuart A. Rose
Payroll Mgr: Sondra Hansen
Employees: 1,966
Jobs Added Last Year: 978 (+99.0%)
Retail - consumer electronics & appliances

THE REYNOLDS AND REYNOLDS CO.

115 S. Ludlow St. Phone: 513-443-2000
Dayton, OH 45402 Fax: 513-449-4416
Chm, Pres & CEO: David R. Holmes
VP HR: Tom Momchilov
Employees: 6,036
Jobs Added Last Year: 558 (+10.2%)
Paper - business forms & computer systems

RISER FOODS, INC.

5300 Richmond Rd. Phone: 216-292-7000
Bedford Heights, OH 44146 Fax: 216-591-2640
Chm & CEO: Anthony C. Rego
VP HR: Frank A. Zeiher
Employees: 5,300
Jobs Added Last Year: 300 (+6.0%)
Retail - supermarkets (Rini-Rego Stop-n-Shop); wholesale food
distribution (American Seaway Foods); private label ice cream
(Eagle)

ROADWAY EXPRESS, INC.

1077 Gorge Blvd. Phone: 330-384-8184
Akron, OH 44310 Fax: 330-258-6042
Pres & CEO: Michael W. Wickham
Mgr HR: Greg Bembenic
Employees: 26,000
Jobs Added Last Year: 708 (+2.8%)
Transportation - long-haul general freight trucking

RUBBERMAID INCORPORATED

1147 Akron Rd. Phone: 330-264-6464
Wooster, OH 44691-6000 Fax: 330-287-2846
Chm & CEO: Wolfgang R. Schmitt
SVP HR: David L. Robertson
Employees: 14,054
Jobs Added Last Year: 1,115 (+8.6%)
Rubber & plastic products - trash containers, storage products,
toys, playground equipment & office products

THE SHERWIN-WILLIAMS COMPANY

101 Prospect Ave. NW
Cleveland, OH 44115-1075
Chm & CEO: John G. Breen
VP HR: Thomas Kroeger
Employees: 18,458

Phone: 216-566-2000
Fax: 216-566-2947

Jobs Added Last Year: 558 (+3.1%)

Paints & allied products - paint stores; coatings (Dutch Boy, Krylon); consumer brands of paints (Ralph Lauren)

TELXON CORPORATION

3330 W. Market St.
Akron, OH 44333
Chm & CEO: Robert F. Meyerson
Dir HR: Meg Pais
Employees: 1,850

Phone: 330-867-3700
Fax: 330-869-2240

Jobs Added Last Year: 200 (+12.1%)

Computers - portable & wireless transaction systems

THE STANDARD REGISTER COMPANY

600 Albany St.
Dayton, OH 45408
Pres & CEO: Peter S. Redding
Asst VP HR: John E. Scarpelli
Employees: 6,439

Phone: 513-443-1000
Fax: 513-443-1239

Jobs Added Last Year: 238 (+3.8%)

Paper - business forms, bar coding & document processing equipment, personalized mail promotional materials & pressure sensitive labels

THOR INDUSTRIES, INC.

419 W. Pike St.
Jackson Center, OH 45334
Chm, Pres & CEO: Wade F. B. Thompson
Chief Admin Officer: Walter Bennett
Employees: 2,945

Phone: 513-596-6849
Fax: 513-596-6092

Jobs Added Last Year: 701 (+31.2%)

Building - motor homes, RVs (Airstream, Ambassador, Four Winds, General Coach) & travel trailers; small & mid-sized buses (El Dorado National)

STERIS CORPORATION

9450 Pineneedle Dr.
Mentor, OH 44060
Chm, Pres, CEO & Treas: Bill R. Sanford
VP Admin: Gerard Reiz
Employees: 560

Phone: 216-354-2600
Fax: 216-354-7887

Jobs Added Last Year: 182 (+48.1%)

Medical products - sterilizers for surgical equipment (Steris System 1, EcoCycle, SafeCycle)

THE TIMKEN COMPANY

1835 Dueber Ave. SW
Canton, OH 44706-2798
Pres & CEO: Joseph F. Toot Jr.
VP HR & Logistics: Stephen A. Perry
Employees: 17,034

Phone: 330-438-3000
Fax: 330-438-3452

Jobs Added Last Year: 832 (+5.1%)

Metal products - tapered roller bearings (#1 worldwide)

Helpwanted.com — http://helpwanted.com/

 An in-depth profile of this company is available to subscribers on Hoover's Online at www.hoovers.com.

273

TRINOVA CORPORATION

3000 Strayer
Maumee, OH 43537-0050
CEO: Darryl F. Allen
Dir HR: Debra Schaefer
Employees: 15,299

Phone: 419-867-2200
Fax: 419-867-2395

Jobs Added Last Year: 275 (+1.8%)

Machinery - general industrial

TRW INC.

1900 Richmond Rd.
Cleveland, OH 44124-3760
Chm & CEO: Joseph T. Gorman
EVP HR & Comm: Howard V. Knicely
Employees: 66,500

Phone: 216-291-7000
Fax: 216-291-7629

Jobs Added Last Year: 2,300 (+3.6%)

Diversified operations - automotive products; space & defense products; systems integration, including automated identification & public safety; consumer credit-reporting service

VALUE CITY DEPARTMENT STORES, INC.

3241 Westerville Rd.
Columbus, OH 43224
Chm & CEO: Jay L. Schottenstein
VP HR: Herbert E. Minkin
Employees: 11,258

Phone: 614-471-4722
Fax: 614-478-2253

Jobs Added Last Year: 1,258 (+12.6%)

Retail - regional department stores in midwestern & eastern states

WENDY'S INTERNATIONAL, INC.

4288 W. Dublin-Granville Rd.
Dublin, OH 43017-0256
Pres, CEO & COO: Gordon F. Teter
SVP HR: Kathleen A. McGinnis
Employees: 47,000

Phone: 614-764-3100
Fax: 614-764-3459

Jobs Added Last Year: 3,000 (+6.8%)

Retail - restaurants

WORTHINGTON INDUSTRIES, INC.

1205 Dearborn Dr.
Columbus, OH 43085
VC & CEO: John P. McConnell
VP Personnel: Thomas L. Hockman
Employees: 8,200

Phone: 614-438-3210
Fax: 614-438-3136

Jobs Added Last Year: 500 (+6.5%)

Metal processing & fabrication - flat rolled steel coils & injection molded plastic products

AAON, INC.

2425 S. Yukon Ave.
Tulsa, OK 74107-2728
Pres & Treas: Norman H. Asbjornson
Mgr HR: Martha Lenard
Employees: 574

Phone: 918-583-2266
Fax: 918-583-6094

Jobs Added Last Year: 136 (+31.1%)

Building products - commercial rooftop air-conditioning, heating & heat recovery equipment & air-conditioning coils for the commercial & industrial new construction & replacement markets

CHESAPEAKE ENERGY CORP.

6104 N. Western Ave., PO Box 18496
Oklahoma City, OK 73154-0496
Chm & CEO: Aubrey K. McClendon
HR & Compliance Mgr & Sec: Janice Dobbs
Employees: 325

Phone: 405-848-8000
Fax: 405-843-0573

Jobs Added Last Year: 75 (+30.0%)

Oil & gas - US exploration & production

EATERIES, INC.

3240 W. Britton Rd., Ste. 202
Oklahoma City, OK 73120-2032
Chm, Pres & CEO: Vincent F. Orza Jr.
HR Mgr: Meline Schwartz-Towler
Employees: 2,421

Phone: 405-755-3607
Fax: 405-751-7348

Jobs Added Last Year: 439 (+22.1%)

Retail - family-style restaurants (Garfield's Restaurant & Pub, Pepperoni Grill) & sports bars

FLEMING COMPANIES, INC.

6301 Waterford Blvd.
Oklahoma City, OK 73126
Chm & CEO: Robert E. Stauth
SVP Assoc Support: Larry A. Wagner
Employees: 44,000

Phone: 405-840-7200
Fax: 405-840-7702

Jobs Added Last Year: 1,600 (+3.8%)

Food - wholesale food & general merchandise distribution to grocers; 350 company-owned retail grocery stores (Baker's, Sentry Foods, SuPeRSaVeR, ABCO, Rainbow Foods, Market Basket)

HALE HALSELL CO.

9111 E. Pine St.
Tulsa, OK 74158-2898
Pres: Robert Hawk
Personnel Mgr: Paul Bradley
Employees: 5,300
Phone: 918-835-4484
Fax: 918-835-3979

Jobs Added Last Year: 19 (+0.4%)

Food - wholesale

HELMERICH & PAYNE, INC.

Utica at 21st St.
Tulsa, OK 74114
Pres & CEO: Hans Helmerich
Dir HR: Todd Sprague
Employees: 3,245
Phone: 918-742-5531
Fax: 918-743-2671

Jobs Added Last Year: 458 (+16.4%)

Oil & gas - US exploration & production, oil field services, chemicals & real estate

MAPCO INC.

1800 S. Baltimore Ave.
Tulsa, OK 74119
Chm, Pres & CEO: James E. Barnes
SVP HR & Admin: Jack D. Maynard
Employees: 6,204
Phone: 918-581-1800
Fax: 918-581-1534

Jobs Added Last Year: 153 (+2.5%)

Oil & gas - production & pipeline; coal mines

PARKER DRILLING CO.

8 E. Third St.
Tulsa, OK 74103
Pres & CEO: Robert L. Parker Jr.
Mgr HR: Gloria West
Employees: 2,360
Phone: 918-585-8221
Fax: 918-585-1058

Jobs Added Last Year: 254 (+12.1%)

Oil & gas - field services

PHILLIPS PETROLEUM COMPANY

Phillips Bldg., Fourth & Keeler Sts.
Bartlesville, OK 74004
Chm & CEO: Wayne W. Allen
EVP Planning & Corp Relations & Svcs: Charles L. Bowerman
Employees: 17,400
Phone: 918-661-6600
Fax: 918-661-7636

Jobs Cut Last Year: 1,000 (-5.4%)

Oil & gas - international integrated

PRE-PAID LEGAL SERVICES, INC.

321 E. Main
Ada, OK 74820
Pres & CEO: Jack Mildren
Mgr HR: Charlene Sanders
Employees: 119
Phone: 405-436-1234
Fax: 405-436-7410

Jobs Added Last Year: 30 (+33.7%)

Business services - legal-expense plans

QUIKTRIP CORPORATION

901 N. Mingo Rd.
Tulsa, OK 74101
Chm & CEO: Chester Cadieux
VP HR: Jim Denny
Employees: 2,501
Phone: 918-836-8551
Fax: 918-834-4117

Jobs Added Last Year: 301 (+13.7%)

Retail - gasoline convenience stores

UNITED VIDEO SATELLITE GROUP

7140 S. Lewis Ave.
Tulsa, OK 74136-5422
Chm & CEO: Lawrence Flinn Jr.
VP HR: Suzanne Shepherd
Employees: 1,100
Phone: 918-488-4000
Fax: 918-488-4979

Jobs Added Last Year: 400 (+57.1%)

TV production & programming - satellite-delivered video, audio & program-promotion services for cable TV & residential satellite dish owners; cable TV program information (Prevue Network)

THE WILLIAMS COMPANIES, INC.

One Williams Ctr.
Tulsa, OK 74172
Chm, Pres & CEO: Keith E. Bailey
VP HR: John C. Fischer
Employees: 9,946
Phone: 918-588-2000
Fax: 918-588-2296

Jobs Added Last Year: 1,719 (+20.9%)

Oil & gas - production & pipeline (#1 in US); telecommunications & technology operations

 An in-depth profile of this company is available to subscribers on Hoover's Online at www.hoovers.com.

275

ASSISTED LIVING CONCEPTS, INC.

10570 SE Washington, Ste. 213
Portland, OR 97216
Pres & CEO: Keren Brown Wilson
Dir HR: Beth Pearson
Employees: 451

Phone: 503-252-6233
Fax: 503-252-6597

Jobs Added Last Year: 384 (+573.1%)

Nursing homes - assisted-living residences for senior citizens

CLAREMONT TECHNOLOGY GROUP, INC.

1600 NW Compton Dr., Ste. 210
Beaverton, OR 97006
Pres & CEO: Paul J. Cosgrave
Corp Mgr HR: Clark Ackerman
Employees: 367

Phone: 503-690-4000
Fax: 503-690-4004

Jobs Added Last Year: 163 (+79.9%)

Computers - information technology solutions for business-wide processes, including customer service, order processing, billing & logistics for large corporations & government organizations

ELMER'S RESTAURANTS, INC.

11802 SE Stark St.
Portland, OR 97216
Pres & CEO: Herman Goldberg
Dir Ops: Anita Goldberg
Employees: 227

Phone: 503-252-1485
Fax: 503-257-7448

Jobs Added Last Year: 53 (+30.5%)

Retail - restaurants

FLIR SYSTEMS, INC.

16505 SW 72nd Ave.
Portland, OR 97224-1206
Chm, Pres & CEO: Robert P. Daltry
Dir HR: Marti Bunyard
Employees: 313

Phone: 503-684-3731
Fax: 503-684-5452

Jobs Added Last Year: 78 (+33.2%)

Electronics - thermal imaging systems for military & commercial applications

FRED MEYER, INC.

3800 SE 22nd Ave.
Portland, OR 97202
Chm & CEO: Robert G. Miller
SVP HR: Keith W. Lovett
Employees: 27,000

Phone: 503-232-8844
Fax: 503-797-5609

Jobs Added Last Year: 0

Retail - regional hypermarts

THE GREENBRIER COMPANIES, INC.

One Centerpointe Dr., Ste. 200
Lake Oswego, OR 97035
Pres & CEO: William A. Furman
Dir HR: Jeannie Wakayama-Onchi
Employees: 2,675

Phone: 503-684-7000
Fax: 503-684-7553

Jobs Added Last Year: 911 (+51.6%)

Transportation - double-stack railcars & intermodal transportation equipment; rail car fleet management services

HOLLYWOOD ENTERTAINMENT CORP.

10300 SW Allen Blvd.
Beaverton, OR 97005
Chm, Pres & CEO: Mark J. Wattles
Dir HR: Mary Geertsen
Employees: 6,723

Phone: 503-677-1600
Fax: 503-677-1680

Jobs Added Last Year: 4,312 (+178.8%)

Retail - video rental superstores (Hollywood Video, Video Central, Eastman Video, Video Park)

JELD-WEN INC.

3303 Lakeport Blvd.
Klamath Falls, OR 97601
CEO: Richard L. Wendt
Corp Svcs Dir: Gloria Aldinger
Employees: 7,100

Phone: 541-882-3451
Fax: 541-884-2231

Jobs Added Last Year: 50 (+0.7%)

Building products - wood windows & doors

LOUISIANA-PACIFIC CORPORATION

111 SW Fifth Ave.
Portland, OR 97204-3699
Chm & CEO: Mark Suwyn
Dir Personnel & Emp Benefits: Gary R. Maffei
Employees: 13,000

Phone: 503-221-0800
Fax: 503-796-0204

Jobs Added Last Year: 0

Building products - dimensional lumber, plywood, gypsum wallboard & wood pulp

MACHEEZMO MOUSE RESTAURANTS

1020 SW Taylor St., Ste. 685
Portland, OR 97205
Chm & Dir Strategic Planning: William S. Warren
Dir HR: Robin Campbell
Employees: 360

Phone: 503-274-0001
Fax: 503-274-4369

Jobs Added Last Year: 96 (+36.4%)

Retail - Mexican-style fast-food restaurants

NIKE, INC.

One Bowerman Dr.
Beaverton, OR 97005-6453
Chm & CEO: Philip H. Knight
VP HR: Sharon Tunstall
Employees: 14,240

Phone: 503-671-6453
Fax: 503-671-6300

Jobs Added Last Year: 4,740 (+49.9%)

Shoes & related apparel - athletic shoes, apparel & accessories;
dress & casual shoes; in-line skates

PACIFICORP

700 NE Multnomah St.
Portland, OR 97232-4116
Pres & CEO: Frederick W. Buckman
VP HR: Michael J. Pittman
Employees: 12,621

Phone: 503-731-2000
Fax: 503-731-2136

Jobs Cut Last Year: 224 (-1.7%)

Utility - electric power

PERCON INCORPORATED

1720 Willow Creek Circle, Ste. 530
Eugene, OR 97402-9171
Pres & CEO: Michael P. Coughlin
Dir HR: Rebecca Plant
Employees: 68

Phone: 541-344-1189
Fax: 541-344-1399

Jobs Added Last Year: 19 (+38.8%)

Computers - bar code reading products, including fixed station
decoders & portable data terminals for automatic identification
& data collection

PRECISION CASTPARTS CORP.

4600 SE Harney Dr.
Portland, OR 97206-0898
Chm, Pres & CEO: William C. McCormick
Dir HR: Mark Damien
Employees: 5,646

Phone: 503-777-3881
Fax: 503-777-7632

Jobs Added Last Year: 480 (+9.3%)

Metal products - complex structural investment castings

R. B. PAMPLIN CORPORATION

900 SW 5th Ave., Ste. 1800
Portland, OR 97204
Chm & CEO: Robert B. Pamplin Sr.
No central personnel officer
Employees: 6,250

Phone: 503-248-1133
Fax: 503-245-1175

Jobs Added Last Year: 522 (+9.1%)

Diversified operations - textiles (Mt. Vernon Mills); concrete &
asphalt

SEQUENT COMPUTER SYSTEMS, INC.

15450 SW Koll Pkwy.
Beaverton, OR 97006-6063
Chm & CEO: Karl C. Powell Jr.
VP HR: Diane M. Williams
Employees: 2,129

Phone: 503-626-5700
Fax: 503-578-9890

Jobs Added Last Year: 319 (+17.6%)

Computers - multiprocessing UNIX-based systems & relational
database management software (RDBMS)

SMC CORPORATION

30725 Diamond Hill Rd.
Harrisburg, OR 97446
Chm, Pres & CEO: Mathew M. Perlot
Dir HR: Dave Bocanegra
Employees: 1,135

Phone: 541-995-8214
Fax: 541-995-1176

Jobs Added Last Year: 280 (+32.7%)

Building - custom RVs

TEKTRONIX, INC.

26600 SW Parkway Ave.
Wilsonville, OR 97070
Chm, Pres & CEO: Jerome J. Meyer
VP Total Quality & HR: Robert W. Phillips
Employees: 7,619

Phone: 503-627-7111
Fax: 503-627-5502

Jobs Cut Last Year: 849 (-10.0%)

Electronics - measuring instruments; color printing & imaging;
video systems; network displays

THRIFTY PAYLESS HOLDINGS, INC.

9275 SW Peyton Ln.
Wilsonville, OR 97070
Chm & CEO: Marty D. Smith
SVP HR: James C. Hamilton
Employees: 31,200

Phone: 503-682-4100
Fax: 503-685-1445

Jobs Cut Last Year: 1,098 (-3.4%)

Retail - drugstores & sporting goods stores

U. S. BANCORP

111 SW Fifth Ave.
Portland, OR 97204
Chm & CEO: Gerry B. Cameron
EVP HR: Judy Rice
Employees: 14,081

Phone: 503-275-6111
Fax: 503-275-3452

Jobs Added Last Year: 3,471 (+32.7%)

Banks - West

An in-depth profile of this company is available
to subscribers on Hoover's Online at www.hoovers.com.

WILLAMETTE INDUSTRIES, INC.

1300 SW Fifth Ave., Ste. 3800   Phone: 503-227-5581
Portland, OR 97201   Fax: 503-273-5603
Pres & CEO: Steven R. Rogel
VP Personnel & Industrial Relations: David W. Morthland
Employees: 13,180

Jobs Added Last Year: 920 (+7.5%)

Paper & paper products - kraft liner, specialty printing & cut
sheet paper; corrugated containers, inks, lumber, plywood, particleboard, fiberboard & laminated beams & veneer products

WILLIAMS CONTROLS, INC.

14100 SW 72nd Ave.   Phone: 503-684-8600
Portland, OR 97224   Fax: 503-684-8675
Chm, Pres & CEO: Thomas W. Itin
Dir HR: Chuck Chambelran
Employees: 500

Jobs Added Last Year: 280 (+127.3%)

Automotive & trucking - heavy vehicle components, automotive
accessories & electrical components; landscape maintenance
equipment

PENNSYLVANIA

II-VI INCORPORATED

375 Saxonburg Blvd.   Phone: 412-352-4455
Saxonburg, PA 16056   Fax: 412-352-4980
Chm & CEO: Carl J. Johnson
Dir HR: Kathy Kinnamon
Employees: 323

Jobs Added Last Year: 91 (+39.2%)

Electrical components - optical & electro-optical components,
devices & materials for infrared, near-infrared, visible &
X-ray/gamma-ray instruments & applications

ADVANTA CORP.

300 Welsh Rd.   Phone: 215-657-4000
Horsham, PA 19044   Fax: 215-956-0268
CEO: Alex "Pete" W. Hart
VP HR: John B. Hofmann
Employees: 2,409

Jobs Added Last Year: 656 (+37.4%)

Financial - credit cards, mortgage loans, credit insurance, equipment leasing & deposit products

AIR PRODUCTS AND CHEMICALS, INC.

7201 Hamilton Blvd.   Phone: 610-481-4911
Allentown, PA 18195-1501   Fax: 610-481-5900
Chm, Pres & CEO: Harold A. Wagner
VP HR: Joseph P. McAndrew
Employees: 14,800

Jobs Added Last Year: 1,500 (+11.3%)

Chemicals - industrial gases & related equipment; specialty &
intermediate chemicals; environmental & energy systems

CareerWeb — http://www.cweb.com/

AIRGAS, INC.

100 Matsonford Rd., Ste. 550   Phone: 610-687-5253
Radnor, PA 19087-4579   Fax: 610-687-1052
Chm & CEO: Peter McCausland
Dir HR: Don Daemer
Employees: 5,200

Jobs Added Last Year: 1,100 (+26.8%)

Wholesale distribution - compressed gases for industrial, medical & specialty uses; welding machines & accessories; protective equipment

ALCO STANDARD CORPORATION

825 Duportail Rd.   Phone: 610-296-8000
Wayne, PA 19087-5589   Fax: 610-296-8419
Chm, Pres & CEO: John E. Stuart
VP Administrative Svcs: Elisabeth H. Barrett
Employees: 36,500

Jobs Added Last Year: 5,900 (+19.3%)

Wholesale distribution - paper, packaging products & office equipment

ALLEGHENY LUDLUM CORPORATION

1000 Six PPG Place   Phone: 412-394-2800
Pittsburgh, PA 15222-5479   Fax: 412-394-2805
Pres & CEO: Arthur H. Aronson
VP HR: Bruce A. McGillivray
Employees: 6,000

Jobs Added Last Year: 0

Steel - specialty & alloy materials, including stainless steel, silicon electrical steel sheet & tool steels

ALUMINUM COMPANY OF AMERICA

Alcoa Bldg., 425 Sixth Ave.   Phone: 412-553-4545
Pittsburgh, PA 15219-1850   Fax: 412-553-4498
Chm & CEO: Paul H. O'Neill
EVP HR: Ronald R. Hoffman
Employees: 72,000

Jobs Added Last Year: 10,300 (+16.7%)

Metal products - aluminum

AMERICAN EAGLE OUTFITTERS, INC.

150 Thorn Hill Dr.   Phone: 412-776-4857
Warrendale, PA 15086-7528   Fax: 412-776-9758
Chm & CEO: Jay L. Schottenstein
VP HR: Michael E. Bergdahl
Employees: 6,122

Jobs Added Last Year: 119 (+2.0%)

Retail - casual apparel, shoes & accessories

AMERIGAS PARTNERS, L.P.

460 N. Gulph Rd.   Phone: 610-337-7000
King of Prussia, PA 19406   Fax: 610-768-7647
Pres & CEO: Robert C. Mauch
VP HR: Annalee C. Bullman
Employees: 5,052

Jobs Added Last Year: 560 (+12.5%)

Oil refining & marketing - propane distribution

AMERISOURCE HEALTH CORP.

300 Chesterfield Pkwy.   Phone: 610-296-4480
Malvern, PA 19355   Fax: 610-647-0141
Chm, Pres & CEO: John F. McNamara
VP HR: Eileen Clark
Employees: 2,600

Jobs Added Last Year: 230 (+9.7%)

Drugs & sundries - wholesale distribution of goods to drugstores & pharmacies

AMETEK, INC.

Station Square   Phone: 610-647-2121
Paoli, PA 19301   Fax: 610-296-3412
Chm & CEO: Walter E. Blankley
Corp Dir HR: Robert Zuzack
Employees: 6,300

Jobs Added Last Year: 100 (+1.6%)

Electrical products - electromechanical devices, process equipment & precision instruments

AMP INCORPORATED

PO Box 3608   Phone: 717-564-0100
Harrisburg, PA 17105-3608   Fax: 717-780-6130
Pres & CEO: William J. Hudson Jr.
Corp VP & Chief HR Officer: Philip G. Guarneschelli
Employees: 40,800

Jobs Added Last Year: 10,400 (+34.2%)

Electrical connectors - splices, connectors, cable & panel assemblies, networking units, sensors, switches, electro-optic devices, touch screen data entry systems & tooling

APOGEE, INC.

1018 W. Ninth Ave., Ste. 202   Phone: 610-992-7670
King of Prussia, PA 19406-9833   Fax: 610-992-0483
Chm & CEO: John H. Foster
VP HR: Jane P. Stanton
Employees: 1,000

Jobs Added Last Year: 319 (+46.8%)

Health care - outpatient mental health group practices

 An in-depth profile of this company is available to subscribers on Hoover's Online at www.hoovers.com.

ARAMARK CORPORATION

1101 Market St.
Philadelphia, PA 19107
Chm, Pres & CEO: Joseph Neubauer
SVP HR: Brian G. Mulvaney
Employees: 140,000

Phone: 215-238-3000
Fax: 215-238-3333

Jobs Added Last Year: 7,000 (+5.3%)

Diversified operations - food services, uniform rentals, child care services & magazine distribution

ARMCO INC.

One Oxford Centre, 15th Fl., 301 Grant St.
Pittsburgh, PA 15219-1415
Chm, Pres & CEO: James F. Will
Corp Dir HR: James W. Edgerton
Employees: 5,900

Phone: 412-255-9800
Fax: 412-255-9883

Jobs Added Last Year: 400 (+7.3%)

Steel - production

ARMSTRONG WORLD INDUSTRIES

313 W. Liberty St.
Lancaster, PA 17603
Chm & CEO: George A. Lorch
SVP HR: Douglas L. Boles
Employees: 11,365

Phone: 717-397-0611
Fax: 717-396-2787

Jobs Cut Last Year: 9,218 (-44.8%)

Building products - resilient flooring, ceramic tile, ceilings, adhesives & insulation

ASPLUNDH TREE EXPERT CO.

708 Blair Mill Rd.
Willow Grove, PA 19090
Pres & CEO: Christopher B. Asplundh
Dir HR: William Hughes
Employees: 18,500

Phone: 215-784-4200
Fax: 215-784-4493

Jobs Cut Last Year: 700 (-3.6%)

Tree trimming

BELL ATLANTIC CORPORATION

1717 Arch St.
Philadelphia, PA 19103
Chm & CEO: Raymond W. Smith
VP HR: Kevin P. Pennington
Employees: 61,800

Phone: 215-963-6000
Fax: 215-963-6470

Jobs Cut Last Year: 10,500 (-14.5%)

Utility - telephone; cellular communications, software, paging services, computer maintenance & business services

BETHLEHEM STEEL CORPORATION

1170 Eighth Ave.
Bethlehem, PA 18016-7699
Chm & CEO: Curtis H. Barnette
VP HR: Dorothy L. Stephenson
Employees: 19,500

Phone: 610-694-2424
Fax: 610-694-6920

Jobs Cut Last Year: 400 (-2.0%)

Steel - production (#2 in US); raw materials; offshore drill rig repair

BIOCONTROL TECHNOLOGY, INC.

300 Indian Springs Rd.
Indiana, PA 15701
EVP & CEO: Fred E. Cooper
Dir HR: Gregory Cornman
Employees: 153

Phone: 412-349-1811
Fax: 412-279-1367

Jobs Added Last Year: 45 (+41.7%)

Medical products - cardiac pacemakers, heart valves & associated accessories; functional electrical stimulators

BOSCOV'S DEPARTMENT STORES

4500 Perkiomen Ave.
Reading, PA 19606
CEO: Albert Boscov
Corp Personnel Mgr: Shirley Holzman
Employees: 6,500

Phone: 610-779-2000
Fax: 610-370-3770

Jobs Added Last Year: 1,000 (+18.2%)

Retail - department stores

CARPENTER TECHNOLOGY CORP.

101 W. Bern St.
Reading, PA 19601
Chm, Pres & CEO: Robert W. Cardy
VP Human & Administrative Svcs: Robert W. Lodge
Employees: 4,068

Phone: 610-208-2000
Fax: 610-208-2989

Jobs Added Last Year: 371 (+10.0%)

Steel - high-performance specialty alloys

C-COR ELECTRONICS, INC.

60 Decibel Rd.
State College, PA 16801
Chm & CEO: Richard E. Perry
Dir HR: Edwin Childs
Employees: 1,494

Phone: 814-238-2461
Fax: 814-238-4065

Jobs Added Last Year: 484 (+47.9%)

Telecommunications equipment - data transmission systems

CENTRAL SPRINKLER CORPORATION

451 N. Cannon Ave.
Lansdale, PA 19446
CEO, Sec & Treas: George G. Meyer
Mgr HR: Charles Whitney
Employees: 900
Jobs Added Last Year: 200 (+28.6%)

Phone: 215-362-0700
Fax: 215-362-5385

Protection - automatic fire sprinkler heads, valves & other components

CERTAINTEED CORPORATION

750 E. Swedesford Rd., PO Box 860
Valley Forge, PA 19482-0101
CEO: Michel Besson
Dir HR: Dennis Baker
Employees: 6,500
Jobs Added Last Year: 126 (+2.0%)

Phone: 610-341-7000
Fax: 610-341-7777

Diversified operations - fiberglass reinforcement, insulation, building materials & pipe

CHARMING SHOPPES, INC.

450 Winks Ln.
Bensalem, PA 19020
VC, Pres & CEO: Dorrit J. Bern
EVP & Corp Dir HR: Anthony A. DeSabato
Employees: 14,200
Jobs Cut Last Year: 2,400 (-14.5%)

Phone: 215-245-9100
Fax: 215-638-6873

Retail - apparel & shoes (over 1,300 units: Fashion Bug, Fashion Bug Plus)

CIGNA CORPORATION

One Liberty Place
Philadelphia, PA 19192-1550
Chm, Pres & CEO: Wilson H. Taylor
EVP HR & Svcs: Donald M. Levinson
Employees: 44,707
Jobs Cut Last Year: 3,593 (-7.4%)

Phone: 215-761-1000
Fax: 215-761-5505

Insurance - property & casualty, health, life & accident

CMAC INVESTMENT CORPORATION

1601 Market St.
Philadelphia, PA 19103
Pres & CEO : Frank P. Fillips
Dir HR: William Marlin
Employees: 420
Jobs Added Last Year: 109 (+35.0%)

Phone: 215-564-6600
Fax: 215-564-5020

Insurance - private mortgage coverage in the US to residential mortgage lenders

COMCAST CORPORATION

1500 Market St., 35th Fl.
Philadelphia, PA 19102-2148
Pres: Brian L. Roberts
SVP HR: Paul Gillert
Employees: 12,200
Jobs Added Last Year: 5,500 (+82.1%)

Phone: 215-665-1700
Fax: 215-981-7790

Cable TV - cable & cellular telephone communications systems & production & distribution of cable programming

COMMONWEALTH BANCORP INC.

70 Valley Stream Pkwy.
Malvern, PA 19355
Chm, Pres & CEO: Charles H. Meacham
VP HR: Ellen L. Benson
Employees: 708
Jobs Added Last Year: 165 (+30.4%)

Phone: 610-251-1600
Fax: 610-993-1742

Financial - savings & loans

CONRAIL INC.

2001 Market St., 2 Commerce Sq.
Philadelphia, PA 19101-1417
Pres & CEO: David M. LeVan
SVP Organizational Dev: Frank H. Nichols
Employees: 23,510
Jobs Cut Last Year: 1,323 (-5.3%)

Phone: 215-209-4000
Fax: 215-209-5567

Transportation - rail

CONSOLIDATED NATURAL GAS CO.

CNG Tower, 625 Liberty Ave.
Pittsburgh, PA 15222-3199
Chm & CEO: George A. Davidson Jr.
VP HR & Administrative Svcs: Joseph S. Usaj
Employees: 6,600
Jobs Cut Last Year: 966 (-12.8%)

Phone: 412-227-1000
Fax: 412-227-1002

Utility - gas distribution

CONTROL CHIEF HOLDINGS, INC.

200 William St., PO Box 141
Bradford, PA 16701
CEO & CFO: Douglas S. Bell
Controller: Steve Pachla
Employees: 123
Jobs Added Last Year: 48 (+64.0%)

Phone: 814-368-4132
Fax: 814-368-4133

Machinery - remote control devices for material handling equipment

 An in-depth profile of this company is available to subscribers on Hoover's Online at www.hoovers.com.

281

CORESTATES FINANCIAL CORPORATION

PNB Bldg., Broad & Chestnut Sts.   Phone: 215-973-3827
Philadelphia, PA 19107-3494   Fax: 215-786-8294
Chm & CEO: Terrence A. Larsen
HR Mgr: Vikram Dewan
Employees: 13,598
Jobs Cut Last Year: 2,147 (-13.6%)

Banks - Northeast

CROWN CORK & SEAL COMPANY, INC.

9300 Ashton Rd.   Phone: 215-698-5100
Philadelphia, PA 19136   Fax: 215-676-7245
Chm & CEO: William J. Avery
VP HR: Gary L. Burgess
Employees: 20,409
Jobs Cut Last Year: 1,964 (-8.8%)

Containers - metal & plastic containers & crowns; packaging & handling machinery

CSS INDUSTRIES, INC.

1845 Walnut St., Ste. 800   Phone: 215-569-9900
Philadelphia, PA 19103   Fax: 215-569-9979
Chm, Pres & CEO: Jack Farber
Mgr Admin: Jacqueline Tully
Employees: 3,910
Jobs Added Last Year: 1,710 (+77.7%)

Paper & paper products - decorative paper products

DAUPHIN DEPOSIT CORPORATION

S Market Sq., 213 Market St.   Phone: 717-255-2121
Harrisburg, PA 17105   Fax: 717-237-6218
Chm & CEO: Christopher R. Jennings
SVP & Chief HR Officer: David L. Brewin
Employees: 2,681
Jobs Added Last Year: 381 (+16.6%)

Banks - Northeast (Bank of Pennsylvania, Valleybank, Farmers Bank)

DAY & ZIMMERMANN INCORPORATED

1818 Market St.   Phone: 215-299-8295
Philadelphia, PA 19103   Fax: 215-975-6666
Chm, Pres & CEO: Harold L. "Spike" Yoh Jr.
VP HR: Anthony G. Natale
Employees: 14,000
Jobs Added Last Year: 200 (+1.4%)

Consulting & engineering

DECISIONONE CORPORATION

50 E. Swedesford Rd.   Phone: 610-296-6000
Frazer, PA 19355   Fax: 610-993-6334
Chm & CEO: Kenneth Draeger
Dir HR: Dwight Wilson
Employees: 5,900
Jobs Added Last Year: —

Computers - computer maintenance & technology support services

DQE INC.

500 Cherrington Pkwy., Ste. 100   Phone: 412-262-4700
Coraopolis, PA 15108-3184   Fax: 412-393-6448
EVP & Interim CEO: David D. Marshall
Asst VP HR: Sally K. Wade
Employees: 4,057
Jobs Added Last Year: 288 (+7.6%)

Utility - electric power

EASTERN MERCY HEALTH SYSTEM

100 Matsonford Rd., Bldg. 3, Ste. 220   Phone: 610-971-9770
Radnor, PA 19087   Fax: 610-688-5443
CEO: C. Kent Russell
Dir HR: Jim Wilson
Employees: 18,982
Jobs Added Last Year: —

Hospitals

FOAMEX INTERNATIONAL INC.

1000 Columbia Ave.   Phone: 610-859-3000
Linwood, PA 19061   Fax: 610-859-3162
Chm & CEO: Marshall S. Cogan
VP HR: Donald Mallo
Employees: 7,700
Jobs Added Last Year: —

Rubber & plastic products - polyurethane foam, automotive textiles & home furnishings

FORE SYSTEMS, INC.

174 Thorn Hill Rd.   Phone: 412-772-6600
Warrendale, PA 15086-7535   Fax: 412-772-6500
Chm & CEO: Eric C. Cooper
Dir HR: John Lawton
Employees: 977
Jobs Added Last Year: 620 (+173.7%)

Computers - asynchronous-transfer-mode networking products; switching systems (Ethernet, Fast Ethernet)

GENERAL NUTRITION COMPANIES

921 Penn Ave.
Pittsburgh, PA 15222
Pres & CEO: William E. Watts
Dir HR: Ilene Scott
Employees: 9,610

Phone: 412-288-4600
Fax: 412-288-2074

Jobs Added Last Year: 1,197 (+14.2%)

Retail - vitamins

GENESIS HEALTH VENTURES, INC.

148 W. State St.
Kennett Square, PA 19348
Chm & CEO: Michael R. Walker
Dir HR: James Tabak
Employees: 16,500

Phone: 610-444-6350
Fax: 610-444-3365

Jobs Added Last Year: 7,877 (+91.3%)

Health care - rehabilitation, subacute care, pharmacy, home care & physician services for the elderly in the eastern US

GENUARDI SUPER MARKETS

805 E. Germantown Pike
Norristown, PA 19401
CEO: Charles A. Genuardi
VP HR: James McCrudden
Employees: 3,500

Phone: 610-277-6000
Fax: 610-277-7783

Jobs Added Last Year: 1,900 (+118.8%)

Retail - supermarkets

GERIATRIC & MEDICAL COMPANIES

5601 Chestnut St.
Philadelphia, PA 19139
Chm, Pres & CEO: Daniel Veloric
VP Legal & HR & Asst Sec: James J. Wankmiller
Employees: 5,300

Phone: 215-476-2250
Fax: 215-748-8862

Jobs Added Last Year: 1,150 (+27.7%)

Medical practice management - health care support services, including medical transport services, medical home care services & pharmacy services

GIANT EAGLE INC.

101 Kappa Dr.
Pittsburgh, PA 15238
Chm & CEO: David S. Shapira
VP Personnel: Raymond A. Huber
Employees: 7,200

Phone: 412-963-6200
Fax: 412-963-0374

Jobs Added Last Year: 0

Retail - supermarkets

GRADUATE HEALTH SYSTEM

2129 Chestnut St.
Philadelphia, PA 19103
Chm & CEO: Harold Cramer
VP HR: Caren Staskin
Employees: 7,000

Phone: 215-448-1500
Fax: 215-448-1500

Jobs Added Last Year: 200 (+2.9%)

Hospital - not-for-profit system serving southern New Jersey, southeastern Pennsylvania (The Graduate Hospital, Mt. Sinai Hospital, City Avenue Hospital) & Delaware

Chicago Tribune Career Finder — http://www.chicago.tribune.com/career/

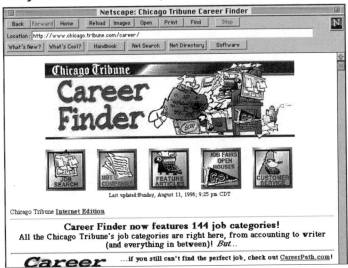

HARSCO CORPORATION

350 Poplar Church Rd.
Camp Hill, PA 17011
Chm, Pres & CEO: Derek C. Hathaway
VP HR: Richard C. Hawkins
Employees: 13,200

Phone: 717-763-7064
Fax: 717-763-6424

Jobs Added Last Year: 200 (+1.5%)

Metal processing & fabrication; industrial services; construction products; defense systems & vehicles

HERSHEY FOODS CORPORATION

100 Crystal A Dr.
Hershey, PA 17033-0810
Chm & CEO: Kenneth L. Wolfe
VP HR: Sharon A. Lambly
Employees: 14,800

Phone: 717-534-6799
Fax: 717-534-6760

Jobs Cut Last Year: 800 (-5.1%)

Food - milk chocolate products (Hershey's Kisses, Hugs, Reese's NutRageous, Kit Kat, Almond Joy, Mounds, York); licorice candy (Twizzlers); pasta (American Beauty, Skinner)

H. J. HEINZ COMPANY

600 Grant St.
Pittsburgh, PA 15219
Chm, Pres & CEO: Anthony J. F. O'Reilly
VP Organizational Dev & Admin: George C. Greer
Employees: 42,200

Phone: 412-456-5700
Fax: 412-237-7883

Jobs Added Last Year: 6,500 (+18.2%)

Food - ketchup, canned soup, tuna (StarKist), pet food (9-Lives) & diet food (Weight Watchers)

IATROS HEALTH NETWORK, INC.

81 Great Valley Pkwy., Ste. 600
Malvern, PA 19355
Chm, Pres & CEO: Robert T. Eramian
No central personnel officer
Employees: 188

Phone: 610-640-0642
Fax: 610-640-4229

Jobs Added Last Year: 95 (+102.2%)

Medical practice management

INNOVATIVE TECHNICAL SYSTEMS, INC.

444 Jacksonville Rd., Ste. 200
Warminster, PA 18947
Pres: William M. Thompson
CFO: Louis J. Desiderio
Employees: 53

Phone: 215-441-5600
Fax: 215-441-3733

Jobs Added Last Year: 14 (+35.9%)

Computers - proprietary computer integrated facilities management (CIFM) software

INTELLIGENT ELECTRONICS, INC.

411 Eagleview Blvd.
Exton, PA 19341-1117
Chm, Pres & CEO: Richard D. Sanford
Personnel Administrator: Sherri Haines
Employees: 2,569

Phone: 610-458-5500
Fax: 610-458-6702

Jobs Added Last Year: 1,407 (+121.1%)

Retail - wholesale microcomputer systems, workstations, networking & telecommunications equipment & software

INTERSTATE HOTELS COMPANY

Foster Plaza 10, 680 Andersen Dr.
Pittsburgh, PA 15220
Pres & CEO: W. Thomas Parrington
VP Manpower Planning: David Rowe
Employees: 18,200

Phone: 412-937-0600
Fax: 412-937-8050

Jobs Added Last Year: —

Hotels & motels - hotel management & related services (154 hotels) in the US, the District of Columbia, Canada, Mexico, Israel, the Carribean, Thailand & Russia

THE ITALIAN OVEN, INC.

11 Lloyd Ave.
Latrobe, PA 15650
VP Ops & COO: Michael B. Understein
Personnel Adminstrator: Denise Cornelius
Employees: 900

Phone: 412-537-5380
Fax: 412-537-6264

Jobs Added Last Year: 250 (+38.5%)

Retail - restaurants

JLG INDUSTRIES, INC.

1 JLG Dr.
McConnellsburg, PA 17233-9502
Chm, Pres & CEO: L. David Black
VP HR: Samuel D. Swope
Employees: 2,222

Phone: 717-485-5161
Fax: 717-485-6417

Jobs Added Last Year: 602 (+37.2%)

Machinery - elevating work platforms & truck-mounted materials-handling equipment for use in the construction, industrial, petrochemical, commercial, sports & entertainment industries

KENNAMETAL INC.

Rte. 981 at Westmoreland County Airport
PO Box 231
Latrobe, PA 15650-0231
Pres & CEO: Robert L. McGeehan
Dir HR: Timothy D. Hudson
Employees: 7,000

Phone: 412-539-5000
Fax: 412-539-4710

Jobs Added Last Year: 400 (+6.1%)

Machine tools & related products - metalworking, mining & highway construction tools

KLEINERT'S, INC.

120 W. Germantown Pike, Ste. 100
Plymouth Meeting, PA 19462-1420
Chm: Jack Brier
VP HR: Denise Hale
Employees: 1,454

Phone: 610-828-7261
Fax: 610-828-4589

Jobs Added Last Year: 453 (+45.3%)

Apparel - children's clothing

KULICKE AND SOFFA INDUSTRIES

2101 Blair Mill Rd.
Willow Grove, PA 19090
Chm & CEO: C. Scott Kulicke
VP HR: Mark H. Heeter
Employees: 1,876

Phone: 215-784-6000
Fax: 215-659-7588

Jobs Added Last Year: 649 (+52.9%)

Machinery - semiconductor assembly systems, including wire bonders, dicing saws & die bonders

MELLON BANK CORPORATION

One Mellon Bank Ctr.
Pittsburgh, PA 15258-0001
Chm, Pres & CEO: Frank V. Cahouet
EVP HR: D. Michael Roark
Employees: 24,300

Phone: 412-234-5000
Fax: 412-234-6265

Jobs Cut Last Year: 700 (-2.8%)

Banks - Northeast

MINE SAFETY APPLIANCES COMPANY

121 Gamma Dr., RIDC Industrial Park
Pittsburgh, PA 15238
Chm, Pres & CEO: John T. Ryan III
VP Personnel: D. E. Crean
Employees: 5,100

Phone: 412-967-3000
Fax: 412-967-3326

Jobs Added Last Year: 600 (+13.3%)

Protection - respiratory, eye, ear & face protective equipment; mining safety equipment; instruments to monitor & analyze workplace environments & control processes

MOTHERS WORK, INC.

1309 Noble St.
Philadelphia, PA 19123
Chm & CEO: Dan W. Matthias
Personnel Mgr: Melissa Eskin
Employees: 2,560

Phone: 215-625-9259
Fax: 215-440-9845

Jobs Added Last Year: 2,074 (+426.7%)

Retail - career, casual & special occasion maternity apparel (#1 in US: Mothers Work, Mimi Maternity, Maternity Works, A Pea in the Pod)

NATIONAL MEDIA CORPORATION

1700 Walnut St.
Philadelphia, PA 19103
Pres & CEO: Mark P. Hershhorn
HR Mgr: Sabrina Childs
Employees: 275

Phone: 215-772-5000
Fax: 215-772-5038

Jobs Added Last Year: 97 (+54.5%)

TV production & programming - TV infomercials

NOBEL EDUCATION DYNAMICS, INC.

1400 N. Providence Rd., Ste. 3055
Media, PA 19063
Chm, Pres & CEO: A. J. Clegg
Dir HR: Karen Bishop
Employees: 2,500

Phone: 610-891-8200
Fax: 610-891-8222

Jobs Added Last Year: 1,000 (+66.7%)

Schools - child-care centers & private schools, preschool through junior high

NOVACARE, INC.

1016 W. Ninth Ave.
King of Prussia, PA 19406
Chm & CEO: John H. Foster
SVP HR: Arthur "Bud" T. Locilento Jr.
Employees: 11,000

Phone: 610-992-7200
Fax: 610-992-3328

Jobs Cut Last Year: 512 (-4.4%)

Medical services - comprehensive rehabilitation services

OWOSSO CORPORATION

One Tower Bridge, 100 Front St., Ste. 1400
West Conshohocken, PA 19428
CEO, Treas & Sec: George B. Lemmon Jr.
SVP Fin, CFO & Asst Sec: John H. Wert Jr.
Employees: 1,345

Phone: 610-834-0222
Fax: 610-834-8664

Jobs Added Last Year: 570 (+73.5%)

Machinery - electric motors & electromechanical timers, heat transfer coils & replacement camshaft bearings for internal combustion gas engines; agricultural equipment

PECO ENERGY COMPANY

2301 Market St., PO Box 8699
Philadelphia, PA 19101-8699
Chm & CEO: Joseph F. Paquette Jr.
SVP HR: William J. Kaschub
Employees: 7,217

Phone: 215-841-5555
Fax: 215-841-4188

Jobs Cut Last Year: 1,835 (-20.3%)

Utility - electric power & natural gas

 An in-depth profile of this company is available
to subscribers on Hoover's Online at www.hoovers.com.

PENN MUTUAL LIFE INSURANCE CO.

Independence Sq.
Philadelphia, PA 19172
Chm & CEO: John E. Tait
VP HR: Catherine B. Strauss
Employees: 2,732

Phone: 215-956-8000
Fax: 215-956-8347

Jobs Added Last Year: 1,622 (+146.1%)

Insurance - life

THE PENNSYLVANIA STATE UNIVERSITY

408 Old Main
University Park, PA 16802
Pres: Graham B. Spanier
Dir Emp Svcs: Robert Kidder
Employees: 16,000

Phone: 814-865-4700
Fax: 814-865-7145

Jobs Added Last Year: 162 (+1.0%)

University

THE PEP BOYS - MANNY, MOE & JACK

3111 W. Allegheny Ave.
Philadelphia, PA 19132
Chm, Pres & CEO: Mitchell G. Leibovitz
VP HR: Roger A. Rendin
Employees: 17,591

Phone: 215-229-9000
Fax: 215-227-9533

Jobs Added Last Year: 1,591 (+9.9%)

Auto parts - retail sales of auto parts and accessories

PNC BANK CORP.

One PNC Plaza, 249 Fifth Ave.
Pittsburgh, PA 15222-2707
Chm & CEO: Thomas H. O'Brien
SVP HR: Daniel F. Gillis
Employees: 25,400

Phone: 412-762-3900
Fax: 412-762-6238

Jobs Added Last Year: 7,400 (+41.1%)

Banks - Northeast

PP&L RESOURCES, INC.

Two N. Ninth St.
Allentown, PA 18101-1179
Chm, Pres & CEO: William F. Hecht
VP HR & Dev: Robert S. Gombos
Employees: 6,661

Phone: 610-774-5151
Fax: 610-774-4198

Jobs Cut Last Year: 770 (-10.4%)

Utility - electric power

PPG INDUSTRIES, INC.

One PPG Place
Pittsburgh, PA 15272
Chm & CEO: Jerry E. Dempsey
SVP HR & Admin: Russell L. Crane
Employees: 31,200

Phone: 412-434-3131
Fax: 412-434-2448

Jobs Added Last Year: 400 (+1.3%)

Chemicals - protective & decorative coatings, flat glass & continuous-strand fiber glass for manufacturing, construction, automotive, chemical processing & other industries

PRIMESTAR PARTNERS L.P.

3 Bala Plaza West
Bala Cynwyd, PA 19004
Chm & CEO: James L. Gray
Dir Emp Relations: Barbara Caprice
Employees: 75

Phone: 610-660-6100
Fax: 610-660-6112

Jobs Added Last Year: 34 (+82.9%)

Cable TV - digital satellite programming (partnership of Comcast, Continental Cablevision, Cox, Newhouse Broadcasting, TCI, Time Warner & General Electric)

R & B, INC.

3400 E. Walnut St.
Colmar, PA 18915
Chm, Pres & CEO: Richard N. Berman
Dir HR: Ardyss Van Horn
Employees: 764

Phone: 215-997-1800
Fax: 215-997-8577

Jobs Added Last Year: 257 (+50.7%)

Automotive & trucking - "hard-to-find" parts for the automotive aftermarket, including window handles, headlamp aiming screws, oil drain plugs & gaskets

RENT-WAY, INC.

3230 W. Lake Rd.
Erie, PA 16505
Pres & CEO: William E. Morgenstern
Dir HR: Joseph Bruzga
Employees: 496

Phone: 814-836-0618
Fax: 814-835-6865

Jobs Added Last Year: 246 (+98.4%)

Leasing - rent-to-own home entertainment equipment, furniture & appliances

RHONE-POULENC RORER INC.

500 Arcola Rd.
Collegeville, PA 19426-0107
Pres & CEO: Michel de Rosen
SVP & Gen Mgr HR: Hadia Lefavre
Employees: 28,000

Phone: 610-454-8000
Fax: 610-454-3812

Jobs Added Last Year: 5,900 (+26.7%)

Drugs - pharmaceutical products, including prescription & over-the-counter medicines, plasma-derived products & bulk pharmaceuticals

RITE AID CORPORATION

30 Hunter Ln.
Camp Hill, PA 17011-2404
Chm & CEO: Martin L. Grass
SVP HR: Jim Talton
Employees: 35,700

Phone: 717-761-2633
Fax: 717-975-5871

Jobs Cut Last Year: 1,000 (-2.7%)

Retail - discount drugstores (#1 in US with approximately 2,700 stores)

ROHM AND HAAS COMPANY

100 Independence Mall West
Philadelphia, PA 19106-2399
Chm & CEO: J. Lawrence Wilson
VP HR: Marisa Guerin
Employees: 11,670

Phone: 215-592-3000
Fax: 215-592-3377

Jobs Cut Last Year: 541 (-4.4%)

Chemicals - polymers, resins, plastics, biocides, automotive fluids & agricultural & water-treatment chemicals

ROYAL BANCSHARES OF PENNSYLVANIA

732 Montgomery Ave.
Narberth, PA 19072
Pres: Lee Evan Tabas
Dir Personnel & Mktg: Lorraine E. Feldman
Employees: 117

Phone: 610-668-4700
Fax: 610-668-1185

Jobs Added Last Year: 34 (+41.0%)

Banks - Northeast

SAFEGUARD SCIENTIFICS, INC.

435 Devon Park Dr.
Wayne, PA 19087
Chm, Pres & CEO: Warren V. Musser
Dir Corp Admin: Gerald M. Hogan
Employees: 3,600

Phone: 610-293-0600
Fax: 610-293-0601

Jobs Added Last Year: 700 (+24.1%)

Financial - venture capital investment in high-tech companies (MulyiGen, Tangram Enterprise Solutions, Cambridge Technology Partners)

SCANGRAPHICS, INC.

700 Abbott Dr.
Broomall, PA 19008-4373
Chm, Pres & CEO: Andrew E. Trolio
HR Mgr: Victoria Franchetti
Employees: 55

Phone: 610-328-1040
Fax: 610-543-6257

Jobs Added Last Year: 32 (+139.1%)

Computers - imaging equipment & software (FRIENDS, SRV/SGE software); scanners, printers, plotters & interfaces

SHANER HOTEL GROUP LTD.

303 N. Science Park Rd.
State College, PA 16803
CEO: Lance T. Shaner
Dir HR: Stephanie Capaccio
Employees: 2,000

Phone: 814-234-4460
Fax: 814-234-3919

Jobs Added Last Year: 200 (+11.1%)

Real estate investment trust - hotels

SHARED MEDICAL SYSTEMS CORPORATION

51 Valley Stream Pkwy.
Malvern, PA 19355
Pres & CEO: Marvin S. Cadwell
VP HR: Doug Lawrence
Employees: 4,826

Phone: 610-219-6300
Fax: 610-219-3124

Jobs Added Last Year: 456 (+10.4%)

Medical practice management - computer-based information-processing systems & services

STRAWBRIDGE & CLOTHIER

801 Market St.
Philadelphia, PA 19107-3199
Pres: P. S. Strawbridge
VP Personnel: David W. Strawbridge
Employees: 12,921

Phone: 215-629-6000
Fax: 215-629-7835

Jobs Cut Last Year: 432 (-3.2%)

Retail - regional department stores in Philadelphia, New Jersey & Delaware

SUBMICRON SYSTEMS CORPORATION

6330 Hedgewood Dr., Ste. 150
Allentown, PA 18106
Chm, Pres & CEO: David F. Levy
Mgr HR: Amy Anderson
Employees: 681

Phone: 610-391-9200
Fax: 610-391-1982

Jobs Added Last Year: 374 (+121.8%)

Machinery - semiconductor manufacturing equipment

SUN COMPANY, INC.

10 Penn Ctr., 1801 Market St.
Philadelphia, PA 19103-1699
Chm, Pres & CEO: Robert H. Campbell
VP HR: Albert Little
Employees: 11,995

Phone: 215-977-3000
Fax: 215-977-3409

Jobs Cut Last Year: 2,573 (-17.7%)

Oil & gas - integrated; commercial real estate development

An in-depth profile of this company is available to subscribers on Hoover's Online at www.hoovers.com.

287

SUNGARD DATA SYSTEMS INC.

1285 Drummers Ln. Phone: 610-341-8700
Wayne, PA 19087 Fax: 610-341-8739
Chm, Pres & CEO: James L. Mann
VP HR: Donna J. Pedrick
Employees: 2,900

Jobs Added Last Year: 400 (+16.0%)

Computers - investment support services; disaster recovery services for computers shut down by natural or man-made catastrophes

TASTY BAKING COMPANY

2801 Hunting Park Ave. Phone: 215-221-8500
Philadelphia, PA 19129 Fax: 215-225-2511
Pres & CEO: Carl S. Watts
VP HR: William E. Mahoney
Employees: 1,300

Jobs Added Last Year: 200 (+18.2%)

Food - cookies, cakes & snack foods (Tastykake)

TECHNITROL, INC.

1210 Northbrook Dr., Ste. 385 Phone: 215-355-2900
Trevose, PA 19053 Fax: 215-355-2914
Pres & CEO: Thomas J. Flakoff
Dir HR: Jim Spangler
Employees: 9,300

Jobs Added Last Year: 6,159 (+196.1%)

Electrical products - scales, measuring equipment, electrical contacts & metallurgical products

TELEFLEX INCORPORATED

630 W. Germantown Pike, Ste 450 Phone: 610-834-6301
Plymouth Meeting, PA 19462 Fax: 610-834-8307
Pres & CEO: David S. Boyer
VP HR: Robert D. Boldt
Employees: 9,800

Jobs Added Last Year: 800 (+8.9%)

Instruments - precision controls & systems for military & commercial use; intravenous catheter tubing & general surgical instruments; mechanical steering systems for power boats

TOLLGRADE COMMUNICATIONS, INC.

493 Nixon Rd. Phone: 412-274-2156
Cheswick, PA 15024 Fax: 412-274-8017
CEO: Christian Allison
VP HR, Safety & Security: Joe Giannetti
Employees: 126

Jobs Added Last Year: 30 (+31.3%)

Telecommunications equipment - products which allow telephone companies to use their existing line test systems to remotely diagnose problems in phone lines

TSENG LABS, INC.

6 Terry Dr. Phone: 215-968-0502
Newtown, PA 18940 Fax: 215-860-7713
Pres & CEO: Jack Tseng
Treas: Barbara J. Hawkins
Employees: 95

Jobs Added Last Year: 32 (+50.8%)

Electrical components - video graphics microchips, adapters & controllers for PCs

Re-Employment 2000 — http://www.inetbiz.com/re-employment2000/

TUSCARORA INCORPORATED

800 Fifth Ave.   Phone: 412-843-8200
New Brighton, PA 15066   Fax: 412-847-2140
Chm, Pres & CEO: John P. O'Leary Jr.
HR Mgr: Irene McAllister
Employees: 1,511
Jobs Added Last Year: 466 (+44.6%)

Containers - custom molded polystyrene foam packaging (#1 in US) for high technology, consumer electronics, major appliances & automotive industries

THE UNIVERSITY OF PENNSYLVANIA

3451 Walnut St.   Phone: 215-898-5000
Philadelphia, PA 19104   Fax: 215-898-9659
Pres: Judith Rodin
HR Mgr: Susan Curran
Employees: 20,500
Jobs Added Last Year: —

University

UGI CORPORATION

460 N. Gulph   Phone: 610-337-1000
King of Prussia, PA 19406   Fax: 610-992-3259
VC, Pres & CEO: Lon R. Greenberg
VP HR: Annalee C. Bullman
Employees: 6,406
Jobs Added Last Year: 2,886 (+82.0%)

Utility - natural gas & propane distribution; electric utilities

THE UNIVERSITY OF PITTSBURGH

4200 Fifth Ave.   Phone: 412-624-4141
Pittsburgh, PA 15260   Fax: 412-624-1150
Chancellor: J. Dennis O'Connor
Dir HR: Darlene Lewis
Employees: 9,000
Jobs Added Last Year: —

University

UNION PACIFIC CORPORATION

Martin Towers, Eighth & Eaton Aves.   Phone: 610-861-3200
Bethlehem, PA 18018   Fax: 610-861-3220
Chm & CEO: Drew Lewis
SVP HR: Ursula F. Fairbairn
Employees: 49,500
Jobs Added Last Year: 2,600 (+5.5%)

Transportation - rail (Union Pacific Railroad Company, Missouri Pacific Railroad Company) & trucking (Overnite)

U.S. HEALTHCARE, INC.

980 Jolly Rd.   Phone: 215-628-4800
Blue Bell, PA 19422   Fax: 215-283-6579
Chm & Principal Exec Officer: Leonard Abramson
VP HR: Rob Rosend
Employees: 4,980
Jobs Added Last Year: 712 (+16.7%)

Health maintenance organization

UNISYS CORPORATION

Township Line & Union Meeting Rds.   Phone: 215-986-4011
Blue Bell, PA 19422-9945   Fax: 215-986-2312
Chm & CEO: James A. Unruh
VP Worldwide HR: David O. Aker
Employees: 37,400
Jobs Cut Last Year: 8,900 (-19.2%)

Computers - network servers, peripherals, workstations, software, & systems-integration & equipment-maintenance services

USX-MARATHON GROUP

600 Grant St.   Phone: 412-433-1121
Pittsburgh, PA 15230   Fax: 412-433-5733
VC Marathon Group & Pres, Marathon Oil: Victor G. Beghini
VP HR & Environment: Kenneth L. Matheny
Employees: 21,015
Jobs Added Last Year: 10 (+0.0%)

Oil & gas - US integrated; natural-gas utility service

UNIVERSAL HEALTH SERVICES, INC.

367 S. Gulph Rd.   Phone: 610-768-3300
King of Prussia, PA 19406   Fax: 610-768-3336
Chm, Pres & CEO: Alan B. Miller
VP HR: Eileen Bove
Employees: 12,000
Jobs Added Last Year: 2,200 (+22.4%)

Hospitals - acute care; behavioral health centers, ambulatory surgery centers & radiation oncology centers

USX-U.S. STEEL GROUP

600 Grant St.   Phone: 412-433-1121
Pittsburgh, PA 15219-4776   Fax: 412-433-5733
Chm & CEO: Thomas J. Usher
VP Emp Relations: Thomas W. Sterling
Employees: 20,845
Jobs Cut Last Year: 465 (-2.2%)

Steel - mill products, coke & taconite pellets; mineral resource management; domestic coal mining; engineering & consulting services; technology licensing; oil & gas production

---

 An in-depth profile of this company is available to subscribers on Hoover's Online at www.hoovers.com.

UTI ENERGY CORPORATION

485 Devon Park Dr., Ste. 112
Wayne, PA 19087
Pres & CEO: Vaughn E. Drum
HR Coordinator: Patricia Pellicciotti
Employees: 650

Phone: 610-971-9600
Fax: 610-964-0141

Jobs Added Last Year: 165 (+34.0%)

Oil & gas - onshore contract drilling services

VF CORPORATION

1047 N. Park Rd.
Wyomissing, PA 19610
Pres & CEO: Mackey J. McDonald
VP Admin & HR : Susan L. Williams
Employees: 64,000

Phone: 610-378-1151
Fax: 610-375-9371

Jobs Cut Last Year: 4,000 (-5.9%)

Apparel - jeanswear, knitwear, intimate apparel, children's play-wear & other apparel

VISHAY INTERTECHNOLOGY, INC.

63 Lincoln Hwy.
Malvern, PA 19355-2120
Chm, Pres & CEO: Felix Zandman
VP & Sec: William J. Spires
Employees: 17,900

Phone: 610-644-1300
Fax: 610-296-0657

Jobs Added Last Year: 1,100 (+6.5%)

Electronics - passive components, including resistors, capacitors & inductors

WEIS MARKETS, INC.

1000 S. Second St.
Sunbury, PA 17801
Pres: Norman S. Rich
Dir Emp Relations: Alan Corcoran
Employees: 16,500

Phone: 717-286-4571
Fax: 717-286-3286

Jobs Added Last Year: 0

Retail - supermarkets

WESCO DISTRIBUTION

4 Station Square, Commerce Ct., Ste. 700
Pittsburgh, PA 15219
Pres & CEO: Roy W. Haley
Mgr HR: Mike Mehagan
Employees: 4,500

Phone: 412-454-2200
Fax: 412-244-2000

Jobs Added Last Year: 1,000 (+28.6%)

Electrical products - distribution

WEST COMPANY, INC.

101 Gordon Dr., PO Box 645
Lionville, PA 19341-0645
Chm, Pres & CEO: William G. Little
SVP HR: George R. Bennyhoff
Employees: 5,210

Phone: 610-594-2900
Fax: 610-594-3014

Jobs Added Last Year: —

Medical & dental supplies - syringe parts & components used in blood sampling, analysis devices & IV-administration sets; packaging products

WESTINGHOUSE ELECTRIC CORP.

Westinghouse Bldg., 11 Stanwix St.
Pittsburgh, PA 15222-1384
Chm & CEO: Michael H. Jordan
SVP HR: David Zemelman
Employees: 77,813

Phone: 412-244-2000
Fax: 412-642-4874

Jobs Cut Last Year: 6,587 (-7.8%)

Diversified operations - broadcasting (CBS network, 16 radio & 5 TV stations); nuclear power; transport refrigeration; environmental services; security products; network & wireless services

YORK INTERNATIONAL CORP.

631 S. Richland Ave.
York, PA 17403
Chm, Pres & CEO: Robert N. Pokelwaldt
VP HR: Wayne J. Kennedy
Employees: 19,000

Phone: 717-771-7890
Fax: 717-771-7440

Jobs Added Last Year: 3,100 (+19.5%)

Building products - commercial & residential heating, ventilation, air conditioning & refrigeration products

RHODE ISLAND

AMERICAN POWER CONVERSION CORPORATION

132 Fairgrounds Rd.
West Kingston, RI 02892
Chm, Pres & CEO: Rodger B. Dowdell Jr.
Mgr HR: Lisa Defruscio
Employees: 2,340

Phone: 401-789-5735
Fax: 401-788-2710

Jobs Added Last Year: 350 (+17.6%)

Electrical products - uninterruptible power supplies, electrical surge protection devices & battery backups for computer systems

BUGABOO CREEK STEAK HOUSE

1275 Wampanoag Tr.
East Providence, RI 02915
Chm, Pres & CEO: Edward P. Grace III
VP Admin & Sec: Corinne A. Sylvia
Employees: 1,050

Phone: 401-433-5500
Fax: 401-433-5986

Jobs Added Last Year: 640 (+156.1%)

Retail - restaurants (Bugaboo Creek Steak House, The Capital Grille)

GTECH HOLDINGS CORPORATION

55 Technology Way
West Greenwich, RI 02817
Co-Chm & CEO: Guy B. Snowden
VP HR: Stephen A. Davidson
Employees: 4,300

Phone: 401-392-1000
Fax: 401-392-3540

Jobs Added Last Year: 300 (+7.5%)

Gambling equipment & services - computerized on-line lottery systems; electronic delivery of government entitlements (e.g., food stamps)

HASBRO, INC.

1027 Newport Ave.
Pawtucket, RI 02861
Chm, Pres & CEO: Alan G. Hassenfeld
SVP HR: Sherry Turner
Employees: 13,000

Phone: 401-431-8697
Fax: 401-431-8535

Jobs Added Last Year: 500 (+4.0%)

Toys - games (Playskool, Tonka, Kenner), puzzles, dolls (Raggedy Ann, Raggedy Andy), action figures (Batman, Star Wars, G.I. Joe), plush products & infant apparel

NORTEK, INC.

50 Kennedy Plaza
Providence, RI 02903-2360
Chm, Pres & CEO: Richard L. Bready
Mgr Personnel: Jane White
Employees: 6,423

Phone: 401-751-1600
Fax: 401-751-4610

Jobs Added Last Year: 1,106 (+20.8%)

Building products - kitchen range hoods, bath fans, a/c & heating units, bathroom fixture & shower doors

PROVIDENCE JOURNAL COMPANY

75 Fountain St.
Providence, RI 02902-0050
CEO: Stephen Hamblett
VP HR: John A. Bowers
Employees: 2,480

Phone: 401-277-7000
Fax: 401-277-7346

Jobs Added Last Year: 980 (+65.3%)

Publishing - newspapers (Providence Journal-Bulletin); network-affiliated & independent TV stations in 11 cities; video programming

TEXTRON INC.

40 Westminster St.
Providence, RI 02903-2596
Chm & CEO: James F. Hardymon
EVP Admin & Chief HR Officer: William F. Wayland
Employees: 57,000

Phone: 401-421-2800
Fax: 401-421-2878

Jobs Added Last Year: 4,000 (+7.5%)

Diversified operations - industrial products; auto parts; finance & insurance (Paul Revere); helicopters (Bell); aircraft (Cessna)

AVX CORPORATION

801 17th Ave. South
Myrtle Beach, SC 29577
Pres & CEO: Benedict P. Rosen
Dir HR: Kathryn Byrd
Employees: 12,000

Phone: 803-448-9411
Fax: 803-444-0424

Jobs Added Last Year: 0

Electronics - ceramic & tantalum capacitors

BOWATER INCORPORATED

55 E. Camperdown Way
Greenville, SC 29602
Pres & CEO: Arnold M. Nemirow
VP HR: Richard F. Frisch
Employees: 5,500

Phone: 864-271-7733
Fax: 864-282-9482

Jobs Cut Last Year: 500 (-8.3%)

Paper & paper products - newsprint (#1 in US) & paper for magazines, catalogs & phone books & continuous-form stock for computer printers

CONSO PRODUCTS COMPANY

513 N. Duncan Bypass, PO Box 326
Union, SC 29379
Pres & CEO: S. Duane Southerland Jr.
Personnel Mgr: Sharon O'Dell
Employees: 1,472

Phone: 864-427-9004
Fax: 864-427-8820

Jobs Added Last Year: 295 (+25.1%)

Textiles - decorative trimmings, including tassels & lace, for the home furnishings industry

An in-depth profile of this company is available to subscribers on Hoover's Online at www.hoovers.com.

291

DATASTREAM SYSTEMS, INC.

1200 Woodriff Rd., Ste. C-40   Phone: 864-297-6775
Greenville, SC 29607   Fax: 864-627-7227
Chm, Pres & CEO: Larry G. Blackwell
Dir HR: Diane Newell
Employees: 211

Jobs Added Last Year: 97 (+85.1%)

Computers - Microsoft Windows-based maintenance management software that tracks facilities & equipment maintenance, parts inventories & personnel

DELTA WOODSIDE INDUSTRIES, INC.

233 N. Main St., Hammond Sq., Ste. 200   Phone: 864-232-8301
Greenville, SC 29601   Fax: 864-232-6164
Pres & CEO: E. Erwin Maddrey II
VP & Sec: Jane H. Greer
Employees: 7,500

Jobs Added Last Year: —

Apparel - casual wear (Duck Head); woven & knitted fabrics; fitness equipment (Nautilus)

FLAGSTAR COMPANIES, INC.

203 E. Main St.   Phone: 864-597-8000
Spartanburg, SC 29319-9966   Fax: 864-597-8780
Chm, Pres & CEO: James B. Adamson
EVP HR & Corp Affairs: Edna K. Morris
Employees: 88,000

Jobs Cut Last Year: 2,000 (-2.2%)

Retail - restaurants (Denny's, Quincy's Family Steakhouse, El Pollo Loco, Hardee's franchisee) & food service (Canteen)

GREENWOOD MILLS

PO Drawer 1017   Phone: 864-229-2571
Greenwood, SC 29648   Fax: 864-229-1111
Chm: James C. Self Jr.
SVP HR: Bill Whaley
Employees: 7,100

Jobs Added Last Year: 100 (+1.4%)

Textiles - denim, other fabrics

HAMPSHIRE GROUP, LTD.

215 Commerce Blvd.   Phone: 864-225-6232
Anderson, SC 29621   Fax: 864-225-4421
Chm, Pres & CEO: Ludwig Kuttner
HR Administrator: Bill Kennedy
Employees: 2,500

Jobs Added Last Year: 765 (+44.1%)

Apparel - sweaters (Designers Originals) & women's hosiery

INSIGNIA FINANCIAL GROUP, INC.

One Insignia Financial Plaza, PO Box 1089   Phone: 864-239-1000
Greenville, SC 29602   Fax: 864-239-1032
Chm & CEO: Andrew L. Farkas
SVP HR & Admin: S. Richard Sargent
Employees: 7,800

Jobs Added Last Year: 0

Real estate operations - property management, partnership administration & mortgage banking services in more than 500 cities in 47 states

THE INTERTECH GROUP INC.

4838 Jenkins Ave.   Phone: 803-744-5174
North Charleston, SC 29406   Fax: 803-747-4092
Chm, Pres & CEO: Jerry Zucker
Dir HR: Al Tiedemann
Employees: 5,000

Jobs Added Last Year: —

Wholesale distribution - sanitation & cleaning products to the food service industry, including disposable shoe covers & nonwoven wipers (PGI Nonwovens)

JPS TEXTILE GROUP INC.

555 N. Pleasantburg Dr., Ste. 202   Phone: 864-239-3900
Greenville, SC 29607   Fax: 864-271-9939
Chm & CEO: Steven M. Friedman
VP HR: Monnie L. Broome
Employees: 5,900

Jobs Cut Last Year: 2,100 (-26.3%)

Textiles - mill products

KEMET CORPORATION

PO Box 5928   Phone: 864-963-6300
Greenville, SC 29606   Fax: 864-967-6800
Chm & CEO: David E. Maguire
SVP HR & Sec: Glen H. Spears
Employees: 9,976

Jobs Added Last Year: 1,586 (+18.9%)

Electrical components - tantalum & ceramic capacitors

MILLIKEN & CO.

920 Milliken Rd.   Phone: 803-573-2020
Spartanburg, SC 29303   Fax: 803-573-2100
Chm & CEO: Roger Milliken
VP HR: Tommy Hodge
Employees: 13,500

Jobs Added Last Year: 0

Textiles - mill products

MOOVIES, INC.

3172 Wade Hampton Blvd.
Taylors, SC 29687
Pres & CEO: John L. Taylor
Dir HR: Kelly McCurley
Employees: 1,875

Phone: 864-213-1700
Fax: 864-213-1706

Jobs Added Last Year: 832 (+79.8%)

Retail - video specialty stores

RESOURCE BANCSHARES MORTGAGE GROUP INC.

7909 Parklane Rd.
Columbia, SC 29223
Pres & CEO: Edward J. Sebastian
SVP HR: R. Michael Watson Jr.
Employees: 880

Phone: 803-741-3000
Fax: 803-741-3583

Jobs Added Last Year: 529 (+150.7%)

Financial - mortgages & related services

RYAN'S FAMILY STEAK HOUSES, INC.

405 Lancaster Ave., PO Box 100
Greer, SC 29652
Chm, Pres & CEO: Charles D. Way
VP HR: James R. Hart
Employees: 15,000

Phone: 864-879-1000
Fax: 864-877-0974

Jobs Added Last Year: 0

Retail - restaurants

SCANSOURCE, INC.

6 Logue Ct., Ste. G
Greenville, SC 29615
Chm & CEO: Steven H. Owings
CFO & Treas: Jeffery A. Bryson
Employees: 52

Phone: 864-288-2432
Fax: 864-288-1165

Jobs Added Last Year: 19 (+57.6%)

Wholesale distribution - bar code equipment, scanners, receipt printers & magnetic stripe readers

SONOCO PRODUCTS COMPANY

One N. Second St., PO Box 160
Hartsville, SC 29551-0160
Chm, Pres & CEO: Charles W. Coker
VP HR: Cynthia Hartley
Employees: 19,000

Phone: 803-383-7000
Fax: 803-339-6078

Jobs Added Last Year: 1,800 (+10.5%)

Containers - paperboard- & plastic-based packaging, paperboard production & recovered-paper collection

SPRINGS INDUSTRIES, INC.

205 N. White St.
Fort Mill, SC 29715
Chm & CEO: Walter Y. Elisha
SVP Growth & Dev & HR: J. Spratt White
Employees: 22,600

Phone: 803-547-1500
Fax: 803-547-1636

Jobs Added Last Year: 2,300 (+11.3%)

Textiles - home furnishings & specialty fabrics, including sheets, comforters, towels & drapes; blinds & decorative hardware

Jobnet — http://www.jobnet.org/

An in-depth profile of this company is available to subscribers on Hoover's Online at www.hoovers.com.

293

THE THAXTON GROUP, INC.

1524 Pageland Hwy.   Phone: 803-285-4336
Lancaster, SC 29721   Fax: 803-286-5770
Chm & CEO: James Thaxton
Dir HR: Dennis Belcher
Employees: 94

Jobs Added Last Year: 31 (+49.2%)

Financial - retail installment contracts for automobiles

UCI MEDICAL AFFILIATES, INC.

1901 Main St., Ste. 1200, Mail Code 1105   Phone: 803-252-3661
Columbia, SC 29201   Fax: 803-252-8077
Pres & CEO: M. F. McFarland III
Payroll Mgr: Renee Adams
Employees: 301

Jobs Added Last Year: 99 (+49.0%)

Medical practice management - nonmedical management &
administrative services for free standing medical centers

ADVOCAT INC.

7108 Crossroads Blvd., Ste. 313   Phone: 615-370-9255
Brentwood, TN 37027   Fax: 615-373-8965
Chm & CEO: Charles W. Birkett
Dir HR: Robert Rice
Employees: 4,000

Jobs Added Last Year: 900 (+29.0%)

Nursing homes & retirement centers

AUTOZONE, INC.

123 S. Front St.   Phone: 901-495-6500
Memphis, TN 38103-3607   Fax: 901-495-8300
Chm & CEO: Joseph R. Hyde III
VP HR: Francis C. Brown III
Employees: 20,200

Jobs Added Last Year: 2,800 (+16.1%)

Auto parts - new & remanufactured auto parts, maintenance
items & accessories (#1 in US)

DAKTRONICS, INC.

331 32nd Ave., PO Box 5128   Phone: 605-697-4000
Brookings, SD 57006-5128   Fax: 605-697-4700
Pres & CEO: Aelred J. Kurtenbach
Dir HR: Carla Gatzke
Employees: 721

Jobs Added Last Year: 285 (+65.4%)

Computers - programmable information display systems for
sports facilities, government & commercial applications

CENTRAL PARKING CORPORATION

2401 21st Ave. South, Ste. 200   Phone: 615-297-4255
Nashville, TN 37212   Fax: 615-297-6240
Chm & CEO: Monroe J. Carell Jr.
VP HR: Brian M. Rettaliata
Employees: 6,500

Jobs Added Last Year: 500 (+8.3%)

Transportation - vehicle parking & transportation services (#1 in
US); valet parking, billing & collection & parking consulting
services

GATEWAY 2000, INC.

610 Gateway Dr.   Phone: 605-232-2000
North Sioux City, SD 57049-2000 Fax: 605-232-2023
Chm & CEO: Theodore W. Waitt
SVP Corp HR: Robert N. Beck
Employees: 9,300

Jobs Added Last Year: 3,858 (+70.9%)

Computers - IBM-compatible PCs; portable computers &
peripheral products

CLAYTON HOMES, INC.

623 Market St.   Phone: 423-970-7200
Knoxville, TN 37902   Fax: 423-595-4395
Chm & CEO: James L. Clayton
Dir HR: Scott Northcutt
Employees: 4,728

Jobs Added Last Year: 773 (+19.5%)

Building - vertically integrated manufactured home company
(builds, sells, finances & insures)

COLUMBIA/HCA HEALTHCARE CORPORATION

One Park Plaza
Nashville, TN 37203
Chm, Pres & CEO: Richard L. Scott
SVP HR & Admin: Neil D. Hemphill
Employees: 240,000

Phone: 615-327-9551
Fax: 615-320-2222

Jobs Added Last Year: 83,000 (+52.9%)

Hospitals - general, acute-care & specialty hospitals (#1 in US)

COMMUNITY HEALTH SYSTEMS, INC.

155 Franklin Rd., Ste. 400
Brentwood, TN 37027-4600
Pres & CEO: E. Thomas Chaney
VP HR & Admin: Linda K. Parsons
Employees: 7,900

Phone: 615-373-9600
Fax: 615-373-1740

Jobs Added Last Year: 900 (+12.9%)

Hospitals - acute-care & psychiatric hospitals (38 units), primarily in smaller cities & towns in the Southeast & Southwest

CORRECTIONS CORP. OF AMERICA

102 Woodmont Blvd.
Nashville, TN 37205
Chm & CEO: Doctor R. Crants
Dir Personnel: Shirley Harbison
Employees: 5,543

Phone: 615-292-3100
Fax: 615-269-8635

Jobs Added Last Year: 2,772 (+100.0%)

Protection - development & management of correctional & detention facilities in the US, the UK & Australia

COVENANT TRANSPORT, INC.

1320 E. 23rd St.
Chattanooga, TN 37404
Chm, Pres & CEO: David R. Parker
Dir Safety: David Frady
Employees: 2,732

Phone: 423-629-0393
Fax: 423-624-7985

Jobs Added Last Year: 700 (+34.4%)

Transportation - long-haul trucking

CRACKER BARREL OLD COUNTRY STORE, INC.

Hartmann Dr., PO Box 787
Lebanon, TN 37088-0787
Chm & CEO: Dan W. Evins
VP Ops Svcs: Frank J. McAvoy Jr.
Employees: 26,299

Phone: 615-444-5533
Fax: 615-443-9480

Jobs Added Last Year: 4,503 (+20.7%)

Retail - restaurants & gift shops in the central & southern US

DIXIE YARNS, INC.

1100 S. Watkins St.
Chattanooga, TN 37404
Chm, Pres & CEO: Daniel K. Frierson
VP HR: W. Derek Davis
Employees: 5,900

Phone: 423-698-2501
Fax: 423-493-7353

Jobs Cut Last Year: 1,000 (-14.5%)

Textiles - yarns, threads & knit fabrics

DOLLAR GENERAL CORPORATION

104 Woodmont Blvd.
Nashville, TN 37205
Chm, Pres & CEO: Cal Turner Jr.
VP Dev: Walter Carter
Employees: 22,000

Phone: 615-783-2000
Fax: 502-386-9937

Jobs Added Last Year: 4,000 (+22.2%)

Retail - discount & variety

EASTMAN CHEMICAL COMPANY

100 N. Eastman Rd.
Kingsport, TN 37660-5075
Chm & CEO: Earnest W. Deavenport Jr.
VP HR, Comm & Public Affairs: William G. Adams
Employees: 17,500

Phone: 423-229-2000
Fax: 423-229-1351

Jobs Added Last Year: 5 (+0.0%)

Chemicals - polyesters, olefins, organic chemistry & cellulose chemistry

FEDERAL EXPRESS CORPORATION

2005 Corporate Ave.
Memphis, TN 38132
Chm, Pres & CEO: Frederick W. Smith
SVP & Chief Personnel Officer: James A. Perkins
Employees: 107,000

Phone: 901-369-3600
Fax: 901-795-1027

Jobs Added Last Year: 6,000 (+5.9%)

Transportation - express air freight

FIRST AMERICAN CORPORATION

First American Ctr.
Nashville, TN 37237-0700
Chm & CEO: Dennis C. Bottorff
EVP HR: John W. Smithwick
Employees: 3,591

Phone: 615-748-2000
Fax: 615-748-2755

Jobs Added Last Year: 318 (+9.7%)

Banks - Southeast (First American National Bank)

FIRST TENNESSEE NATIONAL CORP.

165 Madison Ave.
Memphis, TN 38103
Chm, Pres & CEO: Ralph Horn
VP HR: Bob Zizina
Employees: 5,653

Phone: 901-523-4444
Fax: 901-523-4945

Jobs Cut Last Year: 815 (-12.6%)

Banks - Southeast (#1 in Tennessee)

FRED'S, INC.

4300 New Getwell Rd.
Memphis, TN 38118
Pres & CEO: Michael J. Hayes
VP HR: Paul Upchurch
Employees: 4,800

Phone: 901-365-8880
Fax: 901-365-8865

Jobs Added Last Year: 300 (+6.7%)

Retail - discount general merchandise stores in 9 states (184 units)

GAYLORD ENTERTAINMENT CO.

One Gaylord Dr.
Nashville, TN 37214
Pres & CEO: Earl W. Wendell
Dir Corp HR: Elwyn Taylor
Employees: 10,000

Phone: 615-316-6000
Fax: 615-316-6320

Jobs Added Last Year: 550 (+5.8%)

Leisure & recreational products - musical show park, convention/resort complex; TV & radio stations & cable networks

HARRAH'S ENTERTAINMENT, INC.

1023 Cherry Rd.
Memphis, TN 38117
Pres & CEO: Philip G. Satre
SVP HR & Comm: Ben C. Peternell
Employees: 22,000

Phone: 901-762-8600
Fax: 901-762-8637

Jobs Cut Last Year: 6,500 (-22.8%)

Gambling resorts & casinos in Reno, Lake Tahoe, Las Vegas, Laughlin, NV & Atlantic City; riverboat casinos in Joliet, IL; dockside casinos in Mississippi, Louisiana & Missouri

INGRAM INDUSTRIES INC.

One Belle Meade Place, 4400 Harding Rd.
Nashville, TN 37205-2244
Chm & PR Dir: Martha Ingram
VP HR: Orrin H. Ingram
Employees: 13,000

Phone: 615-298-8200
Fax: 615-298-8242

Jobs Added Last Year: 3,000 (+30.0%)

Diversified - book wholesaler; drilling equipment; barge service; insurance

INSITUFORM TECHNOLOGIES, INC.

1770 Kirby Pkwy., Ste. 300
Memphis, TN 38138
Pres & CEO: Jean-Paul Richard
VP HR: Raymond P. Toth
Employees: 1,342

Phone: 901-759-7473
Fax: 901-759-7500

Jobs Added Last Year: 501 (+59.6%)

Industrial maintenance - wastewater systems repair using a non-disruptive pipeline rehabilitation process (Insituform Process)

THE KRYSTAL COMPANY

One Union Sq.
Chattanooga, TN 37402
Chm & CEO: Carl D. Long
VP HR: Larry J. Reeher
Employees: 9,300

Phone: 423-757-1550
Fax: 423-757-5610

Jobs Added Last Year: 100 (+1.1%)

Retail - fast-food restaurants

LANDAIR SERVICES, INC.

430 Airport Rd.
Greeneville, TN 37745
Chm, Pres & CEO: Scott M. Niswonger
Mgr Emp Benefits: Sharon Susong
Employees: 1,300

Phone: 423-639-7196
Fax: 423-639-8501

Jobs Added Last Year: 260 (+25.0%)

Transportation - freight services

LIFE CARE CENTERS OF AMERICA, INC.

3570 Keith St. NW
Cleveland, TN 37320
Chm & Pres: Forrest L. Preston
VP Professional Dev & HR: Mark Gibson
Employees: 22,000

Phone: 423-472-9585
Fax: 423-339-8337

Jobs Added Last Year: —

Nursing homes

MAGNETEK, INC.

26 Century Blvd., PO Box 290159
Nashville, TN 37229-0159
Pres & CEO: Ronald N. Hoge
EVP HR: Ore Davis
Employees: 14,700

Phone: 615-316-5100
Fax: 615-316-5181

Jobs Added Last Year: 400 (+2.8%)

Electrical products - fluorescent light ballasts, motors, capacitors, uninterruptible power supplies, wire & other electrical products, motors & control systems

MCKEE FOODS CORPORATION

10260 McKee Rd.   Phone: 423-238-7111
Collegedale, TN 37315   Fax: 423-238-7170
Pres & CEO: Ellsworth D. McKee
No central personnel officer
Employees: 5,000
Jobs Added Last Year: 450 (+9.9%)

Food - snacks

MID-AMERICA APARTMENT COMMUNITIES

6584 Poplar Ave., Ste. 340   Phone: 901-682-6600
Memphis, TN 38138   Fax: 901-682-6667
Chm, Pres & CEO: George E. Cates
VP Training & HR: Marilyn Ligon
Employees: 650
Jobs Added Last Year: 185 (+39.8%)

Real estate investment trust - apartment communities

MIDLAND FINANCIAL GROUP, INC.

825 Grossover Ln., Ste. 112   Phone: 901-680-9100
Memphis, TN 38117   Fax: 901-683-6395
Chm & CEO: Joseph W. McLeary
Mgr HR: Debbie Sparks
Employees: 424
Jobs Added Last Year: 144 (+51.4%)

Insurance - property & casualty, primarily auto insurance for high-risk individuals

NATIONAL HEALTHCARE L.P.

100 Vine St.   Phone: 615-890-2020
Murfreesboro, TN 37130   Fax: 615-890-0123
Pres: W. Andrew Adams
VP Corp Affairs: Dave Lassiter
Employees: 13,500
Jobs Added Last Year: 409 (+3.1%)

Health care - long-term health care centers & home health care programs in the southeastern US; specialized care units, assisted living centers & retirement centers

NN BALL & ROLLER, INC.

800 Tennessee Rd.   Phone: 423-743-9151
Erwin, TN 37650   Fax: 423-743-8870
Chm & CEO: Richard D. Ennen
VP HR & Materials: Leonard Bowman
Employees: 467
Jobs Added Last Year: 140 (+42.8%)

Metal products - steel ball bearings & rollers

O'CHARLEY'S INC.

3038 Sidco Dr.   Phone: 615-256-8500
Nashville, TN 37204   Fax: 615-256-8443
CEO & CFO: Gregory L. Burns
HR Officer: Carol Arrowood
Employees: 5,000
Jobs Added Last Year: 228 (+4.8%)

Retail - casual dining restaurants

OLAN MILLS

PO Box 23456   Phone: 423-622-5141
Chattanooga, TN 37422   Fax: 423-624-4815
Chm: Olan Mills II
Dir HR: Terry Blunt
Employees: 5,100
Jobs Added Last Year: —

Retail - portrait photography studios

ORNDA HEALTHCORP

3401 West End Ave., Ste. 700, PO Box 1200 Phone: 615-383-8599
Nashville, TN 37202-1200   Fax: 615-783-1270
Chm, Pres & CEO: Charles N. Martin
VP HR: James Johnson
Employees: 22,000
Jobs Added Last Year: 2,000 (+10.0%)

Hospitals - psychiatric & acute-care medical-surgical hospitals & surgery centers

PERKINS FAMILY RESTAURANTS, L.P.

6075 Poplar Ave., Ste. 800   Phone: 901-766-6400
Memphis, TN 38119-4709   Fax: 901-766-6482
Chm & CEO: Donald N. Smith
VP HR: Jeanne A. Scott
Employees: 9,000
Jobs Cut Last Year: 200 (-2.2%)

Retail - family-style restaurants

PHYCOR, INC.

30 Burton Hills Blvd., Ste. 400   Phone: 615-665-9066
Nashville, TN 37215   Fax: 615-665-9088
Chm, Pres & CEO: Joseph C. Hutts
Office Mgr: Ann Ayers
Employees: 5,300
Jobs Cut Last Year: 200 (-3.6%)

Medical practice management - multispecialty medical clinic management

PLASTI-LINE, INC.

623 E. Emory Rd., PO Box 59043
Knoxville, TN 37950-9043
Chm & CEO: James R. Martin
VP HR: Kathryn C. Wood
Employees: 1,160

Phone: 423-938-1511
Fax: 423-947-8431

Jobs Added Last Year: 317 (+37.6%)

Electrical products - internally illuminated indoor & outdoor signs

PROMUS HOTEL CORPORATION

755 Crossover Ln.
Memphis, TN 38117
Pres & CEO: Raymond E. Schultz
VP HR: Patricia R. Ferguson
Employees: 8,100

Phone: 901-374-5000
Fax: 901-680-7123

Jobs Added Last Year: —

Hotels & motels - national hotel chains (Embassy Suites, Hampton Inn, Homewood Suites)

PMT SERVICES, INC.

2 Maryland Farm, Ste. 200
Brentwood, TN 37027
Chm, Pres & CEO: Richardson M. Roberts
Dir HR: Shannon Morris
Employees: 231

Phone: 615-254-1539
Fax: 615-254-1549

Jobs Added Last Year: 53 (+29.8%)

Business services - marketing & servicing of electronic credit card authorization & payment systems

QUORUM HEALTH GROUP, INC.

103 Continental Place
Brentwood, TN 37027
Pres & CEO: James E. Dalton
VP Corp Svcs: C. Thomas Neill
Employees: 10,300

Phone: 615-371-7979
Fax: 615-371-4853

Jobs Added Last Year: 1,800 (+21.2%)

Hospitals - acute-care hospitals; management, consulting & support services

PROFFITT'S, INC.

115 N. Calderwood
Alcoa, TN 37701
Chm & CEO: R. Brad Martin
SVP HR & Law Gen Counsel: Brian J. Martin
Employees: 14,000

Phone: 423-983-7000
Fax: 423-981-6336

Jobs Added Last Year: 4,600 (+48.9%)

Retail - regional department stores in the southeast (Proffitt's, McRae's)

REGAL CINEMAS, INC.

7132 Commercial Park Dr.
Knoxville, TN 37918
Chm, Pres & CEO: Michael L. Campbell
Payroll & Benefits Administrator: Debbie Robertson
Employees: 3,816

Phone: 423-922-1123
Fax: 423-922-3188

Jobs Added Last Year: 1,100 (+40.5%)

Motion pictures & services - theaters

Marketing Classifieds — http://www.marketingjobs.com

REPUBLIC AUTOMOTIVE PARTS, INC.

500 Wilson Pike Circle, Ste. 115 Phone: 615-373-2050
Brentwood, TN 37027 Fax: 615-373-1629
Pres & CEO: Keith M. Thompson
Dir HR: Mike Bouldin
Employees: 1,300
Jobs Added Last Year: 280 (+27.5%)

Automotive & trucking - replacement parts for automobiles, heavy-duty trucks, snowmobiles, motorcycles & farm & marine equipment

SERVICE MERCHANDISE COMPANY

7100 Service Merchandise Dr. Phone: 615-660-6000
Brentwood, TN 37027 Fax: 615-660-3319
Chm & CEO: Raymond Zimmerman
SVP HR: Robert C. Eimers
Employees: 26,850
Jobs Cut Last Year: 1,986 (-6.9%)

Retail - catalog showrooms that sell jewelry, housewares, small appliances, silver, crystal, home electronics, patio, lawn & garden accessories, cameras, sporting goods & toys

SHONEY'S, INC.

1727 Elm Hill Pike, PO Box 1260 Phone: 615-391-5201
Nashville, TN 37202 Fax: 615-231-2531
Chm & CEO: C. Stephen Lynn
EVP HR: Deborah D. Hollis
Employees: 29,500
Jobs Cut Last Year: 500 (-1.7%)

Retail - family-style (Shoney's), quick-service seafood (Captain D's) & casual (Fifth Quarter, BarbedWire, Pargo's) restaurants

TENNESSEE VALLEY AUTHORITY

400 W. Summit Hill Dr. Phone: 423-632-2101
Knoxville, TN 37902-1499 Fax: 423-632-6783
Chm: Craven Crowell
SVP HR: Wally Tanksley
Employees: 16,559
Jobs Cut Last Year: 2,468 (-13.0%)

Utility - electric power

THOMAS & BETTS CORPORATION

1555 Lynnfield Rd. Phone: 901-682-7766
Memphis, TN 38119 Fax: 901-685-1988
Chm & CEO: T. Kevin Dunnigan
VP HR: David Myler
Employees: 8,700
Jobs Added Last Year: 1,300 (+17.6%)

Electrical connectors - fiber optic & printed circuit board connectors, ceramic-chip capacitors & other electrial products

UNION PLANTERS CORPORATION

7130 Goodlett Farms Pkwy. Phone: 901-383-6000
Memphis, TN 38018 Fax: 901-383-2830
Chm & CEO: Benjamin W. Rawlins Jr.
VP HR: Faye Weakley
Employees: 5,690
Jobs Added Last Year: 330 (+6.2%)

Banks - Southeast

THE UNIVERSITY OF TENNESSEE

305 Student Services Bldg. Phone: 423-974-2105
Knoxville, TN 37996 Fax: 423-974-6341
Pres: Joseph E. Johnson
Dir HR: Joe Fornes
Employees: 15,000
Jobs Added Last Year: 20 (+0.1%)

University

U.S. XPRESS ENTERPRISES, INC.

2931 S. Market St. Phone: 423-697-7377
Chattanooga, TN 37410 Fax: 423-267-9477
Co-Chm, Pres & Treas: Patrick E. Quinn
Dir HR: Steve Cleary
Employees: 3,373
Jobs Added Last Year: 541 (+19.1%)

Transportation - trucking & related information & logistics services

VANDERBILT UNIVERSITY

110 21st Ave. South Phone: 615-322-7311
Nashville, TN 37203 Fax: 615-343-7286
Chancellor: Joe B. Wyatt
Assoc Vice Chancellor HR: H. Clint Davidson
Employees: 12,040
Jobs Added Last Year: —

University

 An in-depth profile of this company is available to subscribers on Hoover's Online at www.hoovers.com.

299

7TH LEVEL, INC.

1110 E. Collins Blvd., Ste. 122
Richardson, TX 75081
Chm & CEO: George D. Grayson
Mgr Personnel & HR: Sherry Denning
Employees: 203

Phone: 214-498-8100
Fax: 214-437-2717

Jobs Added Last Year: 124 (+157.0%)

Computers - interactive software (TuneLand), screen savers (Take Your Best Shot) & games (Battle Beast)

ACE CASH EXPRESS, INC.

1231 Greenway Dr., Ste. 800
Irving, TX 75038-9904
Pres & CEO: Donald H. Neustadt
VP HR: Sherry L. Detwiler
Employees: 1,252

Phone: 214-550-5000
Fax: 214-550-5150

Jobs Added Last Year: 385 (+44.4%)

Financial - retail check-cashing services

ACR GROUP, INC.

3200 Wilcrest Dr., Ste. 440
Houston, TX 77042-6019
Chm & Pres: Alex Trevino Jr.
Dir HR: Carol Russell
Employees: 170

Phone: 713-780-8532
Fax: 713-780-4067

Jobs Added Last Year: 50 (+41.7%)

Building products - wholesale heating, ventilating, air-condition-ing & refrigeration equipment & supplies

ACS COMMUNICATIONS, INC.

1826 Kramer Ln., Ste. M
Austin, TX 78758
CEO: Robby Sawyer
HR Mgr: Sharon Johnson
Employees: 260

Phone: 512-837-4400
Fax: 512-837-6767

Jobs Added Last Year: 62 (+31.3%)

Telecommunications services - cabling for data & voice systems (d/b/a ACS Dataline)

AFFILIATED COMPUTER SERVICES

2828 N. Haskell
Dallas, TX 75204
Chm & CEO: Darwin Deason
Dir HR: Pam McMahan
Employees: 2,800

Phone: 214-841-6111
Fax: 214-821-8315

Jobs Added Last Year: 600 (+27.3%)

Computers - data processing outsourcing; ATM network (MoneyMaker); information management systems

A. H. BELO CORPORATION

400 S. Record St.
Dallas, TX 75202
Chm, Pres & CEO: Robert W. Decherd
Dir HR: Jeff Lamb
Employees: 3,489

Phone: 214-977-6606
Fax: 214-977-6603

Jobs Added Last Year: 407 (+13.2%)

Broadcasting - radio & TV; newspapers (Dallas Morning News)

AIR-CURE TECHNOLOGIES, INC.

2727 Allen Pkwy., Ste. 760
Houston, TX 77019
Chm, Pres & CEO: Michael P. Lawlor
No central personnel officer
Employees: 464

Phone: 713-676-6104
Fax: 713-520-8228

Jobs Added Last Year: 259 (+126.3%)

Pollution control equipment & services - air-pollution-control, air-treatment & air-moving systems, equipment & components

ALAMO GROUP, INC.

1502 E. Walnut
Seguin, TX 78155
Chm & CEO: Donald J. Douglass
Personnel Mgr: Gabrielle Garcia
Employees: 1,306

Phone: 210-379-1480
Fax: 210-379-0864

Jobs Added Last Year: 294 (+29.1%)

Machinery - tractor-mounted farm equipment & replacement parts

ALLWASTE, INC.

5151 San Felipe, Ste. 1600
Houston, TX 77056
Pres & CEO: Robert M. Chiste
SVP Tech & Admin: James E. Reif
Employees: 4,057

Phone: 713-623-8777
Fax: 713-625-7087

Jobs Added Last Year: 423 (+11.6%)

Waste management - waste-handling, -processing & transportation services

ALPHA TECHNOLOGIES GROUP, INC.

330 Barker Cypress Rd., Ste. 270
Houston, TX 77094
Pres & CEO: Lawrence Butler
VP Admin: Steve Chupik
Employees: 693

Phone: 713-647-9941
Fax: 713-647-0587

Jobs Added Last Year: 182 (+35.6%)

Electrical components - standard heat sinks for microprocessors, connectors, back-panels, cables & cable assemblies

AMERICAN GENERAL CORPORATION

2929 Allen Pkwy.	Phone: 713-522-1111
Houston, TX 77019-2155	Fax: 713-831-3028

Chm & CEO: Harold S. Hook
Dir Corp Personnel: Joann Griffith
Employees: 15,300
Jobs Added Last Year: 2,400 (+18.6%)

Insurance - life

ARMY & AIR FORCE EXCHANGE

3911 S. Walton Walker Blvd.	Phone: 214-312-2011
Dallas, TX 75236	Fax: 214-312-3000

Commander & CEO: Allen D. Bunger
SVP HR: Tom Harmon
Employees: 48,219
Jobs Cut Last Year: 11,781 (-19.6%)

Retail - post & base exchanges at military bases

AMERICAN GENERAL HOSPITALITY INC.

3860 W. Northwest Hwy.	Phone: 214-352-3330
Dallas, TX 75220	Fax: 214-351-0568

Chm, Pres & CEO: Steven Jorns
VP HR: Dorothy Wood
Employees: 6,000
Jobs Added Last Year: 400 (+7.1%)

Hotels (franchisee of Best Western, Comfort Inn, Days Inn, Holiday Inn, Hilton, Courtyard Marriott & Ramada)

ARONEX PHARMACEUTICALS, INC.

3400 Research Forest Dr.	Phone: 713-367-1666
The Woodlands, TX 77381	Fax: 713-367-1676

Pres & CEO: David M. Leech
Mgr HR: Connie Stourt
Employees: 58
Jobs Added Last Year: 17 (+41.5%)

Drugs - treatment of cancer & life-threatening infections

AMERICAN HOMESTAR CORP.

2450 S. Shore Blvd., Ste. 300	Phone: 713-334-9700
League City, TX 77573	Fax: 713-334-9737

Chm & Co-CEO: Finis F. Teeter
Payroll Personnel Administrator: Susan Wilburn
Employees: 1,212
Jobs Added Last Year: 323 (+36.3%)

Building - manufactured homes in the Southwest

ASSOCIATES FIRST CAPITAL CORP.

250 E. Carpenter Fwy.	Phone: 214-541-4000
Irving, TX 75062-2729	Fax: 214-541-7420

Chm & CEO: Keith W. Hughes
SVP Corp HR: Kathy Meyer
Employees: 16,647
Jobs Added Last Year: 1,329 (+8.7%)

Financial - home equity lending, retail sales financing, credit cards & commercial financing services

AMERICREDIT CORP.

200 Bailey Ave.	Phone: 817-332-7000
Fort Worth, TX 76107	Fax: 817-336-9519

Chm, Pres & CEO: Clifton H. Morris Jr.
VP & Dir HR: Patricia A. Jones
Employees: 256
Jobs Added Last Year: 73 (+39.9%)

Financial - funding source for franchised & independent dealers to finance their customers' purchases of used cars

ATC COMMUNICATIONS GROUP, INC.

5950 Berkshire Ln., Ste. 1650	Phone: 214-361-9870
Dallas, TX 75225	Fax: 214-361-9874

Pres & Treas: Michael G. Santry
VP HR: Jeff Bearrows
Employees: 2,617
Jobs Added Last Year: 954 (+57.4%)

Business services - telecommunications-based marketing & information services

AMR CORPORATION

4333 Amon Carter Blvd.	Phone: 817-963-1234
Fort Worth, TX 76155	Fax: 817-967-9641

Chm, Pres & CEO: Robert L. Crandall
SVP Corp Svcs: Thomas J. Kiernan
Employees: 110,000
Jobs Added Last Year: 200 (+0.2%)

Transportation - airline (American Airlines, American Eagle)

AUSTIN INDUSTRIES INC.

3535 Travis St., Ste. 300	Phone: 214-443-5500
Dallas, TX 75204	Fax: 214-443-5581

Pres & CEO: William T. Solomon
Dir HR: Rob Brewer
Employees: 5,100
Jobs Added Last Year: 100 (+2.0%)

Building - commercial & industrial

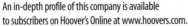 An in-depth profile of this company is available to subscribers on Hoover's Online at www.hoovers.com.

301

BAKER HUGHES INCORPORATED

3900 Essex Ln.   Phone: 713-439-8600
Houston, TX 77027-5177   Fax: 713-439-8699
Chm & CEO: James D. Woods
VP HR: Steve Finley
Employees: 15,200
Jobs Added Last Year: 500 (+3.4%)

Oil field machinery & equipment

BAPTIST MEMORIAL HOSPITAL SYSTEM

660 N. Main St.   Phone: 210-222-8431
San Antonio, TX 78205   Fax: 210-302-3164
Pres & CEO: Callie Smith
VP HR: William McAtee
Employees: 5,500
Jobs Added Last Year: —

Hospitals - not-for-profit system

BAYLOR HEALTH CARE SYSTEM

3500 Gaston Ave.   Phone: 214-820-0111
Dallas, TX 75246   Fax: 214-820-2525
Pres & CEO: Boone Powell Jr.
Dir HR: Beverly Bradshaw
Employees: 11,347
Jobs Cut Last Year: 624 (-5.2%)

Hospitals - not-for-profit system (including Baylor University Medical Center) serving the Dallas area

BAYLOR UNIVERSITY

PO Box 97056   Phone: 817-755-1011
Waco, TX 76798-7056   Fax: 817-755-1490
Pres: Robert B. Sloan Jr.
Asst VP Admin: Cliff Williams
Employees: 1,600
Jobs Added Last Year: 268 (+20.1%)

University - offering 146 undergraduate & 91 graduate degree programs

BENCHMARK ELECTRONICS, INC.

3000 Technology Dr.   Phone: 409-849-6550
Angleton, TX 77515   Fax: 409-848-5270
Pres: Donald E. Nigbor
Dir Corp Admin: Nora Garton
Employees: 568
Jobs Added Last Year: 129 (+29.4%)

Electrical components - printed circuit boards

BJ SERVICES COMPANY

5500 NW Central Dr., PO Box 4442 Phone: 713-462-4239
Houston, TX 77210-4442   Fax: 713-895-5851
Chm, Pres & CEO: J. W. Stewart
Dir HR: Stephen A. Wright
Employees: 4,777
Jobs Added Last Year: 1,997 (+71.8%)

Oil & gas - on & offshore oil field services, including well-cementing, well-stimulation, pipe-laying & leak-detection services

BLUE CROSS AND BLUE SHIELD OF TEXAS

901 S. Central Expwy.   Phone: 214-766-6900
Richardson, TX 75080   Fax: 214-766-6234
Pres & CEO: Rogers K. Coleman
Dir HR: Mike Jarvis
Employees: 4,800
Jobs Added Last Year: 300 (+6.7%)

Insurance - health, hospital & medical service plans

BOLLINGER INDUSTRIES, INC.

222 W. Airport Fwy.   Phone: 214-445-0386
Irving, TX 75062   Fax: 214-438-8471
Chm & CEO: Glenn D. Bollinger
HR Dir: Janice Holden
Employees: 700
Jobs Added Last Year: 260 (+59.1%)

Leisure & recreational products - consumer fitness accessory products, including handheld barbells & dumbbells & aerobic products; sports medicine & safety products

THE BOMBAY COMPANY, INC.

550 Bailey Ave.   Phone: 817-347-8200
Fort Worth, TX 76107   Fax: 817-339-3784
Pres & CEO: Robert E. M. Nourse
VP Store Ops: Jerry Cook
Employees: 5,000
Jobs Added Last Year: 1,000 (+25.0%)

Retail - traditionally styled furniture, prints & accessories

BRINKER INTERNATIONAL, INC.

6820 LBJ Fwy.   Phone: 214-980-9917
Dallas, TX 75240   Fax: 214-770-9593
Pres & CEO: Ronald A. McDougall
SVP HR: John C. Roberts
Employees: 37,500
Jobs Cut Last Year: 500 (-1.3%)

Retail - restaurants (Chili's, Romano's Macaroni Grill, Cozymel's, On the Border)

BROOKSHIRE BROTHERS INCORPORATED

1201 Ellen Trout Dr. Phone: 409-634-8155
Lufkin, TX 75901 Fax: 409-634-8646
Pres: R. H. Brookshire
Dir HR: Tim Hale
Employees: 5,200
Jobs Added Last Year: 200 (+4.0%)

Retail - supermarkets (Budget Chopper, Brookshire Brothers Inc.)

BROOKSHIRE GROCERY COMPANY

1600 SW Loop 323 Phone: 903-534-3000
Tyler, TX 75701 Fax: 903-534-3352
Pres & CEO: James G. Hardin
EVP HR: Tim Brookshire
Employees: 9,600
Jobs Added Last Year: 1,600 (+20.0%)

Retail - supermarkets (Brookshire Grocery Co., Super 1 Food Stores)

BROWNING-FERRIS INDUSTRIES, INC.

757 N. Eldridge Phone: 713-870-8100
Houston, TX 77253 Fax: 713-870-7844
Pres & CEO : Bruce E. Ranck
Divisional VP HR: S. Matt McCoy
Employees: 43,000
Jobs Added Last Year: 6,000 (+16.2%)

Waste management - nonhazardous & medical waste disposal services

BURLINGTON NORTHERN SANTA FE CORP.

3800 Continental Plaza, 777 Main St. Phone: 817-333-2000
Fort Worth, TX 76102-5384 Fax: 817-878-2377
Pres & CEO: Robert D. Krebs
SVP Emp Relations: James B. Dagnon
Employees: 45,655
Jobs Added Last Year: 14,944 (+48.7%)

Transportation - rail

CALTEX PETROLEUM CORPORATION

125 E. John Carpenter Fwy. Phone: 214-830-1000
Irving, TX 75602-2750 Fax: 214-830-1156
Chm & CEO: David Law-Smith
VP HR: E. M. Schmidt
Employees: 7,000
Jobs Cut Last Year: 1,000 (-12.5%)

Oil & gas - refining & marketing (joint venture of Chevron & Texaco)

CAMERON ASHLEY BUILDING

11651 Plano Rd. Phone: 214-860-5100
Dallas, TX 75243 Fax: 214-860-5148
Pres: Walter J. Muratori
VP HR: Thomas R. Miller
Employees: 1,363
Jobs Added Last Year: 212 (+18.4%)

Building products - wholesale roofing, millwork, pool & patio enclosure materials, insulation, siding, steel products & industrial metals

America's Employers — http://www.americasemployers.com

Welcome to America's Employers ...

An in-depth profile of this company is available to subscribers on Hoover's Online at www.hoovers.com.

303

CELEBRITY, INC.

4520 Old Troup Rd., PO Box 6666　　Phone: 903-561-3981
Tyler, TX 75711　　Fax: 903-581-2887
Chm & CEO: Robert H. Patterson Jr.
VP Ops: Roger Craft
Employees: 626

Jobs Added Last Year: 137 (+28.0%)

Wholesale distribution - artificial flowers, foliage, flowering bushes & other decorative accessories for craft stores & wholesale florists

CELLSTAR CORPORATION

1730 Briercroft Ct.　　Phone: 214-466-5000
Carrollton, TX 75006　　Fax: 214-466-9091
Chm & CEO: Alan H. Goldfield
Dir HR: Barbara O'Neal
Employees: 2,008

Jobs Added Last Year: 758 (+60.6%)

Retail - cellular telephones (distribution for Motorola, Nokia, Ericsson, NEC) & auto security systems

CENTEX CORPORATION

3333 Lee Pkwy., Ste. 1200, PO Box 19000　Phone: 214-559-6500
Dallas, TX 75219　　Fax: 214-559-6750
Chm & CEO: Laurence E. Hirsch
VP Fin & Controller: Mike Albright
Employees: 6,500

Jobs Added Last Year: 105 (+1.6%)

Building - residential & commercial; building materials; financial services

CENTRAL AND SOUTH WEST CORP.

1616 Woodall Rodgers Fwy.　　Phone: 214-777-1000
Dallas, TX 75202-1234　　Fax: 214-777-1033
Chm, Pres & CEO: E. R. Brooks
VP Corp Svcs: Venita McCellon-Allen
Employees: 12,000

Jobs Added Last Year: 3,945 (+49.0%)

Utility - electric power; natural gas pipeline

CHIEF AUTO PARTS INCORPORATED

One Lincoln Centre, 5400 LBJ Fwy., Ste. 200 Phone: 214-404-1114
Dallas, TX 75240　　Fax: 214-991-9259
Pres: David H. Eisenberg
Dir HR: Vicki Demas
Employees: 5,600

Jobs Added Last Year: 100 (+1.8%)

Auto parts - retail (over 500 stores)

CINEMARK USA INC.

7502 Greenville Ave., Ste. 800　　Phone: 214-696-1644
Dallas, TX 75231　　Fax: 214-696-3946
CEO: Lee Roy Mitchell
Dir Personnel & Payroll: Peggy McGinnes
Employees: 7,000

Jobs Added Last Year: —

Motion pictures & services - theaters

CLUB CORPORATION INTERNATIONAL

3030 LBJ Fwy., Ste. 700　　Phone: 214-888-7308
Dallas, TX 75234　　Fax: 214-432-0264
Chm & CEO: Robert H. Dedman
SVP HR: Albert Shew
Employees: 24,480

Jobs Added Last Year: 5,280 (+27.5%)

Leisure & recreational services - private club & golf course operations (#1 worldwide) & resorts; bank (Franklin Federal)

THE COASTAL CORPORATION

Coastal Tower, 9 Greenway Plaza　　Phone: 713-877-1400
Houston, TX 77046-0995　　Fax: 713-877-6752
Pres, CEO & CFO: David A. Arledge
Dir Emp Relations: Lloyd Healy
Employees: 15,500

Jobs Cut Last Year: 800 (-4.9%)

Oil & gas - US integrated

COMMERCIAL METALS COMPANY

7800 Stemmons Fwy.　　Phone: 214-689-4300
Dallas, TX 75247　　Fax: 214-689-4320
Pres & CEO: Stanley A. Rabin
SVP Admin: Bert Romberg
Employees: 6,272

Jobs Added Last Year: 1,919 (+44.1%)

Metal processing & fabrication

COMPAQ COMPUTER CORPORATION

20555 State Hwy. 249　　Phone: 713-370-0670
Houston, TX 77070　　Fax: 713-374-1740
Pres & CEO: Eckhard Pfeiffer
SVP HR: Hans W. Gutsch
Employees: 23,884

Jobs Added Last Year: 9,512 (+66.2%)

Computers - PCs (#1 worldwide); peripherals & software (TabWorks)

COMPUSA INC.

14951 N. Dallas Pkwy.
Dallas, TX 75240
Pres & CEO: James F. Halpin
SVP HR, Training & Admin: Paul B. Poyfair
Employees: 7,963

Jobs Added Last Year: 144 (+1.8%)

Retail - computers (#1 in US)

THE CONTINUUM COMPANY, INC.

9500 Arboretum Blvd.
Austin, TX 78759-6399
Pres & CEO: W. Michael Long
HR Dev Mgr: Deborah Stafford
Employees: 4,300

Phone: 512-345-5700
Fax: 512-338-7041

Jobs Added Last Year: 1,300 (+43.3%)

Computers - insurance industry software & data processing services

COMSTOCK RESOURCES, INC.

5005 LBJ Fwy., Ste. 1000
Dallas, TX 75244
Pres & CEO: M. Jay Allison
No central personnel officer
Employees: 54

Phone: 214-701-2000
Fax: 214-701-2111

Jobs Added Last Year: 21 (+63.6%)

Oil & gas - US exploration & production

CONTRAN CORPORATION

5430 LBJ Fwy., Ste. 1700
Dallas, TX 75240
Chm, Pres & CEO: Harold C. Simmons
Emp Benefits Mgr: Keith A. Johnson
Employees: 14,500

Phone: 214-233-1700
Fax: 214-385-0586

Jobs Added Last Year: 0

Diversified operations - refined sugar (Valhi); food & restaurants (Arby's franchisee); chemicals; building products; steel rods, wire & wire products

CONSOLIDATED GRAPHICS, INC.

2210 W. Dallas St.
Houston, TX 77019
Chm & CEO: Joe R. Davis
VP Admin: Janet Swikard
Employees: 998

Phone: 713-529-4200
Fax: 713-525-4305

Jobs Added Last Year: 296 (+42.2%)

Printing - annual reports, product & capability brochures, direct-mail pieces, catalogs & other promotional material for corporate clients

COOPER CAMERON CORPORATION

515 Post Oak Blvd., Ste. 1200
Houston, TX 77027
Pres & CEO: Sheldon R. Erikson
Dir Compensation & Benefits: Jane Crowder
Employees: 7,600

Phone: 713-513-3300
Fax: 713-513-3355

Jobs Cut Last Year: 400 (-5.0%)

Oil field machinery & equipment - valves, wellheads, gas turbines, compressors & turbochargers

THE CONTAINER STORE

2000 Valwood Pkwy.
Dallas, TX 75234
Pres: Garrett Boone
Dir HR: Nancy Donley
Employees: 875

Phone: 214-654-2000
Fax: 214-654-2003

Jobs Added Last Year: 175 (+25.0%)

Retail - household storage & organizational products stores (15 units)

COOPER INDUSTRIES, INC.

1001 Fannin, Ste. 4000
Houston, TX 77002
Chm, Pres, CEO & COO: H. John Riley Jr.
SVP HR: David Sheil
Employees: 40,400

Phone: 713-739-5400
Fax: 713-739-5555

Jobs Cut Last Year: 400 (-1.0%)

Diversified operations - electrical products; electrical power equipment, tools & hardware; automotive products

CONTINENTAL AIRLINES, INC.

2929 Allen Pkwy., Ste. 2010
Houston, TX 77019
Pres & CEO: Gordon M. Bethune
SVP HR: David A. Loeser
Employees: 32,300

Phone: 713-834-5000
Fax: 713-834-2087

Jobs Cut Last Year: 5,500 (-14.6%)

Transportation - airline

COUNTY SEAT STORES INC.

17950 Preston Rd., Ste. 1000
Dallas, TX 75252
CEO: Barry J. C. Parker
Dir HR: Tom Grissom
Employees: 7,714

Phone: 214-248-5100
Fax: 214-248-5214

Jobs Added Last Year: 114 (+1.5%)

Retail - specialty apparel

 An in-depth profile of this company is available to subscribers on Hoover's Online at www.hoovers.com.

CROWN CASINO CORPORATION

2415 W. Northwest Hwy., Ste. 103   Phone: 214-352-7561
Dallas, TX 75220-4446   Fax: 214-357-1974
Chm, Pres & CEO: Edward R. McMurphy
Controller: Mike Cloud
Employees: 361

Jobs Added Last Year: 339 (+1,540.9%)

Gambling resorts & casinos - riverboat gaming casino near New Orleans

CYRIX CORPORATION

2703 N. Central Expwy.   Phone: 214-968-8388
Richardson, TX 75080-0118   Fax: 214-699-9857
Pres & CEO: Gerald D. Rogers
Dir HR: Margaret Quinn
Employees: 389

Jobs Added Last Year: 80 (+25.9%)

Electrical components - IBM PC-compatible microprocessors

DALLAS SEMICONDUCTOR CORP.

4401 S. Beltwood Pkwy.   Phone: 214-450-0400
Dallas, TX 75244-3292   Fax: 214-450-3748
Chm, Pres & CEO: C. V. Prothro
VP HR: Gay Vencill
Employees: 1,078

Jobs Added Last Year: 257 (+31.3%)

Electrical components - integrated circuits & semiconductor-based subsystems

DAL-TILE INTERNATIONAL INC.

7834 Hawn Fwy.   Phone: 214-398-1411
Dallas, TX 75217   Fax: 214-309-4140
Pres & CEO: Howard I. Bull
VP HR: Thomas S. Smith
Employees: 7,100

Jobs Added Last Year: 800 (+12.7%)

Building products - ceramic wall & floor tile (#1 in North America) for residential & commercial use

DELL COMPUTER CORPORATION

2214 W. Braker Ln., Ste. D   Phone: 512-338-4400
Austin, TX 78758-4053   Fax: 512-728-3653
Chm & CEO: Michael S. Dell
VP HR: Julie A. Sackett
Employees: 8,400

Jobs Added Last Year: 2,000 (+31.3%)

Computers - PCs, notebook computers (Latitude) & servers (PowerEdge SP)

DIAGNOSTIC HEALTH SERVICES, INC.

2777 Stemmons Fwy., Ste. 1525   Phone: 214-634-0403
Dallas, TX 75207   Fax: 214-631-8537
Chm & CEO: Max W. Batzer
Dir HR: Marilyn Tortoriello
Employees: 190

Jobs Added Last Year: 65 (+52.0%)

Medical services - diagnostic ultrasound & nuclear-imaging services; cardiovascular laboratory management services; pacemaker-monitoring systems

DIAMOND SHAMROCK, INC.

9830 Colonnade Blvd.   Phone: 210-641-6800
San Antonio, TX 78230   Fax: 210-641-8687
Chm, Pres & CEO: Roger R. Hemminghaus
VP HR: Penelope R. Viteo
Employees: 11,250

Jobs Added Last Year: 4,850 (+75.8%)

Oil refining & marketing

DRESSER INDUSTRIES, INC.

2001 Ross Ave.   Phone: 214-740-6000
Dallas, TX 75201   Fax: 214-740-6584
Pres & CEO: William E. Bradford
VP HR: Paul M. Bryant
Employees: 31,500

Jobs Added Last Year: 2,300 (+7.9%)

Oil field machinery & equipment - well-drilling bits & related equipment; compressors, pumps, turbines, generators & related products

DSC COMMUNICATIONS CORP.

1000 Coit Rd.   Phone: 214-519-3000
Plano, TX 75075-5813   Fax: 214-519-4122
Chm, Pres & CEO: James L. Donald
Dir HR: John O'Loughlin
Employees: 5,860

Jobs Added Last Year: 446 (+8.2%)

Telecommunications equipment - digital switching, transmission & private network system products

ELECTRONIC DATA SYSTEMS CORP.

5400 Legacy Dr.   Phone: 214-604-6000
Plano, TX 75024-3105   Fax: 214-645-6798
Chm, Pres & CEO: Lester M. Alberthal Jr.
SVP Personnel: G. Stuart Reeves
Employees: 71,000

Jobs Added Last Year: 1,000 (+1.4%)

Consulting - outsourcing, consulting & system design services

ELECTROSOURCE, INC.

3800 B Drossett Dr. Phone: 512-445-6606
Austin, TX 78744-1131 Fax: 512-445-6819
Chm, Pres & CEO: Michael G. Semmens
Dir HR: Glenda Massey
Employees: 81
Jobs Added Last Year: 41 (+102.5%)

Automotive & trucking - lead-acid rechargeable storage batteries for electric vehicles

ENSERCH CORPORATION

ENSERCH Center, 300 S. St. Paul St. Phone: 214-651-8700
Dallas, TX 75201-5598 Fax: 214-573-3848
Chm, Pres & CEO: David W. Biegler
VP Ops & Support Systems: Dennis Long
Employees: 5,600
Jobs Added Last Year: 1,400 (+33.3%)

Oil & gas - production & pipeline

EMCARE HOLDINGS INC.

1717 Main St., Ste. 5200 Phone: 214-712-2000
Dallas, TX 75201 Fax: 214-712-2002
Chm & CEO: Leonard M. Riggs Jr.
Dir HR: Michael Lane
Employees: 380
Jobs Added Last Year: 250 (+192.3%)

Medical practice management - physician-services management for hospital emergency departments & urgent-care centers

EQUALNET HOLDING CORP.

EqualNet Plaza, 1250 Wood Branch Park Dr. Phone: 713-556-4600
Houston, TX 77079-1212 Fax: 713-556-4696
Chm & CEO: Zane D. Russell
Dir HR: Kathleen Smalley
Employees: 180
Jobs Added Last Year: 71 (+65.1%)

Telecommunications services - long-distance services

ENERGY BIOSYSTEMS CORPORATION

4200 Research Forest Dr. Phone: 713-364-6100
The Woodlands, TX 77381 Fax: 713-364-6110
Chm, Pres & CEO: John H. Webb
Mgr HR: Marsha A. Nelson
Employees: 96
Jobs Added Last Year: 35 (+57.4%)

Oil & gas - biotechnology-based processes for oil refining & production

EVERGREEN MEDIA CORPORATION

433 E. Las Colinas Blvd., Ste. 1130 Phone: 214-869-9020
Irving, TX 75039 Fax: 214-869-3671
Chm & CEO: Scott K. Ginsburg
HR Mgr: M. Kopel
Employees: 744
Jobs Added Last Year: 159 (+27.2%)

Broadcasting - radio (34 stations)

ENERGY VENTURES, INC.

5 Post Oak Park, Ste. 1760 Phone: 713-297-8400
Houston, TX 77027-3415 Fax: 713-963-9785
Pres & CEO: Bernard J. Duroc-Danner
Office Mgr & Dir HR: Diana Lambert
Employees: 3,800
Jobs Added Last Year: 1,500 (+65.2%)

Oil & gas - field services & equipment

EXCEL COMMUNICATIONS, INC.

9101 LBJ Fwy., Ste. 800 Phone: 214-705-5500
Dallas, TX 75243 Fax: 214-664-3615
Chm, Pres & CEO: Kenny A. Troutt
VP HR: Sandra L. Egland
Employees: 1,200
Jobs Added Last Year: 800 (+200.0%)

Telecommunications services - long-distance telephone services

ENRON CORP.

1400 Smith St. Phone: 713-853-6161
Houston, TX 77002-7369 Fax: 713-853-7920
Chm & CEO: Kenneth L. Lay
SVP Corp Mktg & Resources: Elizabeth A. Tilney
Employees: 6,692
Jobs Cut Last Year: 286 (-4.1%)

Oil & gas - production & pipeline

EXXON CORPORATION

5959 Las Colinas Blvd. Phone: 214-444-1000
Irving, TX 75039-2298 Fax: 214-444-1505
Chm & CEO: Lee R. Raymond
VP HR: Daniel S. Sanders
Employees: 82,000
Jobs Cut Last Year: 4,000 (-4.7%)

Oil & gas - international integrated; chemicals, including poly-olefin catalysts, ethylene & propylene polymers

 An in-depth profile of this company is available to subscribers on Hoover's Online at www.hoovers.com.

307

E-Z SERVE CORPORATION

2550 N. Loop West, Ste. 600
Houston, TX 77092
Chm, Pres & CEO: Neil H. McLaurin
VP HR: Robert L. Howell
Employees: 5,156

Phone: 713-684-4300
Fax: 713-684-4367

Jobs Added Last Year: 2,216 (+75.4%)

Retail - convenience stores, minimarts & gas marts

FALCON DRILLING COMPANY, INC.

1900 W. Loop South, Ste. 1910
Houston, TX 77027
Chm, CEO & Treas: Steven A. Webster
Dir HR: Rick Melancon
Employees: 1,918

Phone: 713-623-8984
Fax: 713-623-8984

Jobs Added Last Year: 409 (+27.1%)

Oil & gas - domestic & international contract drilling & workover
services

FARAH INCORPORATED

8889 Gateway West
El Paso, TX 79985-6584
Chm, Pres & CEO: Richard C. Allender
Dir HR: David Gallardo
Employees: 5,200

Phone: 915-593-4444
Fax: 915-593-4203

Jobs Cut Last Year: 800 (-13.3%)

Apparel - men's & boys' clothing

FIESTA MART INC.

5235 Katy Fwy.
Houston, TX 77007
Chm & CEO: Donald L. Bonham
Dir HR: Juanita Elizando
Employees: 6,500

Phone: 713-869-5060
Fax: 713-869-8210

Jobs Added Last Year: 0

Retail - supermarkets

FIRST USA, INC.

1601 Elm St.
Dallas, TX 75201
Chm & CEO: John C. Tolleson
SVP HR: Daniel C. Barr
Employees: 2,600

Phone: 214-849-3700
Fax: 214-746-8556

Jobs Added Last Year: 800 (+44.4%)

Financial - credit card issuance

FIRSTPLUS FINANCIAL, INC.

1250 W. Mockingbird Ln.
Dallas, TX 75247
Pres & CEO: Daniel T. Phillips
VP & Dir HR: Beverly A. Sharp
Employees: 278

Phone: 214-630-6006
Fax: 214-583-4909

Jobs Added Last Year: 143 (+105.9%)

Financial - home improvement loans

Employment Edge — http://www.employmentedge.com/employment.edge/

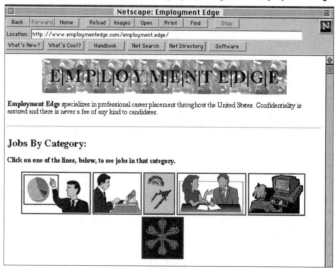

FREEMAN COS.

8801 Ambassador Row
Dallas, TX 75247
CEO: Donald S. Freeman Jr.
No central personnel officer
Employees: 22,800

Phone: 214-638-6450
Fax: 214-638-6454

Jobs Added Last Year: —

Business services - trade show management (#2 in US)

GOLDEN EAGLE GROUP, INC.

120 Standifer Dr.
Humble, TX 77338
Pres & CEO: Patrick H. Weston
No central personnel officer
Employees: 200

Phone: 713-446-2656
Fax: 713-446-6165

Jobs Added Last Year: 50 (+33.3%)

Transportation - international freight transportation logistics services

FROZEN FOOD EXPRESS INDUSTRIES, INC.

1145 Empire Central Place
Dallas, TX 75247-4309
Chm & CEO: Stoney M. "Mit" Stubbs Jr.
Dir Fin: Bart Bartholomew
Employees: 2,553

Phone: 214-630-8090
Fax: 214-819-5625

Jobs Added Last Year: 253 (+11.0%)

Transportation - refrigerated carrier of perishable goods (#1 in US)

GRANT GEOPHYSICAL, INC.

16850 Park Row
Houston, TX 77084
Pres & CEO: George W. Tilley
Mgr HR: Sue Woelfel
Employees: 2,610

Phone: 713-398-9503
Fax: 713-932-4475

Jobs Added Last Year: 931 (+55.4%)

Oil & gas - seismic data services

FURR'S/BISHOP'S, INCORPORATED

6901 Quaker Ave.
Lubbock, TX 79413
Chm, Pres & CEO: Kevin E. Lewis
VP HR: Carlene Stewart
Employees: 6,400

Phone: 806-792-7151
Fax: 806-788-2300

Jobs Cut Last Year: 900 (-12.3%)

Retail - family-style cafeteria restaurants

GREYHOUND LINES, INC.

15110 N. Dallas Pkwy., Ste. 600
Dallas, TX 75248
Pres & CEO : Craig R. Lentzsch
VP HR: Daniel R. Weston
Employees: 10,800

Phone: 214-789-7000
Fax: 214-387-1874

Jobs Added Last Year: 700 (+6.9%)

Transportation - interstate bus line (#1 in US); package delivery service & food service

GARDEN RIDGE CORPORATION

19411 Atrium Place, Ste. 170
Houston, TX 77084
Chm & CEO: Armand Shapiro
VP HR & Ops: Phyllis C. Hink
Employees: 1,800

Phone: 713-579-7901
Fax: 713-578-5379

Jobs Added Last Year: 560 (+45.2%)

Retail - decorative home accessories, seasonal products & crafts

HAGGAR CORP.

6113 Lemmon Ave.
Dallas, TX 75209-5715
Chm & CEO: J. M. Haggar III
VP HR: Sandra K. Stevens
Employees: 6,500

Phone: 214-352-8481
Fax: 214-956-4367

Jobs Added Last Year: 100 (+1.6%)

Apparel - men's clothing

GLOBAL MARINE, INC.

777 N. Eldridge Rd.
Houston, TX 77079
Chm, Pres & CEO: C. Russell Luigs
Mgr Personnel: Don Hansen
Employees: 2,100

Phone: 713-596-5100
Fax: 713-531-1260

Jobs Added Last Year: 400 (+23.5%)

Oil & gas - offshore drilling, oil field services & exploration & production

HALLIBURTON COMPANY

3600 Lincoln Plaza, 500 N. Akard St.
Dallas, TX 75201-3391
Chm, Pres & CEO: Richard B. Cheney
VP HR: Celeste Colgan
Employees: 57,300

Phone: 214-978-2600
Fax: 214-978-2611

Jobs Added Last Year: 100 (+0.2%)

Diversified operations - heavy construction (Brown & Root); oil & gas field services

 An in-depth profile of this company is available to subscribers on Hoover's Online at www.hoovers.com.

HARKEN ENERGY CORPORATION

5605 N. MacArthur Blvd., Ste. 400   Phone: 214-753-6900
Irving, TX 75038   Fax: 214-753-6926
Chm (CEO): Mikel D. Faulkner
No central personnel officer
Employees: 51

Jobs Added Last Year: 11 (+27.5%)

Oil & gas - domestic & international exploration, development, production & marketing

HARRIS COUNTY HOSPITAL DISTRICT

PO Box 66769   Phone: 713-793-2000
Houston, TX 77266   Fax: 713-746-6796
Pres & CEO: Lois J. Moore
Dir Employment: Jenni Carmoucat
Employees: 5,000

Jobs Added Last Year: —

Hospitals - system serving Harris County (Ben Taub General Hospital, Lyndon B. Johnson General Hospital)

HARRIS METHODIST HEALTH SYSTEM

1325 Pennsylvania Ave.   Phone: 817-462-7788
Fort Worth, TX 76104   Fax: 817-462-6135
CEO: Ron Smith
Mng Dir HR: William Witman
Employees: 5,000

Jobs Cut Last Year: 730 (-12.7%)

Hospitals - not-for-profit system & HMO (Harris Methodist Health Plan), primarily serving Tarrant County

H. B. ZACHRY COMPANY

527 W. Harding Blvd.   Phone: 210-922-1213
San Antonio, TX 78221   Fax: 210-927-8060
Chm & CEO: Henry B. Zachry Jr.
VP HR: Steve Hoech
Employees: 10,100

Jobs Added Last Year: 100 (+1.0%)

Building - general contracting

H. E. BUTT GROCERY COMPANY

646 S. Main Ave.   Phone: 210-246-8000
San Antonio, TX 78204   Fax: 210-246-8169
Chm & CEO: Charles C. Butt
VP HR: Louis M. Laguardia
Employees: 40,000

Jobs Added Last Year: 15,000 (+60.0%)

Retail - supermarkets

HEARTLAND WIRELESS COMMUNICATIONS

903 N. Bowser, Ste. 140   Phone: 214-479-9244
Richardson, TX 75081-2858   Fax: 214-479-1023
Pres & CEO: David E. Webb
Dir HR: Bonnie Calamari
Employees: 1,040

Jobs Added Last Year: 670 (+181.1%)

Cable TV - wireless cable TV systems in 35 small to midsize markets, primarily in the southwestern US

HERITAGE MEDIA CORPORATION

13355 Noel Rd., Ste. 1500   Phone: 214-702-7380
Dallas, TX 75240   Fax: 214-702-7382
Pres & CEO: David N. Walthall
Mgr HR: Candi Farley
Employees: 26,200

Jobs Added Last Year: 1,700 (+6.9%)

Business services - in-store marketing (Actmedia, Actradio); broadcasting (5 TV network affiliates & 15 radio stations)

HORIZON MENTAL HEALTH MANAGEMENT

2220 San Jacinto Blvd., Ste. 320   Phone: 817-387-4775
Denton, TX 76205   Fax: 817-387-3593
Chm, Pres & CEO: James K. Newman
Dir HR: Dan Perkins
Employees: 785

Jobs Added Last Year: 229 (+41.2%)

Medical practice management - contract management of mental health programs offered by general acute care hospitals

HOUSTON INDUSTRIES INC.

1111 Louisiana St.   Phone: 713-207-3000
Houston, TX 77002   Fax: 713-207-0206
Chm & CEO: Don D. Jordan
VP HR: Susan D. Fabre
Employees: 8,891

Jobs Cut Last Year: 2,607 (-22.7%)

Utility - electric power; cable TV systems management; power-plant testing

IMCO RECYCLING INC.

5215 N. O'Connor Blvd., Ste. 940   Phone: 214-869-6575
Irving, TX 75039   Fax: 214-869-6585
Pres & CEO: Frank H. Romanelli
VP & Treas: James B. Walburg
Employees: 984

Jobs Added Last Year: 244 (+33.0%)

Metal processing & fabrication - aluminum recycling

INCARNATE WORD HEALTH SERVICES

9311 San Pedro Ave., Ste. 1250
San Antonio, TX 78216
Pres & CEO: Joseph Blasko
VP HR: Sam Buscetta
Employees: 7,600

Phone: 210-524-4100
Fax: 210-525-8443

Jobs Cut Last Year: 235 (-3.0%)

Hospitals - not-for-profit system with 11 hospitals in Texas & one in St. Louis, MO

INDUSTRIAL HOLDINGS, INC.

7135 Ardmore
Houston, TX 77054
Pres & CEO: Robert E. Cone
No central personnel officer
Employees: 263

Phone: 713-747-1025
Fax: 713-749-9642

Jobs Added Last Year: 56 (+27.1%)

Machinery - pipeline valves, metal fasteners & threaded fastener products; retail machine-tool equipment

J. C. PENNEY COMPANY, INC.

6501 Legacy Dr.
Plano, TX 75024-3698
VC & CEO: James E. Oesterreicher
SVP & Dir Personnel & Admin: Gary L. Davis
Employees: 205,000

Phone: 214-431-1000
Fax: 214-431-1977

Jobs Added Last Year: 3,000 (+1.5%)

Retail - major department stores & catalog shopping service; insurance (JCPenney Insurance); consumer banking (JCPenney National Bank); drugstores (Thrift Drug: 645 units)

KAISER ALUMINUM CORPORATION

5847 San Felipe, Ste. 2600
Houston, TX 77057-3010
Chm & CEO: George T. Haymaker Jr.
Dir Corp Personnel: James P. McKnight
Employees: 9,546

Phone: 713-267-3777
Fax: 713-267-3701

Jobs Cut Last Year: 198 (-2.0%)

Mining - bauxite; aluminum production (publicly traded unit of Maxxam, Inc.)

KIMBERLY-CLARK CORPORATION

351 Phelps Dr.
Irving, TX 75038
Chm & CEO: Wayne R. Sanders
VP HR: Bruce J. Olson
Employees: 55,341

Phone: 214-281-1200
Fax: 214-281-1490

Jobs Added Last Year: 12,634 (+29.6%)

Paper & paper products - tissue products (#1 worldwide: Kleenex, Cottonelle, Viva, White Swan), diapers (Huggies), tampons (Kotex), towels & napkins; air-transportation services

KITTY HAWK, INC.

1515 W. 20th St.
Dallas, TX 75261
Chm & CEO: M. Tom Christopher
Dir HR: Lena Knowlton
Employees: 281

Phone: 214-456-2200
Fax: 214-456-2210

Jobs Added Last Year: 77 (+37.7%)

Transportation - air-charter management & cargo services

LA QUINTA INNS, INC.

Weston Centre, 112 E. Pecan St.
San Antonio, TX 78205
Pres & CEO: Gary L. Mead
VP HR: Charles A. McLane
Employees: 6,600

Phone: 210-302-6000
Fax: 210-302-6191

Jobs Added Last Year: 800 (+13.8%)

Hotels & motels

LANDMARK GRAPHICS CORP.

15150 Memorial Dr.
Houston, TX 77079-4304
Pres, CEO & COO: Robert P. Peebler
VP HR: Daniel L. Casaccia
Employees: 910

Phone: 713-560-1000
Fax: 713-560-1410

Jobs Added Last Year: 297 (+48.5%)

Computers - geoscientific exploration software (CAEX) & systems for the oil & gas industry

LANDRY'S SEAFOOD RESTAURANTS

1400 Post Oak Blvd., Ste. 1010
Houston, TX 77056
Chm, Pres & CEO: Tilman J. Fertitta
HR Dir: Rex E. Lee
Employees: 4,300

Phone: 713-850-1010
Fax: 713-623-4702

Jobs Added Last Year: 1,800 (+72.0%)

Retail - seafood restaurants in Texas & Louisiana

LENNOX INTERNATIONAL INC.

2100 Lake Park Blvd.
Richardson, TX 75080
Chm & CEO: John W. Norris Jr.
EVP HR: Harry Ashenhurst
Employees: 8,000

Phone: 214-497-5000
Fax: 214-497-5299

Jobs Cut Last Year: 3,000 (-27.3%)

Building products - air conditioning & heating

 An in-depth profile of this company is available to subscribers on Hoover's Online at www.hoovers.com.

311

LIVING CENTERS OF AMERICA, INC.

15415 Katy Fwy., Ste. 800
Houston, TX 77094
Chm, Pres & CEO: Edward L. Kuntz
Dir HR: Thomas Gillson
Employees: 30,000

Phone: 713-578-4600
Fax: 713-578-4735

Jobs Added Last Year: 12,200 (+68.5%)

Nursing homes - long-term health care services

LOMAK PETROLEUM, INC.

500 Throckmorton St., Ste. 2104
Fort Worth, TX 76102-3708
Pres & CEO: John H. Pinkerton
Dir HR: Sally Hayes
Employees: 281

Phone: 817-870-2601
Fax: 817-870-2316

Jobs Added Last Year: 61 (+27.7%)

Oil & gas - US exploration & production

LONE STAR CASINO CORPORATION

One Riverway, Ste. 2550
Houston, TX 77056
Chm & CEO: Paul J. Montle
No central personnel officer
Employees: 81

Phone: 713-960-9881
Fax: 702-960-9020

Jobs Added Last Year: 18 (+28.6%)

Gambling resorts & casinos in Central City, CO (Papone's Palace)

LUBY'S CAFETERIAS, INC.

2211 NE Loop 410
San Antonio, TX 78265-3069
Chm & CEO: Ralph Erben
VP HR: Raymond C. Gabrysch
Employees: 10,950

Phone: 210-654-9000
Fax: 210-654-3211

Jobs Added Last Year: 850 (+8.4%)

Retail - cafeterias (187 units) in 11 states

MARCUS CABLE COMPANY L.P.

2911 Turtle Creek Blvd., Ste. 1300
Dallas, TX 75219
Pres & CEO: Jeffrey A. Marcus
VP HR: Cindy Mannes
Employees: 2,000

Phone: 214-521-7898
Fax: 214-526-2154

Jobs Added Last Year: 965 (+93.2%)

Cable TV systems

MARY KAY COSMETICS INC.

16251 N. Dallas Pkwy.
Dallas, TX 75248
CEO: John P. Rochon
Pres, US HR: Tim Wentworth
Employees: 2,800

Phone: 214-687-6300
Fax: 214-687-1609

Jobs Added Last Year: 400 (+16.7%)

Cosmetics & toiletries, including fragrances & bath & body products

MAXSERV, INC.

8317 Cross Park Dr., Ste. 350
Austin, TX 78754
Pres & CEO: Charles F. Bayless
VP HR: Steven G. Knowles
Employees: 3,000

Phone: 512-834-8341
Fax: 512-834-1137

Jobs Added Last Year: 2,600 (+650.0%)

Business services - information services for manufacturers & retailers

MAXXAM INC.

5847 San Felipe, Ste. 2600
Houston, TX 77057
Chm, Pres & CEO: Charles E. Hurwitz
VP & Chief Personnel Officer: Diane M. Dudley
Employees: 12,000

Phone: 713-975-7600
Fax: 713-267-3703

Jobs Cut Last Year: 1,860 (-13.4%)

Diversified operations - forest products; real estate development; aluminum

MAXXIM MEDICAL, INC.

104 Industrial Blvd.
Sugar Land, TX 77478
Chm, Pres & CEO: Kenneth W. Davidson
HR Mgr: Beverly Krejci
Employees: 3,605

Phone: 713-240-5588
Fax: 713-276-6299

Jobs Added Last Year: 1,979 (+121.7%)

Medical products - custom procedure trays; guidewires, needles & catheters; hospital supply products, including kits for transfusion, infusion & patient monitoring

MEMORIAL HEALTHCARE SYSTEM

7737 Southwest Fwy., Ste. 200
Houston, TX 77074
Pres: Dan S. Wilford
VP HR: R. Eugene Ross
Employees: 6,428

Phone: 713-776-5484
Fax: 713-776-6978

Jobs Cut Last Year: 572 (-8.2%)

Hospitals - not-for-profit system serving the Houston area, including acute-care hospitals, home health services & retirement centers

THE MEN'S WEARHOUSE, INC.

5803 Glenmont Dr.   Phone: 713-295-7200
Houston, TX 77081   Fax: 713-664-1957
Chm, Pres & CEO: George Zimmer
VP Admin: Julie Maciag
Employees: 4,100
Jobs Added Last Year: 910 (+28.5%)

Retail - men's apparel & accessories

THE METHODIST HOSPITAL SYSTEM

6565 Fannin St.   Phone: 713-790-3311
Houston, TX 77030-2707   Fax: 713-524-6831
Pres & CEO: Larry L. Mathis
VP Admin: Bill Fugauzzi
Employees: 6,650
Jobs Cut Last Year: 50 (-0.7%)

Hospitals - not-for-profit system with 35 affiliated centers serving Houston, Mexico, Guatemala, Italy, Venezuela, Turkey & Peru

MICHAELS STORES, INC.

5931 Campus Circle Dr., PO Box 619566   Phone: 214-714-7000
Irving, TX 75063   Fax: 214-714-7155
CEO: Michael Rouleau
VP Personnel: Donald C. Toby
Employees: 19,330
Jobs Added Last Year: 1,890 (+10.8%)

Retail - arts & crafts

MINYARD FOOD STORES INC.

777 Freeport Pkwy.   Phone: 214-393-8700
Coppell, TX 75019   Fax: 214-462-9407
Pres: J. L. "Sonny" Williams
Dir HR: Alan Vaughan
Employees: 7,100
Jobs Added Last Year: 600 (+9.2%)

Retail - supermarkets (81 units: Minyard, Carnival, Sack 'n Pack) & grocery distribution

MRS. BAIRD'S BAKERIES INC.

7301 South Fwy.   Phone: 817-293-6230
Fort Worth, TX 76134   Fax: 817-568-3690
CEO: Larry G. Wheeler
Dir HR: Mike Stewart
Employees: 3,200
Jobs Added Last Year: 200 (+6.7%)

Food - bread & other baked goods

NABORS INDUSTRIES, INC.

515 W. Greens Rd., Ste. 1200   Phone: 713-874-0035
Houston, TX 77067   Fax: 713-872-5205
Chm & CEO: Eugene M. Isenberg
VP Admin: Daniel McLachlin
Employees: 7,410
Jobs Added Last Year: 2,577 (+53.3%)

Oil & gas - land drilling (#1 worldwide)

Federal Jobs Central — http://www.fedjobs.com

An in-depth profile of this company is available to subscribers on Hoover's Online at www.hoovers.com.

313

NCH CORPORATION

2727 Chemsearch Blvd., PO Box 152170
Irving, TX 75015
Pres: Irvin L. Levy
VP HR: Neil Thomas
Employees: 10,543

Phone: 214-438-0211
Fax: 214-438-0186

Jobs Cut Last Year: 26 (-0.2%)

Chemicals - solvents, insecticides & cleaners; hazardous materials handling equipment; welding supplies & equipment; plumbing & electrical parts

NCI BUILDING SYSTEMS, INC.

7301 Fairview
Houston, TX 77041
Pres & CEO: Johnie Schulte Jr.
Dir HR: Karen Rosales
Employees: 1,431

Phone: 713-466-7788
Fax: 713-466-3194

Jobs Added Last Year: 207 (+16.9%)

Building products - metal building systems, roofing systems & components for the commercial, industrial, agricultural & community-service markets

NEOSTAR RETAIL GROUP, INC.

10741 King William Dr.
Dallas, TX 75220-2414
Chm, Pres & CEO: James B. McCurry
VP Personnel: Michael A. Ivanich
Employees: 7,100

Phone: 214-401-9000
Fax: 214-401-9002

Jobs Added Last Year: 950 (+15.4%)

Retail - personal computer software (Babbage's, Software Etc., Supr Software)

NORAM ENERGY CORP.

1600 Smith, 11th Fl., PO Box 2628
Houston, TX 77252-2628
Pres: Craig Elias
SVP HR & Administrative Svcs: Rick L. Spurlock
Employees: 6,703

Phone: 713-654-5100
Fax: 713-654-7511

Jobs Cut Last Year: 137 (-2.0%)

Utility - gas distribution

NORWOOD PROMOTIONAL PRODUCTS, INC.

70 NE Loop 410, Ste. 295
San Antonio, TX 78216
Chm & CEO: Frank P. Krasovec
Pres & COO: Robert P. Whitesell
Employees: 1,750

Phone: 210-341-9440
Fax: 210-224-5531

Jobs Added Last Year: 668 (+61.7%)

Business services - supply of promotional items imprinted with name or logo of advertiser

NUTRITION FOR LIFE INTERNATIONAL

9101 Jameel
Houston, TX 77040
Chm & Pres: David P. Bertrand
HR Mgr: Robin Bostic
Employees: 78

Phone: 713-460-1976
Fax: 713-895-8929

Jobs Added Last Year: 19 (+32.2%)

Vitamins & nutritional products - nutritional supplements, health foods, weight management products & skin care products; cleaning concentrates; filtration systems

OCCUSYSTEMS INC.

3010 LBJ Fwy., Ste. 400
Dallas, TX 75234
Chm & CEO: John K. Carlyle
Dir HR: Mike Malone
Employees: 1,900

Phone: 214-484-2700
Fax: 214-241-8048

Jobs Added Last Year: 500 (+35.7%)

Medical practice management

OSHMAN'S SPORTING GOODS, INC.

2302 Maxwell Ln.
Houston, TX 77023
VC & CEO: Alvin N. Lubetkin
Dir HR: Mark Groenemon
Employees: 3,700

Phone: 713-928-3171
Fax: 713-967-8254

Jobs Added Last Year: 400 (+12.1%)

Retail - sporting goods

OWEN HEALTHCARE, INC.

9800 Centre Pkwy., Ste. 1100
Houston, TX 77036-8279
Pres & CEO: Carl E. Isgren
SVP Professional Resources: Dennis S. Stepanik
Employees: 3,900

Phone: 713-777-8173
Fax: 713-777-5417

Jobs Added Last Year: 900 (+30.0%)

Medical practice management - pharmacy management & information services for hospitals

PAGING NETWORK, INC.

4965 Preston Park Blvd., Ste. 600
Plano, TX 75093
Pres & CEO: Glenn W. Marschel
VP HR: Levy H. Curry
Employees: 4,676

Phone: 214-985-4100
Fax: 214-985-6711

Jobs Added Last Year: 679 (+17.0%)

Telecommunications services - local, wide-area metropolitan, multistate regional & nationwide paging service (#1 in US)

PANENERGY CORPORATION

5400 Westheimer Ct.
Houston, TX 77251-1642
Pres & CEO: Paul M. Anderson
VP HR: Dan R. Hennig
Employees: 5,000

Phone: 713-627-4600
Fax: 713-627-4652

Jobs Cut Last Year: 500 (-9.1%)

Oil & gas - production & pipeline

PC SERVICE SOURCE, INC.

2350 Valley View Ln.
Dallas, TX 75234
Pres & CEO: Mark T. Hilz
HR Dir: Mary Zapata
Employees: 360

Phone: 214-406-8583
Fax: 214-406-9081

Jobs Added Last Year: 100 (+38.5%)

Electronics - distribution of repair parts for PCs & related peripherals; inventory management & outsourcing services

PENNZOIL COMPANY

Pennzoil Place, 700 Milam
Houston, TX 77002
Chm, Pres & CEO: James L. Pate
Group VP Admin: Terry Hemeyer
Employees: 9,758

Phone: 713-546-4000
Fax: 713-546-6639

Jobs Cut Last Year: 743 (-7.1%)

Oil & gas - US integrated; automotive products, including motor
oil, lubricants & specialty products

PHYSICIAN RELIANCE NETWORK, INC.

8115 Preston Rd., Ste. 300, LB-11
Dallas, TX 75225
Chm, Pres & CEO: Merrick H. Reese
VP HR: Lee Colan
Employees: 803

Phone: 214-692-3800
Fax: 214-692-1637

Jobs Added Last Year: 409 (+103.8%)

Medical practice management - management, administrative &
technical support & ancillary services to cancer doctors (#1 in US)

PIER 1 IMPORTS, INC.

301 Commerce St., Ste. 600
Fort Worth, TX 76102
Chm & CEO: Clark A. Johnson
SVP HR: E. Mitchell Weatherly
Employees: 9,399

Phone: 817-878-8000
Fax: 817-878-7883

Jobs Added Last Year: 728 (+8.4%)

Retail - imported apparel & home furnishings

PILGRIM'S PRIDE CORPORATION

110 S. Texas St., PO Box 93
Pittsburg, TX 75686-0093
Chm & CEO: Lonnie "Bo" Pilgrim
SVP HR: Ray Gameson
Employees: 11,750

Phone: 903-855-1000
Fax: 903-856-7505

Jobs Added Last Year: 1,450 (+14.1%)

Food - poultry products, including prepared, fresh & prepackaged
chicken

PLAY BY PLAY TOYS & NOVELTIES, INC.

4400 Tejasco
San Antonio, TX 78218
Chm & CEO: Arturo G. Torres
No central personnel officer
Employees: 152

Phone: 210-829-4666
Fax: 210-824-6565

Jobs Added Last Year: 35 (+29.9%)

Toys - stuffed toys & sculpted toy pillows using children's entertainment characters (Looney Tunes, Animaniacs) & corporate
trademarks (Coca-Cola)

POLYPHASE CORPORATION

16885 Dallas Pkwy., Ste. 400
Dallas, TX 75248
Chm, Pres & CEO: Paul A. Tanner
Chm, Pres & CEO: Paul A. Tanner
Employees: 832

Phone: 214-732-0010
Fax: 214-732-6430

Jobs Added Last Year: 653 (+364.8%)

Computers - networking & connectivity hardware, inclduing
transformers, inductors & filters; timber & logging equipment
distribution

POOL ENERGY SERVICES CO.

10375 Richmond Ave.
Houston, TX 77042
Chm, Pres & CEO: James T. Jongebloed
VP HR: Louis E. Dupre
Employees: 4,982

Phone: 713-954-3000
Fax: 713-954-3319

Jobs Added Last Year: 533 (+12.0%)

Oil & gas - well servicing & rig operations

POWER COMPUTING CORPORATION

12337 Technology Blvd.
Austin, TX 78727-6104
Pres & CEO: Stephen S. Kahng
Exec Asst: Jeanine Winter
Employees: 300

Phone: 512-258-1350
Fax: 512-250-3390

Jobs Added Last Year: 280 (+1,400.0%)

Computers - Apple Macintosh clones

 An in-depth profile of this company is available
to subscribers on Hoover's Online at www.hoovers.com.

315

PRESBYTERIAN HEALTHCARE SYSTEM

8220 Walnut Hill Ln., Ste. 700
Dallas, TX 75231
Pres & CEO: Doug Hawthorne
VP HR: Vic Vuzachero
Employees: 5,000

Phone: 214-345-8500
Fax: 214-345-4999

Jobs Added Last Year: 43 (+0.9%)

Hospitals - not-for-profit system

PRONET INC.

600 Data Dr., Ste. 100
Plano, TX 75075
Chm & CEO: Jackie R. Kimzey
Dir HR: Martie Chaplin
Employees: 584

Phone: 214-964-9500
Fax: 214-964-9570

Jobs Added Last Year: 263 (+81.9%)

Telecommunications services - medical & business paging
services

R CORPORATION

1000 IH-10 North
Beaumont, TX 77702
CEO: Kenneth E. Ruddy
Emp Benefits Administrator: Jan Thomsen
Employees: 790

Phone: 409-892-6696
Fax: 409-892-7690

Jobs Added Last Year: 440 (+125.7%)

Retail - new & used cars

RANDALL'S FOOD MARKETS, INC.

3663 Briarpark Dr.
Houston, TX 77042
Pres & COO: Robert R. Onstead Jr.
EVP Admin: Ronnie W. Barclay
Employees: 22,000

Phone: 713-268-3500
Fax: 713-268-3601

Jobs Added Last Year: 1,000 (+4.8%)

Retail - Texas supermarkets (121 units, primarily in Houston,
Dallas & Austin)

REDMAN INDUSTRIES, INC.

2550 Walnut Hill Ln., Ste. 200
Dallas, TX 75229-5672
Pres & CEO: Robert M. Linton
Dir HR: Gary Allen
Employees: 3,967

Phone: 214-353-3600
Fax: 214-350-5927

Jobs Added Last Year: 333 (+9.2%)

Building - manufactured houses (#3 in US)

RENTERS CHOICE, INC.

2720 N. Stemmons Fwy., Ste. 300
Dallas, TX 75207
Chm & CEO: J. Ernie Talley
HR Mgr: Robert D. Davis
Employees: 1,700

Phone: 214-638-6633
Fax: 214-638-7711

Jobs Added Last Year: 1,012 (+147.1%)

Leasing - rent-to-own electronics, appliances, furniture &
accessories

REUNION INDUSTRIES INC.

2801 Post Oak Blvd., Ste. 400
Houston, TX 77056
Chm, Pres & CEO: Charles E. Bradley
Dir HR: Judy Dugan
Employees: 411

Phone: 713-627-9277
Fax: 713-627-2069

Jobs Added Last Year: 371 (+927.5%)

Oil & gas - exploration & production

RF MONOLITHICS, INC.

4441 Sigma Rd.
Dallas, TX 75244
Pres & CEO: Sam L. Densmore
Dir HR: Diana S. Handler
Employees: 477

Phone: 214-233-2903
Fax: 214-387-8148

Jobs Added Last Year: 100 (+26.5%)

Electrical components - radio frequency components & modules

SA TELECOMMUNICATIONS, INC.

1600 Promenade, Ste. 1510
Richardson, TX 75080
Chm & CEO: Jack W. Matz Jr.
Dir HR: Robin Cody
Employees: 165

Phone: 214-690-5888
Fax: 214-889-1543

Jobs Added Last Year: 107 (+184.5%)

Telecommunications services - international carrier

SANIFILL, INC.

2777 Allen Pkwy., Ste. 700
Houston, TX 77019-2155
Chm & CEO: Lorne D. Bain
Dir Admin: Ken Rose
Employees: 2,600

Phone: 713-942-6200
Fax: 713-942-6299

Jobs Added Last Year: 1,300 (+100.0%)

Waste management - solid waste disposal

SBC COMMUNICATIONS INC.

175 E. Houston
San Antonio, TX 78205-2233
Chm & CEO: Edward E. Whitacre Jr.
SVP HR: Cassandra C. Carr
Employees: 59,300

Phone: 210-821-4105
Fax: 210-351-2071

Jobs Added Last Year: 550 (+0.9%)

Utility - telephone (Southwestern Bell)

SEACOR HOLDINGS, INC.

11200 Westheimer Road, Ste. 850
Houston, TX 77042
Chm, Pres & CEO: Charles Fabrikant
Personnel Mgr: Rodney Coco
Employees: 1,238

Phone: 713-782-5990
Fax: 713-782-5991

Jobs Added Last Year: 746 (+151.6%)

Oil & gas - offshore exploration support services

SERVICE CORP. INTERNATIONAL

1929 Allen Pkwy.
Houston, TX 77019
Chm & CEO: Robert L. Waltrip
SVP Admin: Jack L. Stoner
Employees: 19,824

Phone: 713-522-5141
Fax: 713-525-5586

Jobs Added Last Year: 1,068 (+5.7%)

Funeral services & related - funeral homes, crematories & cemeteries

SHELL OIL COMPANY

One Shell Plaza
Houston, TX 77002
Pres & CEO: Philip J. Carroll
VP HR: Bert W. Levan
Employees: 21,050

Phone: 713-241-6161
Fax: 713-241-4044

Jobs Cut Last Year: 446 (-2.1%)

Oil & gas - exploration & production of crude oil & natural gas (owned by Royal Dutch/Shell Group); sulfur & carbon dioxide production

SHOWBIZ PIZZA TIME, INC.

4441 W. Airport Fwy., PO Box 152077
Irving, TX 75015
Chm & CEO: Richard M. Frank
VP HR: Catherine Kreston
Employees: 11,290

Phone: 214-258-8507
Fax: 214-258-8545

Jobs Cut Last Year: 2,210 (-16.4%)

Retail - restaurants (Chuck E. Cheese)

SI DIAMOND TECHNOLOGY, INC.

2435 North Blvd.
Houston, TX 77098
Chm & CEO: Marc Eller
Dir HR: Marijane Ensminger
Employees: 113

Phone: 713-529-9040
Fax: 713-529-1147

Jobs Added Last Year: 42 (+59.2%)

Electrical components - thin-film diamond coatings & related products, including flat-panel displays

SISTERS OF CHARITY OF THE INCARNATE WORD HEALTH CARE SYSTEM

2600 N. Loop West
Houston, TX 77092
Pres & CEO: Stanley T. Urban
Mgr HR: Kay Saathoff
Employees: 19,000

Phone: 713-681-8877
Fax: 713-683-2065

Jobs Added Last Year: —

Hospitals - not-for-profit system with acute-care hospitals & long-term health care centers

SMITH ENVIRONMENTAL TECHNOLOGIES

2 Galleria Tower, 13455 Noel Rd., Ste. 1500
Dallas, TX 75240
Chm, Pres & CEO: E. Brian Smith
VP HR: Gail M. Fulwider
Employees: 1,260

Phone: 214-770-1800
Fax: 214-770-0249

Jobs Added Last Year: 1,043 (+480.6%)

Waste management - hazardous waste remediation services

SMITH INTERNATIONAL, INC.

16740 Hardy St.
Houston, TX 77032
Chm & CEO: Doug Rock
HR Dir: Joe Sizemore
Employees: 4,700

Phone: 713-443-3370
Fax: 713-233-5104

Jobs Added Last Year: 600 (+14.6%)

Oil field machinery & equipment - drilling fluids, drill bits, drilling & completion products & services

SOFTWARE SPECTRUM, INC.

2140 Merritt Dr.
Garland, TX 75041
Chm, Pres & CEO: Judy O. Sims
Dir HR: Sue Zurber
Employees: 835

Phone: 214-840-6600
Fax: 214-864-7878

Jobs Added Last Year: 168 (+25.2%)

Retail - computer software

 An in-depth profile of this company is available to subscribers on Hoover's Online at www.hoovers.com.

SOUTHERN FOODS GROUPS INC.

3114 S. Haskell Ave.
Dallas, TX 75223
CEO: Pete Schenkel
VP Personnel: Stuart Bibson
Employees: 2,200
Jobs Added Last Year: 600 (+37.5%)

Food - dairy products

Phone: 214-824-8163
Fax: 214-824-0967

SPAGHETTI WAREHOUSE, INC.

402 West I-30
Garland, TX 75043
Pres & CEO: Phillip Ratner
VP HR: G. Kenna Davidson
Employees: 2,900
Jobs Added Last Year: 1,590 (+121.4%)

Retail - Italian-food restaurants

Phone: 214-226-6000
Fax: 214-203-9594

THE SOUTHLAND CORPORATION

2711 N. Haskell Ave.
Dallas, TX 75204-2906
Pres, CEO & Sec: Clark J. Matthews II
Mgr Compensation & Benefits: Matt Sauer
Employees: 30,523
Jobs Added Last Year: 106 (+0.3%)

Retail - convenience stores (7-Eleven)

Phone: 214-828-7011
Fax: 214-841-6688

SPECIALTY RETAILERS INC.

10201 Main St.
Houston, TX 77025
Pres & CEO: Carl Tooker
VP HR: Jack Chipperfield
Employees: 8,650
Jobs Added Last Year: —

Retail - apparel stores (Palais Royal, Beall's & Fashion Bar)

Phone: 713-667-5601
Fax: 713-669-2708

SOUTHWEST AIRLINES CO.

PO Box 36611
Dallas, TX 75235-1611
Chm, Pres & CEO: Herbert D. Kelleher
VP People: Elizabeth P. Sartain
Employees: 19,933
Jobs Added Last Year: 3,115 (+18.5%)

Transportation - airline

Phone: 214-904-4000
Fax: 214-904-4200

SPECTRAVISION, INC.

1501 N. Plano Rd.
Richardson, TX 75081
CEO: Gary G. Weik
Dir HR: Scott Campbell
Employees: 365
Jobs Added Last Year: 82 (+29.0%)

Cable TV - pay-per-view movies for hotels & motels

Phone: 214-234-2721
Fax: 214-301-9607

JobCenter — http://www.jobcenter.com/

STAGE STORES, INC.

10201 Main St.
Houston, TX 77025
Pres & CEO: Carl Tooker
SVP HR: Ron Lucas
Employees: 9,446

Phone: 713-667-5601
Fax: 713-667-5601

Jobs Added Last Year: —

Retail - men's, women's & children's apparel (Stage, Bealls, Palais Royal: 301 stores) in small markets in 16 central US states

STAR ENTERPRISE

12700 Northborough Dr.
Houston, TX 77067
Pres & CEO: Seth L. Sharr
Dir HR: Floyd M. Chaney
Employees: 7,000

Phone: 713-874-7000
Fax: 713-874-7760

Jobs Added Last Year: 3,000 (+75.0%)

Oil refining & marketing of Texaco-branded products in 26 eastern & Gulf Coast states & Washington, D.C. (joint venture between Texaco & Aramco)

STB SYSTEMS, INC.

1651 N. Glenville Dr.
Richardson, TX 75081
Chm & CEO: William E. Ogle
Mgr HR: Sherri Wolf
Employees: 913

Phone: 214-234-8750
Fax: 214-234-1306

Jobs Added Last Year: 238 (+35.3%)

Computers - graphics adapters for single- & multimonitor configurations, primarily in IBM-compatible PCs

STERLING INFORMATION GROUP

515 Capital of Texas Hwy. South
Austin, TX 78746-4305
CEO: Chip Wolfe
VP HR: Leslie Martinich
Employees: 70

Phone: 512-327-0090
Fax: 512-327-0197

Jobs Added Last Year: 30 (+75.0%)

Computers - software consulting services

STERLING SOFTWARE, INC.

8080 N. Central Expwy., Ste. 1100
Dallas, TX 75206-1895
Pres & CEO: Sterling L. Williams
No central personnel officer
Employees: 3,700

Phone: 214-891-8600
Fax: 214-739-0535

Jobs Added Last Year: 700 (+23.3%)

Computers - software products & services for the electronic commerce & systems & applications management software markets; technical professional services for the federal government

STEWART & STEVENSON SERVICES, INC.

2707 N. Loop West, PO Box 1637
Houston, TX 77251-1637
Acting CEO, Group VP, CFO & Treas: Robert L. Hargrave
VP HR & Risk Mgmt: Bobby Brown
Employees: 4,511

Phone: 713-868-7700
Fax: 713-868-7692

Jobs Added Last Year: 211 (+4.9%)

Machinery - power-generation turbines; industrial equipment distribution

SYSCO CORPORATION

1390 Enclave Pkwy.
Houston, TX 77077-2099
Pres & CEO: Bill M. Lindig
VP Mgmt & HR: Michael C. Nichols
Employees: 28,100

Phone: 713-584-1390
Fax: 713-584-1245

Jobs Added Last Year: 1,900 (+7.3%)

Food - wholesale to restaurants & foodservice companies

TANDY BRANDS ACCESSORIES, INC.

690 E. Lamar Blvd., Ste. 200
Arlington, TX 76011
Pres & CEO: J. S. B. Jenkins
Emp Benefits & HR Mgr: Jan Bland
Employees: 765

Phone: 817-548-0090
Fax: 817-548-1144

Jobs Added Last Year: 215 (+39.1%)

Apparel - accessories, including neckties, belts & wallets (Prince Gardner, Haggar, Bugle Boy, Canterbury) for men, women & children

TANDY CORPORATION

1800 One Tandy Center
Fort Worth, TX 76102
Chm & CEO: John V. Roach
VP HR: George Berger
Employees: 49,300

Phone: 817-390-3700
Fax: 817-390-2647

Jobs Added Last Year: 3,500 (+7.6%)

Retail - consumer electronics (Radio Shack, Computer City, McDuff, VideoConcepts, The Edge, Incredible Universe)

TANDYCRAFTS, INC.

1400 Everman Pkwy.
Fort Worth, TX 76140
Pres & CEO: Michael J. Walsh
No central personnel officer
Employees: 4,200

Phone: 817-551-9600
Fax: 817-551-9795

Jobs Added Last Year: 500 (+13.5%)

Diversified operations - leather (Tandy Leather); books & gifts (Joshua's Christian Stores); office supplies; furniture (Cargo); frames & art; belts & accessories; outerwear & leather products

TECNOL MEDICAL PRODUCTS, INC.

7201 Industrial Park Blvd.
Fort Worth, TX 76180
Chm, Pres & CEO: Vance M. Hubbard
Dir HR: Chris Gonser
Employees: 2,169

Phone: 817-581-6424
Fax: 817-577-6599

Jobs Added Last Year: 382 (+21.4%)

Medical & dental supplies - disposable face masks, ice packs & patient safety restraints

TEMPLE-INLAND INC.

303 S. Temple Dr.
Diboll, TX 75941
Chm & CEO: Clifford J. Grum
VP HR: Herb George
Employees: 15,400

Phone: 409-829-5511
Fax: 409-829-3333

Jobs Added Last Year: 400 (+2.7%)

Containers - containerboard & corrugated boxes, bleached paperboard & building products

TETRA TECHNOLOGIES, INC.

25025 I-45 North
The Woodlands, TX 77380
Pres & CEO: Allen T. McInnes
Dir HR: Linden Price
Employees: 683

Phone: 713-367-1983
Fax: 713-364-4360

Jobs Added Last Year: 250 (+57.7%)

Pollution control equipment & services - environmental engineering & consulting

THE TEXAS A&M UNIVERSITY SYSTEM

Office of the System Comptroller, John B. Connally Bldg., 301
Tarrow, 3rd Fl.
College Station, TX 77843-1118
Chancellor: Barry P. Thompson
VP HR: Patti Courer
Employees: 20,000

Phone: 409-845-2531
Fax: 409-862-1408

Jobs Added Last Year: 3,633 (+22.2%)

University - land-grant system that comprises 7 universities & 8 research agencies, offering more than 300 degree programs

TEXAS INSTRUMENTS INC.

13500 N. Central Expwy.
Dallas, TX 75243
Pres & CEO: Thomas J. Engibous
VP HR: Charles F. Nielson
Employees: 59,574

Phone: 214-995-2011
Fax: 214-995-4360

Jobs Added Last Year: 3,241 (+5.8%)

Electrical components - semiconductors, radar & navigation systems, avionics & surveillance equipment; notebook computers, calculators & printers; electronic sensors & controls

TEXAS TECH UNIVERSITY

250 West Hall
Lubbock, TX 79409
Pres: Robert W. Lawless
Dir Personnel: Jeanette Hodges
Employees: 10,066

Phone: 806-742-2011
Fax: 806-742-1615

Jobs Added Last Year: —

University - system offering 92 undergraduate & 126 graduate degree programs

TEXAS UTILITIES COMPANY

Energy Plaza, 1601 Bryan St.
Dallas, TX 75201-3411
Pres & CEO: Erle Nye
VP Personnel: Pitt Pittman
Employees: 11,729

Phone: 214-812-4600
Fax: 214-812-4651

Jobs Added Last Year: 931 (+8.6%)

Utility - electric power

TRACOR, INC.

6500 Tracor Ln.
Austin, TX 78725-2000
Chm, Pres & CEO: James B. Skaggs
VP HR: Murray Shaw
Employees: 9,400

Phone: 512-926-2800
Fax: 512-929-2257

Jobs Cut Last Year: 300 (-3.1%)

Electronics - fleet weapons & combat systems & weapons testing systems & technical support

TRANSAMERICAN WASTE INDUSTRIES

314 N. Post Oak Ln.
Houston, TX 77024
Pres: Tom Noel
Personnel Dir: Barbara Kaiser
Employees: 160

Phone: 713-956-1212
Fax: 713-956-0262

Jobs Added Last Year: 58 (+56.9%)

Waste management - nonhazardous industrial & municipal solid waste processing, treatment & disposal

TRANSTEXAS GAS CORPORATION

1300 E. North Belt, Ste. 310
Houston, TX 77032
CEO: John R. Stanley
Dir HR: Gerald Barkley
Employees: 2,400

Phone: 713-987-8600
Fax: 713-986-8865

Jobs Added Last Year: 400 (+20.0%)

Oil & gas - production & pipeline

TRINITY INDUSTRIES, INC.

2525 Stemmons Fwy., PO Box 568887
Dallas, TX 75356-8887
Chm, Pres & CEO: W. Ray Wallace
VP HR: Jack Cunningham
Employees: 14,700

Phone: 214-631-4420
Fax: 214-689-0501

Jobs Cut Last Year: 1,800 (-10.9%)

Metal products - railcars, marine products, construction products, pressure & nonpressure containers, fittings & flanges; railcar leasing

TRISTAR CORPORATION

12500 San Pedro Ave., Ste. 500
San Antonio, TX 78216
CEO: Viren Sheth
Corp Dir HR: William Herrera
Employees: 520

Phone: 210-402-2200
Fax: 210-402-2239

Jobs Added Last Year: 409 (+368.5%)

Wholesale distribution - designer alternative & original fragrances, bath & body products & cosmetics

TUBOSCOPE VETCO INTERNATIONAL CORP.

2835 Holmes Rd.
Houston, TX 77051
Pres & CEO: William V. Larkin Jr.
VP HR & Admin: Kenneth L. Nibling
Employees: 2,155

Phone: 713-799-5100
Fax: 713-799-1460

Jobs Added Last Year: 201 (+10.3%)

Oil & gas - inspection & servicing of oil field casing, drill pipes & land pipes

UICI

4001 McEwen Dr., Ste. 200
Dallas, TX 75244
Pres & CEO: W. Brian Harrigan
Dir HR: Linda Flowers
Employees: 1,350

Phone: 214-960-8497
Fax: 214-851-9097

Jobs Added Last Year: 580 (+75.3%)

Insurance - accident, life & health

ULTRAK, INC.

1220 Champion Circle, Ste. 100
Carrollton, TX 75006
Chm, Pres & CEO: George K. Broady
HR Dir: Patty Cramer
Employees: 292

Phone: 214-280-9675
Fax: 214-280-9674

Jobs Added Last Year: 144 (+97.3%)

Video equipment - closed-circuit TV systems

UNITED SUPERMARKETS INCORPORATED

7830 Orlando Ave.
Lubbock, TX 79423
CEO: Robert Snell
Dir HR: Dan Sanders
Employees: 3,000

Phone: 806-791-0220
Fax: 806-791-7480

Jobs Added Last Year: 400 (+15.4%)

Retail - supermarkets (42 units in Texas: United Supermarkets)

UNIVERSAL SEISMIC ASSOCIATES

16420 Park Ten Place, Ste. 300
Houston, TX 77084-5051
Pres & CEO: Michael J. Pawelek
No central personnel officer
Employees: 180

Phone: 713-578-8081
Fax: 713-578-7091

Jobs Added Last Year: 50 (+38.5%)

Oil & gas - 3D seismic data acquisition & processing services

UNIVERSITY OF HOUSTON

4800 Calhoun
Houston, TX 77204-2163
Pres: Glenn A. Goerke
Asst VP: Carol Parmer
Employees: 7,230

Phone: 713-743-1000
Fax: 713-743-8199

Jobs Added Last Year: 33 (+0.5%)

University - offering 102 undergraduate & 65 graduate degree programs

UNIVERSITY OF NORTH TEXAS

PO Box 13767
Denton, TX 76203-6797
Pres & Chancellor: Alfred F. Hurley
Dir HR: Steve Miller
Employees: 5,500

Phone: 817-565-2000
Fax: 817-565-2000

Jobs Added Last Year: —

University - offering 32 undergraduate programs and 52 graduate degree programs

THE UNIVERSITY OF TEXAS SYSTEM

O. Henry Hall
Austin, TX 78701
Chancellor: William H. Cunningham
Dir System Personnel Office: Trennis Jones
Employees: 12,773

Phone: 512-471-3434
Fax: 512-499-4215

Jobs Added Last Year: 77 (+0.6%)

University - system of 9 general academic universities & 6 health institutions offering 108 undergraduate & 179 graduate degree programs

An in-depth profile of this company is available to subscribers on Hoover's Online at www.hoovers.com.

321

U.S. PHYSICAL THERAPY, INC.

3040 Post Oak Blvd., Ste. 222
Houston, TX 77056
Pres, CEO & COO: Roy Spradlin
HR Dir: Kimberly Cox
Employees: 411
Phone: 713-297-9050
Fax: 713-297-7090

Jobs Added Last Year: 95 (+30.1%)

Health care - outpatient physical & occupational therapy

USAA

9800 Fredericksburg Rd., USAA Building
San Antonio, TX 78288
CEO: Robert T. Herres
SVP HR: William B. Tracy
Employees: 15,677
Phone: 210-498-2211
Fax: 210-498-9940

Jobs Added Last Year: 444 (+2.9%)

Multiline insurance for consumers; brokerage services; mutual funds; banking; retirement plans & services

VALHI, INC.

5430 LBJ Fwy., Ste. 1700
Dallas, TX 75240-2697
Chm, Pres & CEO: Harold C. Simmons
Personnel Mgr: Kathy Brownlee
Employees: 11,260
Phone: 214-233-1700
Fax: 214-385-0586

Jobs Cut Last Year: 240 (-2.1%)

Diversified operations - chemicals; refined sugar; forest products; fast-food & hardware

VTEL CORPORATION

108 Wild Basin Rd.
Austin, TX 78746
Chm, Pres & CEO: F. H. "Dick" Moeller
Dir HR: Carson D. Brown
Employees: 463
Phone: 512-314-2700
Fax: 512-314-2792

Jobs Added Last Year: 190 (+69.6%)

Telecommunications equipment - multimedia conferencing systems

WALDEN RESIDENTIAL PROPERTIES, INC.

One Lincoln Centre, 5400 LBJ Fwy., Ste. 400
Dallas, TX 75240
Chm & CEO: Donald R. Daseke
VP : Susan W. Huber
Employees: 514
Phone: 214-788-0510
Fax: 214-392-4417

Jobs Added Last Year: 103 (+25.1%)

Real estate investment trust - multifamily residential properties

WHATABURGER SYSTEMS INC.

4600 Parkdale Dr., PO Box 6220
Corpus Christi, TX 78466
Pres & CEO: Thomas Dobson
VP HR: Peter Oppel
Employees: 9,000
Phone: 512-878-0650
Fax: 512-878-0314

Jobs Added Last Year: 500 (+5.9%)

Retail - restaurants

WHITEHALL CORPORATION

2659 Nova Dr., PO Box 29709
Dallas, TX 75229
Chm, Pres & CEO: George F. Baker
Acctg Mgr: Randy Johnson
Employees: 682
Phone: 214-247-8747
Fax: 214-247-2024

Jobs Added Last Year: 170 (+33.2%)

Electronics - underwater sensing systems & electronic components; aircaft maintenance

WHOLE FOODS MARKET, INC.

601 N. Lamar, Ste. 300
Austin, TX 78703
Chm & CEO: John Mackey
VP HR: Jody Dachtler
Employees: 6,137
Phone: 512-477-4455
Fax: 512-477-1301

Jobs Added Last Year: 837 (+15.8%)

Retail - grocery stores specializing in natural & health foods

WILLIAMSON-DICKIE MANUFACTURING CO.

319 Lipscomb St.
Fort Worth, TX 76104
VC & CEO: Philip C. Williamson
Dir HR: Estelle Lewis
Employees: 5,446
Phone: 817-336-7201
Fax: 817-336-5183

Jobs Cut Last Year: 554 (-9.2%)

Apparel - men's trousers & work clothing

WINGATE PARTNERS

750 N. St. Paul St., Ste. 1200
Dallas, TX 75201
Principal Partner: Frederick B. Hegi
VP Admin: Suzanne Goddard
Employees: 12,000
Phone: 214-720-1313
Fax: 214-871-8799

Jobs Added Last Year: 5,700 (+90.5%)

Diversified - Century Products, Redman Building Products, Loomis Armored, United Stationers, ITCO Tire

WYNDHAM HOTEL CORPORATION

2001 Bryan St., Ste. 2300　　Phone: 214-863-1000
Dallas, TX 75201　　Fax: 214-863-1510
Pres & CEO: James D. Carreker
VP HR: Susan R. Bolger
Employees: 11,400
Jobs Added Last Year: —

Hotels & motels - operation & franchising of 68 hotels in 22 states, the District of Columbia & the Caribbean

ZALE CORPORATION

901 W. Walnut Hill Ln.　　Phone: 214-580-4000
Irving, TX 75038-1003　　Fax: 214-580-5336
Chm, Pres, CEO & COO: Robert J. DiNicola
SVP HR: A. Herschel Kranitz
Employees: 9,000
Jobs Cut Last Year: 500 (-5.3%)

Retail - jewelry stores (1,235 units; #1 in US) under the Zales, Gordon's, Bailey Banks & Biddle names; 202 leased departments in stores

AMERICAN STORES COMPANY

709 E. South Temple　　Phone: 801-539-0112
Salt Lake City, UT 84102　　Fax: 801-531-0768
Chm & CEO: Victor L. Lund
Chief HR Officer: Stephen L. Mannschreck
Employees: 121,000
Jobs Added Last Year: 3,000 (+2.5%)

Retail - supermarkets

BALLARD MEDICAL PRODUCTS

12050 Lone Peak Pkwy.　　Phone: 801-572-6800
Draper, UT 84020　　Fax: 801-572-6999
Chm, Pres & CEO: Dale H. Ballard
Dir HR: Jerri Sterling
Employees: 872
Jobs Added Last Year: 272 (+45.3%)

Medical instruments - catheters, gastrostomy tubes & surgical masks

FIRST SECURITY CORPORATION

79 S. Main St.　　Phone: 801-246-5706
Salt Lake City, UT 84111　　Fax: 801-359-6928
Chm & CEO: Spencer F. Eccles
SVP & Dir HR: Tad Jeppesen
Employees: 7,530
Jobs Cut Last Year: 91 (-1.2%)

Banks - West

JobBank USA — http://www.jobbankusa.com/

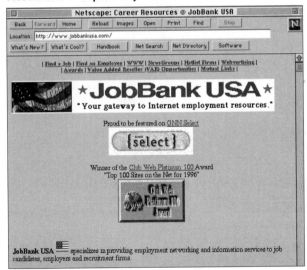

FLYING J INC.

50 W. 990 South
Brigham City, UT 84302
Chm: O. Jay Call
Dir Personnel: Robert O. Langford
Employees: 6,952

Phone: 801-734-6400
Fax: 801-734-6556

Jobs Added Last Year: 1,121 (+19.2%)

Oil & gas - US integrated

FRANKLIN QUEST CO.

2200 W. Parkway Blvd.
Salt Lake City, UT 84119-2331
Chm & CEO: Hyrum W. Smith
HR Mgr: Daken Tanner
Employees: 2,771

Phone: 801-975-1776
Fax: 801-977-1431

Jobs Added Last Year: 753 (+37.3%)

Business services - productivity seminars, business calendars & planners

HUNTSMAN CORPORATION

500 Colorow Dr.
Salt Lake City, UT 84108
Chm & CEO: Jon M. Huntsman
VP HR: Winston H. Conner
Employees: 6,500

Phone: 801-532-5200
Fax: 801-536-1581

Jobs Cut Last Year: 831 (-11.3%)

Chemicals - diversified (#1 privately owned chemical company in the US)

INTERLINE RESOURCES CORPORATION

160 W. Canyon Crest Dr.
Alpine, UT 84004
Pres & CEO: Michael R. Williams
Comm Dir: Mark Fredrickson
Employees: 148

Phone: 801-756-3031
Fax: 801-756-8843

Jobs Added Last Year: 66 (+80.5%)

Oil & gas - exploration & production

INTERMOUNTAIN HEALTH CARE, INC.

36 S. State St.
Salt Lake City, UT 84111
Pres: Scott S. Parker
VP HR: Gary Hart
Employees: 20,000

Phone: 801-442-3587
Fax: 801-442-3728

Jobs Added Last Year: —

Hospitals - not-for-profit system with 24 hospitals in Utah, Wyoming & Idaho (LDS Hospital, Primary Children's Medical Center, McKay-Dee Hospital Center)

INTERNATIONAL TOURIST ENTERTAINMENT

7030 Park Centre Dr.
Salt Lake City, UT 84121
Chm, Pres & CEO: Kelvyn H. Cullimore
No central personnel officer
Employees: 82

Phone: 801-566-9000
Fax: 801-568-7711

Jobs Added Last Year: 43 (+110.3%)

Leisure & recreation services - giant-screen theaters, retail stores & restaurants in selected tourist locations

IOMEGA CORPORATION

1821 W. Iomega Way
Roy, UT 84067
CEO: Kim B. Edwards
Dir HR: Dan Henrie
Employees: 1,667

Phone: 801-778-1000
Fax: 801-778-3190

Jobs Added Last Year: 781 (+88.1%)

Computers - removable data storage products for back-up & storage on personal computers (Zip drives)

MONROC, INC.

1730 Beck St.
Salt Lake City, UT 84110
Pres & CEO: Ronald D. Davis
Dir HR: Frank Metcalfe
Employees: 442

Phone: 801-359-3701
Fax: 801-359-9882

Jobs Added Last Year: 90 (+25.6%)

Construction - ready-mix concrete, prestressed & precast concrete building components & accessories for the concrete trade

NOVELL, INC.

1555 N. Technology Way
Orem, UT 84057
Chm, Pres & CEO: Robert J. Frankenberg
SVP HR: Ernest J. Harris
Employees: 7,272

Phone: 801-429-7000
Fax: 801-453-1267

Jobs Cut Last Year: 642 (-8.1%)

Computers - network software (NetWare) & Internet access tools (Corsair 3D, Ferret)

PST VANS, INC.

1901 W. 2100 South
Salt Lake City, UT 84119
Chm & CEO: Kenneth R. Norton
Dir HR: Brent C. Martin
Employees: 1,601

Phone: 801-975-2500
Fax: 801-975-2402

Jobs Added Last Year: 401 (+33.4%)

Transportation - truck

RESEARCH MEDICAL, INC.

6864 S. 300 West
Salt Lake City, UT 84047
Chm. Pres & CEO: Gary L. Crocker
Dir HR: Janice Barson
Employees: 281

Phone: 801-562-0200
Fax: 801-972-8393

Jobs Added Last Year: 96 (+51.9%)

Medical instruments - cardiovascular catheters, infusers, blood flow control products & other related medical devices; specialty pharmaceuticals

SINCLAIR OIL CORPORATION

550 E. South Temple St.
Salt Lake City, UT 84102
Pres: Robert E. Holding
Dir HR: Wendel White
Employees: 4,800

Phone: 801-524-2700
Fax: 801-524-2773

Jobs Added Last Year: 1,800 (+60.0%)

Diversified operations - oil refineries; ski resorts; hotels; gas stations

SKYWEST, INC.

444 S. River Rd.
St. George, UT 84790
Chm, Pres & CEO: Jerry C. Atkin
VP HR: R. Dale Merrill
Employees: 2,369

Phone: 801-634-3000
Fax: 801-634-2330

Jobs Added Last Year: 290 (+13.9%)

Transportation - airline (SkyWest Airlines, Scenic Airlines); car rental franchises (Avis)

SMITH'S FOOD & DRUG CENTERS, INC.

1550 S. Redwood Rd.
Salt Lake City, UT 84104
Chm & CEO: Jeffrey P. Smith
SVP HR: Richard C. Bylski
Employees: 19,859

Phone: 801-974-1400
Fax: 801-974-1662

Jobs Added Last Year: 1,859 (+10.3%)

Retail - supermarkets

STEINER CORPORATION

505 E. S. Temple
Salt Lake City, UT 84102
CEO & Pres: Richard Steiner
No central personnel officer
Employees: 9,000

Phone: 801-328-8831
Fax: 801-323-5680

Jobs Added Last Year: 0

Business services - commercial dry cleaning services

THERATECH, INC.

417 Wakara Way
Salt Lake City, UT 84108
Pres & CEO: Dinesh C. Patel
Assoc Dir HR: Cheryl C. Doerfler
Employees: 236

Phone: 801-588-6200
Fax: 801-583-6042

Jobs Added Last Year: 49 (+26.2%)

Medical products - controlled release drug delivery products that administer drugs through the skin, by oral delivery to the gastrointestinal tract & through tissues in the oral cavity

THIOKOL CORPORATION

2475 Washington Blvd.
Ogden, UT 84401-2398
Chm, Pres & CEO: James R. Wilson
EVP HR & Admin: James E. McNulty
Employees: 7,200

Phone: 801-629-2000
Fax: 801-629-2420

Jobs Cut Last Year: 800 (-10.0%)

Aerospace - solid rocket motors, propulsion & missile-launching systems; ordnance; fastening systems

ZIONS BANCORPORATION

1380 Kennecott Bldg.
Salt Lake City, UT 84133
Pres & CEO: Harris H. Simmons
SVP HR: Clark B. Hinckley
Employees: 3,075

Phone: 801-524-4787
Fax: 801-524-4659

Jobs Added Last Year: 380 (+14.1%)

Banks - West

BANKNORTH GROUP, INC.

300 Financial Plaza, PO Box 5420
Burlington, VT 05401
Pres & CEO: William H. Chadwick
SVP HR: Richard W. Park
Employees: 1,200

Phone: 802-658-2492
Fax: 802-860-5437

Jobs Added Last Year: 281 (+30.6%)

Banks - Northeast

 An in-depth profile of this company is available to subscribers on Hoover's Online at www.hoovers.com.

BEN & JERRY'S HOMEMADE, INC.

Junction of Rts. 2 & 100
Waterbury, VT 05676
Pres & CEO: Robert Holland Jr.
Dir HR: Keith Hunt
Employees: 703

Phone: 802-244-5641
Fax: 802-244-5944

Jobs Added Last Year: 166 (+30.9%)

Food - premium ice cream

C&S WHOLESALE GROCERS INC.

Old Ferry Rd.
Brattleboro, VT 05301
Chm, Pres & CEO: Richard B. Cohen
VP HR: Mitchell Davis
Employees: 2,000

Phone: 802-257-4371
Fax: 802-257-6727

Jobs Added Last Year: 500 (+33.3%)

Food - wholesale

VIRGINIA

ADVANCED ENGINEERING & RESEARCH ASSOCIATES, INC.

1745 Jefferson Davis, Ste. 800
Arlington, VA 22202
Pres & CEO: Ned Daffan
Dir HR: Metta Vongsanghaier
Employees: 200

Phone: 703-412-7193
Fax: 703-412-7198

Jobs Added Last Year: 89 (+80.2%)

Computers - engineering, multimedia & computer services & electronic performance support systems

THE AES CORPORATION

1001 N. 19th St.
Arlington, VA 22209
Pres & CEO: Dennis W. Bakke
No central personnel officer
Employees: 1,258

Phone: 703-522-1315
Fax: 703-528-4510

Jobs Added Last Year: 578 (+85.0%)

Energy - stem-cogeneration & electricity-generation plants

AMERICA ONLINE, INC.

8619 Westwood Center Dr.
Vienna, VA 22182-2285
Chm & CEO: Stephen M. Case
VP HR & Facilities: Mark Stavish
Employees: 2,481

Phone: 703-448-8700
Fax: 703-883-1532

Jobs Added Last Year: 1,954 (+370.8%)

Computers - Internet access & online services, including e-mail, conferencing, software, computing support, interactive magazines & newspapers & online classes

AMERICAN MANAGEMENT SYSTEMS

4050 Legato Rd.
Fairfax, VA 22033
CEO: Paul A. Brands
VP HR: Judy Tinelli
Employees: 5,400

Phone: 703-267-8000
Fax: 703-267-8555

Jobs Added Last Year: 1,150 (+27.1%)

Consulting - business analysis, information systems management, software programming & systems design & development, for telecommunications, financial & government uses

AMERICAN MOBILE SATELLITE CORPORATION

10802 Parkridge Blvd.
Reston, VA 22091
Pres: Brian B. Pemberton
VP HR: Susan B. Lubert
Employees: 317

Phone: 703-758-6000
Fax: 703-758-6111

Jobs Added Last Year: 125 (+65.1%)

Telecommunications services - mobile voice & data services via satellite to land-, sea- & air-based customers

BASSETT FURNITURE INDUSTRIES, INCORPORATED

PO Box 626
Bassett, VA 24055
Chm & CEO: Robert H. Spilman
VP & Dir Personnel: Jim Philpott
Employees: 7,800

Phone: 540-629-6000
Fax: 540-629-6333

Jobs Cut Last Year: 400 (-5.1%)

Furniture - home furnishings (Bermuda Run, J.G. Hook)

BDM INTERNATIONAL, INC.

1501 BDM Way
McLean, VA 22102-3204
Pres & CEO: Philip A. Odeen
Dir HR: Ron Kinsley
Employees: 7,900

Phone: 703-848-5000
Fax: 703-848-5006

Jobs Cut Last Year: 1,300 (-14.1%)

Computers - systems & software integration, technical services & enterprise management operations

BEST PRODUCTS CO. INC.

1400 Best Plaza
Richmond, VA 23227-1125
Chm & CEO: Daniel H. Levy
VP HR: Wayne Tennent
Employees: 14,200
Phone: 804-261-2000
Fax: 804-261-2250

Jobs Added Last Year: 400 (+2.9%)

Retail - catalog showrooms

BOOZ, ALLEN & HAMILTON INC.

8283 Greensboro Dr.
McLean, VA 22102
Chm & CEO: William F. Stasior
Chief Personnel Officer: Paul F. Anderson
Employees: 6,000
Phone: 703-902-5000
Fax: 703-902-3333

Jobs Added Last Year: 519 (+9.5%)

Consulting - professional management & technology consulting services

BTG, INC.

1945 Old Gallows Rd.
Vienna, VA 22182
Chm, Pres & CEO: Edward H. Bersoff
Dir HR: Winder Heller
Employees: 923
Phone: 703-556-6518
Fax: 703-556-9290

Jobs Added Last Year: 289 (+45.6%)

Data collection & systems - modular, open-information computer-based systems

CAPITAL ONE FINANCIAL CORPORATION

2980 Fairview Park Dr., Ste. 1300
Falls Church, VA 22042-4525
CEO: Richard D. Fairbank
VP HR: Dennis Liberson
Employees: 3,500
Phone: 703-205-1000
Fax: 703-205-1090

Jobs Added Last Year: 871 (+33.1%)

Financial - credit card issuance (spinoff of Signet Banking Corporation)

CARILION HEALTH SYSTEM

1212 Third St., PO Box 13727
Roanoke, VA 24036-3727
Pres: Thomas L. Robertson
Dir HR: Diane Allison
Employees: 9,500
Phone: 540-981-7900
Fax: 540-344-5716

Jobs Cut Last Year: 500 (-5.0%)

Hospitals - not-for-profit system with 13 hospitals serving western Virginia (Roanoke Memorial Hospitals, Community Hospital of Roanoke Valley, Bedford County Memorial Hospital)

CARPENTER CO.

5016 Monument Ave.
Richmond, VA 23261
Chm & CEO: Stanley F. Pauley
Dir Personnel: David Harned
Employees: 6,900
Phone: 804-359-0800
Fax: 804-353-0694

Jobs Cut Last Year: 0

Chemicals - specialty; polyurethane foam

CFW COMMUNICATIONS COMPANY

401 Spring Lane, Ste. 300
Waynesboro, VA 22980
Pres & CEO: James S. Quarforth
Dir HR: Steve Carpenter
Employees: 492
Phone: 540-946-3500
Fax: 540-946-3599

Jobs Added Last Year: 260 (+112.1%)

Telecommunications services - traditional wireline services, wireless services & telecommuncations products

CHESAPEAKE CORPORATION

1021 E. Cary St., PO Box 2350
Richmond, VA 23218-2350
Chm & CEO: J. Carter Fox
VP HR & Asst Sec: Thomas A. Smith
Employees: 5,305
Phone: 804-697-1000
Fax: 804-697-1199

Jobs Added Last Year: 96 (+1.8%)

Paper & paper products - containerboard, linerboard & corrugated packaging materials

CIRCUIT CITY STORES, INC.

9950 Mayland Dr.
Richmond, VA 23233
Chm, Pres & CEO: Richard L. Sharp
SVP HR: William E. Zierden
Employees: 36,430
Phone: 804-527-4000
Fax: 804-527-4164

Jobs Added Last Year: 5,017 (+16.0%)

Retail - brand-name consumer electronics & major appliances (#1 in US) & prerecorded music

CRESTAR FINANCIAL CORPORATION

Crestar Ctr., 919 E. Main St.
Richmond, VA 23219
Chm & CEO: Richard G. Tilghman
EVP Mgmt Resources Group: James J. Kelley
Employees: 6,712
Phone: 804-782-5000
Fax: 804-782-5815

Jobs Cut Last Year: 288 (-4.1%)

Banks - Southeast

An in-depth profile of this company is available to subscribers on Hoover's Online at www.hoovers.com.

CSX CORPORATION

One James Ctr., 901 E. Cary St.
Richmond, VA 23219-4031
Chm, Pres & CEO: John W. Snow
HR Mgr: Linda Amato
Employees: 47,965

Phone: 804-782-1400
Fax: 804-782-6747

Jobs Added Last Year: 1,218 (+2.6%)

Transportation - rail & intermodal services; container shipping
(Sea-Land); barge operations (American Commercial), trucking &
contract services

DIMON, INC.

512 Bridge St.
Danville, VA 24543
Chm, Pres & CEO: Claude B. Owen Jr.
Dir HR: Norma Lutz
Employees: 3,800

Phone: 804-792-7511
Fax: 804-791-0377

Jobs Added Last Year: 1,000 (+35.7%)

Tobacco - leaf tobacco (#2 in US: Dibrell Brothers, Monk-Austin);
cut flowers

DOMINION RESOURCES, INC.

901 E. Byrd St.
Richmond, VA 23219-4072
Chm, Pres & CEO: Thos. E. Capps
SVP Commercial Ops: Larry M. Girvin
Employees: 10,592

Phone: 804-775-5700
Fax: 804-775-5819

Jobs Cut Last Year: 197 (-1.8%)

Utility - electric power & natural gas

DYNCORP

2000 Edmund Halley Dr.
Reston, VA 22091-3436
Pres & CEO: Daniel R. Bannister
VP Labor Relations & Emp Benefits: James A. Mackin
Employees: 17,000

Phone: 703-264-0330
Fax: 703-264-8600

Jobs Added Last Year: —

Business services - engineering, scientific, technology, management & technical support services to US & foreign government
agencies & commercial clients

ETHYL CORPORATION

330 S. Fourth St.
Richmond, VA 23219
Chm, Pres & CEO: Bruce C. Gottwald
VP HR: Henry C. Page Jr.
Employees: 5,500

Phone: 804-788-5000
Fax: 804-788-5688

Jobs Added Last Year: —

Chemicals - petroleum additives, including those for gasoline,
diesel fuels & home heating oils

ETS INTERNATIONAL, INC.

1401 Municipal Rd. NW
Roanoke, VA 24012-1319
Chm & Pres: John D. McKenna
Mgr HR: Amy M. Fulton
Employees: 109

Phone: 540-265-0004
Fax: 540-265-0131

Jobs Added Last Year: 39 (+55.7%)

Pollution control equipment & services - pollution control
systems & testing systems

National Employment Job Bank— http://www.nlbbs.com/~najoban/

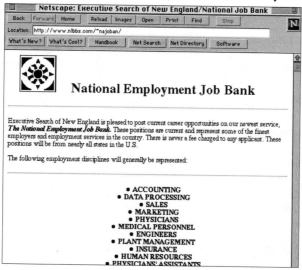

EXCALIBUR TECHNOLOGIES CORPORATION

2000 Corporate Ridge
McLean, VA 22102
CEO: John M. Kennedy
No central personnel officer
Employees: 125

Phone: 619-438-7900
Fax: 619-438-7901

Jobs Added Last Year: 33 (+35.9%)

Computers - document imaging & multimedia information
retrieval software (RetrievalWare)

FARM FRESH INC.

7530 Tidewater Dr.
Norfolk, VA 23505
Chm, Pres & CEO: Michael E. Julian
Dir HR: Debbie Kremers
Employees: 7,000

Phone: 757-480-6700
Fax: 757-480-6399

Jobs Added Last Year: —

Retail - supermarkets & warehouse stores

FORUM GROUP, INC.

11320 Random Hills Rd., Ste. 400
Fairfax, VA 22030
Pres & CEO: Mark L. Pacala
VP HR: Lisa J. Peterson
Employees: 4,000

Phone: 703-277-7000
Fax: 703-277-7091

Jobs Added Last Year: 200 (+5.3%)

Real estate operations - rental retirement communities

GANNETT CO., INC.

1100 Wilson Blvd.
Arlington, VA 22234
Chm, Pres & CEO: John J. Curley
SVP Personnel: Richard L. Clapp
Employees: 39,100

Phone: 703-284-6000
Fax: 703-558-3506

Jobs Added Last Year: 3,100 (+8.6%)

Publishing - newspapers (83, including USA TODAY); broadcasting (7 radio & 15 TV stations); TV programming (Multimedia
Entertainment: Donahue, Sally Jesse Raphael)

GENERAL DYNAMICS CORPORATION

3190 Fairview Park Dr.
Falls Church, VA 22042-4523
Chm & CEO: James R. Mellor
VP HR & Admin: W. P. Wylie
Employees: 27,700

Phone: 703-876-3000
Fax: 703-876-3125

Jobs Added Last Year: 3,500 (+14.5%)

Military equipment - nuclear submarines & armored vehicles

HEILIG-MEYERS CO.

2235 Staples Mill Rd.
Richmond, VA 23230
Chm & CEO: William C. DeRusha
SVP HR & Training: Ronald M. Ragland
Employees: 14,383

Phone: 804-359-9171
Fax: 804-254-1498

Jobs Added Last Year: 1,320 (+10.1%)

Retail - home furnishings & appliances

ICF KAISER INTERNATIONAL, INC.

9300 Lee Hwy.
Fairfax, VA 22031-1207
Chm & CEO: James O. Edwards
SVP HR: Marcy Romm
Employees: 7,500

Phone: 703-934-3600
Fax: 703-934-9740

Jobs Added Last Year: 1,800 (+31.6%)

Engineering - professional services, including engineering, construction & consulting services for public- & private-sector clients
in the environmental, infrastructure & industrial markets

JAMES RIVER CORP. OF VIRGINIA

120 Tredegar St.
Richmond, VA 23219
Chm & CEO: Miles L. Marsh
SVP HR: Daniel J. Girvan
Employees: 27,000

Phone: 804-644-5411
Fax: 804-649-4428

Jobs Cut Last Year: 6,800 (-20.1%)

Paper & paper products - bathroom tissue (Quilted Northern),
paper towels (Brawny), cups & plates (Dixie); packaging for food
& consumer products

K-VA-T FOOD STORES, INC.

329 N. Main St.
Grundy, VA 24614
Chm & CEO: Jack C. Smith
VP HR & Security: William L. Neely
Employees: 4,000

Phone: 540-935-4587
Fax: 540-935-4587

Jobs Added Last Year: 248 (+6.6%)

Retail - supermarkets in Kentucky, Virginia & Tennessee

LAFARGE CORPORATION

11130 Sunrise Valley Dr., Ste. 300
Reston, VA 22091
Pres & CEO: John M. Piecuch
Corp SVP HR: Thomas W. Tatum
Employees: 6,600

Phone: 703-264-3600
Fax: 703-264-0634

Jobs Added Last Year: 100 (+1.5%)

Construction - cement, aggregates & concrete for construction &
paving of roads & sidewalks, hospitals, schools, tunnels, airports,
stadiums & underground utilities

 An in-depth profile of this company is available
to subscribers on Hoover's Online at www.hoovers.com.

MARS, INC.

6885 Elm St.
McLean, VA 22101-3810
Chm, Co-Pres & CEO: Forrest E. Mars Jr.
No central personnel officer
Employees: 28,000

Phone: 703-821-4900
Fax: 703-448-9678

Jobs Added Last Year: 0

Food - confectionery, pet food & rice

MEDIA GENERAL INC.

333 E. Grace St.
Richmond, VA 23219
Chm, Pres & CEO: J. Stewart Bryan III
Dir Administrative Svcs: Edward C. Tosh
Employees: 7,500

Phone: 804-649-6000
Fax: 804-649-6898

Jobs Added Last Year: 200 (+2.7%)

Publishing - newspapers (Richmond Times-Dispatch, Winston-Salem Journal) & business information; broadcast & cable TV; newsprint production; commercial printing & publications

MICRODYNE CORPORATION

3601 Eisenhower Ave.
Alexandria, VA 22304
Pres & CEO: Philip T. Cunningham
Dir HR: Paul Sinclair
Employees: 673

Phone: 703-329-3700
Fax: 703-329-3722

Jobs Added Last Year: 203 (+43.2%)

Computers - LAN adapter cards & concentrators, computer networking hardware & software, aerospace telemetry receivers for data gathering & analysis & technical services

MOBIL CORPORATION

3225 Gallows Rd.
Fairfax, VA 22037-0001
Chm, Pres & CEO: Lucio A. Noto
Mgr HR: Douglas O. Fitzsimmons
Employees: 50,400

Phone: 703-846-3000
Fax: 703-846-4669

Jobs Cut Last Year: 8,100 (-13.8%)

Oil & gas - international integrated

NAVY EXCHANGE SYSTEM

3280 Virginia Beach Blvd.
Virginia Beach, VA 23452
Rear Admiral & Commanding Officer: John T. Kavanaugh
Dir HR: Michael Marchesani
Employees: 21,854

Phone: 757-463-6200
Fax: 757-631-3659

Jobs Cut Last Year: 146 (-0.7%)

Retail - network of retail outlets serving Navy personnel, their families, reservists & retirees

NIMBUS CD INTERNATIONAL, INC.

PO Box 7427
Charlottesville, VA 22906-7427
Pres & CEO: Lyndon J. Faulkner
Mgr HR: Gayle Birckhead
Employees: 871

Phone: 804-985-1100
Fax: 804-985-4794

Jobs Added Last Year: 203 (+30.4%)

Electrical components - audio CDs & computer CD-ROM manufacturing

NORFOLK SOUTHERN CORPORATION

3 Commercial Place
Norfolk, VA 23510-2191
Chm, Pres & CEO: David R. Goode
VP Personnel: Paul N. Austin
Employees: 26,944

Phone: 757-629-2680
Fax: 757-629-2798

Jobs Cut Last Year: 224 (-0.8%)

Transportation - rail & truck (North American Van Lines)

OMNIPOINT CORPORATION

2000 N. 14th St., Ste. 550
Arlington, VA 22201
Chm, Pres & CEO: Douglas G. Smith
VP HR: Arthur A. Pumo
Employees: 234

Phone: 703-522-7778
Fax: 703-522-7747

Jobs Added Last Year: 70 (+42.7%)

Telecommunications equipment - proprietary technologies for digital wireless applications & equipment for personal communications services

ORBITAL SCIENCES CORPORATION

21700 Atlantic Blvd.
Dulles, VA 20166
Chm, Pres & CEO: David W. Thompson
VP HR: Stephen Parker
Employees: 2,729

Phone: 703-406-5000
Fax: 703-406-3502

Jobs Added Last Year: 884 (+47.9%)

Aerospace - aircraft & space launch equipment

OWENS & MINOR, INC.

4800 Cox Rd.
Glen Allen, VA 23060-6292
Chm, Pres & CEO: G. Gilmer Minor III
VP HR: Michael L. Roane
Employees: 3,350

Phone: 804-747-9794
Fax: 804-273-0232

Jobs Added Last Year: 350 (+11.7%)

Drugs & sundries - wholesale distribution of medical & surgical supplies & pharmaceuticals

PRC INC.

1500 PRC Dr.
McLean, VA 22102
Chm & CEO: James J. Leto
SVP HR: Robert Waters
Employees: 6,850

Phone: 703-556-1000
Fax: 703-556-1174

Jobs Cut Last Year: 150 (-2.1%)

Computers - systems integration, primarily for US government clients

PSINET, INC.

510 Huntmar Park Dr.
Herndon, VA 22070
Chm, Pres & CEO: William L. Schrader
VP HR: David Mann
Employees: 625

Phone: 703-904-4100
Fax: 703-904-4200

Jobs Added Last Year: 496 (+384.5%)

Computers - Internet services to businesses

REYNOLDS METALS COMPANY

6601 W. Broad St.
Richmond, VA 23230
Chm & CEO: Richard G. Holder
VP HR: F. Robert Newman
Employees: 29,800

Phone: 804-281-2000
Fax: 804-281-3695

Jobs Added Last Year: 700 (+2.4%)

Metal products - aluminum cans & wrap; plastic shrink film, containers & lids; aluminum wheels & bumper systems; building & construction materials, including siding, doors & roofing

RICHFOOD HOLDINGS, INC.

8258 Richfood Rd.
Mechanicsville, VA 23111
Pres & CEO: Donald D. Bennett
VP HR: Chris S. Zubof
Employees: 1,846

Phone: 804-746-6000
Fax: 804-746-6179

Jobs Added Last Year: 346 (+23.1%)

Food - wholesale to grocers

ROWE FURNITURE CORPORATION

239 Rowan St.
Salem, VA 24153
Pres & CEO: Gerald M. Birnbach
Corp Dir HR: John Clark
Employees: 1,500

Phone: 540-389-8671
Fax: 540-389-8217

Jobs Added Last Year: 200 (+15.4%)

Furniture - upholstered living room furniture including sofas, sleeper sofas & chairs

THE SALVATION ARMY

615 Slaters Ln.
Alexandria, VA 22313
Commissioner: Robert A. Watson
Dir HR: Dorrie DeJong
Employees: 38,999

Phone: 703-684-5500
Fax: 703-684-5538

Jobs Cut Last Year: 592 (-1.5%)

Religious & charitable organization

SMITHFIELD FOODS, INC.

501 N. Church St., 999 Waterside Dr.
Norfolk, VA 23510
Chm: Joseph W. Luter III
Dir Personnel: Herbert DeGoft
Employees: 9,000

Phone: 757-365-3000
Fax: 757-365-3017

Jobs Added Last Year: 1,000 (+12.5%)

Food - pork products (Patrick Cudahy, Gwaltney, Esskay & Smithfield)

TULTEX CORPORATION

101 Commonwealth Blvd., PO Box 5191
Martinsville, VA 24115
Pres & CEO: Charles W. Davies Jr.
Dir HR: Ron Cox
Employees: 6,835

Phone: 540-632-2961
Fax: 540-632-8000

Jobs Cut Last Year: 98 (-1.4%)

Apparel - activewear (Discus Athletic, Logo Athletic)

UNIVERSAL CORPORATION

1501 N. Hamilton St.
Richmond, VA 23260
Chm & CEO: Henry H. Harrell
Corp Dir HR: Mike Oberschmidt Jr.
Employees: 30,000

Phone: 804-359-9311
Fax: 804-254-3584

Jobs Added Last Year: 5,000 (+20.0%)

Tobacco (#1 worldwide); lumber & building products; agricultural products

US ORDER, INC.

13873 Park Center Rd., Ste. 353
Herndon, VA 22071
Chm & CEO: William F. Gorog
Dir HR: Cathy Carney-Peters
Employees: 105

Phone: 703-834-9480
Fax: 703-834-9668

Jobs Added Last Year: 24 (+29.6%)

Business services - home-banking & telecommunication-network services

USAIR GROUP, INC.

2345 Crystal Dr.
Arlington, VA 22227
Chm & CEO: Stephen M. Wolf
EVP HR: John R. Long III
Employees: 39,000

Phone: 703-418-7000
Fax: 703-418-7312

Jobs Cut Last Year: 6,500 (-14.3%)

Transportation - airline

UUNET TECHNOLOGIES, INC.

3060 Williams Dr.
Fairfax, VA 22031-4648
Pres & CEO: John W. Sidgmore
VP HR: Diana E. Lawrence
Employees: 306

Phone: 703-206-5600
Fax: 703-206-5601

Jobs Added Last Year: 119 (+63.6%)

Computers - Internet access services

WLR FOODS, INC.

PO Box 7000
Broadway, VA 22815-7000
Pres & CEO: James L. Keeler
VP HR: Jane T. Brookshire
Employees: 9,000

Phone: 540-896-7000
Fax: 540-896-0498

Jobs Added Last Year: 2,200 (+32.4%)

Food - poultry processing & frozen dinners, turkey burgers & sausage

ACTIVE VOICE CORPORATION

2901 Third Ave., Ste. 500
Seattle, WA 98121-9800
Chm & Pres: Robert L. Richmond
Mgr Personnel & Facilities: Debbie Faulkner
Employees: 177

Phone: 206-441-4700
Fax: 206-441-4784

Jobs Added Last Year: 44 (+33.1%)

Telecommunications equipment - computer-based voice-processing systems (Repartee, Replay, Replay Plus, TeLANophy)

AIRBORNE FREIGHT CORPORATION

3101 Western Ave.
Seattle, WA 98121
Chm & CEO: Robert S. Cline
SVP HR: Richard G. Goodwin
Employees: 19,500

Phone: 206-285-4600
Fax: 206-281-3890

Jobs Added Last Year: 2,100 (+12.1%)

Transportation - express air freight

ALASKA AIR GROUP, INC.

19300 Pacific Hwy. South
Seattle, WA 98188
Chm, Pres & CEO: John F. Kelly
VP Emp Svcs: Dennis J. Hamel
Employees: 7,379

Phone: 206-431-7040
Fax: 206-431-7031

Jobs Cut Last Year: 2,473 (-25.1%)

Transportation - airline (Alaska Airlines, Horizon Air)

ATTACHMATE CORPORATION

3617 131st Ave. SE
Bellevue, WA 98006
Pres & CEO: Jim Linder
CFO: Bill Boisvert
Employees: 2,000

Phone: 206-644-4010
Fax: 206-747-9924

Jobs Added Last Year: 900 (+81.8%)

Computers - supplier of PC-to-mainframe software (#1 worldwide) for building secure intranets

THE BOEING COMPANY

7755 E. Marginal Way South
Seattle, WA 98108
CEO: Philip Condit
SVP HR: Larry G. McKean
Employees: 105,000

Phone: 206-655-2121
Fax: 206-655-7004

Jobs Cut Last Year: 12,000 (-10.3%)

Aerospace - aircraft equipment (#1 worldwide)

EDMARK CORPORATION

6727 185th Ave. NE
Redmond, WA 98052-3218
Chm & CEO: Sally G. Norodick
HR Mgr: Diane Coplentz
Employees: 156

Phone: 206-556-8400
Fax: 206-556-8430

Jobs Added Last Year: 35 (+28.9%)

Computers - children's educational software (Millie's Math House, KidDesk) & books

ERNST HOME CENTER, INC.

1511 Sixth Ave.
Seattle, WA 98101
Pres & CEO: Hal Smith
VP HR: Sue Alford
Employees: 5,150

Phone: 206-621-6700
Fax: 206-621-6837

Jobs Added Last Year: 1,350 (+35.5%)

Building products - retail home improvement & garden products, furnishings & hardware

ESTERLINE TECHNOLOGIES CORP.

10800 NE Eighth St., Ste. 600
Bellevue, WA 98004
Chm, Pres & CEO: Wendell P. Hurlbut
Dir Human Relations: Marcia Greenberg
Employees: 3,499

Phone: 206-453-9400
Fax: 206-453-2916

Jobs Added Last Year: 699 (+25.0%)

Machinery - semiconductor manufacturing equipment; measuring & sensing devices for the aerospace industry; meters, switches & indicators & measurement & analysis equipment

EXPEDITORS INTERNATIONAL OF WASHINGTON, INC.

19119 16th Ave. South
Seattle, WA 98188
Chm & CEO: Peter J. Rose
No central personnel officer
Employees: 2,465

Phone: 206-246-3711
Fax: 206-246-3197

Jobs Added Last Year: 465 (+23.3%)

Transportation - air freight; ocean-freight & import services

GROUP HEALTH COOPERATIVE OF PUGET SOUND

521 Wall St.
Seattle, WA 98124
Pres & CEO: Phillip M. Nudelman
VP HR: Brenda Tolbert
Employees: 9,000

Phone: 206-448-6460
Fax: 206-448-6080

Jobs Added Last Year: —

Health maintenance organization

ITRON, INC.

2818 N. Sullivan Rd.
Spokane, WA 99216-1897
Pres & CEO: Johnny M. Humphreys
VP HR: Paul Boxleitner
Employees: 991

Phone: 509-924-9900
Fax: 509-891-3355

Jobs Added Last Year: 279 (+39.2%)

Instruments - wireless systems to read utility meters

KEY TRONIC CORPORATION

4424 N. Sullivan Rd.
Spokane, WA 99216
Pres & CEO: Fred Wenninger
Dir HR: Keith C. Clement
Employees: 2,925

Phone: 509-928-8000
Fax: 509-927-5248

Jobs Added Last Year: 762 (+35.2%)

Computers - keyboards (#1 independent manufacturer worldwide), including ergonomic & voice-recognition keyboards; mice (ClikMate) & input devices

Reed — http://www.reed.co.uk/

Netscape: Reed Jobnet Homepage

Welcome to Reed Jobnet

An in-depth profile of this company is available to subscribers on Hoover's Online at www.hoovers.com.

333

MICROSOFT CORPORATION

One Microsoft Way
Redmond, WA 98052-6399
Chm & CEO: William H. Gates III
VP HR & Admin: Michael R. Murray
Employees: 17,801

Phone: 206-882-8080
Fax: 206-883-8101

Jobs Added Last Year: 2,544 (+16.7%)

Computers - operating systems (#1 worldwide: Windows 95, MS-DOS); application & language software; CD-ROMs; online service; online publishing (Slate); news services (MSNBC)

NATIONAL SECURITIES CORPORATION

1001 Fourth Ave., Ste. 2200
Seattle, WA 98154
Pres & CEO: Robert I. Kollack
VP Ops: Joanne Salisbury
Employees: 206

Phone: 206-622-7200
Fax: 206-343-6244

Jobs Added Last Year: 95 (+85.6%)

Financial - retail securities brokerage

NORDSTROM, INC.

1501 Fifth Ave.
Seattle, WA 98101-1603
Co-Pres: Blake W. Nordstrom
VP HR: Charles L. Dudley
Employees: 37,000

Phone: 206-628-2111
Fax: 206-628-1795

Jobs Added Last Year: 2,000 (+5.7%)

Retail - major department stores; clearance stores (Nordstrom Rack); men's specialty stores

OMEGA ENVIRONMENTAL, INC.

19805 N. Creek Pkwy., PO Box 3005
Bothell, WA 98041-3005
Pres & CEO: Louis J. Tedesco
VP HR: Jerold O. Gutman
Employees: 1,080

Phone: 206-486-4800
Fax: 206-486-1532

Jobs Added Last Year: 430 (+66.2%)

Pollution control equipment & services - installation & removal of underground storage tanks

PACCAR INC

777 106th Ave. NE
Bellevue, WA 98004
Chm & CEO: Charles M. Pigott
VP Emp Relations: Laurie L. Baker
Employees: 14,000

Phone: 206-455-7400
Fax: 206-453-5959

Jobs Cut Last Year: 600 (-4.1%)

Automotive manufacturing - medium & heavy (Kenworth, Peterbilt) on- & off-road Class 8 trucks; winches & oilfield pumps; auto parts stores (Al's Auto Supply, Grand Auto)

PACIFIC REHABILITATION & SPORTS MEDICINE, INC.

8100 NE Parkway Dr., Ste. 190
Vancouver, WA 98662
Chm, Pres & CEO: Bill Barancik
Dir HR: Rene Neddo
Employees: 554

Phone: 360-260-8130
Fax: 360-260-8131

Jobs Added Last Year: 259 (+87.8%)

Health care - outpatient physical therapy services

PRICE/COSTCO, INC.

999 Lake Dr.
Issaquah, WA 98027
Pres & CEO: James D. Sinegal
SVP HR & Risk Mgmt: John Matthews
Employees: 52,000

Phone: 206-313-8100
Fax: 206-313-8103

Jobs Added Last Year: 5,000 (+10.6%)

Retail - discount membership warehouse clubs

PYRAMID BREWERIES INC.

91 S. Royal Brougham Way
Seattle, WA 98134
Pres & CEO: George Hancock
Payroll & HR Mgr: Jackie Rudd
Employees: 210

Phone: 206-682-8322
Fax: 206-682-8420

Jobs Added Last Year: 105 (+100.0%)

Beverages - specialty beers (Pyramid, Thoms Kemper)

QUALITY FOOD CENTERS, INC.

10112 NE 10th St.
Bellevue, WA 98009
Chm & CEO: Stuart M. Sloan
No central personnel officer
Employees: 4,200

Phone: 206-455-3761
Fax: 206-462-2142

Jobs Added Last Year: 1,000 (+31.3%)

Retail - supermarkets

RED LION HOTELS, INC.

4001 Main St.
Vancouver, WA 98663
Chm, Pres & CEO: David J. Johnson
SVP HR: Steven L. Hubbard
Employees: 11,171

Phone: 360-696-0001
Fax: 360-750-4391

Jobs Added Last Year: 621 (+5.9%)

Hotels & motels - full-service hotels

RED LION INNS LIMITED PARTNERSHIP

4001 Main St.
Vancouver, WA 98663
Pres & CEO: David J. Johnson
VP HR: Steve Hubbard
Employees: 10,000

Phone: 360-696-0001
Fax: 360-750-4371

Jobs Added Last Year: —

Hotels & motels - full-service accomodations

RIDE, INC.

8160 304th Ave., SE
Preston, WA 98050
Interim CEO: Gerald Wasserman
Dir HR: Scott MacIntire
Employees: 361

Phone: 206-222-6015
Fax: 206-222-6499

Jobs Added Last Year: 317 (+720.5%)

Leisure & recreational equipment - snowboards & snowboard boots, bindings, clothing, accessories & related products; retail athletic footwear, in-line skates & other sporting goods (CAS)

SAFECO CORPORATION

SAFECO Plaza
Seattle, WA 98185
Chm, Pres & CEO: Roger H. Eigsti
Dir HR: Teresa Sato
Employees: 7,500

Phone: 206-545-5000
Fax: 206-545-5995

Jobs Cut Last Year: 50 (-0.7%)

Insurance - property, casualty, auto, fire, recreational-property, life & health; real estate, commercial-credit & asset-management services

SIMPSON INVESTMENT CO.

1201 Third Ave., Ste. 4900
Seattle, WA 98101
Chm: William G. Reed Jr.
VP HR: Cynthia Sonstelie
Employees: 8,000

Phone: 206-224-5000
Fax: 206-224-5060

Jobs Added Last Year: 0

Building products - lumber, logging, plywood doors

SISTERS OF PROVIDENCE HEALTH SYSTEM

520 Pike St., PO Box 11038
Seattle, WA 98111-9038
Pres & CEO: Dona Taylor
Dir HR: Sue Byington
Employees: 17,956

Phone: 206-464-3355
Fax: 206-464-3038

Jobs Added Last Year: 594 (+3.4%)

Hospitals - not-for-profit system serving Alaska, Washington, Oregon & California

STARWAVE CORPORATION

13810 SE Eastgate Way
Bellevue, WA 98005
Pres: Michael Slade
Dir HR: Barbara Thompson
Employees: 221

Phone: 206-957-2000
Fax: 206-957-2009

Jobs Added Last Year: 141 (+176.3%)

Computers - online services, including sports (ESPNET Sports Zone), entertainment (Mr. Showbiz) & adventure & travel (Outside Online)

TODD SHIPYARDS CORPORATION

1801 16th Ave. SW
Seattle, WA 98134-1089
Chm & CEO: Patrick W. E. Hodgson
Dir HR: Ludy Marz
Employees: 1,175

Phone: 206-623-1635
Fax: 206-442-8503

Jobs Added Last Year: 475 (+67.9%)

Boat building - repair, overhaul, conversion & construction of commercial & military marine vessels

UNITED SECURITY BANCORPORATION

9506 North Newport Hwy.
Spokane, WA 99218
CEO & Pres: William C. Dashiell
HR Mgr: Edith Dashiell
Employees: 146

Phone: 509-467-6949
Fax: 509-466-0255

Jobs Added Last Year: 38 (+35.2%)

Banks - West (United Security Bank, Home Security Bank)

THE UNIVERSITY OF WASHINGTON

Administrative Offices, AH-30
Seattle, WA 98195
Pres: William P. Gerberding
Dir HR: Margot Ray
Employees: 22,655

Phone: 206-543-8812
Fax: 206-543-3951

Jobs Added Last Year: —

University

WALKER RICHER & QUINN INC.

1500 Dexter Ave N.
Seattle, WA 98109-3051
Pres & CEO: Doug Walker
Dir HR: Norris Palmanleer
Employees: 525

Phone: 206-217-7500
Fax: 206-217-0380

Jobs Added Last Year: 130 (+32.9%)

Computers - software to connect open & proprietary systems

 An in-depth profile of this company is available to subscribers on Hoover's Online at www.hoovers.com.

335

WEYERHAEUSER COMPANY

Tacoma, WA 98477
Phone: 206-924-2345
Fax: 206-924-7407
Pres & CEO: John W. Creighton Jr.
SVP HR: Steven R. Hill
Employees: 39,431

Jobs Added Last Year: 2,766 (+7.5%)

Building products - timberlands & wood; pulp, paper & packaging, including containerboard, fine paper, newsprint & bleached paperboard; recycling; real estate & financial services

WEIRTON STEEL CORPORATION

400 Three Springs Dr.
Phone: 304-797-2000
Weirton, WV 26062
Fax: 304-797-2275
Pres, CEO & COO: Richard K. Riederer
EVP HR & Corp Law: David L. Robertson
Employees: 5,655

Jobs Added Last Year: 90 (+1.6%)

Steel - hot-rolled, cold-rolled & galvanized sheet products

ABT BUILDING PRODUCTS CORPORATION

One Neenah Center, Ste. 600
Phone: 414-751-8611
Neenah, WI 54956-3070
Fax: 414-751-0370
Chm, Pres & CEO: George T. Brophy
Corp Dir HR: Thomas J. Kelly
Employees: 1,669

Jobs Added Last Year: 234 (+16.3%)

Building products - siding, tile board, moldings, shutters & architectural trim

AMERICAN FAMILY INSURANCE

6000 American Pkwy.
Phone: 608-249-2111
Madison, WI 53783-0001
Fax: 608-243-4921
Chm & CEO: Dale F. Mathwich
VP HR: Vicki L. Chvala
Employees: 6,411

Jobs Added Last Year: 46 (+0.7%)

Insurance - multiline

AMERICAN FOODS GROUP INC.

544 Acme St., PO Box 8547
Phone: 414-437-6330
Green Bay, WI 54308
Fax: 414-436-6510
CEO: Carl Kuehne
Dir HR: Roger Wanek
Employees: 1,800

Jobs Added Last Year: 200 (+12.5%)

Food - meat products

A. O. SMITH CORPORATION

11270 W. Park Place
Phone: 414-359-4000
Milwaukee, WI 53224-3690
Fax: 414-359-4198
Chm, Pres & CEO: Robert J. O'Toole
VP HR & Public Affairs: Edward J. O'Conner
Employees: 13,000

Jobs Added Last Year: 900 (+7.4%)

Automotive & trucking - automotive frames, axles, suspension modules & other components; electric motors; water heaters; agricultural feed-storage systems

BANTA CORPORATION

River Place, 225 Main St.
Phone: 414-751-7777
Menasha, WI 54952-8003
Fax: 414-751-7790
Chm, Pres & CEO: Donald D. Belcher
HR Specialist: Cheryl Spindler
Employees: 5,700

Jobs Added Last Year: 792 (+16.1%)

Printing - retail catalogs, direct mail & single-use products; books & magazines; digital imaging services; point-of purchase displays; security products

BRIGGS & STRATTON CORPORATION

12301 W. Wirth St.
Phone: 414-259-5333
Wauwatosa, WI 53222-2110
Fax: 414-259-5338
Chm & CEO: Frederick P. Stratton Jr.
VP HR: Gerald E. Zitzer
Employees: 6,958

Jobs Cut Last Year: 1,670 (-19.4%)

Engines - air-cooled internal combustion engines for original equipment manufacturers of outdoor power equipment (#1 worldwide)

CARSON PIRIE SCOTT & CO.

331 W. Wisconsin Ave.
Milwaukee, WI 53203
Chm & CEO: Stanton J. Bluestone
EVP HR: Roger Gaston
Employees: 12,000

Phone: 414-347-4141
Fax: 414-278-5748

Jobs Added Last Year: 0

Retail - regional department stores (Carson Pirie Scott, Bergner's, Boston Store)

CASE CORPORATION

700 State St.
Racine, WI 53404
Chm, Pres & CEO: Jean-Pierre Rosso
VP HR: Marc J. Castor
Employees: 15,700

Phone: 414-636-6011
Fax: 414-636-6412

Jobs Cut Last Year: 1,200 (-7.1%)

Machinery - tractors, combines, cotton pickers, backhoes, excavators & forklifts

COMMERCE GROUP CORP.

6001 N. 91st St.
Milwaukee, WI 53225-1795
Chm, Pres, CEO, COO, CFO & Treas: Edward L. Machulak
Personnel Dir: Sylvia Young
Employees: 304

Phone: 414-462-5310
Fax: 414-462-5312

Jobs Added Last Year: 79 (+35.1%)

Mining - gold

CONSOLIDATED PAPERS, INC.

PO Box 8050
Wisconsin Rapids, WI 54495-8050
Pres & CEO: Patrick F. Brennan
Dir HR: Kenneth A. Ebert
Employees: 5,930

Phone: 715-422-3111
Fax: 715-422-3469

Jobs Added Last Year: 1,078 (+22.2%)

Paper & paper products

DUNSIRN INDUSTRIES INC.

2415 Industrial Dr.
Neenah, WI 54957
Pres: Brian Dunsirn
Corp HR Dir: Kristine Hackbarth
Employees: 300

Phone: 414-725-3814
Fax: 414-725-9643

Jobs Added Last Year: 80 (+36.4%)

Paper & film products

FIRSTAR CORPORATION

777 E. Wisconsin Ave.
Milwaukee, WI 53202
Chm & CEO: Roger L. Fitzsimonds
SVP HR: Peggy Page
Employees: 9,800

Phone: 414-765-4321
Fax: 414-765-4349

Jobs Cut Last Year: 76 (-0.8%)

Banks - Midwest

FISERV, INC.

255 Fiserv Dr.
Brookfield, WI 53045
Chm & CEO: George D. Dalton
SVP Corp HR: Jack P. Bucalo
Employees: 8,222

Phone: 414-879-5000
Fax: 414-879-5013

Jobs Added Last Year: 2,027 (+32.7%)

Business services - data-processing & information-management services

FORT HOWARD CORPORATION

1919 S. Broadway
Green Bay, WI 54304
Chm & CEO: Donald H. DeMeuse
VP HR: David K. Wong
Employees: 6,800

Phone: 414-435-8821
Fax: 414-435-3703

Jobs Added Last Year: 0

Paper & products - paper towels (Mardi Gras, So-Dri, Page, Green Forest), bath tissue (Soft'n Gentle), wipes & boxed facial tissue made from recycled fibers

GANDER MOUNTAIN, INC.

PO Box 128, Hwy. W
Wilmot, WI 53192
CEO: Ralph L. Freitag
Dir HR: Milton D. Ancevic
Employees: 2,141

Phone: 414-862-2331
Fax: 414-862-2330

Jobs Added Last Year: 702 (+48.8%)

Retail - mail-order sales of hunting, fishing, camping & hiking equipment

HARNISCHFEGER INDUSTRIES, INC.

13400 Bishops Ln.
Brookfield, WI 53005
Chm & CEO: Jeffery T. Grade
VP HR: Joseph A. Podawiltz
Employees: 14,000

Phone: 414-671-4400
Fax: 414-671-7604

Jobs Added Last Year: 2,800 (+25.0%)

Machinery - papermaking (Beloit Corporation), surface (P&H Mining Equipment) & underground mining (Joy Mining Machinery) & material handling (P&H Material Handling)

An in-depth profile of this company is available to subscribers on Hoover's Online at www.hoovers.com.

337

HARRY W. SCHWARTZ BOOKSHOPS

209 E. Wisconsin Ave.
Milwaukee, WI 53202
Pres & CEO: A. David M. Schwartz
Dir HR: Shawn Quinn
Employees: 140

Phone: 414-274-6400
Fax: 414-274-6408

Jobs Added Last Year: 30 (+27.3%)

Retail - bookstores in the Midwest (Harry W. Schwartz, Dickens Discount Books); mail-order business-related books

JOURNAL COMMUNICATION INC.

PO Box 661
Milwaukee, WI 53201
CEO: Robert Kahlor
Dir HR: Daniel Harmsen
Employees: 6,500

Phone: 414-224-2000
Fax: 414-224-2599

Jobs Added Last Year: 2,100 (+47.7%)

Publishing - newspapers (Milwaukee Sentinel); broadcasting; printing; telecommunications

INTREPID CORPORATION

N14 W23833 Stone Ridge Dr.
Waukesha, WI 53188
CEO: Richard A. Burke
No central personnel officer
Employees: 1,900

Phone: 414-523-3000
Fax: 414-523-0700

Jobs Added Last Year: 450 (+31.0%)

Leisure & recreational products - bicycles (Trek)

KOHLER CO.

444 Highland Dr.
Kohler, WI 53044
Chm & Pres: Herbert V. Kohler Jr.
SVP HR: Kenneth W. Conger
Employees: 15,000

Phone: 414-457-4441
Fax: 414-459-1274

Jobs Added Last Year: 500 (+3.4%)

Building products - plumbing products (Sterling Plumbing Group); generators & engines; fine furniture

JOHNSON CONTROLS, INC.

5757 N. Green Bay Ave.
Milwaukee, WI 53201-0591
Chm & CEO: James H. Keyes
VP HR: Susan F. Davis
Employees: 59,200

Phone: 414-228-1200
Fax: 414-228-2302

Jobs Added Last Year: 4,400 (+8.0%)

Diversified operations - automotive products, including seat systems; building control systems; plastic containers & blow-molding machinery systems; automotive & specialty batteries

KOHL'S CORPORATION

N54 W13600 Woodale Dr.
Menomonee Falls, WI 53051
Chm & CEO: William S. Kellogg
VP HR: Margaretta Cullen
Employees: 21,200

Phone: 414-783-5800
Fax: 414-783-6501

Jobs Added Last Year: 3,600 (+20.5%)

Retail - regional department stores in the Midwest

The National Classifieds — http://www.indra.com/ncjobs/

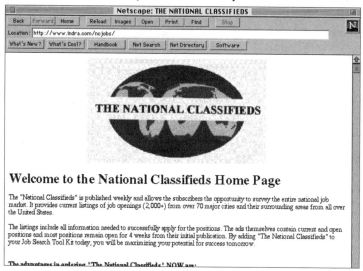

LUNAR CORPORATION

313 W. Beltline Hwy.
Madison, WI 53713
Pres : Richard B. Mazess
VP Fin: Robert A. Beckman
Employees: 191

Phone: 608-274-2663
Fax: 608-274-5374

Jobs Added Last Year: 60 (+45.8%)

Medical products - bone disease treatment products

THE MANITOWOC COMPANY, INC.

500 S. 16th St.
Manitowoc, WI 54220
Pres & CEO: Fred M. Butler
VP HR: Thomas G. Musial
Employees: 3,200

Phone: 414-684-4410
Fax: 414-683-6277

Jobs Added Last Year: 1,300 (+68.4%)

Diversified operations - construction cranes, shipbuilding & repair & ice makers

THE MARCUS CORPORATION

250 W. Wisconsin Ave., Ste. 1700
Milwaukee, WI 53202-4220
Chm, Pres & CEO: Stephen H. Marcus
VP HR: H. Fred Delmenhorst
Employees: 6,800

Phone: 414-272-6020
Fax: 414-272-0669

Jobs Cut Last Year: 700 (-9.3%)

Hotels & motels - economy (Budgetel Inns); movie theatres; resorts; restaurants

MARQUETTE ELECTRONICS, INC.

8200 W. Tower Ave.
Milwaukee, WI 53223
Pres & CEO: Timothy C. Mickelson
Dir Personnel: Gordon W. Petersen
Employees: 2,134

Phone: 414-355-5000
Fax: 414-355-3790

Jobs Added Last Year: 636 (+42.5%)

Medical products - electronic equipment & systems for the diagnosis & monitoring of patients requiring critical care & fetal & neonatal monitoring

MARSHALL & ILSLEY CORPORATION

770 N. Water St.
Milwaukee, WI 53202
Chm & CEO: J. B. Wigdale
SVP HR: Gary Strelow
Employees: 9,079

Phone: 414-765-7801
Fax: 414-765-7899

Jobs Added Last Year: 479 (+5.6%)

Banks - Midwest

MENARD, INC.

4777 Menard Dr.
Eau Claire, WI 54703
Pres & CEO: John R. Menard
Dir HR & Office Mgr: Terri Jain
Employees: 5,800

Phone: 715-874-5911
Fax: 715-876-5901

Jobs Added Last Year: 800 (+16.0%)

Building products - home improvement centers

MIDWEST EXPRESS HOLDINGS, INC.

6744 S. Howell Ave.
Oak Creek, WI 53154-1402
Chm, Pres & CEO: Timothy E. Hoeksema
VP HR: Carol J. Reimer
Employees: 1,809

Phone: 414-570-4000
Fax: 414-520-0055

Jobs Added Last Year: 287 (+18.9%)

Transportation - airlines (Midwest Express Airlines, Skyway Airlines)

MODINE MANUFACTURING COMPANY

1500 DeKoven Ave.
Racine, WI 53403-2552
Pres & CEO: Richard T. Savage
VP HR: Roger L. Hetrick
Employees: 7,561

Phone: 414-636-1200
Fax: 414-636-1424

Jobs Added Last Year: 10 (+0.1%)

Automotive & trucking - heat exchangers

OSHKOSH B'GOSH, INC.

112 Otter Ave.
Oshkosh, WI 54901
Chm, Pres & CEO: Douglas W. Hyde
VP HR: Donald M. Carlson
Employees: 6,500

Phone: 414-231-8800
Fax: 414-231-8621

Jobs Cut Last Year: 100 (-1.5%)

Apparel - children's & men's

QUAD/GRAPHICS, INC.

W224 N3322 DuPlainville Rd.
Pewaukee, WI 53072
Pres: Harry V. Quadracci
VP Emp Svcs: Emily M. Labode
Employees: 8,444

Phone: 414-246-9200
Fax: 414-246-4322

Jobs Added Last Year: 944 (+12.6%)

Printing - commercial

 An in-depth profile of this company is available to subscribers on Hoover's Online at www.hoovers.com.

339

REGAL-BELOIT CORPORATION

200 State St.
Beloit, WI 53511-9940
Chm, Pres & CEO: James L. Packard
VP HR: Fritz Hollenbach
Employees: 2,600

Phone: 608-364-8800
Fax: 608-365-2182

Jobs Added Last Year: 200 (+8.3%)

Machinery - power-transmission equipment & cutting tools for industrial applications

S.C. JOHNSON & SON, INC.

1525 Howe St.
Racine, WI 53403-2236
Pres & CEO: William D. George Jr.
SVP HR & Corp Comm Worldwide: Gayle P. Kosterman
Employees: 13,400

Phone: 414-631-2000
Fax: 414-631-2133

Jobs Added Last Year: 300 (+2.3%)

Soap & cleaning preparations

SCHNEIDER NATIONAL INC.

3101 S. Packerland Dr.
Green Bay, WI 54306
Pres: Donald J. Schneider
Mgr HR: Mary Vogel
Employees: 15,500

Phone: 414-592-2000
Fax: 414-592-3565

Jobs Added Last Year: 200 (+1.3%)

Transportation - trucking services

SHOPKO STORES, INC.

700 Pilgrim Way, PO Box 19060
Green Bay, WI 54307-9060
Pres & CEO: Dale P. Kramer
SVP HR & Sec: David A. Liebergen
Employees: 19,500

Phone: 414-497-2211
Fax: 414-496-4133

Jobs Added Last Year: 0

Retail - regional department stores in the midwest & Pacific Northwest

SNAP-ON INCORPORATED

2801 80th St.
Kenosha, WI 53140
Chm, Pres & CEO: Robert A. Cornog
VP HR: William R. Whyte
Employees: 10,200

Phone: 414-656-5200
Fax: 414-656-5577

Jobs Added Last Year: 1,200 (+13.3%)

Tools - hand-held & power tools & diagnostic & shop equipment

SYBRON INTERNATIONAL CORP.

411 E. Wisconsin Ave.
Milwaukee, WI 53202
Chm, Pres & CEO: Kenneth F. Yontz
Dir HR: Eileen A. Short
Employees: 5,100

Phone: 414-274-6600
Fax: 414-274-6561

Jobs Added Last Year: 1,200 (+30.8%)

Medical & dental supplies - reusable & disposable plastic labware, orthodontic appliances, endodontic instruments & water-purification systems

THE UNIVERSITY OF WISCONSIN

1220 Linden Dr.
Madison, WI 53706
Pres: Katharine C. Lyall
Assoc VP HR: Charles Wright
Employees: 30,410

Phone: 608-262-2321
Fax: 608-265-3175

Jobs Added Last Year: 69 (+0.2%)

University

WISCONSIN ENERGY CORPORATION

231 W. Michigan St.
Milwaukee, WI 53201
Chm & CEO: Richard A. Abdoo
Dir HR: Barbara Braf
Employees: 5,823

Phone: 414-221-2345
Fax: 414-221-3340

Jobs Added Last Year: 1,022 (+21.3%)

Utility - electric power & natural gas

DATA BROADCASTING CORPORATION

3490 Clubhouse Dr., PO Box 7443
Jackson, WY 83001
Co-Chm & Co-CEO: Alan J. Hirschfield
Dir HR: Eileen Gilbert
Employees: 658

Phone: 307-733-9742
Fax: 307-733-4935

Jobs Added Last Year: 282 (+75.0%)

Business services - real-time stock market quotes, customized portfolio tracking & investor information

TOP 2,500 EMPLOYERS

The Indexes

Federal Signal Corporation 151

First Brands Corporation 117

FMC Corporation 152

Follett Corporation 152

GAF Corporation 224

GenCorp Inc. 267

General Electric Company 118

Great Dane Holdings Inc. 195

Griffon Corporation 242

Halliburton Company 309

Harcourt General, Inc. 185

Harris Corporation 130

Harvard Industries, Inc. 130

Hillenbrand Industries, Inc. 166

Honeywell Inc. 203

Ingram Industries Inc. 296

Insilco Corporation 268

ITT Industries, Inc. 245

J. M. Huber Corporation 225

Johnson Controls, Inc. 338

Jordan Industries, Inc. 154

J.R. Simplot Company 144

Knott's Berry Farm 89

Lancaster Colony Corporation 269

Lane Industries, Inc. 155

Litton Industries, Inc. 90

Loews Corporation 246

Lynch Corporation 119

MacAndrews & Forbes Holdings, Inc. 247

Mallinckrodt Group Inc. 213

The Manitowoc Company, Inc. 339

Mark IV Industries, Inc. 247

The Marmon Group, Inc. 155

MAXXAM Inc. 312

Metromedia Company 226

Minnesota Mining and Manufacturing Company 204

NACCO Industries, Inc. 270

National Service Industries, Inc. 141

Newell Co. 157

Ogden Corporation 250

Olin Corporation 120

Parsons & Whittemore, Inc. 251

Penske Corporation 197

Pentair, Inc. 205

Pfizer Inc. 251

Philip Morris Companies Inc. 252

Pittway Corporation 158

The Port Authority of New York and New Jersey 252

Premark International, Inc. 158

Ralston Purina Company 214

Raytheon Company 189

R. B. Pamplin Corporation 277

Renco Group Inc. 252

Rich Products Corporation 253

Rollins, Inc. 142

Ruddick Corporation 261

Samsonite Corporation 134

Sara Lee Corporation 159

Sequa Corporation 254

Sinclair Oil Corporation 325

Tandycrafts, Inc. 319

Teledyne, Inc. 105

Tenneco Inc. 121

Textron Inc. 291

Thermo Electron Corporation 190

Torchmark Corporation 66

Transamerica Corporation 106

Triarc Companies, Inc. 256

Trump Organization 256

TRW Inc. 274

Tyco International Ltd. 220

UIS, Inc. 256

United Dominion Industries Limited 262

United Technologies Corporation 122

U.S. Industries, Inc. 230

Valhi, Inc. 322

Valmont Industries, Inc. 217

Viacom Inc. 256

Walter Industries, Inc. 136

Westinghouse Electric Corporation 290

Whitman Corporation 163

Wingate Partners 322

W. L. Gore & Associates Inc. 124

Drugs

Abbott Laboratories 144

American Home Products Corporation 221

Aronex Pharmaceuticals, Inc. 301

Arris Pharmaceutical Corporation 73

Bristol-Myers Squibb Company 235

Dura Pharmaceuticals, Inc. 81

Eli Lilly and Company 165

Forest Laboratories, Inc. 241

Hoffmann-La Roche, Inc. 225

ICN Pharmaceuticals, Inc. 86

Interferon Sciences, Inc. 225

Jones Medical Industries, Inc. 212

Merck & Co., Inc. 226

Rhone-Poulenc Rorer Inc. 286

Schering-Plough Corporation 229

Warner-Lambert Company 230

Drugs - generic

Royce Laboratories, Inc. 133

Watson Pharmaceuticals, Inc. 109

Drugs & sundries - wholesale

AmeriSource Health Corporation 279

Bergen Brunswig Corporation 75

Cardinal Health, Inc. 264

McKesson Corporation 91

Owens & Minor, Inc. 330

Electrical components - miscellaneous

II-VI Incorporated 278

ACT Manufacturing, Inc. 179

Alpha Technologies Group, Inc. 300

American Power Conversion Corporation 290

Benchmark Electronics, Inc. 302

Kennametal Inc. 284

Machinery - construction & mining
Caterpillar Inc. 149
Harnischfeger Industries, Inc. 337
JLG Industries, Inc. 284
Terex Corporation 122

Machinery - electric utility
McDermott International, Inc. 173
Square D Company 160

Machinery - electrical
Bodine Electric Company 148
Cognex Corporation 182
CyberOptics Corporation 200
Emerson Electric Co. 211
MTD Products Inc. 270
Stewart & Stevenson Services, Inc. 319

Machinery - farm
Ag-Chem Equipment Co., Inc. 199
AGCO Corporation 136
Alamo Group, Inc. 300
Case Corporation 337
Deere & Company 150

Machinery - general industrial
AMSTED Industries Incorporated 146
The Duriron Company, Inc. 266
Goulds Pumps, Inc. 242
IDEX Corporation 153
Inductotherm Industries 225
Industrial Holdings, Inc. 311
Ingersoll-Rand Company 225
The Lincoln Electric Company 269
Owosso Corporation 285
Regal-Beloit Corporation 340
Soligen Technologies, Inc. 102
TRINOVA Corporation 274
Trion, Inc. 262

Machinery - material handling
Control Chief Holdings, Inc. 281

Machinery - semiconductor manufacturing equipment
Applied Materials, Inc. 73
Applied Science and Technology, Inc. 180
Brooks Automation, Inc. 182
Cohu, Inc. 78
Esterline Technologies Corporation 333
FSI International, Inc. 202
Fusion Systems Corporation 176
GaSonics International Corporation 85
KLA Instruments Corporation 89
Kulicke and Soffa Industries, Inc. 285
Lam Research Corporation 89
Mattson Technology, Inc. 91
Semitool, Inc. 216
Silicon Valley Group, Inc. 101
SubMicron Systems Corporation 287
Tylan General, Inc. 106
Varian Associates, Inc. 107

Medical & dental supplies
Becton, Dickinson and Company 221
C. R. Bard, Inc. 222
Gulf South Medical Supply, Inc. 208
Medline Industries, Inc. 156
Sunrise Medical Inc. 104
Sybron International Corporation 340
Tecnol Medical Products, Inc. 320
West Company, Inc. 290
Wilshire Technologies, Inc. 109

Medical instruments
Advanced NMR Systems, Inc. 180
Ballard Medical Products 323
Biomagnetic Technologies, Inc. 75
Biomet, Inc. 165
Boston Scientific Corporation 181
Circon Corporation 77

Endosonics Corporation 82
ESC Medical Systems Ltd. 184
Exogen, Inc. 223
IGEN, Inc. 176
International Remote Imaging Systems Inc. 88
Medtronic, Inc. 204
Research Medical, Inc. 325
Sangstat Medical Corporation 100
Stryker Corporation 197
ThermoTrex Corporation 105

Medical practice management
ABR Information Services, Inc. 127
Access Health, Inc. 71
Allegiance Corporation 145
Clinicorp, Inc. 128
Community Care of America, Inc. 129
CompDent Corporation 137
Crawford & Company 138
EmCare Holdings Inc. 307
Geriatric & Medical Companies, Inc. 283
HCIA Inc. 176
Health Management, Inc. 243
Health Management Systems, Inc. 243
HealthPlan Services Corporation 130
Horizon Mental Health Management, Inc. 310
Iatros Health Network, Inc. 284
Medaphis Corporation 140
Mednet MPC Corporation 219
NMR of America, Inc. 227
OccuSystems Inc. 314
Owen Healthcare, Inc. 314
PhyCor, Inc. 297
Physician Reliance Network, Inc. 315
Safeguard Health Enterprises, Inc. 100
Shared Medical Systems Corporation 287
Sheridan Healthcare, Inc. 134
UCI Medical Affiliates, Inc. 294

Lechters, Inc. 226
Mac Frugal's Bargains -
Close-outs Inc. 90
McCrory Corporation 247
Pamida Holdings
Corporation 217
Price/Costco, Inc. 334
Rose's Stores, Inc. 261
Venture Stores, Inc. 215
Waban Inc. 191
Wal-Mart Stores, Inc. 70
Woolworth Corporation
258

Retail - drug stores
Arbor , Inc. 192
Big B, Inc. 64
Drug Emporium, Inc. 266
Eckerd Corporation 129
Fay's, Incorporated 241
Genovese Drug Stores, Inc.
241
Longs Drug Stores
Corporation 90
Melville Corporation 247
Pharmhouse Corporation
251
Revco D.S., Inc. 272
Rite Aid Corporation 287
Thrifty PayLess Holdings,
Inc. 277
Walgreen Co. 163

Retail - home furnishings
Bed Bath & Beyond Inc.
221
The Bombay Company, Inc.
302
Ethan Allen Interiors Inc.
117
Garden Ridge Corporation
309
Heilig-Meyers Co. 329
Levitz Furniture
Incorporated 131
Pier 1 Imports, Inc. 315
Rhodes, Inc. 142

Retail - jewelry stores
Finlay Enterprises, Inc.
241
Tiffany & Co. 255
Zale Corporation 323

Retail - mail order & direct
Amrion, Inc. 110
Amway Corporation 192
Boise Cascade Office
Products Corporation
148
Celex Group, Inc. 149

Chronimed Inc. 200
Corporate Express, Inc.
111
CUC International Inc. 117
Fingerhut Companies, Inc.
201
Gander Mountain, Inc. 337
J. Crew Group Inc. 245
L.L. Bean, Inc. 174
Lost Arrow, Inc. 90
Pampered Chef Ltd. 157
Roll International
Corporation 100
Spiegel, Inc. 160
Viking Office Products, Inc.
108

**Retail - major department
stores**
Dayton Hudson
Corporation 200
Dillard Department Stores,
Inc. 70
Fedco, Inc. 82
Federated Department
Stores, Inc. 267
J. C. Penney Company, Inc.
311
The May Department
Stores Company 213
Montgomery Ward Holding
Corp. 156
The Neiman Marcus Group,
Inc. 188
Nordstrom, Inc. 334
Saks Holdings, Inc. 254
Sears, Roebuck and Co.
159

Retail - miscellaneous
Army & Air Force
Exchange Service 301
Big 5 Sporting Goods 75
Brookstone, Inc. 220
CML Group, Inc. 182
Cole National Corporation
265
The Container Store 305
The Cosmetic Center 175
CPI Corp. 210
DFS Group, Ltd. 80
Fabri-Centers of America,
Inc. 267
General Host Corporation
118
General Nutrition
Companies, Inc. 283
The Great American
Backrub Store, Inc. 242

Hancock Fabrics, Inc. 208
The Home Depot, Inc. 140
Jenny Craig, Inc. 88
Michaels Stores, Inc. 313
Natural Wonders, Inc. 93
Navy Exchange System 330
Office Depot, Inc. 132
OfficeMax, Inc. 271
Olan Mills 297
Oshman's Sporting Goods,
Inc. 314
PCA International, Inc.
261
Petco Animal Supplies, Inc.
97
PETsMART, Inc. 68
Regis Corporation 206
Rickel Home Centers, Inc.
229
Specialty Retail Group, Inc.
121
Staples, Inc. 190
Supercuts, Inc. 104
Toys "R" Us, Inc. 229
Trend-Lines, Inc. 191
Williams-Sonoma, Inc. 109

Retail - new & used cars
R Corporation 316
RidgeMotors Pontiac/Mize
Import Group Inc. 158

**Retail - regional
department stores**
Ames Department Stores,
Inc. 115
Belk Stores Services, Inc.
258
Boscov's Department
Stores 280
Bradlees, Inc. 181
Carson Pirie Scott & Co.
337
The Elder-Beerman Stores
Corp. 267
Fred Meyer, Inc. 276
Gottschalks Inc. 85
Hills Stores Company 186
Kohl's Corporation 338
Mercantile Stores
Company, Inc. 270
Proffitt's, Inc. 298
Pubco Corporation 272
ShopKo Stores, Inc. 340
Strawbridge & Clothier
287
Value City Department
Stores, Inc. 274

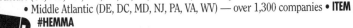